PHYSICAL EDUCATION FOR CHILDREN:

A Focus on the Teaching Process

PHYSICAL EDUCATION FOR CHILDREN:
A Focus on the Teaching Process

BETTE J. LOGSDON — *Professor, Bowling Green State University, Bowling Green, Ohio*

KATE R. BARRETT — *Professor, The University of North Carolina at Greensboro*

MARGARET AMMONS — *Professor, Agnes Scott College, Decatur, Georgia*

MARION R. BROER — *Professor Emeritus, University of Washington, Seattle*

LOLAS E. HALVERSON — *Professor, University of Wisconsin–Madison*

ROSEMARY McGEE — *Professor, The University of North Carolina at Greensboro*

MARY ANN ROBERTON — *Associate Professor, University of Wisconsin–Madison*

Second Edition

Lea & Febiger   1984   *Philadelphia*

Lea & Febiger
600 Washington Square
Philadelphia, PA 19106
U.S.A.

First Edition, 1977
  Reprinted, 1978, 1981

Second Edition, 1984

Library of Congress Cataloging in Publication Data

Main entry under title:

Physical education for children

  Bibliography: p.
  Includes index.
  1. Physical education for children—Study and teaching
—Addresses, essays, lectures. I. Logsdon, Bette J.
GV443.P46   1983   372.8'6044   83-11964
ISBN 0-8121-0892-2

Printed in the United States of America

Print No.:   3   2   1

Preface

This revision has been prepared at a time when critics of the educational system from the angered, exploited athlete to the President of the United States were expressing their dismay at the mediocrity of education and calling for change in the instructional programs of our public schools. The changes in this edition reflect both our personal sensitivity to the needs of college students wishing to acquire knowledge and abilities essential to becoming effective teachers and our growing professional concern for the criticism directed toward education and the need to improve physical education for children to make it an instructional program worthy of being retained as an integral part of the elementary school curriculum.

The educational approach central to this book places a keen responsibility on teachers for developing an instructional program focused on helping children acquire, adapt, and utilize a broad spectrum of games, dance, and gymnastic skills. Important to this educational approach is a scheme for helping teachers organize and develop a teaching/learning progression and a concerted effort to help teachers increase their understanding of movement analysis and teaching strategies. Basic to implementing this approach is a need for perceiving skill development and assessing learning in physical education as on-going processes. We believe this knowledge is important to challenging the individual needs of children in an educational, instructional physical education program.

We are grateful for the continued stimulus and challenge provided us by our undergraduate and graduate students and the many dedicated teachers in the profession who demonstrate a keen commitment to studying and interpreting this approach. It is their efforts, their search that can keep this approach dynamic and responsive to the changes needed to improve physical education.

We wish to acknowledge and sincerely thank the Agency for Instructional Television, Bloomington, Indiana, and the children, teachers, and principals from the following schools—Crim, Conneaut, and St. Aloysius Elementary Schools, Bowling Green, Ohio; Price Traditional School, Greensboro, North Carolina; Linkhorn Elementary School, Lynchburg, Virginia; Glendale-Feilbach Elementary School, Toledo, Ohio—for the many photographs that highlight this edition.

Bowling Green, Ohio　　　　　　Bette J. Logsdon

Contents

Chapter 1

Elementary Education— a Perspective

MARGARET AMMONS

To discuss elementary education in the United States is, in some measure, to discuss the history of the country. If I had to select one word to describe what has happened since colonial times, it would be *change*. From this change has come some progress. One reasonable assumption is that elementary education reflects the changes and the progress in this country. Is this assumption valid? The present chapter explores this question and others that relate to prospects for the future of elementary education in the United States.

First, I have taken a brief look at elementary education "then" in theory and practice. Second, I have looked at elementary education "now" in theory and practice. Third, I have set forth a philosophy of elementary education and its factors in terms of elementary programs today. Finally, I have cautioned those responsible for the planning and implementing of programs in elementary schools.

ELEMENTARY EDUCATION THEN

One way to examine elementary education is to explore what it is or has been in theory and then to compare the theory with current or past practices. Perhaps the prime factor in determining whether education reflects the changes and progress of the United States is the relation of stated purpose to actual practice. Throughout the history of education in this country, the lit-

erature has contained statements of purpose for education in a democracy. Even when such statements are not explicit, they are implied in every proposal for change in education. We must compare those stated purposes, however, with reports of actual classroom practice.

Public education emerged in the colony of Massachusetts in the middle of the 17th century. Since the founding of that colony was based on religious beliefs, its schools were also created for a religious purpose. An important part of the beliefs held by the people who came to Massachusetts centered on the idea of personal salvation. To achieve salvation, one had to read the Bible. As towns grew, it became practical to teach children in ever increasing numbers. Where dame schools had sufficed in earlier times, it was deemed necessary to move to a more formal situation in the 1640s. A purpose of such significance was too vital to be left to the good nature of a townswoman or, worse, to mere chance. Since the schools had a clear purpose, practices to fulfill this purpose were clear. Lessons were assigned, studied, and recited. If students did not master the task in the first attempt, they needed further study and additional recitation. In these schools, perhaps to a greater degree than has existed since, purpose and practice were closely related.

Schools cropped up in other colonies. In New York City, for example, a variety of religious groups established schools for the poor. In most, if not all, the focus was much the same as in Massachusetts. If their purpose had a one-word title, it would be "literacy." There are many reasons for a society to become literate. For the early members of the various towns and colonies, the reason to be literate was intimately entwined with the good of one's soul. It was simply moral to learn the rudiments of the written language. In the minds of many teachers now, those were the "good old days." There were virtually no distractions, no frills, and few attempts to provide for individual differences among students. The only nod in the direction of individualized instruction was that a student could take as long as necessary to complete a given job. The notion of failure and promotion had to wait for a different social climate.

By the mid-19th century, conditions in the United States were quite different. To telescope, two major thrusts were apparent: the Industrial Revolution and the enormous numbers of individuals who were immigrating to the eastern seaboard. This situation, taken with the popular slogan, "The Age of the Common Man," created a climate that resulted in a new stated purpose for the schools. This new purpose was to provide, for all who chose to accept it, the opportunity to better themselves, i.e., to equip themselves to partake of the good life offered by the robust and growing country. Basic to the success of this ideal was the entailed educational purpose, literacy. During this period, literacy was not seen wholly or even significantly as the saving of men's souls. Rather, it was the passport to the good life. With a new reason for literacy, would new practices follow?

In 1848, in Boston, a new kind of school opened.[1] The Quincy grammar school was the first American school organized on the basis of grades—apparently to accommodate increasing numbers of students. The modest claim made for the Quincy school was that it would set the pattern of elementary schools for 20 years. What was different about this school? First, children were assigned to groups according to age. Children entered school at about age 6, remained in one group for the entire school year, and if successful in completing the tasks assigned to them, were promoted to the next grade. If unsuccessful, they repeated the grade. This first major difference gave rise to a new idea in public

schooling: built-in failure was respectable. Second, and of necessity, came two other phenomena. A graded structure required materials that were compatible with the new organization, so graded textbooks appeared in massive quantities. These texts defined the amount of material that a student must master in a school year. These limits were arbitrarily set since there was little information on which to establish norms for children of a particular age.

The other concomitant of a graded structure was the graded teacher. Preparation for this profession meant learning what was to be covered in a given school year by a certain-age child and dispensing that material. Despite these significant changes in the elementary school, the relation between purpose and program was still high. Methods and materials were designed to move students toward literacy.

While education has rarely been without its critics, in the late 19th century, a well-defined movement began to emerge. In 1892, members of the National Education Association (NEA), whose interest was children of kindergarten age, broke with the NEA to form the International Kindergarten Union (IKU). Their grievance against the NEA centered on its failure to support programs that members of the IKU believed to be appropriate for young children. These educators sought to break the lock-step, rigid program that had evolved in the elementary school.

The second substantial critic was John Dewey. In his writings and in the school he established at the University of Chicago, he devised a new way to educate young children. His system centered on the belief that the human organism was not a pitcher to be filled but rather a being with a sense of purpose, with interests, with curiosity. What he saw in schools was inimical to the nature of the child being educated. He wanted the educational program to further the natural inclinations of children rather than forcing them to accept predetermined material.

Dewey, then, articulated a new purpose for education in the 20th century: the opportunity for children to grow through problem-solving experiences. Since such experiences could not occur in a traditional, rigid program, his proposal required a program that would encourage students to inquire, to formulate problems real to them, and to seek data relevant to the problem at hand. He envisioned learning as the goal. Dewey attracted countless disciples, and the educational literature of the 20th century bears the unmistakable mark of this man. Teachers flocked to his classes at Columbia University, and colleagues endeavored to translate their understanding of his purpose into practical programs. Thus, programs in the elementary schools were expected to reflect the Deweyan purpose.

For reasons not yet understood, however, the Dewey influence was limited largely to the printed page. In spite of the sincere attempts of teacher educators, administrators, and teachers themselves, and in spite of the widespread acceptance of a new purpose for elementary schools, business proceeded as usual, with two sets of purposes. One set was Dewey's, or something close to it; the other was the operational set. Operationally, the purpose was much the same as it had been. What transpired in schools differed little from what had been seen in the previous century.

While the foregoing describes education in the early part of this century, what happened in elementary education after 1950? The critics did not lessen their attacks against education in either intensity or number; however, they now charged that education was too soft, that it demonstrated anti-intellectual qualities, and that children were not being taught to read. Many laid the blame at the feet of John Dewey.

How did the targets of those charges respond? The rebuttal was expected to center on the claim that schools had abandoned their earlier role. Instead, researchers rushed to demonstrate that schools were still achieving purposes current in the early part of this century. For example, studies were conducted in 1951, 1952, and 1957, which were designed to prove that children in those years "were doing as well as children in 1921, 1932, and 1937, and which used as measures those tests developed to assess student progress toward purposes in 1920–1931."[2] Such studies do not support the idea that programs of the 1950s reflected the purpose that had seized the imagination of so many who wrote about education. They do suggest that such programs were substantially like those of earlier decades.

Criticism did not abate, but not until October, 1957, did those seeking to make the schools more academically respectable have hard evidence to support their claims. The Soviet Union successfully launched the first Sputnik. America had been beaten in the space race and the fault was that of the schools. Where no amount of pleading had been successful, this event spurred the U.S. Congress to provide millions of tax dollars to upgrade the teaching of science, mathematics, and foreign languages. What resulted from these expenditures is a matter of public record. Teachers were retreaded in countless workshops across the nation. Academicians heretofore uninterested in the programs of elementary schools plunged into program development. Modern math, inquiry approaches in the natural and social sciences, individualized programs, and much more were produced. Avowed purpose and the program designed to achieve it seemed to be positively correlated once again. New evidence did not support this conclusion; operationally, the purpose was still literacy. In 1970, Goodlad and his associates spent hundreds of hours observing in classrooms. They found that elementary education was essentially as it had been.[3]

In working with teachers, I have also found that, particularly in the primary grades, reading and mathematics have achieved such importance that teachers have difficulty working science and social studies into the class schedule. Not teaching, not money, not exhortation have produced changes in practice. *In essence,* the elementary school program is today as it was a century ago. Literacy, not learning, is still the operational goal. Although I am strongly tempted to speculate about or even to analyze the stubborn nature of this educational puzzle, such conjecture is not the purpose of this treatise.

SOME OUGHTS FOR EDUCATION

I have chosen the word "ought" to express my convictions regarding some questions that seem basic to educational decision-making. If one presumes to recommend what ought to be done in any field, one must share the basis for those recommendations. If proposals are inconsistent with basic beliefs, the entire package is, at best, suspect. Therefore, prior to urging a type of education, I will share my basic assumptions about the nature of man, the nature of knowledge, and the nature of the good society and the individual's relation to it.

First, the human beings are rational, in that all can see alternatives and choose among them.

People do not ordinarily act capriciously. Furthermore, all persons can increase their ability to act with reason. Finally, men and women desire to improve and are curious and enthusiastic about topics that have meaning for them.

Much of what I know did not come to me through the five senses, as usually interpreted. I can know what it is like to be lonely or happy, but the way I know is probably different from the way I know that something is blue or hard. If so, what I offer a learner must involve knowing in many ways. Knowledge, then, cannot be limited to what is measured by responses to a paper-and-pencil test, or what is read from a book. Knowledge must allow for empathic knowing. The learner will gain much of worth without my intervention. Finally, knowing and thus learning are deeply personal.

In the good society, people are free to choose, to make of themselves what they will. Such a society encourages independence of mind and spirit. Individuals, in turn, have an obligation to behave as human beings, with the capacity to choose, to add to their knowledge those factors that will let them achieve their potential and contribute to the good of all.

The foregoing summary reflects my stand on the questions that all must answer as they contemplate the task of teaching. If I have been consistent, I can use these assumptions as my criteria for examining projections for the 1980s. What follows is not the only program that could evolve from these basic values, but this program does offer realistic possibilities for progress. Educational aims, organization, activities, and evaluation can now be discussed.

AIMS

Sets of aims of goals have already been discussed; for example, in the section on John Dewey. Although much of what he offered to American educators is consonant with my beliefs, there is a need to go further. If change is integral and inevitable in this country in the foreseeable future, the ability to cope with change is a necessary aspect of personal development. Coping with change entails the ability to choose among the changes available or to choose not to change. The important factor is choice. Human beings will either choose, wisely or unwisely, or have thrust upon them a series

of decisions. Believing as I do, the latter possibility is unacceptable.

Therefore, the most important aim of the elementary school is to enhance each student's grounds for choosing wisely. Certainly, the home and the church, along with countless other social institutions, have a responsibility in the area of improving individual choice. The school, however, has a unique role in this regard, for in the school, at least given current arrangements, children have systematic access to the conventional wisdom of the race. Here they may garner enlightened information regarding how their ancestors have dealt with change and choice. In the school, at least in theory, they learn to weigh, to evaluate, and to compare their own bents, desires, conclusions, and speculations against those of others throughout history. In such an atmosphere, they begin to see the meaning of choice—the ability to project consequences of action—and the relation of their values to their actions.

Such an aim entails others. Children, in order to learn to choose wisely, must move toward literacy in a variety of areas. Two factors must be underscored. First, they *begin* to move toward literacy. As mentioned earlier, with the advent of the graded school, a conviction developed that each school year had about it a finality, an end. Rarely does a school year close with children's having a sense of continuity from one year to the next. The third grade is just that; it bears little relation to the year that precedes or follows it. Too often, teachers expect that certain material has been covered and therefore learned, thus absolving them of any responsibility toward that material. Rather, an elementary education must open, not close, children's minds. It is a disservice to lead them to believe that they have "finished" any aspect of their education.

Second, children must begin to move toward literacy in a variety of areas. As suggested before, literacy has often come to mean the ability to read, particularly in materials designed to teach the skill of decoding new words and the skill of literal translation. Literacy should claim much wider boundaries, but evidence indicates that the foregoing emphases absorb inordinate amounts of children's time in school. Literacy, for example, means also the ability to deal accurately with ideas of quantity and relation. This ability goes far beyond the age-old assignment of numerous arithmetic examples to be worked. Such literacy requires a deep understanding of what ideas numerals represent and how they relate to one another, as well as the ability to apply mathematical operations appropriately.

Literacy includes the capacity to analyze the history of the race as recorded by many observers. This meaning is not to be equated with a knowledge of chronology or with the accumulation of conclusions about historic events as depicted by observers. What is intended is a child's growth toward making critical judgments about man in all his varied developments.

Literacy exists in children's grasp of their natural world and their relation to it. If they are to become prudent choice-makers in the realm of the environment, for example, they must range far beyond the memorization of what specialists have proclaimed. If they are to exercise wise judgments about the conduct of national and international politics, education must help them to become literate in those disciplines that impinge upon such judgments and choices. As members of their society, children must become literate in those areas that affect their physical well-being. No longer can we be content with the ability to play games. Too much is at stake to let games pass as literacy.

Literacy is also involved in the arts—literary, graphic, and performing. Through such literacy comes a bond between the child and the aspirations, despairs, and frustrations of humankind. Such literacy helps children to experience the heights and depths of human emotion at times of failure and success. It enables them to feel the enormity of the act of choosing.

Three aspects summarize literacy in terms of enhancing a human being's ability to make wise choices. First, literacy is much more than the simple accumulation of information about disciplines that are commonly associated with the curriculum of the elementary school. Literacy demands that children internalize information, weigh it, sort it, and use it in making choices about the world and their place in it. Second, literacy must no longer be an end in itself. To demonstrate literacy without the correlative ability and inclination to use it in one's life is to demonstrate pedantry. Third, literacy, as I have discussed it, is an appropriate aim for even the very young. While it may become increasingly

sophisticated in later school years, it cannot be ignored in the elementary school. Assuming that the ability to memorize and return information on demand is a necessary and sufficient condition for later life, literacy is, first, to perpetuate what has occurred for decades and, second, to assume that the human organism at some magical age changes from being sponge-like to being curious and creative.

Thus, elementary education must strive to enhance children's ability to make informed, wise choices about their lives as they relate to the life of others. Essential to this overarching aim is literacy in the areas of human experience.

ORGANIZATION

One aspect of education is relatively clear; there is little relation between school organization and student achievement. In other words, we have not been able to demonstrate that different organizations produce specific differences in pupil performance. It is not that such differences cannot be achieved, only that they have not. What, then, can be said about how schools might be organized?

Historically, the educational scene has witnessed a variety of units: dame schools, Lancasterian schools, graded schools, departmentalized schools, core schools, nongraded schools, platoon schools, track schools, pod schools, cluster schools, junior high schools, middle schools, continuous progress schools, and, recently, open schools. For a time, there was excitement about educational parks as well. One factor seems to have characterized each of these ground swells. As each attracted supporters, these converts held the firm conviction that the organization in which they placed their faith was the type best suited to all students.

One must, however, at least consider Ole Sand's contention: "Human variability demands alternatives." One error that educators seem doomed to repeat is their assumption that an identical set of educational circumstances is equally productive for all students. Evidence to the contrary abounds. Thelen's study is one compelling piece of such evidence.[4]

If student learning is of sincere concern to educators, and if we accept that students have different learning styles, persistence in offering only one pattern of schooling is an act of violence against what we claim to believe. Moreover, students in precollegiate programs are required by law to attend schools that, for some, are sources of legally sanctioned failure. Specifically, if education involves enhancing students' ability to make wise choices, it seems logical to offer honest opportunities to choose. Further, if individual differences are to be considered, then school organizations must reflect this decision. Arguments to the contrary center on the mobility of Americans. Proponents of uniformity claim that, without it, children who move often may miss some portion of content. This argument assumes that every child in the United States must cover identical topics or his opportunity to learn has been diminished by whatever he may have missed. Responding to this issue falls outside the limits of this chapter.

Since considerable evidence suggests that no one pattern of school organization is responsive to the various learning styles presented by individual learners, there is but one admonition. School men and women must be willing to assume the additional burden of assessing the educational requirement of individual students and of providing, within the school's financial limits, the organizational patterns demanded by those differences that can be discerned and described. Suggestions include varying the length of the school day, establishing schools with different academic foci, teaching fundamental information through home-based computer terminals, and holding seminars rather than the usual classes. There is no dearth of ideas; what appears to be missing is a bedrock commitment to the purpose that we claim to support.

ACTIVITIES

Research has revealed that the most regular student activity is "listening to a teacher." For decades, the underlying, although rarely admitted, assumption has been that teaching is telling. We tell students through lecture, we tell them through films, we tell them through books, we tell them through demonstration. While techniques of teacher questioning have recently been given concerted attention, teachers are still inclined to tell and tell for nearly half the school day.

In 1956, Bloom and his associates offered a new way of thinking about educational outcomes and the means for attaining them.[5] From this scheme have come several others designed to help teachers engage students in higher mental activities than simple recall and the paraphrasing of someone else's ideas. Apparently, no movement is assisting teachers in dealing with either intellectual tasks that take students into higher levels of thought or a variety of intangible and imprecisely measured outcomes. If abilities to deal with real problems in critical and creative ways should be developed in the schools, and if knowledge is to be more than material between covers of books, then practice must change.

While extensive examples are not available, a few may be helpful. First, teachers must be clear about the mental, affective, or psychomotor level at which they seek to have students operate. The kind of activity required at the level of memorization is different from the activity needed to help students become involved in analysis. Consider the following questions. (1) What is the street number of your residence? (2) You have two coins that total 55 cents. One of them is not a nickel. What are the two coins? Do you detect any difference in the ease with which you answered the two? Do you feel any different "in your head" as you sort out the answer? Most often the answer to these questions is an unqualified "yes." Therefore, a teacher must at least frame questions according to the mental or affective or psychomotor level toward which he seeks to move students. This approach, while departing from straight recall and paraphrasing, still relies upon the teacher as the source of appropriate questions and responses.

Second, a teacher must be highly aware of individual learning styles. Some learn best through isolated activities, some through the printed media, some through heated but reasoned debate, some through trial and error, some through modeling another, some through graphic or performing arts, some through physical activity. For example, an individual may learn mathematics most readily from working with another student while he learns history best through quiet reading and reflection. A thorough appraisal of each student is mandatory so that a teacher does not misread and decide that a certain child always learns best in isolation.

To restate as a final caution, a single activity is rarely appropriate for all subject matter and/or for all students at any given moment. The nature of the activity must account for the particular subject matter; the intellectual, affective, or psychomotor level one seeks to have students attain; and most importantly the individual's learning style.

EVALUATION

Evaluation in this context describes a student's progress toward one or more specified objectives. It is not judgmental, and is not to be equated with grading or reporting. Evaluation is to be a situation or an activity from which student and teacher can determine what new or similar direction is indicated for the student.

Since objectives differ in intent with respect to the cognitive, affective, or psychomotor domains, so must evaluation differ. As students exhibit different learning styles that require a variety of activities, so do they demonstrate these individual styles in relation to situations where their progress is determined. If true, the ubiquitous paper-and-pencil evaluation syndrome must be relegated to its appropriate place among the appraisal tools.

Too often overlooked, or dismissed as too cumbersome, are such activities as discussion, painting, movement, reading, social situations, shared diaries, revelation of aspirations, or even offhanded comments. To many, these measures are simply not respectable in detecting individual student progress. Effectiveness of the evaluation technique is often judged in terms of its observability and measurability. Emphasis on the latter two factors strongly suggests either that the objectives in which we claim to be interested are only window dressing, or that, while intangible outcomes of schooling are desirable, they are not amenable to clean and unequivocal measures. While their achievement is to be sought, progress toward them is impossible or difficult to determine, according to some; therefore, evaluation will consider only those aspects that lend themselves to neat and precise measurement. Someone once remarked, "Give me control of evaluation and I will control the curriculum."

If evaluation is so powerful and if evaluation becomes a matter of developing techniques only for those aspects of student development that can be observed, the curriculum will be reduced to a series of activities that offer students little hope for deriving much of internal worth from their compulsory schooling. Evaluation, then, must be based on a scale that is as broad as the objectives to which it is supposedly related. It must reflect the enormous variability of the individuals whose progress is to be described and whose school success or failure is at stake. Questions of difficulty, imprecision, disagreement must be put aside in favor of honest attempts to evolve techniques that can be refined after experience provides direction. Instant perfection is not reality; constructive steps toward its achievement are.

A CAUTION

Abroad in this land are examples of an activity that has captured the minds of educators since at least 1900. They have tried to take into the educational sphere the model provided by business. Whereas some claim that educators have discovered the business model only in the past 12 years, Callahan carefully documents attempts that date from the turn of this century.[6] Furthermore, there have been few surceases in such activities since that time. It has all the appearance of another rediscovered wheel.

Why should there be concern over this approach to educational decision-making? Why should there be warnings against such a basis for educational planning? The most significant reason lies in the difference between the purpose of industry and the purpose of education.

Industry, of necessity, seeks to produce, with as much efficiency as feasible, as large a quota of identical items as time, skill, and money allow. Products that deviate from acceptable standards are rejected, discarded, or sold as seconds or irregulars. Means used to produce a particular item are standardized; the relation between process and product is clear, observable, and measurable. If motion X is executed, product Y will result. The purpose of industry is to produce predetermined quotas of specified objects. The purpose of education is diametrically opposite.

Another major difference is the role or the image of those in positions of leadership in business. Such officials are termed management. The implications of the term are clear. The responsibility of managers is to move persons about so that quotas may be met. For many reasons, the relation between management and persons assigned the task of meeting quotas is that of adversaries.

Callahan states that in the 19th century educational leaders viewed themselves, and were viewed by others, as statesmen and philosophers. Since that time, the term manager has often been applied to superintendents. Consultants have recommended that a management team be selected for the purpose of planning educational programs. In some cases, teachers and members of boards of education are to be only tangentially involved in such planning, if at all.[7]

Another difference between business and education is the preparation required for entry. In the case of many workers in industry, on-the-job training is necessary and sufficient. In fact, in many cases within industry, any deviation from established practice can reduce production, which will ultimately be reflected in income. Much has been written regarding the boredom suffered by assembly-line workers as a result of repetition.

Educators, teachers in particular, are prepared to discover alternative ways of approaching problems. They are admonished to analyze student strengths and weaknesses and to plan instructional programs accordingly. Admittedly, once on the job, many teachers are required to produce in much the same way as industrial workers. Some have suggested that a given amount of academic achievement can and should be produced in each student in a given period of time.

The danger inherent in equating education with business lies in comparing students with automobiles, canned goods, bound books, air conditioners, or nuts and bolts. Nor can teachers be compared with workers skilled in some particular function designed to produce the items listed. Nor can superintendents be viewed as managers of plants where those items are produced by workers with such skills. The human personality, graced as it is with emotions and the power to reason, predict, and choose, cannot be developed in whole or in part as though it claimed the attributes of even the most desirable inanimate object. To pursue a path that leads to appropriate ends for the production of things is to violate all that we claim to value about humankind.

This caution is more than sentimental rambling. It stems from a firm belief in what human beings are and can become. A humanist recently wrote:

> . . . Its faculty is devoted to training students so that the essential knowledge may make them free and generous men and women, so that greater clarity of judgment and argument may make them better workers, so that they may refine their understanding of the subtleties and intricacies of the human mind and heart, and so that they may attain the inner coherence which will make them effective persons.
>
> Humanists know that the quality of a culture depends on the sustained cultivation of sensitivities, of refined taste and sound judgment. . . . to cultivate patiently all that makes man worthy of himself, demands devotion, careful craftsmanship, long patience, self-discipline, and the willing help of all who share this ideal.[8]

Can those of us engaged in the education of children in the elementary school accept less?

REFERENCES

1. Goodlad, J.I., and Anderson, R. H.: The Nongraded Elementary School. New York, Harcourt, Brace and Co., 1959.
2. Ammons, M.P.: Purpose and program. Educational Leadership, 22:15, 1964.
3. Goodlad, J.I., et al.: Behind the Classroom Door. Worthington, Ohio, Charles A. Jones, 1970.
4. Thelen, H.A.: Classroom Grouping for Teachability. New York, John Wiley & Sons, 1967.
5. Bloom, B.S.: The Taxonomy of Educational Objectives. New York, David McKay Co., 1956.
6. Callahan, R.E.: Education and the Cult of Efficiency. Chicago, University of Chicago Press, 1962.
7. Handbook for Planning in the Local School System. Raleigh, North Carolina Department of Public Instruction, 1972.
8. Rosenheim, E.W., Jr.: Nostalgia. Chicago, University of Chicago Press, 1974.

SELECTED READING

Borton, T.: Reach, Touch, Teach. New York, McGraw-Hill, 1970.
Fader, D.: The Naked Children. New York, Macmillan, 1971.
Rasey, M.: It Takes Time. New York, Harper and Brothers, 1953.
Zirbes, L.: Spurs to Creative Teaching. New York. G.P. Putnam & Sons, 1959.

Chapter 2

Physical Education— a Design for Direction

BETTE JEAN LOGSDON

How we perceive physical education and its role in a school curriculum is bonded closely to our broad view of education. Bruner reminds us that the most general objective of education is to cultivate excellence.[1] Excellence in education means helping students, irrespective of capabilities, achieve optimal intellectual development. This thought on optimal development of each child has caused us to expand the domain of education and its general objectives. Having a more comprehensive view of the development of the child, we accept the responsibility to work toward excellence in all three developmental aspects. Education is thus perceived "as affecting the total life and lifestyle of the individual, his motivation system and his physical development, as well as his cognitive enhancement."[2]

What is the role of physical education in a school curriculum? Physical education should comply with the same guidelines that justify the inclusion of any subject area within a school's curriculum. One guideline states: ". . . We might ask, as a criterion for any subject taught in primary school, whether, when fully developed, it is worth an adult's knowing, and whether having known it as a child makes a person a better adult."[1]

We recognize the indisputable merit and meaning of movement in the life of the child. Also, increased and continued research concerning the role of motor activity in relief of tension, as a means of self-expression, and in maintenance of cardiovascular and respiratory efficiency is reawakening us to the value of movement in the life of the adult. Thus, physical education is justifiably placed in the curriculum for the meaning it has to both the child and the adult.

The decisive reasons for including physical education in the elementary school program, however, are its unique content and the experiences it can provide, as well as its capacity for enhancing the total education and the life of the child. Movement has been designated as the content of physical education.[3] Physical education can contribute to the curriculum and thus to the education of the child not only because of its unique content but also because of its capability for elaborating, reenforcing, and applying the concepts, skills, and attitudes initiated in other program areas. Furthermore, its potential for producing educational benefits can be enhanced greatly when its learning environments demonstrate the most rewarding educational practices. *The ultimate significance of physical education in the life and education of the child, however, will be proportionate to the importance that principals, physical educators, and classroom teachers attach to movement— and the extent to which the community expects physical education to contribute to the education of the child.*

PHYSICAL EDUCATION—A PART OF THE CHANGE IN EDUCATION

Elementary schools are changing, and their curricula are beginning to reflect more realistic and humanistic approaches to the child and to teaching. These changes have found their way into all fields—language arts, social studies, science, music, art, mathematics. In fact, most fields have undergone some introspective examination. Our concerns resulting from these critical appraisals have indicated that not only do our curricula in elementary schools need to change but teacher preparation in various areas must undergo change also.

Physical education should come under the same scrutiny as all curricular areas if it is to play a vital role in the education of the child. Its programs are financed by the same budget; its faculty is employed as educators; it is housed in the school curriculum; it is a part of education; it is responsible to the same child. *It therefore must contribute meaningfully to the education of this child, or its existence within the curriculum will be challenged.* We must focus attention on the child. This book has been assembled to aid in scrutinizing the content plus the methodologic and evaluative practices in physical education and to stimulate a greater awareness of physical education as a vital, bonafide part of the educational curriculum for children.

Most physical education programs in the elementary school have remained the same over the years. This situation is reflected by the similarity of materials and teaching approaches that have been the focal point in college courses in elementary school physical education. Since the beginning of teacher preparation in colleges and universities, students have been most discerning in describing the content of these courses. They have labeled them "Kiddie Games" no matter what the catalog description. We could cast it off as jargon of the day and the tendency of college students to abbreviate titles, for example, "Kiddie Lit," "Poli Sci," and "Biz Ad;" however, the evidence, the content of the courses, convinces us otherwise. Both our university courses and the elementary school programs have focused largely on "Kiddie Games." Only minimal attention has been devoted to the study of the child, learning, motor development, movement content, teacher behavior, evaluative processes, and educational goals. Rather, the focus has been on "things to do" at the expense of developing an understanding of the processes involved and an appreciation of why children respond as they do when engaged in activity. Nor has there been much stress on understanding movement, the content that provides the framework for structuring the learning activities. Teacher preparation courses also rarely encourage or prepare teachers to design new learning experiences especially for their children. Little importance has been given to the value of helping children create, select, and organize their own ways of pursuing learning in the physical education setting.

If change is to occur in physical education, it has to be negotiated ultimately by each individual teacher. Therefore, a change must take place first in teacher preparation in physical education if we expect the elementary school curriculum or the teachers to change. This much-needed change is beginning to occur—and it presents an exciting challenge. The amount of change possible in each of us is in direct relationship to our ability to see the need for change in ourselves and not be threatened by what we see. Rather than being threatened, we must be challenged. *True change grows from both a commitment to the need for change and a conviction that teachers can be and will be instruments of change.*

If the last sentence in the preceding paragraph holds no meaning, read it again, and then reflect upon how many times you have heard educators make such statements as: "I believe in individualizing instruction, but I can't incorporate it in my room because I have 30 children." "I know children in the same class read at different levels, but our school does not have sufficient materials to accommodate their needs." "We tried that way of approaching behavior once, but it didn't work." You can add to the list. These excuses maintain the status quo; they are all personal barriers constructed unknowingly to combat change. They sound more like reactions to threats than reponses to a challenge. These comments and similar positions nullify the implementation of needed changes in physical education, too. The model of the excuse is the same, irrespective of the subject area. Almost without exception, the stated or implied idea does not get implemented because the one making the statement lacks either the *commitment* to an idea or the *conviction* that the idea can work. Usually the inferred changes are under double jeopardy because the educator giving the excuse lacks *both* the commitment *and* the conviction.

PHYSICAL EDUCATION DEFINED

What is Physical Education?

Sharing the reasoning that prompted this question seems as important as providing the definition itself. Each person reading this question can offer a definition of physical education in terms that reflect his or her perceptions, and each definition may accurately describe one particular program of physical education. The adequacy of the definition is determined by the degree to which the words reflect the perception and experiences of the one who offers the definition.

This situation brings to mind the familiar episode of the blind men who each touched one part of an elephant. One can see readily that each man's description of an elephant would depend largely on what part of the elephant he touched. Each could be accurate, but none would describe the whole elephant or even the part the other man experienced. Likewise, one's definition of physical education depends largely on a personal point of view. This point of view often indicates how a certain physical education program touched the one offering the definition. Care must be taken, therefore, to emphasize that one definition might not be adequate in describing all points of view. Also all physical education curricula are not the same and therefore should not and cannot be defined in the same terms.

The main purpose for offering a definition of physical education at the outset is to acknowledge openly the distinct point of view of this book. *It defines what physical education could be—it may not define what you have experienced.* The definition provides a direction and establishes the basis for judging the relevancy of subsequent positions to be discussed. The definition that establishes the perspective for this study is as follows:

> **Physical education is that part of movement education which has been designated as a re-** **sponsible, educational program (subject) in a school curriculum.**

One of the key phrases is *responsible, educational program.* This point of view concentrates the discussion on the educational goals and the responsibility of physical education as an educating agent.

Physical educators, laymen, and classroom teachers alike can sometimes be heard advocating the purposes of the physical education program, its reason for being, in clichés that cannot be supported on any educational basis. How often you must have heard: "The purpose of physical education is to have fun." "The children need to let off steam." "They need to get outdoors." We agree that children need outlets and that physical education can be an enjoyable experience with the classes often meeting outside; however, if these aspects represent the chief purposes of physical education and the commanding reasons for including physical education in the curriculum, one does not need professional preparation to provide them or a budget and expensive facilities and equipment to accomplish them. Besides, those who say that classroom teachers and the remaining educational experiences of the curriculum do not afford a change, do not offer opportunities for self-expression, do not take the classroom outdoors, do not bring fun and excitement to learning are indicting all good teachers of any subject, who should thus rise in protest. What is more, if physical education is contributing only entertainment and a change of environment, the taxpayers and curriculum specialists should know it and should take steps to use the teaching space, the time in the schedule, and the money devoted to these programs for better purposes.

Physical education must be supportive of the same basic aims as other curricular areas while contributing uniquely to the education of the child. Fortunately, most children do look upon the experiences in physical education as fun. The teaching station in physical education often does vary from the classroom, and the cardiovascular and respiratory systems of the body are stimulated in physical activity, *but we believe that learning how to learn and dealing with meaningful content must be an integral part of physical education before physical education can be justified in our schools on an educational basis.* Learning how to learn requires the stimulation of thought processes, the pursuit of knowledge, and an interaction with others if children are to live effectively with others and at the same time be comfortable with themselves. Thus, a responsible, educational program implies specific educational obligations.

Movement Education ↔ Physical Education

The term *movement education* was used in the definition to focus attention on both movement education and physical education in order to establish a point of view and to place one in perspective to the other. In the past 30 years, it has become increasingly common either to interchange the terms of movement education and physical education or to think of movement education as an activity, a method, or a small part of the physical education program, especially when discussing the instructional programs in elementary schools. Our definition of physical education purposefully accords a more global meaning to movement education than do those that equate it with physical education or designate it as a method or an activity in the physical education program. *Movement education is a lifelong process of change.* This process of motor development and learning has its beginning in the womb and proceeds through a never-ending series of changes until death. Some of this movement education is the responsibility of an inschool program of instruction called physical education; however, much of movement education occurs before the child enters school and continues after he completes formal schooling.

Attempts to enumerate all motor accomplishments and the learning that has accrued through movement before kindergarten would provide a staggering assembly of learning achievements. No other five years of life can boast of so many motor accomplishments as the first five years. Just as movement education does not begin or end with formal schooling, neither is all movement education during the school years confined to the school setting. Many facets of the environment and society contribute to the movement education of the learner. Human beings, regardless of age, constantly need further movement education or reeducation. They need it to cope both with the physical changes of maturation and aging and with the fluctuating interests

and personal desires related to motor activity. The natural play of children, the trees they climb, their environment, life tasks to be performed, Little Leagues, the accidents or illnesses that impair motor style and require relearning or alteration of motor patterns, the processes of maturation, and many more factors make their impact and are a part of movement education. What is said of movement education versus physical education may be said of most subject areas. Much of any aspect of education is a result of experiences gained outside the confines of the school curriculum.

PHILOSOPHY—GUIDEPOST TO CURRICULUM CONTINUITY

Most of the curricula in our schools have resulted from simple mathematics rather than thoughtful pedagogic deliberation and planning. The structure of most curricula has been achieved by *adding to* or *subtracting from* existing practices. What has resulted is a curricular collage that resembles a patchwork quilt devoid of design and constructed from the historic remnants of former generations. Unlike the household warmed by the patchwork quilt, few school faculties can boast of even one teacher or administrator who knows the origin of each piece of their "curriculum quilt." History has designed the fabric of too many of the elementary school physical education curricula in much the same manner.

In order to provide continuity and purpose in physical education curriculum design, a basic philosophy is needed as a guidepost. This philosophy provides a basis for decision-making relative to all aspects of curriculum development: aims, objectives, program, instructional methods, learning experiences, and evaluation. Each of these aspects must interrelate and radiate from the same philosophic position.

To make the statement that a philosophic position is essential to continuity and purpose in education takes little thought or concerted study. To formulate the philosophy, however, requires both thought and study. What is more challenging, once the philosophy takes form and the ideas are expressed on paper, is the implementation of the philosophy. This aspect requires continued scrutiny and thought-provoking assessment to keep the philosophy vibrant and purposeful as the life-giving, life-sustaining element in curricular decisions. To place the philosophic statements in writing provides both the potential for giving direction to curriculum construction and the basis for honest criticism of the curriculum itself. This criticism can be made either internally, by the one who formulates the philosophy and teaches or by the learner who experiences the curriculum, or externally, by those who observe the practices encompassed within the curriculum.

To fail to present a philosophy would be comparable to setting a ship asail without a rudder or judging a beauty contest with specifications used by horticulturists to select an award-winning rose. *We need the philosophy to set and maintain the course and to evaluate the results in relation to the stated purpose of the curriculum.* Besides requiring thought and study, development of a philosophy has another obstacle—writing. One of the reasons why people shy away from committing their philosophy to paper is its vulnerability for attack by oneself or by others. There is an old saying, "Doing nothing attracts no criticism." Similarly, if we do not commit ourselves pointedly in writing, it is easy to waver back and forth on issues and always be on the comfortable or popular side in any de-

bate. We then can be all things to all people. This indecisiveness, however, is likely to breed discontinuity in our curriculum, and both the child and the curriculum can suffer.

Therefore, sharing a philosophy is essential. It provides the basis for both internal and external criticism and further defines the directions for this particular study on elementary school physical education. While I have formulated this philosophy, I have been influenced greatly by Ammons[4] and Barrett.[5] My ideas have been supported further by a broad collection of writings and experiences gained by interacting with colleagues and others. Thus, this point of view cannot be considered original; rather, it is a collection of the ideas that currently are giving zest to education. I have offered suggestions for additional reading at the end of this chapter in hopes that students and teachers using this book might enjoy a more rewarding experience by reading from some of the original materials that influenced the development of this philosophy.

Many writers have noted that a philosophy is always subject to evaluation and open to change. Therefore, although not establishing my position as permanent, I do hope that the material in succeeding chapters is consistent with this philosophy and that continuity is a recognizable characteristic of this presentation.

Statement of Philosophy

Physical education in the elementary school as discussed in this book is based on the following beliefs:

1. **Students are individuals and their individuality varies from day to day, task to task, and moment to moment.**

2. **Teachers must respect the integrity of the student and accept responsibility for the education of this whole being.**

3. **Teachers need a sincere dedication to each child in order to help all children achieve their full potential by permitting them to become increasingly independent learners.**

4. **Students are capable of making decisions, and education is responsible for helping students develop the ability to make reasoned and wise choices so that they can adjust their role appropriately as their social and physical surroundings change.**

5. **Understandings and skills essential to progression can be developed by students at different times through different experiences.**

6. **Physical education, to share meaningfully in education, must provide experiences that improve the ability to move, that engage thought processes, and that contribute positively to the development of a value system and the esteem in which students regard themselves and others.**

Discussion of the Philosophy

The premise is that, to be a complete guide to curriculum development, this philosophy must include beliefs about the child, learning, education's role in society, and the role of physical education in education.

Students are individuals and their individuality varies from day to day, task to task, and moment to moment. The first belief is founded on what has been studied and learned concerning the individuality of growth and development. Every teacher recognizes the uniqueness of the child. Yet dozens of practices that equate all children and place them into expeditiously tidy groups are the basis for most instructional decisions. For example, chronologic age, which is not a valid determinant of readiness, is often the sole basis for initial admittance to public education. From this arbitrary beginning, the educational system seems predisposed to further decisions that tend to whittle down individual characteristics so that the child will conform to preconceived standards and notions.

The first belief recognizes the individuality of the learner. A curriculum espousing this belief must truly accept the unique characteristics of a child and provide many opportunities for pursuits that nurture individuality rather than stunt uniqueness. Criticism of this belief would involve examining the measure to which the child is treated as an individual and the extent to which the child is challenged and served individually. Yet, we cannot and are not denying that society often requires individual tendencies to merge or be subservient to collective group needs. The relatedness and ambiguity between individual needs and responsibilities related to group membership are challenges of public education. Both the individual and the group must and can be served. In elementary school physical education, however, past focus has been too consistently restricted to collective needs, group participation, group norms, and single models of performance to be achieved by all. Perhaps the inclusion of this belief concerning the uniqueness of the child will bring to the physical education curriculum this requisite balance between group and individual needs.

Teachers must respect the integrity of the student and accept responsibility for the education of this whole being. Fundamental to this belief is an acceptance of the unity of the human being. For years the learner has been divided into three separate parts: mind, body, and soul— or, in educational terms, cognitive, psychomotor, and affective.

> There is no behavior pattern, however intellectual, which does not involve affective factors as motives, but, reciprocally, there can be no affective states without the intervention of perceptions or comprehensions which constitute their cognitive structure. . . . It is precisely this unity of behavior which makes the factors in development common to both the cognitive and the affective aspects.[6]

These words by Piaget and Inhelder should motivate us to avoid dividing children into three separate parts and to accept responsibility for stimulating and integrating their total involvement in physical education. While this reference excludes motor behavior, unity does exist among all three areas of development: cognitive, affective, and psychomotor. Development in any of these three aspects depends in part upon experience, and often the earlier the experience, the better. Therefore, elementary school physical education must provide an environment that stimulates development in all three areas.

For too long and almost to the exclusion of the other two aspects, the major focal point in physical education has been physical involvement. Children have been deprived of planned experiences that involve them, and reward them intellectually and affectively while they are engaged in motor-oriented tasks. To unify the three processes of development in physical education requires close examination of the objectives, the content, and the structure of the learning experiences as well as the methods employed while teaching. This second belief keeps the total development of the child in focus. It also embodies the unique contribution of physical education. Physical education is one of the few curricular areas that can educate the total child without diluting its curricular concerns.

Teachers need a sincere dedication to each child in order to help all children achieve their full potential by permitting them to become increasingly independent learners. The third belief provides the avenue to greater independence in development. If the students remain dependent on the teacher for their development, the teacher's capacity rather than the personal potential and capacity of the children often dictates the boundaries for learning and experiencing. Learning becomes deeply personal for children when they develop independency and are provided the freedom to exercise it. Since much development occurs through experiences, children must have those that nurture independency if independency is to be learned. The shaping of this kind of environment requires special aptitudes and attitudes on the part of the teacher. To realize that all that is worth knowing need not come from the mouth of a teacher or from the printed page of a book is a giant step that some educators find difficult to take.

The thrill of discovery and the joy of individual achievement are the rewards and hallmarks of independent learning. It takes a sensitive, secure teacher who can guide without leading, redirect without constricting, and challenge without threatening. That teacher will be successful in providing experiences fundamental to developing independency in learning. This belief involves constant examination of our methodologic decisions in an effort to strive for more fruitful approaches to a variety of end products of learning in physical education, not the least of these being independent learning.

Students are capable of making decisions, and education is reponsible for helping students develop the ability to make reasoned and wise choices so that they can adjust their roles appropriately as their social and physical surroundings change. This basic philosophic point of view is reflected even in our personal, religious life. Some feel that people do not make choices; rather, the environment preempts the decisions. The Judeo-Christian religion is built on the premise that the human being is a rational being capable of choice. Throughout life one is confronted with a continual chain of events in which choices must be made. True, frequently the alternatives may not be self designed, but the choice often is ours and ours alone. Our individual happiness, our contribution to society, our very being are dependent largely on the choices we make and the skill we have in making the choices. Therefore, if we believe decision-making plays such an important role in life, education must nurture the capacity for making reasoned and wise decisions.

The fourth belief influences the methodologic approaches selected. The extent of its presence within the curriculum is discernible through analyzing the teacher's behavior to see to what degree the decision-making role is shared with the learner. For children to learn to make reasoned and wise choices, they must be placed in situations where choices are theirs to make. Also, they must be able to recognize and weigh the consequences of each choice and learn to live with and be accountable for their choices. Often, teachers find it easier just to let children make choices than to help them accept the responsibility for living with their choices. Perhaps, if we can learn to do the latter also, we can help them make wiser choices based on improved reasoning ability.

Understandings and skills essential to progression can be developed by students at different times through different experiences. The implementation of this belief is closely aligned with the acceptance of the learner as an individual. Its essence is that all children do not have to be engaged in the same learning activity at the same time or in the same way. It further indicates that a common understanding or skill might be acquired by different children through diverse experiences. Thus, the teacher must create avenues for individual pursuits while working toward similar educational objectives. We should examine the frequency with which we attempt to require all children to encounter the same concept through identical processes. The doggedness with which we adhere to lesson plans, schedules, and rigid sequencing to activities should come under scrutiny. Teaching should provide diverse opportunities, cater to different learning abilities, encourage varied interests, and promote a variety of end products. Those harboring this belief recognize the value of individual pursuits as motivating stimuli to genuine and long-lasting learning. This belief, when exercised fully, influences both the learning activities and the methodologic approaches reflected in our teaching.

Physical education, to share meaningfully in education, must provide experiences that improve ability to move, that engage thought processes, and that contribute positively to the development of a value system and the esteem in which students regard themselves and others. Underlying this belief is a fundamental position that, when accepted, provides a perspective for examining the entire physical education curriculum. The position is that physical education shares in the responsibility for total education of the learner. This concept appeared first in the definition of physical education as "*a responsible*, educational program (subject area) in a school curriculum." This belief goes further and reflects the harmony and interrelatedness required among all program areas in the school curriculum. It makes physical education responsible for a meaningful role in the total education of the learner. If put into practice, it should influence educators and the public to perceive physical education in this way. As partners in educating the learner, physical education and other curricular areas must pursue their goals jointly, so discontinuity or inconsistency in relating to the learner can be kept at a minimum. Physical education, although educating largely through the medium of movement, must share in stimulating the cognitive processes. It, too, must provide children with experiences which help to develop a value system that will help them achieve respect for themselves and for others.

This belief, which addresses physical education as part of the educational experience, should not only cause close examination of both the teaching approaches and the learning activities but also raise the question and provide the answer regarding the real purpose of physical education. Those who believe that the purposes of recess and recreation are synonymous with those of physical education cannot subscribe to this belief. **Recess and recreation, though extremely important in the life of the child, do not have the same function as physical education and therefore do not fulfill the same developmental and educational needs of the child.**

As stated earlier, it is relatively easy to write a philosophic position; the difficulty lies in trying to live up to it and keep it operant while developing a curriculum and working daily with children. No part of curriculum design or implementation should fail to be influenced by the basic tenets on which the philosophy is built. **Therefore, the philosophy should influence decisions relevant to**

1. **Formulating objectives and goals.**
2. **Developing the program.**
3. **Designing the learning experiences.**
4. **Selecting methodologic approaches used to stimulate learning.**

5. **Delineating the roles and responsibilities of the teacher and the student.**
6. **Evaluating the program, instruction, and learning.**

If this philosophy guides our deliberations, our practices are consistent with our beliefs. If we fail, the value of our efforts in the following chapters are reduced.

GOALS DESCRIBE ASPIRATIONS

Just as a statement of philosophy guides us in our broad curricular decisions, specific goals of a particular subject area are essential in defining our directions. Goals, rather than fixing the perimeters of a program, describe aspirations that should be pursued constantly. Perhaps those who share continually in the pursuit of goals are always in a state of becoming. While there may be no end to learning, there are plateaus of attainment that are self-evident and self-fulfilling and sometimes frustrating. These plateaus make the pursuit of excellence in any field and the constant state of becoming both rewarding and challenging.

Ask yourself the question, "When is a person educated?" The struggle involved in determining the answer is typical of the dilemma in responding to the inquiry, "When is a person *physically* educated?" Neither of these processes is ever finished; there is always more to learn, to achieve, to know, to become. As you read the brief list of goals of physical education, you should perceive readily that these goals are not attainable in the six or seven years usually designated for elementary school education.

GOALS OF PHYSICAL EDUCATION

The goals of physical education are reflective of the three areas of human development: the psychomotor, the affective, and the cognitive. The combined goals prescribe the commitment that physical education has to the education of the total child. Each level—elementary, secondary, and college—can contribute to the attainment of these goals.

Honoring this strong commitment to the total education of the child, we therefore establish that physical education should provide experiences that improve the ability of the learner to

1. **Move skillfully, demonstrating versatile,**

effective, and efficient movement in situations requiring either planned or unplanned responses.

2. Become aware of the meaning, significance, feeling, and joy of movement both as a performer and as an observer.

3. Gain and apply the knowledge that governs human movement.

Discussion of the Goals

Two words in the first goal hold the greatest meaning for the directions we are suggesting in physical education: **versatile** and **unplanned.** Versatility implies having many aptitudes, moving with ease. This word has been selected to bring curricular attention to the need for developing a variety of movement aptitudes along with depth in skill proficiency. Closely associated with versatility is the phrase, **unplanned responses.** Responsibility is hereby focused on developing ways that educate children to cope with the *unexpected in movement situations rather than educate them to rely heavily on predetermined, prescribed motor responses.* Close examination of almost any motor activity shows a special need for versatility and for the ability to move in unpredictable, unplanned ways. **This goal clearly delineates skill development as a goal of physical education.** It goes beyond rote teaching of skills, drills, and stunts and focuses on helping children acquire the facility for varying their movements to meet the needs of the situation.

The *second goal concentrates on the kinesthetic and aesthetic aspects to dictate a direction that requires the expressive, affective characteristics of movement as programmatic goals.* Historically, the greater part of our physical education programs have focused on movement experiences that are function oriented. In other words, most movement taught in physical education is performed to satisfy a functional purpose; for examples, we teach children to move to tag a runner, to catch a ring, to strike a ball. Rarely do we dwell on the feeling created inside the body as the movement is being performed or the attitudes about themselves or movement being developed within them as they move. Even fewer experiences have been provided to nurture the child's ability for using movement as a means of expressing ideas or communicating

with others. This second goal attempts to balance the functional with the expressive and to capitalize on the humanizing effect of affective learning, which can and should be an important part of physical education. For too long, we have reserved this expressive aspect of education in physical education for older secondary school and college students who enroll in dance. Often, only a select few elect to take dance; therefore most people have little experience with the expressive aspect of movement. We should strive to fill this void. Since movement is the young child's first means of communication, expressive movement should have a place in the elementary school physical education program. Dance is the program area that focuses on expressive movement. Therefore, the instructional program in the elementary school should be designed with rather equal emphasis on all three program areas—dance, gymnastics, and games.

The *third goal recognizes the existence of knowledge that can and should be taught, elaborated, and applied in the physical education setting.* We need to give priority to the involvement of the intellect and the acquisition of knowledge and the development of values. Again, traditionally the focus in physical education has been on *doing* rather than on *thinking, knowing, feeling, expressing,* and *doing.*

The consistency within a program is based on the degree to which the practices are in line with its goals. A program to be consistent with these goals must share its learning activities among experiences that nurture all three aspects of learning: cognitive, affective, and psychomotor.

Conviction and Commitment Essential to Achieving Goals

Stating a philosophy that may represent a different approach and establishing meaningful goals are not enough to ensure change in our physical education programs or in any other subject area. These two features must be accompanied by an inner drive to implement the philosophy, thereby compelling us to seek ways to contribute toward achieving the goals. This drive, to be dynamic, persistent, and productive, develops from acquiring and aspiring to certain basic beliefs. Beliefs are the preamble to conviction and commitment—the two essentials if goals are to be realized. Beliefs nurture the desire to accept challenges, to work, to grow, to make the personal sacrifices and take the professional risks that are often a part of change, and to keep searching for greater avenues of fulfillment. One of the biggest deterrents to improvement or change in education is that the route is always made to appear too easy. Oversimplification causes those who could benefit most to flout the need for study, assessment, practice, reevaluation,and reeducation, which are all so much a part of genuine, personal change. Thus, teachers often attempt changes with insufficient background. When they fail, they blame the inadequacies of the new approach or content rather than their own lack of skill, knowledge, and awareness for implementing the new ideas.

In education, it is difficult to make a radical change in what we are doing unless we examine carefully what we are doing and why we do things the way we do. Beliefs, if clear to the believer, can help to provide the stamina needed to become involved in being an instrument of change. "Since what we believe does tend to influence our practice,"[2] we will be more effective practitioners if we know what we believe. Sometimes at the start the end may not be discernible, but if believing exists, a beginning is possible. With a beginning, the probability is improved for continued advancement toward a goal.

The following beliefs about physical education have created a beginning for some who perceive physical education as a responsible, educational subject area.

1. **Physical education must be compatible with and demonstrative of the most desirable practices in education.**

2. **Our teaching approaches should be selected or developed on the basis of our understanding of children, the way they learn, and the purpose for which the content was selected.**

3. **Developing the personal movement potential of children has great value for their total lives.**

4. **The developmental phases of the life cycle are experienced uniquely by each child.**

5. **Movement is the content of physical education.**

6. **Knowledge, attitudes, and motor ability can be developed, strengthened, and applied in the study of movement.**

7. **Observation is central to the process of teaching movement since it makes the teacher aware of both the needs and the accomplishments of the learner.**

8. **Evaluation should be ongoing, and it should be process and product oriented, focused on all aspects of the curriculum as well as on the learner.**

It is possible to develop a commitment to these beliefs or others early in your study. Commitment will occur when you understand why beliefs are formulated and when you can visualize how beliefs relate to your personal point of view, to the aims of education, and to the specific goals and purposes of a subject area. A conviction will often be strengthened when your beliefs are supported in the literature. Also, your commitment can mature faster if you are fortunate enough to be able to observe teachers with similar beliefs working with children. Perhaps genuine enthusiasm for basic beliefs will be reserved for those who have a continuing opportunity to grow in their ability to implement beliefs while personally teaching children.

The purpose of this book, then, is to help

create a commitment and to stimulate a maturing conviction. If possible, we want to arouse your desire to be involved enthusiastically in a personal examination and expression of these beliefs as you receive, seek, and find opportunities to test and implement the ideas while working with children. Your point of view of physical education depends on what happens to you and within you in this process of teaching children and also depends on the nature of the beliefs, convictions, commitments, abilities, and enthusiasm that you develop or accept as your own.

Product Versus Product-Process

Learning how to learn reflects methodology and the way we teach. How we teach, i.e., the methods we employ, should be based on what we believe about learning and the child. The way the learner is approached in physical education should be compatible with and demonstrative of the most fruitful practices in education. Too frequently, our approaches more nearly parallel excerpts from the manuals of master drill sergeants or obedience schools for dogs. With cadences to be maintained, drills to be performed, tricks to be learned, and commands to be obeyed as the focal point of our teaching style, we should not wonder why physical education for many has been a scourge and a plague rather than an educational experience.

Many physical education programs, both past and present, are highly product oriented. With the chief focus resting on products, heavy emphasis is placed on specific skills to be learned, drills to be mastered, stunts to be performed, games to be played, and dances to be danced— each of which are *products* of learning in physical education. What is more, these skills, drills, stunts, games,, and dances have frequently been prestructured with the same end products in mind for all students. With the focus on rather singular end products, insufficient concern has been directed toward the individuality of the learner or toward the development of attitudes and thought processes that should be a part of physical education.

We hope our commitment is based on the belief that physical education can and should be more process oriented, and should provide both individually meaningful and group-stimulating products as viable outcomes of the learning experiences. With the focus shared by both product and process, methods must be selected or developed on the basis of their capacity to stimulate the thought processes and to involve the inner affective qualities of the learners as well as their potential for accommodating the development of motor-oriented end products. This plea for increased concern for processes in the teaching of physical education is supported by research on good and poor teachers. Good teachers are "characterized by broad rather than narrow purposes, seeking to free their students rather than to control them, and concerned with processes rather than ends in their teaching."[7] Both processes and products are critical in achieving fulfillment in education. One without the other can be a dulling experience, and the

result is an unrewarding venture for both the teacher and the learner.

Knowledge About Children and Learning— Basis for Method Selection

For years, lip service has been given to desirable teaching approaches, with unsatisfactory results. Many will expound the ideals of educating the whole child—learning by doing, development of critical thinking, self-actualization, independency in learning, role sharing, personalized learning. Physical education has contributed its fair share to the mounting volumes in these and associated topics. The time has come for more people to face the issue: are we willing to try to practice what we preach? The time of accountability, of humaneness in education is upon us. We need to examine carefully the theories to which we aspire. Then we must get more of our practices in line with our thoughtfully selected theories.

This discussion leads to still another basic commitment. The belief about teaching is that our approaches should be based on what we know about children, how children learn, and what specific children need. We must learn to create the most desirable climates for learning and to create different environments for different children participating in the same class. The type of learning, as well as the quality of learning, is predetermined in part by the methods used in teaching and the environments we create for learning. Sensitive selection of methods has to precede empathetic implementation for gratifying educational experiences to be developed. It has been said that "the teacher does not teach an 'average' or a 'uniform' child, but rather different individuals who vary in terms of their academic potential, personality, and learning styles."[8]

We know that no two children are alike, but how quickly we forget. "Second graders don't do . . ." "Girls shouldn't play . . ." "Mary, I'm surprised; your sister could . . ." "Five-year-olds can . . ." "He's 9 months old and he doesn't . . ." "She's 3 and she still . . ." Teething, pottie training, starting to school, promotion in Sunday school—all children are swooped up and categorized unsuspectingly as if all children were programmed by the same master computer. What is so incomprehensible but true is that, with all our knowledge about individual human growth and development, the lives of children are still full of these computerized boxes that teachers and adults expect them to fit. The child screams out, "But I am me; please, just let me be me. Me with me . . . and nobody else. I can come along; I can learn. Don't push—just help me where I am today." But nobody listens . . . but we can . . . and must.

Study of the child with special emphasis on motor development has great implications for teaching movement. Understanding developmental patterns, being able to analyze and recognize them and to know how they may differ from child to child can be used effectively in teaching children to move. To interpret this information about children and their development on an individual basis while working with children is of paramount importance if the individuality of the child is to receive more than lip service. This concept leads to another commitment that will influence future discussions: while the developmental phases of the life cycle are relatively constant, each child has a unique time schedule through this cycle.

Movement—The Content of Physical Education

Most areas of study, each discipline, in the school curriculum have identifiable content, a body of knowledge, that is associated with them. Movement has been singled out as the common content fundamental to the study of physical education. Basic to the study of human movement are two separate but highly interrelated bodies of knowledge: the laws of motion that govern human movement and the facts associated with the application of mechanical principles[9] and the components of movement—effort, body, space, and relationships—the aspects that together describe and categorize movement and define the qualitative and quantitative aspects of human effort. The former stems from physics, the latter from interpretations of the ideas expressed by Laban.[10]

Both of these bodies of knowledge complement the other and demand concerted study if the full significance of movement is to be realized and understood. The former furnishes the student and teacher with the technical aspects of the knowledge associated with human movement, while the latter contributes knowledge that is helpful in perceiving the individual characteristics of movement and provides a system for the classification of movement. The two combined help to totalize and unify the study of movement, the content of physical education, irrespective of whether the movement is expressive and associated with dance, or functional and a part of gymnastics, games, or aquatics. Morison implies that the study of the components of motion and the mechanical laws helps us to think and observe in a "movement way."

> Experience of movement and a growing awareness and understanding gives people an extra "tool" with which they can "learn to learn." A teacher who understands the basic principles of movement, and who can think and observe in a movement way, is better able to help people to tackle the tasks confronting them, and so enable them to do as they wish, in the way they wish. Through encouraging this personal and individual way, people gain skill and progress is made.[11]

A commitment to movement as the content of physical education permeates this entire study. Through the study of movement, the child grows in awareness. Thought processes, motor and attitudinal development all can be nurtured, stimulated, challenged, strengthened—educated through the study of movement when the study involves personal experiences in movement. The more personally meaningful we can make these movement experiences, the greater the effect physical education will have in the education of today's children. The greater meaning the physical education environment has for the individuality of children, the more they experience the freedom from threat and the greater opportunity they have to achieve and appreciate their full potential in their pursuit of excellence in the mastery of movement.

OBSERVATION—ESSENTIAL SKILL IN TEACHING

Pursuing personal potential in any area is made easier if we know how to learn. Learning how to learn requires active participation in the teaching-learning process by the teacher and the learner alike. Both must develop abilities to share meaningfully in the teaching-learning process. One of the tools that is central to the teaching and learning of movement is observation. Sensitivity and skill in observation are perhaps the most essential keys to teaching physical education. Ease of learning in physical education will be largely based on the teachers' knowledge of the movement content and their ability to observe the responses of children. Observation skill must be based on knowledge of the individual child, the developmental phases of motor development, and the movement content being taught. Observation is the channel that keeps the teacher attuned to both the needs of the learners and their accomplishments.

Observation provides a means to (1) determine content, (2) receive input for instructional insights, and (3) collect data essential to evaluating student-teacher behavior. When the observational skills of the teacher are fully functioning, they play an exciting part in a perpetuating circuit that is created and maintained between the teacher and the learner. In this circuit, the response of the learner becomes the stimulus to the teacher, whose response in turn becomes the stimulus to the learner. Successful communication along this circuit requires both parties to be tuned in. When the learner and the teacher are tuned in to each other, both play two roles: student and teacher—they learn from each other and they teach each other. When either the child or the teacher tunes out, the channel of interdependency in the teaching-learning process is blocked. As a result, the teacher does not teach and the learner does not learn.

Skill in observation, like most desirable qualities of teaching and learning, does not happen overnight and does not occur just because the teacher or the learner recognizes its importance. It, like most skills, has to be based on knowledge, and this knowledge must be applied, practiced, and refined. Courses that teach teachers how to teach any subject, especially physical education, should focus on activities that engage the teacher-to-be in developing and utilizing observation skills. Also, observation is a time-honored means of learning to move and, therefore, is a desirable skill for children to develop, too. This book will continue to stress the role of observation in the teaching and learning of movement because that role is part of the central plan for this book. Since movement is the content of physical education, teachers of that subject must know movement, must be able to observe movement, and must be able to articulate what they have seen in order to facilitate learning through and about movement. Similarly, the observation skills of children need to be developed if all of their faculties are to be used and sharpened in learning.

Value in Evaluation

Evaluation in physical education should be and mean far more than just grading the children. This belief is basic to the view that extends beyond the more familiar summative forms of testing motor skill performance and arriving at a grade in physical education. The emphasis placed on individuality in this philosophy necessitates formative assessment techniques that can be applied frequently and individually to provide instant feedback to the children as they work. Also, because physical education is responsible for the education of the whole child, our evaluative efforts should embrace all three aspects of development—psychomotor, affective, and cognitive. Part of our dilemma in trying to make this belief operative as we teach is the dearth of valid techniques for assessing some of the important objectives in education and in physical education. The following statement by Gordon focuses on one area that lacks sufficient measurement techniques.

> One of the problems is a lack of adequate assessment techniques in the area of self-concept. Virtually all studies pay lip-service to the notion that, either indirectly through some sort of warm environment setting or the improvement of skill, or directly through some forms of affect training which grow out of analytic or encounter orientations, self-concept will be enhanced. Unfortunately, measurement is inadequate.[12]

Combs warns us, "Measuring what we know how to measure is no satisfactory substitute for measuring what we *need* to measure."[7] We must extend our efforts to develop better ongoing assessment techniques and learn to use assessment more broadly rather than focus all our measurement efforts on motor performance . . . the one area in which we know best how to measure. Also, we have overemphasized assessment of the child. We, the teachers, need to devote more time to evaluative techniques that would give us insights about our teaching behavior as well as our program. Perhaps there we will find answers to the reason why, in physical education, ". . . many of the boys and a clear majority of the girls are simply confirmed in their ineptitude. Turned away from the potentialities of their own bodies . . ." as Leonard believes.[13]

Almost any commitment in education requires dedication to make it operative in a curriculum. This need for assessing the behavior of the teacher and the program demands a special kind of perseverance to implement, since both aspects require us to examine our own efforts. Assessing our teaching behavior, if we believe what the results show, persists in making us "see ourselves as others see us" and should help us to keep our practices more in line with our beliefs. It helps put the emphasis in reform where it is needed most . . . on the teacher . . . where change has to start if change in physical education is to occur.

SUMMARY

A concerted attempt has been made to outline and share a specific point of view about physical education—its meaning, its goals, a philosophy to give direction, and beliefs to stimulate and give vitality to commitment and conviction. Since each of us is largely the product of our experiences—and our experiential backgrounds are as varied as the makeup of our genetic structure—no two of us will be the same kind of teacher. We respond differently, we express ourselves differently, we place the emphasis on different objectives—we individualize and personalize our approach to teaching and to living. To a large degree, all teachers ultimately reflect a point of view that is theirs. As you read, contemplate, and perhaps implement some of these ideas, we hope you will find personal meaning in some of the information that has been shared. "Any piece of information will have its effect upon behavior in the degree to which an individual discovers its personal meaning."[14]

Learning, thereby, has been defined as the discovery of personal meaning. To this end, we hope the book is helpful; it is if you discover personally the meaning of physical education as an educational experience for children. We do not want to narrow your point of view but to expand it so that **you will require, expect, obligate physical education to assume an effective,** **unmitigating educational role in the elementary school curriculum.**

To attain compete unanimity in thought and practice, we would have to fill the same moccasins, walk the same mile, be the same person. This we accept as impossible, but I find it even fortunate, because we grow, question, and learn by being able to share varied experiences. Much evidence, however, indicates a need to rally our efforts and collectively direct our pursuits toward improving physical education for the common and total good of the child.

. . . but the GREATEST OF THESE IS CHARITY.

One theologian has interpreted "charity" in these words by St. Paul not to mean almsgiving, as it is thought, but communion, experiential rapport, common consent, and understanding. When we see the current need for better communication, communion, and rapport, it is easy to see why charity, thus defined, becomes "greatest."[15] These thoughts by Earl C. Kelley were also supported by further words from his original source, "Knowledge puffeth up, but charity edifieth." As teachers, to know, to understand, to believe, to be committed ourselves is not enough. We must communicate with others and develop a common cause that focuses on improving physical education if we are going to help each child find greater meaning in movement.

REFERENCES

1. Bruner, J.S.: The Process of Education. Cambridge, Harvard University Press, 1960.
2. Gordon, I.J.: On Early Learning: The Modifiability of Human Potential. Washington, D.C., Association for Supervision and Curriculum Development, NEA, 1971.
3. Barrett, K.R.: Learning to move ↔ moving to learn: a discussion at the crossroads. Theory into Practice, 12:109, 1973.
4. Ammons, M.: Communications: a curiculum focus. In A Curriculum for Children. Edited by A. Frazier. Washington, D.C., Association for Supervision and Curriculum Development, NEA, 1969.
5. Barrett, K.R.: I wish I could fly—a philosophy in motion. In Contemporary Philosophies of Physical Education and Athletics. Edited by R.A. Cobb and P.M. Lepley. Columbus, Ohio, Charles E. Merrill, 1973.
6. Piaget, J., and Inhelder, B.: The Psychology of the Child. New York, Basic Books, 1969.

7. Combs, A.W.: Educational Accountability: Beyond Behavioral Objectives. Washington, D.C., Association for Supervision and Curriculum Development, NEA, 1972.
8. Shumsky, A.: In Search of Teaching Style. New York, Appleton-Century-Crofts, 1968.
9. Broer, M.R., and Zernicke, R.F.: Efficiency of Human Movement, 4th ed. Philadelphia, W.B. Saunders Co., 1979.
10. Laban, R.: The Mastery of Movement, 3rd ed. revised by L. Ullman. Boston, Plays, Inc., 1971.
11. Morison, R.: A Movement Approach to Educational Gymnastics. London, J. M. Dent & Sons, 1969.
12. Gordon, I.J.: On Early Learning: The Modifiability of Human Potential. Washington, D.C., Association for Supervision and Curriculum Development, NEA, 1972.
13. Leonard, G.: Why Johnny can't run. Atlantic Monthly, 236:55, 1975.
14. Combs, A.W.: Personality theory and its implications for curriculum development. In Learning More about Learning. Edited by A. Frazier. Papers and Reports from the Third ASCD Research Institute. Washington, D.C., Association for Supervision and Curriculum Development, NEA, 1959.
15. Kelley, E.C.: Education for What Is Real. New York, Harper & Row, 1947.

SELECTED READING

Association for Supervision and Curriculum Development, Perceiving, Behaving, Becoming, 1962 Yearbook. Washington, D.C., NEA, 1962.

Association for Supervision and Curriculum Development, A New Look at Progressive Education, 1972 Yearbook. Washington, D.C., NEA, 1972.

Ammons, M.: Communication: a curriculum focus. In A Curriculum for Children. Edited by A. Frazier. Washington, D.C. Association for Supervision and Curriculum Development, NEA, 1969.

Barrett, K.R.: Learning to move ↔ moving to learn: a discussion at the crossroads. Theory into Practice, 12:109, 1973.

Barrett, K.R.: I wish I could fly—a philosophy in motion. In Contemporary Philosophies of Physical Education and Athletics. Edited by R.A. Cobb and P.M. Lepley. Columbus, Ohio, Charles E. Merrill, 1973.

Bruner, J.S.: The Process of Education. Cambridge, Harvard University Press, 1960.

Holt, J.: How Children Fail. New York, Pitman, 1964.

Kelley, E.C.: Education for What Is Real. New York, Harper & Row, 1947.

Rogers, C.R.: Freedom to Learn. Columbus, Ohio, Charles E. Merrill, 1969.

Chapter 3

Developing Children—Their Changing Movement

A Guide for Teachers

MARY ANN ROBERTON
LOLAS E. HALVERSON

As parents or teachers, most of us recognize that a program of movement experiences can be beneficial for children. Yet, when we turn to textbooks or guides for help in knowing what kinds of experiences are possible, we must always read with specific children in mind. Are they ready for this experience? How will they react? How will we know if their movement and self-confidence are improving or suffering from a particular practice? Whether we are teachers in formal programs or parents providing informal experiences, all our decisions should stem from where we think children are in their development. A working knowledge of child development, with particular emphasis on motor development, forms the basis for intelligently teaching motor skills to children.

CONCEPTS OF LEARNING AND DEVELOPMENT

Many words imply behavioral or structural change in living organisms over time. Anthropologists study *evolution,* the changes measured across generations. Some psychologists and biologists study *development,* the change within an individual's life span or during several years of that life span. Other psychologists study *learning,* a change within an individual that is measured over days or weeks. Thus, evolution, development, and learning all have similar meanings. We shall distinguish between them only in terms of (1) the time span over which the change is studied (generations, years, days) and (2) the unit showing the change (across individuals, within individuals). Teachers are interested in children's daily changes (learning) that promote long-term progress (development).

Behavioral or structural change is the result of interactions between a child and the environment. Learning and development do not occur solely through features within the individual (as the old term "maturation" implied) or through features solely outside the individual. Rather, they result from the unique coincidence of each acting upon the other. For example, children cannot learn to throw forcefully without an object to throw and without practice in throwing it; however, the presence of that environmental stimulus, even practice with it, does not ensure that children will change their way of throwing. Instead, they may change the object or the task to fit their present throwing behavior, or they may choose to ignore the stimulus entirely. A child's nervous system and mental state must be "ready" for change. The child must then encounter the proper experience for her particular level. Only this unique circle of interaction between the child and the environment will result in learning.

How to detect a child's internal state of readiness and how to determine which environmental experiences will interact with that state are still unknown. We can only say that readiness at any given moment is the result of all the interactions that have formed the child, i.e., readiness is the child's current state of development. We can begin to detect this internal state only by observing the child's outward behavior.

Although we cannot change children's sex, genes, endocrine systems, or past interactions, we can give them many opportunities for acting upon and being acted upon by their environment. We can try to sequence these encounters or help the children sequence them as a result of the behaviors we see. In this fashion, we use children's present readiness as a guide for building their future readiness.

THE TEACHER AS OBSERVER, INTERPRETER, DECISION-MAKER

We have defined learning as the change resulting from a circle of interaction between the child and the environment. Although no teacher is needed to produce learning, teaching occurs when a second person enters the circle as (1) an observer, (2) an interpreter, and (3) a decision-maker.

The teacher first *observes* what the environment demands: what must the child do to succeed at the task being attempted? The teacher then observes what the child is doing in response to that task and how it is being done.

After making these observations, the teacher must *interpret* them. What is the meaning of a child's solution to a particular movement problem? Does it indicate a more advanced form of movement? Does it suggest improved perceptual functioning? Is the solution a cognitive attempt to avoid a balance-threatening position? Does the child's response suggest that the task is too stressful, too complex at that particular moment—that the child is not "ready" for it?

Having interpreted these observations, the teacher then *decides* what to do. Should he take an active role by intervening, or leave the child and the environment alone? If he decides to intervene, in what way should he do so? Should he redesign the physical environment or verbally coach the child or show a possible solution?

After the teacher intervenes or does not intervene, the cycle repeats itself. The teacher again *observes* the child and the environment, *interprets* what is seen in order to evaluate the earlier decision, and makes a new *decision*. Clearly, the soundness of this cyclic approach to teaching depends on the accuracy of both the teacher's observation skills and the interpretation of those observations in terms of developmental progress.

DEVELOPING CHILDREN—SIMILAR BUT UNIQUE

Every child has a sense of "wholeness," a sense of uniqueness, a sense of "me" that remains even as the child continually changes. Children are developing wholes, but within the whole is a pattern interwoven from many strands. At any moment, children are a product of all the changes that have occurred within all parts of their "biopsychology": within their muscle and skeletal systems, their endocrine systems, their nervous systems.

Each of these action systems has its own course of development. Each system proceeds on this course at a different rate. The complex pattern created by the separate developmental levels of all the systems at any given instant comprises the individual child at that point in time. For this reason, every child is unique; in no two children would all aspects of development arrive at the same point at the same time. The special pattern created by the individual action systems within each child, the "me" of that child, clearly supports the adage, "The whole is greater than the sum of its parts."

STAGES OF DEVELOPMENT

Human beings do have a common biopsychologic substrate and environments that are more alike than different. It is logical, therefore, that across the spectrum of uniqueness we should see similarities in development. Each biopsychologic system of the body tends to develop in much the same way across individuals. Sometimes, this common development is charted in "stages." A stage describes a characteristic way of behaving within an action system that is noticeably different from previous or later ways of behaving. These stages are sequenced according to their order of appearance in most individuals. The levels of each sequence form a developmental continuum across the life span.

Since each system proceeds along its continuum at different rates in different people, development is not age-determined. Five years of environment-child interactions will have produced different rates of development in Jim than in Carl. The sequence of stages will be the same for both children, but one child will have passed through more stages within a given action system than did the other child; he will be further along the continuum within that system.

Knowledge of developmental stages provides the teacher with a way to interpret observations of the children whose learning circle has been entered. It is a way to categorize and thus organize the learnings seen. The teacher interprets these observations in terms of the child's progress along the child's own continuum. Each individual's behavior represents "more" or "less" advancement in development. In addition, by knowing stage characteristics, the teacher can better plan experiences to facilitate the child's further development as well as to broaden and enrich that child's encounters at the child's present stage of development.

Looking at one child's behavior in relation to stage sequences that are based on similarities across many children does not ignore the uniqueness of that particular "whole" child. Rather, it provides a way to unravel the pattern of multiple action-system change that makes the child unique. This approach allows the child to be treated as an individual, since it gives the teacher the information necessary to make sound decisions about intervening in that child's learning process. Knowing stage sequences is the first step toward individualizing instruction.

OVERVIEW OF THE DEVELOPING CHILD

The following sections give a selective overview of a few of the biopsychologic systems developing within the child. Since the primary responsibility of the physical education teacher is to promote motor development, that system is discussed in detail later. Children, however, bring their entire selves to the gymnasium, so the teacher of movement needs to recognize and encourage development in all parts of those selves. The research and theories cited have been chosen to provide the "flavor" of current thinking about human development, thinking that stresses the dynamic interactions between actively exploring children and their personal world.

COGNITIVE DEVELOPMENT

Recent research on children's cognitive development has been stimulated by the theories of Jean Piaget.[1] One of Piaget's major contributions has been to demonstrate that children's thinking is *qualitatively different* from that of adults. In addition to differing in the amount of information they possess about the world (a quantitative difference), children and adults also differ in the way they use or understand that information. Following are examples:

If one pours the contents of a transparent beaker of water (A) into another transparent beaker (B) which is taller but narrower, a child under approximately 6 years of age will insist that since the water in B is higher than it was in A, it has increased in amount. Even when the child himself does the pouring and knows no water has been added or subtracted, he is unable to *conserve substance;* that is, to see that although the water has undergone a transformation in height and width, it is the same amount of water.

At age 7 or 8, however, the child readily agrees that the amount of water has stayed the same. The child now conserves substance just as an adult. He will not conserve weight, however, until age 9 or 10; nor volume until age 11 or 12.[1]

An adult places 5 red poker chips in a row on a table. Right below them in another row she places 5 blue poker chips. After that, she asks a 5- or 6-year-old which row has more chips. The child will count, then say the two rows are the same. The adult now spaces the blue chips farther apart so that the blue row is longer than the red row. She asks the child again which row has more chips. The child will now assure the adult that more chips are in the blue row. Again, by age 7 or 8 that same child will just as strongly maintain that the number of chips did not change even though their spacing did.[1]

Young children are also unable to reason simultaneously about wholes and parts. A teacher shows a 5-year-old a group of poker chips, most of which are red and a few of which are blue.

If he asks the child, "Are there more chips or more red chips?" the child will say there are more red chips. The teacher then asks the child to sort yellow or red squares and yellow or red circles into separate piles of yellow squares, yellow circles, red squares, and red circles. She will be unable to do so. She can sort circles from squares, or red objects from yellow objects, but she cannot mentally combine the two classes to form a sorting rule.

Piaget has also pointed out that language usage and mental development are not synonymous. Children use many words in their everyday conversation that they do not understand in the adult sense. A 6-year-old defines a brother as "a boy who lives in my house."[2] Not until that child is in fourth or fifth grade will he understand the kinship relation implied by the word.

Piaget's Stages of Cognitive Development

From his study of the different cognitive operations exhibited by children as they grow older, Piaget hypothesized four major stages of cognitive development:

STAGE 1. SENSORIMOTOR INTELLIGENCE. This earliest level of intellectual development occurs prior to the child's ability to use symbols, e.g., language. Infants "know" the world only as they act upon it. During this stage, objects gradually acquire a permanence, so that the child continues to search for them if they disappear. Gradually, the child also generalizes motor patterns to accomplish new ends, first fortuitously and then purposefully.

STAGE 2. PREOPERATIONAL INTELLIGENCE. When about 2 years of age, children begin to acquire the use of symbols. They start to imitate past occurrences, recognize forms in their scribbles, and use language. Thus, the period from approximately 2 to 7 years of age is a time of movement away from external action toward internal representation. It is a dramatic change from infancy but still a long way from adult thinking. Preoperational children do not realize there are points of view other than their own. They are animistic, attributing life and consciousness to all moving objects, such as the sun and wind. Since their thinking is not organized according to logical rules, they tend to perform as did the children in the preceding examples from Piagetian research.

STAGE 3. CONCRETE OPERATIONAL IN-TELLIGENCE. From about 7 to 11 years of age, children acquire the ability to conserve, to see the relationship between parts and wholes (class inclusion), to form a mental representation of a series of actions, and to order or seriate objects according to different dimensions. These mental operations occur gradually as children develop "reversibility"—the ability to employ mentally the logically meaningful opposite of a given action (adding-subtracting, uniting-separating). As these mental operations occur with experience, they generalize to further concepts. Not until age 12, however, does a child's thinking begin to acquire adult characteristics.

STAGE 4. FORMAL OPERATIONAL INTELLIGENCE. The major characteristic of adolescent and adult thinking is its separation from the concrete and present. Adolescents can deal with hypotheses rather than being limited to concrete observations. They can also use "if-then" and "either-or" propositions. Young children use those words but do not understand their logical implications. Adolescent thinking, in short, resembles formal problem-solving or scientific thinking; it is logical and systematic. The adolescent and adult are also able to think about thought itself: to step aside and view themselves and their ideas from the perspective of another person.

Piaget called the impetus for progression through these stages an *equilibration process*, a continual balance and imbalance between two child-environment actions, assimilation and accommodation. In *assimilation* children incorporate the environment into their present mental structure; they generalize, rightly or wrongly, what they already "know." In *accommodation*, they change their mental structure to better match the environment. Thus, in assimilation, children fit the environment to their view; in accommodation, children change to fit the environment. Movement through stages is theoretically caused by the continual tension between these two processes.

Teaching Implications

Human movement has often been used by both classroom teachers and physical educators as an active means to develop a cognitive concept. It is more meaningful (and fun) to build circles, roll circles, run through, around, and over circles than simply to discuss circles. A problem, however, can occur if it becomes more prestigious in the physical educator's mind to help children learn "through movement" than "just" to help them learn to move. By becoming only another means of reinforcing classroom activities, many well-intentioned physical education programs have lost their emphasis on learning to move efficiently and joyfully, which is their uniqueness in the school curriculum. The well-balanced program, on the other hand, contributes to classroom goals, but retains its unique emphasis on promoting motor development for its own sake.

Thus, the classroom teacher ought to encourage cognitive growth through movement-centered cognitive activities; the teacher of movement, however, will primarily use cognitive developmental information to help children improve and understand their own movement. The equilibration theory, for instance, describes the general environment for developing an intellectual understanding of the world of movement. This environment should allow active knowing on the part of the child rather than passive reception. For both assimilation and accommodation to occur, children must engage in exploring and thinking about the movement problem at hand—in observing, trying, testing, and changing either the problem or themselves. Rather than imposing a concept about movement efficiency on children, physical educators should guide them to discover efficient, effective movement for themselves. Then, they should help the child verbalize why it was efficient and effective. This system of inquiry or problem-solving, through all its phases, engages children in active, directed thinking about their movement. It also helps the teacher to determine both verbally and nonverbally whether the child is understanding basic biomechanical concepts and assimilating more motor tasks to those concepts.

Because most pre- and elementary school children are at preoperative or concrete operative stages of cognitive development, problem-solving must be used carefully. Most teachers treat children as if they were in the stage of formal operations. Instead, they should be presenting problems slowly, concretely, and only gradually chaining them into a series. Children need to be frequently asked whether they understand

their tasks. Their nonverbal answers often give more accurate clues to this question than their verbal ones. Repetition that allows children to assimilate a certain movement answer should also be encouraged before challenging them to produce a variety of answers.

Anytime teachers are talking with children— whether discussing a concept such as absorption of force, giving directions, introducing a new movement word for their vocabulary, or explaining a teacher-developed game— they should be sure the children are "with" them by asking them to rephrase the conversation in their own words. Using concrete illustrations and constantly asking questions rather than giving answers typifies the physical educator who is aware of children's cognitive development.

PERCEPTUAL DEVELOPMENT

Perception is the process through which an individual extracts information from the environment.[3] This definition implies active exploration of, and selection from, the mass of stimuli available. It also implies interpretation of the stimuli selected. While researchers still cannot adequately explain how the perceptual process works, they have made considerable progress in describing the perceptual behavior of both children and adults. From this research, it is evident that adults and children differ in the kind and amount of information they extract from their environment and in the strategies they use to extract the information.

Although Piaget interweaves some perceptual development within his cognitive theory, no one has identified stages of perception. Age differences in perceptual behavior, however, do imply several developmental trends. Three suggested in part by Gibson are (1) increasing discrimination, (2) increasing attention to relevant information, and (3) increasing intersensory integration.[3] While these selected trends are only a few of those possible, they should be useful guides for observing the perceptual behavior of children.

Increased Discrimination

Infants often repond to a generalized stimulus providing sparse sources of information. For example, an infant will smile at a nodding object approximately the size of a human head even if it has no eyes, nose, or mouth. Motion seems to be the sufficient or salient event for the response. While recognizing differences in faces continues to improve to the age of 14 years or beyond, by 8 months the child can discriminate a face from a model and a familiar face from an unfamiliar one.[4]

Four- and 5-year-olds still lump together similar objects with distinctive characteristics that developmentally more-advanced children would use as information. For example, these children may discriminate between open and closed letters such as C and O, but fail to discriminate such properties as straightness or curves, thus confusing letters such as D and O, or U and V. They may fail to notice reversals and confuse the letters b and d, or they may happily accept letters such as M and W or N and Z as the "same."[5]

When contrasted with older children and adults, young children also have more difficulty in accurately discriminating colors, lengths, widths, weights, tones, velocities, and textures.[6] Detection of the spatial directions of up and down, however, appears early. Young children have considerably less difficulty in identifying the top and bottom than the right and left side of an object (including their own body). Some depth perception is present early in development as evidenced in the "visual cliff" experiments. During these experiments infants were unwilling to crawl to their mothers across what appeared to be a drop-off.[7] Even so, not until school age or later does depth perception become relatively consistent and accurate under changing conditions.[3,6]

Increased Attention to Relevant Information

Even into the school years, children's attention may be "captured" by environmental stimuli.[8] The capturing stimulus becomes the stimulus of interest for the young child and may mask or conflict with the less capturing stimuli necessary to accomplish a given task. For example, Suchman and Trabasso observed nursery school children in a two-stimulus (color and shape) sorting task.[9] The children who had exhibited a preference for color as the key feature for sorting made more errors when shape was the "correct" response but fewer errors when color was the "correct" response. The reverse was true for children who preferred to sort by shape. Success in the situation was apparently dependent on the selective attention of the children for color or for form.

Increasing perceptual effectiveness, therefore, also involves the ability to ignore irrelevant stimuli. In an investigation of decision-making speed, Connolly indicated that the amount of irrelevant stimuli increased decision times of 6-, 8-, and 10-year-olds, particularly the 6-year-olds.[10] He concluded that the young child has more difficulty in ignoring irrelevant information, which then causes a "perceptual overload." In another study, 5-year-old children were trained to identify 9 Roman capital letters, 3 each in a different color. When tested on black letters, the children could identify not only the letters but also the colors associated with them. Nine-year-olds in similar tests could not identify the colors associated with the letters and, in some instances, could not even recall what colors had been used. Thus, the younger children had taken in more information than was needed while the older children had selected only the information necessary to the task.[3]

Picking out shapes, designs, or objects from a camouflaging background—for example, finding a lost marble in the grass or detecting a moving red playground ball against the background of a red brick building—is a particularly difficult task for young children. Longitudinal studies by Witkin and his associates indicate that the ability to detect the hidden design in an embedded-figures visual task increases from ages 10 through 17, after which there is a slight decrease through age 21.[11,12] Herkowitz, noting that most figure-ground measures are stationary, devised a moving embedded-figures test using motion pictures.[13] She also found improvement across 5- through 12-year-old children.

Increased Intersensory Integration

The child's environment presents an array of stimuli, which are received through more than one sense modality. Just how the child selects and combines such input is not well understood. One approach in studying intersensory function is to present identical or nonidentical stimuli to two senses simultaneously or sequentially, noting the accuracy of same-different judgments. In studying visual-haptic integration, for example, the visually perceived object must be judged the same as or different from one actively handled. (Haptic refers to the complex of tactile and kinesthetic cues received in handling an object.) Reports have shown increased visual-haptic intersensory accuracy in shape identification from ages 3 through 14.[14,15,16] Birch and Lefford also noted increases in visual-kinesthetic (passive movement) and haptic-kinesthetic intersensory accuracy for 5- through 11-year-olds.[14] Birch and Belmont found auditory-visual integration in reading more or less complete by the fifth grade.[17]

Nash noted that some intersensory relationships may be inherently more complicated than others.[18] For instance, it may be easier to relate information extracted through vision and touch than through vision and audition. He commented that a cross is a cross whether apprehended by sight or by touch. Recognizing the similarity between the seen cat and the heard meow, however, appears to require more abstraction. Further, the similarity between the printed CAT and the spoken word is even more difficult to detect.

Another way to study intersensory functioning is to provide input conflicts between two sense modalities. Witkin et al. measured the ability of subjects to use postural cues to perceive the vertical when the visual frame of reference was distorted.[11,12] They found that young children were strongly influenced by visual "field" cues and were thus field dependent. By age 10, however, children showed a dramatic shift away from the early field dependence, attending more to proprioceptive, kinesthetic, or vestibular postural cues rather than to the distorted visual cues. After age 17, Witkin et al. noted a slight reverse toward field dependence. Other conflicting-input experiments involving visual-kinesthetic (finger position) distortion and visual-touch (size) distortions in 9- through 18-year-olds indicate a developmental trend toward more accurate judgment in the face of conflicting input.[19]

Teaching Implications

Since children are different from adults in level of perceptual development, the teacher should be aware of the perceptual difficulties that environmental settings and movement experiences may pose for children in the gymnasium. To help young children perceive boundaries, for example, lines should be wide and of contrasting colors. The number of lines should be minimal to avoid a perceptually confusing array of intersections. Boundaries of working space should be clearly marked with distinctive shapes, such as rubber highway cones spaced closely enough so that the "line" is easily seen. Young children may not notice "open" space while moving or even when stopped. They need guided experience in "seeing" and then choosing open space away from walls, equipment, and other people.

The research available on intersensory integration suggests the importance of multiple approaches to presenting tasks or in helping young children understand an organizational plan. For example, the teacher can use a visual cue, such as moving to the space set aside for work with balls, while also verbally designating that workspace location. When talking, the spatial orientation of the teacher to the child is also an important way to facilitate an accurate verbal-visual match. The teacher, for example, should face in the same direction as the child when demonstrating a hop on the right foot if the child is going to be asked to try to hop on the right foot. Facing children forces them to reverse the input information—a difficult task even for adults.

Sometimes the planned movement experience requires children to detect the differing sounds of a hard or softly kicked ball striking a wall, or the rhythm of a drum beat, or the teacher's voice. In these cases, the teacher must help the child attend to that contrasting sound among the many background sounds that usually fill a physical education setting. Some children may need a relatively quiet area off the gymnasium where they can have the opportunity to attend easily to the wanted sound without the distraction of irrelevant background noise. This suggestion applies to discrimination in other sense modalities; for example, keeping the visual environment "uncluttered" or having the children close their eyes to concentrate on the feel of a particular movement. Trabasso noted that the effective design of learning environments requires both an impoverishment of the environment by eliminating potentially irrelevant stimuli and an enrichment of the environment by filling it with attention-getting cues of maximum vividness and interest.[20]

PSYCHOSOCIAL DEVELOPMENT

The area of personality development and social interactions covers many aspects of children's behavior. Three are especially relevant to physical education. The first is the moral development of children—the growth of their concept of right and wrong. Usually, moral development is considered part of the socialization process, i.e., the internalization of external social mores. Indeed, in different societies, children do show more of the moral *behaviors* characteristic of their society's expectations as they move toward adulthood. Kohlberg, however, is a developmental psychologist who tried to get beneath behavior to find out what children *thought* was moral. He presented children with an intriguing set of story situations in which obedience to legal-social rules or to authority conflicted with human needs. The following is a paraphrase of one of these stories:

> A man's wife is dying of cancer, but the only town druggist is asking an impossible price for the drug that might help her. The man tries all means to raise the money, fails, and finally breaks in to steal the drug. Should the man have done this? Why?

From children's discussion of the reasons for their answers (rather than the answers themselves), Kohlberg has detected six stages of moral development.[21] He feels that the stages result from the children's internal reorganization of their society's basic prohibitions and commands. Just as Piaget says that the child "knows" the same world differently at different stages, so Kohlberg believes that the child organizes society's moral rules differently at different stages. Since the moral stages result from this reorganization of the environment rather than from the environment "stamping in" its commands, Kohlberg has predicted that the stages would be culture-free.[21] Indeed, when children from the United States, Mexico, Taiwan, and Turkey were tested using stories appropriate to their culture, the same stages of moral reasoning occurred.[22] Kohlberg suggests that this happens because the structures of society—family, social stratification, law, and government—have universal functional meanings, despite different content in different societies.

Kohlberg's Stages of Moral Development

Kohlberg's six stages appear within three levels of development.

LEVEL 1. PRE-MORAL. The child responds to cultural labels of right and wrong, good and bad, but interprets these labels in terms of the physical or hedonistic consequences of action or the physical power of the rule-giver.

Stage 1. Punishment and Obedience. The goodness of an action is determined solely in terms of its physical consequences.

Stage 2. Naive Instrumental Hedonism. Right action is determined by what satisfies one's own needs and, occasionally, those of another. Reciprocity is a pragmatic "You scratch my back and I'll scratch yours."

LEVEL 2. CONVENTIONAL ROLE-CONFORMITY. The child perceives the maintenance of family, group, or national expectations as valuable in their own right regardless of consequences. The attitude reflects both conformity and active loyalty.

Stage 3. "Good Boy–Nice Girl." Good behavior is that which pleases others. It is frequently judged by intention: "He meant well."

Stage 4. "Law and Order." Right behavior is oriented toward authority, fixed rules, and maintenance of the social order.

LEVEL 3. SELF-ACCEPTED MORAL PRINCIPLES. The adult tries to formulate moral values that have validity apart from the groups holding the values.

Stage 5. Social Contract, Democratically Accepted Law. Right action is defined in terms of individual rights and standards agreed upon by the whole society. Personal values are seen as relative, so emphasis is on the "legal point of view," but includes the possibility of changing the law.

Stage 6. Universal Ethical Principle. Right action is a decision of conscience in accord with self-chosen ethical principles appealing to logical comprehensiveness, universality, and consistency.

RELATIONSHIP TO OTHER FACTORS

While the same stages appear in the same order in various cultures, the age at which they appear may differ slightly. In the United States, 10-year-old children operate predominantly at the lower stages and 13-year-olds at the middle stages. Stages 5 and 6 are not reached until adulthood, if they are reached at all.[23]

A parallel exists between these moral stages and Piaget's cognitive stages since moral reasoning (rather than behavior) is their focus. Kohlberg has found that a certain cognitive stage is required for each of the levels of moral reasoning. Being in that cognitive stage, however, does not guarantee that the child will also have the parallel moral stage. For instance, all Level 3 subjects must have formal operations, but many people having formal operations are not at Level 3 in moral reasoning.[23]

While middle-class children seem to move through the stages faster and farther than lower-class children, religion does not affect their moral reasoning.[22] No differences have been found among Catholics, Protestants, Jews, Buddhists, Moslems, or atheists. The concept of God may be employed in any of the stages, but it will be employed in accord with the reasoning of that stage. Kohlberg says that a Stage 2 child may advise, "Be good to God and He'll be good to you."[22]

Teaching Implications

In the course of reacting to Kohlberg's moral conflict situations, about 45% of a child's responses are in the dominant stage; the rest of the responses are in the next higher or next lower stage or in stages adjacent to those.[24] Thus, moral reasoning usually shows vestiges of the stage one has just moved from and intimations of the stage to which one may move. This fact has implications for the teacher. For instance, Rest, Turiel, and Kohlberg have found that people comprehend all stages below their own but not more than one above their own.[25] They tend to prefer the highest stage they can comprehend, although they restate that stage in terms of their own moral reasoning. Teachers who try to resolve conflicts when children feel they have been "wronged" in a game or by a peer are probably wasting time if they appeal to lofty ethical principles. Children who want to hit the person who hit them (Stage 2) have difficulty accepting the teacher's Stage 5 or 6 appeal to "turn the other cheek." The research suggests that reasoning with a child at one stage higher

than the child's stage would be a more useful procedure.

Since movement to the next moral stage is assumed to be the result of active interactions between the child and the social environment, Blatt and Kohlberg have attempted to promote moral development through a 4-month discussion program with 11- through 15-year-old children.[26] As the children actively discussed and sometimes argued hypothetic moral dilemmas, the teacher clarified Stage 3 arguments but refuted arguments below Stage 3. When the children seemed to understand Stage 3, the teacher began to challenge that thinking and to support and clarify Stage 4 arguments. As a result, half the children advanced one stage in their moral thinking, 10% moved up two stages, and the rest remained the same. In a nontaught control group, 90% of the children remained the same, and 10% advanced one stage.

Rather than waiting for skirmishes within the gymnasium, the teacher can try to foster moral development by discussing common social conflicts with the children before they occur. "Right action" for problems, such as what to do if someone takes your ball, your turn on the equipment, keeps infringing on your work space, cheats on your agreed-upon game rules, or wastes the class's time, can be discussed. By listening, the physical educator would learn much about the children's level of moral reasoning and could help them understand the next higher level. At the same time, the gymnasium rules and their reasons would be established by the teacher and children together.

Aggressive Behavior

One source of frequent social-moral conflicts in the classroom and the gymnasium is aggressive children. Little information is available on the development of aggressive behavior, that is, the changing transformations that occur within children's patterns of aggression as they grow older. Most of our information is about the relationship of aggressive behavior to other factors, such as parental discipline and gender. For instance, in examining the environment of the aggressive child, Hoffman has distinguished three types of parental discipline: (1) power assertion, which uses physical punishment, deprivation of material objects or privileges, or the threat of either; (2) love-withdrawal, which includes direct nonphysical expressions of the parents' disapproval, such as ignoring or isolating the child; and (3) induction, in which the parent explains to the child the reasons for requiring a change of behavior.[27] For children old enough to understand the reasoning, induction plus the presence of affectionate parents correlates most highly with indices of internalized moral behavior. Parental power assertion, on the other hand, consistently correlates with more aggressive behavior on the part of the child. It is theorized that, by physically punishing the child, the parent acts as an aggressive model that the child imitates. This modeling theory of aggression is supported by several studies in which children exhibited more aggressive behaviors after seeing an adult act aggressively.[28] Interestingly, aggressive children tend to direct their aggression toward adults outside the home and toward peers rather than toward their parents.[29]

On the other hand, several studies have been able to predict from the first or second year of life certain behavioral disorders of later childhood, such as acting out or antisocial activity.[29] Since not all infants with the predictive symptoms develop these disorders, an important factor seems to be the parents' response to the child's behavior.

Aggression is also related to gender. In animal studies, the male hormone testosterone promotes aggressive behavior in female newborn rats and young monkeys.[30,31] In humans, boys seem to be more physically aggressive; girls tend to use more indirect forms of aggression.[32]

It seems that aggressive behavior cannot be attributed completely to modeling or constitutional factors. Children predisposed to aggression are more likely to imitate aggressive models.[32] Thus, the relationships between aggression and factors such as gender and parental discipline cannot be viewed as cause and effect. Personality and social development result from the interactive process between each child and the environment.

Teaching Implications

Helping children to control physical aggression is a frequent responsibility of teachers. One classic study of aggression by Lewin et al. looked at 10-year-old boys under different teaching methods.[33] The authors worked with the boys in activity clubs, making masks, carving soap, and constructing model airplanes. The clubs rotated adult leaders who used authoritarian, democratic, or laissez-faire methods.

In the authoritarian treatment, the adult leader determined all policy. He dictated the tasks to be done and children's work companions. Within a task, all techniques and activity steps were designed by the leader. While the adult praised or criticized the work of each child, he remained aloof from active group participation.

In the laissez-faire treatment, the boys had complete freedom over what and how they were to proceed in their projects. Various materials were supplied by the leader, but he took no part in work discussions. The leader gave no directions, rarely commented on any individual's activities, and made no attempt to interfere with any of the boys' behavior.

The democratic conditions included having all policies determined through group discussion, which was guided and encouraged by the leader. The adult also sketched the general steps toward the group's goal. When technical advice was needed, he suggested two or three alternative procedures. Members worked with whomever they chose. The division of tasks was left up to the group. The leader tried to criticize individuals objectively and to participate as part of the group.

Observers recording all social interactions among the boys found that the authoritarian atmosphere spawned either high or low levels of aggression. In the high-aggressive groups, the members developed a pattern of dominance toward one another while either submitting to the adult leader or constantly demanding his attention. Scapegoating became so prevalent that the persecuted children finally dropped out of the clubs. The low-aggressive groups under authoritarian leadership were described as dull and lifeless. No joking, little smiling, and little freedom of movement about the room occurred. These boys, however, tended to have an overflow of aggression when they changed to a new atmosphere. They also showed a high rise in aggression when the leader left the room. Under the laissez-faire conditions, aggressive behavior was also high. Under the democratic conditions, the aggressive actions were moderate in number but more than in the low aggressive, authoritarian group.

Several other studies have indicated that authoritarian classes can lower overt aggressive behavior among children, but that aggression tends to show up somewhere else.[32] Some physical education programs have employed methods similar to the authoritarian ones used in the Lewin et al. study.[33] The results of that study suggest, however, that the more democratic atmosphere with its options, participatory decision-making, and guided control by the teacher gives a healthier *balance* to control of aggression in youngsters. Coupling this approach with inductive efforts directed toward the child's moral stage when aggression does occur would provide a more wholesome, normal atmosphere within the gymnasium-classroom.

Competitive and Cooperative Behavior

A third aspect of psychosocial development relevant to the teacher of movement is the growth of competitive and cooperative behavior. Successful participation as a team member in competitive games requires a conscious effort to play as part of a group. Thus, the child must cooperate in order to compete. In many physical education programs, even in the primary grades, competitive games play a dominant role. An implicit assumption in such programs is that children at all developmental levels know how to and will choose to cooperate in order to compete successfully.

A series of between-age and between-culture studies of the cooperative and competitive behavior of children by Madsen and associates is of interest in examining this question.[34-39] In table games designed to bring out cooperative or competitive behavior, pairs of 5- to 10-year-old children were given the option in each game of competing and risking the loss of a prize, cooperating and sharing prizes, or cooperating and each receiving a prize.

One of the games used was the Marble-Pull Game (Fig. 3–1A). In this game, a plastic block that breaks apart is placed on a small table. Each end of the block is attached to a string. The center of the block contains a marble. The object of the game is to pull on the block, without losing the marble, until the center of the block is over the target point. This permits the marble to fall

into the hole in front of either child. If a child chooses to compete by pulling on the string, the block breaks apart and both children lose the prize. They can decide to cooperate, however, and share the prize.

In experiments using this game, Nelson found that in the conflict-of-interest situation (only one prize per game) children, regardless of age, chose to compete even though they both lost the prize.[35] Nelson assumed that finding ways to cooperate so that prizes could be shared might be too difficult for 5-year-old children, but he questioned why the older children would continue irrationally to compete. To explore this problem, he modified the Madsen Cooperation Board Game.[35] In this game, each child had two strings which affected the movement of a plastic pointer on a board having three target circles (Fig. 3–1B). The children could choose to compete by pulling the strings simultaneously. This resulted in a stalemate with both losing the prize. They could also cooperate, together maneuvering the pointer to the middle target, with a resulting prize for each child in each game. Mutual assistance was the only way the pointer could be placed over the middle target. In this experiment, as in the Marble-Pull Game, the younger children tended to compete rather than to cooperate. With a prize for each child for successful teamwork, however, 8- to 10-year-old children cooperated on almost all trials. These findings were also supported in other table games in which the rewards were manipulated between a single prize per game (conflict-of-interest) and a prize for both children per game (cooperation option).

In these situations, as well as in "real-life" situations, cooperation required problem solving, thinking, joint planning, and joint execution of planned moves. The investigators concluded from the second experiment that the capacity to cooperate increased from ages 5 to 10; but surprisingly, this increased capacity was not used by older children in conflict-of-interest situations like those of the first experiment. Rather, the single prize games evoked irrationally competitive behavior that interfered with the demonstrated problem-solving ability of the 8- to 10-year olds.

Teaching Implications

The contrast in the behavior of the children in the two experimental situations should be of

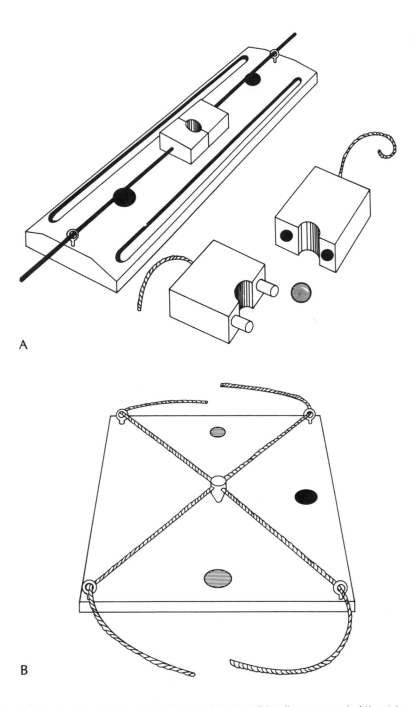

Fig. 3–1.A. Marble-Pull Game. The plastic block pulls apart if each child pulls on one end of the string at the same time (competition). The marble released from the separated block rolls into a groove on the side of the game board. If one child releases one end of the string, the other child may pull the intact block to one end of the game board, permitting the marble to drop in the cup at that end (cooperation). **B. Madsen Cooperation Board Game.** The center plastic marker will not move to either end of the board if the two end strings are pulled by the children with equal pressure simultaneously (competition). The pointer can be pulled to one end of the board over the target circle at that end if one child is stronger than the other (competition). The children can coordinate their pulls on each of the strings on the side toward the middle right circle and at the same time refrain from pulling the strings on the opposite side. This will permit the players to maneuver the plastic center marker over the middle right circle (cooperation). (Redrawn from Nelson, L., and Kagen, S.: Competition: The star-spangled scramble. Psychology Today, 6(4):53, 1972. Reprinted by permission of the American Psychological Association.)

interest to physical educators. Since the results of the studies were obtained in two-person games, they may not be entirely comparable to the demands of larger team games or other cooperative group practices. Yet, many of the conditions that interfered with cooperative behavior were analogous to common physical education environments. For example, single-prize, conflict-of-interest situations are part of programs that stress single winners and best performer standards. Such situations may interfere with a child's perception of success in the class. Despite the teacher's stated goals of cooperation and teamwork, the child may see only the implicit goals of winning or being first in achievement tasks.

These studies on cooperative and competitive behavior illustrate how difficult it is for children to shift from self-centered to other-centered social goals. For example, deciding to share or pass a ball to a teammate rather than keep the ball (prize) to oneself is a decision that taxes many children. It is especially difficult to learn to share, to appreciate others' capabilities, and to want to help others improve their skills in an environment that stresses winning or being best. Even skillful children may at times deliberately make a peer miss with an inaccurate throw or a shift of the hoop as their partner is moving through it. Simply telling the child to share, or asking the child to throw the ball so that the partner can catch it, may be ineffectual if the young child sees the partner as a rival rather than a helper. These studies show that we cannot assume that children will know how to and will choose to cooperate in group activities. Their developmental level, the complexity of the situation, and the stress on conflict-of-interest goals influence their ability to meet the demands involved in a cooperative effort.

COOPERATIVE CULTURES

What then of the commonly held belief that the competitive spirit is deeply ingrained in the nature of man? The Madsen and associates conflict-of-interest and rivalry studies seem to support this view. However, they have also observed the competitive behavior of pairs of children from rural Mexico, rural Canada, and an Israeli kibbutz under experimental conditions similar to those previously cited for the urban children. [40,36,34] The children from cultures where daily living stressed cooperation rather than competition tended to cooperate and share prizes even under the single prize, conflict-of-interest condition. In a rivalry experimental situation, far fewer rural than urban children of similar ethnic backgrounds chose to take toys away from peers. The investigators noted that in some rural cultures the cooperative pendulum may have swung too far. The children showed irrationally cooperative behavior to the point of excessive submission in the face of opposition.

PHYSICAL EDUCATION/ATHLETIC SETTINGS

Research in table game, laboratory settings has provided important insights into the competitive behavior of children. One limitation, however, is that by design such games require little interpersonal behavior. Yet, multiple interpersonal and intrapersonal factors could account for children's cooperative or competitive behavior in physical education game settings.

As indicated earlier, competitive games have traditionally played a dominant role in elementary school physical education programs. Teachers have apparently assumed all children are equally comfortable in competition so the competitive experience will be a positive one for them. The investigations of Solomons, Scanlan, and Scanlan and Passer are of interest in considering these assumptions. [41-44]

Solomons studied how sex roles and perceived ability affected the cooperative and competitive behavior of fifth grade children in physical education games. [41] The children had been in sex-integrated physical education classes throughout their elementary years. Solomons assessed the children's degree of participation and their throwing and catching ability both in a game of Newcomb and in an individual game emphasizing the same throwing and catching skill used in Newcomb. She found that boys made over twice as many attempts to catch balls, almost twice as many successful catches, and received three times as many passes as did girls. Boys also leaped, ran, fell, and collided almost three times as frequently as girls.

Following these initial studies, Solomons formed four-person teams which combined high-ability girls with low-ability boys and high-ability boys with low-ability girls. She devised a game for the children that stressed individual catching and forceful, accurate throwing. In the game, each child had a total of 16 opportunities to score by throwing the ball at a target, or to pass the ball to another member of the same team. The person to whom the ball was passed could either try to score or also pass the ball to another teammate.

In this situation, the highest ability girls gave away twice as many chances to score as the highest ability boys; in turn, high-ability boys received twice as many passes as high-ability girls. Girls who were the second highest ability players on their teams received fewer passes than boys who were the lowest ability players. Thus, low-ability boys were seen by other boys and girls as higher in ability than girls who were considerably more able than they. Girls, even of high ability, responded differently to competition than boys and were treated differently in the competition by both boys and girls.

The effects of competition depend not only on interpersonal factors but also on intrapersonal ones. A competitive experience in games may be perceived by the child as personally enhancing or personally threatening. If the latter, the competition may cause the child to have a high level of anxiety.

In a series of studies, Scanlan[42,43] and Scanlan and Passer[44] used established psychological scales to assess the pre- and postgame anxiety of 11- to 12-year-old boys and 10- to 12-year-old girls in competitive soccer. The investigators found that players who tended to be more anxious about competitive situations, who had low self-esteem, and who expected their team and themselves to perform poorly perceived greater personal threat and higher pregame anxiety than those who were less anxious about competitive situations, had high self-esteem, and who expected their teams and themselves to perform well. Scanlan and Passer also found that postgame anxiety was markedly affected by the experience of winning and losing. Losing players evidenced substantially greater postgame anxiety than winning players even when differences in competitive trait anxiety and pregame state anxiety measures were statistically equalized. Also, when pregame and postgame anxiety scores were compared, losing players demonstrated a significant increase from pregame to postgame anxiety. Winning players showed a marked decrease in anxiety.

Teaching Implications

Confidence in their own ability to meet the requirements of competitive games was a factor both in the behavior of the children in Solomons' study[41] and in the precompetition level of anxiety of children in the Scanlan and Passer[44] investigations. Also, Scanlan and Passer noted that losers in competitive games experienced increased postgame competitive anxiety. Rather than building their confidence, participation in games/sports can be demoralizing for some children. They receive nonverbal signals when teammates lack the confidence to pass them the ball. They experience social pressure "for the good of the team" to give up their own chances to score by passing to players judged to be better. These children are caught in a counterproductive cycle. They lack confidence in their own ability to meet the needs of the competitive game, yet the design of the game is such that those who most need to practice to improve their skills receive the least practice.

Riley and Roberton[45] argue that while teachers intend to teach for developmental progress, the competitive situations they use may cause some children's skills to regress rather than to progress. They suggest that, within one class, children should have the option of practicing the same skills in either a competitive or a cooperative manner. That is, one small group of children may be using striking skills "to keep the ball going." Another group in the same class may be using the same striking skills to try to make the other side "miss." They suggest that children should gradually merge cooperative group work into competitive practice as they feel both the desire and the need for additional challenge.

CHANGING CONCEPTS OF "GAMES"

Riley and Roberton's views[45] parallel the developmental approach to games teaching that is proposed by Mauldon and Redfern.[46] In their insightful book, the authors stress the importance of recognizing that the concept of "game" changes through childhood according to the child's interests and physical, cognitive, and moral development. They note that the young child will play a "game" alone, such as a ball-bouncing game. Even when playing with a ball in a group of three children, the "game" will be more a game of "three ones" than "one three." The authors note that the exploratory play patterns of young children still extend into later group play, and that older children design their own game patterns when given the opportunity. At this level of game development, their games are not contests involving elaborate rules or a high level of cooperative behavior. Rather, they are tests of their own ability with the help of a partner or group. At this point, competition against another team is not stressed. While children 10 through 12 years old become increasingly interested in games with rules, they continue to design their own version of named games, such as basketball or volleyball, unless pressed to play specific adult-designed games. The cooperation demands to keep the game going may become more complex, however, and interest in competing against other teams increases.

CHILD-DESIGNED GAMES

Riley has subjectively observed the game choice, design, and participation of fifth- and sixth-grade urban children in a physical education environment.[47] These children had participated in physical education classes in which the climate for learning was structured to let individuals work at their own rate, feel free to make mistakes in the process of becoming more skillful, and become increasingly independent as learners. The opportunity to make decisions, with guidance in the process of decision-making, and a choice of alternatives were also part of the environment. Development of games cooperatively planned by the teacher and child plus child-designed, original game forms were emphasized.

Riley reported that the 10- through 12-year-old children in this setting did not choose the competitive situations assumed to be a great part of the "needs" of middle elementary school children. Rather, they chose cooperative situations in which they were concerned mainly with making the game "work" so that all could participate. They chose to play in small groups of rarely more than three or four, and they sought others of similar ability. The children chose games that

permitted the use of more than one piece of equipment, e.g., two players, two balls. They also named a game only if asked, and they gave it a simple name like "the striking game." They would keep score also only when asked, and then they tended to score by subtraction. With or without a score, they rarely announced a winner.

It is clear from these observations that the class climate and environment do have a great influence in "freeing" children to choose to cooperate and to define competition at their own developmental level. Freed from adult-imposed competitive stress and given alternative choices for cooperative and competitive patterns in group work, children do not automatically opt for one winner and for beat-the-opponent game patterns even at the 11- and 12-year-old level. We are not suggesting that children will not and do not like to compete. We are suggesting that competitive needs and readiness patterns in children are also developmental and should be viewed in that context.

ART DEVELOPMENT

At one time or another, the developmental changes that occur in children's art have been interpreted to reflect almost every action system discussed thus far. Some writers have studied children's drawings to deduce their stage of cognitive development; others have attempted a psychosocial portrayal from children's art work; still others have thought children's pictures revealed their level of perceptual awareness. Some validity lies in all these approaches, for children's art is clearly a perceptual-motor skill used to communicate subjectively or objectively thoughts, percepts, and feelings. For this reason, we shall use children's art both to close our overview of the developing child and to preview the world of childhood movement, which serves in this case as a tool for the child's expressive self. The perspective we shall take is that of Rhoda Kellogg.[48,49]

She argues that art is more than a reflection of cognition, perception, or personality; rather, it primarily reflects the child's aesthetic development. Rather than learning to draw by copying what they see, Kellogg claims children draw and *then* begin to see forms in what they have created.

Stages in Self-Taught Art

From studying thousands of children's pictures in her role as a preschool educator, Kellogg has identified several stages in self-taught art.

STAGE 1. PLACEMENT. By age 2, children begin to scribble spontaneously if the proper environment (paper, crayon, pencil) is provided. The movement of hand and arm as well as their resulting product give the child great satisfaction, but rarely did intention precede that artistic product. The motor act yields its interesting result solely by virtue of the hand and arm movements available to the child. Children have no prior knowledge of what this result will be, but when they are finished they see a product they begin to remember. Kellogg quotes one child who, when asked what she was drawing, said "How do I know until I have finished?"[48]

Kellogg has identified 20 basic scribbles (Fig. 3–2), which no doubt correlate highly with the muscular actions available to the child's arm. As children perceive their scribbling, aesthetic considerations already come into play, since they show preferred patterns in how they place their scribbles on the paper (Fig. 3–2). All 17 placement patterns identified by Kellogg appear in the drawings of children by about age 3.

Long before children can draw a shape in outline form, shapes will be implied in their scribbles. Roundness hints at circles yet to come; X's and crosses emerge out of oblique, horizontal, and vertical lines purposefully or accidentally colliding. Again, the children perceive these shapes after they have drawn them.

STAGE 2. SHAPE. Three-year-olds will begin to outline the shapes they have seen and remembered from their own work. These outlines or diagrams are less than perfectly executed to an adult, but to the child they are aesthetically pleasing. Adults may try at this time to give representational meaning to the child's outlines, but they are basically still the child's artistic building blocks for later, conscious representation.

STAGE 3. DESIGN. As children expand their repertoire of diagrams, they begin to put two together into a design. When two diagrams are united, Kellogg calls the resulting design a "combine." When three or more are put together, the design is an "aggregate." Again, the child's motivation is aesthetic. Designs are created because they look balanced and pleasing. One combine, the circle or square with a cross in it (Fig. 3–3), is called a mandala. Common even in prehistoric art, the mandala is frequently drawn because of its aesthetic appeal. From it, Kellogg believes children proceed to draw suns and the human figure in universally similar ways.

STAGE 4. PICTORIAL. When children's designs become recognizable to adults, the children have entered the pictorial stage. Early pictorial works are only suggestive of trees or animals. Most drawings of humans done by pre-6-year olds show the basic mandala form with arms and legs radiating from a large, circular body, more to conform with pleasing design principles than accuracy of depiction. If the picture looks a little off-center, an extra radial will be added, not because people have three arms but because the picture "needs it." When human ears get placed on top of the head for variation, an adult says, "Oh, that's a horse," and the child agrees. As adults begin to name objects in children's pictures and the children begin to realize that certain objects do, indeed, resemble their own designs, they move toward representational art, which occurs later in the pictorial stage. Six-year olds have usually reached this final level of self-taught art.

Even in this period, interesting deviations from reality occur although the child may be trying to portray a "real" picture. Lowenfeld[50] has pointed out three common deviations at this time: (1) size exaggeration of important parts of the picture, (2) neglect or omission of unimportant parts of the picture, and (3) shape changes in emotionally significant parts of the picture. For instance, he describes a picture entitled "Searching for the Lost Pencil." The child drew the searching, reaching arms longer than the entire rest of the searcher's body. The hand groping for the pencil is pencil-shaped. A second picture shows the retrieved pencil being inserted in the searcher's pocket. The other hand, no longer involved in the story, has shrunk to only a stub extending from the shoulder.

Teaching Implications

Kellogg's strong message for parents and teachers is to encourage rather than interrupt children's self-taught art. Children are active producers of art rather than passive copiers. Yet,

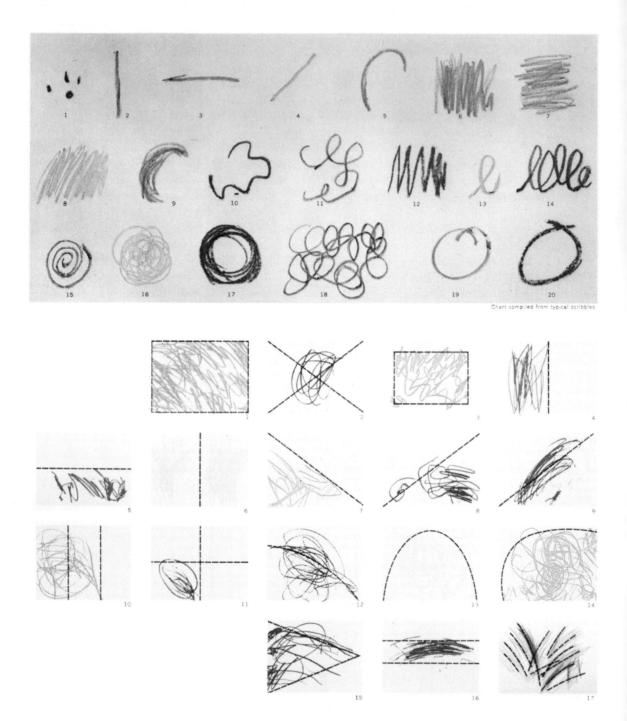

Fig. 3–2.   Scribbles and Placements. The 20 basic scribbles in children's art are illustrated in the top 3 rows. The bottom 4 rows contain the 17 placement patterns recognized in children's scribbling. (From Kellogg, R., and O'Dell, S.: The Psychology of Children's Art. Del Mar, California, CRM-Random House, 1967. Reprinted by permission of R. Kellogg.)

Fig. 3–3. The Mandala. This is the finger painting of a 3-year-old. (From Kellogg, R., and O'Dell, S.: The Psychology of Children's Art. Del Mar, California, CRM-Random House, 1967. Reprinted by permission of R. Kellogg.)

having children color books with pre-drawn outlines or follow stencils of forms forces them into trying to copy. Their own art may appear inadequate in their eyes when, in fact, it is an aesthetic production of some accomplishment.

Teachers of movement can capitalize on the common aesthetics of art and human movement by encouraging early-pictorial children to draw their experiences in movement: Not what they or others "looked like" but, rather, pictures of their pathways through space or their speed of motion. What color will Susan use to show "fast?" Let her contemplate and express her total body movement in art—at her level of creation and enjoyment.

MOTOR DEVELOPMENT

Physical educators' unique responsibility is to promote the motor development of each child. Although they share interest in the child's cognitive, perceptual, psychosocial, and artistic development with every other teacher in the school, they have primary responsibility for the child's growth in the motor domain. For this reason, physical education teachers who believe in individualizing instruction must know how the motor system develops. This knowledge will help them *interpret* the movement they see. From that interpretation, they can *decide* whether and how to intervene in the child's learning.

The following discussion summarizes developmental information for a few dimensions within the Laban movement framework adopted for this book.[76] Research in motor development has not progressed to the level of research in other action systems. No one, for instance, has attempted to identify overall stages of motor development, such as Piaget did for cognition. Instead, what are available are developmental sequences that describe the order of changes both within motor tasks or skills and between skills. When a motor development sequence focuses on the changes that occur within a given skill until that skill is mastered, the sequence is called an *intra-task (or skill) sequence*. When the sequence is made up of different skills ordered along a time span, it is called an *inter-task (or skill) sequence*. We will begin our discussion of motor development by describing the inter-task sequence associated with foot locomotion. Oddly enough, this sequence has not been verified by research. It is our best guess from the information available. In fact, few of the inter- and intra-task sequences we describe are totally validated by research. Validation is a lengthy process involving longitudinal study.[51] We do indicate, however, when the information we are sharing has been validated and when it is our best guess from our own and others' observations while teaching children.

LOCOMOTION ON THE FEET

This introduction to the world of motor development begins with locomotion, which is such an important part of the child's bustling life. Locomotion means to travel or to move from one place to another. Most people think of traveling just on the feet, but there are many forms of locomotion, using other body parts as well, e.g., rolling, crawling, climbing, and scooting. Children use every form they can for the sheer pleasure of moving and exploring their world.

This discussion covers developmental changes in both types of travel, beginning with locomotion on the feet.

Foot Pattern Development

The problem of shifting, projecting, and receiving weight to and from the feet in progressively more difficult situations presents a complex challenge to the young child. There can be only five ways to transfer weight on the feet: from one foot to the same foot, one foot to the other foot, one foot to two feet, two feet to two feet, and two feet to one foot. From these five types, however, come the many temporal and spatial relationships found in locomotor forms. In these many relationships, each foot may perform just a single task, or it may perform more than one task before transferring the weight to the other foot. For example, in walking, each foot completes a single step before the weight transfer; whereas in skipping, each foot completes a step and a hop before the weight transfer.

In early development, the first transfer-of-weight patterns are single-task transfers from one foot to the other foot, from one foot to two feet, and two feet to two feet. As children try to gain more speed and distance, they make increasing use of single-task weight transfers from one foot to the other foot, and less use of a two foot to two foot pattern. Next to emerge are the single-task transfers of weight from one foot to the same foot and from two feet to one foot. These transfer patterns require substantial strength and balance. Also emerging at approximately this level of development are foot patterns requiring each foot to complete two tasks before the weight transfer to the other foot.

SINGLE-TASK FOOT PATTERNS

The pattern of one foot to the other foot observed in *walking* is the first single-task pattern to emerge and is a common element in the locomotor tasks that follow. For example, the *run* evolves from the fast walk, and the *run-and-leap* evolves from a little extra push-off in one step of the run. The latter is, therefore, an early-appearing combination of two locomotor tasks (Fig. 3–4).[52]

Continuous leaping, although an alternating foot pattern, does not appear until much later in development. In fact, this task remains difficult even for adults. Another difficult one foot to one foot relationship is the *hop* (transfer of weight from one foot to the same foot). Hopping seldom emerges before the age of 3[53] and, even then, is often a momentary single hop on the preferred foot.[54] The challenge within the continuous leap or hop is to receive the weight in landing, absorb it smoothly, and again project from the landing foot—a feat that demands considerable strength, balance, and timing.

In early locomotion, an exception to the use of one foot to the other foot is the two-foot *bounce jump*. A two-foot bounce jump is a repetitive bouncing movement that covers little vertical or horizontal distance and requires little force for projection. Once discovered, this form of jumping becomes a game that is repeated time and again, sometimes from low boxes or steps, some-

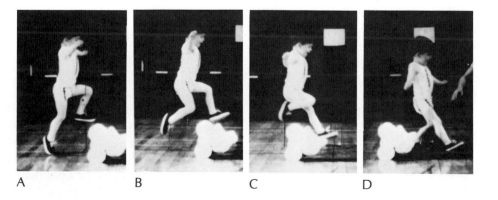

A　　　　B　　　　C　　　　D

Fig. 3–4.　Run and Leap—2 years, 10 months. The environmental challenge to run, get over the rolled towels, and keep on running elicits a beginning run and leap accompanied by reactive arms.

times over obstacles, and most often "just moving around."

The two-foot *jump for distance* from a stationary start is developmentally more complex. In any off-balance position, such as the take-off in the jump for distance, there is a strong tendency to step out automatically with one foot to stop the forward fall. This tendency to use the alternating foot pattern is difficult to inhibit. When the off-balance forward lean at take-off is minimal, as in the two-foot bounce jump, young children can refrain from stepping out with one foot. As the forward lean increases, it becomes more and more difficult for them to inhibit the stepping tendency.[55] Thus, in the early levels of the standing long jump or of *jumping from heights*, children typically shift from two feet to stepping out with one foot as they fall off balance.[56] When the goal is to cover maximal distance, either horizontally or vertically, young children almost always add a run, or at least one step, before taking off from the other foot.

Young children rarely attempt a *vertical jump* from two feet although they can project upward for a minimal distance in a stretched position. For example, a 2- or 3-year-old might use a vertical jump to follow a ball thrown into the air. Poe found that a balloon held overhead, accompanied by a verbal challenge of "Can you jump and touch the balloon?" elicited early levels of a vertical stretch jump in 16 of 22 two-year-olds.[57]

COMBINING SINGLE-TASK PATTERNS

In general, just two combinations of locomotor tasks are observed in early development: the run-and-leap over low obstacles or for short distances and the familiar walk-and-leap of the early *gallop*. Each involves only a single task per foot, but each foot does something different. If the right foot is in the lead in the gallop, it is the "walk" foot, and the left becomes the "leap" foot throughout the gallop. While the gallop with a preferred foot lead may appear as early as 2 years of age, leading with the nonpreferred foot does not come until later.[53]

A *slide* in a sideward direction also uses a step on one foot and a leap on the other, but it appears much later than the gallop. Since the body faces a different direction from the one in which it is moving, the slide is more difficult to control.

Thus, the early slide usually becomes a gallop, with the feet heading in the direction of the movement and the upper torso twisted at right angles trying to maintain the different facing.

DOUBLE-TASK PATTERNS

Skipping combines a walk and a hop, but it requires each foot to accomplish both tasks before transferring the weight to the other foot. The pattern has an uneven rhythm, with the step taking longer than the hop. While some children may manage a skip by the age of 4,[53] many reach only an early level of skipping by age 7. A *step-and-hop* in even rhythm is another locomotor form requiring each foot to perform two tasks. Contrary to what one might predict, it is more difficult for the child to perform this even-rhythm pattern than the uneven rhythm of the step and hop in the skip. The even rhythm requires the child to receive the weight, hold back and balance for the duration of the beat, and then project the body into the air. Holding back, balancing, and projecting require movement control and strength. Thus, the even-rhythm step-and-hop, so much a part of many dance forms, does not appear until well into primary school years.

INTER-TASK SEQUENCE FOR FOOT LOCOMOTION

To summarize this discussion, we will hypothesize an inter-task sequence for eight common forms of foot locomotion. Obviously, an "hypothesized" sequence has not been validated. We will order the skills according to the time when primitive forms of each skill might make their first appearance in a child's repertoire. We stress the word "primitive," which is used in development to mean "early level." Although primitive forms of a task may appear when a child is rather young, the child will not necessarily soon be skillful in that task. A primitive form of the overarm throw, for instance, may be seen when a child is sitting in a high chair, but that throw will not finish developing until the same child is in high school.[58]

Because *walking* lacks a moment of flight, of all the foot locomotor tasks it is the most stable and least demanding of strength. For this reason, walking is the first foot locomotor task to appear in children's repertoires, usually by the first year if not before. *Running* is probably the next to occur, with a single *leap* (Fig. 3–4), *jumping* (down and bounce), and *galloping* coming soon after, although we are unsure of the order. Then the *hop* appears, first on the dominant foot, later on the nondominant foot. When at least a primitive hop can be performed on each foot, the *skip* can occur. Sideways galloping or *sliding* usually differentiates from forward galloping at about this time also.

In their play and practice, children will frequently substitute locomotor forms that appear earlier in the developmental sequence for those they cannot yet perform. The teacher-as-observer can often estimate a child's location in the locomotor sequence by studying these substitutions. For instance, when children cannot jump down, they will step down. When they cannot hop, they will often bounce jump. Those who cannot skip will gallop. Those who cannot jump for distance will leap.

Intra-Task Development

Much better studied than the inter-task sequence for foot locomotion are the intra-task sequences for individual foot locomotor skills. We will examine the specific changes that occur in children's movements as they attempt such tasks as hopping and discuss how to look for these changes in the children we are teaching. First, a few comments about intra-task development.

CROSS-SECTIONAL AND LONGITUDINAL PERFORMANCE DATA. Traditionally, the changes that occurred in specific motor tasks, such as hopping, were studied by looking at how children's performance scores changed as they grew older. Figure 3–5 is a sample graph of how the performance scores for the standing long jump differ across the ages 5 to 17 years. Since the graph compares children of different ages, it is called a *cross-sectional* graph. Most of our performance score information takes this cross-sectional form. Far fewer studies have followed the same children over time to obtain *longitudinal* information. Thus, we have to infer from age differences the kind of curve we would get using data showing age change. Since longitudinal data show age changes directly, they are highly prized in developmental research.

Figure 3–5, then, is a cross-sectional estimate

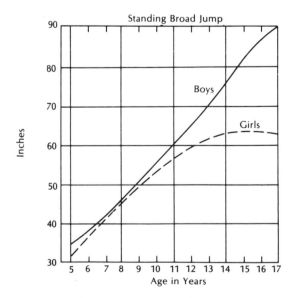

Fig. 3–5. Age Differences in Standing Long-Jump Distance Scores. (From Motor Development, Espenschade, A.: *In* Johnson, W. (ed.): Science and Medicine of Exercise and Sports. New York, Harper & Row, 1960, as modified in Espenschade, A., and Eckert, H.: Motor Development. Columbus, Ohio, Merrill, 1980. Copyright 1960 by W.R. Johnson and 1974 by E.R. Buskirk. Reprinted by permission of Harper & Row, Publishers, Inc.)

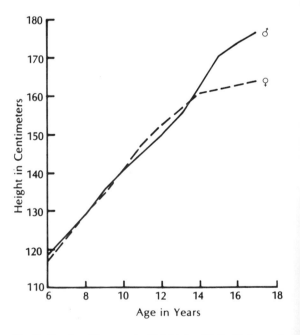

Fig. 3–6. Age Changes in Height for White Males and Females. (From Espenschade, A., and Eckert, H.: Motor Development. Columbus, Ohio, Merrill, 1980. Adapted from R.M. Malina, P.V.V. Hamill, and S.E. Lemeshow: *Body Dimensions and Proportions: White and Negro Children 6–11 Years;* and P.V.V. Hamill, F.E. Johnston, and S.E. Lemeshow: *Body Weight, Statures, and Sitting Height: White and Negro Youths 12–17 Years.* Washington, D.C., U.S. Government Printing Office, Series II (143,126), 1973.

of how boys and girls change in the distance they can long jump. While interesting, such data are not very helpful in visualizing the body movement changes that have also occurred as the child aged. In addition, many of the graphs of performance score changes are strikingly similar to each other and to graphs of growth changes in children during the same years (Fig. 3–6). Peterson, Reuschlein, and Seefeldt suggested that up to 25% of the differences between children's performance scores may be related to differences in their linearity and weight.[59] Their data were only for kindergarten through second grade, but we would not be surprised if their findings were to hold true for older children as well. Thus, performance scores leave it unclear as to whether one is measuring motor development or growth.

MOVEMENT DESCRIPTION. A more direct way of charting the changes that occur in motor skills over time is to film children, then describe the changes verbally or quantitatively. Verbal descriptions will be used in this chapter since they are easier to visualize and since far more verbal than quantitative information is available.

At the verbal level of analysis, recent research[60,61,62] suggests that development occurs at a partial pattern or *body component* level. That is, the notion of an intra-task sequence of development is more valid for parts of the body than for the body as a whole. In the hop, for instance, a separate sequence will be noted for the action of the legs and for the action of the arms. These sequences are surprisingly independent. The level to which a child's arm action has progressed is not directly predictable from knowledge of that child's level of leg action. Of course, the early hopper will be at the most primitive levels in all components. Similarly, when children master the hop, they will have achieved the most advanced levels in both components. How they travel from primitive to advanced—which component develops when and how far in relation to other components—is somewhat particular to the individual. Two children passing through the component sequences may look quite different from each other, depending on the combination or *profile* of developmental levels they exhibit at any one time.

The degree to which intra-task developmental sequences generalize across tasks is only beginning to be studied,[63,64,65] so these sequences can-

not be considered stage sequences analogous to Piaget's cognitive stages. Therefore, levels within intra-task sequences are called *steps* as opposed to stages.[61,66] Sometimes readers feel that the ordinal categories used to delineate steps imply that motor development is discontinuous, with sudden changes occurring from one step to the next with no transitional behavior. Observation of motor development confirms that development is not discontinuous. Each step phases in and out, overlapping with its neighbors.[67]

One way to see this overlapping or *transitional* behavior is to watch children perform a task across trials. On most of the trials they will show the same developmental level. That modal level is used to designate their developmental status. On a few trials, however, they may exhibit the next step toward which they are moving or the developmental step they have just left. Thus, their movement gradually consolidates into a developmental level and then, just as gradually, goes on to a new level. Truly transitional children may show approximately half their trials in one level and half in the next higher level. Another place transitional behavior has been observed is in skills such as the skip. Sometimes, a new developmental level will be observed in one foot before the other foot, even though both feet will eventually show the behavior of the next developmental level. For instance, in advanced foot action in the skip (see Table 3–7) the child's heel never touches down. In the preceding developmental level, the heel always touches down. Some children, however, will touch the heel down on one foot but not on the other. They are in transition between levels 2 and 3. Final evidence for transitional behavior is movement that is hard to categorize because it is "almost" the next level. Instead of agonizing over such a child's level of development ("Is it a 2 or a 3?"), teachers should understand that usually the correct answer is "2½;" i.e., the child is in transition between levels 2 and 3, making the movement difficult to categorize.

Seeing Intra-Task Development

Observing movement is difficult even for those who have taught for many years. It is a constant challenge to see what is happening in various body components as a child performs a motor task. Slow-motion film or videotape is a valuable aid to the observer learning to "see" movement. If it is not possible to use these tools, sequences of still pictures help in capturing the action for study. After one has learned to see key characteristics with these slow motion aids, the faster, "live" action will be easier to assess.

Whether slow motion or live action, the observer cannot see the whole movement of a complex skill at once.[68,69] To assess developmental steps within a motor task, the observer needs to first watch the child make several attempts at the task. This will provide an overall "feel" for the child's movement. Then the observer needs to turn attention to one component at a time. While the components may be assessed in any order, it seems useful for teachers to study the components in the order of their developmental importance, e.g., first the legs in locomotion, or first the trunk action in striking or throwing. We will indicate this order of importance as we describe the developmental steps for various tasks.

Armed with this first strategy for observation,[68] the observer must also be familiar with the particular developmental levels she expects to see. It is impossible to "see" what one does not "know".[68] Therefore, pre-observation study of the definitions of each developmental step and the decision rules for identifying that step is always necessary.

Finally, prior to observing, one must decide where to stand in order to see or, if working with film or videotape, what view to examine. Again, we will try to help with this choice as we discuss the decision rules used for placing movement in different developmental categories.

Ultimately, one learns to see intra-task development only through study and practice. The ease with which successful coaches and teachers seem to spot the movement characteristics of their athletes and students comes from years of hard work. Fortunately, the satisfaction of being able to help children improve their movement because one could see what they were doing is well worth the effort.

Recording Development in the Gymnasium

Although observation is critical for the ongoing process of teaching—the minute to minute interactions with children in the gymnasium—conscientious teachers will also devise some method of periodically recording children's developmental status. This written record serves as a chart of individual children's progress during the year and may be the basis for periodic home reports. To do this kind of record keeping in a nonfrustrating manner requires several additional strategies on the part of the teacher.

First of all, teachers should view developmental assessment as an ongoing project. All children in the school do not need to be evaluated at once. Rather, they should be continually reviewed, a few at a time, throughout the school year. This strategy keeps record keeping a constant but never overwhelming part of the teaching day.

Secondly, the teacher needs to devise some form of checklist, perhaps like the one in Table 3–1, or one containing names of all the children for a given classroom.[121] Whatever its form, the checklist should require a minimum of writing.

Table 3–1   Observation Checklist for Hopping

Child: <u>Jones, Randy</u>   Classroom: <u>S. Johnson</u>
Motor Task: <u>Hopping</u>

Movement Component:	Level Observed		
Leg Action	Jan. 4		
Step 1. Momentary flight			
Step 2. Fall and catch; Swing leg inactive			
Step 3. Projected takeoff; Swing leg assists	✔		
Step 4. Projection delay; Swing leg leads			
Movement Component: _Arm Action_			
Step 1. Bilateral inactive			
Step 2. Bilateral reactive			
Step 3. Bilateral assist			
Step 4. Semi-opposition	✔		
Step 5. Opposing assist			
Overall Movement Profile Legs	3		
Arms	4		
Movement Situation Teacher selected			
Child selected	✔		
Observation Type Direct	✔		
Video-tape			
Film			
Comments:			

Finally, certain types of organization within the gymnasium or out on the playground make it easier to use checklists while teaching. Learning centers or stations, for instance, are useful when a teacher wishes to assess children's developmental levels in a certain task. While most of the youngsters are working independently at other learning centers, the teacher can be observing the children at a particular center. By rotating the children through the centers, an experienced teacher can evaluate a class of 30 children on one motor skill in half an hour.

Hopping Development

Hopping requires the same foot to project the body into the air and catch it. Children do not often choose this mode of travel even after they can successfully accomplish the task. When they do hop, they will choose their preferred foot, seldom using their nonpreferred foot unless challenged to do so. Yet, the hop is often required in combination with other locomotor forms, for example, in skipping, in making rapid changes of sideward direction, in controlling momentum during sudden stops, and in handling unexpected off-balance situations when the other foot cannot move to catch the weight. Thus, both experience and competence in hopping are important for the developing child.

LEG ACTION

In addition to observing children's prehopping movements, we have identified four developmental steps in the leg action of the hop itself. See Table 3–2 for the definitions of these developmental steps.

Although we think of hopping as a one-footed activity, both legs are active in the advanced hop for distance. To distinguish the two, we will call the hopping foot the support leg and the nonhopping foot the nonsupport or "swing" leg. The pattern of change in the support leg from prehop movements to the advanced developmental steps goes from extension in the prehop to flexion in the early hop, and then, back to extension in the more advanced hop. Key changes in the swing leg are from inactivity in the early developmental levels to swinging up and down to produce momentum in the advanced levels. Seefeldt and Haubenstricker[71] note that the level 2

inactive swing leg, which is usually held in front of the body (see Fig. 3–9), is in an ideal position to receive weight in the event balance is lost.

The child's first prehop attempts, when they try to hop but cannot get off the ground, are dominated by extension. The child tries to "lift" off the floor by moving the nonsupport leg as high as possible and, at the same time, extending the hip, knee, and ankle to bring the weight up on the ball of the foot. The idea of "hop" is expressed in the extended, support leg and high position of the nonsupport leg, but the child does not produce the force necessary to project the body off the floor (see Fig. 3–7). When the child is not successful in actually leaving the floor in a hop, a primitive gallop may result as the body falls off balance, or the child may substitute a two-foot bounce jump.

OBSERVING THE LEG ACTION

When the child first manages to hop, there has been a change from the prehop approach to the task. Rather than stretching to get the body high, the child changes to *quick flexion* in the hip and knee to "pull" the foot from the floor in a "momentary flight" (Step 1) (see Fig. 3–8). Occasionally, the child may manage two successive hops at this level, but more often only one hop results.

For the best view of the leg action in Steps 2 to 4, position yourself to the side of the child. To distinguish between Steps 2, 3, and 4, first concentrate on the action of the swing leg. If you decide that the leg action is not at the Step 1 level, the next decision you must make is whether the swing leg is still inactive (Step 2) or whether it is swinging forward to assist in force production (Step 3 or 4). If you decide that the swing leg is inactive, the appropriate developmental step for leg action is Step 2 (see Fig. 3–9). If you decide that the swing leg is pumping up and down to assist in the hop, then check to see if the swing leg appears to pass behind the line of the support leg (Step 4) (see Fig. 3–11), or whether it moves up and down without enough range to pass behind (Step 3) (see Fig. 3–10).

In almost all cases, the action of the support leg will match the developmental step of the swing leg. In Step 2, the action of the knee and ankle prior to takeoff is primarily flexion as the

Table 3–2   Developmental Sequence for Leg Action in Hopping

Step 1. Momentary flight. The support knee and hip quickly flex, pulling (instead of projecting) the foot from the floor. The flight is momentary. Only one or two hops can be achieved. The swing leg is lifted high and held in an inactive position to the side or in front of the body.

Step 2. Fall and catch; Swing leg inactive. Body lean forward allows the minimal knee and ankle extension to help the body "fall" forward of the support foot and, then, quickly catch itself again. The swing leg is inactive. Repeat hops are now possible.

Step 3. Projected takeoff; Swing leg assists. Perceptible pretakeoff extension occurs in the hip, knee, and ankle in the support leg. There is little or no delay in changing from knee and ankle flexion on landing to extension prior to takeoff. The swing leg now pumps up and down to assist in projection. The range of the swing is insufficient to carry it behind the support leg when viewed from the side.

Step 4. Projection delay; Swing leg leads. The weight of the child on landing is now smoothly transferred along the foot to the ball before the knee and ankle extend to takeoff. The support leg nearly reaches full extension on the takeoff. The swing leg now leads the upward-forward movement of the takeoff phase, while the support leg is still rotating over the ball of the foot. The range of the pumping action in the swing leg increases so that it passes behind the support leg when viewed from the side.

Note. This sequence has been partially validated by Halverson and Williams.[70]

Fig. 3–7.   Unsuccessful Hop Attempt—2 years.

body "falls" off balance. In Step 3, extension begins, but it is characterized by limited range and early timing. "Early" extension means that extension begins almost immediately after the flexion from the landing. In Step 4, the extension prior to takeoff is delayed until *just before* takeoff. The action, then, is land, ride, and extend.

If you should encounter a decision problem because the swing leg is at Step 2, for instance, but the support leg is at Step 3, you would identify this as a 2–3 transition. Very likely, the next time you observe the child, the action of both legs will fall in the higher developmental step.

ARM ACTION

Five developmental steps have been identified within the arm action component. They are defined in Table 3–3. As the table indicates, the pattern of development in the arm action changes from inactivity to reactive movement counter to the direction of the hop, to bilateral assisting action, to opposing assisting action.

OBSERVING THE ARM ACTION

The first decision to make in assessing the arm action is whether the arms are in a bilateral or opposing position. If you decide that they are in a bilateral position, then decide whether they are primarily inactive (Step 1) or reactive (Step 2). The key to this decision is whether the arms seem to just "ride" along high or out to the side (Step 1) (Fig. 3–8), or whether they move in a "braking" action counter to the direction of the hop (Step 2). Note that the right and left arms may not be held at the same level. In contrast with the inactive and reactive arm actions, both arms clearly pump up and down together in Step 3 (bilateral assist).

If your first decision was that the arms are working in opposition, then the next decision is whether each arm clearly passes behind the line of the trunk on each swing back (Step 5). If only the arm opposite the swing leg passes behind the trunk while the other covers a limited swing distance or moves very little, the child is in Step 4 (see Fig. 3–10).

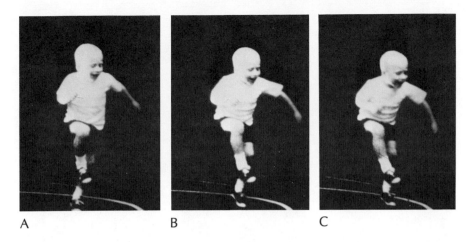

A   B   C

Fig. 3–8.   Hop—3 years, 1 month.
Leg action: Step 1; Arm action: Step 1. Momentary flight occurs in frame B. Note the flexed trunk and high nonsupport leg.

MOVEMENT PROFILE

Once the developmental steps for the leg and arm action have been identified, you have a developmental "profile" of the child's hop. This gives a picture of relative development across components. You will note in Table 3–1 that Randy Jones' movement profile was 3/4. Another child of the same age may have a 3/3, for example, or a 4/3.

Although it is theoretically possible to have any combination of components in a movement profile, some combinations are more likely to occur than others. We have noted that Step 1 (momentary flight) in the legs and Step 1 in the arms (bilateral inactive) always occur together. Also, the most advanced hopping combines the most advanced steps in both components. Another common combination is Step 4 in leg action (projection delay, swing leg leads) and Step 3 in arm action (bilateral assist). Even children who can use their arms at more advanced levels will tend to use this combination when the goal of the hop is height, extreme distance, or accuracy, or when fatigue sets in during continuous traveling.

Teaching Hints

The teacher should first observe whether the beginner is trying to hop in place, since this effort tends to keep the body in an upright position. It is difficult for the young child to project the body directly upward against gravity from

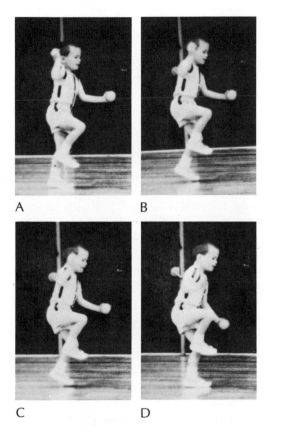

A   B

C   D

Fig. 3–9.   Hop—3 years, 10 months.
Leg action: Step 2. This boy does not let himself fall far off balance before pulling his foot from the surface (frame B).

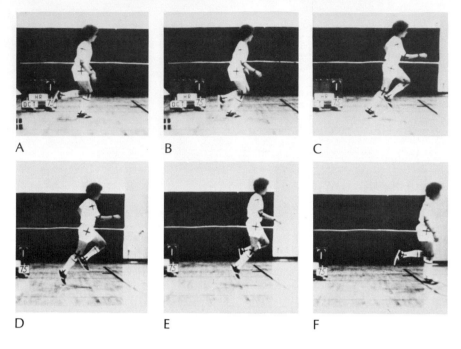

A　　　　　　　B　　　　　　　C

D　　　　　　　E　　　　　　　F

Fig. 3–10.　Hop—16 years.
Leg action: Step 3; Arm action: Step 4. The swing leg leads the upward movement of the hop but does not have sufficient range to swing behind the support leg. The arm opposite the swing leg moves forward and back with that leg. The position of the other arm is variable and not yet working in true opposition. The movement profile of this boy's hop has vastly changed from that illustrated in Figure 3–8.

Fig. 3–11.　Step 4 of Leg Action in the Hop. The range of the swing leg has increased sufficiently to carry it behind the support leg during the hop.

one foot; therefore, the child can do little more than momentary flight when hopping in place. Children having trouble may do better if they try to hop forward. This action shifts their weight off balance so gravity can help produce the hop.

Once the child has begun to move forward

with the hop, the teacher can focus on the leg action to see whether extension in the takeoff phase has begun. At the same time, the teacher should also observe the action in the nonsupport or swing leg. Encouraging use of the swing leg should aid the takeoff phase.

Until children can use their legs to project their bodies effectively in the hop, attempts to change the arm action will probably be ineffective. The balance demands in early movement are too overriding. When the legs do begin to project actively in the hop, the teacher should encourage the beginning of arm and leg cooperation.

Our observations suggest that development in the nonpreferred foot is frequently one step behind that of the preferred foot for both the arms and legs. The teacher should be aware of the child's use of the nonpreferred as well as the preferred foot in locomotion.

Development of the Standing Long Jump

Another common locomotor task, the standing long jump, shows developmental characteristics that are similar to those of hopping. Before two-

Table 3–3 Developmental Sequence for Arm Action in Hopping

Step 1. Bilateral inactive. The arms are held bilaterally, usually high and out to the side, although other positions behind or in front of the body may occur. Any arm action is usually slight and not consistent.

Step 2. Bilateral reactive. Arms swing upward briefly, then are medially rotated at the shoulder in a winging movement prior to takeoff. It appears that this movement is in reaction to loss of balance.

Step 3. Bilateral assist. The arms pump up and down together, usually in front of the line of the trunk. Any downward and backward motion of the arms occurs *after* takeoff. The arms may move parallel to each other or be held at different levels as they move up and down.

Step 4. Semi-opposition. The arm on the side opposite the swing leg swings forward with that leg and back as the leg moves down. The position of the other arm is variable, often staying in front of the body or to the side.

Step 5. Opposing-assist. The arm opposite the swing leg moves forward and upward in synchrony with the forward and upward movement of that leg. The other arm moves in the direction opposite to the action of the swing leg. The range of movement in the arm action may be minimal unless the task requires speed or distance.

Note. This sequence has been partially validated by Halverson and Williams.[70]

footed jumping can be produced, however, the child will substitute a one-footed takeoff with either a one- or two-footed landing. Thus, the step or leap is a frequent substitute for the two-footed jump for distance. This same substitution occurs prior to the ability to jump down.[56] It also persists in the long jumping of some children well into elementary school. Other elementary school children revert back to it when under stress to increase the distance jumped.

When a two-footed takeoff can occur, changes in leg action at takeoff progress from a two-footed, forward "fall," with little or no knee extension, to a two-footed projection takeoff. The first projection takeoff is characterized by incomplete extension of the hip, knee, and ankle. The advanced two-footed takeoff has full extension of the hip, knee, and ankle. In addition to these changes in leg action, the trunk at takeoff shows increasing lean forward from the vertical. The major change in the arms at takeoff is from movement counter to the direction of the jump to a bilateral, forward-upward swing in the direction of the jump.

Leg action changes during the flight and landing phase revolve around the amount of "tuck" during flight, that is the relationship of the thigh with the horizontal. With development, the thigh increasingly approximates a position parallel to the floor. Major arm action changes are from backward movements in flight, to balancing movements, to stabilized, overhead flexion. The need for parachuting reactions on landing also diminishes with advanced development. *Para-*

chuting is a term used to describe protective extension movements of the arms to catch oneself when falling.[72]

These developmental changes have been summarized by Van Sant,[73,69] who hypothesized developmental steps for three movement components within two phases of the jump: the takeoff, and the flight and landing. Tables 3–4 and 3–5 contain a modification by Halverson of the Van Sant sequences.

TAKEOFF PHASE

As in the hop, it is important to observe the standing long jump from the side, opposite the point of takeoff or opposite the flight and landing, whichever phase you are studying. Again, you cannot see both phases at the same time. If you find that you cannot see the action of one of the arms or legs from that side, change to the other side. You may also wish to observe from the front when categorizing some of the arm action. We would suggest first assessing the components involved in the takeoff phase.

OBSERVING THE LEG ACTION. The first developmental level for leg action in the takeoff phase is similar to Step 2 in the hop. The child leans forward enough that gravity can rotate the body over the balls of the feet. Takeoff is achieved mainly because the toes are pulled from the surface in order to catch the off-balance body in a landing. This is why we call it "fall and catch" (Fig. 3–12). The distance of the jump is minimal. If the child has achieved a two-footed takeoff

Table 3–4 Developmental Sequences for the Standing Long Jump
Takeoff Phase

Leg action component

Step 1. Fall and catch. The weight is shifted forward. The knee and ankle are held in flexion or extend slightly as gravity rotates the body over the balls of the feet. Takeoff occurs when the toes are pulled from the surface in preparation for the landing "catch."

Step 2. Two-foot takeoff; Partial extension. Both feet leave the ground symmetrically, but the hips, knees and/or ankles do not reach full extension by takeoff.

Step 3. Two-foot takeoff; Full extension. Both feet leave the ground symmetrically with hips, knees, and ankles fully extended by takeoff.

Trunk action component

Step 1. Slight lean; Head back. The trunk leans forward less than 30° from the vertical. The neck is hyperextended.

Step 2. Slight lean; Head aligned. The trunk leans forward less than 30°, with the neck flexed or aligned with the trunk at takeoff.

Step 3. Forward lean; Chin tucked. The trunk is inclined forward 30° or more (with the vertical) at takeoff, with the neck flexed.

Step 4. Forward lean; Head aligned. The trunk is inclined forward 30° or more. The neck is aligned with the trunk or slightly extended.

Arm action component

Step 1. Arms inactive. The arms are held at the side with the elbows flexed. Arm movement, if any, is inconsistent and random.

Step 2. Winging arms. The arms extend backward in a "winging" posture at takeoff.

Step 3. Arms abducted. The arms are abducted about 90°, with the elbows often flexed, in a high or middle guard position.

Step 4. Arms forward; Partial stretch. The arms flex forward and upward with minimal abduction, reaching incomplete extension overhead by takeoff.

Step 5. Arms forward; Full stretch. The arms flex forward, reaching full extension overhead by takeoff.

Note. These developmental sequences have not been validated. They are modified by Halverson from the work of Van Sant.[73,69]

with some knee, hip, and ankle extension, you must then decide whether the legs are in full extension at takeoff (Step 3) (Fig. 3–14) or whether they are still partially flexed (Step 2) (Fig. 3–13).

OBSERVING THE TRUNK ACTION. To determine the developmental level of the trunk action at takeoff, you must compare the line of the trunk with a vertical line. The smaller the angle between the trunk line with the vertical, the less the forward lean of the trunk. Once you have decided the degree of forward lean of the trunk, then you should concentrate on the relationship of the head and neck to the angle of the trunk. If the trunk is 30° or less from the vertical and the head and neck form a straight line with the trunk, the level is Step 2 (see Figs. 3–12 and 3–13). If the head is back (neck hyperextended or dorsiflexed), the level is Step 1.

If the trunk is inclined forward more than 30° with the vertical, and the chin is tucked into the chest, the child is at Step 3. If the head is aligned, Step 4 is being shown.

OBSERVING THE ARM ACTION. Distinguishing between Steps 1 and 2 in the takeoff arm action is not difficult, since in Step 1 the arms are inactive whereas in Step 2 they clearly move down and back. Distinguishing between Steps 3 and 4 is a matter of deciding whether the forward swinging arms reach shoulder level and move out of plane into an abducted position out to the side (Figs. 3–12 and 3–13) or whether they stay in plane, stopping their forward swing about shoulder level (Fig. 3–14). The position of abduction is frequently called "high guard" when hands are held at about shoulder level or higher and "middle guard" when they are held about waist to chest high.[72] These guard posi-

Table 3–5 Developmental Sequences for the Standing Long Jump, Flight and Landing Phase

Leg action component
Step 1. Minimal "tuck." The thigh is carried in flight more than 45° below the horizontal. The legs may assume either symmetrical or asymmetrical configurations during flight, resulting in one- or two-footed landings.
Step 2. Partial "tuck." During flight, the hips and knees flex synchronously. The thigh approaches a 20 to 35° angle below the horizontal. The knees then extend for a two-footed landing.
Step 3. Full "tuck." During flight, flexion of both knees precedes hip flexion. The hips then flex, bringing the thighs to the horizontal. The knees then extend, reaching forward to a two-foot landing.

Trunk action component
Step 1. Slight lean. During flight, the trunk maintains its forward inclination of less than 30°, then flexes for landing.
Step 2. Corrected lean. The trunk corrects its forward lean of 30° or more by hyperextending. It then flexes forward for landing.
Step 3. Maintained lean. The trunk maintains the forward lean of 30° or more from takeoff to midflight, then flexes forward for landing.

Arm action component
Step 1. Arms "winging." In two-footed takeoff jumps, the shoulders may retract while the arms extend backward (winging)[56] during flight. They move forward (parachuting) during landing.
Step 2. Arms abducted; Lateral rotation. During flight, the arms hold a high guard position and continue lateral rotation. They parachute for landing.
Step 3. Arms abducted; Medial rotation. During flight, the arms assume high or middle guard positions, but medially rotate early in the flight. They parachute for landing.
Step 4. Arms overhead. During flight, the arms are held overhead. In middle flight, the arms lower (extend) from their overhead flexed position, reaching forward at landing.

Note. These developmental steps have not been validated. They have been modified by Halverson from the work of Van Sant.[73,69]

tions are frequently seen in early levels of locomotion, most notably, in the toddler attempting walking. Finally, in contrast with all the preceding levels, Step 5 arms show a fully stretched position at takeoff, making the trunk and arms a straight line.

FLIGHT AND LANDING PHASE

OBSERVING THE LEG ACTION. The key to the three developmental levels of leg action is the angle of the thigh with the horizontal. Envision a horizontal line with another crossing 45° below it (i.e., "half of a right angle"). In flight, Step 1 legs carry the thigh at or below the imaginary line (see Figs. 3–12 and 3–13); Step 2 thighs swing to a position above the line; Step 3 thighs are carried parallel with the horizontal line.

OBSERVING THE TRUNK ACTION. The trunk continues in flight at the same angle as takeoff in Step 1 (less than 30° from the vertical) and Step 3 (more than 30° from the vertical), so it is easy to distinguish between them. Deciding between Steps 2 and 3: the trunk takeoff lean is more than 30°, but in Step 2 the body reacts to this precarious off-balance position by hyperextending the trunk. In Step 3, the trunk maintains the forward lean of takeoff until midflight, when it flexes for landing.

OBSERVING THE ARM ACTION. In Step 1 of arm action, children either hold the winging position of takeoff or continue to move the arms backward during the early part of the flight. They then reach out or parachute forward to catch themselves while landing. The arm action in both Steps 2 and 3 begins by swinging forward and up into a high guard position. The difference is that in Step 2, the arms then laterally rotate (see Figs. 3–12 and 3–13), whereas in Step 3 the arms medially rotate, moving the hands down and back.

Teaching Hints

Action in the takeoff phase substantially affects what is possible in the flight and landing phase;

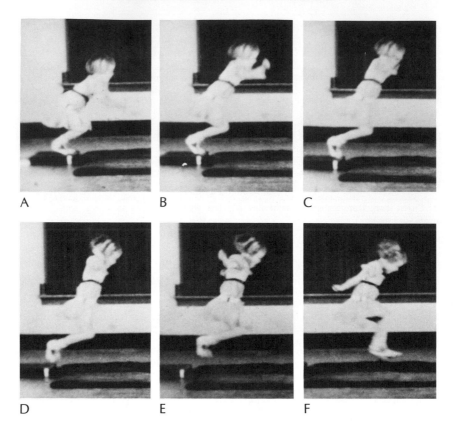

Fig. 3–12.   Fall and Catch—5 years, 6 months

Takeoff phase: Leg action: Step 1; Trunk action: Step 2; Arm action: Step 3. *Flight and landing phase:* Leg action: Step 1; Trunk action: Step 1; Arm action: Step 2. This child performs a standing long jump by shifting her weight off balance, holding her knee and ankle position (frames B and C) as gravity rotates her body over her feet. She pulls her feet from the surface at takeoff (frame D).

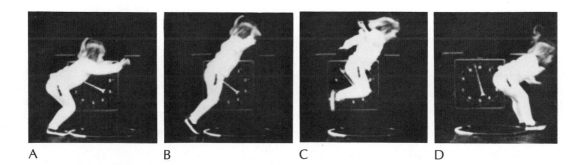

Fig. 3–13.   Project, Ride, and Land—3 years, 4 months.

Takeoff phase: Leg action: Step 2; Trunk action: Step 2; Arm Action: Step 3. *Flight and landing phase:* Leg action: Step 1; Trunk action: Step 1; Arm action: Step 2. Knee extension (projection) occurs from frame A to B in this standing long jump. While more advanced in leg action, the child's arm action remains similar to that of the child in Figure 3–12, illustrating how components within a motor task can develop at differing rates in different individuals.

Fig. 3–14.   Two-foot Takeoff; Full Extension—12 years, 7 months.
Takeoff: Leg action: Step 3; Trunk action: Step 4; Arm action: Step 4. At takeoff, leg action and trunk action show advanced development. The arm action is not yet fully developed.

thus the teacher should first focus on where the child is developmentally in the takeoff phase. One of the first tasks is to help the child achieve a consistent two-footed takeoff. If the child has difficulty resisting the substitution of a one-foot lead, either to help gain distance in the jump, or in reaction to the loss of balance in the takeoff, the teacher may want to change the task slightly. Ask the child to try the standing long jump from a height of about 12 inches and reduce the goal from an all-out jump to a medium distance goal. Marking the desired distance with a piece of tape on the surface will help the child understand how far to try to jump. Reducing the problem of projecting against gravity from the floor and reducing the distance goal frees the child to con-

centrate on keeping the feet together in the take-off. After the child can consistently take off with some extension from two feet, the jump from the floor and increasing distance goals can again be introduced to promote full extension.

As the child gains confidence in the ability to project and land, increasing the distance goal should also bring out an increase in the forward lean of the body. The teacher should monitor what the increased distance goal does to the movement of the child, however, since too much lean too soon may actually cause a protective reaction in both the arm action component ("winging")[56] and in the trunk action during flight (hyperextension). Although the forward-upward swing of the arms is important in assisting the child to project on takeoff, early teaching stress on the arms may be counterproductive. After the child is confident of the ability to use the legs for projection, teaching designed to bring out increased assistance by the arms will be more effective.

Development in Other Locomotor Tasks

Developmental steps have also been hypothesized, although not yet validated, for the locomotor tasks of running[69] (Table 3–6) and skipping (Table 3–7). Study these sequences to pick out the most important changes in each component. Then develop your own decision guides to aid you in categorizing within-component developmental levels. Practice in using your decision guides for observation will enable you to select those which are helpful and to revise the others to aid you in making a clearer categorization.

There are many other locomotor tasks for which we have no hypothesized steps at this time. Through use of film or videotape records of different-aged children in action, you can begin to create your own hypothesized developmental levels for selected tasks. First, decide what components you want to include and then describe the action within each of the components from your filmed or videotaped observations. As you study the components within and across ages, you will begin to pick out movements that seem to be clearly different. By ordering these from least-advanced to most-advanced, you are on your way to establishing beginning definitions of developmental steps. To test the validity of your ordering, graph the frequency of occurrence of your developmental steps across age. If the developmental levels increase in parallel with age, you know that you have detected some potentially key changes in the skill you are studying. If you are interested in the entire process of validating developmental sequences, read the article listed in the Suggested Readings by Roberton, Williams, and Langendorfer.

We would like to stress here also that development can be charted for the many skills in the Laban framework[76] that have no name. By studying the changes in youngsters' responses to the same environmental challenge ("Keep traveling about the gym on different body parts"), developmental sequences can be formulated. Our inability to include such sequences in this chapter underlines the critical need for developmental information on these broader classes of skills.

Developmental Trends Across Foot Locomotion

THE BODY IN RELATION TO GRAVITY

To summarize our discussion of the development of locomotor forms in children, we would like to present two trends we have noticed that seem to generalize across several foot locomotion tasks.

The first is in the way the body projects against or cooperates with gravity as it travels. Most advanced locomotor activities require a "project, ride, and land" sequence of action. The performer (1) cooperates with and then projects against gravity in the takeoff, (2) cooperates with gravity in the flight phase, and (3) opposes gravity in the landing phase. In early development, however, there is little or no projection phase; thus, the sequence is one of fall (cooperating with gravity) and catch (opposing gravity). In the fall, children lean forward with hips and knees flexed, shifting their weight off balance. They then hold the knee position, letting the pull of gravity rotate the body over the ball (metatarsal-phalangeal joint) of one or both feet. While rotating, they often extend at the hips while holding back at the trunk. In the catch, the foot is pulled or withdrawn from the floor through hip and knee flexion as a response to this off-balance position. Thus, the catch begins at takeoff.

The rate of progress from a fall-and-catch sequence to the more developmentally advanced project, ride, and land sequence varies from task to task. A child may have begun to project upward with a one-foot lead but still be in the fall-and-catch sequence in a two foot to two foot pattern. When children do begin to extend actively at the hips and knees in the takeoff phase of a locomotor task, they have taken a significant step in developmental progression. Changes in the manner in which the body is used to accomplish the projection, however, will continue.

Opposing gravity in the landing is also an important aspect in all locomotor activities. Re-

Table 3–6 Developmental Sequences for Running

Leg action component

Step 1. The run is flat-footed with minimal flight. The swing leg is slightly abducted as it comes forward. When seen from overhead, the path of the swing leg curves out to the side during its movement forward. Foot eversion gives a toeing-out appearance to the swinging leg. The angle of the knee of the swing leg is greater than 90° during forward motion.

Step 2. The swing thigh moves forward with greater acceleration, causing 90° of maximal flexion in the knee. From the rear, the foot is no longer toed-out nor is the thigh abducted. The sideward swing of the thigh continues, however, causing the foot to cross the body midline when viewed from the rear. Flight time increases. After contact, which may still be flat-footed, the support knee flexes more as the child's weight rides over the foot.

Step 3. Foot contact is with the heel or the ball of the foot. The forward movement of the swing leg is primarily in the sagittal plane. Flexion of the thigh at the hip carries the knee higher at the end of the forward swing. The support leg moves from flexion to complete extension by takeoff.

Arm action component

Step 1. The arms do not participate in the running action. They are sometimes held in high guard or, more frequently, middle guard position. In high guard, the hands are held about shoulder high. Sometimes they ride even higher if the laterally rotated arms are abducted at the shoulder and the elbows flexed. In middle guard, the lateral rotation decreases, allowing the hands to be held waist high. They remain motionless, except in reaction to shifts in equilibrium.

Step 2. Spinal rotation swings the arms bilaterally to counterbalance rotation of the pelvis and swing leg. The frequently oblique plane of motion plus continual balancing adjustments give a flailing appearance to the arm action.

Step 3. Spinal rotation continues to be the prime mover of the arms. Now the elbow of the arm swinging forward begins to flex, then extend during the backward swing. The combination of rotation and elbow flexion causes the arm rotating forward to cross the body midline and the arm rotating back to abduct, swinging obliquely outward from the body.

Step 4. The humerus (upper arm) begins to drive forward and back in the sagittal plane independent of spinal rotation. The movement is in opposition to the other arm and to the leg on the same side. Elbow flexion is maintained, oscillating about a 90° angle during the forward and backward arm swings.

Note. These sequences have not been validated. They were hypothesized by Roberton[69] from the work of Wickstrom[74] and Seefeldt, Reuschlein, and Vogel.[75]

ceiving and absorbing the force, smoothly slowing the action, and bringing the downward movement to a halt, or shifting it in another direction, present a challenge. In landing, the young child is more controlled by, than controlling, gravity. These early landings are characterized either by a stiff-legged or a collapsing stop. In the stiff-legged stop there is little flexion in the knees, ankles, and hips following the landing touchdown. The weight is stopped suddenly with a jolt rather than slowly absorbed. In the collapse landing, there is little resistance to the action of gravity by the legs, so the mover ends in a heap. In advanced levels, the child effectively opposes gravity, smoothly controlling the landing with an accurately timed reversal from leg extension to leg flexion at landing touchdown. The mover can redirect the movement back into extension or shift the momentum smoothly into a roll or some other task.

LEG DOMINATION TO ARM AND LEG COOPERATION

A second developmental trend in locomotion on the feet is the shift in force production from legs only to the combined action of arms and legs. In early locomotor tasks, the body almost appears to be acting in two parts since considerable movement occurs in the lower body and little in the upper body. The arms are primarily held out to the side and high in readiness for any sudden emergency. As we said earlier, this protective position is termed high guard (Fig. 3–7).[72] A little later, the arms may be carried about waist level, in middle-guard position, or down at the side, but they still contribute little to force production. In early jumping or leaping, the arms may even move in a direction counter to the direction of travel. This action has been termed winging.[56]

When the arms first begin to work with the

Table 3–7 Developmental Sequences for the Skip

Leg action component

Step 1. One-footed skip. One foot completes a step and hop before the weight is transferred to the other foot. The other foot just steps.

Step 2. Two-footed skip; Flat-footed landing. Each foot completes a step and a hop before the weight is transferred to the other foot. Landing from the hop is on the total foot, or on the ball of the foot, with the heel touching down before the weight is transferred (flat-footed landing).

Step 3. Two-footed skip; Ball of the foot landing. Landing from the hop is on the ball of the foot. The heel does not touch down before the weight is transferred to the other foot. Body lean increases over that found in Step 2.

Arm action component

Step 1. Bilateral assist. The arms pump bilaterally up as the weight is shifted from the hopping to the stepping foot and down during the hop takeoff and flight.

Step 2. Semi-opposition. The arms first swing up bilaterally. During the hop on the right foot, the right arm moves down and back only slightly while the left arm continues to move backward until the step on the left foot. Then, both arms again move forward and upward in a new bilateral pumping action. Now, however, the left arm moves back only slightly while the right arm moves backward until the step on the right foot. Although the arm action has the beginnings of opposition, at some time in the arm cycle both hands are in front of the body.

Step 3. Opposition. The arm opposite the stepping leg swings upward and forward in synchrony with that leg and reverses direction when the stepping leg touches the floor. The arm on the same side as the stepping leg moves backward and down in opposition to the stepping leg. At no time are both hands in front of the body.

Note. These sequences, hypothesized by Halverson, have not been validated.

legs in force production, they usually move bilaterally (together) in an outward, or forward and upward movement. Finally, in locomotor tasks with alternating foot patterns, movement in synchrony with the leg on the opposite side of the body appears.

LOCOMOTION ON OTHER BODY PARTS

Although coping with the double- and single-task foot patterns of childhood absorbs much of the young child's time, often the child also moves about on body parts other than or in addition to the feet. While a child has endless ways for moving from one place to another in this fashion, rolling is a common choice. Rolling is also frequently combined with foot pattern activities. The ability to transfer the weight smoothly from a run or a jump into a roll is both a satisfying accomplishment and an important factor in safety.

A child may roll sideward, backward, or diagonally in a curled or stretched position, and he may lead with various parts of the body, such as a shoulder, hip, hands, or knees. Earliest to develop is sideward rolling in a stretched position. In fact, rolling from a supine to a prone position is a "milestone" in an infant's development. Rolling forward in a somersault seems to present an intriguing challenge for the very young child even though it is not the easiest way to roll. Either in imitation of older children, or through self-discovery, the child kneels or squats down, puts the head down and sometimes the hands, extends the knees, and waits to roll. After a while, when nothing happens, the child may attempt to jam over, pushing with everything available and usually ending in a sideward collapse. Often a child associates the word "roll" only with the forward somersault. If asked to roll, the child may not respond with the many other options available. This limited concept of rolling should be expanded, so that the child feels free to choose rolling actions that are effective and comfortable.

Use of Arms and Hands

As in the early developmental levels of locomotion on the feet, the body seems to operate in two parts during early rolling. The arms and hands are relatively inactive at first and only later emerge as important contributors to the total action. Many children do not perceive that the hands and arms are part of a roll. Often children in a stretched roll leave their arms at their sides, making the roll bumpy and their arms useless in assisting. When children do hold their arms overhead in a stretched roll, they seldom maintain active flexion in their shoulders. Instead, their arms flop in a circumductory attempt to compensate for the lack of pelvic lead in their rotation. Often in beginning curled or tucked rolls in a sideward direction, the arms and hands are also used ineffectively. In these early attempts, children are likely to respond to the idea of curl by putting their arms and hands around their knees. While they may achieve a tight curl, the position presents two difficulties: (1) the body usually rocks forward toward the shoulders and head instead of moving sideward, and (2) the body rolls over the hands holding the knees. Both are unpleasant experiences.

In early attempts to roll in a forward direction, children may sometimes put their heads on the mat without using the arms at all. If the arms and hands are placed on the supporting surface, they do little to assist in the roll. When children do begin to use their arms, they may push harder on one side than on the other or, instead of pushing, completely collapse the support in one arm. The strength and timing involved in receiving the weight on the arms and hands and slowly lowering the body against gravity are beyond the young child. In spite of early interest in the roll in a forward direction, many children do not find it much fun. Rolls with other parts of the body leading in different directions may prove more satisfying and more useful to them.

Losing the Curl

A tightly curled (flexed) body position is easy for a young child in a stationary position. Maintaining this position during the rotation presents a different challenge. A common trend across curled or tucked rolls in any direction or with any body lead is to let the body extend or lose the tightness of the curl during rotation.[77]

Sideward rolls lose their curl when the child is on the back, probably because the abdominal muscles are not strong enough, but also because the child does not attach any importance to staying curled. Rolls in a forward direction lose their curl when the individual abandons active work during the roll after the loss of balance. The child pushes to an off-balance position and waits for gravity to bring the body down. As it falls toward

the support surface, the head, shoulders, and arms remain behind. To combat this head and trunk lag, the hips actively extend forming a long leg-lever to assist in righting the body. The roll is completed with trunk and legs in a semipiked position, pivoting over the pelvis and landing with a plop on the floor (see Fig. 3–16). The child cooperates with gravity to get an assist in bringing the trunk and head up against gravity, but then is caught in a sitting position at the end of the roll.

In backward rolls, the curl is lost if the progress of the roll is slowed or stopped by the head and neck. The hips are extended in an effort to keep the action going. O'Quinn commented that some children push the feet upward just before the hips pass the shoulders in the off-balance position in an attempt to take weight off the shoulders and head.[78]

These developmental trends in the use of the arms and hands and in the use of the trunk and legs (losing the curl) are apparent in many forms of rolling. The following developmental sequences have been tentatively determined for the components within forward rolling.

Development of the Forward Roll

Roberton and Halverson have previously hypothesized developmental sequences in the forward roll.[79] Williams partially validated a modification and expansion of these sequences.[80] Based on this work, we have hypothesized sequences within an initial phase (Table 3–8) and a completion phase (Table 3–9) of the roll. The initial phase has been defined as the time from the first movement in the roll to the point when the hips begin moving forward and downward. The completion phase includes the time from that point to the termination of the roll.

INITIAL PHASE

OBSERVING THE HEAD AND ARM ACTION. One of the first decisions you have to make is whether the hands and arms are taking most, or all, of the body weight (Step 3); are only partially supporting the body weight (Step 2); or, are supporting the body weight very little (Step 1). It is usually easy to identify Step 3. It is obvious that the weight is primarily on the arms and hands if the head is free to slide through the

Table 3—8 Developmental Sequences for the Forward Roll
Initial Phase

Head and Arm action component

Step 1. Head support. Little weight is taken on the arms and hands. The hands are often placed on the surface even with the line of the head. The angle at the elbow is approximately 45°. The child may be unable to hold the weight evenly, so the body collapses to one side.

Step 2. Head and arm support. The arms and hands partially accept the body weight. The base of support of the hands tends to be wide from side to side and behind the head toward the feet. The angle at the elbow is greater than 90°.

Step 3. Arm support. The arms and hands now accept the weight as the roll begins, permitting the head, with the chin tucked, to slide through the arms.

Leg action component

Step 1. One-leg push. One leg leads in leaving the surface, then the knee and hip of the lead leg flex while the other leg extends on the push-off.

Step 2. Two-leg push. Both legs push off equally. The knees flex to about 90° as the balance is lost.

Note. These sequences have been modified from Williams[80] and Roberton and Halverson.[79]

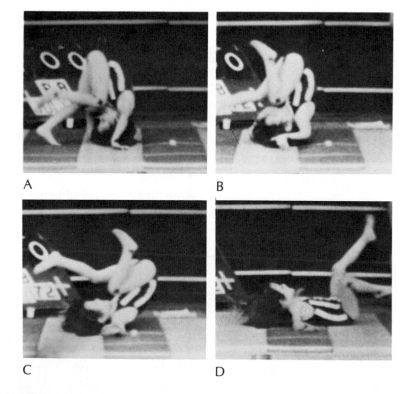

A   B

C   D

Fig. 3—15. Forward Roll—4 years.
Initial phase: Head and arm action: Step 1; Leg action: Step 1. *Completion phase:* Arm action: Step 1; Head and trunk action: Step 1; Leg action: Step 1. Rotation is over the head (frame A). In frame C, the arms fail to move forward and upward to continue the roll. The head and upper back lag even after the middle and lower back have contacted the mat (frame D).

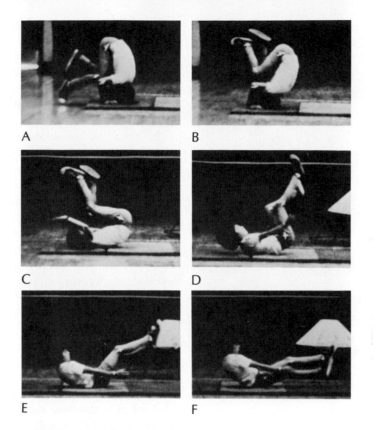

Fig. 3–16. Forward Roll—9 years, 1 month.
Initial phase: Head and arm action: Step 2; Leg action: Step 1. *Completion phase:* Arm action: Step 2; Head and trunk action: Step 2; Leg action: Step 1. Rotation occurs over the head and hands (frames A and B). As the roll continues, the arms partially assist (frames C through E). The head and upper trunk are off the support surface when the lower back touches the mat (frame E). From frames C through E, the knees and hips extend as the child loses the curl.

arms during the early part of the roll (Fig. 3–17). Distinguishing between Steps 1 and 2, however, is more difficult. If you note that the child can easily shift the hand position in the early part of the roll, you can be fairly sure that the weight is mainly on the head (Step 1, Fig. 3–15). You will often see the hands placed in a line perpendicular to each side of the head, sometimes with the fingers pointing forward and sometimes pointing toward the head. You may also see that the arms are ineffective in preventing the body from collapsing to the side. In Step 2, the head is in contact with the surface as in Step 1, but the hands are now placed behind the head toward the feet in a fairly wide base of support (Fig. 3–16).

COMPLETION PHASE

OBSERVING THE ARM ACTION. In Step 1, the arms may stay back by the head where they were in the initial phase. Rather than leading the head and trunk in the forward-upward motion of the roll, you will see that they are pulled off by this motion (Fig. 3–15B). You may also see the arms abducted to the side during this phase. In contrast, in Step 2, the arms swing forward to assist in the forward-upward movement of the head and trunk, but not until the shoulders or the middle back have touched the surface (Fig. 3–16D). Step 3 is not difficult to categorize. The arms and hands push off, beginning the swing forward as the shoulders receive the body weight (Fig. 3–17C). The assisting action of the arms continues through completion of the roll (Fig. 3–17D, E, and F).

OBSERVING THE HEAD AND TRUNK ACTION. It is not difficult to identify Step 1. Note, first, that the weight is supported at least in part by the head. As the hips begin to move forward and downward in the early part of the completion phase, the child "abandons" the body to

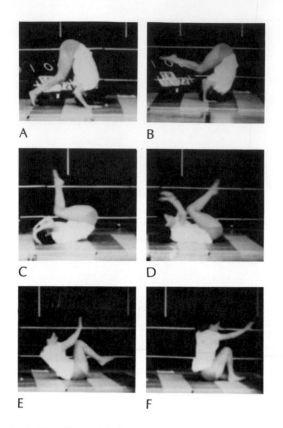

A   B

C   D

E   F

Fig. 3–17. Forward Roll—Young Adult.
Initial phase: Head and arm action: Step 3; Leg action: Step 2. *Completion phase:* Arm action: Step 3; Head and trunk action: Step 3; Leg action: Step 3. Rotation is over the hands, with the head only lightly in contact with the mat (frame B). The arms actively assist (frames D through F). The upper trunk and head are already off the surface as the middle back touches (frame D). The curl is held throughout.

is already off the surface by the time the hips touch (Fig. 3–17E).

OBSERVING THE LEG ACTION. Focus first on the action at the hips as they begin to move forward and downward in the completion phase. If the hips lose the tightly flexed position of the initial phase and extend during the completion of the roll, you can tentatively categorize the action as Step 1 or 2. Concentrate next on the action at the knees. If the knees either maintain an extended position, or increase extension during the roll, the action is defined as Step 1 (Figs. 3–15 and 3–16). If, however, the knees increase in flexion during the roll, it is Step 2. Step 3 is usually fairly easy to categorize because you will see a tightening of the curl with increasing knee flexion through completion of the roll. The flexed hip position of the initial phase is maintained (Fig. 3–17).

Teaching Hints

Rolling in a forward direction is a developmentally advanced task. Before attempting forward rolling, children should have substantial experience in taking and holding their weight on their hands, at least momentarily, in a variety of situations. They should also be experienced in holding a tightly curled position in other developmentally less difficult rolling tasks. Then, if they choose this form of rolling, they may be ready to accomplish it with some control, thus gaining satisfaction from the experience.

Even after experience in taking weight on the hands in other situations, children may still begin the forward roll by putting the head on the support surface. The teacher should immediately work to change this concept by helping the child learn to take weight on the hands and upper back with little or no head contact on the support surface. Then, children need time simply to experience the rapidly changing upside-down position of this form of rolling. When children have had enough experience to know what to expect, they can begin working to keep the curl in their body after the balance point is lost at the beginning of the roll.

NONLOCOMOTION

Bending, curling, stretching, twisting, turning are all movement terms used by Laban[76] and

gravity. With the head on the surface as a pivot point, the trunk is often forced to flatten out (extend) rather than increase the curl (flex). The child is unable to bring the upper trunk and head forward and upward after landing on the flattened back so these are left behind, often just off the surface (Fig. 3–15D). Frequently, the child will end in a supine position or must use the arms and hands to push up to a sitting position.

A key difference between Steps 2 and 3 is that in Step 2 the head and upper trunk just begin to leave the surface as the middle of the back touches (Fig. 3–16D). They are well away from the surface by the time the hips touch (Step 2) (Fig. 3–16E). In Step 3, however, the head is already well off the surface by the time the upper trunk has touched (Fig. 3–17D), and the trunk

Table 3–9 Developmental Sequences for the Forward Roll
Completion Phase

Arm action component

Step 1. Little assistance. The arms may remain back by the head until pulled off by the forward motion of the body.

Step 2. Incomplete assist. The arms swing forward to assist in the completion of the roll when the shoulders and/or middle of the back have touched the surface. The elbows are extended during the assist. The hands may be used to push the body to the feet at the end of the roll.

Step 3. Continual arm assist. The arms swing forward to assist in continuation of the momentum of the roll, as soon as the weight has transferred to the shoulders. The arms continue to assist in a forward-upward direction until the weight is over the feet.

Head and trunk component

Step 1. Head and trunk lag. As the hips begin the forward-downward movement, the child abandons the body to gravity. The upper trunk and hips land on the surface almost simultaneously. As the middle of the back and hips land, the head and upper back lag behind, often remaining close to or just off the surface, even when the lower back has made contact.

Step 2. Partial head and trunk lag. The shoulders touch the surface before the middle of the back and hips, but the head and shoulders do not then leave the surface again until the middle of the back has touched. The body usually continues the roll in a semipiked position over the pelvis.

Step 3. No head and trunk lag. The head leaves the support surface just after the shoulders touch. Both the head and trunk continue moving forward and upward throughout the roll. By the time the lower back contacts the surface, the head and shoulders are well off the mat.

Leg action component

Step 1. Knees extend; hips extend. The legs tend to hold their push-off position until the lower back or pelvis touches the support surface. At this point, extension in the hip increases, contributing to the loss of curl in the roll. The knees either increase in extension or continue in an extended position. The angle at the hip may reach approximately 120° and is then held if the body continues rotating over the pelvis.

Step 2. Knees flex; hips extend. Leg action begins as in Step 1. When the middle of the back touches the support surface, extension at the hips increases also as in Step 1, but the knees flex rather than continuing in an extended position. The roll may continue with the body in this position or the hips may flex.

Step 3. Knees flex; hips flex. The knees begin flexion just after the hips begin the forward-downward movement in the roll and maintain that flexion throughout the roll. The hips continue flexion throughout the roll.

Note. These sequences have been hypothesized from Williams[80] and Roberton and Halverson.[79]

others to describe the anatomic actions of flexion, extension, and rotation. All movements of the body are characterized by complex and changing combinations of these actions. For example, stretching predominates in reaching for an object on a shelf or for a high fly ball, whereas bending predominates in landing from a jump. Twisting is characteristic in sudden changes of direction or in batting a softball. The development of these actions within tasks as well as in isolation is, therefore, of considerable interest to the teacher of movement.

Bending and Stretching

Bending or curling is the dominant posture of infancy. Stretching assumes an important role in the infant's achievement of mobility. Thus, from infancy, curling and stretching movements are familiar and often used in place of the developmentally more difficult rotation movements. Yet, in daily life, stretching and curling seldom proceed through full joint range. While teaching, we have often observed partial stretches or partial curls even when the full stretch or tight curl was the child's goal or was required in the task. Children may assume a position that they think is a full stretch and yet have parts of their body (often arms, fingers, or toes) still partially curled.[81] As we mentioned earlier, those same children may find it difficult to assume a tightly curled position in rolling or to maintain it if their muscles have to work against gravity or centrifugal force.[77] Early in development, the extremes of stretching and curling are often not part of children's repertoire.

Complexity also affects the stretch and curl extremes. For instance, as children begin to combine flexion and extension movements into sequences, they often lapse into a middle range of motion, for several reasons. Children tend to rush their movement when they begin to sequence; thus, they do not allow time for a full stretch or curl. Often, too, they become preoccupied with the problem of sequencing and forget to push themselves for the extremes of movement. Timing difficulties also affect children's ability to show a bend or stretch extreme as they work with movement combinations. To fit a full stretch into a flight period that must end in a flexed landing is developmentally difficult. First, the separate components must be mastered, and then timed perfectly to each other. Anticipation of the landing must be inhibited until the last possible, safe moment.

Stretching and curling frequently alternate in movement; yet, early in development, smooth transitions from one to the other are often difficult, particularly within other motor tasks. For example, in catching, the arms and body stretch forward to reach for the ball. At early levels, bending of the fingers, arms, and body often does not occur until after contact, resulting in a jarring stop of the ball or even a miss. In later levels, the arms and body begin the bending phase before contact. This bending movement continues, slowing as the force of the moving ball is absorbed.

Twisting and Turning

Twisting and turning both involve rotation. Turning means to rotate the entire body around an axis. It is initiated with a briefly resisted twist that is then resolved into a sequentially rotating turn.[77] Twisting itself means to resist the rotation of one part of the body with another part. In twisting, parts of the body may remain stationary while other parts rotate, or body parts may rotate in opposite directions.

Both twisting and turning demand differentiation; that is, different body parts must do different things. Turning, however, requires only brief differentiation during the time the twist initiates the turn; twisting of itself requires either

that a differentiated part fix while the other part rotates or that it rotate in opposition. Twisting also requires a resolution either by untwisting to realign the body or by turning. Developmentally, therefore, turning is the easier of the two and is sometimes substituted for twisting.

In early infancy, the first tendency for the body or segments of the body is to turn in one piece with no sequential resistance. Prior to 4 months of age, the infant moves like a log or "block" when rotated.[72] After that period, the body "derotates" or sequentially untwists when rotary force is applied. If the pelvic girdle of the infant is rotated, the shoulders and head resist and then sequentially rotate to become aligned in an untwisted position.

As voluntary turning occurs, it shows a developmental progression. McGraw studied rolling behavior in infants who were trying to move from supine to prone.[82] She reported that the turn was initiated with a twisting action in the upper body while the lower body lagged behind. Later, the pelvis began to lead with the shoulders lagging. We see this trend repeated often in elementary school children as they attempt a sideward roll in a stretched position. First, they initiate the roll with shoulders and head, often rolling crooked as a result. Only with experience do they initiate the roll with their pelvis.

When children are on their feet, the first twists are usually performed with one of the differentiated parts remaining fixed. Twisting of parts in opposing directions does not occur until later in development. In developmentally early twists, the child is sometimes unable to keep a body part fixed in resistance to the twist. When this happens, the twist gives way to a turn. Beginning batters, for instance, may walk in a circle with the swinging bat because they cannot fix their feet to resist the twist of the trunk during the backswing or its untwist in the forward swing.

As children begin to hold the fixed part so they can twist against it, they still show a developmental progression within the untwisting. First, the derotating parts show a block rotation rather than a differentiation, as illustrated in throwing and striking. The legs may stay fixed during the twist-up of the backswing, but the trunk will then untwist or derotate as a unit or block. Only later will the trunk show a sequential untwist, with pelvis and spine initiating their derotations separately. The developmental order within the initiation of derotation follows generally what McGraw observed in the turning action of infants.[82] At first, the untwist begins in the shoulders, and the pelvis follows suit. Later in development, the untwist begins at the pelvis as the shoulders are still twisting into the backswing.

AVOIDING CONTACT WITH OBJECTS

One way to avoid an object is to dodge it, that is, to change direction while locomoting. This activity forms the basis of many games and correlates highly with subjective judgment of games ability.[83] Dodging also is prerequisite to traveling safely across a crowded playground or avoiding an obstacle in one's path. It has traditionally been considered a good indication of overall body management and is often used as a part of safety work.[84] Dodging may employ either or both aspects of direction change:[85] within a single dodge, one may change body facing or movement direction or both.[77,86]

Tests measuring change of direction, such as the zigzag run, show steady improvement from grades 1 through 6.[87] Boys tend to be faster than girls within their grade level and, after third grade, faster than girls older than they. These findings, however, do not indicate how the movement changes with increasing age. In fact, we are not sure how an advanced performer dodges.

Mauldon and Redfern have suggested that 5-year-olds are usually not able to stop suddenly or to make sharp changes of direction even without the perceptual demand of timing their movement to an outside object.[46] Harper investigated this claim in more detail.[85] She filmed 20 5-year-olds, 10 boys and 10 girls, as they ran along a 30-foot pathway and quickly reversed their direction at her signal. She found no difference between boys and girls in movement reversal time or in running velocities. The children with the fastest reversal times were fast both at decelerating and at changing their facing (Fig. 3–18). Of the 60 reversals studied, 88% were executed with from 4 to 6 steps. Interestingly, the number of steps did not relate to the speed of reversal. Pivots did occur, but always in combination with other steps. Harper believes that the classic pivot occurs only from the isolated standing, forward-stride position.

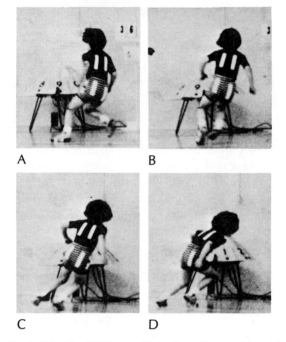

A B

C D

Fig. 3–18. Rapid Change of Direction—5 years. This girl in the Harper[85] study has fast running and reversal times. Initiation of her facing change precedes placement of the left foot in an oblique direction (frame A). The right foot is not placed until frame C. The left foot then pushes off in the reverse direction.

About 75% of the turns were to the child's left, although this finding may have been an artifact of her filming situation. Harper also observed children in several other 180° turning situations, such as running to objects or lines before turning. She noted that 5-year-olds tended to circle 3-dimensional objects but to pivot or reverse turn from a forward stride position when asked to run to a line on the floor and return.

Teaching Implications

Harper's data tentatively suggest that dodging practice should focus on the twisting movements of the upper body, when a facing change is called for, rather than on placement of the feet.[85] Some English field hockey players have suggested this for years: ". . . remember that the head is in charge of balance and often initiates the movement of the feet. . . . Throw head into the lead in the new direction, . . . Think consciously of the head and the push-off."[88]

SENDING OBJECTS AWAY

To generalize the course of development for all motor tasks that involve sending an object away would be premature, given present knowledge. We do, however, have information on the development of forceful throwing and striking with the hands or with a handheld implement. In fact, several similarities exist between the development of forceful overarm and sidearm throwing and overarm and sidearm striking.

Although we will focus this section on those tasks, we will also share some hypothesized developmental sequences for punting, another form of sending an object away.

Development of Trunk Action in Throwing and Striking

The first similarity between throwing and striking tasks is the way trunk action (action of the pelvis and spine) develops. In producing forceful throwing and striking movements of the hand, the trunk acts first as a passive, nonmoving stabilizer and later as an active force producer. When the trunk begins moving, it moves only in a forward-backward direction. Later it moves in a rotary direction. Therefore, both the primitive and advanced performer face their target at ball release, but the advanced child has sequentially rotated to that position. The primitive mover began there. Three developmental steps occur in trunk action.[62,64] They are listed in Table 3–10.

Trunk action needs to be observed from both the side and rear of the performer. The first thing

to look for is the presence of rotary movements. If no rotation is occurring, the child is in level 1. Observation from the side will indicate whether a level 1 child is flexing forward at the hips or whether the trunk is not used at all or is moving only as a result of arm movement. Active flexion is a sign that the child is trying to use the trunk for force production; the child may, therefore, be ready to experiment with the next step, rotation (see Fig. 3–19).

If a child is using some form of trunk rotation to produce force in the throw/strike, then either level 2 or 3 has been reached. To determine which level, the observer must stand to the rear of the child to watch the hips and shoulders as forward rotation begins. If the hips and upper spine start rotating forward at the same moment, the child is in level 2, block rotation (see Fig. 3–22). If only the upper spine rotates, the child is also in level 2. If, however, the hips begin forward rotation while the shoulders are still rotating backward, the child has reached the advanced level 3, differentiated rotation.

Teaching Hints

All forceful throwing or striking movements with the hands must eventually be timed to the action of the trunk. The teacher's first goal, therefore, should be to observe trunk action development within those activities. If children are not yet rotating, they should be encouraged to practice twisting and untwisting, both separate from and within the throwing or striking action. They should be challenged to do so with head and feet *stationary*. As they twist, many young

---

Table 3–10   Developmental Sequence for Trunk Action in Throwing and Striking for Force

Step 1. No trunk action or forward-backward movements. Only the arm is active in force production. Sometimes, the forward thrust of the arm pulls the trunk into a passive left rotation (assuming a right-handed throw), but no twist-up precedes that action. If trunk action occurs, it accompanies the forward thrust of the arm by flexing forward at the hips. Preparatory extension sometimes precedes forward hip flexion.

Step 2. Upper trunk rotation or total trunk "block" rotation. The spine and pelvis both rotate away from the intended line of flight and then simultaneously begin forward rotation, acting as a unit or "block." Occasionally, only the upper spine twists away, then toward the direction of force. The pelvis, then, remains fixed, facing the line of flight, or joins the rotary movement after forward spinal rotation has begun.

Step 3. Differentiated rotation. The pelvis precedes the upper spine in initiating forward rotation. The child twists away from the intended line of ball flight and, then, begins forward rotation with the pelvis while the upper spine is still twisting away.

Note. Validation studies support this sequence.[60,61,62,,64,89]

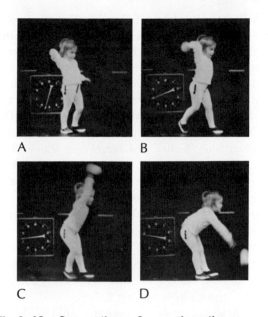

A   B

C   D

Fig. 3–19. Overarm throw—3 years, 4 months.
Trunk action: Step 1; Humerus action and Forearm action: Step 1; Foot action: Step 3. Although her trunk and arm action are primitive, this child does use opposition in her foot action. Note, though, the lack of opening up.

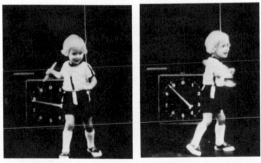

A   B

Fig. 3–20. Undifferentiated Shoulder and Head Movement—3 years, 3 months. By contact, this child's head has rotated with her shoulders past the target. The suspended ball is used to simplify the perceptual demands of striking.

children unconsciously try to keep their heads in line with their shoulders.[90] Their heads follow the movement of their shoulders and arms when they throw, and especially, when they bat. Consequently, they never see the target (Fig. 3–20). With some children, this inability to keep the head stationary while rotating spreads to the feet. As we mentioned in the discussion of twisting, these children cannot rotate their bodies without stepping around to keep their feet in line with their trunks. As batters, they end up

stepping in a circle as they swing the bat. Head and feet need to become differentiated from the trunk to reach intermediate levels of throwing and striking.

When a child has established block rotation with good range, the next teaching goal can be differentiated rotation. Often, a diagonal step to the side encourages the hips to begin rotating earlier than the shoulders.

Opening Up

A second developmental similarity between forceful throwing and striking lies in a phenomenon referred to as "opening up." Harper and Struna use this term to describe the simultaneous movement of body parts in opposite directions in the effort to produce force in the same direction.[91] Primitive levels of throwing and striking with the hands do not exhibit this coordination. Young strikers, for example, first draw the paddle back. Then the hand, trunk, and any stepping actions begin forward movement simultaneously. As they become more advanced, however, they will step forward as the bat or paddle is still going back.[71,91] They appear to stretch out, expand, or open up when observed from the side. This occurrence may relate to the type of back or reverse swing used. Primitive throwers and strikers lift the hand to head level via shoulder abduction, flexion, and lateral rotation. Advanced children swing the hand across the body, back, and then up in a circumductory movement.[92,93]

An extreme prolongation of opening up occurs in the advanced over- and sidearm throw for force. In this example, the reverse arm swing occurs while the forward step is taken, and it continues as forward trunk action begins. As the trunk proceeds in its rotation, the arm starts to rotate laterally (outwardly) at the shoulder. Because of this lateral rotation, the ball in the child's hand remains stationary behind the body as the child moves forward or even drops back or down. When the pelvis and upper spine have rotated to front facing, the arm has rotated laterally to its farthest point back. When viewed from the side in motion pictures, the forearm often appears parallel with the floor (see Fig. 3–25D). Thus, during the entire forward rotation of the trunk, the ball and hand have lagged behind the performer. He/she has opened up to the point of rotating forward and out from under his/her own hand as though someone were holding it as he/she untwists forward.

Development of Arm Action

Until considerable opening up occurs in throwing and striking, we refer to the movement as "arm dominated"; that is, the arm leads the forward movement of the body.[90] As opening up occurs, the arm begins to lag behind the trunk's movement. As this lag increases with development, the body rotates completely to front facing and stops momentarily as the hand follows, swinging around it to contact or release.

Developmental sequences have been validated for the action of the humerus (upper arm) and the forearm in the throw.[60,61,62] They have been hypothesized for the preparatory arm backswing[93,69] and for foot action.[69] These sequences are defined in Tables 3–11 and 3–12. Langendorfer[64] found that the humerus sequence also describes movements used in overarm striking. The forearm sequence describes the action of the rackethead in overarm striking rather than the action of the forearm itself.

OBSERVING THE PREPARATORY BACKSWING. Developmentally young individuals may omit the backswing entirely when they throw. The ball is simply flung from wherever the hand first contacts it. Those children showing some attempt at moving the ball backward in preparation for the throw should be observed from the front or side. If the hand does not drop below the waist, then the child is either in level 2 or 3. Children in level 2 lift the ball directly up to a position above the shoulder. The elbow stays quite flexed. Children in level 3 swing the ball outward, up, and around, extending the elbow to do so. Children in level 4 swing the ball downward below the waist and back using full elbow extension.

OBSERVING THE FORWARD ACTION OF THE HUMERUS. A child's developmental level in humerus action is best observed from the side. The first decision to make is whether the humerus is being carried forward to ball release in a line continuous with the line of the shoulders, thus forming a right angle with the trunk.[94] If the humerus is not in line with the shoulders, that is, it is moved forward obliquely above or below the shoulder line (see Figs. 3–21, 3–19,

and 3–22), the child is in level 1. The elbow will point down toward the floor or up toward the ceiling. If the humerus is aligned with the shoulders, the child is either in level 2 or 3.

Level 2 is distinguished from level 3 by looking at the child's position at the *moment of front facing*. This is the point in the throw when the child has rotated the shoulders to a position parallel with or "facing" the target (see frame D in Figs. 3–23, 3–24, and 3–25). In level 2, the child moves the humerus toward the target independently of trunk rotation. By front facing, the humerus has moved so far ahead of the trunk that the elbow appears to be pointing at the target (see Fig. 3–23). By standing to the side of the child, this configuration is easy to spot: If the elbow is outside the line of the body at front facing, the child is in step 2.

If, however, at front facing the child holds the humerus in line with the trunk so the elbow is pointed toward the observer at the side, the child is in step 3 (see Frame D, Figs. 3–24 and 3–25). The child is able to fix the shoulder joint, allowing the humerus to become an extension of the trunk.

OBSERVING THE FORWARD ACTION OF THE FOREARM (RACKETHEAD). The action of the forearm in throwing and of the rackethead in overarm striking is a fascinating phenomenon, resulting primarily from lateral rotation of the humerus at the shoulder. The first decision to be made in assessing a child's developmental level in forearm action is whether any "forearm lag" occurs as the child throws or strikes. Forearm lag is detected by watching the ball in the child's hand. As the child rotates or flexes forward, the ball may travel steadily toward the target. If it does, no forearm lag has occurred and the child is in Step 1.

If, however, the ball-in-the-hand or the rackethead seems to drop downward or stay stationary as the child rotates forward, then lag has occurred. The child is either in step 2 or step 3. The difference between these two levels is difficult to see without the assistance of slow-motion videotape or film, for the difference is a matter of timing. Children who complete their lag before reaching front facing (see Figs. 3–23 and 3–24) are in level 2. Children who can delay the last moment of lag until they reach front facing (see frame D, Fig. 3–25) are in step 3.

Table 3–11 Developmental Sequences for Backswing, Humerus, and Forearm Action in the Overarm Throw for Force

Preparatory arm backswing component

Step 1. No backswing. The ball-in-the-hand moves directly forward to release from the arm's original position when the hand first grasped the ball.

Step 2. Elbow and humeral flexion. The ball moves away from the intended line of flight to a position behind or alongside the head by upward flexion of the humerus and concomitant elbow flexion.

Step 3. Circular, upward backswing. The ball moves away from the intended line of flight to a position behind the head via a circular overhead movement with elbow extended, or an oblique swing back, or a vertical lift from the hip.

Step 4. Circular, downward backswing. The ball moves away from the intended line of flight to a position behind the head via a circular, down and back motion, which carries the hand below the waist.

Humerus (upper arm) action component during forward swing

Step 1. Humerus oblique. The humerus moves forward to ball release in a plane that intersects the trunk obliquely above or below the horizontal line of the shoulders. Occasionally, during the backswing, the humerus is placed at a right angle to the trunk, with the elbow pointing toward the target. It maintains this fixed position during the throw.

Step 2. Humerus aligned but independent. The humerus moves forward to ball release in a plane horizontally aligned with the shoulder, forming a right angle between humerus and trunk. By the time the shoulders (upper spine) reach front facing, the humerus (elbow) has moved independently ahead of the outline of the body (as seen from the side) via horizontal adduction at the shoulder.

Step 3. Humerus lags. The humerus moves forward to ball release horizontally aligned, but at the moment the shoulders (upper spine) reach front facing, the humerus remains within the outline of the body (as seen from the side). No horizontal adduction of the humerus occurs before front facing.

Forearm action component during forward swing

Step 1. No forearm lag. The forearm and ball move steadily forward to ball release throughout the throwing action.

Step 2. Forearm lag. The forearm and ball appear to 'lag,' i.e., to remain stationary behind the child or to move downward or backward in relation to him/her. The lagging forearm reaches its furthest point back, deepest point down, or last stationary point *before* the shoulders (upper spine) reach front facing.

Step 3. Delayed forearm lag. The lagging forearm delays reaching its final point of lag until the moment of front facing.

Note. Validation studies[58,60,61,89,62] support these sequences for the overarm throw with the exception of the preparatory arm backswing sequence which was hypothesized by Roberton[69] from the work of Langendorfer.[93] Langendorfer[64] feels the humerus and forearm components are appropriate for overarm striking (see text).

Development of Foot Action

Table 3–12 defines a sequence for the action of the feet in throwing and striking that has been hypothesized by Roberton.[69]

Unlike the other components of the throw, foot action tends to be variable across trials and less predictable developmentally. For this reason, developmental categorization is questionable without a number of observations and, even then, it may be less reliable.

Movement Profile

Research is only beginning to chart the developmental relationships across component levels in the overarm throw. This question has not been addressed at all in striking. Roberton and Langendorfer[62] reported that in 7 children whose overarm throwing was followed for 9 to 14 years, trunk action was the first component to develop, progressing to block rotation (step 2). Then the humerus progressed to level 2, followed by forearm action. Humerus action then continued to level 3, being the first component to reach an advanced state. After that, the trunk action and forearm action seemed to progress to their advanced levels at about the same time. Not all children, however, reached those advanced levels by the teen years. In another study,

Fig. 3–21. Step 1 of Humerus Action in the Overarm Throw. The humerus moves forward to ball release in a plane that intersects the trunk obliquely, above or below the horizontal line of the shoulders (depicted by the dashed lines).

Halverson et al.[58] found that most seventh graders had not yet achieved advanced levels in throwing.

Common profiles in the throw, then, are block rotation (Step 2 of trunk action) combined with any of the humerus levels. Level 2 of humerus action frequently combines with level 2 of forearm action. Level 3 of humerus action is usually seen with either level 2 or 3 of forearm action.

The earlier development of trunk action may be why the movements in sidearm striking tasks seem developmentally easier to achieve than the movements in throwing tasks. The advanced tennis forehand drive, for instance, combines block or differentiated rotation of the trunk (Step 2 or 3) with an oblique or horizontal humerus (Step 1 or 2) and an extended elbow. The advanced overarm throw combines differentiated rotation with humeral lag, elbow at a right angle, and a complete forearm lag (Step 3). The advanced thrower, therefore, has more developmental steps to master. Frequently, in fact, children substitute a sidearm sling for an overarm throw when they need to produce force.[90] Their trunk action has developed to a block rotation level, but their arm action remains primitive and not helpful in force production. They change their arm, therefore, to a straight lever and fling the ball via trunk rotation and horizontal shoulder adduction (Fig. 3–26). The movement is similar to a one-handed sidearm strike, such as the forehand drive.

Teaching Hints

It is difficult to attain much range during block rotation, and it is impossible to differentiate one's rotation unless the feet are in contralateral position. For this reason, foot action should be worked on concurrently with rotary forms of trunk action. Even if a child is rotating with the feet in contralateral position, we cannot assume a developmentally advanced throw. As we have indicated, the arm action can still remain primitive, so teachers need to find ways to help children learn to lag their arms as they rotate their bodies. The first step may be to help the child lower or raise the upper arm to the horizontal position. The second step might be to help the child rotate "forward and out from under the ball." The last step may be to work on a long, *diagonal* step to elicit differentiated rotation.

Special Aspects of Striking

In one-handed striking, primitive performers often use a "power grip,"[97] holding the racket or paddle as a club with the broad aspect of the handle placed in the palm.[91] This grip forces the wrist to adduct, making the racket head drop. It is also associated with flexion at the elbow during the swing and supination of the forearm. The latter causes the child to undercut the ball, often missing it entirely. While use of the power

Fig. 3–22. Overarm Throw—6 years, 8 months.
Trunk action: Step 2; Humerus action and Forearm action: Step 1; Foot action: Step 3. This boy's arm action is similar to that of the child in Figure 3–19; however, he has progressed to block rotation of the trunk. Frame D, the corresponding rear view of frame A, illustrates the oblique angle formed by humerus and trunk.

A

B

C

D

grip is frequent regardless of racket type, children must use it when the equipment is too big or heavy. Rackets of appropriate weight, having child-sized handles, will cut down the need for the power grip.

The wrist cock is an interesting developmental phenomenon in batting. With development, children begin to abduct and hyperextend the wrists at the top of the backswing, an action that points the end of the bat up in the air. Previously, they had little wrist cock, sometimes letting the tip of the bat point down at the end of the backswing. Erbaugh has noted that the advanced batter tends to maintain this wrist cock longer into the forward swing than does the intermediate batter.[98]

To close this section on striking, we also include hypothesized sequences for punting development (Table 3–13). As a form of striking, kicking shares some of the perceptual complexities associated with striking; yet, in many ways it is a task unique to itself. The punt, in particular, is a skill young children are often frustrated by as they attempt to time the ball drop with the swing of their leg. Again, we encourage the reader to use these sequences as a basis for formulating observation decision rules.

PERCEPTUAL COMPLEXITIES AND TEACHING

Earlier we suggested that one- and two-handed striking reach fruition before one-handed overarm or sidearm throwing. This statement is true if we make the perceptual aspects of these two activities comparable. Motor tasks have been usefully, if simplistically, divided into "open" and "closed."[99] An open task, e.g., striking, demands that movement be adjusted to coincide with an outside, moving stimulus. The striking movement used, regardless of developmental level, must be timed so that the striking surface meets the ball. A closed task, such as throwing, presumably does not require this perceptual adjustment unless the target is moving. To research the development of striking, we have attempted to control the perceptual problems by employing a suspended, stationary ball (see Fig. 3–20).[90,54] We have chosen to use a stationary ball because the child often regresses to a lower level of movement if the perceptual component becomes more complex. Complexity is a factor when an aerial ball replaces a stationary ball, or when a bounced ball replaces an aerial ball (at least with preschool children). It is a factor for the thrower trying to hit a target, especially when the target is moving.

Thus, teachers of physical education should watch the movement of their students carefully as perceptual components become more complex. If children are regressing in their movement, they are not ready for the added perceptual challenge. This suggestion also implies that

A   B

Fig. 3–23. Overarm Throw—6 years, 2 months.
Trunk action: Step 2; Humerus action and Forearm action: Step 2; Foot action: Step 3. During forward movement, this boy's humerus forms an approximate right angle with his trunk (frame B), but by front facing (frame D), it has moved ahead of his trunk. His forearm lags (frames A to B).

C   D

E

both open and closed tasks should be introduced in as "closed" a manner as possible, by simplifying perceptual components. This view is opposite that of Gentile, who argued that open tasks should be taught as such from the beginning.[100] While we support the need for practice in perceptual tracking, we also feel that such practice should involve tasks in which the child is no longer developmentally primitive. In a few pages, we will suggest a useful way for parents and teachers to identify and simplify the complexities involved in the motor tasks children attempt.

DEVELOPMENT OF OTHER MOVEMENT ASPECTS

This discussion of motor development has dealt solely with what Laban called the "body aspect."[76] His movement framework, however, included three other aspects—effort, space, and relationships. Unfortunately, we know of no developmental research dealing with any of these aspects except Harper's work on change of direction.[85] Yet, each aspect is a vital part of the child's movement repertoire.

Despite this lack of research, we have selected a few dimensions for "educated conjecture." We hope that both researchers and teachers will scrutinize these developmental questions both to support or refute our hypotheses and to generate others. The authors cited did not necessarily state the hypothesis as written; rather, their observations may have suggested the hypothesis to us.

Fig. 3–24. Overarm Throw—7 years, 8 months.
Trunk action: Step 2; Humerus action: Step 3; Forearm action: step 2; Foot action: Step 3. This child's humerus forms a right angle to the trunk (frame C) and stays in line with the trunk at front facing (frame D). The forearm drops down in space from frame B to C as the trunk rotates forward. The child has not reached front facing at frame C, when the forearm reaches its deepest lag. Frame F, the rear view of frame E, shows this block rotator has flexed laterally away from the ball at release.

Developmental Hypotheses

EFFORT ASPECT: TIME. Children's ability to move in a slow, sustained manner develops after their ability to move quickly.[101]

Children can handle sustained movements performed over a wide base of support before they can perform sustained movements that require a great deal of balance.[102]

Children can slowly increase their speed before they can gradually decrease it.[102]

Children can move to their own rhythm before they can adjust their movement to someone else's rhythm.

EFFORT ASPECT: FLOW. Children's ability to stop movement with control develops after their ability to initiate it with control.[102]

Simultaneous initiation of movement precedes sequential initiation.

EFFORT ASPECT: WEIGHT. Strong, forceful movements developmentally precede fine, light movements.

SPACE ASPECT: LEVEL. The extremes of

A

B

C

D

Fig. 3–25. Overarm Throw—6 years, 7 months.
Trunk action: Step 2; Humerus and Forearm action: Step 3; Foot action: Step 3. The point of deepest forearm lag coincides with the moment of front facing (frame D). This child's arm action is advanced, but further development in trunk action and stride length may still occur.

E

F

Table 3–12   Developmental Sequence for Action of the Feet in Forceful Throwing and Striking

Step 1. No step. The child throws from the initial foot position.

Step 2. Homolateral step. The child steps with the foot on the same side as the throwing hand.

Step 3. Contralateral, short step. The child steps with the foot on the opposite side from the throwing hand.

Step 4. Contralateral, long step. The child steps with the opposite foot a distance of over half the child's standing height.

Note. This sequence was hypothesized by Roberton[69] from the work of Leme and Shambes,[95] Seefeldt et al.,[75] and Wild.[96]

movement levels are not experienced until after the middle range.

SPACE ASPECT: EXTENSION. The extremes of movement size are not experienced until after the middle range.

SPACE ASPECT: DIRECTION. Forward movement on the feet develops before backward movement, which develops before sideward movement.

SPACE ASPECT: FLOOR PATTERN. Slanted pathways develop before straight ones, which develop before curved ones, which develop before zigzag ones.

RELATIONSHIP ASPECT: OTHER INDIVIDUALS. As with their thinking, children's movement is at first egocentric. The ability to relate one's movement to that of another begins with dodging or avoidance[102] and only gradually de-

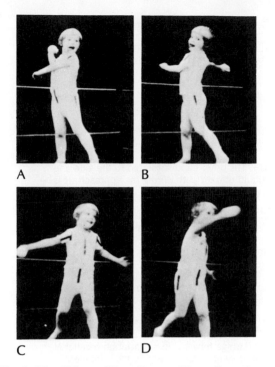

Fig. 3–26. Sidearm Sling—3 years. When attempting to produce force, this child began an overarm throw (frame A), then substituted a developmentally easier movement.

velops to purposeful spatial and timing harmonies.

DEVELOPMENTAL INTERRELATIONSHIPS

As mentioned earlier, the developing child reflects an interwoven pattern of multiple-action system change. Until now, we have discussed the biopsychologic systems separately, so we could focus on developmental change within each. An interesting question, however, is how each developing system relates to motor development.

We have little research on this question. No studies have actually examined the relationship between developmental level in movement and developmental level in another action system. Instead, most have compared the achievement scores produced by different action systems. For example, motor development has been assessed in terms of how many balls children caught, how fast they ran, or how high they jumped. Performance measures, however, may be misleading indicators of development.[55] Despite this limitation, we will explore the relationship between visual-perceptual development and motor

development, a relationship noted in the discussion of striking. Since it is not possible within this chapter to discuss the influence of every biopsychologic system on motor development, we have chosen this topic because of its relevance to teaching.

Visual-Perceptual Development and Motor Development

Most movement tasks involve changing relationships with other movers or with stationary or moving objects. These relationships vary from simple to complex, but even in the simple situations the amount of sensory information is formidable. The accuracy of children's perceptions of such input forms their view of the environment in which their motor response takes place. Thus, perceptual development inevitably facilitates, or limits, the movement response; however, accurate perceptual functioning does not guarantee accurate movement response. Psychologic research has demonstrated a considerable gap between development in perception and in performance.[3,6,37] For example, children make freehand vertical, horizontal, and diagonal lines before they are 2 or 3. Yet, 6- and 7-year-olds encounter difficulty in copying diamonds even through they can recognize a diamond much earlier.[6] The two action systems of perception and performance are intertwined in the child's development, but the nature of that relationship at any one point is still far from clear.

Researchers have only begun to investigate the effect of perceptual development on children's performance in physical education-related tasks. Much of the completed work has centered on the perception of moving balls either in flight or on a surface. These studies have investigated the effects of ball size, ball velocity, and ball path on catching behavior, or on perceptual factors that are presumed to affect catching and striking behavior. It is difficult to directly compare results from these investigations because they vary in scoring systems, age levels, definitions of large and small ball sizes, distances from the ball tosser, ball paths, and ball speeds. Yet the findings do point the way for further research and suggest areas for experimentation by teachers.

Table 3–13   Developmental Sequences for Punting

Ball release: Arm component

Step 1. Hands are on the sides of the ball. The ball is tossed upward from both hands after the support foot has landed (if a step was taken).

Step 2. Hands are on the sides of the ball. The ball is dropped from chest height after the support foot has landed (if a step was taken).

Step 3. Hands are on the sides of the ball. The ball is lifted upward and forward from waist level. It is released as or just prior to the landing of the support foot.

Step 4. One hand is rotated to the side and under the ball. The other hand is rotated to the side and top of the ball. The hands carry the ball on a forward and upward path during the approach. It is released at chest level as the final approach stride begins.

Ball contact: Arm component

Step 1. Arms drop bilaterally from ball release to a position on each side of the hips at ball contact.

Step 2. Arms bilaterally abduct after ball release. The arm on the side of the kicking leg may pull back as that leg swings forward.

Step 3. After ball release, the arms bilaterally abduct during flight. At contact the arm opposite the kicking leg has swung forward with that leg. The arm on the side of the kicking leg remains abducted and to the rear.

Leg action component

Step 1. No step or one short step is taken. The kicking leg swings forward from a position parallel or slightly behind the support foot. The knee may be totally extended by contact or, more frequently, still flexed 90° with contact above or below the knee joint. The thigh is still moving upward at contact. The ankle tends to be flexed.

Step 2. Several steps may be taken. The last step onto the support leg is a long stride. The thigh of the kicking leg has slowed or stopped forward motion at contact. The ankle is extended. The knee has 20 to 30° of extension still possible by contact.

Step 3. The child may take several steps, but the last is actually a leap onto the support foot. After contact, the momentum of the kicking leg pulls the child off the ground in a hop.

Note. These sequences, hypothesized by Roberton,[69] have not been validated.

BALL SIZE

In general, studies support the commonly held assumption that larger balls are easier to catch if catching is defined merely as retaining possession of the ball;[103–105] however, other findings suggest that large balls encourage developmentally primitive catches.[106,107] Victors, for example, reported that ball size did not affect success in catching in 7- and 9-year-old boys, but it did affect the type of catch used.[106] The developmentally primitive "basket" or arm-body catch was more often used with the large ball; the hand catch was used more with the small ball (see Table 3–14).

BALL VELOCITY

Ridenour reasoned that ball size alone probably would not account for differences in a child's ability to judge the path of an oncoming object.[108] In an experiment in which ball size, speed, and horizontal direction were manipulated, she found that ball speed and horizontal direction affected 7-year-olds' accuracy in detecting ball path. Ball size did not. Bruce[109] also found that velocity affected 7- and 9-year-olds' ability to catch, but not 11-year-olds'. The Ridenour study involved balls moving along a pulley system, whereas the Bruce study involved aerial balls. The perceptual and movement demands of each were different. The spatial aspects of the ball trajectory in Bruce's study added another complexity to the perceptual task.

BALL TRAJECTORY

When Bruce investigated the effect of ball trajectory on children's success in catching, he found no significant differences in 7-, 9-, and 11-year-olds' ability to catch a tennis ball projected at 30 and 60° angles from a distance of 20 feet.[109]

H. Williams in a study of 6- through 12-year-olds found a marked difference in the ability of younger children to predict the landing point of balls when compared with older children.[110,111] The children were not required to catch the balls as in the Bruce study, but had to move to the point where they predicted the ball would land.

TRACKING THE BALL

The children in the H. Williams' study viewed only the beginning portion of the ball flight since a canopy interrupted the actual flight. This study raises the question of where children place their attention during ball flight. Kay[112] and Stadulis[113] suggested three distinct stages of learning in an anticipation-coincidence task, that is, in a task that requires perceiving the ball path, predicting its characteristics, and timing movement to coincide with the ball's arrival. In the first or early stage, young children view the tasks in parts rather than in wholes. They direct attention to the source of the object's flight, for example, to the thrower, rather than to the components of the total task. Next they attend to the source of the flight and to their own motor response, but not to the flight itself. Only with response proficiency do children monitor the flight as well. Then they completely ignore their hands and concentrate on the source and the flight of the object.

Recent research challenges Kay's third stage of learning, at least for the task of catching. Kay suggests that advanced performers do not watch their hands.[112] Rather, they are free to focus entirely on the flight of the object. Smyth and Marriott have discovered, however, that catching in adults is much less accurate when they cannot see their hands.[114] They make errors in positioning the hands for the catch, suggesting that kinesthesis is not sufficient by itself to guide the hands to the proper location for intercepting the ball. Thus, Kay's third stage of learning needs to be modified to suggest that proficiency in anticipation-coincidence tasks means the ability to monitor simultaneously both the oncoming object and the body parts moving to intercept that object.

Several studies do support Kay's observation that in the early stages the child is watching only the source of flight.[112] Stadulis found that older children were more accurate than younger children in intercepting a steel ball rolling down a chute at slower rates.[113] He concluded that the older children were more accurate at these slower speeds than the younger because of their greater ability to monitor and use additional information on the ball's rate as it traveled down the chute. The younger children, however, were more accurate at a faster rate, which Stadulis concluded was due to a coincidence between the ball projection speed and the reaction time of the children. Since the younger children reacted as soon as the ball began, it appeared that their response was to the projection of the ball rather than to its path after projection.

H. Williams had a similar interpretation for her findings.[110,111] She commented that all children responded quickly to the moving object, but the younger ones were not able to use the available information as well as the older children. She suggested that young children are aware that the object is moving fast, but that is all. Thus, they proceed to move as quickly as they can in the time allotted.

We have also observed that early in development children apparently watch the ball tosser rather than the ball flight.[90] In striking tasks, we often see them start their swing with the beginning of the arm swing of the tosser (Fig. 3–27). Young children are unable to wait for the ball to arrive, apparently because they cue only on the source of the ball flight.

K. Williams has further investigated this common finding that young children tend to respond too soon to slowly moving stimuli.[115] In her study, children and adults had to move their hands to a target coincident with the arrival of an apparently-moving light. Thus, she focused on the end of the movement rather than the beginning. She found that 5-year-olds arrived *ahead* of the light when it traveled at 1.5 miles per hour. They arrived *late* when the light traveled at 3 to 4 miles per hour. They were most accurate when the light moved at 2 to 2.5 mph. Further study suggested that the 5-year-olds did not have the capacity to vary their movement speed. Their hand traveled at the same rate regardless of the stimulus velocity. Since their preferred movement speed was close to the 2 mph stimulus speed, they performed best at that speed. Even older subjects resorted to a "preferred" speed as the stimulus became too fast. Williams hypothesized that, with development, children

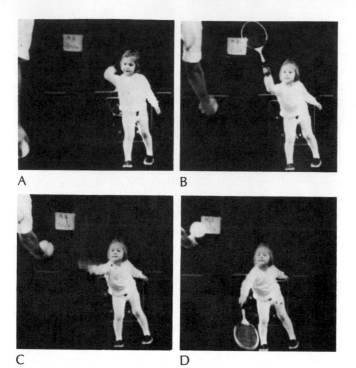

A   B

C   D

Fig. 3–27.   Inability to Hold Back—3 years, 4 months. By ball release (frame D) this child has already completed her swing, which began when the hand of the tosser moved (frames A and B). Her striking shows Step 1 of humeral action and Step 1 of trunk action. Note the step with the homolateral foot (same foot as hand in use).

begin to realize their preferred speed is ahead of a slowly-moving stimulus so they stop to let it catch up. The light then passes them by and they are late in reaching the target. Finally, they achieve a third level in which they can modify their speed as they are moving. This behavior allows them to arrive coincident with the slow stimulus.

INTERACTING FACTORS

All the previous factors affecting visual perception, such as speed of the object, have been discussed individually. To make matters more complicated, it actually appears that factors interact to affect a child's movement.

H. Williams systematically varied speed, direction, angle of projection, skill, and age in an attempt to understand their effect on the visual-perceptual judgments of moving, aerial balls.[116] As in her previously cited study, vision of the projected balls was interrupted by a canopy.[111] Of particular interest was the finding that one could not generalize the effect of the single factors of ball speed, angle of projection, and horizontal direction. For instance, the subjects were more accurate in predicting the landing point when the ball was at a high vertical and a slow speed than at a high vertical and a fast speed.

Yet the low vertical was easier to predict at a faster than at a slower speed. While this study did not involve young children, Ridenour's examination of a striking task did.[117] She found that particular combinations of ball size and speed, as well as the distance, direction, and height of the ball path, produced different results among 7-year-olds. We need more study to determine what combinations of conditions would help children in judging and intercepting moving objects.

FIGURE-GROUND DISCRIMINATION

Earlier, we pointed out that the ability to discriminate a figure from a background improves with age. We know relatively little about how this ability affects the movement performance of children. Only a low positive relationship was reported between children's performance on paper-and-pencil figure-ground tests and their movement performance.[118,119] Gallahue, however, found that, as the figure (a ladder placed on the floor) blended more with the background, and as the figure and ground patterns became more distracting, 5.5- through 6.5-year-old children's sideward walking performance in the ladder deteriorated.[118]

Gallahue's study involved the perceptual task

of picking out a stationary figure against a stationary background. An even more difficult task in a physical education environment is the common challenge of picking out moving objects, such as people or balls, against moving or stationary backgrounds. Morris, studying the effect of ball and background color on catching performance, found significant interactions for grade by ball color, sex by background color, and ball color by background color in 7-, 9-, and 11-year-olds.[120] These findings indicated that combinations of ball colors and background colors produced different catching scores. For instance, blue balls against a white background led to more success than white balls against a white background. However, different-aged children reacted differently to ball color. The sexes reacted differently to background color. Again no single factor was operating.

Teaching Implications

The reported research provides no clearcut answer on the optimal ball size, speed of projection, or ball path to maximize success in interception tasks for the various developmental levels. From our experience, ball size does influence the child's movement, but we do not know what range in ball size may be best for both the perceptual and movement components of interception tasks. Our observations,[55] together with the findings of Victors,[106] suggest that the child is often forced to use a more primitive catching pattern with a large ball; thus, giving beginners only large balls may actually inhibit their progress. Until the facts are known, teachers should let children experiment with different-sized balls and carefully observe what effect the ball size has on the way particular children use their bodies. Table 3–14 lists hypothesized developmental sequences for catching, which may be used to guide your observations.

We know there is a ceiling on the ball speeds that even the most advanced performer can handle and that this ceiling is lower in early development. The teacher should note, however, that in early development the child may also experience difficulty in adjusting timing to a slowly moving object. The acceptable range between "too slow" and "too fast" for each developmental level remains an interesting question.

Previously, we suggested simplifying the perceptual demands within a task; for example, suspending balls in a striking task until the movement response had developed to some extent. Simplifying the task should also continue when the child begins to respond to oncoming, moving objects. For example, ball tosses should, as far as possible, be set to the timing of the child. Only when children are able to attend to and monitor more components of the task will they be able to adjust their timing to the moving object.

It is important for the teacher to note whether children are attending to the ball tosser, the flight of the object, their own movement, or all of these factors when they are catching, striking, or fielding. Young children usually are not ready to attend to more than one factor. They may also not be aware of what to attend to, or not know what to anticipate in the movement of the object. Through questioning or suggestions, the teacher can help children predict what to expect from objects that fly, bounce, or move along the ground. The teacher can also help children by keeping the ball path similar over repeated practices. Primitive catchers or strikers are not ready to adjust to different levels, distances, and speeds on each try. Even if they miss, it is better to keep the path and speed similar on the next try so that they can begin to predict the ball flight. When they are able to monitor more aspects of the flight and when their movement has become developmentally more advanced, they will be ready to respond to changing paths, speeds, and trajectories.

Gallahue and Morris' findings suggest that the movement performance of children may be affected by the lack of contrast between figure and ground as well as the distraction of cluttered wall and floor patterns.[118,120] These findings support the need for designing physical education surroundings to maximize the child's opportunity to pick out stationary or moving figures from their background. As always, observing what happens to the child's motor performance in various settings is essential.

DEVELOPMENTAL TASK ANALYSIS

Herkowitz has designed a simple, practical way for parents and teachers to chart those environmental factors which affect the develop-

Table 3–14   Developmental Sequences for Catching

Preparation: Arm component
Step 1. The arms await the ball toss, outstretched with elbows extended.
Step 2. The arms await the ball toss with some shoulder flexion still apparent but flexion now appearing in the elbows.
Step 3. The arms await the ball in a relaxed posture at the sides of the body or slightly ahead of the body. The elbows may be flexed.

Reception: Arm component
Step 1. The arms remain outstretched and the elbows rigid. Little to no "give" occurs, so the ball bounces off the arms.
Step 2. The elbows flex to carry the hands upward toward the face. Initially, ball contact is primarily with the arms, and the object is trapped against the body.
Step 3. Initial contact is with the hands. If unsuccessful in using the fingers, the child may still trap the ball against the chest. The hands still move upward toward the face.
Step 4. Ball contact is made with the hands. The elbows still flex but the shoulders extend, bringing the ball down and toward the body rather than up toward the face.

Hand component
Step 1. The palms of the hands face upward. (Rolling balls elicit a palms-down, trapping action.)
Step 2. The palms of the hands face each other.
Step 3. The palms of the hands are adjusted to the flight and size of the oncoming object. Thumbs or little fingers are placed close together, depending on the height of the flight path.

Body component
Step 1. No adjustment of the body occurs in response to the flight path of the ball.
Step 2. The arms and trunk begin to move in relation to the ball flight path.
Step 3. The feet, trunk, and arms all move to adjust to the path of the oncoming ball.

Note. These sequences have not been validated. They were hypothesized by Harper.[121]

mental level a child will demonstrate when performing a motor skill.[122] To summarize our discussion of the implications of visual-perceptual development for motor development, we would like to use her approach, called "developmental task analysis." To perform this analysis for any motor task, the teacher creates a chart which lists all those aspects of the environment which might affect performance of the skill. Table 3–15 is our analysis for one-handed striking. Across the top we have listed several of the factors mentioned earlier in our discussion of visual-perceptual development. In each column, we have tried to list relevant environmental situations ordered from least complex to most complex. The particular ordering in Table 3–15 is our best guess from the information we have previously discussed.

The ordering within and across columns allows the teacher to create potential teaching progressions in a systematic fashion, using environ-

mental complexity as a guide. Perhaps the first striking experience would start at the top of the chart by having the child use the hands to hit a large ball suspended from a string. The ball would contrast with the background. No target would be involved; force would be the main goal. As the child practiced, the teacher would note the developmental levels being displayed in this "least complex" environment. When the child showed intermediate levels of movement, the teacher could suggest beginning to make the environment more challenging by changing one of the environmental factors to the next level of complexity. Perhaps the teacher would do this by giving several options: the child could use a smaller ball; keep the same ball, but start it swinging on the rope; or switch to a short-handled implement with a large striking surface. While the child worked in this new environment, the teacher would continue to observe the child's developmental levels. If regression

Table 3–15 Developmental Task Analysis
Task: Striking with an implement

Factor:	Ball Size	Ball Speed	Ball Trajectory	Ball Color	Striking Surface	Length of Handle	Weight of Implement
Level of Complexity	Large	None	None	Contrasting with background	Large	None (use hand or "glove-paddle")	Light
Least (easiest)		Moderate	Aerial, horizontal			Short	
		Slow	Aerial, looping				
			Bounced ball				
Most (hardest)	Small	Fast		Blending with background	Small	Long	Heavy

(After Herkowitz)[122]

occurred, which continued practice did not overcome, the teacher would know that the new environment was too complex for that particular child and should be changed. On the other hand, if the child's movement stayed the same or even advanced under the new complexity, the teacher would know that the new practice situation was a useful one for that child.

Developmental task analysis can thus serve as a way to generate teaching progressions for skills with a high degree of environmental complexity. It also serves as a descriptor of the specific environment within which a child displays certain developmental levels. Combined with knowledge of developmental sequences, developmental task analysis is also an important aid to the observation process.

EQUIPMENT DESIGN

Following upon the ideas presented in her developmental task analyses, Herkowitz has also presented creative and innovative equipment to facilitate the motor development of children.[123] She offers the following principles for the design of play equipment, some of which have already been mentioned in this chapter. They deserve, however, continued emphasis. (1) Accommodate the physical growth characteristics of young children by providing equipment that differs in size or that can be changed by children to fit their size. (2) Design equipment to provide children with feedback regarding their motor performance. Feedback using different colors, sound, timing devices, or movement is particularly salient for children. (3) Encourage children's demonstrations of more advanced developmental levels by designing or placing equipment to encourage force production, specific angles of projection, or specific body actions, such as trunk rotation. (4) Acknowledge children's visual-perceptual capabilities by using ramps or nets to deliver balls at controlled velocities for catching or striking, or by manipulating the color of the ball in relation to its background. (5) Acknowledge children's responsiveness to environmental novelty and complexity by changing equipment periodically and by making equipment interesting, fun, and challenging.

INTERVENTION

One problem in describing developmental sequences is to avoid the impression that the sequences are "automatic"; i.e., if left to their own devices, all children will proceed on their developmental course with no particular help from the environment. The problem is semantic: we tend to use words such as "evolve," or to make statements such as, "Next in development x happens." We should, instead, preface each developmental description with the conditional statement, "If the proper child-environment interaction occurs, the next step will be. . . ." If developmental sequences were automatic for all children, this book would not need to be written. We know that many children never progress beyond the rudimentary levels of certain motor task components.[124,95]

Because their performance is unsatisfactory to them, these children tend to avoid situations that require the components. By avoiding the environment, they form a defeating cycle: the component is not used because it has not developed, and it cannot develop because it is not used. In this way, many components of motor tasks become arrested at early developmental levels, so intervention is often necessary.

SUCCESS

When teachers do decide to intervene, they must find the environmental situation that helps the child move ahead in development. What the particular environment should be for a particular child is always an unknown. Some situations work beautifully; others may cause a child to regress, that is, to move backward within a level or to move backward across levels.[90,54] Experience and research, however, do suggest that, to promote motor development, the movement environment must have an atmosphere of success and satisfaction. It needs to be fun. Success is one of the greatest contributors to development just as failure is one of the prime causes of regression. With success in force-producing situations, for example, the child tends to use more range of movement and to bring more body levers into play. With failure, the child tends to decrease the range of movement and to use fewer levers.[90] Thus, the entire movement environment should be designed so that children can successfully accomplish their individual movement goal. In other words, there should ideally be as many different goals as there are different developmental levels among the children.

THE CYCLE BEGINS AGAIN

Each time teachers set a new goal, change the task, or rephrase a verbal problem for children,

they should step back to observe the result. Sometimes, overemphasis of a force goal may backfire, and the child may regress. Often the excitement, stress, or multiple demands of a game cause the child to use less-advanced movements. Sometimes, when a movement problem is rephrased, children omit the very movement we had hoped they would accent. Many times nothing happens, and children continue at their present movement level.

Whatever happens, however, teachers can observe the worth of their last decision regarding a particular child. The key to all teaching is to know what has resulted developmentally from each child's encounter with the environment, be that encounter teacher-designed or child-designed. In this cyclic manner of observation, interpretation, and decision-making, teachers enter the learning process of the child; in this manner they can explore with that child the joy and challenge of the world of movement; in this manner they are privileged to see each developing child as a unique individual from whom all have much to learn.

REFERENCES

1. Piaget, J., and Inhelder, B.: The Psychology of the Child. New York, Basic Books, 1969.
2. Sigel, I.E.: The Piagetian system and the world of education. In Studies in Cognitive Development. Edited by D. Elkind and J. Flavell. New York, Oxford University Press, 1969.
3. Gibson, E.: Principles of Perceptual Learning and Development. New York, Appleton-Century-Crofts, 1969.
4. Schimmel, S.: Cognition: from sensing to knowing. In Developmental Psychology Today. Published by H. Tilker. New York, Communications Research Machines/Random House, 1975.
5. Pick, A.: Some basic perceptual processes in reading. In The Young Child: Reviews of Research, Vol. 2. Edited by W. Hartrup. Washington, D.C., National Association for the Education of Young Children, 1972.
6. Wohlwill, J.: Perceptual development. In Experimental Child Psychology. Edited by H. Reese and L. Lipsitt. New York, Academic Press, 1970.
7. Walk, R., and Gibson, E.: A comparative and analytical study of visual depth perception. Psychological Monographs, 75:1, 1961.
8. Beadle, M.: A Child's Mind. Garden City, New Jersey, Doubleday, 1970.
9. Suchman, R., and Trabasso, T.: Color and form preference in young children. Journal of Experimental Child Psychology, 3:177, 1966.
10. Connolly, K.: Response speed, temporal sequencing, and information processing in children. In Mechanisms of Motor Skill Development. Edited by K. Connolly. New York, Academic Press, 1970.
11. Witkin, H., et al.: Personality Through Perception. New York, Harper Brothers, 1954.

12. Witkin, H., et al.: Psychological Differentiation: Studies of Development. New York, John Wiley & Sons, 1962.

13. Herkowitz, J.: Moving embedded figures test. Research Quarterly, 43:479, 1972.

14. Birch, H., and Lefford, A.: Visual differentiation, intersensory integration, and voluntary motor control. Monographs of the Society for Research in Child Development, 32:1, 1967.

15. Abravanel, E.: The development of intersensory patterning with regard to selected spatial dimensions. Monographs of the Society for Research in Child Development, 33:1, 1968.

16. Abravanel, E.: Short-term memory for shape information processed intra- and intermodally at three ages. Perceptual and Motor Skills, 35:419, 1972.

17. Birch, H., and Belmont, L.: Auditory-visual integration, intelligence and reading ability in school children. Perceptual and Motor Skills, 20:295, 1965.

18. Nash, J.: Developmental Psychology: A Psychobiological Approach. Englewood Cliffs, New Jersey, Prentice-Hall, 1970.

19. Klein, R.: A developmental study of perception under conditions of conflicting sensory cues. Unpublished doctoral dissertation, University of Minnesota, 1966.

20. Trabasso, T.: Paying attention. In Readings in Developmental Psychology Today. Edited by P. Cramer. Del Mar, California, Communications Research Machines, 1970.

21. Kohlberg, L.: The development of children's orientations toward a moral order. I. Sequence in the development of moral thought. Human Development (Vita Humana), 6:11, 1963.

22. Kohlberg, L.: Development of moral character. In Developmental Psychology Today. Del Mar, California, Communications Research Machines, 1971.

23. Kohlberg, L.: Continuities in childhood and adult moral development revisited. In Life-Span Developmental Psychology. Edited by P. Baltes and K. Schaie. New York, Academic Press, 1973.

24. Turiel, E.: Developmental processes in the child's moral thinking. In Trends and Issues in Developmental Psychology. Edited by P. Mussen, J. Langer, and M. Covington. New York, Holt, Rinehart, Winston, 1969.

25. Rest, J., Turiel, E., and Kohlberg, L.: Level of moral development as a determinant of preference and comprehension of moral judgments made by others. Journal of Personality, 37:225, 1969.

26. Blatt, N., and Kohlberg, L.: Effects of classroom discussion on moral thought. In Moral Education. Edited by C. Beck. Toronto, University of Toronto Press, 1971.

27. Hoffman, M.: Moral development. In Carmichael's Manual of Child Psychology. Edited by P. Mussen. New York, John Wiley & Sons, 1970.

28. Bandura, A., and Huston, A.: Identification as a process in incidental learning. Journal of Abnormal and Social Psychology, 63:311, 1961.

29. Anthony, E.: The behavioral disorders of childhood. In Carmichael's Manual of Child Psychology. Edited by P. Mussen. New York, John Wiley & Sons, 1970.

30. Harris, G., and Levine, S.: Sexual differentiation of the brain and its experimental control. Journal of Physiology, 181:379, 1965.

31. Young, W.C., Goy, R., and Phoenix, C.: Hormones and sexual behavior. Science, 143:212, 1964.

32. Feshbach, S.: Aggression. In Carmichael's Manual of Child Psychology. Edited by P. Mussen. New York, John Wiley & Sons, 1970.

33. Lewin, K., Lippitt, R., and White, R.: Patterns of aggressive behavior in experimentally created "social climates." The Journal of Social Psychology, 10:271, 1939.

34. Madsen, M.C., and Shapira, A.: Cooperative and competitive behavior of urban Afro-American, Anglo-American, Mexican-American and Mexican village children. Developmental Psychology, 3:16, 1970.

35. Nelson, L., and Kagan, S.: Competition, the star-spangled scramble. Psychology Today, 6(4):53, 90, 1972.

36. Shapira, A., and Madsen, M.: Cooperative and competitive behavior of kibbutz and urban children in Israel. Child Development, 40:609, 1969.

37. Kagan, J., and Kogan, N.: Individuality and cognitive performance. In Carmichael's Manual of Child Psychology. Edited by P. Mussen. New York, John Wiley & Sons, 1970.

38. Kagan, S., and Madsen, M. C.: Cooperation and competition of Mexican, Mexican-American, and Anglo-American children of two ages under four instructional sets. Developmental Psychology, 5:32, 1971.

39. Kagan, S., and Madsen, M.C.: Experimental analysis of cooperation and competition of Anglo-American and Mexican children. Developmental Psychology, 6:49, 1972.

40. Miller, A., and Thomas, R.: Cooperation and competition among Blackfoot Indian and urban Canadian children. Child Development, 43:1104, 1972.

41. Solomons, H.H.: Sex role mediation of achievement behaviors and interpersonal interactions in sex-integrated team games. In Children in Cooperation and Competition. Edited by E.A. Pepitone. Lexington, Massachusetts, Lexington Books, D.C. Heath and Company, 1980.

42. Scanlan, T.K.: The effects of success-failure on the perception of threat in a competitive situation. Research Quarterly, 48:144, 1977.

43. Scanlan, T.K.: Sources of competitive stress in young female athletes. Journal of Sport Psychology, 1:151, 1979.

44. Scanlan, T.K., and Passer, M.W.: Anxiety-inducing factors in competitive youth sports. In Psychological Perspectives in Youth Sports. Edited by F. Smoll and R. Smith. New York, Halsted Press, 1980.

45. Riley, M., and Roberton, M.A.: Developing skillful games players: Consistency between beliefs and practice. Motor Skills: Theory into Practice, 5:119, 1981.

46. Mauldon, E., and Redfern, H.: Games Teaching: A New Approach for the Primary School. London, Macdonald & Evans, 1969.

47. Riley, M.: Games and humanism. Journal of Physical Education and Recreation, 46(2):46, 1975.

48. Kellogg, R., and O'Dell, S.: The Psychology of Children's Art. Del Mar, California, CRM–Random House, 1967.

49. Kellogg, R.: Understanding children's art. In Readings in Developmental Psychology Today. Edited by P. Cramer. Del Mar, California, CRM, 1970.

50. Lowenfeld, V.: Creative and Mental Growth, 2nd ed. New York, Macmillan, 1952.

51. Roberton, M.A., Williams, K., and Langendorfer, S.: Prelongitudinal screening of motor development sequences. Research Quarterly for Exercise and Sport, 51:724, 1980.

52. Cooper, J., Adrian, M., and Glassow, R.: Kinesiology, 5th ed. St. Louis, The C. V. Mosby Co., 1982.

53. Sinclair, C.: Movement of the Young Child: Ages Two to Six. Columbus, Ohio, Charles E. Merrill, 1973.

54. Halverson, L., Roberton, M.A., and Harper, C.: Cur-

rent research in motor development. Journal of Research and Development in Education, 6:56, 1973.

55. Halverson, L.: The young child . . . the significance of motor development. In The Significance of the Young Child's Motor Development. Edited by G. Engstrom. Washington, D.C., National Association for the Education of Young Children, 1971.

56. Hellebrandt, F.A., Rarick, G.L., Glassow, R., and Carns, M.L.: Physiological analysis of motor skills. I. Growth and development of jumping. American Journal of Physical Medicine, 40:14, 1961.

57. Poe, A.: A description of the movement characteristics of two-year-old children performing the jump and reach. Unpublished master's thesis, University of Wisconsin—Madison, 1973.

58. Halverson, L.E., Roberton, M.A., and Langendorfer, S.: Development of the overarm throw: Movement and ball velocity changes by seventh grade. Research Quarterly for Exercise and Sport, 53:198, 1982.

59. Peterson, K., Reuschlein, P., and Seefeldt, V.: Factor analyses of motor performance for kindergarten, first, and second grade: A tentative solution. Report to the Research Section, National Convention of the American Association for Health, Physical Education, and Recreation, Anaheim, California, 1974.

60. Roberton, M.A.: Stability of stage categorizations across trials: Implications for the "stage theory" of overarm throw development. Journal of Human Movement Studies, 3:49, 1977.

61. Roberton, M.A.: Longitudinal evidence for developmental stages in the forceful overarm throw. Journal of Human Movement Studies, 4:161, 1978.

62. Roberton, M.A., and Langendorfer, S.: Testing motor development sequences across 9–14 years. In Psychology of Motor Behavior and Sport—1979. Edited by C. Nadeau, W. Halliwell, K. Newell, and G. Roberts. Champaign, Illinois, Human Kinetics, 1980.

63. Breihan, S.: Consistency of arm-leg opposition in performing three tasks. Perceptual and Motor Skills, 54:203, 1982.

64. Langendorfer, S.: Developmental relationships between throwing and striking: A prelongitudinal test of motor stage theory. Unpublished doctoral dissertation. University of Wisconsin—Madison, 1982.

65. Roberton, M.A.: Describing 'stages' within and across motor tasks. In The Development of Movement Control and Coordination. Edited by J.A.S. Kelso and J. Clark. New York, John Wiley & Sons, 1982.

66. Roberton, M.A.: Stages in motor development. In Motor Development: Issues and Applications. Edited by M. Ridenour. Princeton, New Jersey, Princeton Book Co., 1978.

67. McGraw, M.: Neuromuscular Maturation of the Human Infant. New York, Hafner, 1963. (Originally published, 1943.)

68. Barrett, K.: Observation for teaching and coaching. Journal of Physical Education and Recreation, 50(1): 23, 1979.

69. Roberton, M.A.: Changing motor patterns during childhood. In Motor Development During Childhood and Adolescence. Edited by J. Thomas. Minneapolis, Burgess, 1983.

70. Halverson, L.E., and Williams, K.: Pre-longitudinal screening of developmental sequences in hopping. Motor development and child study laboratory, Department of Physical Education and Dance, University of Wisconsin—Madison. Manuscript in progress, 1983.

71. Seefeldt, V., and Haubenstricker, J.: Developmental sequences in hopping: skipping; striking. Motor Development Workshop, Michigan State University, 1974.

72. Milani-Comparetti, A., and Gidoni, E.A.: Routine developmental examination in normal and retarded children. Developmental Medicine and Child Neurology, 9:631, 1967.

73. Van Sant, A.: Development of the standing long jump. Motor development and child study laboratory, Department of Physical Education and Dance, University of Wisconsin—Madison. Study in progress, 1983.

74. Wickstrom, R.: Fundamental Motor Patterns, 3rd ed. Philadelphia, Lea & Febiger, 1983.

75. Seefeldt, V., Reuschlein, S., and Vogel, P.: Sequencing motor skills within the physical education curriculum. Report to the National Convention, American Association for Health, Physical Education, and Recreation, Houston, 1972.

76. Laban, R.: Modern Educational Dance. London, Macdonald & Evans, 1948.

77. Morison, R.: A Movement Approach to Educational Gymnastics. London, Dent, 1969.

78. O'Quinn, G.: Gymnastics for Elementary School Children. Dubuque, Iowa, Brown, 1967.

79. Roberton, M.A., and Halverson, L.E.: The developing child—His changing movement. In Physical Education for Children—A Focus on the Teaching Process. Edited by B. Logsdon, Philadelphia, Lea & Febiger, 1977.

80. Williams, K.: Developmental characteristics of a forward roll. Research Quarterly for Exercise and Sport, 51:703, 1980.

81. Russell, J.: Modern Dance in Education. London, Macdonald & Evans, 1958.

82. McGraw, M.: Neural maturation of the infant as exemplified in the righting reflex on rolling from a dorsal to a prone position. The Journal of Pediatrics, 18:385, 1941.

83. Gates, D., and Sheffield, R.P.: Tests of change of direction as measurements of different kinds of motor ability in boys of the seventh, eighth, and ninth grades. Research Quarterly, 11:136, 1940.

84. Kirchner, G., Cunningham, J., and Warrell, E.: Introduction to Movement Education. Dubuque, Iowa, Brown, 1970.

85. Harper, C.: Movement responses of kindergarten children to a change of direction task—an analysis of selected measures. Unpublished master's thesis, University of Wisconsin—Madison, 1975.

86. Stanley, S.: Physical Education: A Movement Orientation. Toronto, McGraw-Hill, 1969.

87. Johnson, R.: Measurements of achievement in fundamental skills of elementary school children. Research Quarterly, 33:94, 1962.

88. Taylor, E.: The importance of footwork. The Eagle, United States Field Hockey Association, Inc., 26:9, 1965.

89. Roberton, M.A., and DiRocco, P.: Validating a motor skill sequence for mentally retarded children. American Corrective Therapy Journal, 35:148, 1981.

90. Halverson, L., and Roberton, M.A.: A study of motor pattern development in young children. Report to the Research Section, National Convention of the American Association for Health, Physical Education, and Recreation, Chicago, 1966.

91. Harper, C., and Struna, N.: Case studies in the development of one-handed striking. Report to the Research Section, National Convention of the American Association for Health, Physical Education, and Recreation, Minneapolis, 1973.

92. Ekern, S.: An analysis of selected measures of the

overarm throwing patterns of elementary school boys and girls. Unpublished doctoral dissertation, University of Wisconsin—Madison, 1969.

93. Langendorfer, S.: Longitudinal evidence for developmental changes in the preparatory phase of the overarm throw for force. Report to the Research Section, National Convention of the American Alliance for Health, Physical Education, Recreation, and Dance, Detroit, 1980.

94. Atwater, A.: Movement characteristics of the overarm throw: a kinematic analysis of men and women performers. Unpublished doctoral dissertation, University of Wisconsin—Madison, 1970.

95. Leme, S., and Shambes, G.: Immature throwing patterns in normal adult women. Journal of Human Movement Studies, 4:85, 1978.

96. Wild, M.: The behavior pattern of throwing and some observations concerning its course of development in children. Unpublished doctoral dissertation. University of Wisconsin—Madison, 1937.

97. Napier, J.: The prehensile movements of the human hand. Journal of Bone and Joint Surgery, 38B:902, 1956.

98. Erbaugh, S.J.: A longitudinal case study: the developmental changes in the two-handed striking pattern of C. R. with comparisons to a skilled adult. Unpublished paper, Motor development and child study laboratory, Department of Physical Education and Dance, University of Wisconsin—Madison, 1975.

99. Poulton, E.C.: On prediction in skilled movements. Psychological Bulletin, 54:467, 1957.

100. Gentile, A.: A working model of skill acquisition with application to teaching. Quest, 17:3, 1972.

101. Preston, V.: A Handbook for Modern Educational Dance. London, Macdonald & Evans, 1963.

102. Russell, J.: Creative Dance in the Primary School. London, Macdonald & Evans, 1965.

103. Hoadley, D.: A study of the catching ability of children in grades one to four. Unpublished master's thesis, University of Iowa, 1941.

104. McCaskill, C.L., and Wellman, B.: A study of common motor achievements at the pre-school ages. Child Development, 9:141, 1938.

105. Warner, A.: The motor ability of third, fourth, and fifth grade boys in the elementary school. Unpublished doctoral dissertation, University of Michigan, 1952.

106. Victors, E.: A cinematographical analysis of catching behavior of a selected group of seven and nine year old boys. Unpublished doctoral dissertation, University of Wisconsin—Madison, 1961.

107. Gutteridge, M.: A study of motor achievements of young children. Archives of Psychology, 34:5, 1939.

108. Ridenour, M.: Influence of object size, speed, and direction on the perception of a moving object. Research Quarterly, 45:293, 1974.

109. Bruce, R.: The effects of variations in ball trajectory upon the catching performance of elementary school children. Unpublished doctoral dissertation, University of Wisconsin—Madison, 1966.

110. Williams, H.: Perception of moving objects by children. Abstracts: Research Papers of 1967 AAHPER Convention. Washington, D.C.: American Association of Health, Physical Education, and Recreation, 1967.

111. Williams, H.: Perceptual-motor development in children. In A Textbook of Motor Development. Edited by C. Corbin. Dubuque, Iowa, Brown, 1973.

112. Kay, H.: The development of motor skills from birth to adolescence. In Principles of Skill Acquisition. Edited by E.A. Bilodeau. New York, Academic Press, 1969.

113. Stadulis, R.: Coincidence-anticipation behavior of children. Unpublished doctoral dissertation, Columbia University, 1971.

114. Smyth, M., and Marriott, A.: Vision and proprioception in simple catching. Journal of Motor Behavior, 14:143, 1982.

115. Williams, K.: Age differences in performance of a coincident anticipation task: Application of a modified information processing model. Unpublished doctoral dissertation, University of Wisconsin—Madison, 1982.

116. Williams, H.: The effects of systematic variation of speed and direction of object flight and of skill and age classifications upon visuo-perceptual judgments of moving objects in three-dimensional space. Unpublished doctoral dissertation. University of Wisconsin—Madison, 1968.

117. Davis, M. (Ridenour): The influence of object size, speed, direction, height, and distance on the interception of a moving object. Abstracts: Research Papers of 1973 AAHPER Convention. Washington, D.C., American Association for Health, Physical Education, and Recreation, 1973.

118. Gallahue, D.: The relationship between perceptual and motor abilities. Research Quarterly, 39:948, 1968.

119. Torres, J.: The relationship between figure-ground perceptual ability and ball catching ability in ten and thirteen year old boys and girls. Unpublished master's thesis, Purdue University, 1970.

120. Morris, G.S.D.: Effects ball and background color have upon the catching performance of elementary school children. Research Quarterly, 47:409, 1976.

121. Harper, C.J.: Learning to observe children's motor development. Part III. Observing children's motor development in the gymnasium. Paper presented to the National Convention of the American Alliance for Health, Physical Education, and Recreation, New Orleans, 1979.

122. Herkowitz, J.: Developmental task analysis: The design of movement experiences and evaluation of motor development status. In Motor Development: Issues and Applications. Edited by M. Ridenour. Princeton, New Jersey, Princeton Book Co., 1978.

123. Herkowitz, J.: Developmentally engineered equipment and playspaces for motor development and learning. In Psychology of Motor Behavior and Sport—1979. Edited by C. Nadeau, et al. Champaign, Illinois, Human Kinetics, 1980.

124. Halverson, L.: Development of motor patterns in young children. Quest, 6:44, 1966.

SUGGESTED READINGS/FILMS

Espenschade, A., and Eckert, H.: Motor Development, 2nd ed. Columbus, Ohio, Charles E. Merrill, 1980.

Halverson, L. and Roberton, M.A.: Motor Development Instructional Films: Developmental Steps in Hopping; Developmental Steps in Skipping; Developmental Steps in Overarm Throwing. Distributed through the Motor Development and Child Study Laboratory, Department of Physical Education and Dance, 306 Lathrop Hall, University of Wisconsin, Madison, Wisconsin 53706.

Martens, R.: Joy and Sadness in Children's Sports. Champaign, Illinois, Human Kinetics Publishers, 1978.

Ridenour, M.: Motor Development: Issues and Applications. Princeton, New Jersey, Princeton Book Co., 1978.

Roberton, M.A.: Motor development in learning disabled

children. *In* Developmental Theories and Research in Learning Disabilities. Edited by J. Gottlieb, and S. Strichart, Baltimore, University Park Press, 1981.

Roberton, M.A., Williams, K., and Langendorfer, S.: Prelongitudinal screening of motor development sequences. Research Quarterly for Exercise and Sport. *51*:724, 1980.

Thomas, J. (ed.): Motor Development During Childhood and Adolescence. Minneapolis, Burgess, 1983.

Tilker, H. (Publ.): Development Psychology Today. New York, Communications Research Machines/Random House, 1975.

Wickstrom, R.: Fundamental Motor Patterns. 3rd ed. Philadelphia, Lea & Febiger, 1983.

Chapter 4

Basic Mechanical Principles Governing Body Motion

MARION R. BROER

Since the human body is a system of weights (head, trunk, arms, legs) and levers (bones with their adjacent joints), it responds to the mechanical laws of the universe as does any other system of weights and levers. It differs from other leverage systems, however, in that the human body has a *built-in* mechanism for producing force (nervous system) both to move itself and to move objects.

Gravity is a force with which everyone must contend continuously as long as one remains in the earth's atmosphere. The only individuals who have experienced living without the need to contend with gravity are astronauts while in outer space. The closest anyone on earth approaches such a state is when submerged in water; then the effect of gravity is partially or, for some body builds in certain positions, totally offset by buoyancy. *An object is buoyed up by a force equal to the weight of the displaced fluid.* Only while in water or lying flat on a supporting surface do human beings not have to adjust constantly to gravity's pull, and thus it is essential that it be understood.

The teacher must also understand the laws of motion, leverage, and force in order to teach children to move efficiently. The experiences planned to assure the exposure of young children to a multitude of positions and movements in as many different situations as possible must be such that basic mechanical laws become obvious to them. As children grow and begin to realize their movement potential, and as they are guided through experiences that introduce them to fundamental movement patterns, learning situations must be planned to require them to solve movement problems involved in more complex daily life, work, sport, dance, and gymnastic skills. Again, problems must be so structured that the mechanics involved become obvious. Effective teaching of movement involves planning experiences that will present opportunities for children to gain an understanding of the *basic mechanics* involved, the *diversity of application* of mechanical principles and of various fundamental movement patterns, AND the *way to proceed* to *solve new motor tasks*. Only then will they have the background that will enable them to move efficiently regardless of the situations with which they may be confronted throughout their lives. Only then will they understand how to perform effectively any movement task, whether it is a light task or one that demands considerable strength; whether it calls for fine coordination or a gross movement; whether fast or slow motion is involved; whether it must be continued over a long period of time or is of short duration; and regardless of its specific purpose. In other words, only then will their physical education prove to be of real value to them. *It is not enough to teach children selected games and sport skills that can be used only in specific situations*. Children must be given opportunities not only to learn TO MOVE regardless of purpose but also TO UNDERSTAND the basic mechanics applicable to human movement so that they can solve new motor tasks.

The architecture of the human body assures a vast potential for movement, but too many individuals grow to adulthood unaware of the extensive motor vocabulary that could be tapped. For far too long, children and youths were taught a limited number of specific games and/or skills. Many teachers of children taught only the structure of simple games and completely ignored the way children moved, since they themselves had little or no understanding of efficient movement. Those who did attempt to teach any skill described a SPECIFIC way to move the body segments, a way that some individual who had been unusually successful had moved. This procedure ignores several basic facts.

1. No two individuals have exactly the same tools for movement; body builds and thus leverage systems as well as strengths and nervous systems differ. Thus, no two individuals can move in exactly the same way.

2. Every movement made by the highly successful individual may not have contributed to his success; some may actually have been detrimental, necessitating compensatory motions and/or extra energy expenditure.

3. The pattern of movement is NOT THE SAME in the unskilled stage as in the skilled. The process of becoming expert is the process of refining movement, thus *changing* movement. The beginner can NEVER move in the same way that the expert moves. Attempting to do so leads only to frustration.

4. There is not just ONE way to perform any skill. There ARE basic mechanics that must be considered, and adherence to these leads to some general patterns of movement that run through many seemingly different activities whenever the force requirements are similar. There is not ONE way to throw; it depends on the force requirements of the specific task. There is, however, a general movement pattern for producing maximum force underhand. This pattern changes for sidearm force and again for overhead force, although much of the leg and hip movement pattern of a particular individual remains similar for all three arm patterns when the force required

is similar. There is also a general pattern of movement that propels the body upward when it is moving forward. This chapter does not allow full discussion of patterns of movement (for a more complete discussion, see Broer and Zernicke).[1] The teacher of elementary school children must realize, however, that once the child has learned to roll a ball effectively, he has a movement pattern that, with slight adjustments, can be used in other specific skills that also require underhand force. The application of previously learned general movement patterns can make learning more effective when the teacher helps the child realize the possibility of using previously learned movements rather than approaching every specific skill as something completely new.

The realization of the vast movement potential of the human body plus an understanding of the basic mechanical principles relevant to human motion and of the applicability of general basic movement patterns gives the child a broad motor vocabulary on which to build any movement.

The task of the teacher is to plan situations that lead to (1) experiencing a vast variety of movements from basic to complex; (2) realizing the broad applicability of mechanical laws fundamental to efficient performance and of general movement patterns; (3) understanding the method of approach to the solution of new movement problems.

When one considers specific human tasks that involve the large muscles, the number and variety appear endless. However, when they are studied from the standpoint of the force purposes of the movements or positions, they can be organized into four main categories: those that require support of the body or an object (or both), those that involve suspension of the body or an object by the body, those that involve motion of the body (segments or the total body) or an object, and those that require the body to receive a force (see chart, p. 89). Production of force is a factor in all, and the categories listed are not mutually exclusive. The body must be supported to move across a surface. It is rarely suspended just to be suspended; instead the body is moving while suspended. To receive force without injury, either the total body or certain segments of it must move. In spite of some overlapping of these four categories, there are problems unique to each.

ORGANIZATION OF LARGE MUSCLE HUMAN TASKS
(Adapted from Chart I, Broer and Zernicke[1])

I. Supportive Tasks
   A. Supporting the body
      1. On solid surface, e.g., standing, sitting, lying
      2. On water, i.e., floating
   B. Supporting an object, e.g., holding

II. Suspension Tasks
   A. Body suspended, i.e., hanging
      1. From a solid object, e.g., bar, tree
      2. From an object free to move, e.g., rope, ring
   B. Object suspended from body, i.e., holding

III. Tasks Involving Motion
   A. Moving the body
      1. Entire body
         a. On solid surface, e.g., walking, running, skipping, climbing, taking off for jump or vault
         b. On an object free to move, e.g., climbing rope, paddling canoe, rowing boat, performing on ring(s)
         c. Through the air
            (1) With no support, e.g., diving, falling
            (2) While suspended, e.g., pole vault, on rope, trapeze
         d. Through the water, i.e., swimming
      2. Body parts
         a. Neck and trunk, e.g., rotating, bending, stretching
         b. Extremities, e.g., bending, stretching, swinging, rotating
         c. Pelvis, i.e., tilting
   B. Moving objects
      1. Force supplied to object directly by body
         a. Giving initial velocity by keeping object in contact with body, or with object held by body, then breaking contact and allowing object to move under the influence of gravity and other forces such as air resistance and friction, i.e., throwing, rolling
         b. Giving sudden impetus to object by momentary contact with a body part or an object held by body, i.e., striking
         c. Moving object by more or less constant application of force over distance and time, e.g., lifing, pushing, pulling, sweeping, carrying
      2. Force applied indirectly to object. Force of body acts on elastic or some other type structure that in turn supplies force to move an object, e.g., shooting bow, sling shot, gun; bowling (body gives direct force to ball but *indirect* force to pins)

IV. Tasks Involving Receiving Force
   A. Of moving body
      1. Landing ⎱ a. On solid (resistive) surface
      2. Falling (weight out of control) ⎰ b. On only partially resistive surface, e.g., mat, pit, water
   B. Of moving object
      1. Body gains possession of object, dissipates force, "gives" to reduce jar of impact, i.e., catching
      2. Object rebounds from body or object held by body; body resists force of impact so force is returned to object, i.e., striking

SUPPORT OF THE BODY

Because the body must support itself against the pull of gravity while performing movement tasks, children must learn the basic laws of equilibrium. They have been coping with the force of gravity all their lives, but they may not have been aware of it. As they experiment with moving, they should develop two important concepts. First, every object (themselves included) has a *center of gravity, a point about which the weight in all directions is balanced.* Second, the *center of gravity must be above the base or the object will fall downward until a new base is* established under the center of gravity. In other words, *a vertical line downward from the center of gravity (the line of gravity) must cut through the base if the object is to remain upright.* The vocabulary must be adapted to the age of the children, but they can understand these concepts even when they are too young to comprehend such terms as center of gravity. Such terms can become part of physical education lessons when they are introduced into the curricula of other subjects. The wide publicity given the space program and other technologic advances make children today more conversant with scientific terms than any previous generation. Some terms may seem more difficult to teachers than to their small pupils. Physical education teachers should coordinate the concepts and vocabulary of science classes and television programs with movement experiences.

The experience of building with blocks helps young children develop the concept of center of gravity over a base. The child learns that a block must be placed so that its center is above the block below it or it will fall. Blocks weighted so that their centers of gravity do NOT coincide with their geometric centers can then be introduced so that the children begin to learn that not just the CENTER but the CENTER OF THE WEIGHT must be above the base. Experiencing a wide variety of bases that are possible for the human body to use as support can help to make some principles of equilibrium obvious even to the youngest child. As children take various positions with one, two, three, or four body parts supporting their weight, they learn that the effective base is the area encompassed by the points of support. When they test how far they can move above various bases (i.e., when they sway side-to-side and forward-backward) before they fall or have to make a new base, they will begin to realize that the positions that are basically stable as compared to those that are unstable are low and/or have a relatively large base. Thus they see for themselves that, in general, *the wider the base and the lower the center of gravity, the more stable the object.* Since a low center of gravity can move farther than a high center of gravity before the line of gravity falls beyond the edge of the base, and since a larger base makes it possible for the center of gravity to move farther before it falls outside the base, both a low center of gravity and a wide base contribute to stability.

As they experience the movement of one body part leading the total body onto a different base, they develop the idea that an *unstable base can be advantageous* WHEN moving to a new position. They also experience the principle that *the momentum of a body part is transferred to any part attached.* The center of gravity of the child squatting as low as possible is closer to his base. If the heels are kept on the floor (so that the whole soles of the feet remain on the floor, keeping the base the same size), the child can move more without falling than is possible when the center of weight is higher (when standing,

for example). If the child's flexibility does not allow heels to remain on the floor, the base when squatting is diminished and a factor contributing to instability is introduced. If more than one factor is involved, the point to be demonstrated will not be obvious to the child. *If the base remains the same* while the child experiences movement in various levels, increasingly less stability will be encountered as positions that raise the center of weight are taken. In experiencing bases of different numbers of supports (i.e., standing on two feet and on one foot), the child encounters less stability in the position that reduces the size of his base. Such comparisons MUST be experienced *over and over* before the child can grasp a concept. The more experiences that involve the SAME factor and ONLY THAT FACTOR, the more obvious will be the concept involved. If the positions being experienced differ in BOTH size of base AND height of center of gravity (i.e., the child stands on one foot and then moves to hands and knees, both increasing the size of the base *and* lowering the center of gravity), the two concepts become more difficult, in some cases impossible, to grasp.

Regardless of the size of the base, the child whose weight is distributed equally on all parts of the base (centered over the base) has the greatest margin for movement before the line of gravity falls beyond any edge of the base. Thus there is MORE STABILITY *in all directions when the center of gravity is centered above the base.* If the weight is above one edge of the base (for example, the right foot), a wide base contributes to stability ONLY in the direction away from that edge (toward the left). *Degree of stability as related to SIZE OF BASE is a function of the distance that the center of gravity can move before it moves beyond any edge of the base;* the farther it can move, the more stable the object.

Thus the most efficient standing position centers each segment of the body over the segment immediately below (its supporting base), and centers the weight of the entire body over the base made by feet placed directly below the hips (Fig. 4–1A). The body can sway without the line of gravity falling beyond the toes or heels or the outsides of the two feet. When standing, individuals are constantly swaying. This involuntary swaying is important in aiding the return of ve-

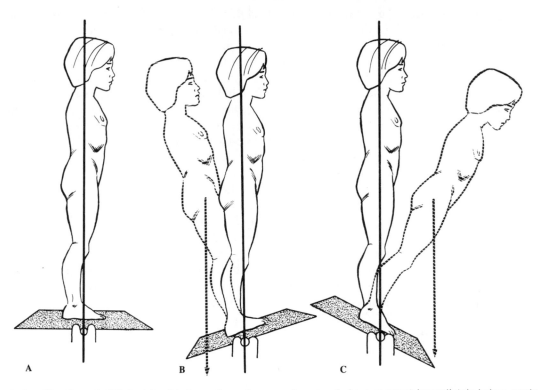

Fig. 4–1. Standing. *A,* Efficient (well balanced); each segment centered above segment immediately below; center of weight of total body over center of base (feet). *B,* Uphill incline; with angle at ankle same as in A (dotted figure), center of weight falls behind base; to maintain balance and keep alignment of body segments total body must lean forward from ankles. *C,* Downhill incline; with no adjustment (dotted figure) center of weight is forward of base; total body must lean back from ankles.

nous blood and assuring adequate circulation to the brain.[2]

When the weight is centered over the base forward-backward, the line of gravity falls forward of the center of the knee and in front of the ankle; therefore, gravity tends to rotate the body forward around the ankles. However, if the line of gravity fell THROUGH the ankles so that this rotating force were eliminated, it would fall precariously near the back edge of the base (the heels). The muscular effort required to maintain a stable posture with the weight centered is imposed on the large and powerful calf muscles, while the weaker anterior group is released from counterbalancing tension.[3] This position is also important when initiating forward movement.

Spreading the feet apart sideward enlarges the base in that direction and thus in general contributes to stability side-to-side; it does nothing to increase stability forward-backward. It also introduces other considerations. When the feet are directly below the hips, the base is larger

than when the feet are together, the legs are vertical, and the force exerted by the weight of the body is straight downward against the floor. This results in a straight upward reaction force to support the body. If, on the other hand, the feet are spread *more* than the width of the hips, the force is applied against the floor in a diagonally outward direction and thus has both downward and outward components. IF there is sufficient friction to resist the OUTWARD component of this force, balance may not be impaired but energy may be wasted and unnecessary force applied against knee and hip joints. When there is NOT sufficient friction between the feet and the surface (i.e., when standing on ice), spreading the feet beyond hip width, which introduces an outward component in the forces against the floor, makes the body *less* stable despite the large base. When the outward component is not resisted by friction, the feet continue to slide apart. The position of feet directly below hips gives the largest base (side-to-side) possible without introducing diagonal forces.

Experiences in standing on a tilt board can demonstrate the need to adjust the body so that the center of gravity is above the base when standing on inclines. The weight must move forward if the incline is upward (Fig. 4–1B) and backward if it is downward (Fig. 4–1C). If the relationship between feet and legs were to remain the same as when standing, the line of gravity would fall outside the base (see dotted figures). Adjustment of the body AS A UNIT from the ankles makes it possible to keep the segments aligned one above the other as in the normal standing position and eliminates lower-back strain caused by adjusting at the hips and waist.

Much of the lower back pain of which a large percentage of adults today complain can be attributed to their lack of education as children in the alignment of the body that maintains the spine in its normal position; the position that provides flexibility but protects nerves from pressure. Since the spine is a flexible rod that must support the upper body, neck, and head while the individual performs each movement task as well as while one stands or sits, low back pain in adult life can be the direct result of years of standing, sitting, and even lying in positions that place the vertebrae in unnatural positions that cause pressure on nerves and strain muscles, particularly in the lower back region.

Because the pelvic girdle forms the base on which the spine rests, any change in its position is immediately reflected in changes in the curves of the spine. The child can experiment with this idea by consciously tipping the pelvis forward* and noting how the lower back arches, the knees hyperextend and the upper body is thrown backward (Fig. 4–2B). When the pelvis is tipped backward† (Fig. 4–2C), the child will find that the lower back flattens and knees tend to flex while the upper back curves forward and the chest drops. NOTE: The child needs to exaggerate these motions of the pelvis so that resulting body adjustments will be obvious. With the pelvis in a balanced, intermediate position (Fig. 4–2A) and the shoulder girdle above the hips, the spine has its normal curves. Very young

children typically stand with the pelvis tipped forward and thus exhibit considerable lordosis and protruding abdomens. This may result from their tendency to hyperextend their knees when they begin to walk. Undoubtedly, hyperextended knees give the baby just starting to walk a greater sense of stability, but as the child grows and develops greater confidence, the knees need to be eased and the pelvic girdle brought to the balanced position rather than tilted forward. The importance of learning early in life to control the position of the pelvic girdle cannot be over emphasized. As soon as possible the child must *understand* the importance of a balanced pelvis to the alignment of the total body and thus to his/her future comfort. Whether supporting the body on the feet (standing, walking, etc.), hips (sitting), or back/front/side (lying), the pelvic girdle must be kept in a straight, well-balanced position so that the normal curves of the spine are not disturbed.

When STANDING, each segment of the body can be centered over the segment below only when the pelvis is in the well-balanced position (Fig. 4–2A), neither tilted forward or backward. This position must be maintained while walking (Fig. 4–2D), sitting, or lying and is extremely important when a task that demands any degree of strength is involved. The danger inherent in performing a heavy task such as lifting with the back in a hyperextended position is well recognized, but the fact that a slight strain imposed continuously over the years (by habitually poor positions while standing, walking, sitting, and lying) may have equally debilitating results, is rarely considered.

When SITTING, the hips must be well back in the seat so that the chair back can support the entire spine in its normal position (Fig. 4–3A); the position of the upper body is the same as when standing, shoulders balanced over hips. The feet flat on the floor with the knees bent so that they are very slightly higher than the hips maintains the pelvis in its balanced position (left-to-right) and removes any pressure from the blood vessels and nerves that pass behind the knees. Obviously, this position will not be maintained at all times when the child (or adult) is sitting; in fact, children should understand that a change of position is always restful. However, in changing position, it is important to balance those positions that lift the left hip (crossing the

---

*FORWARD tilted pelvis—the iliac crest is moved forward-downward.
†BACKWARD tilted pelvis—the iliac crest is moved upward-backward.

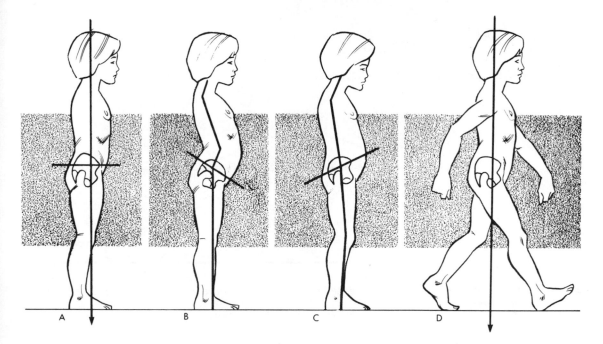

Fig. 4–2. Effect of pelvic tilt. *A,* Pelvic girdle balanced; efficient position. *B,* Pelvis angled forward arches lower back, hyperextends knees, throws upper body backward. *C,* Pelvis angled backward flattens lower back, curves upper spine forward and drops chest; knees tend to hyperextend. *D,* Walking with balanced pelvis, efficient alignment.

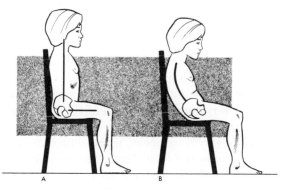

Fig. 4–3. Sitting. *A,* Efficient, back supported in normal position, pelvis balanced, feet flat on floor. *B,* Position causing strain on lower back.

left leg over the right, causing the spine to curve right) with equal time of crossing the right leg over the left to lift the right hip and curve the spine to the left. The opportunity to teach posture is ever present during the school day. It would be well for the physical education teacher to make certain that ALL CLASSROOM teachers themselves understand the mechanics of standing and sitting and to seek their cooperation in reinforcing with their pupils both these concepts and an understanding of their impor-

tance to their future well-being, so that this opportunity will not be wasted.

Because all sections of the body are supported by a surface when LYING, the child (adult also) tends to think that the back cannot be strained when lying down. However, when lying on the back with both legs straight, the pull of hip flexors (which are stretched) on the iliac crest tends to tilt the pelvis forward, arching the lower back (Fig. 4–4A). On the other hand, lying on the front of the body, particularly if the surface is soft, results in gravity pulling the hips (heaviest section of the body) downward, again arching the lower back (Fig. 4–4B). Thus, the position that relieves the strain of the lower back most is on the side with the knees and hips flexed (Fig. 4–4C). This, of course, creates a space between the head and supporting surface that must be filled with a pillow to keep the upper spine (neck) and head in line with the rest of the spine. Rest periods planned for very young children in nursery school offer unique opportunities to begin the teaching of well-balanced lying positions.

The child needs to learn to recognize the feeling of those positions which maintain a balanced pelvic girdle and thus the normal curves of the

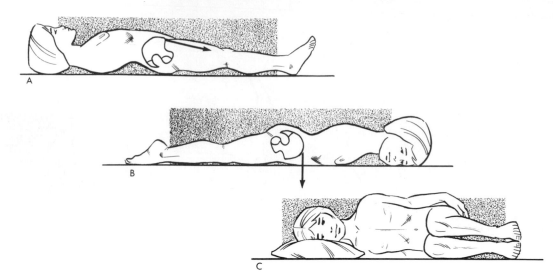

Fig. 4–4. Lying. *A,* On back, weight of legs tends to tilt pelvis forward causing lower back strain. *B,* On face, gravity tends to tilt pelvis forward causing lower back strain. *C,* On side, knees flexed for wider (more stable) base; least strain on back. Note: Pillow needed to support head and keep neck in line with rest of spine.

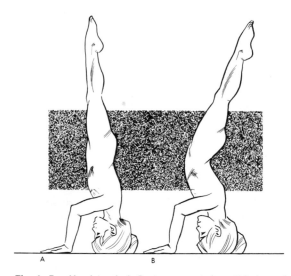

Fig. 4–5. Headstand. *A,* Body segments in well-balanced alignment. *B,* "Aesthetic" arch leads to zig-zag alignment causing lower back strain.

spine (front-to-back) while keeping the spine straight left-to-right. A foundation in efficient body mechanics of standing, walking, sitting, and lying laid in childhood could make the difference between pain and comfort in adult life.

When the child supports himself in an inverted position with the head and hands placed in a triangular relationship, the base is relatively large forward-backward and side-to-side. If the segments are aligned one above the other, as in standing, and the line of gravity falls over the center of the base, the position can be stable. The hands, being forward of the center of gravity, are in a position to apply force backward-upward if the body should start to fall forward. Through use of the fingers and wrists, the hand affords good leverage not afforded by the back edge of the base; thus any tendency of the body to fall forward is more easily controlled than a tendency to fall backward. If the center of gravity is off center at all, it would be better to have it fall nearer the forward edge of the base (the hands) than the back edge (top of back of head). When the hands are placed in line with the head or when only the hands comprise the base of support for the body (handstand), the base is very narrow front to back. In the latter situation, the center of gravity is raised as well, resulting in an extremely unstable position. In addition, supporting the weight on the hands requires that small, relatively weak muscles maintain the wrist angle and thus the vertical position of the body above the hands. Frequently, in teaching the head stand, teachers are tempted to tell children to move their hips forward and legs backward to create an exaggerated arch of the body (Fig. 4–5B) rather than to keep the body segments in straight vertical alignment (Fig. 4–5A). While this may be aesthetically pleasing to some observers, it is NOT mechanically sound. The various segments are in zig-zag alignment which makes balance more difficult as well as putting considerable strain on the muscles of the lower back and causing pressure on the vertebrae in that region. Essentially, the mechanically sound head-stand position is simply the standing position inverted (compare Fig. 4–5A with Fig. 4–2A).

The teacher needs to apply the equilibrium principles when planning certain experiences for the children. For example, if the child is lying or seated when experiencing the movement possibilities for the upper extremities. the problem of balance is eliminated and full attention can be given to determining the scope of possible movements. For the same reason, various movements that cause problems of balance in the standing position should be started in low positions with large bases.

The eyes, ears, and psychologic response to height are factors in balance. Thus, a child needs to walk on a space of limited width (i.e., a board) on the floor or perform certain movements on the floor before trying to walk or complete the movements on an elevated surface. Use of surfaces that are elevated and/or narrowed progressively will help prepare children for performance on the balance beam.

All of the equilibrium and basic body-alignment principles can be taught through many different activities. They are so basic, however, that it may be wise for the teacher to give some time to experiences planned specifically to bring out these concepts and the kinesthetic perceptions of efficient body alignment. They can then be strengthened as the child meets the same principles repeatedly in other activities. The teacher must be aware constantly of the children's body alignment as they participate in all activities.

SUPPORT OF OBJECTS

Having learned that he will fall unless HIS center of gravity is over HIS base, the child can experience the same principle with objects. If an object is supported, the child must provide a base under the object's center of gravity or under a handle attached above the object's center of gravity so that an upward force to offset gravity's downward pull can be applied against the object. It is possible to hold something for a short time by using the fingers and thumb as pincers (thumb and fingers opposing each other)

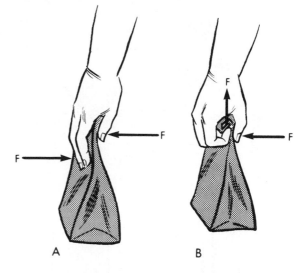

Fig. 4–6. Holding Sack. A, Difficult; dependent on friction caused by pressing thumb and fingers together. B, Easy; top of sack rolled to provide surface for upward force to resist gravity.

if the force exerted causes enough friction to keep the object from slipping downward. Since, in this situation, no force directly opposes gravity, more effort is required AND it is impossible to hold anything any length of time by this method. As children experience various ways of supporting and moving bags (containing light weights), they find that, when the top of a bag is held between thumb and fingers, they cannot support it long; however, if the top is rolled so that the fingers are UNDER the rolled top (force is exerted upward and directly opposes gravity), it is easy (Fig. 4–6).

As the child attempts to hold balls of various sizes in one hand, it will be obvious that a hand *must be under* any ball that is larger than can be grasped (i.e., fingers and thumb cannot curl around the ball).

An upward force to support an object is applied by placing the hands under the object's center of gravity (or under both sides of the bottom so that the two forces balance each other) OR under a handle from which the object is suspended.

When the child supports an object of any weight, it, in effect, becomes part of the child's body, and the center of gravity that must be kept over the supporting base is the center of gravity of the child-plus-the-weight being held. Because the weight cannot be held AT the center of the weight of the body, *the center of grav-*

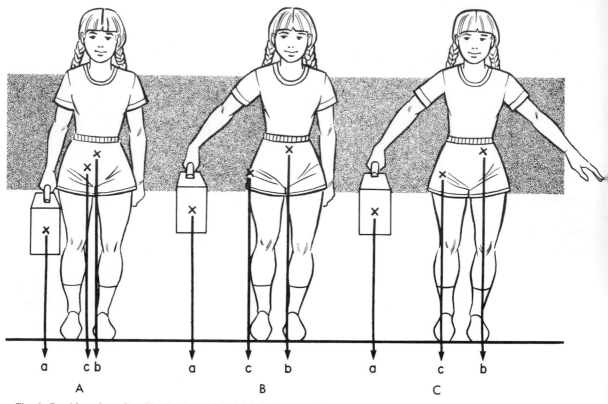

Fig. 4—7.   Line of gravity of body-plus-weight (c) falls between line of gravity of body (b) and line of gravity of held object (a). *A,* Weight held at right side moves center of gravity of total toward right. To keep line of gravity of total centered, body must lean left. Note that this adjustment is made maintaining the straight line of the body segments. *B,* Weight held farther from the body in effect is heavier (see leverage) and thus moves the center of gravity farther right. With the body in the same position as in A, the child would fall because this puts the line of gravity of the total outside the base; to maintain balance, this child would need to lean farther left or counterbalance the weight by weighting the left side (see C). *C,* Lifting the left arm in effect makes it heavier since it is farther from the body (its center of gravity farther from its axis); thus the line of gravity of the total is brought back within the base so that the child is in balance even though the body lean is no more than in A and B. The child is less stable than in A because the line of gravity falls near the right edge of the base.

ity of the total is on a line from the child's center of gravity to the center of gravity of the object and this combined center of gravity must be kept above the base (Fig. 4–7). To keep this new center of gravity above the center of the base to maintain stability, the child's body must shift *away* from the weight. If a child picks up a heavy ball or object of *any weight in his right hand, his center of gravity (body plus object) shifts toward the right (toward the weight) and his body (total or some segment) must shift to the left (opposite direction). The heavier the object and the farther it is held from the body's line of gravity, the farther the shift of the center of gravity (body plus weight) and the greater the adjustment of the body that is required to keep the new center of gravity over the base.*

As children support various weights in the left hand, in the right hand, in front of the body, or

on the back (hung from the shoulders), their bodies must adjust to maintain balance with the added weight. Since *such adjustments are made reflexly,* children may have difficulty feeling their own bodies adjust to an added weight, but they can SEE it in others IF their observation is guided.

As weights are increased or held farther from the body, the greater adjustment required is more readily felt by the child (see Fig. 4–7B). While adjustment can be made in various ways, it causes less strain when the legs, pelvis, and trunk remain in a straight line (as when standing) and move *as a unit* rather than moving separately into various zigzag positions. The zigzag position causes strain at each zig and zag.

As children experience supporting objects in various space relationships to themselves (i.e., holding a light weight close to the body and then out away from the body), they find that an added shift of the body is needed to balance the weight. In addition, the child learns that an object becomes heavier as he holds it farther from his body. In fact, just holding an arm out at shoulder height for any length of time demonstrates that the arm is much heavier when held away from the body than when hanging at the side. This is because of the increase in length of the *resistance arm* (the perpendicular distance from the center of gravity of the arm to the axis for the arm, the shoulder). When a child holds something fairly heavy in one arm, less adjustment of the total body is required if the free arm is lifted than if it is left at the side because the additional weight of the arm held away from the body balances the object (see Fig. 4–7C). Thus the child begins to learn about leverage. *The reaction of a lever is in proportion to its length (perpendicular distance from the center of gravity of the weight, or force, to the fulcrum).*

Exploration with objects of various weights and balance boards of various lengths can lead to experiences that make obvious this principle of the lever. As the child places blocks of various weights on opposite ends of a balance board at different distances from the *fulcrum* (point about which the board balances), it will be obvious that a light weight placed far from the fulcrum can balance a heavy weight closer to the fulcrum. If a balance board is large enough for children to sit on, they can experience this principle as each attempts to balance or to overbalance another child sitting on the opposite end. The heavier child will find that it is necessary to move forward on the board (closer to the fulcrum) in order to successfully "teeter-totter" with a lighter child on the other end (Fig. 4–8). To help children generalize from these experiences, the teacher must help them see the relationship of the balancing tasks to the holding exploration. In such experiences, the teacher must adapt the weights of objects to the particular children involved; objects must be heavy enough to cause observable body adjustment BUT not heavy enough to cause strain.

While adjustment to an added weight is made reflexly, the reflex action may not always be the one that causes least strain. When the adjustment is made from the ankle region, the balance of the body segments is not disturbed, the line of gravity of each segment remains an extension

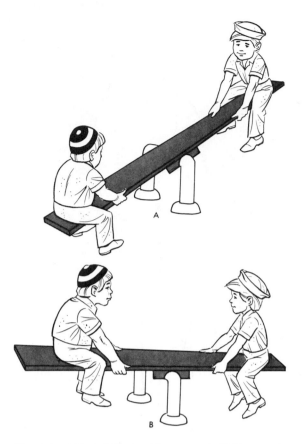

Fig. 4–8. Effect of length of lever arm. *A,* Children equidistant from fulcrum; heavy child overbalances lighter child. *B,* Heavy child moves toward fulcrum to shorten RA and can now be balanced by lighter child.

of the line of gravity of the segment below (see Fig. 4–7), the total body weight is used to counterbalance the lifted or held weight, and the adjustment, unless the load is very heavy, can be slight. When the adjustment is made from the hip and waist area (Fig. 4–9), the lines of gravity of the body segments zigzag, putting strain on the structures of the lower back.

If the teacher helps the child to see the relationship of force problems involved in various activities in a physical education program, the child's *concept of counterbalancing a weight with the least strain, of exerting force through the object's center of gravity to directly oppose gravity (straight upward), and of keeping a held weight as close to the body's line of gravity as possible to reduce its leverage advantage* can be constantly reinforced.

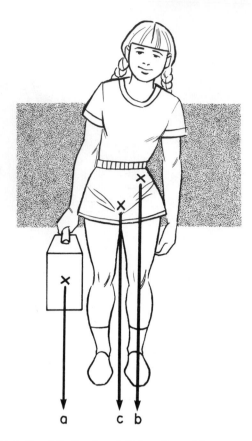

Fig. 4–9. Adjusting to weight from the waist causes lower back strain.

SUSPENSION

A child (or object) is suspended when its center of gravity is BELOW the point of support. A child may suspend himself from a bar or a tree limb by hands or knees just for the challenge of hanging, but most suspension activities involve moving either along a bar or horizontal ladder, up a rope, or swinging on ropes or rings. A child may also hang from a bar for the challenge of pulling the body weight upward against gravity. When hanging, some part of the body, usually the fingers (may be knees) must be ABOVE the supporting surface (i.e., tree limb, bar) or the supporting object (i.e., rope) must be grasped with a strong enough force to cause sufficient friction to keep the hands from sliding down. Because gravity pulls the center of gravity downward FROM the surface, the problems of this type of activity differ from those of tasks that require balancing the many segments of the body against gravity's pull.

During any movement, the ear mechanism and the eyes are active in orienting the body and head in space. In suspension, however, balance is not the same problem since gravity pulls the body straight downward from the point of contact with the supporting object. The first problem is that of applying sufficient force to stabilize the body segment that is above the supporting surface. When hanging by the hands, the child must stabilize the hands in the grasping position with the arms supinated (palms in) or pronated (palms out); muscle action varies with the grip used. In general, the supinated position is easier.

The second problem in a suspension activity is to apply the force to move the body from the straight suspended position. Chinning or climbing a rope involves muscular contraction (upper extremities) to directly oppose gravity and move the body weight upward. Moving along a bar or swinging through the air on a rope(s) or rings is an experience that can increase both the child's understanding of gravity and his concept of the *law of INERTIA—an object at rest tends to remain at rest, and an object in motion tends to remain in motion at the same speed and in the same direction until acted upon by a force* (Newton's First Law of Motion). A child running along the floor holding a rope suspended from a beam or tree learns that, when his feet no longer touch the floor and thus cannot produce further force to move him, he nonetheless continues to move, gradually slowing until gravity stops the forward-upward motion, and he then moves downward-backward faster and faster as gravity acts to pull him down. If he pulls himself up so that his feet are above the floor (or bends his knees to hold his feet up), his speed continues to increase until he reaches the bottom of the arc and then inertia carries him upward again. Thus the child experiences the contest between inertia and gravity which has been called "letting the old cat die." It finally dies when the force of gravity has overcome the tendency to remain in motion. Gravity is the moving force in swinging around a bar. When a child pushes himself *out* from a bar, gravity and inertia cause him to swing around the bar; how far he swings depends on how high he pushes out (or the distance he has to drop and thus the speed attained before reaching the bottom of the arc).

Moving along a bar, from rope to rope or from ring to ring, the child can also experience the effective use of gravity and inertia. To "walk" along a bar when suspended, the child must produce force to remove the weight from one hand so that it can be lifted and moved along the bar and still avoid dropping that side of the body during the fraction of time when the hand is off the bar. The child can do so by producing, immediately before release, *upward* force with the hand and arm to be moved; this is done by flexing that elbow and pulling *down* on the top surface of the bar. The reaction force lifts that side of the body, and as the weight is momentarily removed from the hand, it can be lifted and moved. If a greater upward force is applied, the legs swing to that side and upward. As gravity pulls them downward again, they gain momentum that, because of inertia makes the motion continue beyond the midline, swinging the legs to the opposite side; with very little, or no additional force, that hand is unweighted and can then be moved. This pendular force can be used in moving along a bar, along a horizontal ladder, or from ring to ring.

MOVING THE BODY

As the child moves, whether moving an arm, leg, any body part(s), or the entire body through space, equilibrium problems are compounded. *With every movement of any segment, the body's center of gravity*, and thus that part of the body that must be kept above the base, *shifts within the body.* As the right arm is lifted to the side, it becomes progressively heavier as the perpendicular distance of the arm's center of gravity to the shoulder (the axis for the movement) becomes greater. The right arm and thus the right side of the body, in effect, becomes heavier, and therefore, the center of weight shifts within the body toward the right. Because the arm moves upward as well as to the right, the upper body also has more weight and the center of gravity shifts upward as well as to the right. Thus *as the arms, legs, head, or trunk move away from the body's original line of gravity, the center of gravity shifts WITHIN the body IN THE DIRECTION OF THE MOVING PART; some other segment, or the total body, must move in the opposite direction to keep the moving center of gravity over the base.* Moving the arms from the sides forward-upward to a position straight forward from the shoulders moves the center of

gravity forward and upward within the body, and the body must move backward (adjust the angle at the ankles) to keep the forward center of gravity over the base. These adjustments are made reflexly. Exactly the same principle is involved as when weights are supported by the body.

Since movement causes a shifting of the center of gravity WITHIN the body, adjustment of base may be required to maintain stability. In making the base larger to increase stability, the DIRECTION OF THE MOVEMENT INVOLVED MUST BE CONSIDERED. Standing with feet in a side stride while VIGOROUSLY swinging the arms forward or standing with feet in a forward-backward stride while swinging the arms vigorously from side to side does not increase stability. To increase stability, the child must widen the base forward-backward when the arm swing is forward, and side-to-side when the arms swing sideways.

To be effective, the base must be enlarged IN THE DIRECTION OF THE MOTION, *AND THUS OF THE FORCES INVOLVED.* When swinging the arms vigorously forward and backward, children find that they have to step forward from either the feet together or the side-stride position in order to keep from falling forward, but they are stable in a forward-backward stride. They also note that the forward stride does not reduce the necessity for stepping sideward to keep from falling when swinging their arms vigorously from side to side; they must stand in a side stride.

A child finds it difficult or impossible to roll forward when the feet are in a forward-backward stride because this base is more stable for any movement forward and for THIS TASK a position of INSTABILITY is needed; the center of gravity must pass BEYOND the forward edge of the base. A base with the feet side by side (small forward-backward base) allows the child to easily move the center of gravity ahead of the toes. The base that is enlarged forward (in the direction of the moving force, i.e., the more stable base) interferes with ability to roll. Again the child sees that stability is gained by enlarging the base in the direction of the force (or movement), BUT begins to learn that stability is not ALWAYS desirable since *instability contributes to the performance of some movement tasks.*

With few exceptions, the human body is a

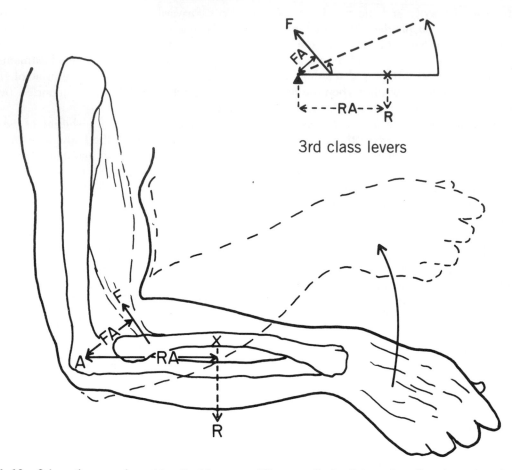

3rd class levers

Fig. 4–10. Schematic comparison of length of force arm (FA, perpendicular distance from line of muscle pull to axis) and length of resistance arm (RA, perpendicular distance from center of gravity of segment to be moved or supported to axis). Example of a third-class lever (FA shorter than RA since force acts between axis and resistance); favors range of motion at expense of force. Note how much farther hand moves than does point of muscular attachment (From Broer[4]).

system of *third-class levers.* The fulcrum (axis) of a *third class lever* is at one end; the force is applied nearer this fulcrum than is the resistance. The various body segments are moved by muscles attached (forces applied) nearer to the joints (axis of rotation) than the center of gravity of the segment to be moved (Fig. 4–10). Therefore, the *force arm* (perpendicular distance from the line of muscle pull to the axis) *is shorter than the resistance (weight) arm* (perpendicular distance from the center of gravity of the segment to the axis). Since *the effectiveness of a force (or weight) depends on the AMOUNT OF FORCE (or weight) MULTIPLIED BY ITS PERPENDICULAR DISTANCE FROM THE AXIS for movement,* the muscular force operates at a considerable FORCE disadvantage. However, during a motion of the arm, the hand at the end of the arm moves much farther than the point of

insertion of the muscles exerting the force causing motion. Thus, since the total arm and hand are moving for the same length of time, *the hand (end of the third-class lever) moves much faster than does the point where the force is exerted* (see Fig. 4–10).

On the whole, the body segments (levers) are long so the distal ends move rapidly. Thus, the human body is a machine that can produce considerable speed but is not effective in moving great weight. To accomplish, without strain, a task that requires considerable force, the human body employs some type of implement that can give a force advantage.

All *second class levers* give a force advantage because, by definition, the resistance (weight) is applied between the point of force application and the axis for the motion. Thus, the force arm (FA) is always longer than the resistance arm

2nd Class Levers

FA longer than RA
Gain Force Advantage

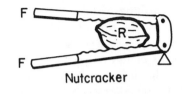

Nutcracker

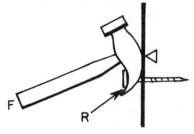

Hammer removing nail

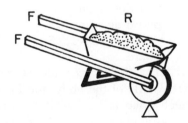

Wheelbarrow with load centered

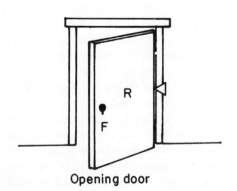

Opening door

1st Class Levers

FA=RA

Balance—no mechanical advantage

FA longer than RA

Gain Force advantage

FA shorter than RA

Lose Force—Gain Speed of motion of R

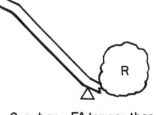

Crowbar   FA longer than RA
Favors Force

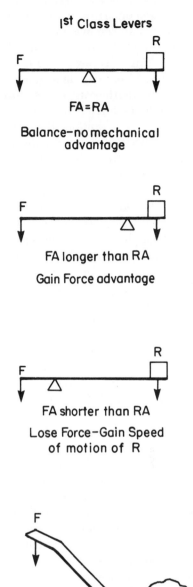

Fig. 4—11.   1st and 2nd class levers.

(RA). A nutcracker is used to crack the hard shell of a nut, a wheelbarrow to transport a heavy load, a hammer to remove a nail, and a door is opened by use of the knob which is located as far from the hinges as possible (Fig. 4–11).

A *first class lever* may favor force or speed, depending on whether its axis is closer to the resistance or to the force (whether the FA or the RA is longer). By definition, the axis is always located between the force and the resistance; when equidistant from them, the lever favors neither because the force arm and resistance arms are equal. When closer to the point of force application, the force arm is shorter than the resistance arm, making the lever useful for gaining speed, but this is at the expense of force. When the axis is closer to the resistance than to the force (longer FA), a force advantage is gained. A crowbar is used to move a heavy rock (Fig. 4–11).

In general, movement of body segments does not involve great weights; however, when a segment is lengthened (straight arm lifted as opposed to an arm with the elbow well bent), its center of gravity is farther from the axis (for arm lift, the shoulder) and thus it takes more force to move it.

Newton's Third Law states: *To every action force there is an equal and opposite reaction force.* This law is all-important in the ability of the human body to move itself along a surface, through water, or into the air. A child lying face downward on the floor must *push down* on the floor to move head, shoulders, and trunk *upward.* When the center of gravity has been moved upward-backward to a position above the feet, the child *pushes down* with the feet against the floor so that extension of the leg joints will straighten *(move)* the body *upward.* When a child stands with back to a wall and a foot up against the wall behind and *pushes backward* against that wall, the *child moves forward.* Standing in a forward stride and *pushing forward*-downward into the floor with the front foot *moves the child backward;* whereas *pushing backward*-downward with the back foot results in *forward movement.* When standing in a side stride, *pushing* downward-*outward* with the *left* foot *moves* the child *right,* and pushing with the right foot results in movement to the left. If, with weight centered above the feet, a child flexes ankles, knees, and hips and quickly ex-

tends them so that force is exerted straight downward, the body is projected straight upward, but if the child leans forward while extending, the push against the floor is downward-backward and the resulting movement is forward-upward. *The direction of the body movement is opposite to the direction of the force applied against the surface.* As the child moves across a surface, whether walking, running, hopping, or jumping, the angle of the body determines the direction of the force applied against the floor by the pushing or takeoff foot (feet), and thus determines the direction of the force that moves the body along the surface or projects it into the air. If the center of gravity is directly above the feet, the force is applied straight downward and the reaction against the body is straight upward. If the center of gravity is forward of the pushing feet, the force is diagonally downward-backward.

A *diagonal force has two components, one vertical and one horizontal.* This downward-backward force has vertically downward and horizontally backward components and results in a force against the body (upward-forward). This force has a VERTICAL COMPONENT (Fig. 4–12E), which is upward and thus supports or moves (depending on the amount of force exerted) the body upward against gravity, and a HORIZONTAL COMPONENT (F), which moves the body forward.

Because in walking, the *forward* foot strikes the ground FORWARD of the body, the force produced at heel strike is FORWARD-downward against the ground (see Fig. 4–12 a). The body receives a force that is BACKWARD-upward and *resists* forward progress (Fig. 4–12 d), making it possible to stop the body's forward motion at any moment (to overcome inertia). When moving fast enough that the period of double support is eliminated (running), the foot strikes under or almost under the body, and the resistive phase found in the walk is eliminated. Thus it takes less energy to run easily (jog) than to walk fast, BUT the ability to stop forward motion suddenly is sacrificed.

Moving forward across a surface can be relatively easy if gravity is used to advantage. As indicated earlier, when the center of gravity is centered above the base, the line of gravity falls forward of the ankles, so gravity exerts a forward rotating force on the body as a whole. Relaxation

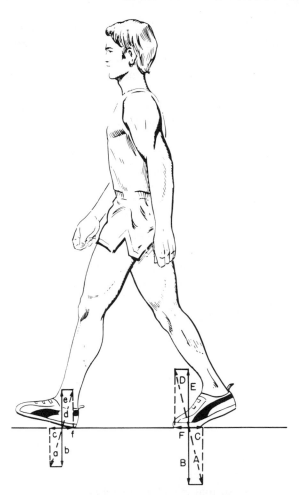

Fig. 4—12. Diagonal force has horizontal and vertical components. Force produced by the back foot to move the body forward *(A)* is applied against the surface in a backward-downward direction. Given force A, the backward force component is C and the downward, B. The reaction force effective against the body *(D)* has forward component F and upward component E. Force from forward foot heel strike *(a)* being diagonally forward-downward will resist (retard) forward movement. Forward component c results in backward reaction force against body *(f)*. For movement to occur, F must be greater than f.

is a time when both feet are on the floor (i.e., walking). A forward lean at the instant of push-off enlarges the FORWARD component of the reaction force against the body, since the pushing foot is farther behind and therefore pushes at a greater BACKWARD angle against the floor.

As the right leg swings forward, the forward motion is transferred to the pelvis (motion of a segment is transferred to any segment attached), and this force tends to rotate the pelvis toward the left. To balance this rotation and thus keep the total force against the body FORWARD, the left arm swings forward, rotating the shoulder girdle toward the right. This opposition of arms and legs takes place at the reflex level and is present in all activities that involve a straight forward force applied to the body by one leg and arm at a time, e.g., crawling, walking, running, jumping, and leaping. Unless a nervous system problem interferes with the normal functioning of this reflex, there is no need to teach this opposition of arm and leg motion. Many a child has had great difficulty in learning to skip because well-meaning teachers have stressed swinging the right arm forward while lifting the left knee. The effort of concentration can cause tension that interferes with the smooth functioning of the reflex. Normally, if children are stimulated to experience various ways of moving across a flat surface, eventually, in each child's own time, a step hop step hop pattern will develop and the swing of the arms in opposition will materialize without interference.

The more directly forward the leg and arm swing, the more effective their force for forward motion of the body. As the child speeds up leg and arm swing to move forward faster, these long levers must be shortened by flexing elbows and knees (reducing the weight by shortening the lever). Some children, girls more frequently than boys, may resist the forward lift of the knee, turning the knee inward and "flinging" the lower leg out-forward. These children also tend to "hug" their upper arms to their sides, allowing the lower arms to "flap" outward. Since any forces from such movements are outward, they interfere with smooth progress forward instead of aiding it. Children who tend to run this way need to think about LIFTING their KNEES FORWARD and keeping their upper arms relaxed with their elbows well bent, allowing the arms to swing as they will in response to the

of the leg extensor muscles results in movement of the center of gravity forward. By allowing the center of gravity to shift forward of the edge of the base, gravity can be used to assist in overcoming the inertia of the body, and a relatively small force is required to cause forward motion. Since FORCE IS MORE EFFECTIVE THE MORE IT IS EXERTED IN THE DIRECTION OF DESIRED MOTION, the body's center of gravity is carried farther forward of the pushing foot when moving forward fast (i.e., running) than when moving slowly enough so that there

motion of the legs. RELAXATION of the arms is the key.

The position of the feet as the child moves across a surface is another factor in the direction of force against the floor and thus the reaction upon the body. When toes are forward, the backward component of the force exerted is straight backward, but when they turn outward or inward, the force is applied at an angle, and therefore the reaction is not totally effective in moving the child forward. Even MORE IMPORTANT is the effect of such forces on the arches of the feet, ankles, and knees of young developing bodies. When toes are turned out or in, the reaction force to the push of the foot against the floor is exerted diagonally across the arch, ankle, and knee. This force puts considerable strain on these joints which are not constructed to withstand heavy forces against their sides, and injury may result. The greater the force applied, the more the chance of instant injury. However, a small force applied constantly over considerable time can be just as dangerous, although the pain or disability is delayed. One forceful jump with the feet in a toed-out position may cause strain or injury, but also the child who consistently walks with feet in this position is storing up problems for the future.

The child can project himself into the air at various angles from one or from two feet. The relationship of center of gravity to takeoff foot determines the angle of the force against the floor and the reaction force that projects the child. When the center of gravity is vertically above the takeoff foot, the child is projected straight upward, since the force exerted against the floor at takeoff is straight downward and thus the reaction force (the force effective in moving the body) is straight upward. When the center of gravity is forward of the takeoff foot (feet), the reaction force against the body is forward-upward. The downward force of gravity acting against the upward component of this force causes the path of the child's center of gravity to curve, and when gravity has overcome the upward component, the path curves downward. Thus, the center of gravity of the child, like any projected object, follows a parabolic curve (Fig. 4–13). The path of the center of gravity depends on the forcefulness of the takeoff and the angle of projection. Although the position of various body parts may change while the child is in the air and thus shift the location of the center of gravity WITHIN the body, *the path of the center of gravity itself cannot be altered after takeoff* since it depends on the force applied and the *angle* of takeoff.

When the arms swing vigorously in the direction of desired projection, the force of the swing, if timed with the takeoff, is added to the force from the leg extension and increases the distance that the child moves through the air (the momentum of a part is transferred to any part attached). Maximum UPWARD distance is gained when the center of gravity is directly above the takeoff foot (feet) and the greatest effort of the arm swing is upward. Since gravity is constantly acting to pull the child downward at a constant acceleration that is independent of any horizontal force applied to the body, maximum FORWARD distance results when half the projecting force is effective against gravity (upward) and half is effective in moving the body forward. (Note: 45-degree angle is theoretical; several complex factors modify this somewhat.) The child leans forward at takeoff and the arm swing is forward-upward so that force is applied both backward and downward against the floor. The forward component of the reaction force moves the child forward and the upward component causes upward motion and resists gravity's pull so that the child remains in the air for the forward motion. If, as the child flexes hips, knees and ankles in preparation for the jump, the "lean" is from the feet (Fig. 4–14A), the center of gravity is carried forward, and the force on extension is in the desired direction (forward-upward); however, frequently a child leans well forward from the hips with less flexion of the knees and the center of gravity remains further back (Fig. 4–14B). This results in a higher angle of takeoff as well as reducing the force possible. The child can lean farther forward without loss of balance when the arms are held well back (weight of arms balances forward lean). If the arms are then swung forcibly forward during the leg extension, both their momentum and the change in their position move the center of gravity well forward of the feet at takeoff so that force is applied against the floor BACKWARD-downward and the reaction force (effective in moving the child) is FORWARD-upward.

A child running across a surface can transfer forward momentum to upward momentum by a

A

B

Fig. 4–13. Self-projecting activities: child's center of gravity follows a parabolic path.

forceful lift of one knee while the other leg is applying the takeoff force. The knee lift serves a *dual purpose:* it not only supplies UPWARD momentum (transferred to body parts attached) but also retards the forward movement of the center of gravity (caused by momentum) to keep (or move) the center of gravity over, or more nearly over, the takeoff foot. Thus, force from that foot is exerted DOWNWARD instead of downward-backward (UPWARD against the body instead of forward-upward).

Children find that they can twirl faster when they "hug" their arms to their bodies, shortening the radius of rotation (the distance from the center of the body to the point of the body mass to left [or right] of body center). This idea confuses

some because it seems to be in conflict with the fact that, given a certain force, the longer the lever, the faster the distal end (farthest out point) moves (see p. 100).

Given a force sufficient to move lever A (Fig. 4–15) at a certain speed, point Z moves twice as far in a given time as point X and thus moves twice as fast; however, this speed is gained at the expense of force. Since in moving level B (see Fig. 4–15), which is half as long as A, the resistance to be moved is only half as great (resistance to be moved is the resistance times its resistance arm or R·RA, see p. 100, it takes only *half* as much force to move lever B that same distance in that time. IF the SAME FORCE as was applied to lever A were applied to lever B,

Fig. 4–14. Preparation for jumping forward for distance. *A*, Center of gravity well foward from feet. *B*, Center of gravity remains back; will result in higher takeoff angle and reduced forward force.

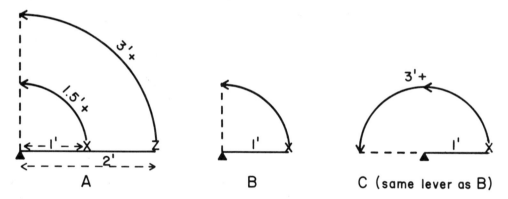

Fig. 4–15. Comparison of Effect of Lever Length and Speed of Rotation. *A*, Point Z moves twice as far as X in a given time and thus twice as fast. *B*, Lever half as long as A and thus resistance is half as great (R·RA); only half as much force required to move same speed as A. *C*, Lever same length as B (thus half as long as A) will move twice as far, thus twice as fast IF SAME FORCE applied to it as applied to A.

B would move twice as far in that time and thus twice as fast. Thus the figure skater pulls arms close to speed the twirl and spreads arms and sometimes moves one leg outward to slow motion. The child finds that, when taking off into the air and attempting to rotate the body forward, tucking into a small ball (reducing the radius of rotation) results in much faster body rotation than if the child tried to flip over with a straight body.

MOVING OBJECTS

When attempting to move a wide variety of objects, the child finds that force can be applied in three general ways.

1. Contact with the object can be maintained and force applied to the object constantly over a given distance and for a given time (see pp. 107–109).

2. The object can be held, the hand moved rapidly (object moving with the hand), and then contact broken suddenly. (The object continues to move at the same speed, in the same direction, under the influence of gravity and other forces that may act on it—law of inertia. See pp. 109–115.)

3. Some body part can be moved and then contact an object momentarily (see pp. 115–118).

In all of these situations the child applies force directly to the object. The arm may be lengthened by the addition of some object such as a racket, but it is used simply as an extension of the body part and can be considered a part of the body since it moves as the arm moves. If, on the other hand, the child moves some object and this object, independent of the child, then applies force to a second object, the child's force is applied to the second object indirectly. For example, if the child rolls a ball which then contacts and moves some other object, perhaps a second ball, the child has applied force indirectly to the second ball. If the rubber of a slingshot is pulled and released, the child applies force directly to the rubber BUT indirectly to an object projected by the slingshot.

Constant Application of Force

The child will find that an object can be moved from one position to another by supporting it (lifting and carrying), by placing hands against it and moving it in front (pushing), or by grasping some part of it (or a rope that is around it) and moving the object behind as the child moves (pulling).

The problems involved in moving an object by supporting it while moving (carrying) have been covered in the discussion dealing with support (pp. 95 through 98). If the object is to be moved upward from the floor (lifting), new problems are introduced. A child can get down to an object on the floor in many ways and if the object is very light in weight, it is immaterial which is used; however, back strain can result from leaning over to pick up an object that has any weight. Also an object that is relatively light for an adult may be a danger to the child. When a child bends forward from the hips (knees straight), the weight of a lifted object is magnified since it is added to the child's body far from the axis for the lifting motion (distance from shoulders to hips). In addition, the force is exerted backward toward the body as well as upward rather than directly upward. Finally and most importantly, the major lifting effort must be supplied by the relatively weak back muscles. If the child squats (flexes hips and knees to lower buttocks close to floor) to contact the object, the burden of the major lifting effort falls on the strongest muscles of the body (legs and hips), the object's weight is supported close to the body, reducing the leverage effect, and the force to lift the object is exerted almost straight upward (in the direction of desired motion) (Fig. 4–16).

As the child squats, the feet may be together or only slightly apart, in which case the object to be lifted is in front of the feet; they may be in a side-to-side stride so that the object can be between them, or in a slight forward-backward stride with the object close to the side. With the object forward of the feet, the weight must be taken farther from the body and will, in effect, be greater (weight multiplied by distance from axis) than when it is between the feet or at the side; thus the strain will be greater. Often when squatting with a side stride, the heels are lifted from the floor. This results in a smaller base forward-backward and means that balance is precarious when a weight is added in front of the body. The forward-backward stride (object at side), with feet *slightly* separated sideward as well, gives a larger base and thus greater stability. If the foot closer to the object to be lifted is back, the foot position rotates the pelvis *toward* the object and little or no spinal rotation is required to grasp the object at the side.

When attempting to move a heavy object from a table, the child will find that, by first pulling it close to the edge (so that as the weight is taken it will be close to the body), it will be easier to lift than it would be from a position farther on the table (leverage, shorter resistance arm). The child who stands in a forward-backward stride close to the table (one foot under the table) can remove the object by simply transferring the weight from the forward to the back foot; thus again the strongest muscles (legs) are used for moving the weight.

If an object that the child wishes to move forward is light and high enough to reach a point behind its center of gravity without having to assume a position in which it is difficult to move forward (i.e., a low squat) or if it is on wheels that turn easily, pushing is no problem. If, however, the object is heavy and there is considerable friction between it and the surface, pushing is more difficult than pulling. (*Friction depends on the types of surfaces and the force pushing the surfaces together.*)

A pushing force applied to an object above its center of gravity and exerted in a forward direction (direction of desired motion) tends to rotate the object around its base since friction

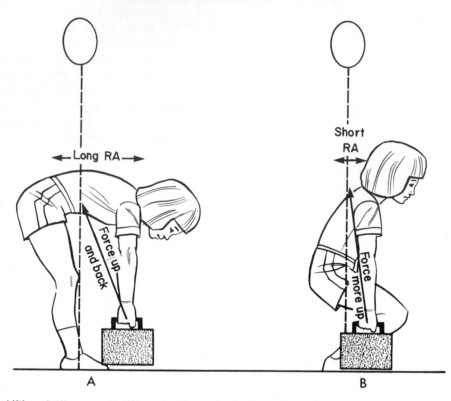

Fig. 4–16. **Lifting.** *A,* Wrong; major lifting effort by weaker back muscles under conditions of disadvantageous leverage (long RA). *B,* Efficient; major lifting effort by strong leg muscles, RA of weight reduced considerably, force nearly in direction of desired motion (upward).

resists the forward motion of the base across the surface. Also, some of the pushing force is effective *downward* as well as forward and thus increases friction further (greater force pushing surfaces together) and interferes with forward motion. On the other hand, if a rope is put around the object's center of gravity or lower, and the hand grasping the rope to pull the object is higher than the object's center of gravity, the force exerted against the object is forward-upward and thus has a component that is effective in reducing friction. The heavier the object the child is trying to move, the greater the friction and the greater the upward component of the pulling force required. A shorter rope, which increases the angle of the rope (Fig. 4–17B), increases the upward component of the force and thus reduces friction and makes such a task easier. If friction is not great, however, pulling is more effective with a longer rope, which results in a greater horizontal (forward) component of the pulling force (in the direction of desired motion) (Fig. 4–17C). If, when pushing a heavy object, the child stands away from it, leaning toward the

object from the ankles, knees and hips somewhat flexed (Fig. 4–17A), by setting the muscles of the trunk, arms, and shoulders, the heavy work can be accomplished by the strong leg muscles. Actually, whether pushing or pulling, the most efficient position for moving a heavy object is the same, except that the arms are forward to push and backward to pull (Fig. 4–17). The legs do the work and the force is transferred through the trunk and arms to the heavy object (or rope attached to it).

As more tasks involving heavy objects are experienced, the child finds that it is more difficult to start a heavy object moving than to keep it going (inertia). Therefore, when pushing or pulling, it is easier to keep an object moving than to start and stop and start again.

Frequently, a child can move a heavy object by rotating it around one corner; in other words, knowledge that a force applied above the center of gravity of an object tends to rotate the object (tip it) is applied to this task. The child applies second-class leverage; the force arm (perpen-

Fig. 4–17. Pushing and pulling. Well aligned body allowing for major force production by strong leg muscles. *A*, Trunk and arms stabilized to transfer pushing force from legs to object. *B*, Pulling with shorter rope results in greater proportion of force upward; effective if friction is considerable. *C*, Pulling with longer rope results in greater proportion of force forward (direction of desired motion); effective if friction NOT a problem.

dicular distance from the point at which the child pushes to the corner around which it rotates, opposite corner) is long compared with the resistance arm (the perpendicular distance from the center of gravity of the object to the corner about which it rotates). Thus the force required to rotate is less than the weight of the object. The child pushes as high as possible (to lengthen the force arm to its maximum) against one corner, rotates that corner forward, then repeats against another corner. In this way, an object that would be too heavy to be pushed or pulled by the child can be moved forward.

If the child's experiences include moving light, long objects, particularly those on wheels, control is a greater problem than the production of sufficient force to produce motion. Unless force is applied exactly opposite the center of gravity of the object, the child finds that the object rotates. Since it is difficult to push or pull through this one point (center of gravity) and, even then, slight differences in friction at the two ends (i.e., more dirt on the floor in one place) may cause

rotation, control is easier when the child spreads the hands as far as possible to both sides of the object's center of gravity. This increases the length of the force arm on each side and thus the force that is effective in preventing rotation around the end on that side. If the motion of the object's right end is retarded so that the object tends to rotate toward the right, the right hand is in a strong position to produce force to cause counter rotation and thus keep the object moving straight. (The force arm for the right hand, its distance from the left end, is long, and its force for rotation to the left is multiplied by this distance.)

Grasping, Developing Motion, and Releasing (Throwing or Rolling)

Children are constantly trying out various motions with their arms, and they inevitably swing them in large circles. As they speed up this movement, their fingers begin to tingle. They are beginning to learn about a phenomenon which has been called "centrifugal force." Actually, centrifugal force is the inertia (tendency to move in a straight line) of an object which another force (centripetal, or force holding the object in) causes to move in a circle. The blood in the child's arm is forced toward the fingertips and pressure is increased, causing the tingling sensation.

Children have many games that use this principle. As they swing each other around in a circle and then let go, the child who has been forced to move in a circle by contact with the child turning him moves off in a direction that is tangent to the circle; this is the direction that the released child was moving at the instant of release. Long ago, children discovered that the longer the line of children being turned in a circle, the faster the child on the end would move; and the game "crack the whip" was born. This game applies the leverage principle that the longer the lever, the faster the distal end moves for a given speed at the axis (see pp. 100 and 105).

Children use these same principles as they experience moving small objects in various ways. Just as another child can be swung in a circle and released, so too can a ball or other small object held in the hand. It too, because of inertia (tendency to maintain its state of motion), keeps moving in the direction and at the speed it was moving at the instant of release. This direction is tangent to that arc through which it was being moved; this is the same arc through which the hand was moving when it released the object. Thus the child finds that the faster the hand(s) move(s), the faster the object moves at release and the farther it travels after release. Speed of movement of the hand (or the distal end of any body segment) depends on (1) the time and distance over which the speed can be developed, (2) the speed of muscular contraction, (3) the length of the lever being moved, (4) the number of body levers involved, and (5) the sequence of the action.

The child can increase the time and distance for the development of speed by lengthening the backswing, in other words, by carrying the hand(s) backward as far as possible through action of the arm, shoulder, trunk rotation, and transference of weight to the back foot. Because a two-handed throw greatly curtails trunk rotation and thus backswing, it cannot develop as much force as one-handed projection. More force is possible in a two-handed sidearm than a two-handed overhand movement because more trunk rotation is possible. The faster the child's muscular contraction, the greater the speed potential. The longer the lever, the faster the distal end moves for a given movement at the joint, and maximum speed results from combining many parts of the body into a system of levers. To gain maximum speed of the final lever, each lever of the system must come into the action when the part below is approaching its maximum speed. This is known as SEQUENTIAL ACTION. The greatest speed can be developed with an overhand pattern because it allows for the use of the maximum number of body levers in sequence. For a sequential throwing action, a right-handed child starts the forward motion by rotating the pelvis toward the left and, as this gains speeds, beginning trunk rotation. As the trunk approaches top speed, shoulder girdle action begins, followed by elbow, wrist, and fingers each coming into the action as the preceding part approaches its greatest speed. This combining of body parts also results in the use of more muscles and thus contributes to the production of more force.

Some children, usually more girls than boys, tend to throw overhand with the elbow low and close to the side—a "push" rather than a "throwing" motion. All segments of the arm tend to extend at the same time, and the whipping action of the sequential levers is eliminated; thus much less speed can be developed and the throw lacks force. Also, in this type of throw, trunk rotation is usually minimal.

The movement pattern must be changed as the object to be projected varies in size and weight. The sequential action of the overhand pattern can be produced only when the elbow is well away from the side, and this places the hand under the ball rather than behind it at the moment that the hand reverses its direction from backswing to forward swing. Thus, unless the object is small enough to be grasped with the fingers around the *back* of the ball, the hand is not in position to stop the ball's backward motion and, as the hand reverses, the ball continues backward (inertia) and is dropped.

Also, a heavy object cannot be controlled when held far from the body, as is a ball when the overhand or sidearm pattern is used (weight is multiplied by distance from axis—leverage). With the pushing action (elbow low and close to side), the hand is close to the shoulder, minimizing the weight arm and thus the weight, and it can be behind the ball to apply forward force. This is the reason some children use this movement pattern; it is impossible for them to use a sequential overhand motion with objects that are too large for their small hands to grasp or too heavy to control far from the body.

The sidearm pattern allows the hand or lower arm to be behind the object as the backswing is reversed to start the forward swing, and thus large objects can be controlled. Considerable speed can still be developed because maximum trunk rotation is possible and the full length of the arm results in a long lever. The sidearm pattern with balls too large to be grasped lacks the full potential of sequential action that is present in the overhand pattern, however, because the total arm acts as one lever rather than a system of levers. Thus, a child cannot produce as much force with this sidearm throw as with a sequential overhand, provided the object is small enough to be grasped and light enough to be controlled far from the body.

The underhand pattern also uses the total arm as one lever, and if the arm moves in line with the desired projection throughout the swing, it also minimizes trunk rotation. This pattern lacks the force potential of either the overhand or sidearm pattern; however, the child can control a larger ball with this motion than with the overhand because it rests on the hand and the lower arm is *behind* it in position to apply *forward* force. A greater weight can be manipulated with this pattern than with either of the others since gravity and inertia can be utilized to accomplish most of the backswing and the forward swing. The weight can be held close to the body to reduce leverage, and when pushed out away from the body, gravity acts to cause the ball to drop; its inertia causes it to continue to move backward and upward until gravity stops it and starts it moving downward and forward. It requires relatively little muscular strength to lengthen the backswing beyond that which would result from inertia alone (takes less force to keep an object moving than to start it moving). In addition, the underhand pattern makes it possible to move the arm straight back and straight forward along the line of desired flight for the object, and this

makes accuracy (right-left) less a problem when the underhand pattern is used. Lengthening the backswing to a complete circle increases the possibility for developing considerably more speed but, because of this, control of angle of release and direction become somewhat more difficult.

Because any object continues to move in the direction it was moving at release (inertia), *whenever an object is moving in an arc, it continues to move in the direction that is tangent to that arc at the point of release.* The flatter the arc through which the hand moves, the less divergent the tangents drawn at various points on that arc. Thus, anything that flattens the arc of the hand contributes to control of the flight of the object. The arc of the arm in the underhand pattern is vertical, whereas that for the sidearm pattern is more horizontal; therefore, the problem of left-right accuracy is minimized in the underhand pattern. The vertical arc can be flattened by transferring the weight from the back to the forward foot. In the overhand pattern, the sequential action of the segments of the arm contributes somewhat to a flatter arc of the hand as it moves forward. Although right-left accuracy is not as easily controlled as with the underhand, it is easier to control with the overhand than the sidearm movement in which the arc is more horizontal (right-left). Forward weight transference does help flatten this arc to some degree.

Continuing arm and hand motion in the direction of desired ball flight well after release (follow-through) contributes to BOTH accuracy and speed. It increases the possibility that the hand will be travelling in the direction of desired flight of the object AT THE INSTANT OF RELEASE and makes possible the release AT THE TIME THAT THE HAND (and thus the object) IS MOVING AT ITS FASTEST. Any attempt to stop movement at or right after release not only means that the hand is actually slowed BEFORE release in anticipation of stopping, but also results in a jerking of the hand, making it impossible to predict the direction of the object. It requires time and distance to decelerate just as it requires time and distance to build up speed of motion. The greatest speed of the object results from its release near the center of the arc of the movement. Although follow-through takes place AFTER the object has left the hand, it still affects the object because of its effect on the movement that precedes release.

If a ball is released along a surface, the child finds that friction slows and eventually stops its motion; if released in the air, gravity immediately acts to pull it downward. If the child simply drops it, gravity pulls it straight downward with a uniform acceleration (32 ft/sec/sec). Thus the length of time the ball remains in the air depends on its height above the surface when released. If the child gives a ball straight downward force, that force is added to gravity and the ball drops faster. If the ball is given straight upward force, gravity gradually slows the ball, stops it, and then pulls it down with uniform acceleration. If it is given forward force, gravity causes it to curve downward as it moves forward. The distance the ball travels forward depends on the forward force given the ball and the time it takes gravity to pull it to the surface. The time it takes gravity to pull the ball down to the surface depends on the height and angle of release.

As the child releases the object at various angles forward, it becomes obvious that the flight curve is high when the angle of throw is more upward-forward and flattens as the angle is lowered toward the horizontal. For the projected object to travel the greatest distance, the angle of projection must be halfway between straight up and straight out, 45 degrees (air resistance neglected). If there is little air resistance, an object travels farthest when approximately half the projecting force is exerted upward to withstand gravity and keep the object in the air longer and half is forward to carry it in the direction desired. This is the same as when the child projects his own body into the air. A higher angle results in greater force to keep the object in the air a longer time but less force to move it forward, so it travels in a higher shorter arc. A lower angle moves an object forward with more force, but because little force resists gravity, it hits the ground before this greater forward force has had time to be effective.

One question is whether it would be preferable for a deviation of angle from 45 degrees to be high or low. In other words, when attempting to throw as far as possible, if a child is unable to project at 45 degrees (air resistance neglected), would it be more effective to throw at 30 degrees or at 60 degrees? The answer depends on the purpose of the throw. So long as the deviation above 45 degrees is EXACTLY THE SAME as the deviation below, objects projected with the same force travel *exactly the same distance* BY THE TIME THEY ARE OPPOSITE THE POINT OF PROJECTION. Thus, objects projected with a given force FROM THE GROUND TO THE GROUND at 60 degrees and at 30 degrees (both deviating 15 degrees from 45) travel exactly the same distance. This would also be true of balls released 5 feet above the ground AND caught 5 feet above the ground. In both cases, while there is no distance advantage for one angle over the other, the lower angle would result in a faster flight. In addition, if the thrown balls were not caught BUT ALLOWED TO CONTINUE UNTIL THEY HIT THE GROUND, the ball projected at the lower angle would hit farther out than the one projected at the higher angle because of the angles of approach to the ground (Fig. 4–18).

Because of the vertical arc of the hand in the underhand pattern, the point on the arc at which the ball is released is all-important in determining the angle of projection and thus is important in the distance that an object travels (*distance depends on angle of release and speed*). If a child steps forward onto a BENT knee in attempting to project an object with the underhand action, the shoulder (the center of the arc made by the hand) moves both forward and downward, somewhat flattening the arc through which the hand moves and increasing the possibility of release at the angle desired.

As the child learns to apply more and more force to various objects to be projected, it is quickly apparent that stability becomes a problem unless a foot is placed forward to widen the base in the direction of the force. A wider base in the direction of the force (forward-backward) allows the child to transfer the weight in the direction of the desired force without loss of balance and also adds the strong leg muscles to the action. The child may try enlarging the base with the right foot or with the left foot forward; either improves balance, BUT it will be obvious that the object will travel both farther and straighter when the foot placed forward is opposite to the arm and hand with which the object is grasped and projected. Just as swinging the right leg forward in walking and running rotates the pelvis to the left, standing with the right foot forward (or stepping onto it) rotates the pelvis to

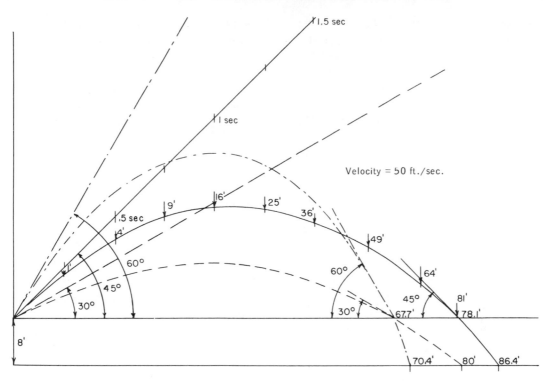

Fig. 4–18. Paths of Objects Projected at Various Angles (Air Resistance Neglected). Note that a deviation of 15 degrees above 45 results in the same distance as a deviation of 15 degrees below 45 *at the point opposite the point of projection* (From Broer and Zernicke[1]).

the *left*. The backswing (which allows time to develop momentum) of a child projecting an object with the right hand rotates the shoulder girdle to the *right;* this trunk rotation of the backswing is restricted when the pelvis is in a position of left rotation (right foot forward); thus less force can be developed.

When enlarging the base, BOTH the direction of the force being produced AND the possible restriction on joints involved must be considered. Moreover, the purpose of the particular throw is all-important. WHEN SPEED OR MAXIMUM FORCE IS DESIRED, the supporting base should be enlarged by putting the foot OPPOSITE the throwing arm forward to allow for maximum backswing. WHEN LITTLE FORCE IS REQUIRED, which foot is forward is immaterial so far as force is concerned; in fact, the base does not need to be enlarged to the same extent for a less forceful throw. A toss may require NO widening of the base; however, which foot is placed forward may be important to accuracy even in a throw requiring little force. With the same foot as throwing arm forward, both the pelvis and shoulder girdle are rotated

in the same direction as the arm swings through, and there is a tendency to project the object in that direction rather than straight forward. The rotation of the hips to the right when the left foot is forward tends to balance the rotation of the shoulder girdle to the left as the right (opposite) arm moves forward to project the object, and makes it easier to throw straight forward.

Rather than being told to "always place the opposite foot forward when throwing or striking," the child needs to understand not only the contribution of a wide base to balance and to the force of a throw or strike but also the direction of pelvic rotation resulting from the different foot positions and the effect of this rotation on both force and accuracy. The child then begins to develop a basis for judgment about the type of base required for movements involving different purposes.

Whenever a foot is placed forward of the body, it pushes forward-downward against the surface, which applies a reaction force backward-upward against the body and resists its forward motion. This resistive force can be removed by allowing the forward knee to bend as the body moves forward over the base. When the child rolls a ball or slides a bean bag or other object along the surface, this bending of the forward knee makes an additional contribution to the efficiency of the total movement. The child must lower the projecting hand to the surface to release the ball, and this can be done without the problem of precarious balance by bending the hips, knees, and ankles. This keeps the center of gravity of the body low and over the base as the child moves forward. Bending forward from the hips to lower the hand leaves the center of gravity high, and as the arm swings forward, the body can be pulled off balance. If the hand is not lowered and the ball is released above the surface, it gains downward momentum as gravity pulls it down and it hits the surface with downward as well as forward force. The reaction force is upward and forward and it bounces; how high, depends on the height of release and the degree of *restitution* of the object (*its ability to retake its shape after being flattened by impact*). This downward force as it hits the floor also increases friction, which reduces the forward force and also may change the direction of the ball.

When less than maximum speed is desired, some of the preceding factors are modified. The DEGREE of modification depends on the SPEED DESIRED; the WAY in which they are modified depends on the INDIVIDUAL CHILD. One child may choose to reduce the speed of his hand by cutting the length of the backswing through elimination of trunk rotation, another by lessening the arm and shoulder action, and still another by slowing the muscular contraction. NO TWO CHILDREN have the same leverage system or the same strength, so no two will ADJUST IN EXACTLY THE SAME WAY. The important factor is that each understands the problems of controlling direction AND the contribution of various movements to both speed and direction as well as the relationship of speed and angle of release to the distance an object travels through the air.

There is not ONE WAY to throw; there are certain factors that contribute to speed and accuracy, and there are general patterns of movement that employ all of these factors, and thus produce *maximum force*. These patterns must be adjusted as less force is required, and the teacher must understand that numerous adjustments are possible.

Seldom does a ball move through the air with no spin. Some off-center force at release or as its surface encounters air resistance causes the ball to spin around its axis. It may spin forward or backward around a horizontal axis (top spin or back spin), or it may spin right or left around a vertical axis. (The direction of motion of the TOP of the ball indicates whether it is forward spin or back spin. The direction of motion of the FRONT of the ball indicates whether it is right or left spin.) These spins carry a layer of air around the ball, and as the ball moves forward through the air, pressure builds where the airflow around the ball is in a direction opposite to the airflow caused by the ball's forward motion, and lowers where they are in the same direction. The flow of air forward over a top (forward) spinning ball is in opposition to the wall of air into which the ball is moving, and air pressure builds up at the front top of the ball. The top-spin airflow below the ball is backward (same direction as air resistance to the forward motion of the ball), and pressure below the ball decreases. Thus, *a ball with top (forward) spin tends to drop more rapidly than one with no spin*. It follows that a ball with back spin (top moving away from the direction of the ball flight) carries air around it which is moving backward on top and forward under the ball. This results in an increase in air pressure below the ball (upward) and a decrease in pressure above the ball; this offsets gravity to some extent and thus tends to keep the ball in the air longer (Fig. 4–19).

A ball spinning to the right (front of the ball— or side facing the direction in which the ball is moving—moving to the right; back moving left) carries air backward on its right side and forward on its left. The air moving forward on the left side of the ball is in opposition to the wall of air into which the ball is moving, while that moving backward on the right of the ball is in the same direction. Thus, pressure builds on the front left of the ball and is reduced on the right, and the ball *tends to curve right. A left spinning ball tends to curve left*.

Air resistance is a lesser factor in modifying the direction of a rolled ball, but friction is a considerable factor. The *friction depends on the weight of the ball (force pushing the two surfaces together) and the types of surfaces involved*. The harder the ball and the surface over which it is rolling, the less the rolling friction.

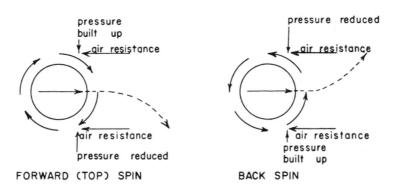

FORWARD (TOP) SPIN   BACK SPIN

Fig. 4–19. Effect of Top (Forward) Spin and Back Spin on Ball Flight (Looking at Side of Ball). (From Broer and Zernicke[1])

A ball with *top spin* as it rolls forward pushes backward on the surface (bottom of top-spinning ball moves back), and friction results in an opposite (forward) force against the ball; this is added to the forward force given the ball at release, and *it rolls forward faster.* If the *ball is spinning backward* when released along a surface, the bottom of the ball pushes forward against the surface and the resistive force from the surface is backward, *slowing the ball's forward motion.* If the spin force is slight, friction quickly overcomes this force, reversing the spin and causing the ball to roll forward. If it is great, the ball slides along the surface until friction finally overcomes the spin force and the slowed ball begins to roll forward. A *rolling ball with left spin curves left,* and *one with right spin curves right.*

Developing Momentum, Sudden Contact (Striking)

Whenever two objects collide, a "striking" situation is involved. A stationary object may be struck, or a moving object such as a ball may either strike a more or less solid surface that is stationary (i.e., floor, court, wall, backboard) or be struck by a moving surface (i.e., some body part, bat, racket).

When an object strikes a solid horizontal surface (floor or court), *it rebounds at an opposite angle equal to that at which it approached the surface (Law of Rebound).* Thus a ball thrown straight down (or straight up so that it then falls straight down) bounces straight up. The bottom of the ball is depressed equally on all sides of its center, so the rebound forces are equal on all sides. If it is thrown to the floor at an angle,

Fig. 4–20. Child tenses neck muscles to make head a resistive surface for striking soccer ball.

it rebounds at an equal angle, if it has no spin. The angle is less if there is any "give" in the surface or if the object does not immediately retake its original shape. An old tennis ball rebounds at an angle lower than its angle of approach to the floor or court, and any ball rebounds lower from grass than from a wooden or concrete surface. The old tennis ball does not retake its shape immediately and the grass "gives" with the force of impact (in essence, some of the impact force is absorbed). The same law of rebound operates when a ball strikes a vertical surface (wall or racket), but gravity immediately acts to pull the ball downward, thus modifying the rebound angle. If a ball strikes a child (i.e., head, hands, held object) and the child contracts muscles, stabilizing the body segment so that there is no "give" on impact, the ball will rebound as from any other surface (Fig. 4–20).

Whether a child strikes an object with hand, foot, knee, head, or any other body part, motion of the striking body part must be developed *before* making contact; the greater the momentum of the body part used as the striking implement at the time of contact, the greater the force imparted to the struck object. All the general movement patterns used to throw or roll objects are used also to strike objects; thus all of the principles of force production and control of direction apply (see pp. 110 through 114).

Just as in throwing, the greater the time to develop speed of motion (longer backswing), the greater the momentum. (*Momentum is the product of the moving object's mass and its velocity.*) In throwing, the direction of the object depends on the direction of the motion of the hand at the instant of release, but when *striking, direction depends not only on the direction of motion of the striking body part at the moment of impact, but also on the point of contact on the object and the angle of the striking surface*. If the point of contact is in line with the object's center of gravity, the struck object moves in the direction of the motion of the striking part; if it is off center, it moves in a direction between the direction of the motion of the striking body part and the direction of the line from the point of contact through the object's center of gravity. Thus, an object struck with a forward motion but hit off center to the right (right of the object's center of gravity) moves diagonally forward and left rather than straight ahead; an object hit forward but below its center of gravity travels higher than one hit through its center, whereas one hit above its center of gravity travels lower. The angle of the striking surface affects the angle of rebound and thus the direction of the struck object.

A child may strike an object that is stationary or one that is moving. Since *to every action force there is an equal and opposite reaction force,* striking situations differ from throwing in that they involve a force applied by the object against the striking body part. This is illustrated when a child, swinging a bat (or other implement) rapidly, misses the ball; there is no force against the bat to slow its forward motion, and the bat's momentum may carry the body completely around in a circle frequently upsetting the child's balance. In any kick, the force from the leg swinging forward, which tends to rotate the body lever, must be balanced by forward motion of the upper body around the hips to exert a counter rotating force. But even when this is done, if a child attempting a forceful kick misses the soccer or football, the momentum of the leg swinging forward, not being resisted by the impact, can rotate the body around its center of gravity and the child falls backward.

When two objects collide, as in any striking situation, *the total momentum after impact equals the total momentum before impact (Law of Conservation of Momentum),* and *the resultant motion is in the direction of the greater force.* If the object contacted is moving, its force against the body is greater than if it is stationary; the faster it is moving, the greater this force (momentum = mass × velocity). Thus, when a child wishes to reverse the direction of an oncoming ball, the momentum of the body part with which the ball is struck must be greater than the momentum of the ball. Because of action-reaction, the striking surface must be firm to apply maximum force to the object. If the child does not stabilize the striking body segment so that it resists the force of impact, some force will be dissipated in the "giving" of the striking segment. For example, when a child striking a ball with the hand allows the wrist to be extended by the force of the impact with the ball, the ball cannot be hit as far as if the child had been able to resist the force of the ball against the hand so that all of the force of impact (that from the mass and velocity of the moving hand and body plus that from the ball's mass and velocity) would be effective in moving the ball. While the flat hand with its many small bones does not afford a firm surface for striking, various techniques can make the hand firmer. For example, with the fist clenched, the child can hit the ball with the heel of the hand (hand facing forward) or with the surface of the curled first finger and thumb, the thumb side of the hand. The latter, since it affords a smaller striking surface, increases the difficulty of hitting the point that will apply force *through the center of gravity of the ball in the desired direction* and thus makes control of direction more erratic. For the "dig" (volleyball), the two hands are interlocked to form a firm surface to resist the force of the oncoming ball.

When strings of a racket are loose, much of the force of impact is lost in the "give" of the strings. Force of impact can also be lost through a loss of restitution of the object being struck. An old tennis ball that has lost some restitution rebounds with less speed than a new ball hit with the same force. Of course, a child does not always wish to hit a ball as far or as fast as possible. The bunt in baseball is an example of using a "giving" of the bat to reduce the force of the approaching ball.

The child may lengthen the striking lever by adding some implement (a bat, racket, stick) to the body. While this makes possible greater speed at the end of the striking lever, control is more difficult. Because the end of the longer lever is moving faster, the force of impact is greater and thus reaction force to be resisted, if advantage is to be gained from the greater speed, is increased. Also, this additional force is applied against the striking implement farther from the wrist, lengthening the resistance arm and further increasing the difficulty of resisting the reaction force.

In addition, lengthening the striking lever makes *spatial judgment* more difficult. Early in life, the child becomes familiar with the distance that can be reached with the hand(s). As the child grows, this distance lengthens gradually and it is easy to adjust. However, the addition of an implement suddenly increases considerably the "reach distance," and it takes time for most children to form a new distance concept. Too often, teachers take it for granted that children develop a new spatial concept immediately and automatically when they pick up a new implement, but children differ considerably in this ability as in other abilities. Adjustment is easier when children are exposed gradually to progressively longer implements that they might use to strike objects (i.e., hand to paddle to racket) rather than starting with an instrument such as a racket or a bat.

Weight of the implement is another factor to be considered. Although it is true that the heavier the striking implement, the greater the force potential (momentum = mass × velocity), heavier implements are more difficult to move AND to control. Also, the longer the implement, the more the weight is magnified. If the greater weight cannot be manipulated as rapidly, force will be lost by use of a heavier striking implement. Even if it can be moved as fast, direction will be sacrificed if it cannot be controlled. The length and the weight that can be manipulated successfully depend on the strength of EACH INDIVIDUAL child.

SPIN on a ball complicates any striking situation; it affects a ball's rebound from the floor or racket because another force is introduced. A rapidly spinning ball that strikes the floor applies force against the floor in the direction of the movement of the BOTTOM of the ball (part of ball making contact with the floor), and *the floor applies a reaction force against the ball in the opposite direction. The rebound is the resultant of this force (reaction to spin) and the normal rebound force.* When a horizontal surface (floor) is involved, the bottom of a ball with TOP spin pushes backward against the surface, and the reaction force from the surface against the ball is forward. (Top spin: top is moving forward; therefore bottom is moving backward.) The resultant of this forward force and the force of impact is at a lower angle than the angle of approach to the surface. A ball with top (forward) spin dropped straight down to the floor no longer bounces straight up but in the direction of the resultant of the upward force from the impact and the forward force caused by the floor's reaction force from the backward push by the bottom of the ball against the floor. In other words, it rebounds at an upward-forward angle. A ball with BACK spin rebounds upward-BACKWARD because the bottom of the ball pushes forward against the floor and thus the reaction force is backward.

When a *top-spinning ball strikes a horizontal surface at an angle*, the forward reaction to the backward force from the bottom of the ball against the floor causes *the bounce to be at a lower angle than the angle of approach* to the floor; *a back-spinning ball rebounds at a higher angle than it approached* (Fig. 4–21). How much spin changes the angle of rebound depends on the speed of the spin in relation to the speed with which the ball is traveling, since the latter affects the force of impact. A fast spin in combination with a relatively slow ball considerably modifies the rebound angle, but a slow spin has little effect on the rebound of a fast ball. These changes of rebound must always be considered IN RELATION TO THE ANGLE AT WHICH EACH BALL APPROACHES THE SURFACE. Since spin alters flight, it also changes the angle of approach (see p. 114).

When a ball with either RIGHT or LEFT spin is thrown straight down, it rebounds straight up because the front of the ball is moving (and thus pushes against the floor) in one direction and the back is moving in the opposite direction. Thus the forces are neutralized. If a right-spinning ball strikes AT AN ANGLE to the floor, however, it rebounds forward-RIGHT because the impact depresses the BACK of the ball more than the front and the BACK is spinning left (pushes left against the floor; reaction force is to the right against the ball, Fig. 4–22). A left-spinning ball bounces forward-LEFT. (This discussion considers side spin around a vertical axis only. Right spin means that the FRONT of the ball is moving right and the BACK is moving

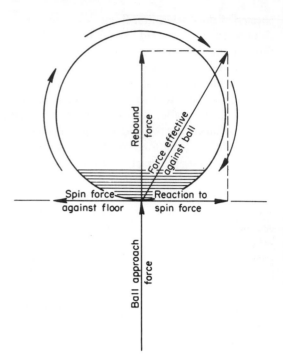

Fig. 4–22. Direction of Bounce of Right-Spinning Ball (Vertical Axis) Approaching the Surface at an Angle (Looking Down on Ball). Since BACK of ball approaching surface at an angle is depressed more than front, the direction of spin of the back determines the effect of spin on bounce; ball bounces toward right. (From Broer and Zernicke[1])

left. For more detail concerning the effect of spin, the reader is referred to Broer and Zernicke.[1]

Against a VERTICAL surface, the direction of spin of the FRONT of the ball affects the rebound since this part of the ball makes the contact. Thus, a ball with top spin (front moving down, reaction force up) rebounds higher than normal; one with back spin comes off the surface at a more acute angle (lower); right spin (front moving right, reaction left) causes a left rebound and left spin a right rebound.

Thus, a struck ball reacts differently if the ball is spinning as it approaches the striking implement. The *effect of the spin depends upon the relation between the speed of the spin, speed of the approaching ball,* and *force of the hit,* which in turn depends on the *speed* and *weight of the striking implement.*

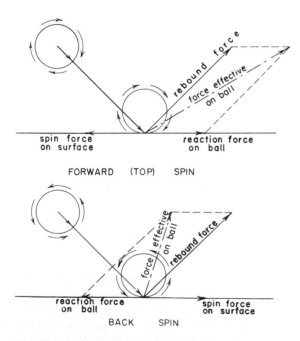

FORWARD (TOP) SPIN

BACK SPIN

Fig. 4–21. Effect of Top Spin and Back Spin on Bounce of Ball Approaching Surface at an Angle (Looking at Side of Ball). (From Broer and Zernicke[1])

RECEIVING FORCE

In all of their activities, children are constantly receiving force. It may be the force of their own moving bodies that must be dissipated, or they may need to stop a moving object. The way in which the force of the movement of the child's body or some object is dissipated determines whether injury results and, in the case of an object, whether it rebounds from the child. When the purpose is to reverse the direction, as in striking (pp. 115 through 117), the force is resisted rather than dissipated. When the child wishes *to maintain contact* with an approaching object, *he must dissipate the force* of its movement.

Whether the child is landing from a fall (weight out of control) or landing following a jump, leap, or even a step when running, the force of impact must be dissipated gradually. If the motion is stopped suddenly, all force is exerted at once against the surface contacted and the REACTION force against the body may cause injury. Even landing from a VERY SMALL jump causes considerable jarring of the entire body and particularly the spine if, as the feet hit the floor, the hips, knees, and ankles are kept rigid so that the downward motion of the body is stopped suddenly. On the other hand, if the ankles, knees, and hips flex sequentially as the feet hit, the motion stops gradually and no jarring occurs even when landing from a jump of considerable height. The higher the jump, the greater the force that must be dissipated on landing since the acceleration caused by gravity increases rapidly. A *controlled* bending of the joints of the legs allows the body to keep moving and gradually slows it. This controlled bending is commonly called "giving," and the gradual force dissipation is called "force absorption." *The greater the time and distance over which force is "absorbed," the less the chance of injury.*

Gradual force dissipation is equally important when the child attempts to catch a moving object. If, as a moving object is contacted, the hands are held firm against the impact, a large portion of the force that the object exerts against the hands is returned to the object and it is difficult or impossible to control (it rebounds); also the force of impact against the hands is great. If the object's momentum is reduced gradually by moving the hands in the direction the object is moving, resisting its movement with a force only sufficient to slow its motion gradually, contact can be maintained easily. This is accomplished by reaching forward to contact

the object so that there is space through which the hands can be moved in the direction of the object's motion after contact is made; thus the object is allowed to move toward the body and its motion is gradually resisted and finally stopped. If the child transfers weight to the back foot, the time and distance for force absorption can be increased. The faster the object to be caught is moving, the longer the time required to stop its momentum gradually, and the greater the distance the hands must move in the direction of the object's motion.

Balance becomes a problem when the child must receive any amount of force, so the base should be widened in the direction of the force to be received (pp. 91 through 99). Leverage is also involved; the farther out to the side or the higher above the head an object is contacted, the more it tends to rotate the body. A fast ball caught far out on the right exerts considerable force to twirl the body in a clockwise direction, and it is difficult to keep from falling backward when catching a fast ball high overhead.

Normally, when jumping, leaping, or running the child's body is under control and he lands with a foot (feet) below or only slightly ahead of the center of gravity, so that the gradual force dissipation can be accomplished by controlled "giving" of the leg joints. This is really a matter of allowing gravity to flex the joints while controlling the speed of their bending. This does not mean that the muscles of the lower limbs relax; if so, the body would crumble and the total force would be taken on whatever parts hit next. Rather, it means that the muscles of the legs resist slightly at impact and gradually increase their contraction.

Although, when the child is leaping and running, the center of gravity may be slightly behind the landing foot (feet), the forward momentum of the body (its inertia) carries the center of gravity forward over the base. If a child jumping forward for distance (projecting himself forward-upward) reaches the feet well forward of the trunk for the landing, the force of impact by the feet against the surface is downward-forward, and the reaction force against the body is upward-backward, creating considerable force resisting forward body motion. If the joints of the legs are allowed to flex, not only is the force of impact gradually dissipated, but also the radius of rotation of the trunk around the feet is shortened (distance from center of gravity to feet), and the forward momentum of the body rotates the trunk over the feet more rapidly. If there is little forward momentum or the joints of the legs are NOT flexed on landing, the child is not only jarred but falls backward because the center of gravity remains behind the feet. Flexing the joints of the legs when landing from a forward jump is important for two reasons.

1. It contributes to a gradual reduction of motion and thus reduces the reaction force against the body, minimizing the jar of landing.

2. It reduces the radius of rotation for the trunk around the feet and thus makes it easier for the center of gravity to move to a position above the base (feet) so that balance can be regained. When momentum is great, the trunk may continue forward beyond the feet, but the child can then go into a roll.

When considerable force is involved, a partially nonresistive surface should be provided for the activity. Any nonresistive surface allows for gradual force absorption by BOTH the SURFACE and the BODY and thus provides greater reduction of jar on impact. A mat is somewhat nonresistive; a jumping pit (area filled with soft material) has much more "give."

The child does not always land on the feet and the motion cannot always be controlled; however, many things can be done to slow the movement gradually in order to reduce the force of impact. Any way of making the body into an object that can roll rather than hit flat results in a more gradual loss of momentum and thus less injury. When falling forward or sideward, the hands and arms can be used to absorb some of the force as well as redirect it. The wrists, elbows, and shoulders must flex, *gradually* resisting motion in the same way that the joints of the legs slow motion when landing on the feet. A child can tuck the body more or less into a "ball" so that it rolls and can slow gradually. Some of the force may be taken on the hands and redirected to the back of rounded shoulders; the child rolls forward or sideward. When falling backward, the child has more difficulty absorbing force gradually although the same general procedure can be used—the hands and arms taking some of the force and redirecting it so that the body goes into a backward roll.

Children have an advantage over adults in that they are closer to the surface and thus are not moving as fast when they hit; momentum being less, the force of impact is less. Very small children fall backward onto their large soft buttocks with relatively little jar. Since the buttocks, particularly of small children, are larger and softer than other body parts, they absorb force more gradually than hard surfaces. Bony surfaces such as the elbow and knee are both hard and small; they have no inherent "give," and thus landing on these points almost always results in injury. Since *the force of a moving body is distributed over the total surface contacted, the larger the area contacting a surface, the less the force per unit of the area.* Thus a force against one hand is twice as great as the same force against both hands. The redirection of the movement into a roll not only dissipates the force gradually BUT ALSO spreads the force over a large area as it is taken by the back of the shoulders, following a preliminary "give" of the joints of the arms. Although no injury results from contacting a fast moving ball with both palms, this same force applied against the end of one finger injures the finger. The force is concentrated on a very small area and is in the direction that jams the bones of the finger together. This is an additional factor causing injury. Thus the palms of the hands rather than the tips of the fingers MUST face an approaching ball.

The *two important principles* in dissipating the force of impact when a more or less *resistive surface* is contacted are:

1. The more gradual the force dissipation, the less likely is injury to the body or rebound of an object. The greater the time and distance over which motion is slowed to a stop, the less the reaction force from the impact with a resistive surface.

2. The greater the area contacting a resistive surface, the less force per unit area.

When the child lands on a *NONresistive surface, one that will part* so that the body can pass through (water), the problems are different from those of landing on a resistive surface or one that gives to a slight degree, as discussed previously. For example, any effort to cut a cake, loaf of bread, or piece of cheese would be unsuccessful if the broad surface of a knife were used; however, the task is easily accomplished when the edge of the knife is used. In the same way the body passes easily through water if the surface of the water is contacted by a SMALL area of the body such as the fingertips, but if the child lands flat on his body, the force of impact resisting the passage of the body is great. Thus when diving, jumping, or falling into water, the force against the body can be reduced by approaching the water with a small area of the body (the fingers or feet) that can in effect, make a hole for the body to pass through. Also, the arms (or legs) must be kept rigid rather than "giving" as they do when the surface contacted is resistive. If they are not kept rigid, they do not part the particles of water and the full force of the impact is taken on a larger surface, the head in the case of a dive in which the arms are allowed to "give." A nonresistive surface can be parted, and the water friction then slows the body gradually. A resistive surface, as the name implies, stops the body's motion suddenly, and thus the gradual slowing of the body must be accomplished by the body itself. In instances where the surface is partially nonresistive (jumping pit), both the surface and the body absorb force.

The principles for reducing force against the body when contacting a NONresistive surface are, therefore, the opposite of those for contacting a resistive surface:

1. The smaller the area contacting a NONresistive surface, the less the force against the body.

2. The more rigid the small body part contacting the water, the more it parts the particles of water, so the body meets less resistance.

If the child wishes to stop the body faster when jumping into water, the surface contacting the water must be enlarged. By spreading the legs forward-backward and holding the arms out sideways at shoulder height, a greater surface area of the water resists the body and slows its downward motion more rapidly than if the child jumps in with feet together, arms at sides.

Some attention must be given to the problem of *stopping the motion of a moving body part*. When a body part is put into motion, the force of its inertia (tendency to keep moving at that speed and in that direction) must be overcome to stop it. If the movement is slow and upward, gravity may be sufficient to overcome its inertia, but when it is fast or downward, inertia and gravity both act to keep it moving; muscular effort is needed, and to avoid injury and/or loss of control, the motion must be slowed and stopped gradually. This is one purpose of the

follow-through in throwing and striking. If there were no follow-through, stopping the motion would have to begin BEFORE release or impact and maximum speed could not be transferred to the object; force of projection would be lost. The follow-through gives time and distance for gradual stopping of the motion AFTER release or contact. Thus it is possible to accelerate UNTIL release or impact in order to impart maximum force, and still have time to decelerate gradually to avoid injury.

SUMMARY

If physical educators and classroom teachers understand the *basic* mechanical principles and their application to human motion and if they think in terms of movement education rather than in terms of specific game or sport skills, knowledge important to *all* human motion can be taught through *any* specific situation. Children can be put into movement situations that demonstrate similarities both in basic movement patterns and in mechanical principles.

Rowing a boat, riding on a teeter-totter, lifting a shovel of dirt, prying up a rock are very different activities; yet all are essentially first-class leverage problems. The car stops suddenly and the child who did not fasten the seat belt lands on the floor; the rider attempts to take a jump but the horse refuses and the rider goes over his head; the child steps off a merry-go-round that has not quite stopped, and falls; these are a few of the endless examples of the principle of inertia. In fact, why does a ball continue to move after the child has broken contact with it? Each of the basic mechanical principles discussed in this chapter is met repeatedly in a wide variety of seemingly different situations. Wise teaching can make these repeated exposures lead to generalizations so that these principles can become a base for the child's understanding and for use in the solution of future movement problems.

Also, patterns of movement are widely applicable, although slight adjustments may be required by a specific purpose or equipment. For example, many different situations involve force applied with an *underhand* pattern of motion. Study of several sport skills has indicated that, while degree of muscular activity varies with specific purpose or equipment involved, the timing of muscular activity is almost identical for those situations using an underhand pattern.[5] Furthermore, it appears that essentially the same *overhand* (or *sidearm*) pattern is used for many different specific skills. In fact, the leg activity for underhand, overhand, and sidearm patterns was found to be similar whenever considerable force was the objective.

In this age, widespread attention to, and respect for, the human body are evident on every front. A high percentage of adults are groaning with lower back pain and other muscular strains, many because of poor body mechanics throughout their younger years and a lack of understanding, even as adults, of *basic* mechanical principles that could make obvious to them the dangers of certain positions and movements and the effectiveness of others. Certainly, in such a climate, those entrusted with the physical development of children must themselves understand the laws of motion, force, and leverage, so that they can intelligently plan experiences that will assure a wide exposure in varied movement situations, situations that will make obvious to children the basic mechanical laws and their wide and varied application to human motion and that will help children understand the way to go about solving a new movement task.

Might it be possible to teach widely applicable movement patterns in such a way that they would become the base of a movement vocabulary for children? A teacher who can guide children in the development of a wide movement vocabulary and an understanding of the applicability of both various movement patterns AND basic mechanical principles makes a *lasting* contribution by giving them tools for determining for themselves effective ways to move in any situation with which they may be faced in the future.

REFERENCES

1. Broer, M.R., and Zernicke, R.F.: Efficiency of Human Movement, 4th ed. Philadelphia, W.B. Saunders Co., 1979.
2. Hellebrandt, F.A., and Brogdon, E.: The hydrostatic effect of gravity on the circulation in supported, unsupported and suspended positions. American Journal of Physiology, 123:95, 1938.
3. Morton, J.D., and Fuller, D.J.: Human Locomotion and Body Form. Baltimore, The Williams & Wilkins Co., 1952.
4. Broer, M.R.: An Introduction to Kinesiology. Englewood Cliffs, New Jersey, Prentice-Hall, 1968.
5. Broer, M.R., and Houtz, S.J.: Patterns of Muscular Activity in Selected Sport Skills: An Electromyographic Study. Springfield, Illinois, Charles C Thomas, 1967.

Chapter 5

Movement—The Content of Physical Education

BETTE J. LOGSDON
KATE R. BARRETT

Teachers of children must have a thorough understanding of the content of the curricular area for which they are responsible. Movement has been established earlier as the content of physical education. If movement is the content and we are to teach children to move, we must know how to observe, analyze, describe, and teach movement.

There are several ways of describing movement, and each contributes toward a greater appreciation of movement. Some systems use an anatomic approach for studying movement. The terminology utilized in the anatomic system reflects the vocabulary of physics and anatomy and focuses chiefly on body actions. This method of analyzing movement is highly useful in the fields of kinesiology, anatomy, and other allied sciences where the interest is especially on the mechanical analysis of movement (see Chapter 4). It also continues to be a useful tool in analyzing movement in elementary school physical education.

LABAN: HIS INFLUENCE ON THE STUDY OF MOVEMENT

In recent years, interest has developed in expanding our awareness of movement; thus, a more comprehensive description of movement has emerged, and is used along with the mechanical analysis discussed in the previous chapter. This approach, with a broader, more inclusive perspective for viewing and describing movement, was initiated and influenced by the work of a Hungarian, Rudolph Laban.[1] He made perhaps his greatest contribution, especially to education, during his residency in England, where he lived from 1938 until his death in 1958. Laban's study of movement represents a systematic way of describing all four aspects of movement: body, space, effort, and relationship. Respectively, these four aspects describe:
What the body is doing, Where the body is moving, How the body is performing the movement, and the Relationships that are occurring as the body moves.

This scheme provides a means of scrutinizing each aspect of movement singularly; and when used collectively, the four aspects describe more nearly the totality of movement. The independence of each aspect and the interrelatedness of the four aspects make Laban's system uniquely useful in physical education. Its completeness provides the structure for determining the content. It also is used extensively in the instructional aspects of the program in designing the learning experiences, analyzing movement, and discussing with students ways to improve their movement.

Laban's study of movement is broad in both scope and application. Only the rudiments of his classification of movement have been adapted for presentation here. Many people who are not just being introduced to this material may benefit from a more comprehensive study of his writings, especially those that deal with spatial orientation. This detailed spatial phase of his work is omitted in this book because it was deemed too advanced for the elementary school child. Further reading will reveal the extent to which he has examined movement, and his influence in the study of human movement. Broader study of his writings will demonstrate the impact of his work: in the study of personality, on the theater, on dance, in industry, as well as in physical education. The understanding of his basic system for categorizing movement is essential for those who wish to implement a physical education curriculum as it is described in this book.

Laban's System for Categorizing Movement

In understanding Laban's basic ideas, it is helpful to visualize a framework illustrating how he viewed movement. This framework is not dissimilar from those introduced by Stanley,[2] Russell,[3] and others. The framework for looking at and thinking about movement is developed and simplified by centering our observations and our thoughts on answers to the following questions:

What is the body doing? Where is the body moving? How is the body performing the movement? What relationships occur as the body moves?

Seeking answers to these questions forces us to focus on the four specific movement aspects. These questions and the four movement aspects they represent help us to perceive the totality of movement. By looking at all aspects, we can become more consciously aware of movement. This more thorough perspective can create greater sensitivity for identifying, differentiating, describing, and teaching movement. Similarly, if the four aspects help teachers to gain a greater awareness and appreciation for the totality of movement, the program content developed from these same four aspects can provide children with experiences to make them more aware of their bodies and help them achieve their individual potential for movement.

A Framework for Classifying Movement

Figure 5–1 is a basic framework for classifying movement. It shows the four broad aspects of movement in the left-hand column. In the right-hand column, the dimensions for each of the four aspects are identified. These dimensions and the broad aspects comprise the scheme for classifying all movement. Once this framework is understood, it can be elaborated to have meaning for the study of human movement no matter what the purpose or nature of the movement.

Throughout the ensuing discussion on movement as the content of physical education, the content is conceived broadly to be applied and experienced in all three learning domains: motor, knowledge, and feeling—or psychomotor, cognitive, and affective. The extent to which the learner can gain from learning experiences built from this movement content depends to a measurable degree on the teacher's capacity to understand, interpret, and implement the movement content. The goal for the teacher is to develop sufficient knowledge about movement to help the child develop skill in executing all aspects of the movement content. In so doing, the teacher should strive to create within the children an inner feeling for their bodies as they move as well as an understanding for the movement principles involved.

To assist you in the development of a more thorough appreciation of the framework of the movement content, we have examined each aspect separately to illustrate how the dimensions are interpreted. In addition, the basic framework for examining movement content has been expanded in Chapters 6, 7, and 8, specifically for classifying dance, games, and gymnastic movement.

THE BODY ASPECT—WHAT IS THE BODY DOING?

The body aspect has four dimensions: *actions of body, actions of body parts, activities of body,* and *shapes of body.* Each of the four dimensions of the body aspect either:

1. Categorizes the actions.
2. Describes the roles different body parts play in movement.
3. Names the activity being performed
   or
4. Defines the shape of the body during the activity.

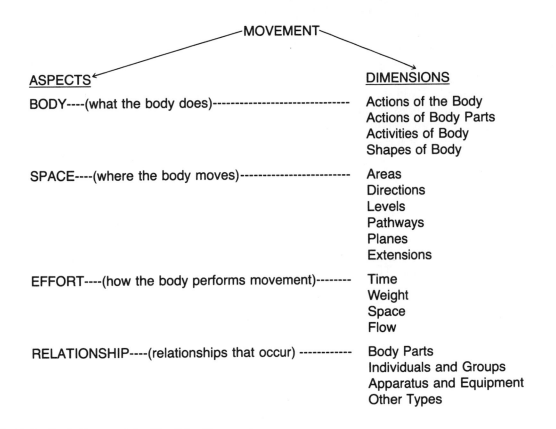

Fig. 5–1. **Basic Framework for Classifying Movement.**

Naming the activity being performed seems to be the dimension that is identified most readily, perhaps because we have used it more extensively before in describing movement. Uninitiated observers of movement tend only to name the activity when asked, "What is the body doing?" All four dimensions must be noted to develop an adequate description of movement.

Actions of the Body

Three actions—curl, stretch, and twist—constitute all movement. Some writers call these the basic actions, since the action in movement cannot be classified more finitely. As the body moves, curling, twisting, and stretching may occur continuously. (The word bending is often used interchangeably to express the curling action.) Perhaps the term bending is used more commonly to connote the action of flexion that occurs in an isolated joint, whereas curling represents a more total involvement of many joints. Curling or bending makes the body become more compact. In the curling action, the body parts are drawn toward the center of the body. As one would expect, stretching is the opposite of curling. Stretching, therefore, lengthens and extends the reach of the body and its parts. The stretching action moves away from the body center and elongates the body or spreads the body parts away from the center. Twisting results when a part of the body is kept still while other parts turn or rotate about the fixed part to face a new direction.

In addition to curling, stretching, and twisting, swinging can be considered a basic action. In swinging, a body part (or entire body) is restricted at one end while the opposite or free end is set in motion either by muscle action working against gravity or by the weight of the body (or a body part) yielding to gravity.

Actions of Body Parts

This dimension of the body aspect, although crucial to movement, is often overlooked in observing and analyzing movement, as well as when constructing physical education content. To become attuned to this aspect of movement, you should focus attention on specific body parts. It is essential, therefore, to determine the roles the various body parts play in the action. Many body parts play different roles at various times. They can support the body weight, lead the action, receive the weight or force, or apply the force.

SUPPORTING THE BODY WEIGHT

The action of supporting the body weight is frequently called weight bearing. The actions that characterize this group may be classified as simple actions of balancing. The experiences built on weight bearing or on supporting the body weight focus on the different body parts that serve as the base of support and not on the act of balancing per se.

LEADING THE ACTION

Another factor that may be overlooked is the body part that leads the action, i.e., the body part that *initiates* the movement or the body part *responsible for the change in direction* once a movement has been started.

RECEIVING WEIGHT OR FORCE

Another role body parts play in activities is to receive weight or force. This force may be generated by the body itself, as apparent in landing from a jump, or it can be the force of an object that must be controlled, such as a ball. At times, it could also be receiving the force of another person's body, which is experienced in many different settings in gymnastics, games, and dance.

When the body is in the air, the control of the force of landing can be demonstrated in two general ways. One way is to absorb the force by sequentially giving in the joints and retaining balance on the same body parts that touch the ground first in the landing. The other method is to absorb the force by giving in the joints sequentially, and then immediately sending the weight back into the air or onto new bases of support. The control of this landing is thus the ability to keep the body in action, following the landing, rather than bringing the body to a moment of stillness. In both instances, great stress is placed on the sequential giving in the body parts (feet, ankles, knees, and hips) if landing occurs on the feet with sufficient muscle tension to prevent a complete crumbling or collapsing of the body as in a fall. Regaining and maintain-

Photo from the Agency for Instructional Television.

ing appropriate muscle tension in the landing is essential to retaining the body weight over the original base formed on landing, controlling the body when projecting it upward in a springy, resilient landing, or transferring the weight immediately onto different body parts.

The same principles of absorbing force of the body in landing are exercised in absorbing the force of a ball or other objects with different body parts or with sport equipment. The body part or equipment receiving the force usually is extended toward the approaching object. Elongating the body before the moment of contact increases the available distance and thus the time for absorbing the force. Immediately upon contact with the object, the body part or piece of equipment is retracted along the path of the force until the force of the object is stopped or controlled sufficiently to be redirected. Again,

in catching as in landing, the joints tend to bend and to retract sequentially until the force is absorbed. At the same time, muscle tension is retained or recovered sufficiently to maintain possession of the object or to redirect it.

APPLYING FORCE

Body parts play another role in actions: applying force. You will recall that, in receiving force, the body parts retract to absorb the force. The opposite action, a stretch, usually occurs in applying force. On the other hand, the body parts can retract or bend to apply force, for example, when pulling the body up to a horizontal bar. To pull up to a bar requires power to overcome the pull of gravity and to lift the weight of the body. In producing the power or applying the force essential for this maneuver, the elbows

Photos from the Agency for Instructional Television.

must bend rather than extend. In general, the parts of the body recoil or retract in preparatory movement and then extend or elongate in the actual action of applying force.

Force may be applied to a stationary object, like the floor or vaulting apparatus, as a means of transferring one's weight or gaining or maintaining one's balance. Force can also be applied to a stationary object for the purpose of moving the object, e.g., striking a held ball or kicking a ball lying on the ground. Body parts may also apply force to moving objects for the purpose of changing the direction of the object or adding to the momentum. Shuttlecocks and balls of all kinds when struck in flight or when rolling are examples of applying force to moving objects. Also, at times in gymnastics, dance, and even in games, one person may apply force to others to add impetus to or restrict their movement.

Activities of the Body

Activities of the body are classified into three broad categories.

1. Locomotor activities—those activities that cause the body to travel from space to space or from one base of support to another.

2. Nonlocomotor activities—those activities that can be executed in a single space without moving the base of support or without the intent to travel from space to space.

3. Manipulative activities—those activities used to manipulate or avoid equipment.

Keep in mind that the basic actions mentioned earlier—curl, stretch, and twist—are combined in various ways to form these activities.

LOCOMOTOR ACTIVITIES

The five broad forms that categorize all types of locomotion are: *step-like actions, rocking, rolling, sliding,* and *flight.* In the first four, at least one part of the body is always in contact with the floor. In the last form, flight, there are moments when all parts of the body are off the floor.

Step-like actions tend to make us think first of walking, but such actions can also be executed on body parts other than the feet, such as hands, hips, and knees. Especially significant may be step-like actions that are performed by transferring weight onto a series of a variety of body parts. The one qualifying characteristic for step-like actions is that at least one body part must be on the ground at all times; however, the various body parts used in step-like actions can alternate or change so no one body part remains in constant contact with the floor.

Rocking and rolling are two more forms of locomotion where contact with the floor or ground is not lost. *Rocking* occurs when the body weight is transferred back and forth along the same body surfaces or on changing surfaces. The body surfaces must be round or made rounded to facilitate rocking. Usually, an increase in muscle tension is used to keep the surfaces rounded and firm and to redirect and distribute the tension and the muscular action back and forth along the body parts used as the base of support. *Rolling* is defined as continual transference of weight along adjacent body parts or body parts that are made adjacent. Rolling differs then from rocking in that rocking requires a transfer of weight back and forth on the same body parts in reverse order, while the rolling activity continues onto the next adjacent body part. The body can be made to roll in several different directions while in various shapes. Likewise, many surfaces of the body can be used as rockers; feet, fronts, seats, and sides are some of those surfaces used most frequently in rocking.

Sliding is the one form of locomotion that does not require transference of weight from one base of support to another in the activity itself. It does involve transfer of *body weight,* but from one *place* to another rather than from one body part to another. Momentum must be generated for sliding to occur. This momentum can be built up by transference of weight, such as in running before the body starts the slide, or it can be generated by the weight of the body as it slides down a smooth, inclined surface. It also can be produced by other body parts pushing, pulling, or pressing against other surfaces to make the body slide. Once the activity of sliding begins, if momentum is sufficient, the body can travel from one place to another place without additional momentum. Various surfaces of the body can be used as the base of support in sliding: backs, fronts, feet, hips, seats, legs, and thighs. The smaller the base and the smoother the sliding surface, the less friction is developed. The body slides farther when less friction exists.

Flight or elevation occurs whenever there is

a momentary loss of contact with the floor or ground. Jumping is the major locomotor activity associated with flight. Here are the five basic jumps. Each is performed differently by varying how the weight is transferred.

one foot to the same foot
one foot to the other foot
one foot to two feet
two feet to one foot
two feet to two feet

While all five combinations are classified simply as jumps, two have specific names. Taking off from one foot and landing on the same foot is called a hop, whereas running and leaping involve taking off from one foot and landing on the other foot. These five basic jumps are used in achieving elevation and flight. To develop a feeling of flight, we stress the momentary time the body is suspended in the air. We often think that, in games, dance, and gymnastics, the momentum essential for flight comes solely from the individual; however, frequently partners,

equipment, and apparatus assist or give impetus to the flight. Still, most flight is initiated by the individual through jumping. At times, flight can be initiated by springing from other body parts such as the hands, knees, or body parts used in combination, such as the shoulders and the hands.

Many movement variations can be devised from these simple locomotor activities. Also, many other locomotor activities are merely combinations of those already mentioned; for example, skipping combines a walking step with a hop. You can see it would be impossible to list all of the many possible combinations. By keeping the simple definition of locomotor activities in mind, you can add to the list and make it as complete as you wish.

MANIPULATIVE ACTIVITIES

Some activities related to games involve the use of equipment. These manipulative activities can be classified in three broad categories. Maul-

don and Redfern have identified these categories to be sending an object away, gaining possession of an object, and traveling with an object.[4]

SENDING AN OBJECT AWAY. Two main activities send an object away: throwing and striking. *Throwing* can be executed with the hands, different body parts, or objects. Throwing patterns include underhand, overhand, and sidearm. Each of the throwing patterns can be used in specialized ways, often with different equipment to develop other specific forms of throwing. For instance, the overhand throw pattern is refined in a specific way in performing the overhand pass in football, in lacrosse, or with a scoop.

Striking can be performed with different kinds of bats and racquets, or with different parts of the body. What was said in throwing is true also in striking. There are various striking patterns: forehand, backhand, underhand, and overhand. Many of these, when used with different kinds of sports equipment, are known by specific names, such as lob, clear, smash, serve, and drive, and have specialized identifying characteristics. Some may be executed with one hand, others with two, and all in a variety of styles. When the striking body part is a foot, we classify the action as kicking. Both striking and kicking take on different characteristics according to whether the object being struck or kicked is stationary, rolling, or airborne. Striking and kicking also can vary according to individual styles, the object involved, and the purpose for the activity. For example, you have the punt, place kick, and the drop kick. Each is different; all are forms of kicking, and the technique used in kicking may vary, depending on the situation and the kind of ball used.

GAINING POSSESSION OF AN OBJECT. Catching and collecting are the two broad types of activities listed under gaining possession of an object. Although they are often used interchangeably, they can imply two different kinds of activity. *Catching* in this context connotes grasping or holding, when the object caught could be retained if desired. Catching is most frequently associated with the gathering in of aerial balls or other objects. *Collecting* refers mainly to gaining control of objects moving along the ground in order to redirect them. Both involve reducing the speed of the object by bringing it toward the body. Although we may rec-

ognize all forms of catching with the hands, we may fail to identify trapping the ball with the legs or feet as a form of catching. Likewise, we might omit drawing in the hockey ball with the stick or giving with the body to check the speed and change the direction of a soccer ball.

TRAVELING WITH AN OBJECT. Items under this category involve keeping an object (frequently a ball) under control as one travels with it, i.e., *propelling* and *carrying*. Propelling includes such activities as dribbling a ball with the hands, feet, or a hockey stick. It implies a repeated contact with an object by the same person. The object can be tapped repeatedly into the air or along the ground, or it can be bounced. In addition, children have devised games where tossing and catching to themselves were a means of maintaining possession of a bean bag or a ball as they traveled. In one game setting of this type, they used small paddles for catching.

Carrying activities occur in football and other games where players with the ball can run with it in their hands. Carrying can also be accomplished with equipment, such as when cradling in lacrosse.

Photo from the Agency for Instructional Television.

NONLOCOMOTOR ACTIVITIES

Unlike traveling actions, the nonlocomotor activities are executed on a fixed base of support. *Turning* is the one nonlocomotor activity that does involve moving the base of support, since the entire body moves to face a new direction. Another activity often coupled with turning is twisting; however, these terms should not be used interchangeably.

Twisting, unlike turning, requires different body parts to face in opposite directions. Twisting is identical to the twisting listed as a basic action of the body. One part of the body remains fixed while other parts continue to turn about it. Unlike turning, which requires little body tension, twisting cannot be accomplished without muscle tension. The greater the degree of the turn over the fixed base, the greater the torsion. The torsion, which increases when a part of the body is stabilized and other parts of the body move to face in different directions, can be used to develop the momentum essential for making jump turns, quickly changing directions, righting oneself, or catching oneself to prevent a fall.

Spinning is an activity that involves turning on the floor without lifting the supporting body parts. The entire body turns on a central axis to face new directions. Spinning also can take place while in the air. Unlike turning, momentum in spinning can be the result of a single action. The same body surfaces used in sliding can be used in spinning.

Bending and *stretching* are two nonlocomotor activities that represent opposites on a continuum. They are identical to stretching and curling listed as basic actions of the body. As the body parts move away from the body center, various stages of stretching ensue. Likewise, when the body parts are drawn toward the center of the body, varying degrees of bending or curling occur. Bending and stretching, when coupled with twisting, can be accomplished to some degree in most regions of the body and in all directions about the body. When stretching occurs in the backward or sideways direction, the opposite side of the body contracts. Awareness for and ability and versatility in bending and stretching are essential to achieve the full potential of the body for movement. Much of the movement of our daily routines does not involve a full stretch, a full bend or curl, or a complete twist, especially movements within the spinal and neck regions. Consequently, we have become very limb oriented and often fail to attain the range of movement, flexibility, and agility that the joint structure affords. Children benefit from continued emphasis on these areas to keep them flexible when their bodies are more supple.

Pushing and *pulling* are further examples of direct opposites in movement. Pushing, with few exceptions, focuses on directing force away from the body, whereas pulling usually is typified by directing the force toward the body. In both instances, to exert maximal force in either pulling or pushing requires extreme firmness and muscle tension throughout the body, with the force applied in the direction that the weight is being pushed or pulled.

Another form of nonlocomotor movement is *gesturing*, which is usually accomplished with the arms and legs, although the head and the body may be used effectively too. Gesturing in expressive movement is often used to demonstrate an idea or a mood, and the actions may create different patterns or shapes in the air. This activity is usually associated with dance content, but the feint used in games to distract or trick a wary defenseman and some of the movements of the body parts not used as the base of support in gymnastics can be classified as gestures also.

Rising and *sinking* are two additional nonlocomotor activities. They are associated with dance. Like most of the other nonlocomotor activities, they can be and are done usually in conjunction with forms of locomotion. Rising has the quality of reaching upward or stretching, while sinking portrays the opposite. Sinking suggests giving into gravity, as in dropping or collapsing; however, when speed in the movement is controlled, dropping and collapsing do not coincide with sinking. The focus is to rise to the utmost and sink to the lowest point. In making a quick equation between rising and stretching and sinking and curling, one must realize that rising and sinking always give an up-down, high-low effect while stretching and curling may be negotiated in any direction, at any level, and on any plane.

Other forms of nonlocomotor movement associated with dance content are *opening* and *closing*. Again, similarities exist between these forms and stretching and curling. In opening, the body parts move away from the body to increase the space used by the body and to show openness of the body and to increase the size of the movement. In closing, the body parts are brought toward the body or toward each other.

Nonlocomotor activities are frequently categorized as weight-bearing activities in gymnastics, for example, balance, counterbalance, and countertension. Some will add off balance to this list; however, as soon as off balance occurs, weight transference and locomotion follow.

Balancing is a fundamental skill of body management in gymnastics. Although *balance* is present in most of our daily activities, *balancing* is considered more of a skill, which is developed by improving the ability to align and maintain the body in a still position over smaller and more difficult bases of support. Balance is easier to achieve on wider and symmetrical bases than it is on narrow and asymmetrical bases.

Once the body weight is assembled and maintained over the base of support, a state of balance exists. Muscle tension to a degree is essential to maintain a state of balance. The shape of the body can be changed and balance can be retained as long as the center of gravity remains near enough to the vertical line over the center of the base. Muscle tension can compensate for a certain degree of freedom of movement away from the base of support. Balance can be lost either through the lack of muscle tension or by body weight shifting too far away from the base of support. The willful ability to lose balance and to control the speed with which it is lost is another skill associated with balancing. Learning to gain, maintain, and intentionally lose balance, although interrelated, have different sensations and can be and often are treated as separate movement content, especially in gymnastics.

Off balance is discussed with nonlocomotor activities, but it should be noted again that off balance always creates locomotion. *Off balance* as a skill or activity is a willful act in which the performer intentionally moves the center of gravity outside the base of support. This activity can be accomplished in three ways: (1) by leaning away from the base, carefully letting new body parts become a part of the base until the weight arrives onto a stable base once again, (2) by making the free body parts (parts of body not included in the base) move quickly to bring about a sudden change in the base, and (3) by pushing or thrusting against the supporting surface with the body parts that comprise the base itself. The sensation of off balance is felt when the center of gravity moves far enough away from the base to develop momentum that cannot be checked until the body weight arrives on a new base. In other words, the body moves so far it gets to a point of no return. Off balance occurs at the moment when the body cannot return to its former base. Creating a feel for off balance and developing skill in using it are basic to many activities, especially in gymnastics.

Counterbalance is another activity that is outlined in the movement content. Counterbalance, as an activity for program development, involves two or more people. Partners, or small groups, working together, form a wide base and then lean against each other so as to support their weight over their mutually formed base. Balance of all people in the group depends on the weight of others. The force applied in counterbalance is recognized as pushing. A feeling of counterbalance can also be experienced by an individual who leans (presses) a part of the body against a piece of apparatus and becomes dependent on the apparatus to maintain balance. Once the state of counterbalance is attained, the partners or small groups, through practice, can learn to push in different directions to change the level of their balance and to change the body parts that press against each other. Throughout, those working together must remain interdependent for support, with the force of the pushing, pressing actions directed toward the center of their mutually formed, wide base.

Countertension is similar to counterbalance inasmuch as it often involves at least two people working together to create a balance over a mutual base. The action in countertension, however, is pulling, with the force exerted away from a narrow base. Those working together must attach themselves in some way that allows them to resist the weight of each other. This is accomplished most frequently by beginners by clasping hands but is also possible by hooking other body parts together. Throughout countertension, the balance of all people upon each person remains interdependent and pulls away from the mutually formed small base of support.

A feeling of countertension can also be created by the performer securing a body part onto a piece of apparatus and by leaning or pulling away from the base to make the apparatus responsible for maintaining the balance.

Shapes of the Body

The body outlines four general shapes while still or when moving: *straight* (or angular), *wide*, *round*, and *twisted*. The shapes of the body are specifically related to the actions of the body. Stretching takes the body into straight, wide shapes, while curling yields rounded shapes, and twisting results in twisted shapes. *Symmetrical*

Photo from the Agency for Instructional Television.

shapes are made when like body parts on both sides of the body are placed in identical positions to make both sides of the body identical. Any shape that does not have this exact similarity in relationship of body parts is called an *asymmetrical* shape. Other names can also describe the shape; for instance, *narrow, pin-shape,* or *arrow-like* may be interchanged with straight; *wall-like* or *star-shape* can be used instead of wide; *ball* or *tucked* are terms describing a round shape; while *screw-like* is frequently used in conjunction with the twisted shape. Children often invent more descriptive terms to designate various shapes.

THE SPACE ASPECT—WHERE IS THE BODY MOVING?

The responsibility of the space aspect is to outline where the body moves in space. The following six dimensions delineate the special categories: areas, directions, levels, pathways, planes, and extensions.

These six characteristics of the space aspect focus collectively on the space available for movement and describe the spatial intricacies of the movement. This aspect assigns to movement describable, spatial orientations with precise mental images that can be defined, interpreted, and reproduced. It identifies where the action is located, where the movement is going, and where the movement has been.

Areas—General and Personal Space

The area in which movement takes place can be described in two ways: general space and personal space. General space is the total area available for movement, e.g., a hallway, gymnasium, a dance studio, the designated part of a playground, a classroom, or a multipurpose room. Whereas general space is usually perceived as the entire space, personal space is that which immediately surrounds the individual body, not only when it is still but also while it is traveling. The limits of this personal sphere are determined by extending body parts to their furthermost reaches in all locations about the body. Working in personal space usually connotes staying on a fixed base of support to do nonlocomotor movement.

While personal and general space are recog-

nized as the two main areas in this movement classification system, another area is often included in movement tasks. (It is discussed here, but is not included on any of the movement analysis charts.) This area is referred to as *working space*. Frequently, individuals working alone or in a group are neither asked to move only on a fixed base of support nor required or permitted to move about the entire area or general space. Rather, they are asked to select and confine their movement to a portion of the general space.

Directions

Another observable trait of the space aspect is direction. The five simple directions are forward, backward, sideward, upward, and downward. Their names relate to the front of the body that faces in the direction of the movement being executed. This concept is made more difficult because a directional change can be made in two ways: (1) by changing the body front and (2) by maintaining the same front but turning to face a different direction.

Levels

This dimension of the space aspect focuses attention on the location of the movement in relation to the floor or supporting surface. The three levels of movement are *low, medium,* and *high.* Often, low is referred to as deep, especially in dance literature and content. Low movement occurs close to the floor, whereas high movement means the complete body rises off the floor in elevation. Medium level is the area of space through which the body passes as it moves from low to high. In some situations, the movement that occurs beneath knee level is classified as low, between knees and shoulders, medium, and above the shoulders, high. While seeming to have clearly defined perimeters, levels in movement can also be relative. For example, high level involves the body rising off the floor, but high level may be interpreted also as lifting a single body part high or as placing a body part or the total body higher in relation to something or someone.

Pathways

Another distinguishing characteristic of the space aspect is the path the movement takes as

it moves through space. This movement pathway may be inscribed by the body, its parts, or by objects such as balls, racquets, or musical instruments. In any case, pathways made by objects or the body can be inscribed either on the *floor* or in the *air*. The two simple lines from which all pathways are constructed are straight lines and curved lines. By incorporating these in various combinations, you can, for example, make zigzag and twisted pathways.

Planes

The three different planes in movement are each characterized by a pictorial term: wheel, door, and table. The *wheel* or *sagittal plane* refers to the circular pathway inscribed by passing through four directional points in space about the body. These four points are forward-deep (low level), forward-high, backward-high, and backward-deep. Envisioning a tire rolling or a forward or backward roll are ways to gain an image of the wheel plane. The *door* or *frontal plane*, too, makes reference to a surface that is outlined by movement passing through four directional points in space about the body. These four points in the door plane are high-right, high-left, deep-left, and deep-right. A cartwheel, in which weight is transferred sideward from hand to hand to foot to foot, is an activity performed in the door plane. The outer limits of the surface of the *table* or *horizontal plane* are determined by a pathway that connects four directional points in space: right-forward, right-backward, left-backward, and left-forward. This plane is parallel with the floor, whereas the door and wheel planes are perpendicular to the floor. An activity performed more nearly in the table plane is the swing associated with batting in softball and baseball.

This discussion of the planes in which movement is performed has been included to make the analysis of the space aspect more complete. Although the concept of planes is not difficult, planes are not given priority in the development of content in either dance, games, or gymnastics. As a concept, it is not usually taught in the elementary school physical education program. Understanding planes, however, is important in observing and analyzing the motor responses that occur in all three program areas.

Extensions

Extensions refer to the size of the movement: large or small. Extensions not only show the limits of the movement but also identify whether it is executed near the body or far from it. Naturally, many movements fall between the extremes of large and small or near the body and far away.

THE EFFORT ASPECT—HOW IS THE BODY PERFORMING THE MOVEMENT?

All movement is either expressive or objective. Movement that is expressive communicates feelings and ideas. Experiences in the physical education program that focus primarily on this type of movement usually fall within the dance area, where the body is used as an instrument for the purpose of conveying thoughts, feelings, and moods. The main purpose of objective or functional movement is to accomplish a task or job. Experiences that are included in the gymnastic and game areas of the program involve this type of movement. Although there may be overtones of expression when performing in gymnastics or playing in a game, the major purpose is to accomplish a task, not to express a feeling or thought.

The effort aspect of movement refers to the way we use our bodies. Four motion factors—time, weight, space, and flow—make up this aspect, and the way these factors are blended makes movement effective and gives it quality. How effort is used as content specific to each program area—dance, games, gymnastics—is described in detail in the next three chapters.

Each motion factor has an expressive or qualitative aspect and an objective or quantitative aspect. When the purpose of the movement is more expressive than objective, the qualitative aspect of the motion factor is stressed; when the movement becomes more objective in nature, the quantitative aspect of the motion factor predominates.

The Four Motion Factors and Their Elements

TIME. Movement can be either *sudden* or *sustained*. Sudden movement is quick, abrupt, hasty, hurried, and of short duration. Qualitative examples could be sudden, dart-like actions with different parts of the body or a series of sudden jumps used in a dance to convey excitement. Quantitatively, sudden change in direction to avoid a collision in a basketball game or quick passing of a ball with a hand, foot, or implement are examples.

Sustained movement, on the other hand, is prolonged, continuous, unhurried, leisurely, and of long duration. An unhurried walk accompanied by a slow arm gesture in a dance sequence would exemplify using sustained movement in a qualitative way, whereas taking aim in archery and executing a very slow roll in gymnastics are by nature quantitative.

WEIGHT. Movement can be either *firm* or *fine*. Firm movement is strong, energetic, forceful, and resistant. The qualitative aspect could be demonstrated in a dance expressing anger by stamping feet or clenching and gripping fists. A push pass in field hockey and an effort to send a basketball down the court, beginning the passing action in close to the chest, are examples of using weight quantitatively. A strong, forceful movement is needed in both these instances.

Fine movements characteristically are delicate, fragile, weak, and buoyant. A qualitative example could be a gentle bringing together of hands as in a group dance communicating a feeling of peace; holding a shuttlecock in preparation for serving in badminton could be a quantitative example.

SPACE. Movement uses space in either a *direct* or an *indirect* way. Direct movements are straight, penetrating, and threadlike. A group of dancers walking directly toward another group of dancers can express a feeling of accusation. Using movement in this way would be considered qualitative. On the other hand, a forceful jump for height, either off a vaulting box or for a head shot in soccer, would be considered quantitative.

Indirect movements are flexible, wavy, pliant, and supple. A group of dancers mingling in, out, and around each other to convey a feeling of constant motion is an example of using the space factor qualitatively or expressively. Quantitatively, the body action needed in lacrosse to keep the ball in the crosse is one example. Another quantitative example, this one related to gymnastics, is the movement needed to negotiate through apparatus that is designed to elicit twisting actions.

FLOW. All movement is characterized by a control factor; it can be either *bound* or *free*. Bound movements are cautious, hesitant, restrained, and stoppable. Movements such as small controlled jumps suggesting surprise, or careful stepping, expressing fear, are examples in the qualitative aspect. Quantitative examples are walking a balance beam and putting in golf.

Free movements, on the other hand, tend to be fluent, rushing, abandoned, and unstoppable. The qualitative aspect is exemplified by the wild gestures of a person communicating anger; and the quantitative aspect, by movements such as fly-casting, running in field games such as soccer, or executing an overhead smash in tennis.

RELATIONSHIP ASPECT—WHAT RELATIONSHIPS ARE OCCURRING?

The final aspect of movement focuses specifically on the relationships that occur as the body moves in and through space. This aspect of movement brings ideas together in a unified whole and acts as a major source for making experiences increasingly challenging in all parts of the physical education program. Movement does not take place by itself, but in relation to the surrounding environment. Thus, all individuals should develop their movement ability so they readily may adapt to or change the environment. For the purpose of this discussion, three basic types of relationships will be examined briefly:

1. Relationships of body parts to other body parts.

2. Relationships of individuals and groups to each other.

3. Relationships of individuals and groups to objects, apparatus, equipment, rules, and boundaries.

Body Parts to Other Body Parts

As you observe the body in motion or in stillness, the relationships between and among different body parts become evident. Basically, there are two factors to consider: the relationship itself and the way in which the relationship occurs.

Body parts can come *together* and go *apart;* i.e., they can *meet* and *part*. They can be placed in space so they are *above, below, behind, in front of, beside, on, alongside, over,* and *under*—their positional or spatial relationship.

Besides observing the relative position of body parts to each other, one can observe how these relationships take place: at the same time or at different times. When they occur at the same time, we call this *matching, mirroring,* or *contrasting*. Matching movements require that the individuals involved face the same way and move at the same time while attempting to make their movements identical. Mirroring also implies a type of identical and simultaneous movement, but in this situation, the individuals are facing each other and give the illusion of being the same. In actuality, the right side of one individual is "mirroring" the left side of the other individual. When contrasting movements, the movements of one individual are intended to be as different as possible from those of the other.

When movements occur at different times, they can happen successively or alternately.

move *apart;* *meet* and *part;* and/or *advance* and *retreat.* In this type of relationship, movements such as *circling, mingling,* and *passing through* may be considered part of it, thus giving richness and variation to the original action of coming together and separating. In addition, individuals can create relationships between themselves that are *above, below, in front of, behind, beside, on, alongside, over,* and *under* each other.

As previously discussed, there are various ways that relationships can occur. They can be done simultaneously or at different times. Individuals can match, mirror, or contrast each other's movement as well as move in ways that are both successive and alternating. Additional relationships can develop, such as questioning-answering, acting-reacting, and following or copying. In addition, relationships can occur by *supporting* (or being supported) and *lifting* (or being lifted). The former implies a stillness in the movement, and the latter is more of a continuous action. Individuals may rest or balance on another individual or be assisted through the movement in some way. As content and focus for lessons, these ideas are used primarily in the gymnastic area and are considered advanced.

In addition to these forms of relationships, the *nature* of the situation may vary. It can emphasize cooperation, competition, or collaboration. Cooperation implies working with another person to achieve a common goal. Competition, on the other hand, implies that one individual or group of individuals should achieve a goal better than another and both set out to exceed the ability of the other. Collaboration refers to those competitive situations where two or more individuals are working together as a "team" in an attempt to outwit their opponents. It requires trusting each other's ability in such a way that the strengths of each can be blended together for utmost effectiveness.

When body parts move fairly quickly, one right after the other, the movements are called *successive.* The term *alternate* is used to describe a slower action where body parts almost seem "to take turns."

In addition, these two time sequences can be "played with" subtly to effect still other relationships. *Questioning-answering, acting-reacting,* and *following* or *copying* all deal with successive-type movements. The first two are similar in that one movement follows another; it "answers" or "reacts" to the first. The movements may or may not be alike. To follow or copy a movement means to reproduce it as closely as possible.

Individuals and Groups to Each Other

Relationships not only occur among different body parts but also among the movers themselves. Three such possibilities are (1) individuals to individuals, (2) individuals to groups, and (3) groups to groups and groups to individuals.

INDIVIDUALS TO INDIVIDUALS

The types of relationships and the way they might occur (discussed previously with reference to body parts) also pertain to individual movers. Individuals can move *together* and

INDIVIDUALS TO GROUPS

A natural outgrowth of an individual relating to another is an individual relating to a group. Group, here, means two or more people. Consequently, it will be important to consider the group size because, as the size increases, the complexity of the relationship does also. The types of relationships and the way they might occur between individuals and groups are similar to those just discussed except that more people are involved.

GROUPS TO GROUPS AND GROUPS TO INDIVIDUALS

Little more can be said when discussing the relationships that might develop between two or more groups and between groups and individuals. The actual relationships are more complex, because whenever groups of individuals must work together in any way (cooperatively, competitively, or collaboratively), the challenge is greater. In all areas of physical education—games, dance, or gymnastics—groups have to function in relation to each other or in relation to an individual; however, the *way* they function and their *purpose* may differ, thus becoming key ideas to remember when designing learning experiences that focus on relationships.

Individuals and Groups to Objects, Apparatus, Equipment, Goals, and Boundaries

Up to this point, the discussion about relationships has centered primarily on the types that involve people, both as they move alone or as they form part of a group. The final type of relationship involves individuals to objects, apparatus, equipment, goals, and boundaries. For example, you can be *above, below,* or *alongside* a vaulting box or you can be *in front, behind,* or *to one side* of a soccer ball as you prepare to pass it. You can be moving in relation to a rhythmical beat or an oncoming ball, both different tasks, but both requiring a change in relationship.

When you are dealing with this type of relationship in any area of the program, you are in reality *relating to the environment.* Understanding the nature of this environment, whether stable or dynamic, is a key factor in understanding this portion of the relationship aspect. Briefly, a stable environment is one in which the object, implement, or apparatus involved is *fixed.* Throwing a ball against a target on the wall (the target does not move) or balancing on top of a vaulting box (the box is stationary) are examples of tasks to be performed in a stable environment. In a dynamic environment, the object, equipment, or apparatus is not fixed; it is in motion. For example, striking a ball among four players

(ball and players are in motion) and mounting a swinging rope have environments that are characterized by an object, players, or apparatus that is moving.

Relating to music, words, apparatus, equipment, goals, and boundaries is a critical part of the relationship aspect in each of the program areas and often is not well understood. Since this type of relationship is so important and unique to each area of the program, further discussion of it will occur in the separate chapters on dance, games, and gymnastics, Chapters 6, 7, and 8.

UTILIZATION OF THE MOVEMENT FRAMEWORK

The framework for classifying movement, illustrated in Figure 5–2, has to be studied from several vantage points and applied to various situations with different purposes in mind before its full impact on the teaching of physical education can be recognized. It is hoped that, concurrent with this reading about the framework, the student is involved in the study of movement both in observing and analyzing movement and in participating in movement. To be truly meaningful, the framework has to be experienced, and experienced in many ways. Each word in the framework remains just a word until personal understandings, feelings, visual images, and experiences can be associated with it.

Distinguishing Characteristics of the Framework

THOROUGHNESS. The thoroughness with which the framework approaches the study of movement has set this scheme apart from others. As mentioned before, it makes us look for not only *what the mover does* but also what occurs in the *movement itself.* As we said earlier, those who describe movement frequently stop after naming the activity. Those who stop here analyze movement by saying, "The man *walked* into the room." Naming the activity does not describe the man's body in motion. Visualize for a moment a 15-month-old baby boy as he *walks* into the room. Recapture the look of a drum major *walking* in front of the band—an inebriated derelict *walking* by a bus station—a college couple *walking* hand in hand across campus—a

MOVEMENT FRAMEWORK

BODY ASPECT
(What Body Does)

Actions of Body
- Curl
- Bend
- Twist
- Swing

Actions of Body Parts
- Support Body Weight
- Lead Action
- Receive Weight or Force
- Apply Force

Activities of Body
- Locomotor
- Nonlocomotor
- Manipulative

Body Shapes
- Straight
- Wide
- Round
- Twisted
- Symmetrical–Asymmetrical

SPACE ASPECT
(Where Body Moves)

Areas
- General
- Personal

Directions
- Forward
- Backward
- Sideward
- Upward
- Downward

Levels
- Low
- Medium
- High

Pathways
- Straight
- Curved
- Zigzag
- Twisted

Planes
- Wheel—sagittal
- Door—frontal
- Table—horizontal

Extensions
- Large
- Small

EFFORT ASPECT
(How Body Performs the Movement)

Time
- Fast–accelerating–sudden
- Slow–decelerating–sustained

Weight
- Firm–strong
- Fine touch–light

Space
- Direct–straight
- Flexible–indirect

Flow
- Bound–stoppable
- Free–ongoing

RELATIONSHIP ASPECT
(Relationships that Occur in Movement)

Body Parts
- Above–Below
- Apart–Together
- Behind–In front of
- Meeting–Parting
- Near–Far
- Over–Under

Individuals and Groups
- Mirroring–Matching
- Contrasting
- Successive–Alternating
- Questioning–Answering
- Acting–Reacting
- Following–Copying
- Lifting–Being lifted
- Supporting–Being supported

Apparatus and Equipment
- Over–Under
- Near–Far
- Above–Below–Alongside
- Behind–In front of
- Arriving on
- Dismounting

Other Types
- Goals, Boundaries
- Music, Sounds
- Poems, Stories, Words
- Beat Patterns
- Art Work

Fig. 5–2. Movement Framework.

bride *walking* down the aisle. To describe each of their movements only as *walking* tells just part of the study. You need to know more to describe their movement and differentiate among their walking styles. The framework makes and helps us tell more. It makes us look for and see more. The framework forces us to pay equal attention to the effort and efficiency of the movement, makes us become aware of the space aspect, and causes us to observe the relationships that exist in movement, along with naming the activity being performed by the body.

Look back at each of the walkers—the baby's walk is characterized by the speed, flow, path, and relationship of arms to his body and the relation of one leg to the other. His rather fast, toddling gait seems unstoppable. He appears to have neither the desire nor the ability to stop. His path is straight and he has difficulty in negotiating a turn or a change of direction. His arms are likely to be bent at the elbows with his hands held up at the sides of his body at head height. His legs are about shoulder width apart. You can continue to describe the walk of this one baby and the other walkers. With every new descriptive addition, it becomes easier for someone to replicate precisely the walking style of that individual. To show the importance of discriminating in selecting and identifying particular styles of walking, can you imagine the hysteria that would fill a church if the bride walked in like a drum major? Can you perceive the cadence and pathway of a marching band who followed and copied the walk of an inebriated drum major? The framework helps us to be more thorough by guiding us in examining all four aspects of movement: what the body does, where it moves, how it moves, and what relationships exist as it moves.

UNIVERSAL APPLICATION. The second distinguishing characteristic of the framework is its universal application in studying all forms of movement. As we differentiate between the walk of a drum major and the walk of a bride, we can apply this same framework when describing all movement in physical education, be it in games, dance, gymnastics, or aquatics. The adaptability of the framework to the study of all movement to all ages is an important attribute that serves as a unifying thread in developing continuity in physical education. Think of its effect on the learner. Ideas or concepts introduced in one area

of the program at one level can be elaborated or strengthened in another phase. This approach represents a change in how learners are confronted and what is expected of them. Historically, students in physical education classes learned separate terms in each new activity at each grade level. The student and the teacher often failed to recognize the same movement feeling, actions, or principle when they confronted it in a different situation. When integration in elementary school physical education was even considered, it usually meant trying to work closely with art, music, or other regular classroom experiences to unify experiences and elaborate concepts. Now, meaningful integration can be a deliberate curriculum goal within the specific physical education content as well.

Ways to Use the Framework

Basically, this scheme for categorizing movement has four different uses.

1. Structuring content in physical education.
2. Observing and analyzing movement.
3. Communicating with others.
4. Evaluating the content of the program.

STRUCTURING CONTENT IN PHYSICAL EDUCATION

The movement framework is used to structure the program at all levels of content development from broad topics (themes) to be studied, to units, to individual lessons, down to the design of one learning experience for a single child. That the framework is used at all levels in structuring content is basic to the belief that *movement is the content of physical education*.

The framework can be used rather quickly by teachers to structure isolated content. It can be used so fast that implementation of the framework appears simple to teachers who are uninitiated to its total implications. The true complexity involved in implementing the framework seems to grow through each encounter with it.

Authors' Note: Many uses of Laban's movement classification are far more sophisticated than those listed. The bibliography at the end of the chapter, which provides references for deeper study of Laban's work, includes entries that demonstrate different and distinctive uses of the movement classification.

The more you study it, the more you realize what there is to know about movement and the more respect you gain for the value associated with a genuine understanding of movement. The intriguing characteristic of the framework and the associated study of movement is that both continue to present new challenges no matter how long you continue to study them.

OBSERVING AND ANALYZING MOVEMENT

Discussing the initial existence of the chicken and the egg differs from discussing observation and analysis of responses and communication with the learner. The order of events is clearer in the teaching of movement than in the dilemma of the chicken and the egg. Observation has to precede instruction if instruction is to be personalized. The more the teaching process and the content are studied in this book, the more fully the role of observing, analyzing, and evaluating the response of the learner is appreciated. Until there is a continuing interaction between the student and the teacher, continuous learning about movement, by either the teacher or the student, is not likely to be long-lived.

The teacher needs to have a framework with which to observe the response of the child. Accurate and complete information derived from sensitive observation is essential if the teacher is to intervene meaningfully in the child's learning environment—whether the teacher needs to give praise and encouragement or to change or extend the movement challenge. What better or more logical framework is there to observe the movement response of the child than the framework used to formulate the learning activity that provided the original stimulus to the children. Therefore, another strength of the framework is its use in observing and analyzing the responses of the child. Once the teacher observes, the teaching role becomes one of communicating with the child about what has been observed.

COMMUNICATING ABOUT MOVEMENT

To further extend use of the movement framework, teachers when communicating with students about their work can continuously incorporate the movement vocabulary from the framework in providing verbal guidance to the students. Likewise, when the children are involved in verbal interaction with other students, they can use the same vocabulary in their discussions. This ability for teachers and children to communicate with a common movement vocabulary plays a meaningful role in the teaching-learning process in physical education. It is so much easier to understand and to communicate when everyone speaks and understands the same language. In addition, both the teacher and the learner need to have a growing understanding of the terms and the concepts they represent for the framework to be used effectively.

EVALUATING THE PROGRAM

The framework can also be used when assessing the program to see what ideas or concepts have been taught in order to determine both scope and sequence in the program. A quick checklist can reflect the recurring concepts and the time when new ideas are introduced. Thus the movement framework can be instrumental in all phases of curriculum development in physical education. It can help us examine what we believe about physical education, it can serve in structuring content, it can be a tool in analyzing responses, it can be incorporated in the methodologic approach when communicating with the learner, and it can serve as a means for assessing the scope and sequence of the program.

If movement is the content of physical education, it follows that those preparing to teach physical education must be knowledgeable about the construct of movement. All teachers must be able to observe and analyze movement. They must be discriminating in developing learning experiences as well as skillful and sensitive in intervening in the learning environment if the ability of the child to move and to learn through movement is to be enhanced by teaching. Teachers who accept the responsibility to teach movement must know what to look for and how to look at movement, and they must be able to interpret what they know and observe to those they teach. Chapter 10 will assist you in developing the skills of observing, analyzing, and interpreting movement responses.

This scheme for categorizing movement initiated by Laban, if coupled with experiences to develop a functional understanding for it, and with understanding for how the child grows, develops, and learns, can improve the potential of teachers to teach movement to children. If we improve our ability to teach, perhaps more children will learn to move better and will learn more from and while moving.

REFERENCES

1. Laban, R., and Lawrence, F.: Effort. London, Unwin Brothers, 1947.
2. Stanley, S.: Physical Education—A Movement Orientation, 2nd ed. Toronto, McGraw-Hill of Canada, 1969.
3. Russell, J.: Creative Dance in the Primary School, 2nd ed. London, Macdonald & Evans, 1975.
4. Mauldon, E., and Redfern, H.B.: Games Teaching, 2nd ed. London, Macdonald & Evans, 1981.
5. North, M.: Personality Assessment Through Movement. London, Macdonald & Evans, 1972.

SELECTED READING

Boorman, J.: Creative Dance in the First Three Grades. Ontario, Longmans Canada Ltd. 1969.
Department of Education and Science: Movement—Physical Education in the Primary Years. Westerham, Kent, Her Majesty's Stationery Office, 1972.
Holbrook, J.: Movement Activity in Gymnastics. Boston, Plays, Inc., 1973.
Laban, R.: Mastery of Movement, 3rd ed. Revised by L. Ullman. London, Macdonald & Evans, 1971.
Laban, R., and Lawrence, F.: Effort. London, Unwin Brothers, 1947.
Morison, R.: A Movement Approach to Educational Gymnastics. London, J.M. Dent and Sons, 1969.
Russell, J.: Creative Dance in the Primary School, 2nd ed. London, Macdonald & Evans, 1975.

Further Readings for Those Interested in More Advanced Study of Laban's Influence

Hutchinson, A.: Labanotation. New York, New Directions Books, James Laughlin, 1961.
Laban, R.: Modern Educational Dance. London, Macdonald & Evans, 1948.
Laban, R.: Choreutics. Annotated and edited by L. Ullman. London, Macdonald & Evans, 1966.
Lamb, W.: Posture and Gesture. London, Gerald Duckworth and Co., 1965.
Thornton, S.: Laban's Theories: A New Perspective. Boston, Plays, Inc., 1973.

Note: Most books published by Macdonald & Evans, Ltd., are available in the U.S. from Plays, Inc., Boston.

Chapter 6

Educational Dance

KATE R. BARRETT

Movement experiences for children have long been a part of our schools' curriculum. While gaining significantly in acceptance during the last two decades, those experiences that are mainly concerned with expressive movement are now beginning to come into their own. Dance in the schools, particularly dance for children, is not a new idea but one that is finally being recognized as vital to the total development of the individual. The essence of children's dance lies in a commitment to using movement as a medium for expression, that is, helping children gain control over their bodies in order to use the language of movement expressively and inventively. Using movement in this unique way, children have the opportunity to increase their aesthetic sensitivity.

As evidenced by the increasing number of recent publications and workshops focused on dance, a revitalization of interest in the area of children's dance is occurring. Many different emphases are emerging, once again leaving readers and observers to decide in what direction to go with their children. No matter what the emphasis, however, the basic thread that binds all approaches to children's dance is the belief that movement plays a crucial role in the education of children, and that when movement is used as a language for communication, the essence of dance is discovered and experienced.

The approach taken in this book supports this belief totally. As in the other two areas of physical education, gymnastics and games, implementation is guided by how a child views dance; i.e., the ideas for experiences grow directly from the children's personal movement or individual way of moving. Children love to move—they jump, run, turn, whirl, and spin—expressing their very nature. This natural inclination for movement is the beginning of all experiences in children's dance. To use it as the major thrust for the direction of subsequent experiences, we must understand children and their movement in a unique way. For children to become their own "dancers," they must be able to be themselves. As this approach focuses on the children's way of moving, and not that of adults it follows that the dance experiences will be characterized by movement responses that are spontaneous, unique, and natural to each child. When spontaneous expression is the core of each experience, we have the dance of children—and the dance for children.

"MOVEMENT EDUCATION" AND DANCE EDUCATION

Since the formal introduction of the concept of movement education into the physical education programs of the 1950s, its relationship to children's dance has been interpreted in various ways. The following discussion orients the reader to how this relationship is perceived so the rest of the material can be interpreted within this frame of reference.

When examining alternative approaches to physical education, such as the one this book is proposing, it is important to know how the approach views the relationship between movement education and physical education since that is often the key to understanding why the approach supports certain program directions but not others.

In the second chapter, physical education was defined as ". . . that part of movement education which has been designated as a responsible, educational program in the school." Therefore, children's dance in this book is considered an integral part of the total physical education program as well as a *part*, a vital part, of a child's life-long movement education. As a part of the total physical education program, dance, as well as gymnastics and games, takes its direction from a particular philosophic viewpoint and not from methods and content considered "special" to it, as is so often the case. If each had a special program, each area would have different content and different methods.

In this approach to physical education, both the content and ways of teaching stem from common rationales. The content for *all* areas of the program is movement, which derives from four major aspects: body, space, effort, and relationship. The development of the learning environment for *all* areas emerges from a commitment to the individualistic nature of children and the belief that movement plays a crucial role in their lives. What makes dance experiences for children look and feel different from either gymnastic or game experiences is *not* its methods or content but the way and the purposes in which the content is used by the child. Movement, as the content of the dance experience, is used for expressive and aesthetic purposes—as a means for communication. This communication aspect gives dance its uniqueness and separates it from games and gymnastics.

TEACHERS OF CHILDREN'S DANCE

Today the area of children's dance is exciting, and many school systems are looking for ways to include it in their curriculum. Some teachers of children's physical education appear hesitant, however, and say they "cannot teach dance." Why do they have this reaction? Perhaps those who do *not* feel this way had a dance educator in their undergraduate professional preparation who helped them see that dance could be taught, and taught well, by anyone who truly believed it had a place in a child's education.

The use of movement as a crucial aspect of a child's education, whether its purpose is expressive or functional, is central to the physical education approach taken by this book. Where gymnastics and games structure movement for functional, task-oriented purposes, dance structures it for expressive and aesthetic purposes. Teaching dance to children is one of the most exciting and privileged experiences a teacher can have, and one of the most rewarding for each child. I hope that more and more teachers reach out for this privilege.

SCOPE OF THE PROGRAM

The experiences to be suggested as appropriate for a program of children's dance focus entirely on helping children study movement to discover for themselves its potential for expression and communication. Special adult-style forms of dance, such as jazz, tap, and ballet, are not included as they are considered inconsistent with the philosophy of the program. Folk dances of the simplest kind could be included as part of the program but only if the movements of children can remain natural and informal. Children love to respond to the gay and lively nature of folk tunes and, when they have had considerable experience in discovering what they can do in movement, can often create their own "folk dances" or handle the simplest forms.

DANCE-MAKING

Throughout the discussion of the program there is reference to the actual making up of dances by children. In this approach, the experiences that create movement phrases and sequences are the beginning of dance-making, regardless of the number of children involved. A dance is a series of movements that has a beginning, middle, and end. It is structured in space and time, and "There must be something present that pertains to the spirit of the performer, and the movement must communicate that spirit."[1] When talking about a child's dance or a dance composed by a group of children, the structure is probably simple in comparison to a dance designed by an adult. But it is the child's dance, and that is what is important.

In this approach to children's dance, the transition from guided experimentation with movement ideas to their organization into some type of structure should be a smooth one. As soon as the children begin to join movements together, the process of dance-making begins. How important this aspect becomes in a total program once again is a decision for the teacher and children. For what purpose are the dances being made? Will they be shown to others, or will they be made up purely for the children who created them? Probably both purposes will be important.

From this natural relationship between the movement experiences and the making of dances, one can generalize that children approach the creation of dances through the movement ideas they have experienced. In other words, the movement material is the major stimulator for the direction the dance may take. Ideas from sources such as imagery, words, music, and songs are also influential. Still, whenever ideas for dances come from places other than movement, a careful translation into ". . . the language of action" must occur.[2] For example, if children have become interested in the movement of animals and want to use some of the ideas as a stimulus for a dance, they must first examine carefully the movements of specific interest. The teacher can ask questions such as "What was in the shape of the movement or in the quality that was of particular interest?" From this study, ideas for the type of movements that could form the core of their dance might result. The ideas are not the dance, however, for that has yet to be created. To do so, the child, or group of children, must experiment with the ideas fully to discover their potential, then select the motifs they wish to use and the rhythmic and spatial structure. They must determine the sequence of events and engage in a constant process of selection, refinement, and reselection of movements.

Creating a dance is exciting and hard work, but its values are many. Sometimes, the difference between a movement experience designed to help children learn about movement and themselves and the experience of dance-making may be difficult to discern. But with experience, both teachers and children will come to respect both for what each has to offer.

ORGANIZING DANCE CONTENT

To design dance experiences for children, teachers must have an understanding of movement as content that allows them imaginative flexibility in planning and implementation. They must be able to view movement as a totally dynamic phenomenon while simultaneously being able to sense the logical relationships among its parts. This way of understanding movement cannot be overemphasized, for it is essential if the content for dance experiences is to be selected and developed truly in accord with the children's needs.

Many different ways of looking at movement have been devised, each offering a different perspective into its structure. While the way movement is being viewed here reflects strongly the work of Rudolf Laban, his is not the only one that could be used. It has been chosen because of its comprehensiveness and ability to be used consistently and effectively throughout *all phases* of the physical education program: gymnastics, games, and dance. Figure 6–1 shows this view of movement as adapted for children's dance.

Laban's Movement-Themes

Historically, the earliest application of Laban's work to education was in the field of dance; hence, much information is available in both current and past literature. Valuable insight can be gained from reading both Laban's writings and the more recent interpretations by his advocates. Since the area of dance in education was where Laban first experimented with application of his ideas, some of his most salient points on progression and teaching are briefly discussed here. While the present-day work in all areas of the field is a result of experimenting with and expanding his original ideas, it is not always possible to implement them or to discover new meaning in them without some knowledge of their initial form.

Laban, when applying his ideas to the teaching of dance in an educational environment, organized the way he viewed movement into "Sixteen Basic Movement-Themes." The purpose of these themes was to give teachers of dance a "methodical foundation" on which to build educational dance. These themes, their combinations and variations, became the tools for dance teachers rather than the previously used ". . . sets of standardized exercises."[3] Laban stated: "Each of the basic movement-themes represents a movement idea corresponding to a

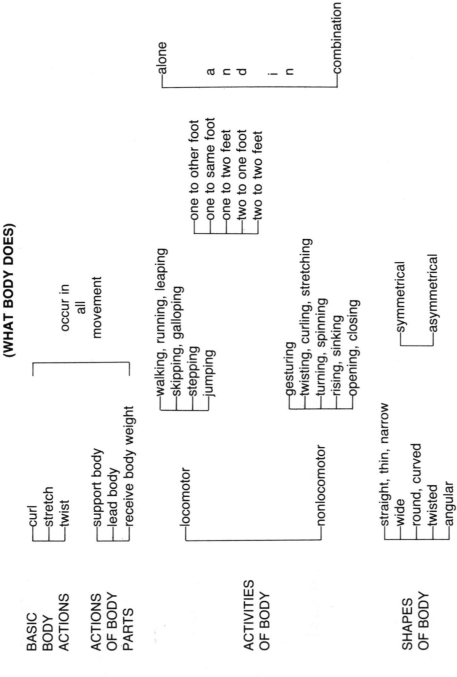

Fig. 6—1. Movement Framework for Educational Dance.

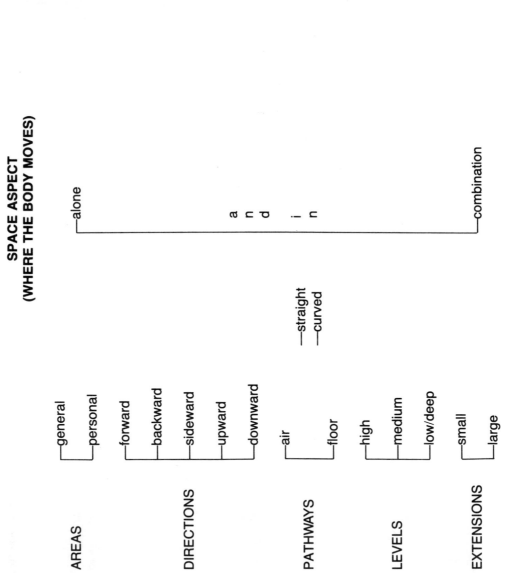

SPACE ASPECT
(WHERE THE BODY MOVES)

AREAS
- general
- personal

DIRECTIONS
- forward
- backward
- sideward
- upward
- downward

PATHWAYS
- air
- floor
  - straight
  - curved

LEVELS
- high
- medium
- low/deep

EXTENSIONS
- small
- large

alone — and in — combination

EFFORT ASPECT
(HOW BODY PERFORMS THE MOVEMENT)

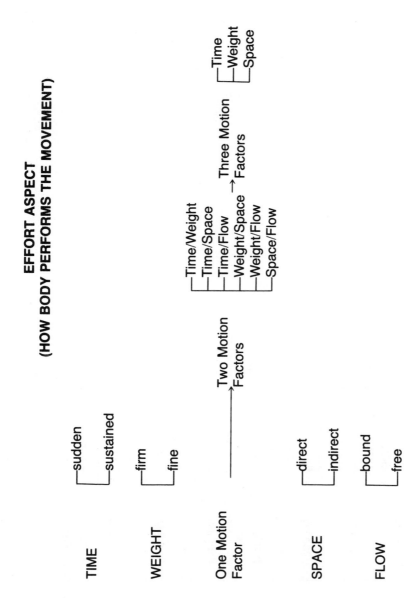

TIME ─ sudden
     └ sustained

WEIGHT ─ firm
       └ fine

One Motion Factor → Two Motion Factors ─ Time/Weight
                                        ├ Time/Space
                                        ├ Time/Flow
                                        ├ Weight/Space
                                        ├ Weight/Flow
                                        └ Space/Flow
                                        → Three Motion Factors ─ Time
                                                               ├ Weight
                                                               └ Space

SPACE ─ direct
      └ indirect

FLOW ─ bound
     └ free

thrusting — sudden, firm, direct
floating — sustained, fine, indirect
slashing — sudden, firm, indirect
gliding — sustained, fine, direct
wringing — sustained, firm, indirect
dabbing — sudden, fine, direct
pressing — sustained, firm, direct
flicking — sudden, fine, indirect

alone — and in — in combination

RELATIONSHIP ASPECT
(RELATIONSHIPS THAT OCCUR IN MOVEMENT)

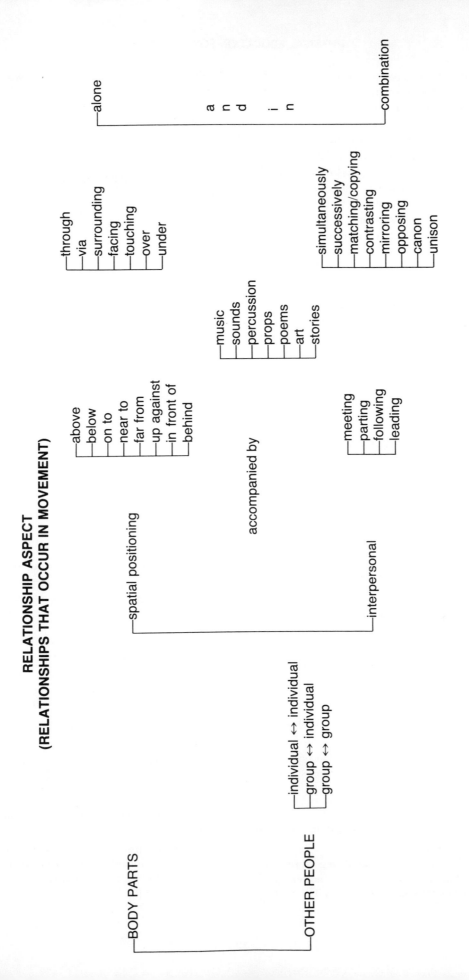

BODY PARTS

OTHER PEOPLE
- individual ↔ individual
- group ↔ individual
- group ↔ group

spatial positioning
- above
- below
- on to
- near to
- far from
- up against
- in front of
- behind

through
via
surrounding
facing
touching
over
under

accompanied by
- music
- sounds
- percussion
- props
- poems
- art
- stories

interpersonal
- meeting
- parting
- following
- leading

alone

and in combination
- simultaneously
- successively
- matching/copying
- contrasting
- mirroring
- opposing
- canon
- unison

stage in the progressive unfolding of the feel of movement in the growing child, and in later stages to the development of his mental understanding of the principles involved."[3]

Since the original identification of these basic themes, much experimentation has gradually uncovered the richness that was inherent in each theme but undiscovered in Laban's time. The themes are listed next as Laban *first* expressed them.[3] Underneath each one is Preston-Dunlop's most recent interpretation of their major emphases.[4]

Elementary Movement-Themes

1. Themes concerned with the awareness of the body.

Theme 1: The possible ways of using the body in movement are introduced in connection with the development of the kinesthetic sense.

2. Themes concerned with the awareness of resistance to weight and time.

Themes 2: The concentration is on the dynamics and rhythm of movement.

3. Themes concerned with the awareness of space.

Theme 3: Movement of individuals on their environment is the major emphasis—general principles of space awareness.

4. Themes concerned with the awareness of the flow of the weight of the body in space and time.

Theme 4: Attention is on the transitions between movements, how they follow one another—an *integration* of Themes 1, 2, and 3.

5. Themes concerned with the adaptation to partners.

Theme 5: Social awareness is introduced through dance and movement responses to a partner—an *expansion* of the individual's environment.

6. Themes concerned with the instrumental use of the limbs of the body.

Theme 6: The bodily skill required for gestures, stepping, locomotion, turning, and jumping is developed—an *expansion* of Theme 1.

7. Themes concerned with the awareness of isolated actions.

Theme 7: The combinations of movement qualities that form the eight basic effort actions are introduced—an *expansion* of Themes 2 and 4.

8. Themes concerned with occupational rhythms.

Theme 8: The movement vocabulary is here used in connection with work rhythms and actions that have been the inspiration for dancers since dancing began—an *integration* of Themes 5, 6, and 7.

Advanced Movement-Themes

9. Themes concerned with the shapes of movement.

Theme 9: The ability to make movement patterns in the kinesphere and with the body is developed and used in dance—an *expansion* of Theme 3.

10. Themes concerned with combinations of the eight basic effort actions.

Theme 10: Abrupt and gradual transitions between the eight basic effort actions are experienced and used in dance—an *expansion* of Theme 7.

11. Themes concerned with space orientation.

Theme 11: The general principles of space awareness are developed further—an *expansion* of Theme 3.

12. Themes concerned with shapes and efforts using different parts of the body.

Theme 12. The link between effort and shape in movement is developed—an *integration* of the work in Themes 9, 10, 11.

13. Themes concerned with elevation from the ground.

Themes 13: The bodily skill required for elevation is developed, and the significance of it in dance is experienced.

14. Themes concerned with the awakening of group feeling.

Theme 14: Social awareness is furthered in dance and movement by participating in the common rhythms, actions, and aims of a group.

15. Themes concerned with group formations.

Theme 15: Form is given to the content of work in Theme 14.

16. Themes concerned with the expressive qualities of moods of movements.

Theme 16: The content of work in the previous themes is here integrated, and compositional forms necessary for choreography are studied.

Once the basic idea of Laban's movement-themes becomes familiar to you, further study reveals an inherent and sophisticated concept of progression. The way Laban introduced the movement-theme concept has a tendency to oversimplify his idea about progression. He merely stated that the themes taken as a whole were ". . . built up along a scale of increasing complexity corresponding roughly to the development of a child from the infant stage to the highest age-group."[3] Preston-Dunlop's analysis of Laban's work, however, makes this concept of progression more meaningful by showing the specific relationship among and between the different movement-themes. Her analysis shows that the 16 themes actually fall into groups, with the latter groups being developments of the first, and the last theme in each group serving as an integrator of some kind.[4]

    a. Themes primarily concerned with the Body:
          Themes 1, 6, and 13
    b. Themes primarily concerned with Effort:
          Themes 2, 7, and 10.
    c. Themes primarily concerned with Space:
          Themes 3, 9, and 11.
    d. Themes primarily concerned with Social Relationships:
          Themes 5, 14, and 15.
    e. Integrating themes:
          Theme 4, combining Themes 1 through 3 while introducing the flow of movement.
          Theme 8, combining Themes 5 through 7 while introducing working actions.
          Theme 12, combining Themes 9 through 11.
          Theme 16, combining all the previous themes.

The "Themes" Today

You will notice that the themes used in this chapter differ somewhat from Laban's original ones in both title and emphases. In Laban's original work, he stressed a flexible use of the themes, encouraging teachers to use in their lesson (when appropriate) simple forms of the more advanced themes. In relation to the titles used for each theme, Preston-Dunlop has recently stated that the term "awareness" used in Laban's original themes 1 through 4, 7, and 9 is ambiguous and inaccurate in light of dance (aesthetic) education today. She states: "In all these themes the work includes perceptual sensitising, skill development, making, and the appreciation of dances. I cannot see that awareness goes far enough."[4] These interpretations have added richness to the idea and use of themes and have influenced the way they are identified and used in this chapter and in the chapters on games and gymnastics. Serious students are encouraged to read Preston-Dunlop's recent work.[4]

SEVEN MOVEMENT-THEMES FOR ORGANIZING AND DEVELOPING EDUCATIONAL DANCE CONTENT

    Theme 1—INTRODUCTION TO THE BODY
    Theme 2—INTRODUCTION TO WEIGHT AND TIME
    Theme 3—INTRODUCTION TO SPACE
    Theme 4—THE FLOW OF MOVEMENT
    Theme 5—INTRODUCTION TO RELATIONSHIPS
    Theme 6—INSTRUMENTAL USE OF THE BODY
    Theme 7—THE BASIC EFFORT ACTIONS

The remainder of this chapter identifies and develops the substance of each theme. Understanding each theme is the key to designing appropriate learning experiences. Concluding this chapter is a suggested progression for dance content.

DANCE THEME 1—INTRODUCTION TO THE BODY

Theme 1 focuses on the use of the body as a whole and the use of individual parts. It should

help children become increasingly aware of their bodies and at the same time gain a feeling for producing motion and maintaining stillness. The central idea in this theme is similar to the beginning theme in both gymnastics and games. How it is ultimately handled depends on the children and what they have already experienced. Although the themes are similar in intent, the responses could be quite different. In the dance area, the children will be working with the material in ways that will encourage the expression of feelings. In gymnastics and games, there is a more functional or objective purpose.

No matter what the age of the children working with ideas derived from this theme, they need to understand their role in making the environment a learning one and one that is safe for all involved. The fact that little equipment is used in dance at this stage does not exempt the teacher and children from focusing on this major responsibility. Movement experiences that are designed to encourage traveling, jumping, turning, and spinning are exciting for children, and they must see their responsibility in creating a productive learning environment.

Development of Theme 1

> **Basic Content**
> Total body: locomotion—walking, running, skipping, galloping, leaping, stepping, jumping
>   nonlocomotion—rising-sinking, opening-closing, turning, spinning
> Body parts: leading, supporting, receiving

TOTAL BODY. When the teacher first emphasizes the use of the total body, the main purpose is to have the children experience motion and stillness in such a way that they learn to control the flow of movement by hesitating, by pausing or stopping, or by letting it emerge in a free unhindered way. They need to develop an ability to stop movement as it will help them to make clear phrases of movement.

Both locomotor movements and nonlocomotor movements offer a variety of ways to design experiences that help children learn how to control the flow of movement. Once children have achieved some feeling for this control, focus can be redirected toward the locomotor and nonlocomotor movements, for they provide an additional emphasis important to the dance education of children.

At this stage, locomotion primarily refers to "traveling" with emphasis on *walking, running, skipping, galloping, leaping, stepping,* and *jumping.* It further involves experimenting with and exploring all the different ways that a person can walk, run, or step in a spontaneous, inventive, and exuberant way. Children already know how to walk, run, step, and jump, but the teacher should encourage further exploration of *their* way of doing it. Given ample time to explore what they can do with the different forms of locomotion, children will discover that they can take steps of various sizes, that they can keep their feet together or apart, that they can let their feet pass one another or not, and that they can stop their feet simultaneously or one after the other. The variations are endless, and with each new way of moving discovered, the children find out more about their bodies and the way they move.

While walking, running, skipping, galloping, leaping, stepping, and jumping are familiar, stepping, as a variation of walking, may not be. In this form of locomotion, the steps are more deliberate, exact, and obvious. Where the feet are placed can be varied more easily as there is more time to decide where they might go. In a way, stepping is a special form of weight transference since there are movements when the body transfers from one foot to the other, and the feeling one gets when weight is being shifted is so obvious.

The term nonlocomotion refers to those movements that do not have traveling as their focus but rather involve moving on the spot. In this theme, focus is on the total body, as in *opening-closing, rising-sinking, turning,* and *spinning.*

Opening and closing are movements that cause the body to extend or broaden out, as well as to contract, or draw in all parts of the body toward its center. In rising and sinking, the body is first trying to reach upward, getting as far away from the ground as possible (moving against gravity), and then trying to sink or collapse into the ground as far as possible (moving with gravity). When children have become sensitive to their bodies as they move, all four movements

can express different feelings, both to those performing them and to those observing them. Children can express a feeling of hopelessness or despair when sinking toward the ground or drawing inward all parts of the body, or they can express confidence or exhilaration when lifting away from the ground or extending outward all parts of the body.

Turning, spinning, whirling, and pivoting describe movements used when constantly changing the direction the body is facing. Turning is an everyday action: we turn to face our friends, we turn to change the direction in which we were moving, or we turn to avoid bumping into someone or something. In dance, the sensation of turning becomes an added focus: what does a turn feel like, can a turn be executed at different times and in different ways to provoke different feelings? What happens when turning is done on one foot, two feet, quickly, slowly? Again, children already know the movement and do it many times each day, but teachers can encourage them to use it to find out more about themselves in movement.

Sample Learning Experiences
1. Move freely throughout the space, using different ways to travel (e.g., walk, run, skip, hop, or leap).
2. Rise and sink, using the whole body while remaining in one spot.
3. Open and close, using the whole body while traveling short distances.
4. Combine different forms of traveling into short phrases (e.g., running followed by jumping and jumping followed by stepping).
5. Combine different forms of traveling with different movements on the spot (e.g., running and turning followed by opening and closing).

Discussion. Traveling as a dance experience means using the locomotor activities such as walking, running, skipping, galloping, leaping, stepping, and jumping freely and spontaneously. In a sense, it means "open exploration" of ways to cover space. The intent is to have children do what they already know how to do, while helping them become more aware of their bodies through movement. Whether the specific forms of locomotion are included in the experiences depends on the children's background and the teacher's view of their needs. As we try

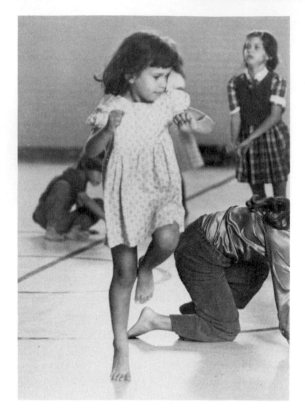

to help children learn how to explore more on their own, we may have to change the structure of the experience often, because children in the beginning have difficulty taking much responsibility in the decision-making process.

Because traveling movements are vigorous and energetic, these experiences should alternate with those of a calmer nature. Focusing directly on opening-closing or rising-sinking has this effect. At first, the children's responses lack variety, for they have to concentrate on the activities themselves, getting a feel for them, before being able to show many variations. In addition, working with these movements together is helpful to show the contrast: rising–*then* sinking, or opening–*then* closing.

The last two sample learning experiences focus on combining ideas from the earlier ones. In this way, the experience is made more difficult, and the idea of movement phrases is introduced. At this stage, the way the children put together the movements is important, not whether they can all respond, for example, to a rhythmic phrase designed by the teacher. The emphasis is on helping the children move freely and naturally,

focusing on simple combinations of traveling movements and movements that remain on the spot.

The body actions of stretch, curl, and twist have deliberately not been identified as separate content since they are inherent in all movement and are particularly useful concepts for description. Furthermore, the movement ideas of rising-sinking and opening-closing are directly related to these concepts. Rising and opening movements *cause* the body to stretch, and sinking and closing movements *cause* the body to curl. When different body parts are used to lead an action, twisting movements often result. As the body actions themselves are specifically involved, their connection to the movement in question will be brought out. Taking this position does not mean that using the basic actions of stretch, curl, and twist as content is incorrect; rather, that their meaning and essence are being developed from a different perspective.

The learning environment that needs to be established is one in which children are free to be themselves, experiment, and continuously discover the different ways their bodies can move. Children must have respect for one another and be self-directed in their learning to profit from this experience. Without this type of learning atmosphere, the ideas suggested become too difficult to implement.

BODY PARTS. All movements, no matter what their purpose, involve the use of body parts. Using "body parts" as content focuses on them specifically. In Figure 6–1, three factors relate to the study of body parts as content. Body parts can *support the body*, *lead the body*, and *receive the body's weight*. For this discussion, body parts used as content will center around the idea of leading or being emphasized. The other two aspects will be used primarily for descriptive purposes and not for content.

With very young children, using body parts as content could begin with expanding the idea of traveling to include use of different parts of the body, e.g., hands and feet, one foot and two hands, and hips. Closely allied to this focus would be emphasis on different body parts, such as knees, feet, heads, and shoulders. As they travel, they can lift these parts high, reach out with them, or shake them. Gradually, as the children become aware of different body parts and the way they can move them, experiences can focus on a more sophisticated concept—body parts that lead a movement. For example, shoulders, elbows, wrists, hands, and chests can lead a movement, as can hips, knees, and feet.

Once the children have become aware of individual body parts and their role, combining the idea of body parts leading with rising-sinking or opening-closing can do two things: (1) heighten the children's awareness of their body parts and (2) produce a greater variation within the movement activities of rising-sinking and opening-closing.

Sample Learning Experiences
1. Travel freely throughout the space, using different body parts (e.g., hands, feet, and backs).
2. Emphasize (make important) different body parts as you alternate skipping with slow stepping.
3. Explore the different body parts that can lead the movement as you rise and sink while staying in one spot.
4. Lead with different body parts (e.g., wrists, elbows, hips) while opening and closing and traveling short distances.
5. Combine different forms of traveling on the feet while emphasizing a variety of body parts (e.g., jumping, turning, with elbows high).
6. Combine traveling with movements on the spot while emphasizing different body parts (e.g., running, turning, rising, and sinking, with wrists important).

Discussion. With the additional emphasis of body parts, all movement experiences immediately become richer, for two reasons. First, the experience is more complex; second, the effect on the body is more comprehensive. For example, rising and sinking with the additional focus of leading with different body parts is much harder than rising and sinking alone. In addition, emphasizing different body parts while rising and sinking gives the movement a totally new feeling.

Basically, these experiences are the same as those first suggested, with the additional focus of different body parts; however, developing clarity in the way body parts are used is not easy, especially for the very young child. Teachers need to evaluate the progress the children are making with this factor in mind. Knees and feet shooting high into the air while jumping and

leaping are movements that young children can understand, whereas leading a movement with elbows, shoulders, or hips is a more appropriate concept to teach older children. When children become aware of what it means to lead a movement with different body parts, they often tend "to carry" the part at first. Instead of allowing the elbows, for example, to lead their movement, they put them in a particular spot in space and then travel with them. It gives the observer the feeling that the part is being carried with the body, not leading the body. This phenomenon tends to occur when the child is covering space rather than when he is moving on the spot.

The experiences suggested offer a lot of latitude for choice by the children. They have decisions regarding the method of traveling and the selection of body parts to use. This number of choices is too many for some of the children, especially at the beginning. It is not easy to design early experiences because, on the one hand, the children need to experience a variety of movements or they will not know what they can do; on the other hand, the children are trying to learn how to take responsibility for some of their own learning. What is essential is a balance between different types of experiences.

The concept of relationship as a major theme or series of themes has been omitted, except in Theme 5, to avoid an inflexible use of this idea. Basically, relationship refers to movement in relationship to music, sounds, poems, and percussion instruments, for example, when their purpose is to enrich the dance experience. At this point, and with the movement ideas considered thus far, it is recommended that the children work primarily alone. They seem to need a period of independence while they build their own rhythm, phrases, and sequences. Simple relationships, such as all moving in toward the teacher, rising and then sinking as a group, but in their own time, followed by everyone moving back into the space, are fun and give the children the beginning feelings associated with working with others. Since children differ from class to class, teachers must be alert to their needs and structure the experiences accordingly.

SAMPLE UNIT PLAN THEME 1

Theme. Introduction to the Body—Theme 1.

Unit Focus. Traveling, with rising and sinking.

Appropriate For. Children with no experience in dance.

Length of Unit. Two 30-minute lessons.

Content

       Body—walking, stepping, skipping

       Space—

       Effort—

       Relationship—

Student Objectives. Children should be willing to try to

1. Explore the body activities of walking, running, skipping, jumping, and rising and sinking—alone and in combinations.

2. Enjoy the feeling of combining rising and sinking with "traveling."

3. Find ways to make hands and elbows "dance" while traveling.

Teaching Area. Indoors—medium to large.

Accompaniment. Tambourine, drum, or teacher's voice.

Learning Experiences (Tasks)

1.0 Find as many different ways as you can to travel throughout the space using just your feet. Keep your traveling movements soft and quiet and watch carefully where you are going.

1.1 Try just running and walking, but this time have your feet close together, then far apart. Maybe you could add a turn?

1.2 Travel with skips and jumps; bring your feet away from the floor, close to the floor. Put your feet in front of you, behind you, to the sides.

1.3 Choose two ways of traveling that you enjoyed doing and do them one after the other. Repeat this four times and stop.

2.0 Either sitting or kneeling, draw shapes in the space above your head with your hands and elbows: big shapes, little shapes. Lightly punch (or polka-dot) the space above your head and all around you.

2.1 When ready, let the movements of your

A Suggested Progression for Sample Dance Unit/Theme 1

	Lesson 1		Lesson 2
Tasks	**Teaching Tips**	**Tasks**	**Teaching Tips**
1.0	Encourage children to find different ways to travel; suggest some if it looks as though they need it.	1.2	Encourage more variation in the jumps. Go over the five basic jumps if this would help. Continue to encourage soft, resilient feet.
1.1	Stress spacing and the use of *both* running and walking. Observe for the feet close, far apart; if this is not happening, remind them. Demonstrate it if they need to see it to understand it.	2.0	Same task, should be familiar. Help them find more places their hands and arms can go.
1.2	Stress same ideas as above; keep observing for lightness and resiliency. You could have one half of the class work and one half rest.	2.1	Stress greater use of space and light, soft, "footwork." "Do this long enough (give rests) for children to enjoy doing it.
1.3	Stress that the two ways are smoothly linked and clear. Before repeating it, give them time to choose the two ways.	2.2	Take them through the sequence so they know the order ("talk them through it"). After they know what *to do*, then begin developing skill in their movement. Have children feel good, confident in doing this sequence before moving to next task.
2.0	Encourage use of *all* the space, *lots* of space. Their upper bodies should be forced to move.		
2.1	Stress *full* use; let body react to arms and hands. Keep traveling light and free.		
3.0	Help them find different ways by suggesting ones you do *not* see happening. Stress the ongoingness of both rising and sinking, and the feeling of going up and going down inherent in these actions.	3.0	Encourage children to find *new* ways of rising and sinking; different than previous lesson. Demonstrate (you or other children), if it would help. Demonstrate to give children *ideas*, not to "copy."
3.1	Stress *short* travel; full stop before starting sequence again. Encourage variation in the way they rise and travel, sink, and travel. Suggest variations if necessary.	3.3	Stress traveling and the idea of continuous movement. Give them rests, this task is tiring! If children cannot handle this task, go back and work with tasks 3.1 and 3.2. Help children "get back" clarity in rising and sinking and rising and sinking *and* traveling.
3.2	Encourage a continuity between the rising and traveling.		

Note: Not every task needs accompaniment with a drum or tambourine. Your voice can be very helpful. *Practice,* however, *how* you plan to say the tasks—this is part of the "accompaniment"—AND, when possible, move with the children; it will motivate them and help you pace how you give the tasks.

hands help you get up; with hands and elbows "dancing," begin to travel into the open space; keep hands and elbows "dancing" above you, at the sides, in front of you.

2.2 Begin in a position low to the ground. Start hands dancing, add elbows; let body come up as a result of hands and elbows "pulling" or "lifting" you; travel; begin to slow down; let body lower (keep hands and elbows moving); slowly stop all movement and hold position. Repeat (throughout this task there should be an accompaniment designed to help the children phrase this sequence).

3.0 Find as many different ways as you can of rising away from the floor and sinking (*not* collapsing) onto the floor.

3.1 As you are rising, travel a short distance and stop. Sink while staying in one place. Repeat enough times to get a rhythm in your rising and traveling, stop; sinking and stop.

3.2 Begin in a tall, stretched, open position and as you are sinking, travel a short distance and stop. Continue traveling while rising.

3.3 Find different ways to rise and sink as you travel. Keep your body continuously moving, traveling while rising and traveling while sinking.

Note: It is recommended that an outside accompaniment be used during these lessons. This accompaniment will have to be designed to match the children's movements and used when it would be most helpful in bringing out the desired responses.

Evaluation. Refer to Chapter 10 and either select or adapt one of the evaluative tools or develop a tool that can be used to help assess a specific aspect of the unit that is important to the needs of your students.

DANCE THEME 2—INTRODUCTION TO WEIGHT AND TIME

This theme is the first one dealing with the quality of movement or how the body moves. Earlier in this book, when discussing the four aspects of body, space, effort, and relationship, it was pointed out that the four motion factors of time, weight, space, and flow made up the

aspect of effort. Furthermore, each factor comprised both an expressive phase and a functional or objective phase. In dance, the use of these motion factors for expressive purposes is the emphasis, and Theme 2 focuses on the factors of weight and time specifically. In so doing, it involves the children with the dynamics of movement, and all experiences are designed to help the children gain control over them with increasing sensitivity.

Development of Theme 2

> **Basic Content**
> Time: sudden, sustained
> Weight: firm, fine touch

Time. Movement can be *sudden* or it can be *sustained*. Sudden movement gives a feeling of urgency, excitement, and spontaneity. Continuous use of a sudden quality results in quivering and vibrating movements and is extremely tiring over extended periods of time. Movement that is prolonged, unhurried, and continuous has a sustained quality. The sensation is unlike any other when the children achieve a leisurely, smooth feeling.

Weight. Besides being sudden and sustained, movement can be either *firm* or *fine*. Firm movements are strong, forceful, and often resistant. They require energy and a strong use of the body's muscle in two ways: (1) moving away from the body into the surrounding space, and (2) holding in toward the body, as in gripping.

Movements that are light, delicate, and fragile are considered fine. The tension employed by the muscles is "sensitive" and slight. Fine movements can also be projected into the surrounding space or held very gently, as if holding one's breath.

Sample Learning Experiences
1. TIME. Open and close, contrasting a sudden movement with a sustained movement. (Rising-sinking, traveling, or leading with different body parts could be the focus of the body action instead of "open and close.")
2. WEIGHT. Rise with a firm movement and sink with a fine movement. (Opening-closing, traveling, or leading with different body parts could be the focus of the body action instead of "rising and sinking.")

3. TIME-WEIGHT. Show a firm-sustained opening contrasted with a fine-sustained closing. Stay on the spot when opening and travel when closing.

Discussion

TIME. Many possibilities exist for learning experiences when time and weight qualities are the focus. Basically, when designing experiences using these two motion factors, the content of Theme 1 needs to be used (e.g., methods of locomotion, use of body parts, rising-sinking). Whether to use single ideas or combinations of ideas from Theme 1 depends entirely on the children for whom the experiences are being developed. The amount of experiences contained within each of the ones listed is vast. For example, if contrasting sudden and sustained movement is the focus, the following tasks may be used:

1. Travel, using just your feet, first very quickly, then very slowly.

2. Make quick lively jumps and turns with your feet while you travel throughout the space.

3. Focus on the idea of rising and sinking very slowly—create within yourself a feeling of calmness and quietness.

4. Lead with different body parts as you slowly and carefully open and close your body.

5. Travel, turn, rise, and sink, contrasting sudden movement with sustained movement.

Again, the question of structure of the experience must be discussed. Within these five tasks is a range of specificity—the first two being quite specific and the last three quite open. All tasks imply that the children will experiment to find the potential within each. Otherwise, the task(s) in question may have to be reworded so that the children know more specifically what is expected of them. For example, Task 4 might be reworded accordingly:

> Beginning in an opened position, slowly close your body with your elbows leading the movement; then, quickly open your body, with your elbows still leading. Repeat, trying to vary the way you are doing it each time.

Even though this variation is more specific, there still is ample opportunity for individual interpretation. As the children become more aware of their bodies in movement, this ability improves.

WEIGHT. Little more can be said when discussing the second experience: contrasting firm movements with fine. Although the construction of the experiences is not difficult, the challenge comes in developing observation ability to assess progress. When is a movement firm, fine? How do you know when children have gone as far as they can go with the particular quality or combination of qualities? All are good questions with no pat answer. From experience and hard work, teachers gradually can tell what are firm and fine movements, and thus become more flexible in the way they plan subsequent experiences.

TIME–WEIGHT. Combining elements of the qualities of time and weight begins to give children experience in the richness available in Laban's theory of effort. Each movement now becomes something quite different and unique in terms of the sensation that accompanies it. There are four combinations:

1. *Firm-sustained movement:* a strength persistently evident throughout the entire body.

2. *Fine touch-sudden movement:* a gaiety, a liveliness about the way the body moves.

3. *Firm-sudden movement:* a vigorous, energetic, vitalized quality to the movement.

Photo from the Agency for Instructional Television.

4. *Fine touch-sustained movement:* a soothing, serene, peaceful expression.

As explained previously, the experiences are derived from either taking an idea by itself, such as firm-sustained movement, or by combining ideas, such as firm-sustained and firm-sudden. Because the logistics of designing experiences focused on helping children to gain control over movement qualities are relatively easy, one must guard against going so fast (covering material) that the purpose of the experiences is not met. Careful observation of the children's responses and study of the experiences can prevent this problem.

Depending on the progress of the children, the material in this theme can be used to design both simple relationship experiences and short individual sequences. In the first instance, children can work in pairs or as a total group in relation to the teacher. For example, children can come together in twos with light, lively traveling movements; slowly travel around each other; and separate with the same light, quick traveling movements used in the beginning. As another example, teachers can stand in the center of the room and with sharp, firm drum beats have all the children move toward them with strong, firm stepping movements. While they gently rub their hands across the surface of the drum, the children take slow but firm stepping movements back to where they started.

These experiences, using the familiar material in simple relationship patterns, are the beginning of creating a dance. In these early situations, movement is being structured into a pattern that has both temporal and spatial dimensions. The purpose, however, is solely for the children. Emphasis is not on having them remember what they did for others to see but rather on trying different ideas within a particular "structure for action." In the first example just given, the structure for action was simple: the children were to *meet, mingle,* and *separate,* using light, lively movements. What traveling actions they used or how they used their body parts was left to their individual interpretation. Refining these "dances" will come, but at a later time.

Besides designing experiences that have a relationship concept as their core, the teacher can encourage children to make up individual sequences of movements, getting their ideas from the lesson's material. For example, sequences emerging from experiences associated with this theme could involve the following:

1. Movement that travels continuously (e.g., jumping and turning, stressing a sudden quality).

2. Movement that stays on the spot (e.g., rising-sinking, while contrasting firm movement with fine movement).

3. Movement that combines traveling and staying on the spot (e.g., quick and lively, jumping and turning, and sustained rising and sinking).

Observers viewing children working with the ideas discussed thus far often remark, "Don't you ever use music, or do rhythms?" The answer is yes, but the manner in which these ideas are incorporated, into the program may have variations not found in some of the other approaches.

Rhythm is of two kinds: metric and nonmetric. Metric rhythm is expressed in the legs whenever step-like actions occur. Nonmetric rhythm, or free rhythm, is associated primarily with gesturing. Both forms of rhythm are important and need to be included throughout.[4]

In this approach to children's dance, designing experiences that help them gain sensitivity to the rhythms of their bodies is of major importance. Movement combined with music, as well as movement performed without music but with the climaxes and hesitations coming from the feeling of the natural phrasing of movement, are both integral parts of the rhythmic and dance education of children. Knowing which direction to take with children, and when, comes from understanding their individual needs in movement. The following two learning experiences focus on rhythm, using material from Theme 2.

1. Create a free rhythmic phrase while opening and closing the body, using sudden-firm movements as the body contracts and sustained-fine movements as the body opens.

2. Using stepping actions, create a metric time rhythm, varying the amount of weight used.

The rhythmic education of a child cannot be achieved in a single lesson or even a series of lessons. This component of a child's dance education needs to be blended carefully throughout all experiences. Because rhythmic movement involves the mastering of the weight-time qualities in all their variations, it seems most appropriate to introduce the concept at this point; however, rhythm, as a concept in children's dance, is an aspect of all the themes presented.

SAMPLE UNIT PLAN THEME 2

Themes. Introduction to Effort—Theme 2 (selected content from Theme 1).

Unit Focus. Contrasting the difference between firm, strong movement and fine, delicate movement.

Appropriate For. Children who can handle the basic locomotor and nonlocomotor activities easily and who can understand how to work safely as an individual in a large group.

Length of Unit. Three 30-minute lessons.

Content

> Body—stepping, jumping, skipping, running, opening, closing
> body parts: hands, arms, elbows, knees
> Space—
> Effort—weight: firm, fine
> Relationship—group to individual (simple form)

Student Objectives. Children should be willing to try to

1. Contrast strong, firm movement with light, free movement.

2. Be aware of others as they move.

3. Concentrate on the feel of firm and fine movement.

4. Visually see the difference between movement; that is firm and strong and movement that is fine and light.

Teaching Area. Indoors—larger and small.

Accompaniment. Tambourine, drum, triangle, or teacher's voice.

Learning Experiences (Tasks)

1.0 Firmly grip hands, arms, and legs in toward center of your body; slowly release the tension, letting arms move away from your body. (Children are well spaced out and working alone.)

1.1 Run (a short distance) stop and grip firmly in toward center of body; slowly release tension, feeling lightness in arms, hands, upper body (body will rise and open a little) and travel to another place, stop and grip (watch spacing when traveling). Re-

peat. (Gripping and stopping are done simultaneously.)

1.2 With light, quick, jumps, skips, and runs, travel in and out of the class; be careful not to touch (teacher can accompany this with short taps on the triangle, edge of drum, shake of the tambourine, or with own voice).

1.3 Begin with light, quick steps and suddenly (on drum beat) grip the floor firmly with feet and total body (body slightly curled; hands and arms firm and flexed and close to body's center). Release tension and repeat.

2.0 Begin standing up, think about your position. On the drum beat, sink quickly with a firm gripping movement of your whole body (children will be curled, but balanced on feet). BEAT DRUM. Hold position; now slowly release the tension, letting your body rise as far as it will go and still feel light. Hold, and relax. Let us try it again. Keep repeating this until they get a good feel for the idea.

2.1 As you sink, sink with lightness, and as you rise, rise with firmness. Release tension and gently, lightly let your body sink. Do all this without traveling and enough times to feel the rhythm.

2.2 Easy, light running to an open space; stop with a firm gripping action; release the tension and gently sink; then rise. When you are almost up, begin running and repeat sequence, stopping the run when you hear the drum.

2.3 Practice rising and sinking in your own space, sometimes showing a firm, strong, and powerful use of your body and sometimes a delicate, gentle, fine use. When you can, emphasize different parts of your body: arms, hands, head, knees; you choose. Add traveling when ready.

3.0 On the drum beats, take firm steps (grip with hands, arms as foot touches) toward the center of the circle. Teacher is in center of space (has tambourine and triangle) and children around him/her about 15 feet away. Stop and hold a firm position. Rise with lightness (teacher strikes triangle), sink with lightness (triangle), hold. With light, quick jumps travel back to your starting place. (Teacher uses drum to bring out

A Suggested Progression for Sample Dance Unit/Theme 2

	Lesson 1		Lesson 2		Lesson 3
Tasks	**Teaching Tips**	**Tasks**	**Teaching Tips**	**Tasks**	**Teaching Tips**
1.0	Encourage children to grip with all parts of their bodies. The whole body should be firm.	1.0 / 1.1 / 1.2	Repeat same tasks and help children improve and expand their responses. Stress clear contrast between firm and fine qualities, use a greater variety of body parts.	2.3	Work individually now, help children refine *their* sequences. Be sure you know what they are trying before you help. If children want to, you could put two groups together and they could share their work with each other.
1.1	Stress easy lifting of arms when releasing tension.	1.3 / 2.2	Help them discover which ones are still not in use.	3.1	Work on the body parts that are "pulling" up or "pulling" down. Help children make these parts clear.
1.2	Watch spacing as children should be moving quickly.	2.3	Help them make the decisions necessary by directly asking them what qualities they are using and when. Then observe and respond. Try to have them make the choices, but help those who specifically need it.	3.2	Explain variation in coming together, practice this. Do entire sequence through observing for clarity in firm, fine qualities, use of different body parts, and clear rising and sinking. Design additional tasks if they need specific work on any one part (e.g., rising and sinking *with* variation).
1.3	Stress that whole body grips, and whole body should feel light.	3.0	Review for them the basic sequence. Begin stressing firm steps (body into floor), lightness in rising and sinking, and sudden quick jumps back "home." (*Hold* final position at least 4 seconds.)		Conclude lesson, doing sequence three to four times without stopping.
2.0	Stress concentration on selves before beginning task. Encourage *still* starting positions.				
2.1	Make rising and sinking actions clear.				
2.2	Be sure they understand: run, firm stop, sink, rise. This is a four-part sequence.				
3.0	Let them just try it to get idea. Work for good spacing and knowing when to start, stop, etc. Keep refinement of movements until next lesson.				

"light, quick jumps.") Hold position, and rest. (Repeat several times.)

3.1 As you sink and rise, see if you can make different parts of your body pull you up (rise) or take you down (sink). Make it clear which part you are using. You choose.

3.2 Listen to the drum and begin traveling to the center when you want to—not all together this time. Remember, firm steps to center; a light, fine quality when rising and sinking; and quick, light jumps back to place.

Evaluation. Refer to Chapter 10 and either select or adapt one of the evaluative tools or develop a tool that can be used to help assess a specific aspect of the unit that is important to the needs of your students.

DANCE THEME 3—INTRODUCTION TO SPACE

Theme 3 is the first to focus specifically on the environment rather than on the children. In this theme, the way space can be used is the major emphasis. As previously noted, all three areas of the physical education program stress learning how to use space, with the *way* space is used being the distinguishing feature among the areas. This point is important because if teachers cannot distinguish these differences, parts of gymnastics, games, and dance will appear to be too similar, and some of the advantage of using this particular movement framework might be lost.

In games and gymnastics, the space is used functionally. Individuals must be able to use it effectively in accomplishing the task at hand. Games players keep attempting to restructure the space so they can manipulate themselves or an object into a more advantageous position. Gymnasts use it to help them discover more variations in the way they move. In all areas, space is considered the medium in which all movement must take place.

In dance, space is sculptured rather than restructured as in games and gymnastics. When handled inventively, space helps to create a particular mood or feeling. Space can be "felt." Once children become interested in space, as content, and develop some degree of mastery in using it, they have taken a great step forward.

Development of Theme 3

> **Basic Content**
> Areas: general, personal
> Directions; forward, backward, sideward, up, down
> Pathways: air, floor
> Levels: high, medium, low (deep)
> Extensions; small-large, near-far

AREAS. The first concept with which children need familiarity in terms of space is the *use* of it—both personal and general space. The space around an individual is referred to as *personal space* and includes all the space within the range of that individual. *General space* is all the space available to the mover at any given time. Depending on the situation, the amount of general space can vary greatly. Use of this space (general and personal) can be achieved by the body (1) *exploring* it (moving into it; playing with it); (2) *penetrating* it (dividing it); (3) *filling* it (leaping and spreading); (4) *surrounding* it (gathering it in toward the body); and (5) *repulsing* it (pushing it away from the body).[4]

Sample Learning Experiences
1. Extend different body parts into space as far as they will go while remaining on the spot (personal space emphasized); travel while extending (general space emphasized).
2. Surround a "piece" of space using your arms (legs, head) and bring it into your body; gently push it away (on the spot and traveling).
3. Fill the space by leaping, turning, spinning; stop, and gather it in (repeat).

Discussion. At first, the experiences must be comprehensive in nature so that the child gets the feeling of what it means to "use the space" (e.g., exploring, penetrating, filling, surrounding, repulsing). Sometimes the transition between the way they have already been using the space (traveling and watching out for others) and this new use is not easy. Because it is crucial to the development of all subsequent experiences, children need to understand the difference—and take an interest in it.

Exploring personal space is enriched considerably when time and weight qualities are added as well as when the use of different body parts is emphasized. As already brought out, there are limitless directions in designing experiences once the children understand the basic idea. Whenever the teacher designs new experiences, especially when adding past movement material or combining it in unique ways, the children's progress and developmental needs must serve as major criteria for the final decisions.

DIRECTIONS AND PATHWAYS. These two space concepts are being considered together because they are related and are often handled simultaneously.

When observing movement, it is possible to identify the direction in which it is occurring. For purposes here, only five of these directions will be considered: *forward, backward, sideward, upward* and *downward*. Furthermore, the part of the body that is leading will identify the direction the movement is taking. If an individual's chest or front of the body goes first, a forward direction results; if the back of his body leads, the direction is backward. Likewise, if the body's side leads, the individual is moving sideward (right or left). When the body rises or lowers, it is using the directions of up and down.

In addition to "knowing" what constitutes the different directions, being aware of the relationship between certain body activities and directions is particularly useful, so experiences can be designed in a slightly different manner from those in gymnastics and games. The body activities of rising and sinking move in an up-down direction, whereas opening and closing are movements in a sideward direction, either to the right or to the left. Movement in the forward and backward directions is often referred to as advancing and retreating. Laban's eleventh theme develops this idea further by combining activities, such as a movement with the right side leading, while rising and opening simultaneously. In this instance, we would describe the directions as upward and sideward (Laban would describe this direction as high-right). Becoming intricately involved with directions as a highly sophisticated concept of space orientation is not necessary when thinking in terms of children's dance; however, children must have experiences that allow them to become both adept with movements that use the five basic directions and sensitive to the concept of direction as an integrator of movement.

The concept of pathways is related to the pattern of the movement along the floor or in the air. No matter where the pattern is created, all

are derivations of either straight or curved, lines. *Angular patterns* emerge from the manner in which straight lines are combined, and *twisted* or *circular patterns* are variations of curved lines.

Sample Learning Experiences
1. Advance and retreat (forward-backward directions), using quick, lively steps contrasted with slow, sustained steps, or rise and sink (up-down directions) in place of advance and retreat.
2. Carve different pathways in the air with different body parts as you rise and sink, or use different pathways as you *travel* while rising and sinking.
3. In twos, advance and retreat, sometimes using quick, light steps, sometimes slow, firm steps. When together, rise and sink together, or one after the other.

Discussion. Many of these experiences may seem similar to past ones, but as their focus is specifically on the use of directions and pathways, they are quite different. When children begin to put more and more movements together, thus creating more phrases and sequences, the need for clarification of their movements becomes more obvious. For instance, showing the direction of a movement often takes much work to refine the way specific body parts are moving.

The idea that a sequence of movement has a starting position as well as an ending position should not be new to the children. The challenge is the combination of the new movements the children are discovering, coupled with the true difficulty children have in achieving positions of pure stillness.

In examining the sample learning experiences, once again, the manner in which they are designed is the same. New ideas are either taken alone or combined with material from past themes. In suggesting that experiences may involve another person or even a small group, we are using the simplest forms to integrate ideas from some of the more advanced themes into the experiences (Laban's Themes 14 and 15 in particular). A more detailed discussion regarding relationships and the development of sequences and dances appears in Theme 5; its major purpose is to have the children explore simple relationships with others and subsequently create simple dances.

LEVELS AND EXTENSIONS. In order to indicate some of the logic and potential relatedness in movement, levels and extensions are discussed together.

In dance, the concept of levels occurs primarily in relation to the total body. Movements above the shoulders are referred to as *high*, whereas movements below the hips are considered *low* or *deep*. Any movements that take place between the hips and shoulder area are said to occur at a *medium* level.

Similarly, the concept of extension also relates to the total body. This concept focuses on whether the movement is *large (far from the body)* or small *(near the body)*. Once an understanding of this concept becomes well developed, its relationship to the body activities of opening and closing should be obvious. Opening involves reaching as far from the body's center as possible and closing involves the opposite. As teachers become more familiar with the ideas and more comfortable teaching dance to children, deeper insights into movement should begin developing. Ultimately, these under-

standings are the greatest help in designing experiences that are naturally developmental, since the understandings relate to both movement itself and the child's learning how to move.

Sample Learning Experiences
1. Travel and stop at a medium level; slowly change to a high level; and suddenly change to a low level, and hold. Vary the way different body part are used during the changes between levels.
2. In response to every drum beat, make a firm-sudden movement, each time at a different level. Add when appropriate a variety of body parts, a range of musical accompaniment, so different time-weight qualities can be stressed (firm-sustained, fine-sudden, fine-sustained), traveling as well as moving on the spot.

Discussion. No matter what the movement experience, the space concepts of levels and extensions are automatically present. The experiences, however, highlight these concepts and build them in as specific foci. By the time teachers have designed material from this theme and used it in any way, they should have at their fingertips the means to design many experiences. With this ability, however, comes a potential danger, *that of making the experiences too complex.* Beginning teachers often have this problem when they first realize how easily they can manipulate the material. In the process, they forget to look at the children and their level of development or at the logic of what they have put together. If every possible combination of movement ideas is presented, there will be too much material. How much material the children "experience" is not of major importance, but what they do with it is.

A lot of material is inherent in the learning experiences just described. To have children gain fully from these experiences, they will need time—time to explore *and* time to develop a degree of quality in their work. As in all experiences, whenever we add a new idea to a familiar one, we experience a moment of regression. For example, if the children are working alone with rising and sinking, emphasizing body parts near to them or far from them, the additional idea of contrasting weight qualities may make them lose the clarity they had either in rising and sinking or in the way they were using different body parts. This momentary regression is a natural part of the learning process.

To help teach spatial concepts, words that initiate "spatial" movement should be used. Use them alone or in combination, as children respond easily to them and enjoy the results. Here are a few: *in front, behind, to the side* (right, left), *over, below, beside, under, on, through, towards, away* (far) *from, near* (close) *to, via, around, up against. . . .*

SAMPLE UNIT PLAN THEME 3

Themes. Introduction to Space—Theme 3 (and selected material from Themes 1 and 2).

Unit Focus. Using levels and directions in space while opening and closing, showing changes in speed.

Appropriate For. Children who have worked with the basic means of traveling and body actions of rising and sinking and opening and closing. They are able to contrast sudden and sustained movement and firm and fine. They can initiate movements with hands, arms, elbows, and knees. Their ability to stay on task is improving.

Length of Unit. Three 30-minute lessons.

Content

Body—opening and closing

Space—levels: high, medium, low/ deep; directions: forward, backward, sideward

Effort—time: sudden, sustained

Relationship—

Student Objectives. Children should be willing to try to

1. Link movement taking place at high, medium, and low levels with traveling in forward, backward, and sideward directions.

2. Design a short sequence of actions that has a beginning, middle, and an end.

3. *Feel* space, by exploring each level to its fullest.

4. Gain confidence in their ability to improvise.

5. Concentrate inwards.

Teaching Area. Indoors—medium to large.

Accompaniment. Tambourine, drum, or teacher's voice.

Learning Experiences (Tasks)

1.0 Begin by combining in ways of your choice, running, skipping, opening, and closing.

Use all the available space; keep your feet light and bouncy.

1.1 When you are opening, open quickly; close slowly. Show a clear contrast.

1.2 Now reverse this. When you are opening, open slowly; close suddenly.

1.3 Now, mix your changes in speed when running and skipping as well as when opening and closing.

2.0 In a standing position, take your arms and hands and move them *all about* in the space way above your head. Feel what a high level feels like; move (reach) in all directions: forward, backward, and sideward.

2.1 Now, do the same thing, but move in all directions at a medium level.

2.2 Keep searching the space in all directions, but now near the floor (low level).

2.3 Repeat the same idea of moving your arms and hands in all directions, but now use all three levels: low, high, and medium. Mix the order, but use all three.

3.0 As you reach with your arms and hands forward, sideward, and backward at *one* level, let your body travel in the same directions. (Let children choose level.)

3.1 Repeat same task at another level. (Let children choose level.)

3.2 Repeat same task at third level. (Let children choose level.)

4.0 Make a sequence of actions that
   a. starts in a high position,
   b. travels in different directions,
   c. uses opening and closing,
   d. finishes in a low position.

5.0 Suddenly open your body and be at a high level (drum beat excellent stimulus); slowly close your body and be at a low level; repeat until you get the feel of high/low and sudden/sustained.

5.1 Find different levels into which you can open and close your body while contrasting a quick with a slow speed. As you are working, be sure to travel forward, backward, or sideward.

6.0 *Demonstrate through movement*, to another member of the class, the difference between
   a. high, low, medium levels,
   b. forward, backward, sideward directions,

A Suggested Progression for Sample Dance Unit/Theme 3

Lesson 1		Lesson 2		Lesson 3	
Tasks	**Teaching Tips**	**Tasks**	**Teaching Tips**	**Tasks**	**Teaching Tips**
1.0	Stress opening *while* running and closing when still. Encourage full use of space.	2.0} 2.1} 2.2}	Let them get comfortable with these ideas again. Stress that *where* in the space they put their arms and hands must *continuously vary*.	4.0	As they come into class, encourage them to begin working where they left off. When you think they have worked enough, have all of them go through their sequence three times. You start them.
1.1} 1.2}	Stress clarity of quality: quick, over in a flash; slow, lingering.	2.3	Encourage the children to decide on the order of levels used and repeat it.	5.0	Stress clarifying the time factor: *sudden, sustained*. Use drum to aid them get this feeling.
1.3	Clear contrasts in speed. This may disappear because of the change in task. Go back to 1.1 or 1.2 if this happens.	3.0	Stress traveling because of reach. Let reach pull children off balance into traveling. You might have to demonstrate this—as an idea it is difficult to explain.	5.1	Make sure they know the parts to this task. Ask them, so you are sure. You are looking for clarity in body action (opening/closing), time quality (sudden/sustained), and directions used (forward, backward, sideward).
2.0	Use *lots* of space. Reach *everywhere*.	3.1} 3.2}	Same as in 3.0. This is a difficult concept but a lovely feeling when achieved.	6.0	As children are working, make notes (mental or written) related to their progress with these ideas. Notice how they go about showing they know these differences. Keep all children working on the same request; you pace the experience.
2.1} 2.2}	Stress lots of space, and in all directions. If they are having trouble, break it down again.	4.0	Give out entire sequence and let them work alone. Encourage them to ask for help if they need it. Observe entire group and try to select major problems everyone is having before going to individuals.		
2.3	Stress that all three levels are to be used and they must use them without help from you.				
4.0	Let them try different starting positions; combining them with traveling in different directions. Leave the rest of the sequence until next lesson.				

c. a change in speed,

d. opening and closing.

Evaluation. Refer to Chapter 10 and either select or adapt one of the evaluative tools or develop a tool that can be used to help assess a specific aspect of the unit that is important to the needs of your students.

DANCE THEME 4—THE FLOW OF MOVEMENT

Theme 4, like Theme 2, emphasizes the quality of movement. In so doing, it introduces new material as well as integrating material from Themes 1, 2, and 3. The new ideas relate to the motion factors of flow and space. Integration of the three preceding themes primarily results from combining ideas from them into movement phrases, while at the same time, helping the children become more aware of what a movement phrase (sometimes called sequence) is.

Development of Theme 4

> **Basic Content**
> Flow: bound, free
> Space: direct, indirect

FLOW. Movement can be either *bound* or *free*. Bound movements are hesitant, restrained, and capable of being stopped, whereas free movements are unrestrained, fluent, and often difficult to stop. In order to design experiences that help children become sensitive to the feeling of flow, teachers must recognize the type of tasks or body activities that have this potential. Experiences that cause the children to stop, to hesitate, to pause, and to move slowly contribute to a child's awareness of bound flow. In contrast, to develop a child's awareness of free flow, activities such as jumping, leaping, whirling, and traveling in a continuous manner are the focus of the experiences. Children can also feel free flow when they pause yet let the movement continue a bit longer. This subtle use of flow is not easy for most children.

Two ideas associated with flow are helpful when teaching. These are continuity, or the transition between movement and body flow, and the way the movement flows through the body.[4] Being aware of these ideas should aid

teachers in helping children handle experiences focused on bound and free flow, for no matter which flow quality is stressed, the way children handle the ideas of continuity and body flow will influence the quality of their responses. Specific experiences emphasizing continuity of movement and body flow could be developed if it seems necessary. For example, practice rising and sinking as one continuous ongoing movement; practice moving different body parts in sequence (e.g., shoulder, elbow, wrist, and fingers; upper back, shoulder, and head). To be meaningful and helpful to children, these "practices" should relate directly to some identified problem the children are having.

Sample Learning Experiences
1. Travel throughout the space, turning and running; be as continuous and ongoing as possible (free flow). (Have small groups of children at a time doing this.)
2. Move forward, backward, and sideward, using slow, hesitant steps (bound flow).
3. Develop a short sequence that involves rising and sinking while traveling and that clearly shows a contrast between bound flow and free flow.

Discussion. All the experiences encourage the children to feel the sensation of flow, bound or free. In structure, the first two experiences are fairly specific and permit the children only to decide when to change the activity (turning and running) or the direction (forward, backward, and sideward). Until the children become skillful in handling the flow concept, especially free flow, this limited opportunity for making decisions may be ample. It is not easy to make decisions when trying to experience the sensation of free flow—for free flow implies there is no time to make them!

SPACE. When considering the motion factor of space, concern is for the actual amount of space a movement takes. Movement can be *indirect* or *flexible*, using vast amounts of space, or it can be *direct* or *straight*, using space sparingly. As before, ideas from Themes 1 and 3 in particular can help children become aware of how much space their movements use. To experience a direct use of space, traveling in straight pathways or cutting through space with a hand or foot are possibilities. Activities such as turning, twisting, and creating wavy patterns in the air give children experiences in feeling indirect or flexible movement. Whatever the experience, it should be designed to focus on the amount of space used in relation to either a large amount, where the space is used abundantly, or a small amount, where the space is used economically.

When teachers first use the movement framework of body, space, effort, and relationship, they often confuse the *major aspect* of space with the *motion factor* of space. In the former, the emphasis is on *where* the body moves in space; in the latter, the emphasis shifts to the *amount* of space that a movement takes. To allay this potential confusion, it often helps to think of the space aspect, the larger of the two concepts, as space *awareness*, and the motion factor as dealing with space *quality*.

Sample Learning Experiences
1. Walk across the floor, penetrating the space (a direct use of space), forward, backward, sideward. Feel as though you are cutting through the space, separating it into two halves. (This task could be redesigned to include contrasting time qualities, contrasting weight qualities, or contrasting weight-time qualities.)

2. In twos, one after the other, rise with arms and hands using as much of the surrounding space as possible as they lead you up to a fully extended and still position (an indirect use of space with the arms and hands). Sink, using as little space as possible (a direct use of space). You may travel or remain on the spot. (As suggested above, time, weight, or time-weight qualities could be included in a redesigning of the task.)

Discussion. Each of the experiences just listed focuses on one or the other element of the space factor, direct or indirect. The teacher can also combine both elements in a single experience; for example, you might say, "As you rise, use as little space as possible; as you sink, use as much of the space as you can." The child will feel two very different sensations within the same experience.

In helping children get a feeling for traveling using as little space as possible, the idea of making "straight pathways" brings out a direct use of space. Even though technically this concept is one of space awareness (pathways), its use in this experience helps give the children a sensation of "directness." The idea of using pathways in curved, twisted ways, on the other hand, helps children focus on using space in a free and flexible way. The important point is to be sure the children know what concept they are trying to understand.

The first experience suggested could also incorporate the idea of a contrasting use of space quality. Instead of always traveling in a direct manner, resulting in straight pathways, the experience can be redesigned to include alternating pathways; first straight, then curved, wavy, or twisted, the latter experience focusing on the use of the space in a more flexible way than the former.

It may also be possible to design experiences that involve small groups of children (2 to 4) moving in relation to each other. For example, advance toward each other, using straight pathways. Upon meeting, mingle in and out of the group, using curved pathways; then return to your starting place, again using straight pathways.

In this example, the emphasis is on moving toward and away from each other, using space both economically and abundantly (space quality). There is no specification of other qualities.

Once the children understand the basic idea, the teacher can add other qualities. Time qualities can be used alone or in combination with weight qualities. Decisions regarding which qualities to use, and when, can be made by the teacher alone, by the teacher with the children, or by the children alone. In addition, each group may make its own decisions with the possibility that different qualities will be evident in each group.

MOVEMENT PHRASES

Throughout each theme's discussion, the idea that different movements can be joined together to form a sequence or phrase has been suggested. Making or designing a movement sequence implies joining together a series of movements that have logic in their selection as well as clarity in their performance. A sequence or phrase of movement has a definite beginning, a middle, and an end. The idea of sequences and phrases is on the threshold of dance-making. In fact, Murray believes ". . . that the simplest combination of movement phrases, say only two, which a child puts together and performs may be legitimately called a dance." She goes on to

ask, "Who can say when random experimenting with an art medium ends and expression of an idea begins?"[5]

When sequences or phrases are introduced as possible experiences, connected with Themes 1 and 3 in particular, they are farther from this threshold of dance-making than when associated with Themes 2 and 4, because Themes 2 and 4 deal directly with the expressive aspect of movement whereas the other themes do not. The material in Themes 1 and 3 begins to take on expression when combined with material from Themes 2 and 4.

In this approach to dance, phrases and sequences are considered preliminary to dances and are considerably shorter in length. When children first begin to design phrases and sequences, whether they are expressive is a personal matter—personal to the child. As movement vocabulary increases and ability to work sensitively with the movement qualities improves, expressing or communicating a specific feeling should begin to be more evident.

No specific pattern exists regarding when and how long movement phrases should be a part of lessons. Teachers must make this decision in relation to the needs of the children. The ex-

perience is meaningful when it helps children synthesize aspects of their quest to understand movement; however, if indiscriminantly tacked on at the end of a lesson, the experience can be useless and frustrating for all involved. Used sensitively, the idea of having children develop and refine personal sequences that say something special to them can be most meaningful.

SAMPLE UNIT PLAN THEME 4

Themes. The Flow of Movement—Theme 4 (and selected material from Themes 1 through 3).

Unit Focus. Experiencing free flow and bound flow and sensing the difference; integrating material from Themes 1, 2, and 3.

Appropriate For. Children who have self-control in the way they use general space and to whom the concept "flow" is new. They can use material from Themes 1, 2, and 3 easily, but there is still much room for improvement.

Length of Unit. Four 30-minute lessons.

Content

> Body—running, skipping, jumping
> Space—general, pathways: curve, zig-zag
> Effort—flow: free, bound
>   weight: firm, fine
> Relationship—to a drum (as focal point), "follow the leader"

Student Objectives. Children should be willing to try to

1. Contrast bound flow with free flow while doing a variety of different movements.

2. Work together in a short sequence and take responsibility for their *own* actions in the group.

3. Show, by pointing to pictures on a bulletin board, people who are moving freely or with hesitancy, quickly or slowly, in an open or closed position, or at a high, medium, or low level.

Teaching Area. Indoors—preferably large.

Accompaniment. Tambourine, drum, or teacher's voice.

Learning Experiences (Tasks)

1.0 Explain meaning of bound flow and free flow (be brief). Give examples with explanation and let the children experience (or mime) them. Examples:

Bound	Free
carrying a full bucket of water	turning the rope for jump the shot
an older person walking (on ice)	whirling
crouching back in fear	sliding down a slide

1.1 Have children give other examples by DOING THEM (in pairs: one does, other observes). As you watch your partner, can you tell whether the movement is bound or free?

A Suggested Progression for

Lesson 1		Lesson 2	
Tasks	**Teaching Tips**	**Tasks**	**Teaching Tips**
1.0	Study material so you can explain it easily. Practice demonstrating the differences.	5.1	Place pictures wherever you wish.
1.1	Observe for problems. Let them go; this is just introductory.	1.0	Ask children to tell you what bound and free flow are.
2.0	Encourage discussion related to feeling the difference.	1.1	Observe children's interpretations (examples) for purpose of gaining insight into their progress.
2.1	Keep going back to 2.0 if children lose quality.	2.1	Discuss which locomotor skills are hardest/easiest when trying to show bound/free qualities. Review the five basic jumps if necessary.
3.0	Stress use of *all* the space and *clear* pathways. Work specifically on them if needed.	3.0	Encourage use of arms, elbows, when "freely" traveling; a calmer, more contained body when "carefully" traveling.
3.2	Stress *leading* not *carrying*.		
3.3	Change the body part that is leading *often*.	3.2	Stress a clearer use of elbows, hands when leading. Start with body part close to you, begin to travel as soon as it moves away and "leads."
5.0	Show some examples. Encourage them to bring pictures of people of *all* ages.	3.3	Try a new part every time you change path. Make paths short.

2.0 Travel (use any means you would like), first *cautiously*, then *freely*. Change the way you are traveling, but always *cautiously* (b) first and freely (f) second. Discuss *feeling* of both.

2.1 Repeat task 2.0 but select specific loco-motor movements; for example: running, skipping, jumping (one or more of the five basic jumps).

3.0 Run or skip "freely," then "hesitantly" throughout the space, following curved pathways, then zig-zag pathways. Discuss which type of pathway is easier for movement to be "free" or for movement to be "bound."

3.1 Repeat the task, using more space: ½ of the class or even ⅓ of the class.

3.2 As you travel in curved pathways, see if your elbow can lead you, then your hand.

3.3 Try this as you travel in zig-zag pathways.

3.4 Play follow the leader with another person.

4.0 In threes, beginning about 10 feet apart, with a drum in the center of the space:

a. Take a starting position that is *open* and at a *high* level.

b. Cautiously move toward the drum with firm, sudden, steps (bound).

c. Upon reaching the drum, stop, and hold individual shape: still.

d. In turn, freely play on the drum with lively, light finger tips while others re-spond in movement on the spot; *short* turns.

e. After all have had a turn, *rush* (free) back to your starting place, twirl a few times, and *freeze*. You should be in your starting position, ready to repeat sequence.

5.0 Bring in pictures of people moving that you think show free and bound qualities, sudden and sustained qualities, firm and fine qualities.

5.1 Put your pictures on the board any place you would like.

5.2 Choose a picture and say whether the movement shows bound or free flow; sud-den, sustained, firm, or fine quality; and whether the body of the person is open, closed, high, low, or medium.

Evaluation. Refer to Chapter 10 and either select or adapt one of the evaluative tools or develop a tool that can be used to help assess a specific aspect of the unit that is important to the needs of your students.

DANCE THEME 5—INTRODUCTION TO RELATIONSHIPS

This theme is an outgrowth of Theme 3, In-troduction to Space, as its focus is again the en-vironment. Now, however, the environment be-comes a person or a small group of people, not

Sample Dance Unit/Theme 4

Tasks	Lesson 3 Teaching Tips	Tasks	Lesson 4 Teaching Tips
5.1	Place pictures wherever you wish. Encourage children to look at board and discuss what they notice with friends.	5.1	Same as in Lesson 3.
		5.2	Start class with children talking in partners or as a group. Continuation from Lesson 3.
3.2 3.3	Clarify the body part leading; make sure it leads. Show a clear difference between curved and zig-zag pathways. Have children find new body parts that can "lead."	3.4	Stress clearer movements in both leader and fol-lower. Encourage children not to repeat the same movements over and over when they lead—select different ones if they can.
3.4	Have leader make clear movements for partner to follow. Change leaders often.	4.0	Walk through sequence again. Clarify the se-quence, making certain children know "order of events." Take each part and help them find new ones to include. Slowly build sequence a, b, ab, c, abc, d, abcd, e, abcde. When ready, perform entire sequence three to four times. Stress con-centrating throughout. Help them by verbalizing what comes next, if necessary.
4.0	Walk (talk) the children through entire sequence. Suggested approach: do a, b, c, three to four times; do d, e three to four times; go through a-e slowly. Purpose: to get feel of sequence and basic actions involved.		
5.2	Bring children together and discuss selected pic-tures. You select some to show the range of move-ments studied.		

just the space. Up to this point, most of the work has been done by children as individuals, with the idea of relating to each other kept at a minimum. When working together was suggested, the primary emphasis was more on spontaneous occurrences than on any careful development of the relationships that were or were not happening.

This theme's focus is specifically the concept of relationship, stressing the relationships that can occur among body parts as well as among people. If this approach to dance were to continue into the secondary physical education program, Laban's fifteenth theme would take the work begun here and develop it further. Theme 5 primarily emphasizes two kinds of relationships: body parts to each other and individuals and groups to each other. The use of music, sound, poems, and props will be discussed briefly; they are considered special forms of the relationship concept.

Development of Theme 5

> **Basic Content**
> Relationship of body parts to each other
> Relationship of individuals and small groups to each other

BODY PARTS. Whenever movement occurs, parts of the body are in motion and their relationship to each other can readily be described. The words used to describe these relationships are familiar to us all: *above, below, behind, in front of, on,* and *alongside* to mention the most common. As words, they are good descriptors and communicate quickly the relationships observed. As *ideas*—movement ideas—they are also useful. When considered as content, they can often enrich the learning experience. This idea of relationships helps children develop greater awareness of individual body parts. Theme 1 began to develop this idea by building on the way body parts can lead movement, this theme capitalizes on the relationships that can occur between and among them.

Besides this spatial-type relationship, body parts can relate in ways that are usually associated with relationships among individuals and groups. For example, body parts can move *si-multaneously,* or at the same time. In the former time sequence, body parts can *match* or *copy* each other's movement by trying to duplicate it exactly or *mirror* it. In the latter time sequence, they can move in *opposition* as one hand reaching above the head seeking a high level and the other reaching toward the ground as far as possible. Furthermore, body parts can move at *different times,* sometimes in quick succession and at other times in a manner similar to taking turns. Body parts can also move so that they *come together* and *separate,* also called *meeting* and *parting.*

Sample Learning Experiences
1. In your own space, standing or sitting, find different ways to bring your hands together and then apart; use other parts such as elbows, hands and elbows, knees, knees and elbows. (Material from Themes 2 and 4 could be used to design additional experiences.)
2. By yourself, traveling or remaining on the spot, bring your hands and arms together suddenly while moving from a medium level to a low then high level. Hold the high level before repeating. (Hands and arms may be above, below, alongside, or around each other.)
3. Slowly advance toward another person with one set of hands arriving below the other; keep changing the relationship of one set of hands to the other; separate quickly and then repeat the sequence; then add:
   —rising and sinking as you advance.
   —using as little space as possible when coming together; filling the space with arms, knees, and hands when separating.

Discussion. These experiences are of two types. The first focuses on individual movers working by themselves and concentrating specifically on the different relationships that can be made with body parts. The first two examples are of this nature. The last example, while still focusing on body parts and their relationship, is designed with two people working together. In all examples, the ideas suggested for possible variations come from the material of previous themes. As discussed in all other themes, the way in which the experiences are further developed depends on the situation, which ultimately becomes each teacher's responsibility.

In the examples just given, the first experience is open. Using the first experience, or one similar to it, observe the children's responses carefully *before* trying to design additional experiences.

The question of how much decision-making is appropriate becomes an important one in such experiences. What is done in relation to this question depends on the progress the children are making toward becoming increasingly self-directed in their learning. If they need help, they should receive it; i.e., the teacher can make the experiences more specific. Yet, this approach offers no guarantee that they will become more self-directed. There are times when teachers need to leave a child or a group of children alone "to keep exploring" on their own, for without opportunity to practice being "self-directed," children will have difficulty improving. Sometimes, the results are not what was hoped for, but as mentioned earlier, if aspects of learning are as important as the movement content, they, too, must be allowed to develop.

INDIVIDUALS AND SMALL GROUPS. The ideas that can be used to stimulate different relationships among people are similar to those previously mentioned in terms of body parts.

Individuals can relate to other individuals, *alone* or as *part of a group*, by being *above* or *below* them, *behind* or *in front of* them, or *on* or *alongside* them. Other words that are space-like in their orientation and that could be used to stimulate movement ideas are over, under, onto, into, through, via, around, mingling with, and up against.

Besides creating relationships primarily through positioning, deciding how these relationships occur offers additional ideas for developing learning experiences. For example, individuals can move with other individuals or small groups at the same time or at different times. They can copy each other's movement, concentrating on duplicating as clearly as possible the shape and level of the movement. In addition, they can try to emulate the qualities used and the way the different body parts are stressed. While copying movement is always fun for children, it also helps them become more aware of what they are trying to do. This benefit relates more to the child being copied than the child copying, since the one being copied must make all movements to be copied very clear.

In addition to copying movement, other movements that occur at the same time can be contrasting. For example, a child could reach high into the space above him, while another child (or a group) could move low, toward the ground.

Movement in relation to others does not have to occur simultaneously; it can happen successively. Carrying on a conversation in movement exemplifies this type of relationship. The following brief interchange illustrates this point.

> *Child 1* jumps high in the air, lands in a position that is semi-crouched, with a feeling of excitement portrayed through the way he holds his body.
> *Child 2* slowly steps away in an opposite direction with sustained and direct movements; she hesitates and then suddenly curls her entire body, covering her face as well as turning away from Child 1.
> Child 1 releases some of the tension in his body, then advances toward Child 2 slowly, letting his body and arms in particular freely weave through space. Upon reaching Child 2, he takes a position above her, gently encircling her but not touching with his arms.

This type of "conversation" can occur with any number of movers. With too many people, however, the advantages of such an experience may be lost.

Another example of a relationship that involves movement at different times would be individuals in a group, moving one after the other in quick succession. This pattern could occur (1) at the beginning of a group sequence with each individual arriving at a designated spot one after the other; (2) during a sequence when a small movement or gesture is "passed along" through the group; or (3) at the conclusion of a sequence when each member of the group travels back to his starting place at a different time.

When designing experiences that have the relationship concept as their major focus, the teacher must remember their purpose. First, for example, these experiences can orient the children to the fun of working with others, awaken their interest, and let them "feel" the meaning of the relationship. When the children can use basic relationship ideas easily and spontaneously, they can approach relationships at a more complex level through short movement studies or the creation of individual dances.

Sample Learning Experiences

1. By yourself, travel quickly toward someone in the room and stop suddenly; draw away slowly from each other, and then quickly find another person; repeat.
2. In twos, copy each other's body shape every time you hear a drum beat.
3. In twos, carry on a "movement conversation" by first one person moving and then the other reacting. Try to change the levels used and the time, weight, or flow qualities.
4. In a group of three, four, or five keep moving, by passing by one another or moving above, below, behind, or alongside each other.

Discussion. The major purpose of the preceding experiences is "to have fun with others." They should be considered the starting point in helping children learn about others through their movement. Often, at the start of such experiences, children feel self-conscious and silly; they may even laugh and giggle. As the children become more aware of what they are trying to learn and begin to recognize the challenge in the substance of the material, they will settle down and be able to show amazing concentration. The inherent excitement of working with others in movement must be accepted by the teachers and

reflected in the way the class atmosphere is handled. Children are children, and they see working with others in a child-like way.

Experiences such as these can be incorporated into the earlier work when using the content from previous themes. What is known about children who are approximately 5 through 7 years old indicates that they prefer and need to work alone, rather than in relation to each other. They may seek to do things together, but not *in relation* to each other. On the other hand, children may often surprise us with what they are able to do, so there are no hard, fast rules. Observe the children carefully and let their actions help you in the decision-making process.

The next group of learning experiences could be developed into dances or could be considered forerunners of dances. Children who are ready for experiences of this nature have a good movement vocabulary and are able to work productively as members of a group. All examples can be performed with groups of two to five.

Sample Learning Experiences

1. Beginning in a circle, well away from each other, come together, using sudden-firm movements. Hold a group shape; then, mingle in and out; hold a second shape. Part one at a time with sudden quick jumps and turns. Hold shape. Repeat.
2. One person has a tambourine. The group decides the formation to use (e.g., a circle moving in and out, or a straight line in "Indian style"); the group responds freely to the rhythm of the tambourine.
3. Starting together as a group, twist in and out with firm and flexible movements; release tension and establish a group rhythm by rising and sinking with flexible and fine movements. Complete the sequence by moving as a group to a predesignated spot with firm and direct movements.

Discussion. All three examples require that the children be comfortable working in groups and that they have ideas for a variety of individual movements. In addition, their ability to vary qualities of movement must be fairly well developed. If any factors are missing, the teacher can redesign further experiences.

As children begin experiences of this type, they need plenty of time to practice or refine the various sections of the sequence. Various ways of helping them recognize which parts need work are possible, but the children should have the chance to make the decisions if you agree with the approach to physical education taken by this book. This approach does not mean "hands off"; it means helping the children develop their ability in self-assessment. Purposeful dialogue between the teacher and the children should be closely aligned to what is occurring in their work.

Two of these experiences have been designed with no outside rhythm. The only rhythm to be used results from the children's movements; however, adding an accompaniment would be a good variation. An outside person (i.e., another child) or a child within the group could be used. Both cases would probably entail alteration of the original ideas. This variation would add significantly to the experience, as the children would gain additional insight into movement and its relation to rhythm and vice versa.

Identifying a specific theme dealing solely with relationships could be misleading when trying to develop a program of children's dance. Experiences of this nature and of this particular focus need to be blended throughout the program. One of their major uses is to synthesize movement ideas. If they help the children pull together the ideas that they have experienced singly, the experiences gain new meaning for them. Many teachers use this relationship concept in almost every lesson because they value it highly. When this type of experience occurs successfully, teachers can focus on designing relationships that show great complexity and respond to the developmental needs of the children in question.

SPECIAL FORMS OF RELATIONSHIP

Music, poems, props, sound, art work, and percussion instruments can have a place in teaching dance to children. While opinions on how to use them may vary, the predominant reason for their use is to help the children understand a movement idea better as well as have a richer experience. For example, music that is sustained, quiet, and soothing can help children feel more deeply the essence of sustained movement. On the other hand, music that is loud and brisk, when played for a short duration, can help children understand better the energy needed to perform firm, sudden movements.

Similar effects could come from carefully selected poems, sounds, and props. Imagine children trying to keep a sheet of newspaper up in the air with elbows, fists, and knees. They could learn much about their bodies (as well as about the properties of newspaper) and the motion factors of time, weight, space, and flow, particularly sudden, firm, and direct movement. Using sources outside movement itself carries a potential danger. Children can be carried away with the idea and let the movement learnings disappear. In other words, they can forget the reason for using the sheet of newspaper and retain only the idea of hitting the newspaper rather than gaining added insight into knowledge about movement.

Any of the experiences in all the themes thus far considered could profit from using these special forms of relationships. Let your imagination be your guide, with selection based on whether new relationship movements would give children a more meaningful movement experience. Remember that newspapers are not taught; they are used to *help* teach children about movement and ways to move.

SAMPLE UNIT PLAN THEME 5

Themes. Introduction to Relationships—Theme 5 (and selected material from Themes 1 through 4).

Unit Focus. Meeting and parting as it relates to individual body parts and to other persons.

Appropriate For. Children who can work with others and still maintain their concentration and own interest in the task. Their movement vocabulary is steadily improving, but they still have difficulty exploring movement possibilities without teacher help.

Length of Unit. Three 30-minute lessons.

Content

    Body—body parts

    Space—levels

    Effort—time: sudden-sustained

                weight: firm-fine

    Relationship—meeting-parting

Student Objectives. Children should be willing to try to

1. Show relationship of meeting-parting (advancing-retreating with hands as well as other body parts).

A Suggested Progression for Sample Dance Unit/Theme 5

	Lesson 1		Lesson 2		Lesson 3
Tasks	**Teaching Tips**	**Tasks**	**Teaching Tips**	**Tasks**	**Teaching Tips**
1.0	Stress light use of feet and free use of arms and upper body. If necessary, remind them that it is two directions, not just one and then another; e.g., F-B, F-B, or B-F, B-F, or B-S, B-S, etc.	2.0 2.1	Have them start right off. You speak the task as they start. Lively music is helpful.	2.2	Pick new class moves and start right off. By now this should be fun for them and a good way to start. Little explanation should be needed.
1.1	Make body parts clear.	2.2	As soon as they are organized, let them start. Encourage light, free skipping.	3.2	Switch this to threes and again let them start. Stress different levels when meeting, different hand positions (crossed, behind each other).
1.2	Stress careful touching if they choose to do so.	3.1 3.2 3.3	Go into these tasks fairly quickly to see what they remember. Keep stressing key idea in each task. If they do not remember them, go through them again, carefully, giving the children time to be involved.	6.0	This should take the majority of the class time. Let them work on this long enough to gain confidence in how they do it. If all groups have something finished, they could be shown and discussed. If you do this, be sure to finish the class with all groups going through *their* sequence (dance) at least two times without stopping. Stress: concentration and focus on own group's work.
2.0	Light, resilient feet, encourage use of all directions. See Task 1.	4.0	Have them get the feeling back. Stress that they do not repeat the same movements each time they "meet and part." Encourage exploring different ways to travel—you might suggest they change their speed.		
2.1	Easy traveling, do not touch partner—*just up to* her/him.	4.1	When it looks like this would open up new responses, suggest it. Encourage them to try different parts, not always the elbow.		
3.0	As you give them this task, do what you are saying. Then, do it with them, helping them understand the different ways hands can meet (e.g., come together at same time or one and then the other).				
3.1	Have them spread out as they do this. Encourage change in time and weight. Specifically lead them if necessary.				
4.0	Encourage variation after they have "the idea." Remind them about levels, different locomotor patterns as well as body activities (e.g., opening-closing).				

2. Hold concentration when working alone or with others—use eye contact where possible.

3. Observe in others when changes in speed and level of their movement is clear.

Accompaniment. Tambourine, drum, triangle, folk dance records.

Learning Experiences (Tasks)

1.0 Travel freely, skipping, sliding, galloping, throughout the space forward-backward, forward-sideward, sideward right–sideward left or any other combinations of two directions. (Use a skipping rhythm with either a drum, tambourine, folk dance, or popular record to accompany the children.)

1.1 Emphasize elbows, knees, head as you travel.

1.2 Do this with a friend. You may hold onto each other if you can do it gently and it does not change the way you are traveling.

2.0 Pick a spot on the floor. Begin traveling (skipping, galloping, sliding) toward it and away from it. Do this a few times then find another one and travel toward it and away.

2.1 Without saying anything (class is still, well spread out) travel toward another person and away from them; do it again.

2.2 Sit down in groups of three. Learn who is in your group. Scatter all over the room well away from each other. Begin skipping when you hear the drum (or music) and
   a. skip throughout the room "watching your partners;"
   b. skip toward each other (on signal) and meet—almost touching;
   c. skip away and scatter. REPEAT.

3.0 Seated informally fairly close together; using just your hand, find different ways that your hands can come together (meet) and separate (part).

3.1 Bring your hands together and apart, using the space around you, above you, and under you (they will now have to get up): slowly, quickly, firmly, gently.

3.2 Face a partner and let your hands meet (do not touch) and part. As your hands meet, travel some place before you separate.

3.3 Change the level at which your hands meet.

4.0 With a partner, stand about 10 feet away. Using different ways to travel, move toward each other and separate ("meet and part").

4.1 Lead with different body parts as you meet, change and lead with another part as you separate.

5.0 In groups of 4 or 6, begin facing each other about 20 feet away. Select a starting position, and
   a. Advance quickly to the center.
   b. Slowly rise and sink, not all going at the same time.
   c. One at a time suddenly jump away from the group and go back to your starting place and hold your finish.
   (Entire sequence accompanied by teacher: drum to center, triangle for rising and sinking, drum at end, four times.)

6.0 In groups of 6 or 7, facing another group of equal size (20 to 30 feet apart):
   a. Both advance with strong, firm, steps until face to face. Hold still (drum accompaniment).
   b. One group rise suddenly and hold a high, firm shape; other sink suddenly and hold a low, firm shape. Both groups emphasize arms and hands. Keep looking at each other.
   c. Both groups relax tension; come to medium level; with light running steps, go back to starting position, turn suddenly and hold still (groups should be facing each other again).

Evaluation. Refer to Chapter 10 and either select or adapt one of the evaluative tools or develop a tool that can be used to help assess a specific aspect of the unit that is important to the needs of your students.

DANCE THEME 6—INSTRUMENTAL USE OF THE BODY

Theme 6 is the second theme to focus on the use of the body. It expands and refines the work begun in Theme 1 through a more precise look at jumping, at the shape of the body in stillness, and at the movements of the arms and legs in gesturing.

Development of Theme 6

> **Basic Content**
> Jumping: five basic jumps
> Body shape: straight, wide, twisted, round
> Gesture

JUMPING. In Theme 1, the idea of jumping is inherent in the concept of locomotion; however, it is developed in a spontaneous, free way, with little attention to how the feet are used. In fact, all the forms of locomotion (e.g., walking, running, skipping, and stepping) are handled in the same way. The emphasis in Theme 1 is on traveling, covering the space, and using different forms of locomotion naturally and spontaneously—without practicing precise foot patterns.

Jumping, as developed in this theme, focuses on helping children to leave the floor with the intention of traveling upward, into or through the air. In some instances, the movement skill of jumping is considered to have occurred only if the individual lands on both feet. In this theme, jumping is said to happen whenever individuals get into the air no matter what foot pattern they use. There are *five different ways* for individuals to project themselves into the air: (1) from *one foot to the same foot* (1–1s); (2) from *one foot to the other foot* (1–1o); (3) from *one foot to two feet* (1–2); (4) from *two feet to two feet* (2–2); and (5) from *two feet to one foot* (2–1).

Children love to experiment with these jumps and will find many variations if given the time. With enough opportunity to experience these jumps in a variety of situations, children should be able to gain valuable insight into their nature. For example, jumps that use one foot in the takeoff can achieve more height than jumps that begin with two feet. Furthermore, jumps done in double time are bouncy, buoyant, and close to the floor. In triple time, the jumper can go higher as arms and legs have more time to influence the body. For the more advanced children, combining steps and jumps will bring out

many familiar patterns, such as the skip, polka, or set.

Even though Theme 1 focuses on using the basic locomotor patterns, do not hesitate to review them. With new emphasis on the five basic jumps, the children can create many more variations than previously. Adding music, particularly the kind associated with folk dances, enriches these experiences immeasurably.

Sample Learning Experiences

1. Do a series of light, quick jumps, combining at least three different uses of your feet (the children know the five basic foot combinations); use a large amount of space; use a small amount of space.
2. Facing a partner, come together suddenly by running and jumping towards each other—*do not touch*. Hold your shape. Separate by slowly stepping, using forward, backward, and sideward directions. Hold your finish. Repeat.

Discussion. When first working with this idea, the children need time to find out how the different ways of jumping feel. The amount of time depends on the age of the children and their readiness for this type of work. Children thoroughly enjoy this work as it creates a mood of gaiety and freedom; but remember that it can be fatiguing if done too long. Observation and discussion sessions, carefully blended throughout the experiences, can review and summarize what the children are learning. In addition, the lesson will be more balanced between vigorous and less vigorous movement if the children build short dances in which using the jumping ideas are only a part.

All kinds of accompaniment can be used in various ways with these experiences. Music, words, poems, and percussion instruments are possibilities, and either the teacher or the children can use them. Dancing to the rhythmic nature of names, words, and poems has long been a favorite of children, and the focus of these experiences lends itself naturally to this activity. In addition, children find new meaning in these jumping variations when accompanying themselves with drums, rhythm sticks, tambourines, small cymbals, and rattles.

Children enjoy the music of folk dances and respond easily to their lively nature. By this time, the children should be free and skillful in the way they use their feet, so they can respond spontaneously to the folk tunes. As they become more familiar with the tunes, they can begin responding to the phrasing and then possibly developing short sequences. Depending on the children, these sequences can be designed by small groups or by themselves.

Whether to take this work into the teaching of folk dances depends on the children's ability. Most folk dances have such complicated movement patterns representative of a country's culture that they prove to be too difficult for many children. Although eager and willing to try them at first, the children often become rigid, making it impossible for them to catch the meaning and significance of the dance. If you teach specific folk dances, choose the simpler ones in which the children can take part with confidence and ease.

BODY SHAPE. All movement has shape, and the shape of the body is particularly noticeable when it is completely still. The material considered thus far, while not directly focused on the shape of the body, has been indirectly related. For example, whenever the children are working with activities such as rising-sinking or opening-closing, shapes that are *straight*, *wide*, or *round* result. *Twisted* shapes appear with a flexible, indirect use of space (Theme 4).

The emphasis of this work is on helping children sharpen or heighten their awareness for the shape of the body, primarily through improving their ability to achieve stillness. In complete stillness, the children have a greater opportunity to become aware of the relationships among their body parts. In concentrating more on stillness as a "movement" itself, the ability to balance becomes an additional focus of importance. To maintain a good position of balance, children must become increasingly aware of producing the right amount of muscular tension. Early experiences that focus on achieving stillness and balance have some similarities in both gymnastics and dance, in that they help children become more aware of what it takes to achieve complete stillness. Depending on the direction of the program, there are a variety of ways to take advantage of this situation.

The four basic shapes are straight, or arrowlike; round, or ball-like; wide, or wall-like; and twisted, or screw-like. In working with shape as material, do not perceive yourself as "teaching shapes" and do not have the children perceive themselves as "making shapes" because working this way often results in artificial posing. If the children have a rich movement vocabulary, merely having them "stop" and "go" should bring about a variety of shapes. By asking questions relevant to the concept of shape, you are providing the foundation for subsequent experiences.

Sample Learning Experiences
1. Travel quickly and stop—hold your shape very still; make it very clear. Change it slowly; hold. Repeat.
2. On the signal (gong, triangle, drum, hand clap), change the shape of your body as well as its level. Sometimes show round, twisted, straight, or wide shapes. Make the position of your hands, arms, and legs clear. Do this while traveling. (Have one "sound" meaning to travel and one "sound" meaning to change shape. Remember to vary the type of sounds used so you can have children vary the way they use time, weight, space, and flow.)

Discussion. There are two different ways to implement these experiences. In the first way, the teacher (or child) gives an outside signal; in the second, the movers stop themselves. Both are effective, with the second one placing greater responsibility on the learner. In both situations, either vocal or instrumental signals are possibilities, e.g., a single short sound or a series of sounds ended abruptly.

As the different shapes begin to appear, questions and comments by the teacher can help the children learn what the different shapes are and identify what relationships are occurring among their body parts. For example, a question relating to the type of shape would be "Is your shape a twisted one or a straight one?" In addition to asking about the type of shape, the teacher might ask whether it is symmetrical or asymmetrical. In fact, these concepts can be used most effectively as content themselves, especially when focusing on relationships between body parts. Further questions might relate to where different body parts are placed: "Are they near, far apart, or alongside each other?"

Having the children change their position every time they hear a signal offers an interesting variation. Using an instrument that has an "after sound," like a gong or triangle, offers children the possibility of experiencing a sudden shift of position followed by a slow, easy settling into a new one. This type of experience can help children obtain a good feeling for stillness and an awareness of position and shape.

In addition to working alone, children can create group shapes designed in a number of ways and with groups of various sizes. Most experiences can use the basic relationship patterns discussed in Theme 5; then the groups stop their movement and try to achieve stillness, as in the following examples.

1. *In groups of three, four, or five:* using sudden, quick, lively jumps, move toward the center, one at a time. When you reach the center, *stop,* and hold your position until everyone else is there. Repeat to return to your starting place.

2. *In groups of three:* slowly approach each other with fine-sustained movements. Upon reaching each other, twist in and out of the group (mingle) and *hold* very still when you hear the gong. Then with quick, sudden movements, go back to your original place, and when you get there, hold your final position very still.

Both experiences use the basic relationship pattern of meeting and parting but with variations in how the children get there, what they do when they arrive, and how they return to their starting points. By concentrating on stillness and position in experiences of this nature and in those already discussed, the children's ability to show clarity in their movement should improve greatly.

GESTURE. As content, gesture or gesturing relates closely to the emphasis on individual body parts introduced in Theme 1. In essence, gesturing is *shaping movements in the air with those body parts not supporting any weight.* An example would be someone bringing his hands together while his weight is supported on the knees. As pointed out earlier, the rhythm created by gesturing is nonmetric and cannot be measured as can the metric rhythm created by the use of feet.

Gestures can be made with many parts of the body, but the legs and arms are the easiest and the best for children to use because they have the greatest range of motion as well as having individual parts that can be stressed alone and in combination.

Gesturing as an idea is not new; it has been an integral part of many experiences previously discussed. After specifically focusing on it and body shape together, the children should have increased clarity of movement. In the previous concept of gesture, emphasis was on making body parts "important." Being able to add the basic relationship concepts *plus* ideas from past themes can give the experiences many new directions.

Sample Learning Experiences
1. Travel by running, spinning, and jumping. Stop and gesture with arms. Follow your hand (or hands) with your eyes. Repeat, changing the gesture each time. Concentrate on the flow of the movement, making it continuous and on the levels at which it occurs (high, medium, low).
2. Select different parts of the body to support your weight; then explore the kinds of gestures possible with the free parts. Develop a sequence: take a still position; gesture; change position; gesture. Repeat.
3. Design a short sequence with at least two others in which the use of the arms, elbows, and hands plays a dominant role.

Discussion. The children's movement vocabulary should be such that they have little difficulty taking any task designed from these ideas and exploring all the variations. As the children focus on gesturing, be careful not to let them lose the idea that individual body parts can lead a movement as well. The end of a gesture (e.g., a gathering movement of one arm coming across the body) might lead or be the stimulus for the next movement (e.g., a turn of the body followed by traveling). As you become more and more familiar with this content and the ways to develop it with children, you may wish to introduce this particular aspect earlier; however, concentrated work on positioning and repositioning (gesturing) of body parts is quite advanced.

Of all the possibilities, the arms are the natural body parts for gesture. Their positioning, with the help of the shoulders, trunk, and head, can influence the balance of the body over the legs. In the second learning experience, this idea has been somewhat reversed by suggesting that the body's weight is supported by parts other than the legs. In this situation, both the legs and arms are used to gesture. The experiences suggested have been chosen to give children an opportunity to experiment fully with the idea of gesture. They need to realize that the arms will probably be used predominantly, but other parts, although not quite so natural, are equally important and also need to be used.

As stated in the beginning of this theme, Themes 1 and 6 are closely related. Both focus on the development of the body. Theme 1 being more introductory in nature and Theme 6 more advanced. In addition, Theme 6 begins to emphasize the process of refinement—helping the children bring greater clarity and shape to their movement.

SAMPLE UNIT PLAN THEME 6

Themes. Instrumental use of the Body—Theme 6 (and selected material from Themes 1 through 5).

Unit Focus. Clarifying shape of the body alone and in relation to a group.

Appropriate For. Children who are familiar with the content from earlier themes and who can improvise it; they know how to explore the movement possibilities of their body without constant direction from the teacher.

Length of Unit. Four 30-minute lessons.

Content

> Body—shapes, traveling (all forms)
> Space—general, levels
> Effort—time: slow, quick
> Relationship—meeting; parting; successive; simultaneous; copying

Student Objectives. Children should be willing to try to

1. Show clearly a variety of body shapes, using different levels in space, alone and in a group.

2. Contribute ideas in a group setting when designing a short movement sequence.

3. Hold their concentration when working on their own and when in a group; can focus on themselves in both situations.

4. Know why working at all levels will help their ability to find new and different body shapes.

Teaching Area. Indoors: large or small.

Accompaniment. Tambourine, drum, and other percussion instruments.

Learning Experiences (Tasks)
1.0 Without traveling, explore all the twisted shapes you can make with your body.
1.1 Explore all the rounded shapes.
1.2 Explore all the angular shapes.
1.3 Explore all the wide and narrow shapes.

	Lesson 1		Lesson 2
Tasks	**Teaching Tips**	**Tasks**	**Teaching Tips**
1.0 1.1 1.2 1.3	Allow them to find different shapes on their own. If needed, you could suggest using different levels; this should bring out additional responses.	1.4	Stress concentration on task. Make clear the change in speed just before a shape is held. (Speed change should occur between body shapes.)
3.0 3.1 3.2	Repeat these tasks enough times to give children time to find different "low, wide" shapes. Let them do it on their own time, no tambourine.	2.0 2.1	Help them focus and stay on task. Stress that they should experiment without talking except if absolutely necessary.
4.0	Help them find different ways to interpret the task. Stress that they should keep changing (improvising) methods of traveling and shapes.	5.0	Stress not to look for partner, but sense his/her presence—*no touching* (implies slow, careful stepping).
4.1	Make sure they know what to do and are safe. Let them freely play with their idea. Observe carefully their responses to help you assess progress in their ability to improvise.	5.1	You make up one, or let children suggest one. Be sure it is logical and relates to previous work.

1.4 Explore making different shapes with your body, changing the speed at which you move into them.

1.5 Play follow the leader with 1.4.

2.0 In threes, make different group shapes that stress "twistedness" (no traveling).

2.1 In threes, make different group shapes that stress "roundedness," "angularness," "wideness," and "narrowness." (2.1 is really *four* tasks.)

3.0 Travel quickly to an open space and hold a high, wide shape; go in a new direction and repeat. (Quick shaking of the tambourine during the run and a firm sharp hit when you want them to hold will help give the children the feel of the rhythm.)

    3.1 . . . a low wide shape

    3.2 . . . a medium wide shape

    3.3+ . . . tasks designed to include types of shapes as well as level in space.

4.0 Alone and on your own time (or accompanying yourself with a percussion instrument) travel and stop, changing your method of traveling (skip, jump, step, etc.) and the shape of your body when still (twisted, rounded, etc.).

4.1 In groups of four or five, and with a drum or tambourine, travel as a group (skipping or jumping), and on the sound of the drum, face each other and form a group shape. Do not plan the shapes, just let them "happen," being sensitive to where you are in space and where other people are. Repeat.

4.2 Instead of traveling together as a group,

travel all over the room. On the signal, come toward each other and make a group shape. Repeat.

5.0 In twos or threes, begin facing away from each other about 10 feet apart. Slowly come together, without looking, using sustained careful stepping actions. Feel when you are near, then suddenly face each other and create a group shape that shows clearly both high and low levels and is characterized by angular shapes of your body and body parts.

5.1 Repeat basic actions (travel and make shape), but design new tasks, changing the method of traveling and nature of shape. (Use material from earlier themes.)

5.2 Using the same idea, begin away from each other. Travel to meet, making a clear shape together, but change your starting position (back to back, one in front of the other, etc.), methods of traveling, and nature of shapes. Focus on changing one idea at a time.

5.3 Select a sequence you like and practice it, making clear all shapes of your body (beginning position, during traveling, and final shape).

6.0 In groups of six or seven, facing a designated spot (as a group) or facing inward toward the center of the space (in a circle). One child with a drum or tambourine who plays the accompaniment throughout (may participate with group or may choose not to).

    a. One at a time, quickly travel to des-

Sample Dance Unit/Theme 6

	Lesson 3		Lesson 4
Tasks	**Teaching Tips**	**Tasks**	**Teaching Tips**
1.4 1.5	Have them choose, alone or with a partner. Stress clarity in whatever shapes they choose (wide, narrow, twisted, etc.). You should be able to tell shape type by observing; if this is not clear, go back to tasks 1.0 to 1.3.	3.3	Design a task that has in it specific shapes and levels with which they need practice. This information will be available at the end of Lesson 3.
5.0	Have them do what they did in the previous lesson, stressing clear levels and angular body shapes. See if children can use more body parts in angular shapes.	6.0	Take a group and walk them through it to show class basic idea. Make sure all groups know what they are going to work on. Go around after all groups are focused, and give individual help. Focus the children on starting position (clear? are you concentrating?), order of moving (clear?), clear rhythm (practice with child if necessary), interrelatedness and clarity of group shape, clear, *still* ending position. Group shape may need help in getting level contrasts—children tend to stay at the level of first child.
5.2	Explain clearly that the outline or structure of the task is the *same,* only now they can select different starting positions, etc. Support them while they make these decisions. Take one idea at a time.		
5.3	Only move on to this if you have at least 10 minutes. Stress the refinement process, what it means. Tell them they will finish next lesson.		

ignated spot and make a clear shape. (As other children come toward shape, stress that they should relate their shape to one already there. No touching.)

b. When group shape is complete, all move slowly into the same shape. (Children pick one, e.g., tall with arms outstretched in a "V" position, heads up.)

c. Return to starting place in same order and in same manner. Hold finish position.

Evaluation. Refer to Chapter 10 and either select or adapt one of the evaluative tools or develop a tool that can be used to help assess a specific aspect of the unit that is important to the needs of your students.

DANCE THEME 7—THE BASIC EFFORT ACTIONS

Theme 7 continues the emphasis begun in Themes 2 and 4 on the effort aspect of movement. When looking at the three themes in order—Theme 2, Theme 4, and Theme 7—consider them as a progression, with each theme focusing on a further distinction of the quality in movement. Whereas Themes 2 and 4 clarify two motion factors within the same movement, Theme 7 clarifies the three motion factors of time, weight, and space within the same movement. The result is termed an action—an effort action. When these three motion factors have been combined in all possible ways, eight basic

effort actions result. All movement contains them, or variations of them, and the purpose of Theme 7 is to gain skill in their use. These effort actions are called thrusting, slashing, floating, gliding, wringing, pressing, flicking, and dabbing.

The format used for discussing the effort actions is similar to that used in Theme 4 when presenting the various combinations of motion factors. In discussing these actions, there is a brief orientation highlighting the essence and structure of each. After all the effort actions have been presented, suggestions for teaching effort actions to children are given and discussed. The development of this material was influenced by the work of Preston–Dunlop.[4]

Development of Theme 7

Basic Content	
Thrusting	Wringing
Slashing	Pressing
Floating	Flicking
Gliding	Dabbing

THRUSTING. Movements that are *sudden, firm,* and *direct* are called thrusting actions. They are vigorous, powerful, forceful, and energetic. Punching gestures of the arms, knees, and elbows and stamping of the feet are examples.

SLASHING. Slashing actions are similar to thrusting actions in that they are *sudden* and *firm.* Their difference lies in the way they use space. A slash uses space in an *indirect* way, and a thrust uses space in a direct way. When slashing, arms and legs whip about the body causing it to twist and turn, whereas when thrusting, the body remains fixed and firm as arms and legs penetrate the space with quick, sharp, punchlike movements.

FLOATING. Floating movements are sensitive, gentle, buoyant, and soothing and use the motion factors of time, weight, and space in a *sustained*, *fine*, and *indirect* way. Using space this way causes the body to twist and turn, and the arms and legs to move freely in the surrounding space.

GLIDING. The gliding action maintains the same serene and quiet mood as did the floating action, but again the space factor is used differently. Where floating movements are roundabout, causing twisting and turning of the body, gliding movements are direct and cut sharply through the space. Movements that are *sustained*, *fine*, and *direct* are considered to be gliding actions. When gliding is continued over any length of time, a feeling of inner peace and quietness develops.

Gliding and floating are related in the same way as are thrusting and slashing: both use time and weight in the same way but differ in the way they use space; however, the relationship between gliding and floating and thrusting and slashing is quite different. Thrusting and floating are complete opposites as are slashing and gliding: each pair uses the motion factors of time, weight, and space in totally opposite ways. Figure 6–2 illustrates this relationship.

WRINGING. Wringing actions are *sustained*, *firm*, and *indirect*. They are powerful, twisted, knotted, and askew. They are mainly created by the shoulders and hips moving in opposition and toward each other. Arms, in particular when the elbows lead the movement, play a major role in producing the twisting, undulating movement so characteristic of wringing.

PRESSING. When the twisting, undulating use of space so evident in wringling changes to a direct penetrating use, the action of pressing results. As in wringing, pressing uses *sustained*, *firm* movement, but it uses space *directly.* The feeling expressed by the pressing action is one of sustained power and deliberate force.

FLICKING. Flicking movements are frisky, lively, spirited, and bubbly and use *sudden*, *fine*, and *indirect* movements. Lively hops, springy jumps, and hands fluttering all about the surrounding space are examples of this action. The feeling or mood associated with these movements is excitedness, playfulness, and gaiety.

DABBING. Where flicking uses the surrounding space freely and abundantly, dabbing does just the opposite: it uses space sparingly and economically. Dabbing actions are *sudden*, *fine*, and *direct*. To experience dabbing, the body must move in a dart-like fashion, quickly to one spot and then quickly to another, punctuated by sudden pointed movements of the hands, feet, knees, and elbows. The whole body gives a feeling of being alert, ready and poised for quick action.

The relationship between wringing and pressing and flicking and dabbing is similar to the relationship between thrusting and slashing and floating and gliding: they use time and weight in the same manner but differ in the use of space. As with the first four effort actions discussed, the relationship between wringing and dabbing and pressing and flicking is completely opposite

Action	Time	Weight	Space
Thrusting and Floating	Sudden | Sustained	Firm | Fine	Direct | Indirect
Slashing and Gliding	Sudden | Sustained	Firm | Fine	Indirect | Direct

Fig. 6–2. Relationship Between Thrusting and Floating and Slashing and Gliding.

Action	Time	Weight	Space
Wringing and Dabbing	Sustained | Sudden	Firm | Fine	Indirect | Direct
Pressing and Flicking	Sustained | Sudden	Firm | Fine	Direct | Indirect

Fig. 6–3. Relationship Between Wringing and Dabbing and Pressing and Flicking.

Action	Time	Weight	Space
Thrusting	Sudden	Firm	Direct
Slashing	Sudden	Firm	Indirect
Floating	Sustained	Fine	Indirect
Gliding	Sustained	Fine	Direct
Wringing	Sustained	Firm	Indirect
Pressing	Sustained	Firm	Direct
Flicking	Sudden	Fine	Indirect
Dabbing	Sudden	Fine	Direct

Fig. 6–4. The Eight Basic Effort Actions.

in the way the motion factors of time, weight, and space are used. Figure 6–3 summarizes this relationship.

In summary, the emphasis of Theme 7 is on a more differentiated use of quality in movement by stressing clarification of the motion factors of time, weight, and space in the same movement. When making all the combinations among these actions, eight basic effort actions result. Figure 6–4 summarizes these actions and identifies for each the manner in which the motion factors of time, weight, and space are used.

When teaching the basic actions to children, no matter how carefully you plan the experience, they may have difficulty with it. When teaching effort actions, you have probably given too much at once, and the children are having trouble clearly differentiating all the motion factors at the same time. Alter the way the effort action is taught so that it *gradually* emerges. In other words, the children should experience each effort action separately, and then take the entire action. For example, if thrusting is the effort action being taught, the first movements of the children could focus on the sudden aspect (e.g., quick, lively jumps). Then, they might be asked to do movements that are firm (e.g., stamping into the ground with the feet or piercing the air with fists, knees, or elbows). With this last experience, the children are close to thrusting; in fact, all they need is a clarification of the way they are using the space. To be a thrusting action, the space must be used in a sharp, pointed way with all movements piercing and cutting the air decisively

Sample Learning Experiences
1. *EFFORT ACTIONS:* Thrusting (sudden, firm, direct), and Floating (sustained, fine, and indirect).

Move with strong, vigorous, and powerful movements, piercing the space all about you (thrusting); contrast this with easy, gentle, twisting, and spiraling movements (floating).

2. *EFFORT ACTIONS:* Pressing (sustained, firm, direct) and Flicking (sudden, fine, indirect).

Begin by moving on the spot, using palms, different surfaces of the arms and legs, and the soles of your feet, with slow, strong, penetrating movements (pressing); contrast this with quick, lively, sparkly jumping, turning, and twisting movements (flicking).

3. *EFFORT ACTIONS:* Gliding (sustained, fine, direct) and Floating (sustained, fine, indirect).

Penetrate the space about you with slow, gentle, and delicate movements (gliding). Change the way you are using space to one in which you use it more freely: use it in a roundabout twisting way (floating); traveling or on the spot.

When appropriate, all the above experiences could be expanded to include material from past themes. For example, use of different body shapes could be stressed, or directions in traveling, or levels of the movement, or pathways, or the size of the movement. Be careful when considering this, for combining more than one movement idea often makes the task too difficult for many children.

Discussion. The first sample learning experience approaches the teaching of effort actions by focusing on paired opposites, in this sample, thrusting and floating. No specific reference is made to body activities or the use of individual body parts; however, while the children are working, it may be necessary to redesign the experience to include one or both of these aspects.

The second learning experience again focuses on effort actions that are paired opposites: pressing and flicking. The manner in which the experience is designed differs from the first in that it reaches the effort actions through the use of body activities and body parts. When introducing pressing, it is suggested that the movement be tried with ". . . palms, different surfaces of the arms and legs, and the soles of the feet." Jumping and turning movements are suggested as movements through which flicking might be experienced. With experiences of this nature, the children may have difficulty in directing themselves to use all the ideas suggested. If so, the experiences may have to be redesigned so the children have less to think about at one time.

The effort actions in the third experience use the motion factors of time and weight in the same manner, but use the space factor differently. The experience begins with the children working with gliding, and then, while maintaining the sustained and fine quality to their movement, they are asked to use the space freely in a ". . . roundabout, twisting way." From using the space in this roundabout, free way, the children would again change and use the space as before, in a direct manner. As in the first experience, the teaching of the effort actions is approached directly—through the actions themselves.

When teaching the effort actions, and approaching them through body activities, certain activities have a natural relation to particular effort actions. Jumping can be used readily with thrusting, slashing, flicking, and dabbing actions, whereas turning can be used with all the effort actions that use space in an indirect and flexible way: slashing, wringing, flicking, and floating. Locomotor patterns, such as stepping, can be used to help experience gliding when the steps are slow and the pathway straight. Thrusting actions in the legs result when firm, strong steps are taken. Traveling movements that are quick and emphasize twisted, curved pathways lead to flicking; if the speed of travel changes, floating results. To get a feel for pressing in the legs, the children can make deep stepping movements in all directions. Gesturing can accompany all effort actions but particularly floating and flicking.

When working with content of this nature, which is part of the most advanced theme, the development of sequences and dances of varying lengths is considered an integral part of the process of designing learning experiences. The following sequences could be done by children individually or in groups of two, three, four, or five.

1. Two children work together in a question-answer pattern where one is the "flicker" and the other the "presser."

2. A group of five children could meet together with thrusting movements; mingle, using floating movements; and part, one after the other, with flicking movements.

3. A group of children could be given the relationship pattern of meeting, circling, mingling, and parting with the choice left up to them as to which effort actions they would use. This situation could also be reversed; the effort actions would be predesignated, and the children's task would be to decide the relationship patterns.

Percussion rhythms are excellent stimuli when working with effort actions, alone or in combinations. For example, a sequence of two short flicking actions, followed by a series of flicks and a long press, could be accompanied by a bell and a drum or a tambourine used in two different ways. In addition, the percussion instruments can be played by the children when they are dancing. Within a class, one group could do a "flicking" dance, another a "thrusting" dance, and another a "floating" and "dabbing" dance. Each group would have the appropriate instruments to accompany its dance.

In designing experiences where the emphasis is on the eight basic effort actions, care must be taken not to be preoccupied with them in "name" only and to remember that the purpose behind studying them is advanced work in differentiating the quality in movement. If the material in Themes 2 and 4 is well developed, there should be little difficulty. If the effort actions are introduced too soon, however, meaningless experiences can often result. Through the work with effort, children's ability to express through movement, ideas, feelings, and moods should be greatly enhanced.

SAMPLE UNIT PLAN THEME 7

Themes. The Basic Effort Actions—Theme 7 (and selected material from Themes 1 through 6).

Unit Focus. Thrusting, slashing, floating, gliding.

Appropriate For. Children who are ready to handle three motion factors, time, weight, and space, in the *same* movement. Their movement vocabulary is good and they can work on tasks that have a range of decision-making ability without constant teacher help.

Length of Unit. Three 30-minute lessons.
Content
      Body—traveling/nontraveling actions of
        choice
      Space—levels, general

A Suggested Progression for Sample Dance/Unit Theme 7

Lesson 1		Lesson 2		Lesson 3	
Tasks	**Teaching Tips***	**Tasks**	**Teaching Tips***	**Tasks**	**Teaching Tips***
1.0	Encourage movements that are short in duration. Sudden = over in a flash. Look for use of all these levels. Sustained movements can be longer. (Design yourself an appropriate accompaniment. Drum for sudden, firm and triangle for sustained and fine are good.)	4.1} 4.2} 5.1} 5.2}	See what they remember. State the effort action and see what results. Stress concentration on *own* work. After observing responses from 4.1–5.2, select from 1.0–3.1 those tasks needed to bring clarity to sudden, sustained, firm or fine quality.	4.1} 4.2} 5.1} 5.2}	Encourage children to practice on their own. If this does not work at the start, you suggest which effort action and accompany them. They should be getting familiar with them.
1.1	Encourage focused work.	4.1} 4.2} 5.1} 5.2}	Let them try again. Observe and stress use of space (quality).	4.3	Set up rhythms like THRUST THRUST SLASH, stop; repeat. Keep stressing the three qualities: use of time, weight, and space.
1.0} 1.1}	You will need to go back. They need this work as a base for the rest of the lesson. Getting the qualities is important.	4.3} 5.3}	Stress just trying to do this; it is very difficult. Some children might like to "show" their attempts to see if others can guess.	5.3	Set up rhythm—FLOAT, FLOAT, GLIDE. Again stress qualities.
2.0} 2.1}	Stress that they are trying to use very little space.			6.0 or 6.1	Allow the majority of class time for this. Help children make decisions and after they have made them and begun work, observe for clarity in the three factors within the effort actions chosen. Help groups or entire class whenever you think it is needed. Tasks 1.0–3.1 are always useful. Have groups or individuals perform their sequences at least twice through before ending; half at a time (others could look for effort actions) or all together.
3.0} 3.1}	Stress the opposite, use *lots* of space, freely.				
4.0	Stress the quickness and the firmness; use of space.				
4.1	Stress the direct use of space. Stress it but do not worry if they cannot get it right away. It will come.				
4.2	Stress indirectness, the flexible use of space.				
5.0} 5.1} 5.2}	Same as in 4.0, 4.1, and 4.2. Help them if they forget the delicateness of fine and ongoingness of sustained.				

*Whenever specific body actions need to be stressed (i.e., children's movement shows no variation), to enrich their work, do so. Suggest specific locomotor activities (run, skip, step, jump) and nonlocomotor activities (open-close, rise-sink), and use of specific body parts (elbows, knees, heads).

Effort—time: sudden-sustained
weight: firm-fine
space: direct-indirect
Relationship—

Student Objectives. Children should be willing to try to

1. Show the difference between thrusting and slashing, and gliding and floating.

2. Know the differences between thrusting and slashing, gliding and floating, thrusting and floating, and slashing and floating.

3. Describe how they feel when thrusting, slashing, floating, and gliding.

Teaching Area. Indoors: large or small; blackboard.

Accompaniment. Tambourine, drum, triangle, Listen More and Dance Volumes 1 to 11,[6] teacher's voice.

Learning Experiences (Tasks)

1.0 Using your arms, hands, legs, feet make sudden, firm movements. Use high, medium, low levels (teacher accompanies this with drum, tambourine, or voice); then, contrast this with sustained, fine movements.

1.1 With no accompaniment, keep working: sudden, firm movements followed by sustained, fine.

2.0 Standing or walking, have your hands and arms cut through, penetrate, the space in front of you, behind you, to your sides (space quality—direct). Use finger tips, edge of hands, elbows to initiate movement.

2.1 Rise and sink as you continue to use the space in this manner (travel).

3.0 Standing or walking, using hands and arms, cut through the space above you, below you, in front of you, and at your sides in free, weaving patterns. Circle, twist, weave your hands in and out of the space.

3.1 Rise and sink as you keep using the space in this indirect, flexible manner (travel).

4.0 Again, using your arms, hands, legs, elbows, heads, do a series of sudden firm movements.

4.1 Now, let us clarify the space. Do the *same* or similar movements but *add* a direct use of space. Your movements should feel and look *sudden*, *firm*, and *direct*. This is THRUSTING.

4.2 Same as 4.1 but add an indirect use of space. Your movements should feel and look *sudden*, *firm*, and *flexible*. This is SLASHING.

4.3 Try to THRUST and SLASH.

5.0 Traveling (walking is good to start with), use arms, hands, knees, feet, showing a sustained and fine quality to your work.

5.1 As you are traveling, use space in a *straight*, *direct*, *penetrating* way. This is GLIDING.

5.2 Now use the space in a flexible, roundabout way. This is FLOATING.

5.3 Try to GLIDE then FLOAT.

6.0 Alone, make up a short sequence that
   a. has a clear starting position and ending position;
   b. has THRUSTING *or* SLASHING, *and* GLIDING *or* FLOATING;
   c. has traveling in two different directions. You may use outside accompaniment or you may not.

6.1 Same, but with two or three in the group.

Evaluation. Refer to Chapter 10 and either select or adapt one of the evaluative tools or develop a tool that can be used to help assess a specific aspect of the unit that is important to the needs of your students.

PROGRESSION

The acceptance and use of Laban's first seven themes (with slight modifications) as a means for organizing the dance content entail certain ideas about progression, which were examined carefully in the introductory part of this section. Additional points will be made in relation to their actual application.

Even though these themes are considered progressive in nature and the key ideas are clearly identified within each one, teachers must always be ready to respond to the emerging situation with any variation of progression that seems necessary, yet appropriate. Being open, ready, and able to change the experience is a major characterstic of a child-oriented program.

By organizing the content into themes, Laban intended to give teachers a set of guidelines, not a rigid prescription. He never implied that they must be firmly followed, nor did he expect children to "master" all aspects of a theme before working on material from the next theme. Rather, he encouraged an easy shifting between

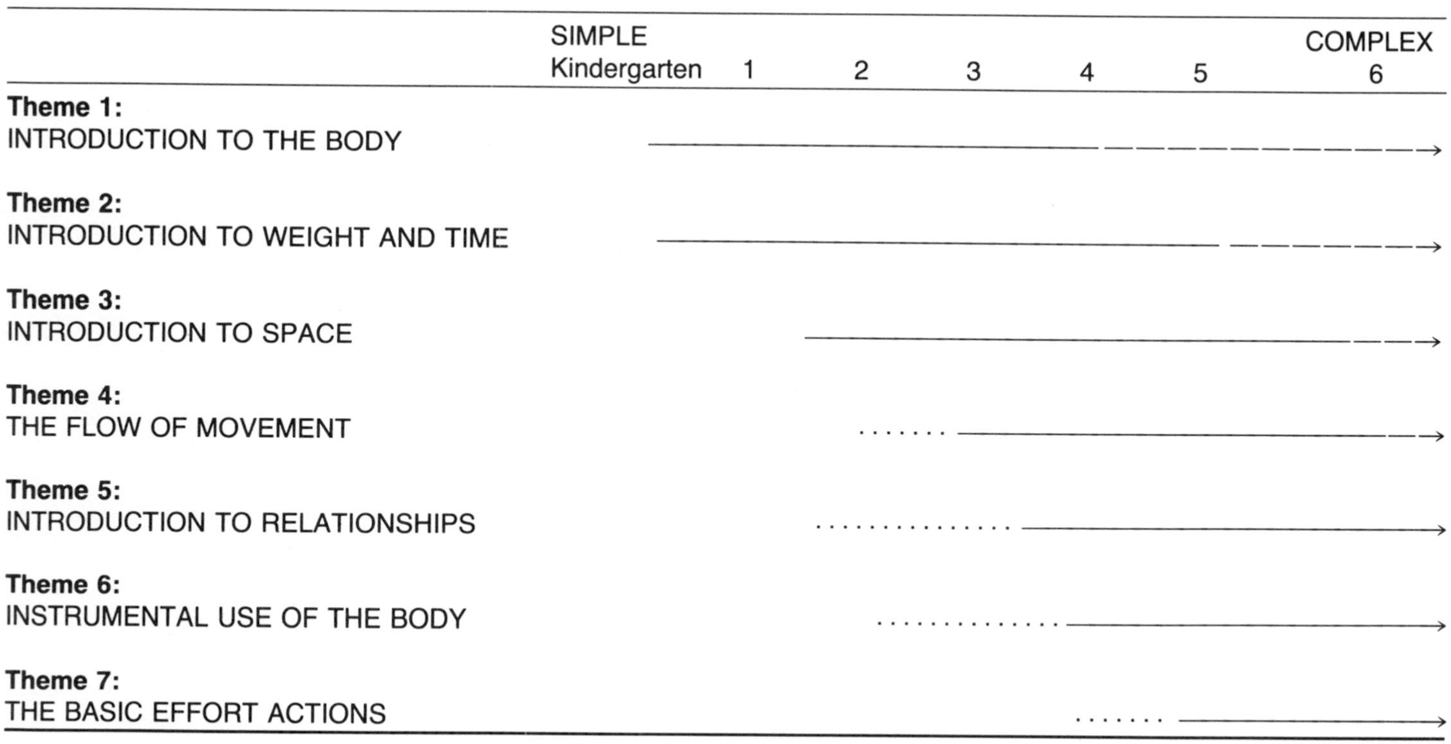

	SIMPLE					COMPLEX
	Kindergarten 1	2	3	4	5	6

Theme 1:
INTRODUCTION TO THE BODY

Theme 2:
INTRODUCTION TO WEIGHT AND TIME

Theme 3:
INTRODUCTION TO SPACE

Theme 4:
THE FLOW OF MOVEMENT

Theme 5:
INTRODUCTION TO RELATIONSHIPS

Theme 6:
INSTRUMENTAL USE OF THE BODY

Theme 7:
THE BASIC EFFORT ACTIONS

Fig. 6–5. Theme Progression for Educational Dance Program.

and among themes so the best possible experiences could result. Each of the seven themes was discussed with this idea in mind. Careful study will show that in almost all the experiences suggested, both in the themes and in the planning guides, this interrelation of material from more than one theme is present.

Figure 6–5 represents a dance program that begins in the kindergarten and continues through the sixth grade. The suggested use of themes is based on a physical education instructional program in which educational dance is approximately one third of the total program. To show the flexible nature of these suggested progressions, the themes have been coded in a special way. The solid lines indicate when a theme may be most important in the development of a lesson or a series of lessons. The broken lines connote times when the material may still be appropriate but is used less frequently. The dotted lines suggest times for presenting material from more advanced themes to increase the complexity in some experiences. In other words, while a general thematic progression is suggested, its effectiveness depends on each teacher's ability to sense when to alter it for the benefit of the children.

REFERENCES

1. Fleming, G.A. (ed.): Children's Dance. Washington, D.C., American Association for Health, Physical Education, and Recreation, 1973.
2. Russell, J.: Creative Movement and Dance for Children, 2nd ed. London, Macdonald & Evans, 1975.
3. Laban, R.: Modern Educational Dance, 2nd ed. Revised by L. Ullman. New York, Frederick A. Praeger, 1963.
4. Preston–Dunlop, V.: A Handbook for Modern Educational Dance, 2nd ed. Boston, Plays, Inc., 1980.
5. Murray, R.L.: Dance in Elementary Education, 3rd ed. New York, Harper & Row, 1975.
6. Gray, V.: Listen, Move and Dance. Vols. I and II. Capitol Recordings.

SELECTED READING

AAHPERD: Elementary Curriculum: Theory and Practice—Educational Dance. Reston, VA, AAHPERD, 1982.
Bartenieff, I., with Lewis D.: Body Movement. New York; Gordon and Breach Science Publishers, 1980.
Boorman, J.: Creative Dance in the First Three Grades. Ontario, Longmans Canada, Ltd., 1969.
Boorman, J.: Creative Dance in Grades 4–6. Ontario, Longmans Canada, Ltd., 1971.
Dell, C.: A Primer for Movement Description, 2nd ed. New York, Dance Notation Bureau Press, 1977.
Department of Education and Science: Movement Physical Education in the Primary Years. London, Her Majesty's Stationery Office, 1972.
Fleming, G.A. (ed.): Children's Dance. Washington, D.C., American Association for Health, Physical Education, and Recreation, 1973.
————: Creative Rhythmic Movement. Englewood Cliffs, New Jersey, Prentice-Hall, 1976.
Laban, R.: Modern Educational Dance, 2nd ed. Revised by L. Ullman. New York, Frederick A. Praeger, 1963.
McKittrick, D.: Schooling in the Middle Years—Dance. Basingstoke, Macmillan Education Ltd., 1972.
Murray, R.: Dance in Elementary Education, 3rd ed. New York, Harper & Row, 1975.
North, M.: Movement Education. London, Temple–Smith, 1973.
Preston–Dunlop, V.: A Handbook for Modern Educational Dance, 2nd ed. Boston, Plays, Inc., 1980.
Russell, J.: Creative Movement and Dance for Children, 2nd ed. London, Macdonald & Evans, 1975.
Stanley, S.: Physical Education—A Movement Orientation, 2nd ed. Toronto, McGraw-Hill Co. of Canada, 1977.

Chapter 7

Educational Games

KATE R. BARRETT

The approach to teaching games is called educational games because it is committed to HELPING ALL CHILDREN TRY TO REACH THEIR FULL POTENTIAL AS SKILLFUL GAMES PLAYERS and ACCOMMODATING THEIR INDIVIDUAL DIFFERENCES. Helping *all* children means meeting the needs of the gifted and talented, the slow learner, the less mature, the handicapped, the culturally deprived, the motivated, the disinterested, and the average. Accommodating their individual differences means knowing about development—motor, cognitive, perceptual, affective, psychosocial—as it applies to *teaching children*.

Currently, many physical educators are renewing their efforts to change the teaching of games in school physical education programs and sport programs for children. All such efforts center around commitments similar to those expressed above, a sincere desire to reach more

children and release their individual potential for learning. The approach taken in this book is one such approach.

TERMINOLOGY
Game
Game-like experience
Game form: conventional, original
Skillful games player

In this chapter, a GAME is being defined as *an activity in which one or more children engage in competitive or cooperative play with a moving object within the framework of certain rules.* GAMES are unique in that the environment in which they are played is always changing—it is *dynamic*, not static. A GAME-LIKE experience is a task (or learning experience) designed *specifically to reflect this type of environment.* The term GAME FORM is used to identify the type of GAME, CONVENTIONAL or ORIGINAL. A CONVENTIONAL game is predetermined; it is already in existence and available for use. An ORIGINAL game is not predetermined; it is created by the teacher, the teacher and child together, or by the children alone.[1] SKILLFUL GAMES PLAYERS are children who have a large repertoire of movement skills that they can use in a variety of situations, planned as well as unexpected, with confidence, freedom, and individuality.[2] In other words, they are versatile movers and quick thinkers.

Fundamental skills
Game skills

A FUNDAMENTAL SKILL *is a common motor activity with a general goal and is the basis for more advanced skills specific to a particular game.*[3] The basic locomotor skills of walking, running, hopping, skipping, and jumping and the manipulative activities of catching, collecting, throwing, striking, carrying, and dribbling are examples of fundamental skills. A GAME SKILL *is an advanced and refined version of a FUNDAMENTAL SKILL that is used in a particular way in a particular game.*[3] For example, in an original game, where four children are trying to keep a plastic or volley ball in the air by striking it with the upper parts of their bodies while in the air, a GAME SKILL would be the jump (timed at a particular point), the hit (strike with finger tips of both hands) to a specific person, and the landing (handled so player was balanced, ready to move to a specific spot if necessary), all timed to fit the particular games situation.

The ability to get to the ball had its beginnings in the FUNDAMENTAL SKILLS of running and jumping and the ability to hit the ball had its beginnings in the FUNDAMENTAL SKILL of striking. GAME SKILL, in most instances, implies *a combination of* FUNDAMENTAL SKILLS used in a particular way in a particular game.

Therefore, FUNDAMENTAL SKILLS are the *roots* of GAME SKILLS, and with guided practice *over time* they have the potential to become GAME SKILLS. The more complex the game, the more complex the GAMES SKILLS required. Central to this approach to games is the assumption that the closer tasks can be designed to reflect the "games environment," the more potential there is for this transfer process to occur.

Open skills
Closed skills

GAME SKILLS are of two types: OPEN SKILLS and CLOSED SKILLS. OPEN SKILLS are those skills which require children *to respond in a variety of unpredictable ways because the environment is always changing.* CLOSED SKILLS require children *to respond in a consistent way because the environment is not changing.*[4] The approach to games teaching presented in this chapter is influenced strongly by the concept of the OPEN SKILL.

QUESTIONS
"This approach is fine, BUT . . . do you ever teach sport skills?"

Based on the previous discussion, and using Wickstrom's definition of a sport skill,[3] the answer to the question is "Yes, we do teach sport skills, but we call them GAME SKILLS."

The answer is yes because the definition of sport skill given by Wickstrom is the same definition as the one used for GAME SKILLS. Thus, when you use this definition *and* (a) accept that the nature of the game environment requires children to use OPEN SKILLS, and (b) design experiences that reflect this nature, there is no way you cannot be teaching "sport skills."[5]

"When using this approach do you ever refer to some of the game skills by name, e.g., the forehand drive, the lay up shot, etc.?"

When approaching the teaching of games through this approach, many of the game skills used by children will have familiar names, but some will not (encourage the children to create names). This fact does not make one set of skills "better" or "more important" than another. Identifying game skills by name is not new: we use them frequently, such as the cradle in lacrosse; we change them, such as the bump in volleyball to the forearm pass; and we create new ones, such as the stretch volley or the fly volley in tennis (Wimbledon, 1982).

It is sensible to refer to what children are doing by a familiar name, if there is one, or by one that has been especially created. Just remember, *using the Wickstrom definition of game skill, a game skill is a game skill only when it is being used in a game or in a game-like environment.*

"The approach is fine, BUT . . . do you ever have the children play real kickball or real volleyball?"

Again, based on the previous discussion and interpreting "real kickball" and "real volleyball" to mean the *regulation* version, the answer is "No, we do not teach real kickball or real volleyball. If we taught them, we would teach a modified version."

The answer is no because of the term *regulation*, not because kickball and volleyball are by definition conventional, competitive games. The rules and boundaries of *regulation* kickball and volleyball prohibit accommodating individual differences of children, a basic goal to which this approach is committed.

The question asked is one that is asked frequently. It reflects a view of games that is often narrower than the one being presented here. This games approach acknowledges both game forms, conventional and original, as viable options to include as part of a games program *so long as children's individual differences are accommodated.* This requires that most games, conventional and original, go through a modification process, the number of players involved, the size and weight of equipment, the size of the playing area, and the rules in particular.

The issue here is not one of competitive versus cooperative, with competitive implying conventional games and cooperative implying original, but one of accepting the fact that children develop at different rates, and for all of them to have a chance to develop their full potential for skillful games playing, their individual needs must be accommodated. It is harder and takes longer than we like to admit.

ORGANIZING GAMES CONTENT

In Chapter 5, the content of physical education was identified as human movement, and an adaptation of Laban's framework for classifying movement was given. Historically, Laban's framework was first used in relation to teaching dance, then gymnastics, and then games. His work is useful in games because analyzing movement from this approach gives a comprehensive picture of the dynamic nature of games and, thus, what it takes to be a skillful player. This means, of course, that those using this framework are able to analyze and describe games, using the language of the framework and its implied meaning and to recognize that the resulting description is the major resource for identifying games content and designing actual learning experiences or tasks.

A problem facing many teachers when using this framework as the major resource for designing experiences in games is knowing where to begin and how to continue. In other words, what is the progression? To arrive at a suggested progression, the movement framework as described in Chapter 5 was adapted to games, see Figure 7–1 and then organized into seven themes. The themes as designed are central to this approach and give it progression as well as unity. The order and substance of each theme

BODY ASPECT

BASIC BODY
ACTIONS
- curl
- stretch
- twist

ACTIONS OF
BODY PARTS
- support body
- lead action
- apply force
- receive force

hands
feet
shins
knees
hips
head
shoulders
chest

ACTIVITIES
OF BODY

locomotor
- walking
- running
- jumping
- sliding/sidestepping
- rolling

manipulative
- sending away
  - traveling and stopping
- gaining possession
  - striking
  - throwing
  - catching
  - collecting
- traveling with
  - carrying
  - dribbling

nonlocomotor
- bending
- extending
- twisting

SPACE ASPECT

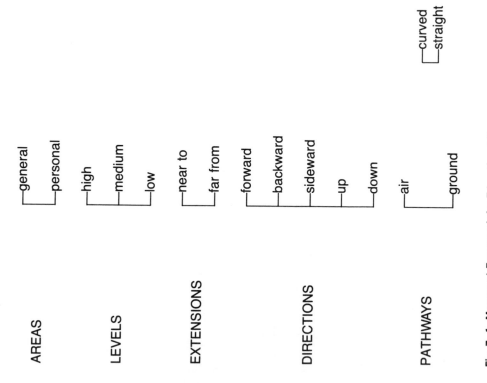

AREAS
- general
- personal

LEVELS
- high
- medium
- low

EXTENSIONS
- near to
- far from

DIRECTIONS
- forward
- backward
- sideward
- up
- down

PATHWAYS
- air
- ground
- curved
- straight

Fig. 7–1. Movement Framework for Educational Games.

EFFORT (QUALITY) ASPECT

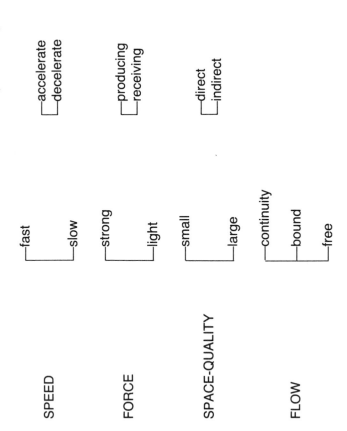

SPEED ⎡fast
      ⎣slow
      ⎡accelerate
      ⎣decelerate

FORCE ⎡strong
      ⎣light
      ⎡producing
      ⎣receiving

SPACE-QUALITY ⎡small
              ⎣large
              ⎡direct
              ⎣indirect

FLOW ⎡continuity
     ⎡bound
     ⎣free

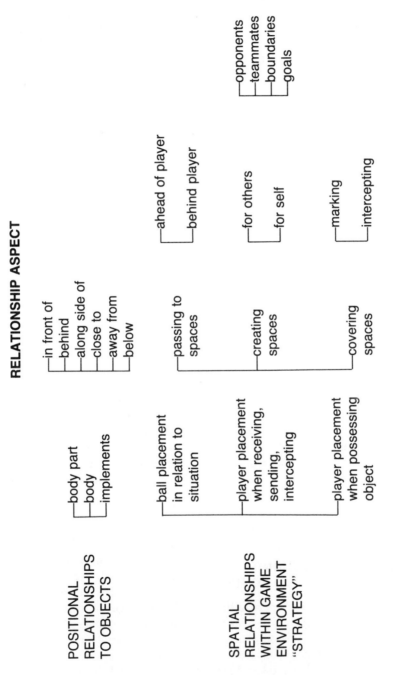

RELATIONSHIP ASPECT

POSITIONAL RELATIONSHIPS TO OBJECTS
- body part
- body
- implements

SPATIAL RELATIONSHIPS WITHIN GAME ENVIRONMENT "STRATEGY"
- ball placement in relation to situation
  - in front of
  - behind
  - along side of
  - close to
  - away from
  - below
- player placement when receiving, sending, intercepting
  - passing to spaces
    - ahead of player
    - behind player
  - creating spaces
    - for others
    - for self
- player placement when possessing object
  - covering spaces
    - marking
    - intercepting
      - opponents
      - teammates
      - boundaries
      - goals
      - rules

Fig. 7–1. *Continued.*

was influenced by Laban's original set of themes as further explained and analyzed by Preston-Dunlop.[6]

SEVEN MOVEMENT THEMES FOR ORGANIZING AND DEVELOPING EDUCATIONAL GAMES CONTENT

Theme 1—INTRODUCTION TO BASIC BODY AND MANIPULATIVE CONTROL

Theme 2—INTRODUCTION TO SPACE

Theme 3—INTRODUCTION TO MOVEMENT QUALITY (EFFORT)

Theme 4—MOVEMENT FLOW

Theme 5—INTRODUCTION TO BASIC RELATIONSHIPS

Theme 6—ADVANCED BODY AND MANIPULATIVE CONTROL

Theme 7—INTRODUCTION TO COMPLEX RELATIONSHIPS

The material that follows includes a discussion of each theme accompanied by a sample unit plan. You will notice that only in the unit plan for Theme 5 is there an actual game included as an integral part of a unit. Not including more games, original or conventional, was done intentionally. Unit plan 5 serves as "an example" of how a game might be "planned" as part of a unit. It has a definite purpose, it makes sense being there. Rather than showing other ways in which games could be integrated into a unit plan and, therefore, take away from illustrating more learning experiences, game play as an integral part of the program is discussed separately, following the themes and unit plans.

GAMES THEME 1—INTRODUCTION TO BASIC BODY AND MANIPULATIVE CONTROL

Games players have to gain mastery over their bodies as well as manipulative control over objects (balls, pucks, bean bags) or implements (rackets, bats, sticks). The level of mastery required to become a games player takes TIME TO DEVELOP. It is the purpose of Theme 1 to suggest content appropriate for children in the beginning stages of gaining this type of skill.

Development of Theme 1

> **Basic Content**
> Manipulative activities: striking, throwing, catching, collecting, carrying, dribbling
> Locomotion: traveling and stopping, running, jumping, sliding, sidestepping
> Body parts: hands, feet, shins, knees, hips, head, shoulders, chest

MANIPULATIVE ACTIVITIES. Central to games in which an object is manipulated with an implement or part of the body are six basic manipulative activities: *striking, throwing, catching, collecting, carrying,* and *dribbling.*[5] When designing tasks specifically related to the manipulative activities, it is suggested that these activities be considered as fundamental (motor) skills rather than their advanced and refined version, game skills. Children need to be confident in the basic, yet skillful use of these activities before they can be expected to modify them in relation to different game situations. The content of the later themes is designed to aid the development of these manipulative activities into more advanced and refined skills appropriate for all game forms, conventional and original. No further information about these manipulative activities will be given here, as this is well handled in detail in other places in the book. See Chapter 5 for a basic discussion of each of them, Chapter 3 for a description of how they develop over time, and Chapter 4 for the mechanical principles that govern skillful use of them. This material is considered basic and essential for this approach to games teaching.

Sample Learning Experiences
1. Throw a yarn ball against the wall; quickly retrieve it; go back to your starting place; and throw it again.
2. Find different ways to manipulate the ball (PG 5 inches).
3. Strike a plastic ball (8 inches) with arms, knees, and head. Strike it so it goes just above your head and up toward the ceiling. Try to stay in one spot.

Discussion. Task 1 focuses on the manipulative activity of throwing as well as running. While running is not directly stated, retrieving a ball quickly requires it. The purpose here is to let the children throw and "collect." Asking the children to throw the ball high and hard will allow you to assess the development of their throw.

Task 2 is an example of a task that is open, completely exploratory in nature. It is meant to be. It is a task designed to encourage children to experiment and not be afraid of what results. Stressing safe use of the space is a must.

The last task stresses striking as a fundamental skill—the goal being to strike it upwards with selected body parts. A key focus here would be to get the striking surface directly under the ball. The concept of how a ball can be directed is used in all striking skills, fundamental and specific. Fairly quickly after the children begin working, this task should change: e.g., try to keep the ball in the air without letting it bounce, or let it bounce between strikes.

LOCOMOTION. Most games require players to travel, stopping momentarily to assess where to go next or what to do. Stopping, in this case, is more of an "active pause" than a "full stop" as you must often reposition quickly to go after or avoid an opponent. This requires a constant state of alertness or readiness; weight is up, not down into the ground. Watch a skilled tennis player wait for a serve; watch a skilled dodger in a dodgeball game adjusting to where the ball is being tossed.

Traveling implies being able to *run, jump, slide,* and *sidestep when the situation requires it.* Skillful games players can use these ways of traveling in many different situations; they can use them interchangeably in a short period of time or separately in a long period of time. In this theme, running, sliding, sidestepping, and jumping are used as basic means to travel, to cover space, to get somewhere. Specific practice and advanced use of them is more the focus of Theme 6.

Sample Learning Experiences
1. Travel throughout the space, mixing running with sliding, stopping on a signal (active pausing), but ready to go again.
2. Tossing a bean bag gently out of reach, run and catch it. Repeat this traveling throughout the entire space. Keep bean bags at eye level.

Discussion. Both tasks specifically include traveling, and that is what the children should sense. Agile body control, weight up, ready to go, a spring in the legs are all important to achieve if this task is going to be beneficial. Task 2 is not as easy as it appears. Children must be able to (or willing to) toss the bean bag *slightly forward* and then go after it. Children will often run and then throw; this task is trying to bring out the run as a result of the toss. If the children can toss it sideward as well as behind them, sliding and sometimes jumping (caused by a poor toss) results. Sometimes, children cannot see any connection between this type of task and actual games playing, so this relationship may have to be explained. Suggest they watch how games players travel; this is often helpful.

BODY PARTS. Many games require that players are versatile with different parts of the body, not just their hands and feet: *hands, feet, shins, knees, hips, head, shoulders, chest.* Thus, early emphasis is on helping children begin to use a variety of body parts as they learn to manipulate objects. In addition, using body parts skillfully means surfaces of parts: *inside, outside, back, top* of foot.

Sample Learning Experiences
1. Dribbling a slightly deflated 8-inch PG rubber ball, using all surfaces of your foot. Travel throughout the space, trying to avoid contacting other people or other balls.
2. Toss a bean bag so you can catch it on different parts of your body. Try many different parts.

Discussion. Both tasks are designed to have the children focus their attention on parts of their bodies in manipulating a ball. Task 1 specifically identifies surfaces of the foot and Task 2 is designed so the children make this decision. Some of the responses to Task 1 could be very soccer-like; the basic difference being the use of a deflated ball (deflating the ball slows it up a bit). If any children are skilled with this task, change the ball to a soccer ball (or the closest thing to it) and help those children with the "soccer dribble," remembering that dribbling in a soccer game, modified or regulation, is an open skill. Asking children to use different surfaces of their feet will bring out change in direction. How much running and sliding occurs will depend on how fast they go.

The second task requires a concept basic to catching in general: getting the part of your body going to receive the ball behind it (in this case *under* it). Encourage the children to experiment with all body parts. This will help them to understand the important concept that they will not be successful 100% of the time and that this is normal. A discussion with them about which parts are easy and which hard is helpful.

GENERAL COMMENT

From the examples and discussions given, it is obvious that there is no end to tasks that can be designed using this content. Two reasons for this are that the theme itself includes six manipulative activities and the knowledge that every time a different object or implement is used, it becomes a new task. It is also a theme that needs to be revisited anytime one of the basic manipulative activities is being presented in an unfamiliar or new context. This theme is introductory in nature; it emphasizes getting the feel or idea of objects being manipulated with implements as well as with different body parts.

In making decisions as to what to include in tasks, remember, because of the size of the playing area, type of equipment available, and the developmental level of the children, *not all manipulative activities will be appropriate all of the time.* For example, having small children trying to dribble a ball with a normal-sized plastic hockey stick is not appropriate. They will look like they are sweeping the floor, not dribbling a hockey ball. Nor is asking 28 children to

quickly dribble balls in a small space or rough playground area appropriate.

Theme 1 is one of the most important themes; it will have to be revisited often.

SAMPLE UNIT PLAN THEME 1

Theme. Introduction to Basic Body and Manipulative Control—Theme 1.

Unit Focus. Dribbling (as a basic manipulation activity) with feet, hands, and hockey stick.

Appropriate For. Children for whom this approach to games is new and who have had beginning work in either Educational Gymnastics or Educational Dance.

Length of Unit. Two 30-minute lessons.

Content

> Body—manipulative activity: dribbling
> locomotion: traveling and stopping; running, sidestepping, sliding
> body parts: feet, hands (hands with a hockey stick)
> Space—
> Effort—
> Relationship—

Student Objectives. Children should be willing to try to

1. Dribble a ball, using feet, hands, and a hockey stick.

2. Concentrate on taking care of themselves so as not to bump into others.

3. Know when they are going too fast, and stop.

4. Know the purposes of "dribbling" as a manipulative activity when playing games.

Teaching Area. Indoors, outdoors, medium to large. (This unit can be adapted to smaller spaces by careful organization.)

Equipment

Objects. 8-inch plastic, PG rubber ball (slightly deflated): 1 per child.

Implements. Plastic (field/ice) hockey sticks, cut to fit children: 1 per child or 1 per 2 children; 3-inch yarn balls, pucks, or soft softballs: 1 per child (for use with hockey sticks).

Other. Cones.

Learning Experiences (Tasks)

1.0 With your own ball (8-inch plastic) and using either your hands or your feet, take the ball anywhere you would like to go. Move (travel) slowly so you do not bump into other balls or other people. Easy running.

1.1 With either hand, dribble the ball (a bounce-type dribble) anywhere you would like to go. Remember, go carefully. If you think your ball is going to get away from you, stop it (and you) and start again. Easy running.

1.2 Same task as 1.1 but with the other hand.

1.3 As you dribble your ball, now try to keep changing hands. Give both hands plenty of practice.

2.0 With just your feet, dribble the ball (slightly deflated 8-inch rubber) anywhere you would like to go. Stop the ball if it begins to go too fast. Be careful of others. Easy running.

2.1 Still using your feet, begin to find all the parts of your feet with which you can make the ball move. Keep watching out for others and their balls. Easy running.

3.0 With your stick, gently dribble (tap) the

A Suggested Progression for Sample Games Unit/Theme 1

	Lesson 1		Lesson 2
Tasks	**Teaching Tips***	**Tasks**	**Teaching Tips***
1.0	Stress: watch where you are going; find different ways to use your hands and feet; use hands and feet gently. Keep ball close to you. *Only stress these points if needed.	9.0	Help them decide if needed and encourage them to start right away. Have them watch their speed, spacing, and "strength" of tap. End with everyone with an 8-inch plastic ball, everything else away.
1.1	Help them select a hand if necessary. Stress same as above in Task 1.0.	1.0	Have them do this just long enough to get the feel of it.
1.2	Make sure they switched. Stress same as above in Task 1.0.	1.3	Stress: just use your hands, keep changing them.
1.3	Observe carefully to see whether they are changing hands. Help them with this decision if needed. Stress same as above in Task 1.0.	4.0	Stress: go a little faster, but only as fast as you can keep your body and ball under control. (Can you stop when you need to?) Teach children how to rotate, from watching (off) to working (on). Stress quick change. Stress easy, alert running.
2.0	Stress gentle "taps" with feet; go only as fast as you can stop quickly.		
2.1	Encourage complete exploration of parts of the feet. Be aware that using heels often makes the ball shoot away from the children.	4.1	Stress: mix a sideward dribble with forward. Keep stressing a ready body and resiliency in the feet and ankles.. Suggest taking ball backwards, *if* they have not already done it.
3.0	Make sure stick fits children first. Help them know what that means and why it is important. Stress easy taps, no need to rush, watch others.	2.1	Do this only as long as they need to use space well and truly use all parts of their feet. If certain parts of feet are not being used, suggest them and work on them.
3.1	Encourage the use of both sides of the stick, and not always in the same pattern.	5.0} 5.1}	Same as Tasks 4.0 and 4.1.
7.0	Arrange obstacles: some close together and some apart. Stress dribbling in and out, around, up to, and away. Always stress gentle taps, careful traveling.	3.1	Stress: keep ball close to stick, stay away from other balls and people.
		6.0	Same as Tasks 4.0 and 4.1.
8.0	To finish the class, have them put away their hockey sticks and take a plastic ball. Keep the cone arrangement as for Task 7.0. Stress as above for Task 7.0.	7.0	Design an arrangement that would fit the needs of the group (one half on; one half off) based on their work observed from Task 6.0.

*Comment. Always encourage an easy, resilient running motion. Energy should be up and "ready" to go. Alertness.

ball anywhere you can take it without getting in anyone else's way. Easy running.

3.1 As you dribble the ball, try to use both sides of your stick.

4.0 (One half of the children on the side of the area and one half of the children working: switch groups every 1 to 2 minutes.) Dribbling with your hands, using first one then the other, travel a little faster (this should bring out "fast" running if the children have not already been doing it; most will have, but not all).

4.1 Same as Task 4.0, but adding: sometimes take the ball sideways (should bring out slipping/sidestepping).

5.0 Same as Task 4.0, but changing to feet and the deflated ball.

5.1 Same as Task 5.0, but adding: use all parts of your feet, heels, sides, and toe. Careful that you only go as fast as you and the ball can stay safe; no bumping into anything.

6.0 Same as Task 4.0, but changing to a hockey stick and ball.

6.1 Same as Task 6.0, but adding: use both sides of your stick.

7.0 This task number, 7.0, represents adding cones (or other obstacles of choice) in some arrangement in the space to serve as "obstacles" for the children. When using them, stress that children dribble *in and out, up to and away,* or *around.* With the added challenge of cones, a different "dribbling" task results. It should help children broaden the ways they can dribble.

8.0 As you dribble the ball, dribble first with your hands, then your feet, then your hands again, etc. (8-inch plastic ball).

9.0 Select whether you want to dribble with your hands, feet, or with a hockey stick. Go ahead and practice.

Evaluation. Refer to Chapter 10 and either select or adapt one of the evaluative tools or develop a tool that can be used to help assess a specific aspect of the unit that is important to the needs of your students.

GAMES THEME 2—INTRODUCTION TO SPACE

Theme 1 focused on the basic manipulative activities as fundamental skills, as well as using them while traveling and where appropriate with different body parts. The focus was on the individual child as a mover. Theme 2 shifts this focus by introducing the child to the *environment,* the *games environment*—SPACE. When children gain confidence and skill with the material in this theme, much improvement toward becoming skillful games players is noticed.

Development of Theme 2

> **Basic Content**
> Manipulative activities: striking, throwing, catching, collecting, dribbling, carrying
> Areas: general, personal
> Levels: high, medium, low
> Extensions: near to, far from
> Directions: forward, backward, sideward, upward, downward
> Pathways: ground, air, curved, straight

GENERAL SPACE. If one were asked to identify the factor most essential for skillful games playing, it would probably be the way players use the general or *available space.* Skillful games playing always requires a sophisticated use of the general space. Theme 2 *begins* the development of this ability by focusing on the individual who has to handle the available space. As soon as children start working in relation to one or more persons, whether cooperatively or competitively, their ability to use the existing space *effectively* always influences the success of their efforts. Ability to use the available space for specific reasons is not easy and should not be looked upon as "covered" when Theme 2 is no longer the central focus. It begins here and should be continued throughout all themes.

PERSONAL SPACE. As general space focuses on the use of the available space while traveling, personal space focuses on the use of the space that *surrounds* the individual, whether he or she is traveling or stationary. For example, players catching a ball with their feet touching a base or on the run often have to reach well out in front or to the side to catch it. How far the players can reach without losing contact with the base or falling over is the outer limit of their personal space. Watch a skilled tennis player go for a ball that seems (to you) to be out of reach.

Sample Learning Experiences

1. Quickly collect (pick up, gather) a soft soft-ball that you have rolled into a space. Keep doing this. You can roll the ball forward, backward, or sideward; watch that you do not roll it into someone else's space.

2. In one quarter of the space (area designated by clear boundaries), travel dribbling (bounce dribble with hand) a PG 8-inch ball throughout the space; be careful, no touching. When you hear my hand clap, move throughout the entire space; another clap, small space.

3. Toss and catch a small ball then a larger ball in all the space around you. Take your time and see whether you can find many different places in which to toss it. You may change the size of the ball when you wish; be sure to change, however.

4. With a plastic field hockey stick (cut to size to fit child's height), move the small yarn ball along the floor all around you. Find all the places into which you can tap the ball without its getting out of your reach. Keep at least one foot stationary.

Discussion. Tasks 1 and 2 include focused work on the general space with Task 1 using the larger amount of space. Task 2 has the children dribbling their balls in a much smaller area, but having to use all of it. In both tasks, emphasis should be placed on *seeking* spaces and filling them, not just moving through them trying to avoid others. While stress is on the use of space, continued observation and guidance should be directed to the specific manipulative activities as well. In this case, helping children improve the way they "tossed" and "caught" the ball, the way they "quickly collected" it, and the way they "dribbled" the ball should be a continuous and thoughtful process.

In the third and fourth tasks, the use of space shifts to the use of personal space. Children need to know the space that is around them and the different ways they can use it. They need to find this out by using different body parts as well as implements. Both the concept of extensions and levels, also material in this theme, are related to personal space. Together, they help teachers help children become skillful at using it.

Please note that listed as part of the "content" for Theme 2 are the six manipulative activities: striking, throwing, catching, collecting, carrying, and dribbling. They are listed there as a reminder that they are to be considered as content in *all themes*. They serve as the focus of most tasks, and it is by practicing them, integrated with material from the other themes, that

allows the children to become skillful with them. This revisiting of content from previous themes is an example of the spiral approach to progression.

LEVELS. The concept of levels implies using all the space around a person or around yourself, from the lowest point to the highest point. As game players, children must be able to react to situations that cause them to handle objects and implements at different levels as well as to cause other children to do the same.

When thinking in terms of levels, it is helpful to think of areas of space, vertical areas, and not specific points in space. The high level becomes, then, the area of space from your shoulders up; the medium or middle level becomes the area between your shoulders and knees; and the low level becomes the area from your knees down. To become versatile in the way they use space, children need to be adept at handling objects and implements in all these spatial levels (vertical areas). It is true that the body or selected parts of it does change levels when playing games, but it is because the object being manipulated is *causing* the change. Because of this, it is suggested that, when designing learning experiences, place the emphasis on what the object should do to bring out (elicit) at what levels the body will have to move.

Sample Learning Experiences
1. Toss the ball (choose one from a collection, including a small one, a medium-sized one, and a large one) just above your arm's reach and catch it (gather it) before it starts to come down. Do this so your arms have to reach up and out (forward, backward, sideward: right/left).
2. Dribble a PG 8-inch rubber ball (hand) so the ball changes levels, but all below your waist. Use different hands and travel throughout the space, clearly looking for spaces into which you can go.
3. Throw a PG 5-inch rubber ball against the wall so it hits the wall at different levels. Watch it closely, having your body in readiness ("active pause" from Theme 1) to catch it. Keep changing the levels.

Discussion. All three tasks, if able to be done by the children, should cause them to catch (Tasks 1, 3) balls at various levels. This would be most clearly seen by observing where in space the hands contact the ball—at a low, medium,

or high level. The same would be true for Task 2. Observe the hand: as it gets closer toward the floor, the body will be closer as well.

In Task 1, the child is free to choose the size of the ball. If children cannot toss the ball to bring out this high catch (using the high area), they will first need help doing this. Stressing a toss "just out of reach" often helps. This task can also be redesigned to use lacrosse sticks (very difficult) and scoops (less difficult) as well as be done with partners. One person stands near the other and tosses the ball into the "high" space, and the partner reacts to the toss. Observe to see whether the purpose of the task is being met—to catch the ball at different levels.

Task 2 can be changed to include material from Theme 1 if the children are responding well. For example, have them stop ("active pause") and start quickly, as well as change the size of the area in which they are traveling. Cones or other pieces of similar equipment can be placed out on the floor, adding obstacles that the children have to negotiate (while changing levels, remember).

Task 3, if done well, should bring out good use of different levels. If this does not occur, you may have to focus only on the fundamental skill of throwing, it may not be mature enough for this task. This task can also be done using scoops, but because of the scoop's structure, it is often difficult to use.

EXTENSIONS. Inherent in some of the experiences suggested thus far is the idea of extension. When developing a child's ability to use personal space, you are beginning to deal with extension. Extension implies a spatial relationship of body parts and objects to the body: they can be either *far from it* or *near to it*. In game play, this situation happens all the time. Leading passes force players to reach well away from their bodies, whereas passes that have been thrown poorly often involve catching that is close to the body. Implements serve as an addition (or "extension") to body parts and increase the length of reach. Although extension implies a spatial relationship, it is not limited to the front of the body; the concept includes all the space around the body, over it, and underneath it. Acknowledging the similarities between personal space and extension does not exclude the differences, which are equally important. Developing an awareness of personal space means concentrating on it, determining how to use it and what it is. Extension focuses on how far away from your body or how close to it you can throw, strike, catch, collect, dribble, and carry the object effectively.

Sample Learning Experiences

1. In twos, toss a bean bag back and forth so your partner has to reach away from his/her body to catch it. Try to have your partner reach forward, upward, as well as sideward.
2. Strike a plastic 8-inch ball, using your arms and feet, sometimes with the ball close to your body and sometimes farther away.

Discussion. As the children begin responding to both these tasks, or tasks similar in nature, the teacher must observe carefully to see if the desired movement is coming out. Task 1 requires a child "to set up the ball" for another (this is often the cause of Task 1 not working). In Task 2, the children involved have the responsibility of seeing that the ball is sometimes close to their bodies or away from them. Both tasks can be redesigned, keeping the same focus, easily; but remember, every time this is done it is a *new* task. For example, using Task 1 as the basic structure or pattern, the bean bag could be changed to balls of various *sizes, shapes,* and *textures;* instead of two children doing this you could have one setting the object up to himself or herself. The basic idea in this task can be used again in later themes. Changing the weight and type of ball used in Task 2 also changes the challenge. Skilled and well-developed children might be able to use a volleyball or a ball close to it in weight and texture.

DIRECTIONS. Talking about direction implies both changing direction and using different ones (*forward, backward, sideward, up, down*). This difference may seem subtle, but both are vital in skillful games playing. Often, players find they have to alter their direction. For example, players running forward may have to move suddenly backward or sideward. At other times, they must decide which direction to take. In addition, players may encounter a situation in which they have to send a ball in one direction while moving abruptly in still another. As games are almost totally unpredictable, little can be planned ahead, so the teacher is responsible for designing experiences that develop this ability. If children are to have the greatest opportunity for

choice, when choice becomes necessary, they must be skillful in moving in all directions with and without objects—so they can make a choice.

Sample Learning Experiences

1. With a plastic hockey stick (field/ice *and* appropriate length), dribble the ball so you have to move forward, sideward, and backward.
2. Using all surfaces of your feet, travel throughout the space (outside, inside), traveling in different directions. Use all of them; you decide the order.

Discussion. Both these tasks place the emphasis on *the mover* initiating the direction change. If the children can change their directions, the ball will also. These tasks could also be written so the children would focus on making *the ball* change directions; then, they would have to change directions to keep up with the ball. Both ways get at the same thing. Related to decision-making, Task 1 has more specific information to guide the children's responses. Task 2 is designed assuming the children know the basic directions they can move while dribbling a ball and giving them the job of using them all. Again, changing the object or implement or both changes the task.

PATHWAYS. Taken in their broadest sense, pathways can occur *along the ground* and *in the air.* Players travel using different pathways, and players cause objects to travel in different pathways. Pathways, whether along the ground or floor or in the air, can be *straight, angular, curved,* or in various combinations.

Most pathways used by both players and objects result from a response to a particular situation. Two opponents are between you and your teammate, so you throw a ball over their heads (curved pathway). You weave in and out of two soccer opponents in an attempt to get free to cut for a pass.

As content to be included in tasks, pathways related to objects in the air are difficult and may not be appropriate for some children until they have experienced content included in later themes. Focusing on pathways taken by individuals and objects along the ground is not that difficult when kept at a simple level and, as you will see, is closely related to tasks designed to help children change their directions when they travel.

Sample Learning Experiences

1. Dribble the ball, using all the available space, making the ball move first in a curvey pathway, then in a straight pathway (the word line could be used instead of pathway).

2. Strike the ball (appropriate in size and weight) against a wall, sometimes reaching the wall quickly (a direct pathway or line) and sometimes making it take more time (a curved, arched pathway).

Discussion. In both tasks, the emphasis is on the pathway taken by the object, in this case a ball (ground/floor; air). Task 2 can present some problems to children if their "striking with different body parts" is not developing. If this should be the case, do not hesitate to design another task that focuses on striking and body parts (material in Theme 1). Task 1 will bring out similar, although not exactly the same, responses to Task 1 under "Directions." Comparing these tasks should help you see how the ideas of directions and pathways are related.

SAMPLE UNIT PLAN THEME 2

Theme(s). Introduction to Space—Theme 2 (selected content from Theme 1).

Unit Focus. Using directions and extensions while catching, throwing.

Appropriate For. Children who can toss (light throw) and catch bean bags and plastic 8-inch balls in their own space with minimum wandering (due to throw), and who are being introduced to these ideas for the first time.

Length of Unit. Three 30-minute lessons.

Content

      Body—manipulative activity: throwing, catching

      Space—areas: general, personal; directions: forward, sideward; extensions: far from

      Effort—

      Relationship—

Student Objectives. Children should be willing to try to

1. Begin using different directions and extensions while throwing and catching, alone and with another person.

2. Watch carefully their spacing throughout the lesson.

3. Feel what the meaning is of a full extension.

4. Know why their tosses/throws are or are not helping their partner with the given tasks.

5. Know how to pick up and put away equipment.

Teaching Area. Indoors, outdoors, medium to large.

Equipment

Objects. Bean bags; 5-inch yarn balls, 5-inch PG balls; 8-inch plastic balls; deck tennis rings: 1 per child.

Implements. Scoops or scoop-like: 1 per child.

Other. Wall space (enough for one-third or one-half the class to work at one time).

Learning Experiences (Tasks). NOTE—This unit has purposely used a number of space concepts and not only one or two. To help you understand how this was planned, the specific space concept is indicated in the early tasks.

1.0 Toss and catch your bean bag in all the space around you. Make sure you use the space in front of you, behind you, beside you, and over you (personal space).

1.1 Keep tossing and catching it, but now toss it a little farther (and farther) away from you. Toss it so that, when catching it, you feel you have to reach away from your body (extensions: far from).

1.2 Now toss it just far enough so you have to leave your spot to catch it. (A *small* distance.) Keep doing this all over the space. (Extensions: far from; general space.)

2.0 Same as Task 1.0, but using a 5-inch yarn ball, then a 5-inch PG ball, and then an 8-inch plastic ball.

2.1 Same as Task 1.1, but using a 5-inch yarn ball, then a 5-inch PG ball, and then an 8-inch plastic ball.

2.2 Same as Task 1.2, but using a 5-inch yarn ball, then a 5-inch PG ball, and an 8-inch plastic ball.

3.0 Same as Task 1.0, but using a scoop or scoop-like implement. Use a bean bag.

3.1. Same as Task 1.1, but using a scoop or scoop-like implement.

3.2 Same as Task 1.2, but using a scoop or scoop-like implement.

4.0 Select either a plastic or rubber ball (8-inch or 5-inch). Find an empty wall space, and at a good distance for you, toss/throw and catch the ball. Throw it so you *can catch it,* keep it for now right in front of you.

A Suggested Progression For Sample Games Unit/Theme 2

	Lesson 1		Lesson 2		Lesson 3
Tasks	**Teaching Tips**	**Tasks**	**Teaching Tips**	**Tasks**	**Teaching Tips**
1.0	Help children find all this space as well as explaining to them what space is and why it is important in games. Draw examples from current sports.	6.0	Encourage them to start right off with what they were doing at the end of the last class. Stress careful spacing and controlled speed.	6.1	Let the children select their equipment and focus and begin right away. Stress clarity of focus. You should be able to tell what they chose. Suggest and work in "directions" and then "extensions." Stress careful throws, throws that cause direction change and full extensions.
1.1	Show them what a "little" farther means. Do not let them throw it so far they create a dangerous situation. Stress soft catches.	3.0} 4.0}	Same organization as before and same emphases. Let them get the feel of the Tasks. Switch at least twice. Keep same organizational pattern, but introduce new tasks to entire group.	5.0	Let the children get organized and started. Stress safe organization, balls under control.
1.2	Stress that it is where the bean bag is placed in space that pulls them off balance. You may have to show them what this is. Stress as they get moving (they will pick up speed), to travel only a *short* distance, and *watch* where you are going. Seek *empty* spaces.	3.1	Encourage "just" a little farther, in different places away from you. Toss with hand if needed.	5.1	Make partner *move* to left and right. An underarm throw is suggested. The practice is on catching while moving *into* space. Stress and help them get ALL DIRECTIONS.
2.0} 2.1} 2.2}	Handle these the same as three previous tasks. You may want to select an order for them, or you may let them select it. If you have one ball per child, you can let them select. If not, you will have to organize differently. Change the ball type fairly quickly as this unit is introductory.	3.2	When ready, begin to let yourself travel.	5.2	Stress the importance of the throw. Help them understand how to position scoop under or behind ball. Catch softly. If they seem ready, let them travel as they toss and catch.
	It is suggested that the class be divided into half and that Tasks 4.0, 4.1, 4.2 and Tasks 3.0, 3.1, 3.2 be going on at the same time. The groups would have to switch at least twice. Tasks 3.0 to 3.2 in the middle of the space and Tasks 4.0 to 4.2 around the outside.	4.1	Encourage *slightly* left, and *slightly* right—too far in either direction causes collisions. Have them use their most accurate way of throwing.	6.2	Make sure they have made a decision as to what content they want to use. Stress traveling slowly at first. Watch spacing. You may find letting one half of the group go first and then the second half, necessary.
3.0	Stress good spacing, soft catching. If any children have difficulty tossing with the scoop, have them use their hands for now.	4.2	Careful with this one; only do it if you have space enough. Stress getting palm of hand behind the ball and not being afraid of missing it. Trying to catch a ball away from you is hard and takes lots of practice. Switch groups at least twice.		
4.0	Have children well-spaced out *before* they start. Let them begin so you can check spacing. Encourage different throws overarm, underarm. If you feel the time is right, help children with less mature throws. This may have to come later, however, because you need to observe the entire group.	5.0	Let them get organized (partners and balls) and spaced out well away from others. Encourage tossing so partners can catch it. Stress focusing on own task and amount of space; get the feel of the distance you have.		
6.0	Let them choose and observe carefully to see what progress is evident, and whether they do use anything that was covered in the lesson. Stress safety in terms of speed, and use of space.				

4.1 Throw the ball against the wall slightly to your right and slightly to your left. Catch it after one bounce or no bounce. (Directions: sideward). Throw it gently to the wall and catch it. (Directions: forward).

4.2 Same as 4.1, but throwing it farther left and right so children have to reach to catch it. (Extension: far from; directions: sideward.)

5.0 With one other person, select which ball to use (8-inch plastic, 5-inch PG rubber) and begin by tossing and catching between you. Partner *must* be able to catch it. Stay in your own area.

5.1 Throw the ball now to either side of your partner so he/she has to move to catch it. Throw it short in front, so your partner has to run forward to catch it. (Directions: sideward, forward.) Watch spacing.

5.2 Same as Task 5.0, but one person with a scoop or scoop-like implement. The "thrower" is the one without the scoop.

6.0 With either a bean bag, a 5-inch yarn ball, or an 8-inch plastic ball, travel throughout the space while you toss and catch to yourself. Keep both youself and the ball under control. Use the wall space if you want to.

6.1 With same object, select a special focus as you work, directions or extensions. Toss your ball so you have to move forward, backward, sideward to catch it; or toss your ball so you have to reach away from your body to catch it. Use all the space.

6.2 Same as Task 6.0, but you may select someone to do this with if you wish to.

Evaluation. Refer to Chapter 10 and either select or adapt one of the evaluative tools and develop a tool that can be used to help assess a specific aspect of the unit that is important to the needs of your students.

GAMES THEME 3—INTRODUCTION TO MOVEMENT QUALITY (EFFORT)

Theme 1, introduction to basic body and manipulative control, and Theme 2, introduction to space, have focused specifically on the games player and the games environment (the space in in which games take place). Theme 3 begins

specific focus on the *quality of the movement*—how the movement is being performed; how "efficient" it is.

In this theme, the phrase "quality of movement" is being used instead of the term "effort" because it seems more appropriate when discussing the movement content of games—and it means the same thing. Quality of movement refers to both the "economy of effort" (Laban's approach[8]) or the "efficiency of movement" (Broer's approach[9]). Both the motion factors of time, weight, space, and flow (Laban's conceptualization) and the basic mechanical principles (Broer's conceptualization) refer to the broader concern of efficiency, the quality of movement, or how the movement is being performed. Both concepts are integrated in this theme, with the concepts of time, weight, space, and flow (Theme 4) serving as the major means for designing learning experiences. How these two approaches to the efficiency/economy of movement are being used in this book is discussed in greater detail in Chapter 10, Teaching As Observing, Integrating, and Decision-Making. Time, weight, space, and flow, the four motion factors associated with effort, or the quality of movement, will be referred to as speed (time), force (weight), space-quality (space), and flow throughout the games chapter.

Development of Theme 3

> **Basic Content**
> Manipulative activities: striking, throwing, catching, collecting, carrying, dribbling
> Force: strong ↔ light
> Speed: fast ↔ slow
> Space-quality: small ↔ large

Force. Force implies the energy, or *amount of strength* or *lack of strength*, used in performing a movement. In game play, the ability to vary skillfully the amount of force used is critical to success. Force as content means more than learning how to produce it; it means learning how to absorb it as well. Successful games players, when catching (air) and collecting (ground), are able to control the force of the object so they can redirect it immediately. Children need continuous opportunities to "play" with force, producing it as well as absorbing it.

Speed. Speed relates to *how fast* or *how slowly* the individual is moving. It refers to the speed of the total body action as well as the speed of individual body part and parts. The coverage of space in games, accomplished more often by running, has to be done with varying speeds. Effective acceleration and deceleration in relation to the emerging situation are well-known characteristics of good games players. All players need this trait, not only those "with the ball." The challenge is in determining the optimal moment for that sudden burst of speed or that subtle slowing down *and* being able to execute it.

Besides having to alter their speed when traveling, players must be able to change the speed of the object with which they are playing. Whenever children are working with different traveling speeds while manipulating objects, the control over the object should be appropriate.

Space-quality. Space used as space-quality focuses solely on the amount of space used. Does the body or the body parts involved use a *small amount* of space or a *large amount* of space. Sometimes using more space (an indirect use of space) is important to the quality of the movement and sometimes using less is (a direct use of space). A shot for goal in most games needs a quick arm, hand, or leg action that uses a small amount of space; the body part should cut through the space quickly, not weave all around it. On the contrary, a serve in tennis needs to use a greater amount of space to produce the necessary amount of force.

To be skillful games players, children need to be able to vary

(1) the AMOUNT of FORCE they use from:

STRONG $\longleftrightarrow$ LIGHT

(2) the AMOUNT of SPEED they use from:

FAST $\longleftrightarrow$ SLOW

(3) the AMOUNT of SPACE (QUALITY) they use from:

SMALL $\longleftrightarrow$ LARGE

BECAUSE

MOVEMENT(S) WITH THE RIGHT

AMOUNT OF

FORCE, SPEED, AND SPACE (QUALITY)

FOR

THE PARTICULAR SITUATION RESULTS

IN EFFICIENT MOVEMENT

Sample Learning Experiences and Discussion
Because of the nature of this content, the sections on "Sample Learning Experiences" and "Discussion" will be combined.

FORCE. When children are beginning to develop ability in producing different amounts of force, they need to be certain of what they are trying to do. Some children interpret this work as how high or how far they can throw (hit, kick), entirely forgetting their responsibility for a safe and productive learning environment. The atmosphere must be one of total involvement in the individual challenge of gaining skill in using different amounts of force, from "lots" to "little." To obtain this focus, initially use demonstrations and fairly structured experiences.

Throwing, striking, dribbling, catching, and collecting are manipulative activities with which to develop skillful force production (throwing, striking, and dribbling) and force absorption (catching and collecting). Early experiences should concentrate on purposely producing and absorbing varying amounts of force. For example:

1. Throw a ball against a wall so when it returns *you can catch it.* Start close to the wall first, and then gradually and in your own time, move farther and farther away. Remember, you must be able to catch the ball. Be careful you do not bump into anyone behind you. (Additional tasks could focus on a larger ball; encouraging the throw to be overarm, sidearm, underarm.)

2. Same as Task 1, but with a partner.

3. Toss bean bags to different levels (heights) in the space above you, then catch them on different parts of your body WITHOUT A SOUND.

4. Toss a heavy ball (soccer, PG 8-inch) into the air and "catch" it, using different body parts. Catch, absorbing the ball's weight by going with the ball on contact and redirecting it to the ground. There cannot be an actual catch.

All these experiences lend themselves well to discussion of the principles that govern the concept of force (Chapters 3 and 4 address this information specifically). The children can then apply these principles to their movement and thus continue gaining insight into their progress. Children's interpretations of what is strong and light movement differ widely, and discussions on this topic are of much value. In addition to discussing the "technical" aspects of force, discussing the children's preferences for forceful and less forceful movement can be explored. In this type of discussion, no value judgments should follow anyone's comments, since the purpose is for the children to find out about themselves—what they seem to like and dislike and why.

Experiences can center on striking and dribbling. Both these skills are difficult, and the children will have to be comfortable with them *before* adding purposeful variations in force production. (Earlier themes were designed with this objective in mind.) Featuring work in striking does not always mean doing it continuously, for this action involves an extremely complex series of movements. Striking, using body parts

(as opposed to a bat or racket), can include: one strike (hit) followed by a catch; two strikes and then a catch; a bounce between strikes, etc. Children need to be aware of these options, because otherwise, they have difficulty in contin-

uously challenging themselves in a progressive manner.

Applying the concept of force production to dribbling is not easy in the beginning stages, especially when using a smooth surface. It primarily involves increasing and decreasing the distance the object is hit. This activity can be done freely throughout the space or against a wall of some type. Equipment arrangements can be designed to elicit (bring out) different uses of force. For example:

1. Moving in a straight path (children are at one end of the space; only five or six will go at one time), sometimes dribble your ball close to your stick (field hockey) and sometimes away from your stick. Keep it and you under control.

2. Pass the ball (soccer or slightly deflated PG 8-inch) back and forth between you and your partner. Pass to a space, but a space near him, *while* changing the distance between you. (This is a challenging task.)

As stressed in the development of every theme, the selection of objects, implements, and equipment is crucial to the success of the experiences. You must be alert to how certain types of equipment work in differing situations and what exactly you want to have happen. For example:

1. Yarn balls, bean bags, and deflated rubber balls do not rebound as much as a tightly blown-up ball.

2. Blankets or similar materials hung away from a wall or just hung freely deaden any object thrown against them.

3. Implements that are heavy cause light plastic-like objects to travel fast. Light implements need light to medium-light objects to hit.

4. Equipment placed too close or too far apart may not allow the desired movements to emerge.

5. Implements and balls, like clothes, MUST FIT THE CHILDREN!

All these examples have one implication. *Observe carefully* what and how the children are moving in relation to the task, and adjust accordingly.

SPEED. Remembering that speed includes the ability to accelerate (go faster and faster) and decelerate (go slower and slower), safety is of utmost concern when designing tasks focusing on this idea. Organizational patterns allowing safe use of speed are major criteria.

Encouraging children to go fast is potentially dangerous if they have not developed the ability to direct their work and if they have not gained a responsible attitude toward personal safety and the safety of others. Once children can and do take the responsibility to work *only as fast as they can control themselves*, productive learning experiences can develop.

To design a task that focuses on speed, the task can be structured to vary the speed of the *object* or the *mover*. For example:

1. With a partner, roll the ball back and forth and (slightly) to the sides as well as in front of your partner. As you do this, change the speed at which you roll (or low bounce) the ball.

2. With a partner (both with a field/ice hockey stick), begin to pass the ball back and forth; then

  2a. as you collect it (gather it), move into an empty space, keeping the ball close to your stick (dribbling with short taps). After you have traveled a short distance, locate your partner and pass it back. Keep this up; then when ready,

  2b. accelerate, as you collect the ball and move into a space.

Accelerate only when you have control over the ball, and look where you are going.

As in past examples of learning experiences, teachers must observe carefully to see whether or not the purpose of the task is being met. Task 1 focuses on (a) passing (throwing) along the ground with different speeds and (b) catching (absorbing force) balls of different speeds (and force). Task 2 focuses on the same ideas, but in this task, an implement is used instead of a hand. The task is also made harder by the fact that the receiver is going to accelerate at some point. Two examples of less complexity that use content from Theme 2 follow:

1. Travel throughout the space, changing the directions you are traveling quickly, then slowly.

2. Dribble a soccer ball in, out, and around the cones (no special order) accelerating and decelerating when the space permits (or requires you).

SPACE-QUALITY. Because space-quality is often confused with the spatial concepts in Theme 2, it is being suggested here that the concept space-quality be used primarily to help children refine the quality of their movement-response and not to design tasks. For example, if a child is having difficulty hitting a ball from a batting tee, because the bat does not stay parallel with the ground long enough, a teacher might say: "Bring your bat through in a straight, direct line, cut through the space sharply." Similar difficulties with hitting a ball against a wall with a plastic tennis racket might be helped with this statement: "Let your racket move in a direct line between here (point) and here (point)." Asking children to evaluate their own movements results in statements like these: "My racket is all over the place" (the child is saying my racket head is moving through too much space); or "I did not take my arm back far enough" (the child is saying my arm used too little space). Teachers know that with more trunk rotation, the arm would have a greater chance to use more space and that should produce more force.

REMEMBER

THE RIGHT AMOUNT OF FORCE WITH

THE RIGHT AMOUNT OF SPEED WITH

THE RIGHT AMOUNT OF SPACE-

QUALITY

RESULTS IN

EFFICIENT MOVEMENT

SAMPLE UNIT PLAN THEME 3

Theme(s). Introduction to Movement Quality (selected content from Themes 1 and 2).

Unit Focus. Striking with emphasis on force production.

Appropriate For. Children who have had introductory work with striking (work associated with Themes 1 and 2) and who are beginning to get comfortable using a number of different body parts, in particular forearm, upper arm, and thighs.

Length of Unit. Two 30-minute lessons.

Content

  Body—manipulative activity: striking body parts: forearms, upper arms, fists, head, thighs, shins, feet
  Space—levels (as a result of force variations)
  Effort—force: strong ↔ light
  Relationships—

Student Objectives. Children should be willing to try to

1. Strike with different parts of the body while varying the amount of force given.

2. Know the factors that govern force production.

3. Take responsibility for working cooperatively with a partner so both gain productive practice.

4. Sense the difference between strong and light amounts of force when striking a ball.

Teaching Area. Indoors, large. (This can be adapted to outdoors and a medium space with careful organization.)

Equipment

Objects. 8-inch plastic balls; 8-inch foam balls: 1 per child or equal numbers of each, 1 per 2 children.

Implements. None.

Other. Wall space (enough for at least one fourth of the class to work at one time).

Learning Experiences (Tasks)

1.0 With your own ball (8-inch plastic or foam), begin by striking the ball with as many parts of your body as you can. For example, forearms, upper arms, fists, head, thighs, shins, feet. Try to keep it going as long as you can without stopping (it may bounce).

1.1 Work for a while with your forearms, fists, and head. Keep it going straight up.

1.2 Work now, just with your forearms and fists, striking the ball continuously in an upward direction.

1.3 Begin to change the force (or power) you are using and strike the ball to different heights in the air.

1.4 Observation/discussion session. Topic: what do you have to do to accomplish this and why? (See Chapters 3 and 4 for supportive material.)

2.0 Now shift to body parts below the waist: thighs, shins, feet. Still striking in an upward direction, keep the ball going. Let it bounce if it has to, but try to keep it going.

2.1 Same as Task 1.3.

2.2 Same as Task 1.4.

3.0 Using your fists and/or forearms, strike the ball against a wall. Get so you can keep it going with a sidearm pattern: both sides with both arms ("backhand" and "forehand").

A Suggested Progression for Sample Games Unit/Theme 3

	Lesson 1		Lesson 2
Tasks	**Teaching Tips**	**Tasks**	**Teaching Tips**
1.0	Encourage striking part directly under the ball and firm at contact; use of different parts. (If they need help here, identify specific ones to use.)	1.0 3.0	½ class ⎫ Stress same points as in previous lesson. ½ class ⎭ Switch groups (one at wall space other in center) even, 2 to 3 minutes.
1.1	Stress an "alert" body position; use of both forearms and wrist (together and separated).	1.3 3.1	½ class ⎫ Stress those points needed to help them ½ class ⎭ change amount of force used: e.g., speed of body part, distance body part
1.2	Same as Task 1.1 .		moved before contacting ball.
1.3	Stress "alert" body position, striking part under ball with a firm, direct, quick hit. Help them notice the height on their ball, is it changing.	3.2	Another group discussion/observation session might be necessary.
1.4	Discuss/demonstrate factors affecting production of force: magnitude, direction, point of application, impact. Prepare this discussion/observation ahead of time.	4.0	This task is only appropriate if above work was handled well. Stress safe spacing; ball hit *up* (to give it an arc); bounce in between hits; "alert" body positioning.
1.3	Observe for understanding of discussion. A good time to ask them questions to test understanding.	4.1	Same as for Task 4.0.
2.0	Stress active body position, etc. See above.	4.2	Guide the children into summarizing. Ask them to select the most critical factor to remember when they are working.
2.1 2.2	Same as Tasks 1.3 and 1.4. Encourage a bounce in between strikes, they probably will need the time this gives.	4.1	Stress: what they answered to above question. Have them try to apply their own evaluation.
3.0	Stress point of contact, path of arm parallel to floor; follow through at wall.		

NOTE. This unit will be difficult if the children do not have the ability to strike a ball in an upward direction or in a sidearm (forehand) pattern. If this is true, you will have to work on that until they do. This unit, depending on the children's skill, could go anywhere from two to six lessons.

3.1 Using a sidearm, strike, sometimes hitting it with a lot of force and sometimes with a little. Experiment with this until you can keep the ball going, applying different amounts of force.

3.2 Observation/discussion sessions: review main points from earlier discussions. What do you have to do to accomplish this and why?

4.0 In twos or alone, strike the ball to your partner, using upper body parts, sometimes being close together, sometimes farther apart. Let the ball bounce in between. (The ball must be hit up so it can bounce high enough for the next to get under it.) If alone, use a wall.

4.1 Same as 4.0, but add lower body parts when appropriate.

4.2 Summarizing discussion based on question: what are some of the key ideas you must remember when you strike a ball hard or soft. What do you see that is different?

Evaluation. Refer to Chapter 10 and either select or adapt one of the evaluative tools or develop a tool that can be used to help assess a specific aspect of the unit that is important to the needs of the students.

GAMES THEME 4—MOVEMENT FLOW

In Preston-Dunlop's interpretations of the relationship of Laban's 16 basic movement themes, she identified several that had as their major purpose *integrating* material from previous themes.[6] In adapting the theme structure to games, it was decided to have one theme, the mid-point theme, to serve this purpose. Theme 4 focuses on the flow of movement specifically as it relates to games playing. The motion factor of flow as it relates to movement describes its continuity and whether its quality is perceived as bound or free.[10]

Development of Theme 4

> **Basic Content**
> Manipulative activities: striking, throwing, catching, collecting, carrying, dribbling
> Flow: bound—free
> continuity

BOUND FLOW/FREE FLOW. Movement that is hesitant, tense, and restricted is said to be characteristic of *bound flow.* *Free flow* is characterized by movement that is often described as free, easy, relaxed. All movements have a flow characteristic, and skillful games players have control over the flow of their movement. The flow of their movement can be free or bound, according to the game situation. The swift, abandon-like running so characteristic of some players in field games or a well-hit overhead smash in a racket game are examples of free flow. The toss of a ball prior to serving in games like tennis and volleyball demonstrates the use of bound flow. Contrast the way players have to cover space in games like soccer, field hockey, baseball, and lacrosse with the way they cover space in tennis, badminton, squash, and racket ball. Although all games demand quickness and speed, the player needs more free flow in the field games and a more bound flow in the net games. If, in the net games, players could not stop quickly and change direction, they would often be ineffective. In field games, if the players could not accelerate and cover large amounts of space quickly, they would be ineffective.

CONTINUITY. In addition to the concepts of bound flow and free flow just described, there is another characteristic of skillful games players that is related. When playing a game, these players have the ability to keep the game going. In observing these games, the players seem to "keep the ball alive," they "hustle," the game has an exciting atmosphere. In games where the object might be to keep the ball off the ground, these players will do *everything* in their power to do that—they never seem to give up, they always "have a go." Tasks designed with content from this theme are of two types: tasks with content specific to flow and tasks with content from Themes 1, 2, 3.

Sample Learning Experiences

1. As you are running, catch a ball tossed slightly ahead of you; at the moment you catch it, travel (straight line) as fast as you can across that line. (The line is well away from the wall or, if outside, no one is standing where the "runner" could bump into them.)
2. Traveling as quickly as you can throughout the given space, stopping on the signal. Be sure to go everywhere and do not touch anyone. Be in control of yourself at all times.
3. With a plastic 8-inch ball and using different parts of your body, keep the ball in the air by striking upward. You may let it bounce if necessary, but keep it going.
4. You may use a plastic hockey stick (ice/field) or your feet. While dribbling the ball, you are to try to accelerate and decelerate *and* keep changing your direction.

Discussion. Whenever designing a task that involves asking children to move *fast* (free flow), they must be organized to do it safely. It is rare when the whole class can work at once. Task 1 is such a task. This task is more appropriate for outdoors, but could be organized for inside as well. This task needs all children working in the same direction, with some setting up the pass. It is easy to have six children at a time have a turn and the next six immediately following. Movement of this type is necessary to experi-

A Suggested Progression For

Lesson 1		Lesson 2	
Tasks	Teaching Tips	Tasks	Teaching Tips
ALL	Stress: keep the ball going, go after everything, keep the ball alive.	4.0	Stress: catch and toss, one continuous motion; give leads into catch.
NOTE: Because of space restrictions, you may have to have two groups working simultaneously on different tasks. SPACING IS CRITICAL—children have to have *room*: they will be going after balls harder.		4.1	Stress: go to meet object, then give with it; get body position behind object, give, then throw right back. ALL ONE MOTION. Change object and implement if desired.
1.0	Use any pattern that is called for: sidearm, (forehand/backhand), overarm. Let it bounce, volley it.	3.0	Based on observations, discuss what is needed (e.g., factors affecting receiving and producing force with a smooth transition = continuity).
1.1	Same as Task 1.0	4.2	Same as Task 4.0. When ready, have partners change bean bag to 8-inch plastic or PG; scoop. Let them choose, or if a space problem requires it, organize it formally on a rotation basis.
3.0	Discuss what is needed based on your observation of the group.		
1.2	Same as Task 1.0		
2.0	Stress: let it bounce to give you more time if needed. Be in position to strike it.	3.0	Use this whenever you think they have lost the purpose of "continuity."
2.1	Same as Task 2.0.		

ence and everyone cannot go at once. It will take, on the teachers' part, some careful and clever organization.

Task 2 is not unlike some previous ones, but the emphasis is stopping quickly and in control, balanced and ready to go again. The children are being asked to check their flow of movement unexpectedly (the signal); therefore, they may have to hold back their speed a bit.

The third task focuses on helping children get the feel of "hustling" after something (so it does not go out of bounds) and keeping the ball "alive." They will have to be motivated or "cheered" along at first; this ability does not seem to be natural to many children at first. When they catch on, however, your games program turns around and takes on a new look. At this point, children will have to be reminded to, yes, go after everything, but not to get into anyone else's way. It is at this point that the dynamic nature of games should be evident in everything they do. It suggests they are ready now to focus on relationships that lead to teamwork, strategies, and the like.

The final task represents the type of task that includes content from Themes 1, 2, and 3 and integrates them into one task. All content is assumed to be of equal importance. The purpose here is to begin integrating the ideas, resulting in more complex movements (and often more game-like ones).

There are different ways, all of which are potentially useful, to integrate content from Themes 1, 2, and 3. The resulting experiences are challenging, so children need plenty of time to work with them. If children seem uninterested or bored with the task, perhaps it is *too* difficult for them, or they really do not know what they are trying to do or what is expected of them. The task probably needs to be reexplained or redesigned; usually the latter.

There are also ways to combine Themes 1, 2, and 3 *illogically*. When this happens, the movement demands are usually next to impossible or so novel they have little relation to game-like movement. An example might be dribbling (Theme 1) a ball with different body parts (Theme 1) while changing speed (Theme 3) and directions (Theme 2). Have you ever tried dribbling a ball with you knee under these conditions? It is next to impossible. The selection of content from different themes needs to be made carefully, being guided by what is game-like and appropriate for the children for whom it is being selected.

A FINAL COMMENT. This theme is a critical one, but difficult to handle from both the teacher's and child's point of view. Selection of objects and implements appropriate for each child's developmental level is essential as are organizational patterns that will allow the desired movement to emerge. Tasks designed with this Theme's content are challenging for the children, if done well.

Sample Games Unit/Theme 4

Lesson 3		Lesson 4	
Tasks	Teaching Tips	Tasks	Teaching Tips
4.0	Continue practicing, using the more difficult parts: feet, shins, thighs, head. Encourage a rhythmic catch and toss, catch and toss. (Difficult.) Have children work with both bean bags and larger ball.	ALL	Stress: focus of tasks—to get feeling of bound and free flow. To achieve this purpose, they may not be as active as they have been in past lessons.
2.0	Review purpose of continuity—keep it alive—do not let ball stop.	6.0	Stress: clear understanding of task and when to go, where to go, and when to slow down and stop. All going in one direction, a few at a time, is suggested. BEFORE adding speed, have them do task at easy speed. Then slowly work them up to it. Use deflated 8-inch PG, soccer, and hockey stick so they can feel difference.
5.0	Let them just try it. Stress: use catching, striking, throwing in different combinations, trying to change them continuously.		
5.1	Same as Task 5.0.		
3.0	Use whenever you think the class needs to be refocused or to discuss problems associated with the task.	3.0	Use often, both to give them a rest and to help them understand the concept.
		6.1	Build up speed gradually. You may want to begin with this task rather than 6.0. Stress: watch spacing and control speed *(the latter is what flow is all about—purposeful control of energy)*.

NOTE: Some or many of the children may "regress," at first, in their ability to throw, catch, strike. This should be expected as they are using them in new situations. Go back to easier tasks if they consistently have trouble.

SAMPLE UNIT PLAN THEME 4

Theme(s). Movement Flow (selected material from Themes 1, 2, and 3).

Unit Focus. Controlling the flow of movement when striking, throwing, catching, and dribbling.

Appropriate For. Children who have good control over the basic manipulative activities while working alone on the spot and *while* traveling. Past work in Themes 1, 2, and 3 is critical to the success of this unit. This unit is considered an *introduction* to the idea of "flow."

Length of Unit. Four 30-minute lessons.

Content

> Body—manipulative activities: striking, throwing, catching, dribbling
> Space—
> Effort—flow: bound, free, continuity
> Relationship—

Student Objectives. Children should be willing to try to

1. Show continuity in the way they throw and catch, strike, and throw, catch, and strike in combination.
2. Experience free flow and bound flow when dribbling.
3. Know what the concept "flow" means related to games playing.
4. Feel in their movement continuity and the difference between bound and free flow.

Teaching Area. Indoors, large. (This unit can be adapted to a smaller area with careful organization. As the concept of movement flow is being *introduced*, indoors is more appropriate; the children can hear better and hold their concentration more easily.)

Equipment

Objects. 8-inch plastic balls: 1 per child; 8-inch foam balls: 1 per 4 children; 8-inch PG balls, slightly deflated: 1 per child; bean bags: 1 per child; 5-inch PG balls: 1 per 4 children.

Implements. None.

Other. None.

Learning Experiences (Tasks)

1.0 Hit the ball against the wall with the purpose of KEEPING IT GOING (plastic tennis racket, and sponge ball).

1.1 Same as Task 1.0, but with a partner.

1.2 Hit the ball back and forth between you and your partner with the purpose of KEEPING IT GOING.

2.0 Strike the ball in an upward direction, KEEPING IT GOING CONTINUOUSLY. Use any body parts. (8-inch plastic or sponge ball.)

2.1 Strike the ball back and forth between you and your partner, KEEPING IT GOING CONTINUOUSLY. Use only body parts you wish.

3.0 Observation/discussion session focusing on concept of continuity of action (trying for everything; keeping ball alive).

4.0 Tossing and catching a bean bag with continuous motion.

4.1 Same as Task 4.0 and adding contact with the bean bag at all levels: high, medium, low.   } Could change object here; large ball, scoop, or scoop-like implement.

4.2 Same as Task 4.1, but with a partner.

5.0 Handle the ball, alternating between catching, throwing, and striking. Whatever you do, keep it in an upward direction and keep it CONTINUOUS.   } 8-inch PG rubber, plastic or sponge ball; could change to 5-inch rubber or soft softball.

5.1 Same as Task 5.0, but with a partner (threes?).

6.0 Dribble a ball as fast as you can (cannot "lose" it) over "this line." AMPLE space for child to slow down after crossing line. (Not all children will be moving at once.) *Free flow* emphasis.   } deflated 8-inch PG rubber or soccer ball and hockey stick and ball (yarn, soft softball).

6.1 All together, dribble the ball in and out of everyone as fast as you can, BUT be ready to STOP immediately on the signal. *Bound flow* emphasis.

Evaluation. Refer to Chapter 10 and either select or adapt one of the evaluative tools or develop a tool that can be used to help assess a specific aspect of the unit that is important to the needs of your students.

GAMES THEME 5—INTRODUCTION TO BASIC RELATIONSHIPS

In Theme 2, the space as the game environment was introduced. It was shown to have *areas* and *levels* into which you could move, *extend* into, make *pathways* in, and use in many different *directions*—all while manipulating an object. Theme 5 expands the understanding of space by introducing the child to the space as something to *relate* to. It focuses on two kinds of relationships needed for skillful games playing: (a) the kinds of relationships that your body, your body parts, or an implement have to an object, and (b) the kinds of relationships you set up within the games environment.

Development of Theme 5

> **Basic Content**
> Relationships to objects: body, body parts, implements
> Basic relationships within game environment

RELATIONSHIPS TO OBJECTS. When manipulating objects with implements or different parts of the body, it is often where your body, body parts, or implement are in relation to the object that allows for effective movement to result. For example, when striking or hitting a ball straight against a wall with your forearm, your forearm should contact the ball directly *behind* it and your body should be far enough *away* from the ball to allow your arm to swing through easily and contact the ball with the right amount of force, speed, and space (quality). Likewise, when passing a soccer ball backwards into the space behind you, your body must be *in front* of the ball and in such a place as to allow your heel to strike the ball directly in line with the direction you want it to go. In short, much of the effectiveness of our catching, collecting, carrying, dribbling, throwing, and striking ability is because of the relationship that the body part, or the body, or the implement has to the object AT THE MOMENT OF CONTACT. Improving this awareness helps children improve their skill.

Sample Learning Experience
1. Travel throughout the space, dribbling a ball with your feet, changing directions quickly

and often. Before you contact the ball, be in the best possible position in relation to the ball to hit it in the desired direction. Think in terms of your body as well as your foot.
2. With your hands, run and collect the ball that is being rolled to you (bounced, thrown) at different speeds and in different directions. As you go to collect it, only attempt to get it if you think your body/or hands are in the best position to do so (behind it).
3. As you strike the ball with your hands (other parts are equally appropriate), strike under it, on top of it, and on its sides. Learn where the ball goes when you contact it in different places.

Discussion. The first two tasks should be familiar as they use content from Themes 2 (directions) and 4 (speed). The difference, however, is the stress on the *position* of the body and body parts involved *before* contacting the object. As a focus, this should be used as soon as children can handle it, because it is critical to skillful movement. Adding to tasks challenges such as "ONLY catch it, strike it, or make other contact when you are in what you think is a *good* position," is an excellent way to help children sharpen their concentration on the focus of the task—positioning in relation to an object.

Task 3 is different. This task gives children an opportunity to think about the different relationships possible and then to try them out. At the start, it is wise to let them explore these different positions so they find out for themselves what happens to a ball when struck from "on top," "underneath," and "on the sides." Remember, however, the purpose of the task is to help children experience the meaning of in front of, behind, etc. when manipulating an object. If you think they need more guidance, you will have to add structure to the experience.

RELATIONSHIPS WITHIN THE ENVIRONMENT. This type of relationship is not easy, either for the child or for the teacher. For teachers, it means that they must be familiar with a number of basic concepts of strategy *common* to games.[11] This will allow the teacher to help children figure out strategies specific to any game they might ultimately be playing, conventional or original. For the children, it means they must now *relate* their movement to others, with others, and against others as well as objects and boundaries, and adjust because of rules. This is difficult because the games environment is an open one, one that is constantly changing as the game is played. Three ideas to which children should be introduced are particularly helpful. The first idea focuses on the *individual child as a player* in a game or game-like situation, the second focuses on the *importance of knowing where the ball is or should be*, and the third focuses on knowing *where to take the ball when you are in possession of it and why*. The development of these ideas has been influenced by some of the "common strategy concepts" identified by Seidel, et al.[11]

1. Throughout a game or game-like experience, children have to be aware of where they are in relation to everyone else, the ball, and the boundaries. In net-type games, this is often called "court sense;" in field and goal-oriented games, it does not have a name, but it means the same thing. This implies that players must constantly *position* and *reposition* themselves; for example, when waiting to receive a ball, when preparing to send a ball away, and when planning to intercept a ball. In other words, constant observation of the entire area is needed to know how the game or game-like experience is developing, and hence, where to position yourself.

2. A second idea to which children need to be introduced is that when a ball is sent to a space it should not be sent to just any space, but rather to one that is important to the flow of the game. Children need to know that thinking where to put the ball when passing is *basic* to becoming a skillful games player.

3. Finally, the third idea to which children should be introduced is that when in possession of the ball during a game or game-like situation, they need to be able to take it where they want to go. Being able to maneuver the ball by quick changes in direction and speed (carrying or dribbling), in order to gain some advantage, is a skill we must introduce to children early.

Sample Learning Experiences
1. As you move throughout the space, toss a ball (a variety of types are appropriate) among your group (three to four), always staying the same distance away from each other. Do not move in a circle, but cut across the space frequently and toss the ball so your teammates can catch it. (Add a person to try to tag the ball.)

2. As you move down the space, pass the ball (a variety of types are appropriate) to your teammate (two per group), making your passes go directly to him/her or slightly ahead. (After they get this idea, you could change the formation and make it similar to Task 1.)
3. Set up a couple of cones with different distances between them. With a soccer-type ball (or hockey-type stick), plan your route, beginning from where you want to start and ending where you want to finish. Dribble the ball according to your plan, increasing your speed each time. Make a new plan and repeat.

Discussion. First and most important, a word about "game-like" experiences. All experiences in this theme *should be considered as game-like*. They are like games, but are not games. Their purpose is to simulate the dynamic nature of games by involving more than one person so children have to relate to each other—cooperatively, or competitively, or both. In other words, the idea of manipulating a ball in an environment that is constantly changing begins to be stressed. The intent of this type of experience is to begin focusing on relationships as something tangible as well as using the manipulative skills in a more dynamic environment (e.g., more "game-like"). In designing this type of experience, and for it to meet the purpose for which it was designed, the size of the group must match the developmental level of all its members. To gain maximum benefit from experiences such as these, children need to

1. understand the idea of the task and what it means *translated into action* (demonstrations are needed);
2. begin slowly; and
3. make it more challenging by gradually increasing the speed, the distance between players, and the object or implement being used (playing with them yourself is another good way to challenge them).

Task 1 has the children focusing on the other players, where they are in relation to them. This takes a lot of concentration, especially as the throws must be such that they can be caught. Adding a "ball tagger" makes keeping that distance even more of a challenge. Task 2 has the children shift their attention now to the ball and where it should go, specifically. Should it go

ahead of the player, behind the player, or what? This is difficult as it involves timing a pass in relation to a moving player (some of whom, in this case, may not be certain where they are going). The emphasis here should be on the idea only, helping children realize its importance and "having a try." Theme 7 will focus on this again. Task 3 asks the children to think where they are taking the ball, *ahead* of time. The point here is to introduce children to the idea that traveling with a ball in a game needs to be planned; one does not just go.

As these ideas are common to games of all forms, it is critical that children begin to understand them and their importance. For without

them, becoming a skillful games player is questionable. No matter how skilled children may be in catching, collecting, throwing, striking, carrying, and dribbling as "fundamental skills," it is only how they can refine and adapt them in game play that ultimately will decide their skill at playing games. These experiences represent the first phase of a fundamental motor skill "becoming" a game skill.

SAMPLE UNIT PLAN THEME 5

Theme(s). Introduction to Relationships— Theme 5 (selected material from Themes 1, 2, 4).

Unit Focus. Positioning and repositioning, as it relates to teammates and opponents.

Appropriate For. Children who can handle balls easily with feet (dribbling) or upper body parts (striking, throwing, catching), and who can easily handle a given amount of space. When playing together, they are not aware that they are part of a group.

Length of Unit. Three 30-minute lessons.

Content

> Body—manipulative activities: dribbling, striking, throwing, catching body parts: feet, arms, head, fists
> Space—areas: general
> Effort—flow, continuity
> Relationship—positioning in relation to teammates and opponents

Student Objectives. Children should be willing to try to

1. Observe and adjust their position in relation to teammates and opponents in different situations.

2. Recognize when they are successful at "positioning" and when they are having difficulty.

3. To play a familiar game modified to help them practice a "specific skill"—positioning (circle dodgeball).

Teaching Area. Indoors, outdoors, medium to large (in a medium-sized space you may have to have some children take turns, for which this could easily be planned).

Equipment

Objects. 8-inch plastic, PG rubber and soccer balls (or deflated 8-inch PG).

Implements. Hockey (field/ice) sticks and balls.

Other. None

Learning Experiences (Tasks)

1.0 Everyone travel throughout the entire space, trying to keep an equal distance between yourselves. Watch very carefully.

1.1 Same task, but pass a ball among the group. Try to get a feel for where everyone is.

1.2 Same as Task 1.0, but starting with five children, spread out then add one at a time until all are moving. Keep looking and adjusting.

2.0 Discussion: review the purpose of most recent task and ask them to evaluate their progress.

3.0 In groups of three (four if necessary), keep the distance between yourselves equal (as possible) and toss a ball around while traveling. Cut across the space frequently, no circling.

3.1 Same as Task 3.0, but use your feet as you pass the ball among yourselves.

3.2 Same as Task 3.0, but use a hockey stick (field/ice) and ball.

4.0 In a circle formation (3 to 4) and using upper body parts, strike (hit, volley) a ball (8-inch plastic or sponge) back and forth among your group. Every time someone hits the ball, the rest must reposition themselves to "reform" the "circle." Try to keep the ball in the air, but use a bounce when necessary.

4.1 Same as Task 4.0, but with eight people.

Task 5.0 is designed specifically to lead up to a *modified* version of the conventional game of "Circle Dodgeball." This game is selected because awareness of one's position in a group is central to its success. Remember, the *reason* this game is being played as part of this unit is to help children focus on their position in relation to a group.

5.0 Arrange your 8 people with 4 in the middle of a 4-person circle (25 feet across). (The children know the object of the game; if they do not, it should be explained here.)

Task for "Throwers": pass the ball across and around the circle, but always to a person close to a "dodger." Do not try to hit the dodgers, yet. As you do this, try to maintain your circle by repositioning in relation to the person about to catch the ball.

Task for "Dodgers": keep as far away from the ball as possible, being careful not to bump or trip your teammates. Sense where everyone is *at all times.*

REMEMBER TO HAVE GROUPS SWITCH: THROWERS BECOME DODGERS

5.1 Same as Task 5.0, but letting "Throwers" aim at the "Dodgers" (below waist). (If they are hit, have them indicate this by raising a hand, but have them *stay in* so they can get the full practice of positioning within the group.)

5.2 Same as Task 5.0, but having those hit *become part* of the outer circle. This makes the task of positioning and repositioning

A Suggested Progression for Sample Games Unit/Theme 5

	Lesson 1		Lesson 2		Lesson 3
Tasks	**Teaching Tips**	**Tasks**	**Teaching Tips**	**Tasks**	**Teaching Tips**
1.0	Stress easy traveling; look all about you and reposition yourself accordingly.	3.0	(Use a plastic ball) Warm yourselves up, getting back the feel of where you are and where everyone else is. Keep this going until everyone seems "focused."	4.0	Use this as a warm-up and let them keep at it until everyone is "on task" and active. Keep stressing key points related to their positioning in relation with others.
1.1	Stress same points. This will be harder for them—fun, but harder.	4.0	Explain task and let everyone try it. Clarify any points that need it. Stress quick repositioning as soon as you can tell where ball is going.	5.0	Let them get themselves started so you can see what they remembered. Stress same points. Stop play to help them, if necessary.
1.2	Stress: as you go in, be sure to pick a place that will balance the group. Stop the task if they begin to crowd. Let them reposition and start again. Do this whenever this happens.	2.0	If needed.	5.1	Explain modification and why it is being made. As they shift their focus on hitting someone out, they will most likely lose their focus on positioning. Help them bring it back.
2.0	If needed. The children must know why this idea is so important. Relate it to current sports. Suggest they observe for it on TV, etc.	4.1	Stress: everyone "alert" and reposition immediately. (Circle may have to be larger to make task challenging.)		*Comment.* You will notice lots of "other things" that need work, but leave them alone until another time. The idea of positioning will get lost if too much other information is now given.
3.0	Encourage safe spacing as they begin. After they have settled, stress their positioning; keep circle balanced. Have them speed up their throws.	5.0	Explain to children the purpose of using "Circle Dodgeball," and do not let them take you away from this purpose. Demonstrate task with one group and then let other groups get started.	5.2	Explain this modification and why. As they play this, keep helping them with their positioning. As they get better, you probably will need to point out:
2.0	If needed.	2.0	REMEMBER, STOP ALL GROUPS IF PURPOSE IS NOT BEING MET. Explain to children that they will continue with this, next lesson.		To "Throwers": only throw at people who have one of your team behind them; throw quicker.
3.1 } 3.2 }	Explain to groups that you want them to try this in two other situations. Let them select the order and begin. Stress: watch all your teammates, be aware of where they are and reposition yourself.	5.0	As they work, help both "Dodgers" and "Throwers." Stress: look about, reposition. Stop "game" if they need to see what they are *not* doing.		To "Dodgers": watch the ball and move away from it.
2.0	If needed. This might be good to end the class with—summarize the purpose of the lesson.				*Comment.* You may notice that some of the throwing, catching, and dodging is weak. Give only essential help, and use information gained for future lessons. You want the children in these lessons to really look like they know something about positioning.

harder as both groups are now changing in size.

Evaluation. Refer to Chapter 10 and either select or adapt one of the evaluative tools or develop a tool that can be used to assess a specific aspect of the unit that is important to the needs of your students.

GAMES THEME 6—ADVANCED BODY AND MANIPULATIVE CONTROL

Theme 6 is the second theme designed to help children gain skillful use of their bodies. Theme 1 was introductory in nature and stressed that *the level of mastery or body control required to become a skillful games player TAKES TIME.*

Theme 6 revisits this idea and begins to extend the work begun in Theme 1 by expecting more skillful use of the body in game-like situations. This improvement in skill can be expected if the children can handle well the work in Themes 1 through 5. The placement of Theme 6 is purposeful; it is placed between the two relationship themes, Theme 5—Introduction to Basic Relationships—and Theme 7—Introduction to Complex Relationships. Although Themes 1 and 6 are separated by Themes 2 through 5, ideas associated with Theme 6 should be used whenever a child or group of children are developmentally ready.

Development of Theme 6

```
Basic Content
   Manipulative activities: striking,
   throwing, catching, collecting, car-
   rying, dribbling
   combined with
            ↓
   Locomotion: running, jumping, slid-
   ing, sidestepping, rolling (for recov-
   ery of balance)
   combined with
            ↓
   Nonlocomotion: extending
                   twisting
                   bending
```

MANIPULATIVE ACTIVITIES COMBINED WITH LOCOMOTION COMBINED WITH NONLOCOMOTION. By now, the children should be comfortable using the basic manipulative activities while handling a range of objects and implements. Teachers designing tasks and using material from this theme should consider these activities as getting closer to what a game skill really is.

Tasks may have to be focused on one or more of the ideas contained in this theme because individual children or groups of children may need less difficult work. The purpose of the theme, however, is to design tasks that use manipulation activities in a more risk-taking situation. To do this involves greater skill in the way the body travels and the way it can twist, bend, and extend itself in relation to a moving object. For example:

1. Catching a ball way out in front while traveling fast, and recovering if balance is lost.

2. Throwing a hard, direct pass to a player who is running into a space quickly.

3. Running forward prior to jumping high into the air to catch a high, softly thrown ball.

4. Fully extending a leg in an effort to keep a ball passed along the ground from getting past you, while traveling at top speed.

To be able to move like this, children need the options offered them by achieving or being close to the mature stage in the manipulative activities (see Chapters 3 and 4 for help in evaluating this) as well as an agile use of their bodies. This means children need to be able to FULLY *twist, bend,* and *extend* WHILE *traveling* (in air or along ground with feet and other body surfaces) AND *strike* (volley, hit, bat), throw, collect, catch, carry, and dribble EFFECTIVELY and EFFICIENTLY.

All the content in this theme, except "rolling," has been discussed in earlier themes (see Themes 1 and 2) and should be familiar. What is DIFFERENT now is the WAY it will be used.

Sample Learning Experiences
1. *Purpose of task:* to create a situation in which children can practice running and catching a ball, which makes them extend their arms in front of them, out to the sides of them, and over their heads (eventually at top speed).

   Task for runner: run past the thrower and catch the ball.

   Task for thrower: throw the ball so the runner has to catch it out in front, overhead, and behind.

For children to develop skill in catching balls that come in different places around them, the thrower must be able to toss them there. While this task focuses on the runner, the thrower is getting practice at timing a throw. To achieve the intent of the experience in this task, a list of suggestions are given to help make it (and others similar to it) meet the criterion of "risk taking."

1. Show the formation of the task. Use children as "demonstrators" and walk them through it. Make sure it "works."
2. Let other children set themselves up and do that much. (They are showing you they understand the organization of the task.)
3. Tell the thrower where to pass the ball. Tell them to begin. Have them keep working, encouraging the thrower to make his/her partner reach out *a little* farther each time; runner will begin to run faster and jump higher.
4. Tell thrower next place, and repeat 3.
5. Tell thrower next place, and repeat 3.
6. Let thrower select place to pass and let runner react. (You could begin with 6 if children were ready and then if needed use 3, 4, 5.) Work out a way for the children to switch roles, or let them decide.

Task 1 is a basic task that can be redesigned in several ways: (a) the ball being thrown can be changed to another size, weight, or texture; (b) both children could use a hockey stick (field/ice),

the runner could have the stick with the thrower using his/her hands to throw; (c) a plastic tennis racket or short-handled racket could be used, and instead of catching being the focus, hitting/striking could be. Remember, though, it is the extra speed, the extra reach that is important here.

2. Working by yourself, toss a ball so you have to catch it *in the air* and *off balance*. As you land, gently lower your body and roll over to a standing position. Repeat, changing where you throw the ball (forward, backward, sideward).
2a. When ready, have a partner throw it to you to bring out the same off-balance catch (off balance can be forward, backward, sideward).

This task should only be done when the children are skilled in rolling-for-recovery purposes. Because this is part of Educational Gymnastics, no discussion is needed here.

Children need to experience falling off balance because of over extending. They will enjoy this if the "rolling" movement is well developed. This task unites both Educational Gymnastics and Educational Games for a moment and can be used to help children realize the relationship between them.

3. Strike the ball back to your partner, using tops of feet, thighs, forearms, fists; try hard to get everything back. (Partner keeps sending ball toward partner's feet, thighs, fore-

arms, and fists, slowly making partner reach a little farther each time.) Remember, in observing the children doing this task, be sure the striker *is* being continuously extended, stretched out.

Discussion. Task 1 and Task 3 are both tasks that will need help from the teacher, particularly at the beginning. Children will have to learn specifically what the role is of the "thrower," and it may take more control than some children have. It is the accuracy of where the ball is placed that brings out the desired movement response.

As the children are working, it may become evident that some may need added practice with certain parts of the task because it is too challenging. For example, if it is too difficult for some children to do Task 1 as designed, they might just toss an object to themselves so they have to jump to catch it, only traveling when they can. When children seem to be having difficulty, the following three steps may be helpful:

1. Identify the major problem.
2. Find which theme deals directly with it.
3. Redesign a task or series of tasks accordingly.

One of the major challenges in designing tasks truly representative of this theme is that children need *space* in which to do them. This is because in order to capture the dynamic nature of games, more speed is necessary and more speed needs more space to handle the new safety considerations. To handle this problem, careful organizational patterns must be designed, with the children learning why certain ones are being used. These patterns should seriously consider not having all children participating at once, but on some quick rotation scheme. This level of work needs space to develop; it is a problem that has to be faced. If children can handle themselves responsibly, they will waste little time in "switching places." When their turn comes, they will be able to use more space and go "harder," both essential to becoming skillful.

SAMPLE UNIT PLAN THEME 6

Theme(s). Advanced Body Control—Theme 6 (selected material from Themes 1, 2, 3, 4, 5).
Unit Focus. Catching balls that force running,

jumping, and reaching into space at the same time.

Appropriate For. Children who can catch and throw, using the space around them with some confidence. They use space well when traveling and are improving in their ability to catch balls that make them jump. They use space well when traveling and are improving in their ability to "sense" each other.

Length of Unit. Two 30-minute lessons.
Content
    Body—manipulative activities: catching, throwing combined with running, jumping combined with extending, twisting
    Space—extensions: far from; levels: high, medium
    Effort—right amount of speed, force, and space-quality for efficient and effective "jumping and catching"
    Relationship—position in relation to each other

Student Objectives. Children should be willing to try to

1. Catch balls when in the air, using all the space around them.
2. Throw the type of pass that will make a person jump to catch it.
3. Evaluate their own progress as well as the progress of others in relation to the task.
4. Enjoy the feeling of going "out into space" to catch a ball.

Teaching Area. Indoors, outdoors, medium to large. Ground surface should be smooth.
Equipment
Objects. 8-inch plastic, sponge, or PG rubber balls; 5-inch PG rubber of soft softball; bean bag; 1 per child.
Implements
Other. "Boundary" markers: tape, cones, ropes. (Use with Tasks 5.0, 5.1 in particular.)
Learning Experiences (Tasks)

1.0 By yourself and with a bean bag to start with. Toss the bean bag in the space above your head and jump to catch it. Catch with your right as well as your left hand. Now use a ball.
1.1 Same idea, but now toss the bean bag out to the sides. Toss it so you must leave the ground to catch it. Remember, both left and right hands. Now use a ball.

1.2 Same as Task 1.1, but with traveling. Now use a ball. Travel only short distances.

2.0 Observation/discussion session(s) focused on helping the children understand the importance of the toss to bring out the jump and the importance of giving in hips, knees, and ankles to cushion the landing.

3.0 Working with partners, toss the ball in all the spaces around them so they HAVE TO JUMP TO CATCH IT. Change size of ball.

3.1 Same idea as in Task 3.0, but now have your partner travel into a space as you throw the bean bag. Watch that your partner does not always move in the same direction. Change size of ball.

4.0 Both traveling (within a designated area), toss and catch the bean bag, keeping it off the ground. Change the direction you are traveling often and quickly. Watch carefully where others are going and adjust your movements to fit.

4.1 As you get the feel of this task, toss the bean bag so your partner has to jump up to catch it.

4.2 Toss it so your partner has to jump and reach forward, sideward, and even backward.

4.3 Same task but with balls of different sizes.

5.0 In a group no larger than five (they choose the size), toss and catch while traveling, getting the feel of the different-sized group. Group choses object.

5.1 Same as Task 5.0, but emphasizing different points: (a) tossing so player has to jump and reach forward, backward, sideward to catch it; (b) even spacing between all players; (c) running across the space, not around it.

A Suggested Progression for Sample Games Unit/Theme 6

Lesson 1*		Lesson 2*	
Tasks	**Teaching Tips**	**Tasks**	**Teaching Tips**
1.0	Let them get feel of toss and jump-to-catch before you "stress" anything in particular. Stress type of toss (one that hangs above your head) and when to jump (ask them this). Discuss differences when using a ball. (Let them choose ball.)	4.3	Have them quickly get a partner, *different* than last class, and begin immediately. Observe carefully and go back to Tasks 4.2 or 4.1, if needed (keep ball).
		6.0	Stress selecting one point to work on.
1.1	Same as for Task 1.0 with increased attention on the toss and where it should go.	4.3	Work on the point selected in Task 6.0. You may have to ask them what it was to observe results.
2.0	Pose questions and help children seek the answers.	5.0	Help them get organized. As soon as they are ready, let them start. Have them just get the feeling of the space and group size first; use tosses that are easy to catch.
1.1	Stress what they suggested.		
1.2	Stress the control of the flow of their movement (Theme 4), especially their speed and use of general space.		
3.0	Stress the accuracy of the toss so partner really has to jump.	5.1	Select a, b, or c and help them with it. Add a new idea whenever group seems ready.
3.1	Encourage looking where you are going and changing to a ball of your choice when ready.	6.0⎫ 5.1⎪ 6.0⎬ 5.1⎭	Use this pattern, and if group is skilled enough, let them pace themselves as to when to evaluate, when to move.
4.0	Make sure they know the area in which they have to work. Let them get the feel of it before stressing specific parts of the task. Stress: watch how you are positioned in relation to each other; try to be in the best place to toss as well as to receive the ball (Theme 5).		
4.1⎫ 4.2⎭	Gradually add each idea as you think they are ready. This may have to be done with individual pairs, for the group may not be ready all at the same time.		
6.0	When finished, encourage them to start again, trying to use their suggestions.		
4.3	If time permits and they would like to shift to a ball, let them select one and try it.		

*Comment. Estimating the length of this unit is difficult without knowing specifically the children's experience. Remember: discussions often take more time than planned; all the children will not be moving all the time—for some of these tasks they will need more space as well as rests: Tasks 3.1, 4.2, 4.3, and 5.1 in particular.

6.0 Group evaluation session: group stops, evaluates its progress with task, suggests improvement, and tries to put it into practice.

Evaluation. Refer to Chapter 10 and either select or adapt one of the evaluative tools or develop a tool that can be used to help assess a specific aspect of the unit that is important to the needs of your students.

GAMES THEME 7—INTRODUCTION TO COMPLEX RELATIONSHIPS

In Theme 5, two forms of relationships were introduced, relationships with objects and relationships within the game environment. Theme 7 takes the latter idea farther by focusing on three specific forms of relationships: passing to spaces, creating spaces, and covering spaces.

Development of Theme 7

> **Basic Content**
> Relationships within the environment: passing to spaces, creating spaces, covering spaces

RELATIONSHIPS WITHIN THE ENVIRONMENT: PASSING TO SPACES. Passing to spaces, one of the most basic principles associated with game strategy, means *passing to a space in relation to someone*—a teammate or an opponent. We speak of passing *ahead of, behind,* or *even with* your teammate or opponent, but in reality, we pass into a space that is ahead of, behind, or even with your teammate or opponent. For example:

1. *Passing ahead of a teammate:* used in games like soccer, field hockey, or basketball to move the ball forward down the field or to put the ball in a good position for "a shot at goal." This type of pass is often called a "lead pass."

2. *Passing ahead of an opponent:* used in games like dodgeball to move the ball into position for "hitting" the runner (opponent) out.

3. *Passing behind a teammate:* used in games like soccer, lacrosse, field hockey, or basketball when a teammate is being closely marked or there is a sudden shift in a team's positioning.

4. *Passing behind an opponent:* not usually used unless by mistake.

5. *Passing even with a teammate:* used in games like field hockey, soccer, or basketball to allow *you* to dodge an oncoming opponent. (Making a "flat" pass to a teammate who is free at the same moment a defense player is approaching, allows you to go around the oncoming player and receive a pass back from your teammate. This "pass" is the classic "triangular" or "give and go" pass so basic to many games.)

Although the idea of passing to spaces can be applied to most games, for net games such as tennis, volleyball, and newcomb, it is used for a different purpose. As long as the ball is on your side of the net, players need to be able to toss the ball ahead, even, or behind their teammates (not tennis). When the ball is sent over the net, however, the main objective becomes to send it to the *open spaces* to force the opponents out of position. It is not sent to a specific place in relation to a specific player.

RELATIONSHIPS WITHIN THE ENVIRONMENT: CREATING SPACES. This is a difficult idea for beginning games players to understand and is considered too hard to be handled with a total class. A basic understanding of what it means by the teacher, however, is necessary, for it could be introduced to individual children or groups of children as they demonstrate a need for it.

Creating spaces is just what it sounds like—*making spaces.* Players create spaces usually for two reasons: (a) to make a space for another player to move into or through and (b) to make a space for themselves to cut back or through. Offensive players rather than defensive players usually use this strategy. It is a well known strategy in games such as lacrosse, field hockey, soccer, basketball, and the like. There are many game-like experiences as well as original and conventional games that would be handled better by children if they could use this strategy. It takes a long time to develop, but if some children seem ready, it could be introduced.

RELATIONSHIPS WITHIN THE ENVIRONMENT: COVERING SPACES. As a strategy or special form of relationship, covering spaces is usually associated with defense players. It refers to the players when they position themselves in a space *between* the person they are responsible for and another opponent or opponents. It is often referred to as a loose form of marking or guarding. This "loose" positioning often helps

the players intercept a pass because they are often closer to the ball if they have positioned themselves well. Covering requires constant positioning and repositioning in relation to the emerging flow of the game and because it is so situational it is difficult to teach out of context.

For beginners, it is suggested that close marking be encouraged as the way to be introduced to guarding. Then, as the children need it and are ready, covering, per se, could be introduced.

Sample Learning Experiences

1. Passing to spaces.

In a designated spot, in twos, pass a ball (hands, feet, implement) *ahead* of your partner. (Give a lead pass.) Both of you should be constantly moving. (When they are ready, increase the group size.)

Using a 2 v 2 formation, play "keep away." As you play, focus on cutting soon enough so your partner can give you a lead pass. Concentrate on giving lead passes. Stop periodically to discuss how well you are handling the task and what could be improved.

In a 3 v 3 formation, strike an 8-inch plastic or sponge ball back and forth (hands, arms, head), *always* trying to strike it to a space (not to a person) when it passes over the "net" (a string, net, or line). When sending it to your teammates, put it in the best place for them to handle it.

Discussion. In Task 1, the focus is on passing ahead of the player, giving lead passes. A lead pass pulls a player forward into an empty space. This is not an easy idea to develop with children, because when they are the receiver, they have difficulty in knowing when to "cut" for the pass; and when the thrower, they have difficulty in knowing when to release the pass. These two ideas, cutting or moving into a space "at the right time" and passing ahead depend on each other and should be developed as such.

Task 2 focuses on the same idea as Task 1, but with opposition. If children have difficulty with Task 1, Task 2 may be too hard. To make Task 2 easier, you could add an extra person to the "offense." In doing this experience, children will feel as if they are playing a game. In the excitement, the receiver will probably stand waiting for the pass rather than cutting into an open space and the thrower will probably throw directly at the receiver. This is all normal when first working with this type experience, but with

practice, they should improve. If this does not happen, you may have to break it down for them.

Task 3 focuses on the idea of hitting or striking a ball to a space when sending it over a "net." The focus is on making the opponents move out of position to return it. This is a lot to keep track of, visually, because as the players are getting ready to hit the ball, they must observe where their opponents are as well.

2. Creating/covering spaces.

No sample learning experiences are being given here, since introducing these ideas in context when needed was suggested to be more meaningful. This allows the children to relate the ideas immediately to a real situation. For example: imagine children in a game-like experience where two sets of partners are doing a task that requires each pair to keep the ball away from the other. They are using plastic hockey sticks. One child, instead of moving to receive a pass, stands in the center of the playing area waving his stick. Stopping the experience and showing the child (and letting him do it a few times) how to move out of that spot, thereby "opening" a space for a teammate to use or "creating" a space for himself to run back into, could be demonstrated. The assumption is that when this child finds himself in this situation again, he might try that particular move.

A FINAL COMMENT

The material discussed in both Themes 5 and 7 is not easy to understand or to apply when playing in a game or game-like experience. You might well ask is it too hard for children? The answer is yes, no, and it depends.[1] What is certain, however, is that few children are being introduced to these ideas in elementary school physical education classes and they need to be. By keeping the groups small enough and accommodating to children's individual needs, many of these concepts can be introduced.

SAMPLE UNIT PLAN THEME 7

Theme(s). Introduction to Complex Relationships—Theme 7 (selected material from Themes 1, 2). The tasks in this unit are such that they can only be accomplished with a solid base of work from Themes 1 through 6.

Unit Focus. Passing to spaces, emphasizing the placement of the pass in relation to the receiver.

A Suggested Progression for Sample Games Unit/Theme 7

Lesson 1		Lesson 2		Lesson 3	
Tasks	Teaching Tips*	Tasks	Teaching Tips*	Tasks	Teaching Tips*
1.0	Help them get settled and have them begin working right away. Stress careful spacing and knowing what they are working on. (Focus on their work.) Stop activity and organize into 8 groups. Have every group sit as a group. Go over organization, showing where each group will be, what direction they will rotate (clockwise), and with what equipment they will start. Explain that everyone will get to use all the equipment.	2.0} 5.0}	They will start with the next set of equipment. Follow same pattern as the previous lesson. Two rotations.	2.0	Have them begin with the last set of equipment. As soon as they are ready, they can begin.
3.0	Give out task 2.0, stressing only part (a) passing ahead. *Show* them what this means with one group. Review for them the organization and let them begin.	3.0	Observe a different group (using different equipment). Discuss where pass is being sent and if ready, discuss the receiver's role in timing the cut (move for pass).	6.0	Stress looking at *where pass went* in relation to receiver and *when* receiver cut. Two turns each, remember they have to share their observations this time.
2.0	Stress good spacing in group; passing ball *ahead* of receiver.	2.0} 5.0}	Rotate to third type of equipment. Help children waiting their turn in the process of self-evaluation.	3.0	Observe a group (different equipment) and have them comment on *where pass went* and *when* receiver cut.
5.0	Group coming off to self-evaluate. Change until each group has had two turns.			2.0} 4.0}	Give them a choice—to add opponents or not (use same equipment). If using opponents, have them mark closely. Help children *time* cut to receive pass and pass *ahead* to receiver.
3.0	Bring class together to observe a group under your guidance. Stress discussion of *pass* and where it went. Tell them that when they come in the next time, they will begin with the next type of equipment.				

*Common to all the manipulative activities needed in this unit is the idea of the position of the implement or body part in relation to the object at moment of contact. While focus here is on passing to a space, or ahead of the player, some of their problems will be because of the *way* they hit the ball or threw it. Help them focus on this as they work; it will help them improve their passing as well. If they cannot handle both ideas, have them focus on the passing to a space.

Appropriate For. Children who are experienced using hockey sticks, plastic tennis rackets, feet for dribbling, and hands for throwing and catching. They understand what it means when you talk about "a player's position in relation to people, boundaries, etc.," but they still cannot always adjust in a game-like situation. They tend to "crowd" each other. They can direct themselves in group work.

Length of Unit. Three 30-minute lessons. (This has been written up for three lessons but could easily be extended to one or two more.)

Content

Body—manipulative activities: throwing, catching, striking, dribbling, collecting

Space—areas: general

Effort—

Relationships—relationships within environment: passing to spaces

Student Objectives. Children should be willing to try to

1. Pass ahead of a moving player, using a variety of implements and objects.

2. Self-evaluate their group's progress, with the concept of passing ahead to a receiver.

3. Suggest to other groups what they might practice after a direct observation of their work.

4. Accept the suggestions for improvement given them from their peers.

Teaching Area. Indoors, ourdoors, large (although this unit needs a large space, the basic tasks are possible to adapt for use in other units).

Equipment

Objects. 8-inch PG rubber, plastic, soccer, and 5-inch PG rubber balls, soft softballs (minimum 10 each).

Implements. Plastic tennis rackets and sponge ball, field hockey sticks and soft softballs.

Other. Boundary markers (if children want these).

Learning Experiences (Tasks)

1.0 In groups of twos or threes, select your equipment and use it in some way together. Decide together the focus of your activity and then begin.

2.0 Pass a ball among yourselves (four per group) working on two things:
(a) when you pass the ball, pass it *ahead* of the receiver, and } major emphasis

(b) when you want to receive the ball cut (move) quickly into an open space. } minor emphasis

3.0 Class discussion/obervation, using one group as the focus.

4.0 Same task as Task 2.0, but with defense players added.

5.0 Group self-evaluation of work: identification of strengths and weaknesses and suggestions for improvement.

6.0 Observation of another group, followed by a discussion with them of their strengths and weaknesses.

Basic Organization beginning with task 2.0. (Adaptations will have to be made according to individual situations.)

1. 8 groups, 2 each with hockey sticks and balls, tennis rackets and balls, 8-inch PG rubber balls, and soccer balls.

2. Four groups will work simultaneously, with one group waiting safely out of the way. If more than four groups can work, have like groups near each other.

3. Groups will keep taking turns. Once both have had a chance to work with the task(s), their waiting time will become observation and evaluation time.

4. If inside, make sure "tennis" group has a corner, so when ready, it can "use" the walls.

Evaluation. Refer to Chapter 10 and either select or adapt one of the evaluative tools or develop a tool that can be used to help assess a specific aspect of the unit that is important to the needs of your students.

PROGRESSION

Organization of the content of games into seven themes helps give the games program unity and direction. The themes, while possessing an internal progression, are not the only way to organize this content. Rather, they are suggestions, to be used in the way most helpful to the particular situation. When you give suggestions in a hierarchical format, they may be used in too rigid a fashion. For example, you may think you should use certain themes for the kindergarten, certain themes for the first grade, and the like. For these themes to be of any value, they must be used in relation to each situation, with the basis for selecting when to

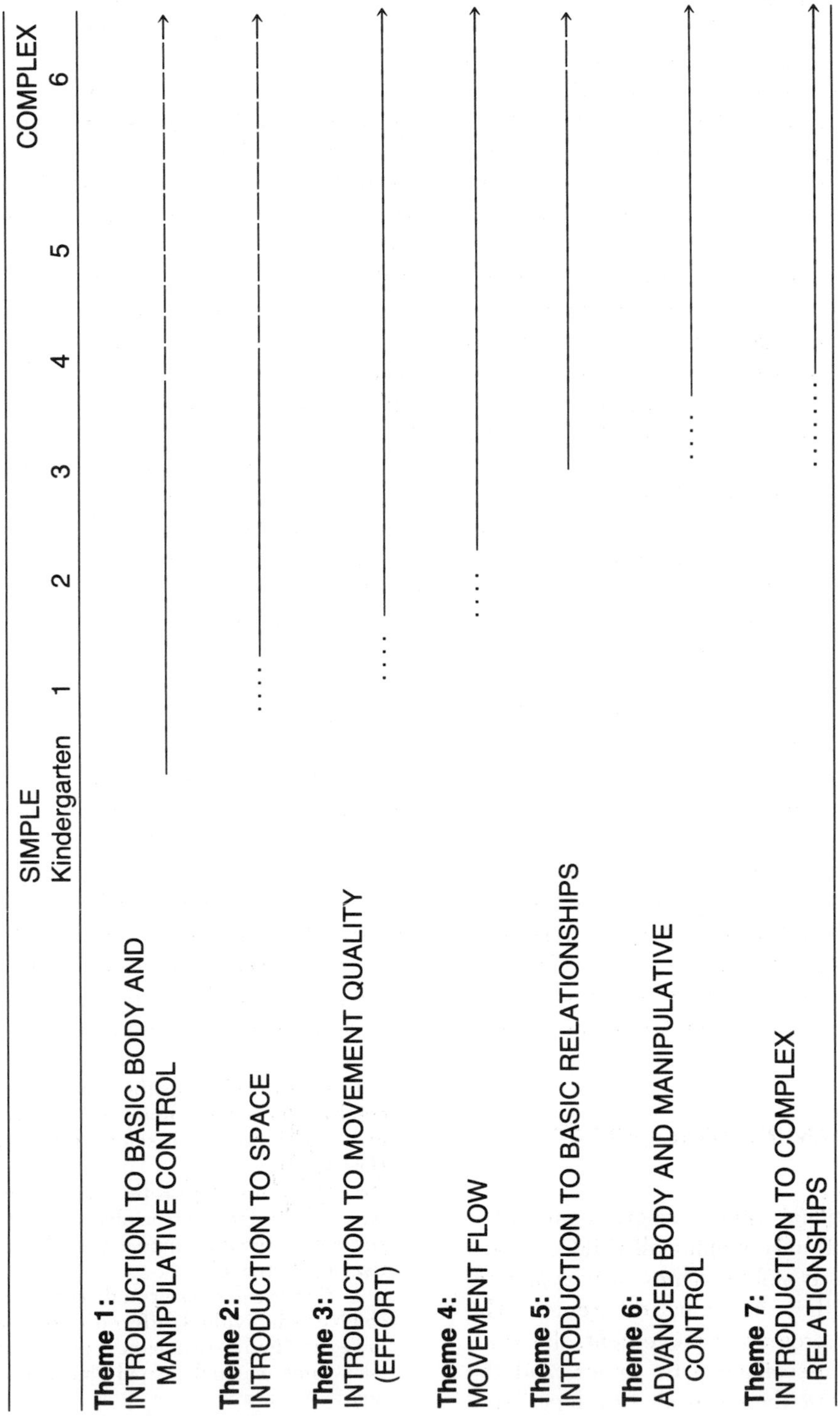

	SIMPLE					COMPLEX
	Kindergarten	1	2	3	4	5	6

Theme 1:
INTRODUCTION TO BASIC BODY AND
MANIPULATIVE CONTROL

Theme 2:
INTRODUCTION TO SPACE

Theme 3:
INTRODUCTION TO MOVEMENT QUALITY
(EFFORT)

Theme 4:
MOVEMENT FLOW

Theme 5:
INTRODUCTION TO BASIC RELATIONSHIPS

Theme 6:
ADVANCED BODY AND MANIPULATIVE
CONTROL

Theme 7:
INTRODUCTION TO COMPLEX
RELATIONSHIPS

Fig. 7–2. Theme Progression for Educational Games Program.

use which ones and how long to use them dependent on a clear and logical understanding of movement and children.

To give additional guidance to the development of a game program, a suggested progression of themes has been designed. Figure 7–2 illustrates this progression. The purpose of the suggested progression is to show how themes may overlap and how ideas from past and future themes may be used throughout the games program.

Figure 7–2 represents a program that starts in the kindergarten and continues through the sixth grade. The suggested use of the themes is based on an instructional program of physical education, in which educational games comprise approximately one third of the total program for all children.

The solid lines suggest when the content inherent in the themes might be used as the major emphasis in designing the lessons. The broken lines suggest when the content in the themes might be used less frequently, with the primary purpose being to revisit prior content ideas if particular experiences were too difficult for a class or if you need to help individual children within it. The dotted lines indicate that the content in particular themes may be used to increase the complexity of an experience for a particular group of children. Certain children's needs may exceed the general direction of the class, and this approach personalizes their experience. Although a suggested progression of themes is given, introduction and development of them must be left with the teachers as they are the only ones who truly know how to pace the work.

GAME PLAY—AN INTEGRAL PART OF THE PROGRAM

The educational games program presented here is committed to helping all children reach their potential as skillful games players and accommodating their individual differences. The content of the program is movement, the kinds of movement associated with games, and the seven movement themes were developed specifically to give the program progression and unity. The program is perceived as having a broad set of experiences, a "liberal education in games," designed to help all children develop

the degree of skill level needed to allow them true options for personal choice during and after elementary school. This approach tries to see the playing of games as children see it, not as do adults.

A program based on these commitments should include both game forms, conventional and original. What games to include and how to teach them as an integral part of the program are important questions to ask yourself. Although answers to these questions may differ slightly among physical educators, all experiences designed within this part of the program must show *clearly* and *consistently* that individual differences are being accommodated, that all children do have a chance to improve their skill level when playing, and that how the experiences are designed is based on knowledge about children. Consider using these steps to help you plan the game experience as an integral part of the total games program: (a) GAME SELECTION: (b) GAME INTRODUCTION; and (c) GAME COACHING.

GAME SELECTION

As previously stated, there are conventional and original games. Both forms can be competitive or cooperative, both forms can be modified by the teacher, the teacher and child together, or the child alone, and both forms can be related to a specific game, a combination of more than one game, or a combination of elements in many games (e.g., dodgeball). In selecting a game, you need to ask yourself these questions:

1. How closely does the game "fit" what the children have been doing in class up to this point? The game you select needs "to fit" *as closely as possible*.
2. How important is the game in relation to meeting the stated lesson objectives? The game you select should support your lesson objectives *very strongly.*
3. Can the game selected accommodate the children's individual differences or will it have to be modified? Most games, conventional and even some original, usually have to be modified in some way.
4. In playing this game, will *all* children have an opportunity to improve their game-playing ability? The game selected should extend the children, but not frustrate or bore them.

If after asking yourself these questions, your answer to question 1 was "very close," to question 2 "very important," to question 3 "yes," and to question 4 "yes," you have probably made a good and timely selection.

If on the other hand, your answer to question 1 was "not too close," to question 2 "related, but vaguely," to question 3 "no," and to question 4 "no," you have probably made a poor selection or possibly a good selection but at the wrong time.

GAME INTRODUCTION

The less adjustment the children have to make in the type of skills they will use from their previous experiences to playing the game, the smoother and easier the transition will be. If you have made a careful selection based on answering the questions just suggested, this should not be a major problem.

For CONVENTIONAL GAMES, consider these ideas as one way to start the children playing a game:

1. For a less complex game, plan the previous learning experiences (tasks) carefully, so when the game is introduced, the children almost "feel" they have played it before.

2. For a more complex game, design some modified versions of it and have the children play them first. For example:

. . . reduce the number of players recommended, increasing it only if the children request it and can handle the new size—maximum six . . .

. . . change the rules: where a bounce was not allowed, allow it; where one player was designated a "goalie," play without one . . .

. . . alter the size of the playing area: make it smaller, eliminate boundaries . . .

. . . change the equipment: use a lighter ball, a shorter stick, a lower net, a larger target . . .

For ORIGINAL GAMES, consider these ideas as one way to start the children playing a game:

1. Time the moment you want the children to "make up a game" when they have just experienced a number of game-like tasks with some confidence.

2. Give the children a framework within which to make up their game that includes the same movement ideas with which they have *just* been working. Keep the framework simple.

3. Limit the group to three or four children per game group, increasing it only if children request it and can handle the new size—maximum six.

GAME COACHING

Coaching a game means *helping children improve the way they are playing it*. If your are committed to helping children reach their potential as skillful games players, they have to have experience, educational experience, in playing games. Many games played by children in physical education settings are not educational because they do not accommodate their individual needs. Coaching a game so that *all* children can learn while playing it is a skill we all need to cultivate. This is not easy because children in physical education classes will always show a wide range of development.

Coaching a game involves coaching it when *it is not working* and coaching it when *it is working*. A game is not working when the skills (motor, cognitive, affective) the children are using are ineffective. The game, because of this, begins to deteriorate. A game that is working is the opposite—the skills the children are using are effective.

IF A GAME IS NOT WORKING, the first thing you have to do is STOP it, and then start right in helping the children help themselves improve it. For some reason, many teachers are not willing or do not know how to stop a game and improve it "on the spot." Reasons vary from not knowing what should be happening to being intimidated by the children themselves. Whatever the reason, it is critical that you learn how to stop a game while it is going on and then "coach it."

To stop an entire class, agree on a signal before the children begin to play, which, when they hear it, will let them know to stop playing and listen. *To stop an individual group*, "intercept" the ball, or have the children pass it to you. Before stopping the game, however, be sure you have a definite plan in your mind as to what you intend to do once the children have stopped and are quiet. This includes how you want to organize them if different from their present pattern, as well as what you want to say once they have stopped and are listening. Here are several "plans" that have been useful when the game the children were playing WAS NOT WORKING.

PLAN A:
—Stop all groups.
—Make a comment based on your observations; e.g., "As I watched you play, all groups were having difficulty in passing ahead of the receiver."
—Ask them for suggestions as to how to improve this.
—Select a suggestion from their contributions or let them make the selection and let them work on it.
—Begin observing; look specifically for what was decided they would work on.

PLAN B:
—Stop one group (keep your eyes on the others).
—Make a comment based on your observations; e.g., "You are having some difficulties with this game, what do you think is the major problem?"
—Listen to their answers.
—Ask them to select a "difficulty" and let them work on it.
—Begin observing; look specifically for what was decided they would work on.

PLAN C:
—Stop all groups (the class is playing a dodgeball-type game).
—Keep one group up and bring all others in close enough for them to "see" them.
—Make a comment based on your observations; e.g., "I have noticed that every time you try to hit out a 'dodger,' no one from your team is behind him or her and the ball gets away."
—Show them what you meant by this comment, making sure they know what it is they are supposed "to see," guide their observation specifically.
—Ask them how they might handle this situation so the ball does not get away from them.

—Let them demonstrate their answer; you make sure the important points are made and that all can see the demonstration.
—Have the group play the game while you and the others comment on how well they are applying the ideas just discussed.
—Have the children make comments to the group that was just playing.
—Let all groups go back and work.
—Move from group to group, stopping them every time they throw without someone behind the "dodger." Ask them what should be done; have them do it; and let the game go on. Try to get around to all groups as quickly as possible.

IF A GAME IS WORKING, get excited for the children and let them PLAY IT. Too often, children reach a point in playing a game where it finally comes together—and we stop them. We go onto something else or we have them focus on "getting it better" immediately. There is a time when playing a game well, a simple or complex one, is important for the development of a skillful games player. There are special feelings and special learnings that come with playing a game *well* that can never be realized if it is never allowed to happen.

Obviously, you cannot play the same game all the time, and you will have to make a decision when to stop it and go on. Here are two options you might find helpful; both have worked well with children.

1. Let them play, and when you think they have had a good experience with it, begin new work in the *next* class; dance, gymnastics, or a completely different focus in games.

2. Let them play, and when you think they have played enough or the children request it, discuss with them how the game might be played better or modified for a greater challenge.

3. Take their suggestions and plan accordingly.

To help visualize how some of these ideas might be used in a lesson or a series of lessons, two real-life descriptions are given. In the first description, the game form used is original, and in the second description, the game form is conventional.

DESCRIPTION 1

BACKGROUND INFORMATION. The children have been working for several lessons with the manipulative activity of striking. Their ages range from 9½ years to approximately 11 years. There are 28 children in the class. The majority of the children can handle striking fairly well, using different body parts and a variety of implements with some confidence. The last class focused on striking, emphasizing a continuous change in levels while working in small groups. The children were free to choose whether to use paddles, short-handled tennis rackets, or parts of their bodies for striking. All three options were used.

The children grouped themselves and handled the method of striking as follows:

Group	Size	Method of Striking
A	1	racket
B	2	hands and head
C	2	different body parts
D	3	rackets
E	3	different body parts
F	3	different body parts
G	4	different body parts
H	4	paddles
I	6	upper body parts only

NEXT CLASS EXPERIENCE. Upon entering the room, the children form their groups from the last class and continue working with striking, trying to vary the level of the ball. After approximately 5 minutes, the teacher stops them and says, "In addition, try to hit the ball so you make your teammates move. In other words, see if you can force your teammates, or yourself if working alone, to have to move to get the ball each time; however, still keep the ball within reach."

The teacher calls all the children together after another 5 minutes and has them sit down while an explanation is given as to how to take current group work into a game. It is not the first time they have done this kind of activity, so they are familiar with the idea.

The children are given certain limitations. First, they must use striking as the major idea in their game, and they must have boundaries. As the children are already in groups, the teacher suggests that they begin with that number and change later if they wish. The teacher lets the children decide rules.

The teacher concludes by saying, "There are tape, cones, bean bags, and rope that can be used for boundaries, and if you need net-like equipment, you can use the chairs or posts. In addition, there are shredded newspaper and old material available, if some of you want to make a more realistic net." For the next 5 minutes or so, the children are getting their equipment and setting up the areas in which they will play their game.

The "setting up" and "get going" period is over, and all groups are busily playing. The groups have set themselves up in the following ways:

Group A (1): tape against wall approximating the height of a tennis net; rectangular boundaries affording enough space to move in all directions.

Groups B (2), E (3), F (3), G (4), and H (4): rectangular boundaries with a "center line" and enough space to move in all directions.

Group C (2): two chairs with a rope tied across, approximately 2-feet high; rectangular boundaries with enough space to move in all directions.

Group I (6): two posts with a rope tied across, 6-feet high; rectangular boundaries with enough space to move in all directions.

The teacher circulates from group to group, helping them clarify their games and improve the way they are playing them. *Comment:* Helping children clarify their games involves discussions about the rules and boundaries in particular. To help children improve the way they are playing their games involves discussions about the movement skills needed and the concepts of strategy.

As these children are fairly advanced, the teacher is primarily helping all groups with concepts of strategy. Basically, the children are asked to figure out how to place balls in relation to opponents to make it more difficult. Most of the children's games have a competitive aspect in that points are scored when their opponents "miss." *Comment:* These children have had quite a bit of experience with game playing prior to this lesson, so it is not surprising to have a number of them now playing in a competitive direction. Although all groups are not using a competitive aspect, all groups *are* demonstrating a high enough level of movement ability to challenge everyone involved. The strategy concept of ball placement either to catch an opponent off balance or to make a teammate able to handle the ball easily is beginning to show improvement.

The teacher ends the class by asking the children to get together and summarize the basic structure of their games. In addition, they are asked to identify one or two aspects on which they will concentrate their attention in the next game lesson. The children put all the equipment away and go back to their classroom.

Comment: The next few lessons would build from this one, with the teacher helping the children further refine the structure of their games as well as the way they play them. Most of the children are at the stage where they need to practice playing their game. They will have ample opportunity for this in the lessons to come.

DESCRIPTION 2

BACKGROUND INFORMATION. The children have been working in past lessons with the manipulative activities of throwing and catching, using just their hands. Dodging, as a body management activity, has been integrated throughout all experiences. Previous learning experiences have been developed with the following content-ideas:

Alone:
—throwing-catching while traveling and constantly changing directions (the way the ball was thrown was to force the mover to change directions).
—throwing while changing levels of the ball (walls).
—catching while falling off balance; jumping in the air.

In groups of three or four, moving and passing so teammates have to

—reach to catch it.
—jump to catch it.
—move in different directions to catch it.

In all experiences, the area of space used was changed continuously. (*Comment:* this often brought out sudden changes in direction or dodge-like actions.)

The children, 32 in all, are between the ages of 10½ and 12. They handle throwing and catching in relation to directions, levels, and the available space well, but many of the children still

have difficulty throwing to others and making them either jump or almost fall off balance to catch it.

NEXT CLASS EXPERIENCE. As the children come to the areas on the playground that are designated for physical education classes, they begin working with a ball of their choice. The teacher has put out a selection that includes rubber balls (5, 7, and 8 inches), volleyballs, plastic and sponge (8 inches), and tennis balls. Directions to the children are: "For the first 5 minutes or so, work with a ball of your choice on anything that involves throwing, catching, traveling, and a change of levels. You may work alone or with others." All types of balls are used, and all of the children but four are working in groups. The groups range in size from two to five, with the majority in groups of two.

The teacher asks the children to stop, put all balls away, and arrange themselves in groups of four. The teacher's plan is to have the children eventually play a modified version of a game called field dodge. In making the transition to the actual game, two intermediate steps have been planned: (1) a game-like experience that is familiar to them and (2) a game the teacher has made up specifically to help them in playing field dodge.

Step 1
In groups of four, all moving and tossing the ball.
Purpose: Keep the ball moving quickly and in such a way that everyone *can catch it.* Use all of the space.
Step 2
The group is now divided into a "team" of three (fielders) and a "team" of one (runner). The team of three must keep the ball constantly moving in relation to where the runner is moving.
Purpose: The "runner" is to move in, out, and among the "fielders," trying to stay as far away from the ball as possible. The "fielders" are trying to catch the runner, so to speak, by getting the ball as close to him as possible.

Comment: Step 2 is considered a game (teacher-designed original) and grew out of Step 1, which was a learning experience familiar to the children; only this time, they experienced it in a larger group. There are eight groups of children, all working at the same time. The groups would choose the type of ball; five groups chose the rubber (8-inch) one and three groups chose the plastic (8-inch) one.

The teacher moves among the eight groups, helping them play the "game" better. Moving in relation to a ball and passing a ball in relation to a runner was not easy to do well. When helping the children, the teacher is having them figure out what needs improvement by asking questions such as:

> To a "runner": "How were you running?" or "Where was the ball when you were over there?"
> To the "fielders": "Was there a reason you threw the ball over there?" or "Where do you have to throw the ball so it's the most difficult for the runner?"

After working with all the groups, the teacher stops the whole class and says, "When you think your group understands the basic idea of this game, and you can control the ball well, you may try to hit the 'runner' out below the waist." They are asked to figure out their own way to change "runners."

Comment: From this "game," the teacher would introduce the children to field dodge, which is a conventional game (Fig. 7–3). Briefly, field dodge is played with two even teams, with the boundaries comprising a restraining line and a base. Rules regarding additional boundaries and fouls must be devised in relation to the type of space being used. The idea of the game is easily understood, but playing it well is difficult. The first person "at bat" puts the ball in play by throwing it into the field of play. The player then tries to touch the base (being on base is not safe) and return across the restraining line without being hit below the waist and on the fly. To be safe, the player may cross the restraining line at any place. If the runner is hit out, the next person at bat begins immediately and tries to do the same thing. If a runner makes it safely over the restraining line, then the next person at bat starts. This pattern continues until all members of the team at bat have had a chance to try to make a run. Then, the two teams change sides and play resumes. Success in this game depends on understanding the concept of running in relation to the ball (*away* from the ball) and passing in relation to the runner (*ahead* of the runner).

The teacher shows the game to the class by having two groups of four "walk it through." The

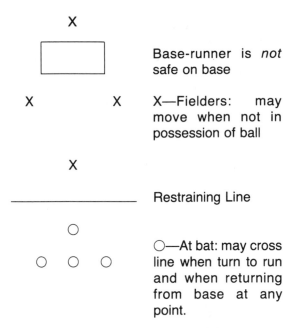

Fig. 7–3. Modified Field Dodge Ball.

game has been modified, primarily by reducing the number of players and the size of the playing area. When there are no more questions, the teacher tells them all to start their own game. Markers are available for both the bases and restraining lines. Again, they have a choice of which ball they will use.

The teacher continues as before, helping each group identify its weaknesses and figure out how to overcome them. By the end of the class, one group of eight has broken up into two groups of four, and each group is practicing again with one runner and three throwers. They found they were having too much difficulty when in the field dodge situation and decided to go back to the previous "game." The other groups remain with the modified field dodge and are slowly improving. They play until the end of the period. After the equipment is put away, everyone goes back to the classroom.

Comment: The structure of both games was designed by the teacher; however, the evaluation of what the children were doing and the suggestions given for improvement were decided by the children. The next lessons would be built upon this one, with any one of the following directions possible.

1. Continued playing of field dodge, with the

possibility of larger groups or additional modification.

2. New learning experiences based on the difficulties encountered with the movement demands of field dodge.

3. Development of an original game (child-designed) using field dodge as the starting point.

In these examples, cooperative and competitive play are all occurring simultaneously, yet at different levels of complexity. If true personalization of the games program is to happen, this variety is necessary.

REFERENCES

1. Riley, M.: Games and humanism. JOPER, 46:46, 1975.
2. Barrett, K.R.: Games teaching: adaptable skills, versatile players. In Elementary Curriculum: Theory and Practice—Games Teaching. Reston, Virginia, AAHPERD, 1982.
3. Wickstrom, R.L.: Fundamental Motor Patterns, 3rd ed. Philadelphia, Lea & Febiger, 1983.
4. Stallings, L.M.: Motor Learning: From Theory to Practice. St. Louis, The C.V. Mosby Company, 1982.
5. McKinney, E.D.: But can game skills be taught. In Elementary Curriculum: Theory and Practice—Games Teaching. Reston, Virginia, AAHPERD, 1982.
6. Preston-Dunlop, V.: A Handbook for Modern Educational Dance, 2nd ed. Boston, Plays, Inc., 1980.
7. Mauldon, E., and Redfern, H.B.: Games Teaching, 2nd ed. London, Macdonald & Evans, 1981.
8. Laban, R., and Lawrence, F.: Effort. London, Unwin Brothers, 1947.
9. Broer, M., and Zernicke, R.: Efficiency of Human Movement, 4th ed. Philadelphia, W.B. Saunders Co., 1979.
10. Bartenieff, I. with Lewis, D.: Body Movement. New York, Gordon and Breach Science Publishers, 1980.
11. Seidel, B.L., Biles, F.R., Figley, G.E., and Neuman, B.J.: Sport Skills a Conceptual Approach to Meaningful Movement, 2nd ed. Dubuque, Iowa, Wm. C. Brown Company, 1980.

SELECTED READING

Hardisty, M.: Education Through the Games Experience. Bellingham, Washington, Educational Designs and Consultants, 1972.
Mauldon, E., and Redfern, H.B.: Games Teaching, 2nd ed. London, Macdonald & Evans, 1981.
Morris, G.S.: How to Change the Games Children Play, 2nd ed. Minneapolis, Minnesota, Burgess Publishing Company, 1980.
Martens, R., and Seefeldt, V.: Guidelines for Children's Sports. Washington, D.C., AAHPERD, 1979.
Riley, M., Barrett, K.R., Martinek, T.J., and Roberton, M.A.: Children and Youth in Action: Physical Activities and Sports, Washington, D.C., U.S. Government Printing Office, 1980.
Riley, M.: Games and humanism. JOPER, 46:46, 1975.
Seidel, B.L., Biles, F.R., Figley, G.E., and Newman, B.J.: Sport Skills a Conceptual Approach to Meaningful Movement, 2nd ed. Dubuque, Iowa, Wm. C. Brown Company, 1980.
Stallings, L.M.: Motor Learning: From Theory to Practice. St. Louis, The C.V. Mosby Company, 1982.
Wagonvoord, J.: Hangin' Out—City Kids, City Games. Philadelphia, J.B. Lippincott, 1974.
Wickstrom, R.L.: Fundamental Motor Patterns, 3rd ed. Philadelphia, Lea & Febiger, 1983.

Chapter 8

Educational Gymnastics

BETTE JEAN LOGSDON

Movement associated with gymnastics is functional or objective rather than expressive. This description implies that gymnastic movement is done primarily to perform a task rather than to convey an idea or mood. The name, educational gymnastics, originated in England where it characterized an educational approach distinctive from formal gymnastics and other forms of gymnastics in that country, as well as the Olympic gymnastics and the stunts and tumbling programs in the United States.[1] The *educational* approach to gymnastics, as in games and in dance, focuses on the individuality of the learners and the unique style in which each one moves, learns, and develops. Closely aligned with recognizing, encouraging, and developing the child as an individual is a commitment to involving and educating the whole child. The educational approach focuses on helping and permitting the child to know, to understand, and to feel movement and to develop decision-making abilities, so that each can achieve full and personal gymnastic potential.

This approach, rather than emphasizing designated stunts to be performed and specific tumbling feats to be mastered by all children at the same time, centers its attention on awakening children to the full potential of the body as an instrument for movement and helping them develop individuality and versatility in gymnastics as they pursue their skill potential. Although known stunts and recognized tumbling and gymnastic feats do become a part of the movement vocabulary of the children, most frequently, the specific gymnastic stunts come at the discretion of the learner rather than being imposed by the teacher as rigid requirements for each child to achieve. Because children differ widely in their physical structure, abilities, development, levels of achievement, and motivation, versatility and personal satisfaction are as desirable and perhaps more realistic educational objectives than specific gymnastic stunts. Also, when we build our requirements and programs around such specific responses, we often find ourselves teaching to the middle of the class. Those who lack experiences and specific ability fail to find success and are discouraged, while the more highly skilled go unchallenged and fall victim to monotonous repetition of elementary gymnastic stunts.

Children who learn in the environment of the educational approach often are encouraged to develop a variety of general gymnastic responses or ways they can solve the tasks rather than being shown and taught one way of performing a stunt or skill. They then experience a selection and refinement period, whereby a response is practiced, assessed, and refined. This refinement stage often is followed by tasks that focus the work of the children on adapting the response to new situations; for example, taking a refined roll while working on a mat and adapting it for execution on a bench or vaulting box. Also, the refined response (the roll) might be incorporated into the development of a gymnastics sequence. The nature of the stages of student challenges in educational gymnastics are as follows:

Stage 1—Seeks variety of gymnastic responses, develops a broad repertoire of gymnastic movement, or develops an awareness of a concept.

Stage 2—Focuses on refinement of skills through selection, practice, and assessment.

Stage 3—Focuses on adaptation of response to different environments or on incorporation of the response into movement sequences.

It is important to note that even the very young elementary school child can be challenged to work successfully in all three stages. NO ONE STAGE IS THE FOCUS FOR ANY AGE GROUP OR EXPERIENTIAL LEVEL. Although the stages are sequential, they frequently need not be approached in 1–2–3 order. For example, a teacher may work in stage 1 and stage 2 for long periods of time, moving back and forth between these two stages without approaching stage 3. At other times, a teacher might move from stage 1 to 2 to 3 in the same lesson.

This practice not only can help to yield an expanded gymnastic program and variety among the responses of the children but also can produce an environment that can develop an *"I can"* attitude and reward the ability of all children at their own level, enhance self-worth, and develop versatility and skillful gymnastic movement. We feel the *earlier versatility* is stressed, the greater the possibility for the children to realize their full movement potential and to gain some degree of freedom for learning on their own. Also, the more versatile the children are and the wider the range of movement they experience in gymnastics, the greater the chance each child will discover ways to move that are unique and satisfying.

Versatility, individual inventiveness, and originality are nurtured in educational gymnastics from the beginning along with skill development. In the more traditional approaches to formal gymnastics and to stunts and tumbling programs, these qualities are often not required of the learner. In Olympic gymnastics, these qualities are reserved for advanced experiences when importance is placed on originality in creating competitive gymnastic routines.

Special teaching styles and attitudes are associated with the teaching of educational gymnastics. Basic to these styles is the divergence between versatility and conformity and the differing teaching-learning environments conducive to the development of each. Actually, conformity and versatility are both important aspects in becoming a skillful, versatile gymnast. Moreover, both the content and the way we teach as well as our objectives distinguish educational gymnastics from other forms of gymnastics. People who are interested in this approach recognize and value its potential as compatible with the goals of education, the goals of physical education, and the philosophy and beliefs stated earlier in the book. When implementing this approach, one is not faced with dichotomy and inconsistency in dealing with the learner when teaching gymnastics while promoting physical education as a viable part of education. Our earlier statements, made in Chapter 2, which could have been viewed as highly theoretic and philosophic, should become more practically oriented as you see them applied in the teaching of educational gymnastics, games, and dance. As we approach the study of the content in gymnastics, you will become aware of the methodologic directions that characterize the educational approach. Chapter 9, The Teacher as Observer, Interpreter, and Decision-Maker, will strengthen your awareness for the teaching-learning process.

ORGANIZING GYMNASTIC CONTENT

In Chapter 5, a basic framework for classifying movement was developed (Fig. 5–1). A movement framework for gymnastics is illustrated in Figure 8–1 to simplify interpreting and utilizing the classification system when teaching gymnastics. You recall that Laban's framework has been chosen to give order to movement—because it can be applied to all facets of the program, because it can be used to observe and analyze movement and when communicating with the learner, and because it can be used to create new and varied learning experiences. In spite of this inspiring list of attributes associated with the movement framework, often the features are not easily implemented in program planning. Since you have already seen its elaboration and development for dance and games in Chapters 6 and 7, you may more fully understand its application in gymnastics. You may have the same experience I had in finding it easier, at first, to use the framework in gymnastics than in either

BODY ASPECT   **WHAT BODY DOES**

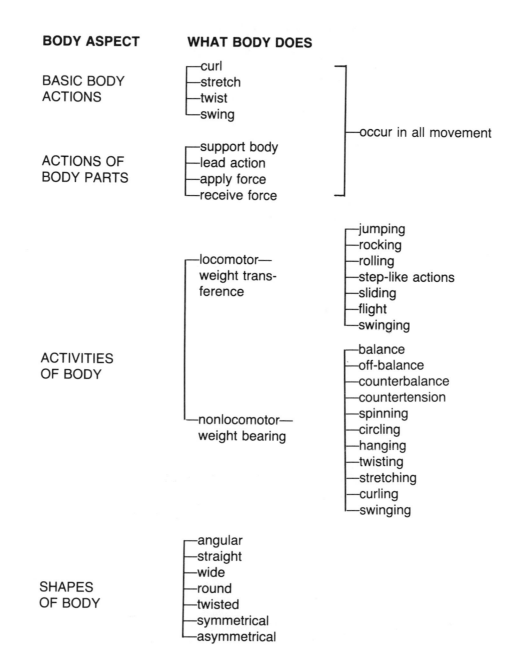

BASIC BODY
ACTIONS

- curl
- stretch
- twist
- swing

ACTIONS OF
BODY PARTS

- support body
- lead action
- apply force
- receive force

occur in all movement

ACTIVITIES
OF BODY

locomotor—
weight trans-
ference

- jumping
- rocking
- rolling
- step-like actions
- sliding
- flight
- swinging

nonlocomotor—
weight bearing

- balance
- off-balance
- counterbalance
- countertension
- spinning
- circling
- hanging
- twisting
- stretching
- curling
- swinging

SHAPES
OF BODY

- angular
- straight
- wide
- round
- twisted
- symmetrical
- asymmetrical

Fig. 8–1. Movement Framework for Educational Gymnastics.

SPACE ASPECT	WHERE BODY MOVES
AREAS	general personal
DIRECTIONS	forward backward sideward up down
LEVELS	high medium low
PATHWAYS	air — straight, angular, curved, twisted, zigzag floor
PLANES	wheel (sagittal) door (frontal) table (horizontal)
EXTENSIONS	small large
EFFORT ASPECT	**HOW BODY PERFORMS THE MOVEMENT**
TIME	fast, accelerating, sudden slow, decelerating, sustained
WEIGHT	firm, strong, tension soft, light, relaxed
SPACE	direct, straight indirect, flexible
FLOW	bound, stoppable free, ongoing

RELATIONSHIP ASPECT   **RELATIONSHIPS THAT OCCUR IN MOVEMENT**

BODY PARTS
- above-below
- apart-together
- behind-in front of
- meeting-parting
- near-far
- over-under

PARTNERS/SMALL
GROUPS
- contrasting
- alternating
- successive
- canon

- mirroring-matching
- following-copying
- above-below
- behind-in front of
- near-far
- over-under-alongside

- supporting-being supported
- lifting-being lifted

APPARATUS
- near-far
- over-under-on
- behind-in front of-alongside
- above-below

- arriving on
- dismounting

OTHER TYPES   beat pattern (rhythm)

dance or game teaching; however, I am sure this must be a personal experience and one that cannot be predicted. I hope that use of the movement framework in one program area will come more easily and more quickly so you recognize its value and become more open and able to apply it to the other two areas.

Developing learning experiences utilizing the movement framework (body, space, effort, and relationship) is not a difficult task. The root of the problem is to order these experiences in a logical, progressive, and interrelated manner so increased versatility and skill development in gymnastics can be a growing challenge as a child of any age or ability moves, learns, and matures. A plan must be formulated so that continuity, essential to meaningful learning, exists in gymnastic programs and so that the child can experience the entire physical education program, dance, games, and gymnastics, as an integrated whole.

Laban outlined a scheme for expressive movement by creating 16 movement-themes for dance[2] (see Chapter 6). The first 7 or 8 are thought to be most appropriate for the elementary school child. His idea to use a thematic scheme for organizing experiences in a progressive manner has prompted us to use this approach as an organizing scheme to provide for progression and to interrelate all content in physical education, in gymnastics, games, and dance. Barrett was motivated by Laban's scheme and the interpretation given to it by Preston-Dunlop[3] when she developed the dance content and game content around 7 themes. All three of the thematic schemes are interrelated and facilitate progression and integration of dance, game, and gymnastic experiences for the learner. The integration of all movement experiences can provide for greater continuity in the total physical education program.

The thematic plan developed here for organizing the elementary school program in gymnastics consists of the following eight themes:

EIGHT MOVEMENT THEMES FOR ORGANIZING AND DEVELOPING CONTENT FOR EDUCATIONAL GYMNASTICS

Theme 1—INTRODUCTION TO THE BODY

Theme 2—INTRODUCTION TO SPACE
Theme 3—INTRODUCTION TO TIME
Theme 4—INTRODUCTION TO RELATIONSHIPS OF BODY PARTS
Theme 5—INTRODUCTION TO WEIGHT
Theme 6—FLOW AND CONTINUITY IN MOVEMENT
Theme 7—RELATIONSHIPS TO OTHERS
Theme 8—INTRODUCTION TO RHYTHM

GYMNASTICS THEME 1—INTRODUCTION TO THE BODY

The first gymnastics theme centers on creating environments in which children are encouraged to try, discover, invent, see, practice, refine, learn, and develop a movement vocabulary appropriate to gymnastics. Not incidental to this purpose is the development of general body control and responsibility for the movements made by the body in gymnastics. This includes the development of a variety of locomotor activities (*rocking, rolling, step-like actions, sliding, jumping, swinging*), which have been identified as basic to the general movement repertoire of gymnastics, as well as the awareness of the body and its various body parts while performing in a gymnastic setting.

Since this theme is the initial one, the emphasis is largely on developing body awareness by getting the children to demonstrate great variety in traveling. This variety in gymnastic ability develops through first permitting them to find different ways to travel. In expanding their awareness of how variety is achieved, you can direct their work toward traveling on different body parts. The emphases include developing a feeling for the body parts involved in weight transference. They learn to know and to change the body parts that touch the floor as they travel. More advanced work focuses on the seven forms of weight transference—rocking, rolling, step-like actions, sliding, jumping, swinging, and flight. In the initial stages of this theme, the children are encouraged and helped to achieve variety in the way they move as a means of increasing their movement vocabulary. The children should begin to perceive the limitations as well as the capabilities of the human body. As the work in this theme progresses, the children should become more adept at willfully selecting and controlling their movement. Greater variety in the way they

Photo from the Agency for Instructional Television.

riences that challenge them to improve their responses. Also, when working with this theme (and all others for that matter), teachers must learn to encourage individuality while stressing that children do their best work and find ways to move that are increasingly more difficult. Frequently, if we are not aware of each child, some can lollygag and not extend themselves. WE THEN ARE QUICK TO CRITICIZE THE EDUCATIONAL OR MOVEMENT APPROACH FOR NOT YIELDING SKILLFUL MOVEMENT RATHER THAN FOCUSING THE RESPONSIBILITY FOR SKILL DEVELOPMENT ON BOTH THE TEACHER AND THE CHILD. Both must do their part if the full movement potential of the child in relation to this theme and others is to be realized.

Development of Theme 1

> **Basic Content**
> Locomotor movement (weight transference): rocking, rolling, sliding, step-like actions, jumping, swinging, flight.
> Alert stillness
> Body parts: hands, feet, shoulders, for example

LOCOMOTION (WEIGHT TRANSFERENCE). Movement performed by transferring weight from one body part to another or back to the same part while traveling is called locomotor movement. Certain forms of locomotor movement in gymnastics are executed with part of the body always in contact with the floor, e.g., *rocking, rolling, sliding,* and *step-like actions. Swinging,* an action of the body, can also result in traveling. Swinging when coupled with step-like actions or flight may be classified broadly as a form of locomotion. Movement that takes the body into the air is categorized under the broad umbrella of flight. Most movements involving flight are achieved by taking off from the feet, as in jumping; but other body parts, such as hands, knees, and shoulders, can be used as takeoff points for springing into flight under certain conditions, especially when these body parts are used in various combinations.

The more familiar forms of locomotion—running, skipping, and hopping—are not highlighted in the content of gymnastics except as

travel should also be evident. If it is not, the teacher needs to work harder in motivating and stimulating the children. As a result of work initiated in Theme 1, children should begin to develop not only invented, unnamed forms of locomotion in gymnastics but many of the more familiar named forms, for example, forward rolls and cartwheels.

Although the early emphasis in this theme is on variety, you should help all children become committed to developing skill by doing quality work and taking pride in their accomplishments. For example, children often need to be motivated to manage their bodies so as not to fall. Thus, they need opportunity even in this first theme to go beyond the exploratory stage to selection, refinement, and application of skills. We can help them progress by including expe-

they are preparatory for other movements. These, as content, are usually reserved for dance. Jumping is the exception.

In gymnastics, rather than emphasizing traveling on the feet, teachers should encourage children to change the body parts that are touching the floor. Through this activity, they become accustomed to transferring their weight onto all parts of the body while rolling, rocking, and performing various step-like actions. Special attention is given to traveling on the hands and feet so that children can experience inverted positions and add to their arm-shoulder strength. Here, cartwheels, round-offs, walk-overs, and other such movements can be encouraged.

Work in the area of locomotion may at times be directed toward each of the specific locomotion forms to aid children in developing specialized gymnastic skills as well as to ensure increasing their movement repertoire in gymnastics. Therefore, rolling, step-like actions, rocking, jumping, swinging, and flight may be studied independently in tasks. As the work in some of these selected forms progresses, the children and/or the teacher can choose specific examples from these categories to be developed, practiced, and refined. For example, rather than always studying general step-like actions, if the child seems ready or groups of children are ready, the focus of a portion of a lesson might center specifically on cartwheels as a form of locomotion. *IN SELECTING SPECIFIC EXAMPLES OF THE VARIOUS CATEGORIES AS CONTENT, THE TEACHER MUST DEVISE WAYS TO ACCOMMODATE AND CHALLENGE INDIVIDUAL DIFFERENCES OR THE PHILOSOPHIC BASIS OF THE EDUCATIONAL APPROACH CENTRAL TO THIS BOOK WILL BE VIOLATED.*

Sample Learning Experiences

1. Travel freely about the room, trying to keep from touching anyone, and listen for the signal to stop.
2. Find movements that make you travel on different body parts.
3. Select two different traveling movements; do one movement for a while and then do the other.
4. Each get a block and newspaper, place these in your own space, and see how you can travel about your equipment.

Discussion. In these four sample experiences, the children are free to select their means of traveling even though the tasks from 1 to 4 become a bit more structured. Most commonly, children go into the usual forms of locomotion on their feet: walking, running, skipping, jumping, and hopping. At first, as long as the very young children move safely, you should make few movement restrictions. Stopping and starting becomes the major emphasis. During this brief experimentation stage, you should stop them frequently to help establish early a pattern for teacher control, to help them develop personal control over their movement, to maximize safety, and to minimize speed if running is the mode they choose for traveling. Soon, for safety reasons, as well as to nurture more gymnastic-like responses, you should add more structure to the tasks by having them think of other ways to travel *BESIDES* running if running is the prime way they choose to move. (At an early age, their *ability* to generate speed exceeds their *agility* in dodging others.)

You probably will choose just "traveling" for only brief periods, except with the very young child. Soon the focus shifts from mere locomotion to traveling on different body parts or perhaps to different numbers of body parts or specified body parts such as hands and feet. These shifts may come if the teacher adds new content to the task, or they may be natural responses from the children. For example, when responding to any of the four sample tasks, the children or a single child may choose to travel on different body parts. The teacher then makes the choice to focus on traveling or directs the children's attention to body parts also.

The initial work on locomotion is important because it brings the teacher and the children together in establishing an environment that is conducive to learning. Children need sensitive help in recognizing the role each individual plays in the learning environment of others when they work in the same room. They must learn not only to stop and control their momentum but also to move more skillfully and to remain quiet and attentive so they and others can receive full benefit from the learning experience. Success in establishing a learning environment that is mutually rewarding is dependent largely on the teacher's ability to help each child value the roles the teacher and each child share in making it possible for all to learn.

When the children demonstrate some ability

in traveling on different body parts, their work can concentrate on specific forms of traveling. Tasks devoted to the seven forms of locomotion can increase their body awareness as well as their ability to travel. Although the progression sounds specific, it is not a lock-step procedure. Each teacher is free to select from within the movement content of the theme and to design tasks that fit the needs of a particular child or group of children. Progression for the gymnastics program is discussed at greater length at the end of the chapter.

ALERT STILLNESS. The initial lessons in physical education for young children are frequently developed around this first gymnastics theme. When they are, moments of stillness preceded by starting and stopping are included. This stillness is essential to initiate self-control, body awareness, and responsibility for safety, which is associated with working in a space that must be shared by other children. As the children start and stop, their focus when stopped is not on balancing but on creating an alert stillness and willful control of momentum. In alert stillness, muscle tension is present, and the children are in control of their bodies. Muscle tension and control are both vital components of body awareness. Irrespective of how apparent this idea seems, children need help to recognize, to feel, and to be aware of the importance of muscle tension. Teachers are often shocked to discover that children show great glee when falling and often choose to flop to stop. You can show the value of controlled stopping with muscle tension by drawing attention to children who are quick to demonstrate alert stillness when asked to stop.

One way to demonstrate this ability to control movement is great fun for the 4-, 5-, and 6-year-old. I have found that trying to move a child's arm or foot or picking little ones up, commenting on how firm and strong they are, brings giggles from the class but also brings an amazing number of alert positions the next time the class is stopped. This technique aids tremendously in developing both a visual and kinesthetic awareness for muscle tension. Many times simple, fun-giving ways motivate the child's desire to respond. Once the desire is present, learning is usually enhanced.

BODY PARTS. When body parts are introduced as content in relation to traveling, the purposes are

1. to get children off their feet if this mode has been their only means of locomotion.
2. to bring variety into traveling.
3. to make them more aware of the different body parts, especially those that support the weight in traveling.

How soon more structure (body parts) is added to the task depends on the variety of movement the children create in a more open task, their safety (if they insist on running and do not have control), and the need for variation to pace, motivate, or enrich the learning experience.

While developing awareness for body parts, some teachers have children name the body parts or give the number of parts touching the floor. At other times, they are asked to observe or think about their movement or the movement of others and tell what body part(s) left the floor first or last—which touched first or last. These and other cognitive tasks given along with motor tasks can help children to see and to feel movement, to start gaining an awareness for where their body parts are, and to know and control what their body parts are doing in movement.

Sample Learning Experiences

1. Travel, letting different body parts touch the floor.
2. Travel on three body parts (four, two).
3. See how you can travel on your hands and feet.
4. With a partner, one be a leader and the other copy the different things the leader does traveling about the room.

Discussion. Although adults tend to be limb oriented, young children are not. By emphasizing weight transference onto different body parts, we can widen the possibilities for movement and develop the ability to utilize more parts of the body as the base of support in traveling. This is one of the keys to introducing children to gymnastic movement.

In these four samples, the awareness of body parts is the focal point for the movement experience. The greater the specificity required in the task, the more the decisions are made by the teacher. As more structure is added to the tasks (specifying number of body parts, naming specific body parts, or giving precise ways to travel), the child must find more specific solutions appropriate to these limitations. The first task is more open than the second; however, in both tasks, the children are free to choose the body parts on which they wish to travel. In the third task, the teacher selects the body parts that must be touching the floor. These three examples illustrate how the choices of the child are limited by the way tasks are stated. In the fourth task, the leaders are free to move while the followers must restrict their movement to coincide with the movement of their leader. Limitations, although narrowing the type of response, can serve to sharpen creativity and expand versatility.

Be sure to make suggestions relative to safety when taking weight on the hands. Safety is important, since tasks similar to the second one are likely to elicit various styles of "handstands." Whenever children begin to support weight fully on their hands, even momentarily, help them to recognize the following ideas relevant to managing the body in inverted positions while on the hands.

1. Head should be lifted with eyes focused outward toward the space in front of the hands (increases arch in back, getting center of weight over the base of support).

2. The closer their feet come back to the floor in relation to their hands, the more slowly they can lower their feet.

3. It takes muscle tension and personal effort to make the return slower or faster than the normal pull of gravity.

4. Twisting in the hips when the feet are over the head and bringing both feet down close to the side of one hand can help to prevent an overthrow.

In following and copying the movement of another, i.e., perceiving a response and attempting to duplicate what is seen, the children wed the cognitive and motor processes because they must think before and while doing to be successful. The uniting of thinking with doing is a vital part of the educational approach. This fourth sample also introduces early partner work, although the content or purpose is to develop body awareness by looking at and copying the movement of a partner. Although partner and small-group work are not the content focus until Theme 7, experiences with partners and small groups can be an organizational feature of every unit of study centered around any theme. When partner or group work is included in work from Themes 1 through 6 and in Theme 8, purposes other than content-focus prompt their use, e.g.,

socialization, utilization of limited apparatus or space, motivation, or movement observation. Here, in the fourth task, copying was introduced primarily to sharpen movement observation skills.

It will be said and reiterated that these experiences are only a small sample of the numerous ways in which content for this first theme can be developed. Children need both time and practice to acquire a vocabulary of locomotor movement in gymnastics and control and awareness for the body parts used as the base of support in traveling.

APPARATUS. Small apparatus such as individual mats, ropes, hoops, blocks, and newspaper rolls can be a part of any lesson. These objects may be selected, arranged, and used at the discretion of the child, or the choices of what, when, how, and where to use the apparatus can be the teacher's. The purposes for adding apparatus in the early themes are much the same as those for adding additional movement content. These are

—to increase the challenge.
—to motivate.
—to elicit more varied or explicit movement responses.
—to restrict the movement of each child.

A hyperactive, uninitiated class, unable to cope safely with a large space, can often be calmed and prepared to handle larger spaces effectively and efficiently through the use of tasks requiring them to work at their own equipment in their own space.

By giving each child, or letting each child select, a piece of equipment to travel about, the teacher focuses the movement of a child in a smaller space rather than about the whole room. When children learn to manage their bodies alone, they are more able to move and share space safely with others. Also, certain locomotor activities are evoked by the presence of equipment. For example, you may be able to motivate children more quickly and with greater purpose when you ask them to jump over something rather than just to jump. Equipment tends to spice up the environment, and frequently, a child responds with longer working periods and greater achievement. Also, much of the movement in gymnastics is done in relation to apparatus, and this facility for using apparatus must start early. In Figure 8–2, a rope has been used to help this

Photo from the Agency for Instructional Television.

Fig. 8–2. A Jump Rope Used to Isolate Working Space and to Motivate Taking Weight on Hands

first-grade boy transfer weight from his feet to his hands and back to his feet.

SAMPLE UNIT PLAN THEME 1

Theme. Introduction to Body—Theme 1.

Unit Focus. Traveling on different body parts with emphasis on variety.

Appropriate For. Children who have had previous experiences in traveling on different body parts in more open tasks where rolling was not required.

Length of Unit. Five 30-minute lessons.

Content

Body—weight transference on different body parts; rolling

Space—

Effort—

Relationships—

Student Objectives. The students should be willing to try to

1. Combine traveling and intentionally changing the body parts touching the floor with a roll and coming to feet quickly.

2. Share small equipment and space with others by willfully managing their body to avoid getting into the space of others.

3. Seek a variety of solutions to each task.

4. Do their best work and not distract others.

Teaching Area. Indoor space large enough to accommodate class size.

Apparatus and/or Equipment. Block and paper wand for each child; a mat for each four to six children.

Learning Experiences (Tasks)

1.0 Carefully, without touching anyone, see how many different body parts you can travel on. Really travel on your own into open spaces, avoiding others.

1.1 Keep changing the body parts that are touching the floor as you travel about the room.

1.2 Try to think ahead, so your traveling is continuous as you change body parts touching the floor.

1.3 As you make different body parts touch the floor while traveling about the room, take care you do not let them flop or fall—you take charge of those body parts especially as they touch the floor.

1.4 Select one way of traveling and keep repeating it, making the same body parts touch the floor.

Now keep changing the body parts—making very different ones help you travel. Do you feel the difference when you keep changing the body parts that touch the floor?

1.5 Let only your hands and feet be the body parts you travel on.

2.0 See what body parts you can travel on, going over and under the newspaper roll placed on your wooden block. Take care in working to keep the newspaper roll on the block.

2.1 After you go under the newspaper, see how quickly you can come back over the newspaper.

2.2 Most of you are jumping as you go over the block. When you jump, work on making those landings soft and springing up immediately after you land.

2.3 Try to do something other than jump as you go over the newspaper—remember you are working on making different body parts touch the floor.

2.4 Some of you might like to try to travel from your feet to your hands as you go over the block. If you do, take care not to let the

A Suggested Progression For Sample Gymnastics Unit/Theme 1

Lesson 1

Tasks	Teaching Tips
1.0	Emphasize traveling to open spaces. Stop and start frequently, check spacing. Get them back to work quickly.
1.1	Stress: keep changing body parts; do not let them scoot on backs—name body parts touching floor.
1.2	Encourage constant movement—no stops. Might see if all can do their best work for 45 seconds without stopping.
2.0	Watch to see whether children move far away from block. Keep them close so the approach does not become a 25-yard dash.
2.1	Still stress different body parts touching floor.
2.2	May be able to suggest one- then two-foot takeoffs and landings as a means of developing more variety in their takeoff.

Lesson 2

Tasks	Teaching Tips
1.1	Emphasize spacing blocks away from walls and other blocks, and traveling on variety of body parts.
1.3	May need a demonstration of children who are changing body parts.
1.4	This task is given to show contrast—to teach difference between repeating the same solution and seeking new solutions.
1.5	Stress not letting hips or thighs touch floor—making feet land.
2.0	Emphasize changing body parts touching floor.
2.2	Watch how far they start away from blocks. Keep them close, working in their own space.
2.3	Again, keep asking them to make different body parts touch the floor (could suggest specific body parts).
2.4	Encourage them to land only on their feet, not letting hips or thighs touch the ground.

Lesson 3

Tasks	Teaching Tips
2.1	Again, keep them close to block. Avoid long running starts.
2.2	Stress backs perpendicular to floor on landing—pop-up and land in same spot.
2.4	Begin to emphasize taking feet high—full stretch.
3.0	Look carefully at kinds of rolls. Begin to stress tight body parts. Encourage one roll and standing up after roll is completed.
3.1	After they roll, stress trying to get to feet without having their hands help them.
3.2	Have them check the amount of mat behind their feet after they stand up. Encourage them to tighten up or tuck up to make their roll look better and to reduce space needed for rolling.

Lesson 4

Tasks	Teaching Tips
3.1	Same as Lesson 3.
3.2	Encourage variety of rolls.
3.3	Ask individual children what they are thinking about. Check to see if you see what they have mentioned improving.
3.4	Caution the observer to watch all parts of the roll—beginning, middle, and end—BEFORE copying the roll.
4.0	The block placed in the path in front of the mat should be far enough away to allow movement under the newspaper roll before rolling.
4.1	Watch individual children to see whether responses vary for each child. Too frequently, we see different children doing different things and we assume each child is showing variety.
4.2	Check to see whether children are getting the sequence accurately. (A good check for listening skills.)
4.3	Refine landing in jump over first block as well as the last. No falling.

Lesson 5

Tasks	Teaching Tips
4.1	Strive for even greater variety. Encourage them not to repeat.
4.4	Refine all parts of the task. Refine work going under block. Refine rolling. Refine work going over block.
4.5	Stress for leaders to take pride in their work. Show tight muscles, clear body lines throughout. For followers—copy work carefully—do not just do their own thing. BE "LOOK-ALIKES."

thighs or seats touch the floor, just hands and feet.

3.0 Rolling is a way that helps us to travel on lots of different body parts. Be thoughtful, to give each other time and space to roll before starting your roll. Roll two at a time, traveling across the mat one near each end. Be sure to carry mats to an open space. In groups of four, get a mat and begin.

3.1 See how quickly you can come to your feet after you roll.

3.2 Try to complete your roll on as little of the mat as you can—making your body tight as you roll.

3.3 If you have a favorite kind of roll, begin to practice it and make it your very best work. Be ready to tell me what you are trying to do to make your roll even better.

3.4 You might enjoy copying other people's best rolls. Try to make your roll look just like their very best roll.

4.0 Let us see if you can combine traveling over and under the blocks on different body parts with rolling. Listen carefully as to where the blocks and newspaper rolls are to go, then you may get them and place them in your working space. At least one block with newspaper roll on it must be placed on the floor slightly away from the side of the mat to make you go over or under it before you roll and one block and newspaper roll are to be placed right next to the side of the mat to be used immediately after you roll. Quietly place blocks and begin.

4.1 Work on making each turn you take different by intentionally making difficult body parts touch the floor or mat.

4.2 Try to go under the first block, roll, and go over the second block.

4.3 Let only your feet take you over the first block, roll, and then hands and feet take you over the last block.

4.4 Now select your best work going under the block, rolling, and going over the block . . . and . . . work to make it even better by really taking care and thinking about what you are doing.

4.5 Play follow the leader. One person, do your best work and all others watch carefully; then try to copy the best work of the leader. Take turns being leader so all get to copy the best work of everyone at your mat.

Evaluation. Refer to Chapter 10 and either select or adapt one of the evaluative tools or develop a tool that can be used to help assess a specific aspect of the unit that is important to the needs of your students.

GYMNASTICS THEME 2—INTRODUCTION TO SPACE

The second theme focuses on using space and developing an awareness of where the body is in space as it moves. As the facility for varying and controlling the use of space develops, children extend their versatility in efficient and effective movement. Thus, when the focus is on space, children are learning to be responsible for and understand where their bodies are in space.

Although the children used space when responding to experiences in the first theme, the teacher did not structure the dimensions of space in the content of the experiences. The children were not asked to think about the space being used as they moved except when placing restrictions, e.g., to travel using all the space in the room while avoiding contact with others or, for organizational purposes, to place equipment in their own space. In other words, the interpretation in the first theme is on *spacing* for safety or convenience rather than on *space* content.

Space has six dimensions: *areas*, *directions*, *levels*, *pathways*, *planes*, and *extensions*. The first three are of greatest importance in this second gymnastics theme, with some work focusing on pathways and extensions. The study of planes involves more advanced space concepts introduced in conjunction with Theme 4. It is used almost exclusively in elementary school gymnastics when observing movement rather than when structuring gymnastic content.

SPACE CONTENT IS NOT TAUGHT ALONE. LIKE CONTENT FOR EACH OF THE REMAINING THEMES, SPACE IS ALWAYS TAUGHT IN CONJUNCTION WITH CONTENT FROM THEME 1. Space content may also be combined with content from all other themes. The early combination with the body aspects offers children an extended opportunity to expand their gymnastic locomotor vocabulary. If you stress space awareness, children as they travel can learn to manage their bodies and extend movements originally executed in one direction, level, area, or pathway to others, thus increasing their versatility.

We do not exhaust content ideas in one theme before we introduce subsequent themes. Because all movement involves the same aspects (body, space, effort, and relationships), there is constant opportunity to gain greater facility and awareness for the use of space as we focus our content and the attention of the learner on other aspects of movement. This reenforcement and elaboration happen not only as we move from theme to theme in gymnastics but also as we teach in the other program areas of games or dance.

Space awareness is a critical aspect of learning in gymnastics. The ability to negotiate space must be developed fully if one expects to work effectively in space that is often limited by the shape, size, and arrangement of apparatus, and also if one expects to blend personal movement with that of others.

Development of Theme 2

> **Basic Content**
> Areas: general, personal
> Levels: high, medium, low
> Directions: forward, backward, sideward, up, down
> Pathways: floor, air; straight, curved, zigzag
> Extensions: small, large
> (In conjunction with content from Theme 1.)

AREAS—GENERAL SPACE. General space is the total space available for activity. Its purpose as content is to develop the understanding that general space is large, the total space must be shared safely by all, and it is utilized by means of locomotion. General space also is included as content to help the children develop the facility for using it. Learning to use the total room space is not as simple as it seems. Some children are sharing activity space with a large number of children for the first time in physical education classes. The aggressive child or the child unconcerned for personal safety or the safety of others may have no trouble covering the total space, but may have a problem in controlling movement to avoid others. Timid or overcautious children may avoid others (as they find comfort in the quiet corners), but need help in venturing into the mainstream of activity and negotiating spaces along with the class. *When general space becomes content, emphasis is on the child moving and learning to use the total space.* Helping children to assume responsibility for their movement and to avoid collisions was initiated in the first lesson and reenforced as long as needed in subsequent lessons on any theme. This emphasis on safety does not and should not subside. In fact, the children's ability to control movement grows as lessons on Theme 2 focus explicitly on the use of general space.

AREAS—PERSONAL SPACE. *Personal space is that space which surrounds the individual—the space the body parts can touch as they extend in all directions.* This personal space surrounds the body while it travels or when it is stationary. Nonlocomotor movement is emphasized most frequently to develop a feeling for the extent of one's personal space. Therefore, the purpose for introducing personal space as content is to help children grasp the scope of this sphere, extend it, and gain and make full use of it in gymnastics. Because nonlocomotor movement is so appropriate to acquainting children with personal space, it is often a part of a lesson that involves locomotor movement through general space to help in pacing that lesson. This practice keeps the children working, yet provides a rest by changing the nature of the activity. *More important, when teaching most concepts, it is helpful to learning if we teach the contrast involved within the concept.* For example, since space is being taught, a clearer perspective of both general and personal space is developed when the child can contrast one with the other within the same lesson.

Sample Learning Experiences

1. As you travel about the room, see how close you can come to one another without touching. Then move far away.
2. On your own, combine traveling with movement in your personal space.

Discussion. This theme is one that can be experienced by very young children. It is added early in the program and can be coupled most effectively with the content from the first theme. When introducing this theme to older children who have had little or no educational gymnastics background, you may want to combine the first two themes immediately. The emphasis in either case is on helping the children to use the general space freely and to recognize either how their movement may need to be restricted when the area is small or how they are freer to move in larger spaces. The nonlocomotor movement is added to help them recognize the amount of space their movement can encompass and to help them use personal space more effectively.

When children are working on this theme, you may find it a continuing challenge to help them focus their attention on their movement while avoiding others. The distractable child tends to look about and follow friends, and forgets to take control of his or her movement. This child often makes responses that are not on a par with his or her capabilities. Sometimes it helps to add more structure, e.g., changes of levels, directions, activities, or body parts, to help children remain more attentive to the task at hand.

LEVELS. In gymnastics, levels as space content are introduced primarily to challenge children to get off their feet and to use the extremes in levels—*high and low.* Levels also add another means of varying movement while controlling the body. As they come off their feet into the air and experience elevation (flight), children go into the high level. When they get down close to the floor, they are in the low level. The level between low and high is referred to as medium. *Remember that levels are relative.* For example, a child may be in a low balanced position and understand the level concept by elevating one body part higher than the rest.

When the high level becomes a focus, children associate it with jumping, especially if they are traveling. The emphasis should also encompass safety and efficiency in landing. (See page

269 for a discussion on controlling force in landing.) The movement of the children can be enhanced greatly by helping them differentiate between and develop ability in resilient landings and fixed (glued) landings where the feet remain on the floor. They need continuing opportunities to practice both types, and to recognize that the former is used especially when continuing momentum is desired and the latter is appropriate when momentum is to be curtailed.

Sample Learning Experiences

1. As you do step-like actions, constantly change levels.
2. Select one way to travel and see whether you can do it in all three levels.
3. As you travel, see how high you can take your feet.
4. Jumping high over your block and newspaper, make one landing very soft and still and let the next landing pop you straight up into the air.

Discussion. Notice all of the samples given involve traveling (content from Theme 1). Rather than having the children focus on the content of locomotion, we shift their attention to the concept of levels. In this way, they expand and continue to practice former concepts while encountering new material. As the children grow in their ability to both move and think through the problems, it is customary for the learning experiences to become more complex. Children eventually can focus on more than one movement concept at a time. Care should be given not to give too many at one time.

In combining levels with general space, some children tend to enjoy scooting aimlessly on their backs while others run and jump continuously, moving at a faster speed than they can manage safely. In challenging both to alter their behavior and to make their movement more gymnastic-like, the teacher can add frequent changes of levels to the task.

DIRECTIONS. In the second gymnastic theme, the children learn to change directions. They can change directions while maintaining the same pathways—*a change of front.* They can also change direction with *no change in front*—this must result in a change in pathway. Including directions as content helps children learn to move in a variety of ways in all directions—*forward, backward, sideward, up, and down*—and they become more responsible for choosing and con-

trolling the direction of their movement. Learning to change direction willfully and to execute the same movement in different directions is critical to the development of skillful, versatile, safe, and agile movement in gymnastics. Early in gymnastics, children are encouraged to negotiate general space, changing directions as they travel. Later, the children change directions while focusing on forms of traveling such as rolling. In these situations, children can develop both confidence and skill in specific locomotor forms.

I have found that young children at first manage movement at different levels more safely than they change direction when working in general space. Therefore, you may want to introduce levels before directions.

Even the most simple locomotor movements take on a new challenge when children try to do them in different directions. The purpose of being able to change direction is closely associated with being able to take care of oneself in unexpected or unplanned situations. When large groups of people (irrespective of age) are asked to move in general space, their usual procedure is to travel in a forward direction in a circle. We have been programmed by traffic laws and our pedestrian codes to conform. It is not difficult, or at least it is easier, to follow along and avoid others in environments where everyone follows specific rules and regulations. Children who are taught to move in such sterile settings in physical education, however, may not learn to cope with the natural movement in games or the safety hazards that develop when another child in front swerves or falls. A more realistic directional challenge is to be able to travel in an area where the direction and the starting and stopping of movement of each person are unpredictable and self-regulated. Thus, one has to look for empty spaces and be able to adjust speed, direction, and path quickly and often, because of the movement of someone else and not because of personal choice.

Sample Learning Experiences

1. See how you can change direction as you travel, being careful to avoid others.
2. Keep the way you move the same, but try to move in all different directions.
3. As you roll across the mat, see how you can roll in different directions.
4. Travel over the box (bench or block and newspaper roll); work on being able to land, facing in different directions.

Discussion. The four tasks were designed to move from the simple to the more complex. The complexity of the learning experience depends on the nature and number of concepts contained in the experience as well as on the ability of the learner. Entire lessons or units can be developed around a single concept. We believe it helpful to learning for the child to experience a movement concept such as directions in many different movements and in different lessons and settings before going on to a new concept.

Even though the list of examples shows a simple form of progression, it is not a series of experiences appropriate for a single lesson. None of the lists of sample learning experiences was written with this purpose. When the children begin to demonstrate an awareness for one concept and show some ability to work with it in gymnastics, you can combine it with concepts already learned. Using this theme of space awareness along with body awareness gives children not only opportunities to develop new ways to move but also situations that should help them to utilize space effectively and efficiently as they move in a greater variety of ways. The space aspects can be combined to form the content of an experience, and each can be combined with modes of traveling. All can be altered by sharing the decisions with the child. For example, one experience is: "As you roll across the mat, see how you can roll in different directions." *Travel* instead of *roll* could have been the choice, thereby letting the child select the form of locomotion. Likewise, a change of levels or pathways could have been included.

The teacher must and should move on to the next theme long before the children encounter all of the possible experiences in space awareness. Since space is a part of all movement, however, it will be used again and again in each of the next themes, if only in subtle ways. You can and often should return to a theme and use its content as a major focus for a unit of study after advancing to the next theme.

PATHWAYS. The pathways entered as content in Theme 2 are limited to those on the floor. A floor pathway is created as the body travels across the floor; it is the route taken in traveling. Since a change of pathways is one method for changing direction, some study of pathways may be included previously in the work on directions. Children learn that pathways may be *angular,* *straight, curved, twisted, zigzag,* or combinations of these, and they gain ability in recognizing and controlling the path the body takes as it travels.

Sample Learning Experiences

1. Think of a pathway and see how you can keep moving in that pathway, but change the direction in which you are traveling.

2. As you travel across the mat, show a definite change in your pathway.

3. Arrange hoops, blocks, or newspaper rolls to help you work on changing pathways. Then show a variety of ways to travel as you move about your apparatus changing pathways.

Discussion. Being able to change pathways is important not only in safe body management but also in the creation of gymnastic sequences that are visually and personally appealing. Change of pathways is also important in negotiating apparatus, especially when the apparatus is not arranged in linear fashion. Children too frequently are faced with working in straight pathways because either they or the teacher lacks imagination in setting up the apparatus. Also, many times children approach and leave apparatus in a straight, unaltered pathway because teachers fail to recognize the value of having them experience a willful change in pathway.

EXTENSIONS. Initiating an awareness and control of the size of movement *(large and small)* is the purpose of including extensions in Theme 2. Developing a feeling and control for the body parts in relation to their position in space is crucial to body management and skill development in gymnastics.

The focus is on experiencing the full range of movement of each body part in diverse locomotor and nonlocomotor situations. The farther the body parts are taken away from the body center, the greater the extension and the more space used; therefore, the greater the size of the movement. Conversely the closer the body parts to the center of the body, the smaller the movement.

Children find locomotion and balancing a new challenge when focusing their attention on increasing or diminishing the size of their movement and the amount of space used. Also included is an appreciation for how big is big in one's personal spectrum of space and the kinesthetic sensation of full extension when it reaches the farthest fiber of the body part being extended. Children can often see the full pres-

ence or lack of extension in others before they can feel and accomplish it personally. For this reason, partner work or brief periods of observation are often part of the lessons involving extension.

Sample Learning Experiences

1. As you keep part of your body glued to the floor, see how much of the space you can reach with your other body parts.

2. Touching only your hands to the bench as you travel back and forth down the bench, sometimes make your body big and use great amounts of space and sometimes make it small and use small amounts of space. Really work on extending legs and back and taking care to land softly.

3. Watch your partner move, making his or her body first very big, then very small. See whether you can see the muscle tension that is used to be very big and very small.

Discussion. The comments you make about being able to see the tension in the extremes of extension often cause the children to exert greater effort. Many times, we seem more prone to praise full extension and deemphasize tightly tucked positions, failing to remember that both require tension and are important in gymnastics. These emphases should be continuous as we observe and respond to the movement of the children and not reserved only for instructional periods when the content is focused on extension. Children need help in developing the feeling in gymnastics for tension that is so much a part of the tightly tucked, near positions of the body and the fully extended body part(s). Emphasize the feeling of tension in the child's movement and the ability to see it in the movement of others.

APPARATUS. Simple, large apparatus such as benches, boxes, or mats as well as any small apparatus can be added at any time. Learning to appreciate the amount of space used by another person when working in a small group sharing a piece of equipment like a bench is an essential aspect of space awareness in gymnastics. Also, learning to cope with space restricted by apparatus provides meaningful challenges. *Usually anything that is to be done on apparatus is first done on the floor.* Either you or the children can arrange the apparatus in terms of the kinds of spatial demands in the movement. For example, you can get the children to tuck tightly while rolling by carefully placing apparatus to decrease the amount of space available to them.

You can place a newspaper roll on a block midway on a mat. As the children dismount from a box and roll, they have to adjust the size of the roll to accommodate the space restricted by the block. Many times we can develop these kinds of situations and have the children work on the space concept without focusing the content on space itself, but letting the environment pose the task.

SAMPLE UNIT PLAN THEME 2

Theme(s). Introduction to Space—Theme 2 (and selected content from Theme 1).

Unit Focus. Balancing, rolling, and step-like actions, with emphasis on changing levels and directions.

Appropriate For. Children who have started to refine some step-like actions and forms of rolling and have demonstrated ability to manage their body in inverted balances in an instructional setting.

Length of Unit. Four 30-minute lessons.

Content
　　Body—(continued work on balancing, rolling and step-like actions)
　　Space—change in directions and levels
　　Effort—
　　Relationship—

Student Objectives. The students should be willing to try to

1. Understand that step-like actions can be performed on a variety of body parts and occur whenever the weight of the body is kept in contact with the floor and transferred from one body part to another.
2. Know that changes in levels and direction can be used to develop variety in gymnastics movement.
3. Show distinct changes in levels and directions when combining rolling and step-like movements.
4. Accept responsibility for refining personal responses by working to achieve greater constant tension in the body and its parts.
5. Willfully attempt to place body parts over the base in balancing and, when bringing them back down to the floor, to avoid collapsing or falling.

Teaching Area. Indoor space large enough to accommodate class size.

Apparatus and/or Equipment. One mat and a bench or box for each four to six children.

Learning Experiences (Tasks)

1.0 Remember that step-like actions are performed by lifting your weight from one body part to another. Staying in your own space, work on inventing step-like actions on different body parts.

1.1 Try to involve body parts you do not usually think about for stepping in gymnastics, such as the lower leg, arms, or knees.

A Suggested Progression For

	Lesson 1		Lesson 2
Tasks	**Teaching Tips**	**Tasks**	**Teaching Tips**
1.0	Emphasize that a step-like action is like walking, only they walk from one body part to another or to different surfaces, such as *front* of leg.	2.2	Quality of performance can sag. Recall any good work observed in previous lesson. Stress showing a "performance attitude."
1.1	Try to encourage as much upness, "gymnastic posture," as possible. Try not to accept grovelling.	2.3	You need to be ready to give specific cues to help here; e.g., squat—do not sit; hands flat, thumbs pointed in. Know your class—do not make backward roll a must if some are not ready.
1.2	Work toward getting some body parts high—feet especially—cartwheeling, weight on hands; activities will emerge.	2.4	Try to emphasize going into the second roll with no "extra" movements. Encourage variety so they do different combinations.
2.0	This can be done safely on the floor without mats by most classes. In all cases, strive for refinement of each roll.	1.2	Step-like actions here offer a nice change. Really observe landings, stress intentional placement of new body part on floor—muscle tension—no falling.
2.1	You might ask children to observe a nicely tucked roll where muscle tension is observable before sending them to work on this task.	1.3	Repeat this several times; be ready to comment on progress made. This is a good time to stress working without making a sound.
2.7	Coach to get rid of extraneous movements between roll and step-like actions and go for quality here too. Do not let them get floppy.	1.2	Ask for their best work. Stress a feeling of upness in upper part of body.

Combine these with an occasional hand or foot.

1.2 Work on involving many different body parts in your stepping actions, and try to show a clear change in levels.

1.3 Thinking about doing only step-like actions, see if you can make your stepping actions continuous for 30 seconds. When I say stop, either hold the position you are in or go into a position you can hold.

1.4 This half of the class, sit and observe the other half and see what body parts are taking the weight in step-like actions.

1.5 Let us see how you can make step-like actions (just plain walking on feet is illegal) take you onto, along, and off a bench. Remembering to lift bench with your arms and backs straight, get into groups of four to six, get one bench, and quietly show your best work.

1.6 As you approach and as you travel away from the bench, strive to change your direction as you make step-like actions.

2.0 Trying to keep body tucked tightly as you roll, begin to show your best rolls. Travel one at a time down the length of a mat. How do we get the mats to our working space? (Carry them, do not drag them—in groups of four to six.) Quietly, see how you can manage this.

2.1 No matter what kind of roll you are doing, think about the muscle tension needed to make nice firm arms and bodies and tight lines in our legs. Really begin to show these clear lines.

2.2 Begin to vary your roll by changing your direction. Try not to roll two times in the same direction.

2.3 Work on rolling backwards, if you would like; remember to push with your hands flat on the mat.

2.4 Try to combine two directions while rolling down the mat.

2.5 Those of you who have been tucking your head in the forward roll or have been successful in getting both hands to push you straight while rolling backwards may find it fun to see whether you can start your roll from a medium high level. Try rolling from a standing position, in which your knees are straight instead of bent.

2.6 Roll from any level in any direction and go *immediately* into a balance on completion of your roll. Then take care to *intentionally* come out of the balance—*do not flop or fall.*

2.7 Roll at a low level in any direction and, immediately on completing the roll, finish with a series of step-like actions in a new direction.

3.0 We are going to be combining rolls with step-like actions, trying to develop greater

Sample Gymnastics Unit/Theme 2

	Lesson 3		Lesson 4
Tasks	**Teaching Tips**	**Tasks**	**Teaching Tips**
2.5	Encourage others to refine roll from a low level, but observe them carefully—they may find this not as hard as it sounds.	2.6	Let them tell you how they group and how mats are to be carried; see if they can get them out (if age and size of children are appropriate for mat size). Refine work from Lesson 3.
2.6	Stress getting base ready as they finish roll; holding balance a short time; coming out of balance by preparing a body part to take weight.	3.0	Add bench. Really stress tight muscles—always . . . not just for moments. Have them feel the difference in relaxed and strong muscles.
1.5	Getting benches can be catastrophic unless you have worked with children to help them learn a safe, quiet way. Take time to get benches in an orderly fashion.	3.2	Stress safety, watching, moving away from work of others; use space away from bench and mat.
1.6	Focus your attention both on observed changes of direction AND on quality of step-like actions. Stress their entire series of movements should look like a gymnastic performance.	3.3	Can have a demonstration anytime to show *thoughtful,* careful gymnasts. Slow them down— it is not a race. Stress *constant* movement, but *quality*—clear body shapes, lines of legs firm.
3.1	Children often avoid using floor. If step-like actions are controlled and not floppy, the floor is safe.	3.4	Encourage balances that can be held *and* then coming out of them with care and going into roll or step-like action. (Let one half the class show, then the other half.) A sharing demonstration can be placed anytime it seems appropriate.

variety by skillfully changing our levels and directions. Your mat can be placed anywhere near your bench, but once you have placed it, leave it for today. Show your sharpest clear body shapes and planned, gymnastic movement. Carry your bench to your working space, then get your mat. Get into groups of four to six and begin.

3.1 Make the floor a part of your gymnastic scene. Begin to show changes of direction, doing step-like actions on the *floor* after you leave the bench or mat.

3.2 Starting your work from different places on the mat, on the bench, and on the floor, see how all of you in your group can continuously demonstrate safely your best step-like actions and rolls, clearly showing a change in levels and directions. Take a moment to decide where each of you is going to begin.

(Children can number off in their groups. Then teacher can ask number 1s to begin, then 2s start safely, 3s, until all in each group are in motion. Stopping children, then starting again, may help them manage this task safely.)

3.3 Let us see if every group can be in continuous movement for 1 minute. Try to make each movement planned and show clearly change of directions and levels.

3.4 Add some of your best balances to your work, but make them by moving into them immediately following a roll or a carefully planned step-like action.

Evaluation. Refer to Chapter 10 and either select or adapt one of the evaluative tools or develop a tool that can be used to help assess a specific aspect of the unit that is important to the needs of your students.

GYMNASTICS THEME 3—INTRODUCTION TO TIME

The third gymnastics theme concentrates work on *how* the body performs the movement, with specific attention to the time factor. The chief purpose of this theme is to improve the efficiency or effectiveness of movement by creating experiences that involve the production and regulation of speed.

It is essential in gymnastics to be able to change speed from movement to movement as well as within a single movement. One must also be able to set and maintain a continuous speed as well as to accelerate and decelerate. Also basic to skillful, versatile performance in gymnastics is the ability to bring the speed of the movement to a sudden, momentary stop, maintaining alert stillness—an important aspect of the first theme where the idea was introduced at an elementary level. The more simple characteristics of time—fast and slow—are dealt with first in this theme, with others coming in when awareness for the first two becomes evident in the movement responses of the children. Although sometimes unknowingly, each person shows a definite preference for moving fast or slow. Most children find it more difficult to move slowly than to move fast (perhaps partly because speed is more exhilarating).

Although all content covered in the first two themes can be revisited, emphasis is on combining time with the various activities of the body (locomotor and nonlocomotor) or body actions (twist, stretch, and curl). The body actions may have been experienced somewhat superficially when extensions were examined in the second theme. They occurred because the children were using the full range of personal space, not because the content centered on body actions. Also, some initial teaching might have been directed toward control of speed; again, the content focus was not on the time factor but on safety.

Work with the time aspect in gymnastics focuses primarily on its association with rolling and step-like actions, especially those that combine hands and feet. Children can develop an appreciation for the role acceleration plays in the approach run used before flight and when vaulting.

As you approach the content and the development of this theme on time, remember that you are introducing the material and will revisit the time aspect often as both real and incidental content in the remaining themes.

Development of Theme 3

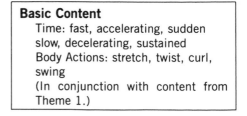

Basic Content

Time: fast, accelerating, sudden
slow, decelerating, sustained
Body Actions: stretch, twist, curl, swing
(In conjunction with content from Theme 1.)

TIME. Time describes the speed of a movement. Time refers to the speed with which the movement is performed. The speed or time of the movement may be *fast or slow, accelerating or decelerating, sudden or sustained.* Obviously, much of the movement of the gymnast is performed somewhere between the extremes of these three dimensions of time. Do not confuse time with *timing,* which involves the meshing and interplay within and among movements.

Children should begin to gain a keen sense of inner responsibility when developing, regulating, and redirecting speed is the goal. In gymnastics, the mover is often solely responsible for all three of these. (Much later in their experiences, they can use trampettes, hanging ropes, or force applied by being lifted by someone else to add to or generate personal speed.) Success and beauty of movement in gymnastics are directly related to the ability to change speed. *If a single ability holds the key to the mystic mastery of movement—in dance, gymnastics, or games—it would be the ability to produce and regulate speed.*

As you work with children, you will observe that some children move quickly with facility whereas others seem to enjoy and be more at ease while doing slow, sustained work. It is critical for both to work on the speed that is more difficult, and each should have freedom to improve skills using the speed that gives the greatest satisfaction. Include both ends of the time spectrum in all lessons concentrating on time since a lesson involving all sudden, fast, quick movement can be exhausting, whereas one with slow, sustained movement can be just as exhausting and taxing as well as somewhat boring.

Throughout the study of time, some children need considerable help to recognize that their responsibility with time is threefold:

1. They must be helped to realize that the ability to *produce speed* is a personal challenge.

2. They need help in developing a personal commitment to *selecting the appropriate speed.*

3. They need feedback relevant to the content that will motivate a growing ability to *control speed.*

Sample Learning Experiences

1. Take a gymnastic movement and, working in your own space, try to see how fast and then how slowly you can do it.

2. Select a way of transferring your weight from your feet to your hands to your feet; first do it slowly, then fast.

3. Concentrate on making the speed of your run build as you approach the box, pause momentarily on the box, then dismount quickly.

4. While rolling, see if you can change the speed of your roll.

5. Develop a short gymnastic sequence that shows distinct and frequent changes in speed.

Discussion. Usually, the study of the speed or time factor begins with selecting one movement and repeating it, varying the speed, making it very *fast* and very *slow.* This movement can be either teacher selected or child selected. The choice can be an activity, such as rolling, or it can be the use of specific body parts such as feet or hands and feet, with the way the body parts are moved left up to the child. Frequently, these first experiences can be done in confined portions of general space, i.e., working space. (Working space permits traveling about in a small area that is free from the work of others.) Thus, fast movement need not be curtailed because of safety reasons and the need for focusing on the movement of classmates. The addition of small apparatus, such as ropes, to these simple tasks helps to confine the work in gymnastics to a smaller area and gives the child something specific to travel over. This feature helps some execute their responses with more dedication; however, what helps one might hinder or restrict others. Therefore, often let the addition of apparatus be the student's choice.

Speeding up and slowing down—*acceleration and deceleration*—can be introduced in much the same way as the teaching of fast and slow. Once these time concepts are taught, help the children use them in a purposeful way to improve past performances in the takeoff, as in sample 3, and begin to join these concepts with the space aspect introduced in Theme 2, as well as with all of the remaining themes. DO NOT HAVE CHILDREN JUST WORKING ON TIME. Always have them doing something from Theme 1 as they sensitively regulate time. The emphasis in these examples is on combining time with locomotor activities (step-like actions, rolling) as well as with flight.

The complexity of experiences develops in terms of the nature and number of requisites within the experience. Experiences similar to the first two examples with few simple content ideas can be introduced early, whereas those like the last two examples are reserved for students who are maturing in their ability to control their speed of movement. Never believe that you have *taught* time. Provide continuing experiences in it and frequently revisit the concept because there are always ways to improve the ability to produce, regulate, and redirect speed. The needs of the children, other content, and program priorities force you to leave each theme or concept, not the belief that there is no more to teach or to be learned.

BODY ACTIONS. Three body actions comprise all activities the body performs: *twist, stretch,* and *curl.* Some analysts also add *swing* to the list. Focusing on stretch, twist, curl, and swing elaborates on the use of personal space introduced in the second theme. As children develop the ability to perform these four actions in combinations, in all different directions, levels, and speeds, and in general as well as in personal space, they become more aware of the body as an instrument of movement.

So much of our movement in adult life involves primarily the space immediately in front of us. While the child's body is young and more supple, you should develop the ability to utilize the full range of motion—the maximum stretch, twist, curl, or swing the child can produce. These actions should be experienced over and over while moving through the air, in flight, and while traveling on the floor or when balancing by moving the parts of the body not responsible for supporting weight.

Sample Learning Experiences

　1. Just where you are, see how you can twist, stretch, curl, and swing. Keep changing the body parts or body surfaces that touch the floor.
　2. Take a balance in any way you are comfortable—then see how you can twist the free body parts that are not a part of the base. (Later add speed in the twist.)
　3. Travel on and off the bar by swinging, curling, and stretching. (Later add a change in speed.)
　4. As you come off the apparatus, show exaggerated twisting, curling, and stretching while in the air and when making step-like actions on hands and feet on the floor after you land.

Discussion. Children need ample opportunity to work on the new content of twisting, curling, stretching, and swinging before they consider and learn to control the speed with which they perform these movements. In introducing curling, twisting, and stretching, use the concept of extension, and elaborate upon it. Also, give the children practice in experiences that share the focus with the space concept as well as the seven locomotor forms. Some children can work enthusiastically and satisfyingly with the actions of the body as isolated content, such as in the first sample experience. Others may need to have the actions combined with other content almost immediately to keep them motivated.

Twisting requires one part of the body to remain fixed while other body parts move around to face a new direction. Turning requires no fixed body parts—the entire body moves around to face a new direction. Children may need help in differentiating between twisting and turning.

As the twisting, stretching, curling, and swinging actions become bonafide content, you should notice increased flexibility, range, versatility, and mastery of the body in movement. The children gain more complete sensations if you can motivate them to exaggerate their actions—to go another inch or two in their efforts to feel the tension that should exist when the body is more fully stretched, curled, twisted, or swinging.

APPARATUS. Apparatus is used freely in this theme because the nature of apparatus itself as well as its spatial arrangement help to dictate certain conditions of speed. In other words, apparatus is often a meaningful, external motivator of speed. Therefore, be sensitive as you arrange equipment to create the space essential to the development and the reduction of the speed appropriate to the task. A young man I know said, "The only problems I have in teaching are those I create myself." Keep this confession in mind when you arrange equipment for use in lessons built from this theme. If you want the children to be able to accelerate for height after takeoff,

you must provide the space essential to acceleration. Likewise, if children have been permitted to generate speed, they often need space to reduce it, so their path may have to be free of other apparatus and they should not be working close to a wall or other obstructions. Thus, the decisions relevant to arranging apparatus have to be checked to ensure that the arrangement creates the environment essential to learning.

SAMPLE UNIT PLAN THEME 3

Themes. Introduction to Time—Theme 3 (and selected content from Theme 1).

Unit Focus. Contrasting slow and fast movement while traveling on hands and feet.

Appropriate For. Children who have demonstrated a learning attitude in a gymnastic setting and who have developed some arm-shoulder strength.

Length of Unit. Three 30-minute lessons.

Content

Body—transferring weight: hands to feet, giving attention to controlling feet in the air; landing

Space—

Effort—slow, fast, contrasting speed

Relationship—

Student Objectives. The students should be willing to try to

1. Willfully change their speed while performing a variety of locomotor and nonlocomotor movements.
2. Know that muscle tension must be exerted in the hip/abdominal area to slow or speed the descent of the feet when in an inverted position.
3. Acquire the ability to change speed through attending to coaching cues and practice in order to show greater versatility and skill in movement.
4. Pace their movement to allow others about them to alter their speed.
5. Discover movements that are easier for them to do faster and that are easier to do slower to help them gain an appreciation for producing and controlling speed in gymnastics.

Teaching Area. Indoor space large enough to accommodate class size.

Apparatus and/or Equipment. One mat and a bench for each four to six children.

Learning Experiences (Tasks)

1.0 Place your hands on the floor near a line on the floor and see how you can take your feet back and forth, up and over the line.

1.1 Try to think about the speed you are making your feet travel when you are taking them back and forth over the line—is it slow, medium, or fast? Get rid of medium movement, make your speed either very fast or very slow, but never collapse.

1.2 Make both feet land at the same time as you go back and forth over the line and try to bring your feet down very slowly. Feel the muscles up where your legs attach to your trunk really begin to tighten. Remember, you have to work to tighten those muscles to slow your feet down.

2.0 Clearly show a change in speed, traveling down the mat, being free to change your pathways and your directions.

2.1 Select one way of traveling—repeat it two or three times and make a distinct change in speed as you travel.

2.2 Think of a gymnastic movement you usually do rather fast—try to do it much slower. Is it harder or easier when you slow down your speed?

2.3 Same as above, only select a slow movement and speed it up.

2.4 Combine two or more different kinds of gymnastic movement, making at least one movement very slow and one very fast . . . and feel what you do to control your speed.

A Suggested Progression For Sample Gymnastics Unit/Theme 3

	Lesson 1		Lesson 2		Lesson 3
Tasks	Teaching Tips	Tasks	Teaching Tips	Tasks	Teaching Tips
1.0	Emphasize straight elbows, strong arms, and making feet land close to hands.	1.2	See Lesson 1—really get back parallel to wall.	3.0	Select different balances or let children choose their own.
1.1	Encourage them to make fast speed very fast or slow speed very slow—have them experience both.	2.4	See Lesson 1—work on greater clarity in speed, refinement of what they choose to do.	3.2	Work to make this response continuous . . . *and* focus their attention on clearly showing variety in speed.
1.2	Sometimes, children get more success here if they do not straighten legs in the air but keep them bent—back in a straight line over hands.	2.2	Have them try several. Get them to talk about why speed helps or hinders what they are doing.	4.0	Same as Lesson 2—work on refinement. Get feet to land close to bench.
2.0	Caution other children not to start so persons on mats do not have to alter speed for anyone else.	2.3	Same as above. Work to get the contrast between fast and slow.	4.1	Ropes are parallel to bench about 6 feet away. Work toward step-like actions, with feet high.
2.1	Seek variety here. Get them to experience forward, backward rolls, step-like actions, etc., all with a definite contrast in speed.	3.0	You can select any other balances children can do or children may select balance.	4.2	After experimentation, have them select, put into a sequence, and refine a specific series of movement. Stress care in showing clarity in speed and maintaining a performing posture throughout. Firm, clear, strong body lines.
2.4	Encourage quality performance—light, springy movement, upness in upper torso.	3.1	Stress placing of feet—discourage *falling* feet.		
		4.0	(Watch straight arms, backs when carrying bench, avoid having anyone walk backwards.)		
			Again, check backs; urge they get hips over hands on bench by pushing with both feet against floor.		

3.0 Go into weight on hands or a shoulder stand and try to make your feet come down slowly, controlling exactly where they land and then stand up. If in a handstand, try to make your feet land very close to your hands.

3.1 In your handstand or shoulder stand, think about speed and bring your feet down fast by your hands or shoulders and pop up. Keep playing with your speed and see whether the speed begins to help you get to an upright position.

3.2 Try to come out of your balance, going from one balance position to another, letting different body parts or surfaces support you. Each time you change balance positions, show a clear change in speed. (Urge children to make different balances as their starting position.)

4.0 Taking care to give the other people room and time to change their speed, see how you can change your speed, traveling on your hands and feet back and forth over the bench trying to intentionally make both feet take off and land at the same time. Get in groups of four to six, and get one bench.

4.1 After you travel down the bench changing speed, do the same thing back and forth over the rope alongside the bench on the floor, only make your feet land one at a time. (Be sure rope is far enough to the side of the bench to allow room so no one gets kicked.)

4.2 Develop a series of fast and slow movements back and forth over the bench, and rope, and on the mat. Decide where you will put the mat in your working space. Carry it carefully and safely begin.

Evaluation. Refer to Chapter 10 and either select or adapt one of the evaluative tools or develop a tool that can be used to help assess a specific aspect of the unit that is important to the needs of your students.

GYMNASTICS THEME 4—INTRODUCTION TO RELATIONSHIPS OF BODY PARTS

The fourth gymnastics theme places full attention on the relationships of body parts as a child performs in gymnastics. These relationships may be the *relationship of one body part* to another or the *relationship of body parts to the floor or apparatus.*

It is possible to approach this theme in several ways. Perhaps the most simple is the study of body shapes, then relationship of body parts to each other, followed by actions of the body. Each of these content areas may be couched in simple or complex learnings, as illustrated in the list of sample experiences. When the learner is being introduced to the idea, the experiences deal with the more simple concepts (balance; base of support; wide, round, straight, and twisted shapes), with fewer and less demanding movement ideas. As the learner matures and the theme is revisited, the more difficult concepts (off-balance, body parts leading action, symmetry, asymmetry) are studied, and the movement involved in responding becomes more demanding. NO ONE THEME IS "COVERED" IN ANY ONE GRADE LEVEL OR YEAR. The variety of experiences appropriate for full development spans 3 or more years of work and, in fact, is never covered.

Concept Development in Gymnastics

Nothing has been mentioned in gymnastics about how to introduce movement concepts (e.g., shapes, off-balance, relationships, body leads). Now is the time to discuss this important aspect of teaching, since so many special concepts occur in the content of this theme. Movement concepts have underlying facts, knowledge, or principles. Becoming familiar with or understanding the concept that underlies the movement content is often a prerequisite for responding appropriately to a task on any theme.

When the educational approach was introduced in the United States, many people (myself included) thought you always had to let the boys and girls discover for themselves the concept being studied; however, many children failed to develop the understanding underlying the concept. We have looked more closely at learning and at children and realize that different children learn in different ways from many kinds of experiences. Discovery, therefore, remains *one meaningful way*—but *not the only way*. For example, I have used various objects (cup, saucer, pictures of a butterfly, children's art) to teach the concept of symmetry and asymmetry, showing the objects after explaining symmetry and asymmetry and asking the children to select those of one classification or the other. These experiences, given before setting children off to work on symmetry and asymmetry, have hastened the children's understanding of the concept, so the thrill of discovery could be attached to reproducing and reexperiencing the concept in movement. You can think of ways to develop an understanding for the concepts introduced in this theme and others by remembering that the "appropriate" way to introduce the concept depends on the objectives, the children who are to be involved in the learning, and the concept to be taught. Also, you can use several approaches for the same concept at various times to initiate, elaborate, and apply the level of understanding appropriate to the experience and the maturity of the children.

Development of Theme 4

Basic Content

Relationship of Body Parts to Each Other:
    above–below–alongside
    apart–together
    behind–in front of
    meeting–parting
    near–far
    over–under
Relationship of Body Parts to Apparatus:
    over–under–on
    near–far
    above–below–alongside
    behind–in front of
    arriving on–dismounting from
Actions of Body Parts:
    support body
    lead action
    apply force
    receive force (weight)
Body Shapes:
    angular
    straight
    wide
    round
    twisted
    symmetrical
    asymmetrical
(In conjunction with content from Theme 1 or with 1, 2 and/or 3.)

RELATIONSHIP OF BODY PARTS TO EACH OTHER. The relationship theme is developed first by creating learning environments to study control of the relationship of one body part to another. This control can be developed in both locomotor and nonlocomotor situations through traveling or balancing in a variety of ways while focusing on the relationship of one body part to another. Later work can involve relationships of body parts to each other while moving on or in relation to apparatus. All the possible relationships of one body part to another are examined specifically as content or incidentally in movement by individual children: *above–below–alongside; apart–together; behind–in front of; meeting–parting; near–far; over–under.* As is always the case in content selection, either the student or the teacher can select the relationships.

To appreciate the vital role relationship of body parts plays in movement, think of gymnastic movements that involve weight transference from feet to hands to feet, such as when traveling over a box. In gymnastics, this motion has traditionally been called vaulting. The relationship of the legs and feet to each other, to the hands, and to the box primarily makes one response or one vault different from another.

Sample Learning Experiences

1. Travel about the room on your hands and feet, noticing when you bring your feet and hands close together or far apart.
2. Think about your legs and feet as you roll. Try to show different relationships at the beginning, in the middle, and at the end of your roll.
3. As you vault over the box, try to take your feet far away from the box.

Discussion. Whether to start with teacher-selected structure or with students playing a greater role in decision-making depends on the objectives of the experiences as well as the needs and level of achievement of the children. Sometimes, you may start with great specificity, as evident in the second example, or you may start with a more open task such as number 1. You must realize, however, that both structure and the lack of structure can be restricting to different children in different ways.

Children who are being introduced to this theme have found tremendous satisfaction in foretelling what their feet (or other body parts) are going to do in movement, then doing the movement, and showing others they can make their predictions come true. This technique gets children to think before and while doing. The experience can be shared with a partner or small group. One person can tell what relationships are to occur, and the other(s) can observe to see whether they do. Both the mover and the observer sharpen their ability to observe the relationships of body parts during movement. The partner work can develop into one person copying the observed relationships of the other. Being able to predict the relationships of the body parts in movement requires the learners to know where the body parts are to be as they move. Knowing where the body parts are is basic to and instrumental in the refinement of movement and is

an asset in demonstrating greater versatility and skill in gymnastics.

RELATIONSHIPS OF BODY PARTS TO APPARATUS. The ability to control different body parts can be enhanced by developing tasks in which the children perform gymnastic movement, intentionally making specific body parts assume the various relationships to the apparatus: near–far; over–under–on; behind–in front of–alongside; and above–below. The focus is drawn to creating, observing, selecting, practicing, and perfecting specific relationships of body parts to the apparatus.

As the learner develops and matures in gymnastics and in the ability to deal with concepts, the complexity of the relationships can be expanded. Also, the challenge created by the apparatus can become more challenging by in-

creasing the height and amount of apparatus as well as by making the arrangement of the apparatus more complicated.

Sample Learning Experiences

1. Arrange any two or three pieces of small apparatus and see how you can go over it. Try to take different body parts close to the apparatus or far away.

2. See how many relationships you can make with your legs to the bench and one leg to the other while your legs are in the air as you travel back and forth over the bench.

3. As you come over the box, try to land with your feet in different relationships to the box (heels closest to the box; feet side by side, with feet parallel to the box; toes pointed toward the box).

Discussion. As work begins with very young children on relating the body or its parts to apparatus, it often starts at an exploratory level so that the learners can see how they move in relation to a piece of apparatus. Once they find and experience the various alternatives (e.g., over, under, above, below, around), they can choose, as in example 1, a specific body part (feet, hands, or legs) and see how they can move, keeping that body part near to or far from the apparatus. Later, various body parts are controlled in relation to apparatus as the children spring over it, move along on it, or do general work with it, as in example 2. Attention shifts to the relationship of the body parts to the apparatus during takeoff, flight, and landing (see example 3). Often, relationship to the apparatus is studied while combining both locomotor and nonlocomotor movement.

This theme has extensive content for different degrees of complexity and can be used repeatedly during the entire gymnastic program. Since you can include content from previous themes, you need this word of caution. Avoid making the task so complex that the learners end up focusing on nothing. WHEN MOVEMENT CONTENT BECOMES MULTIVARIED, ANY RESPONSE SEEMS TO SATISFY THE TASK AND THE CHILDREN DO NOT HAVE TO BE SELECTIVE IN THEIR MOVEMENTS.

BODY SHAPES. A natural outgrowth of, or adjunct to, the study of relationships of body parts to each other is the work devoted to creating body shapes: *angular, straight, wide, round, twisted, symmetrical, and asymmetrical.* In this theme, you should devote attention to the shapes created by the body when the relationship of the body parts changes. As the content of lessons on this theme shifts to body shapes, the experiences are likely to include opportunities to create body shapes in the air as well as on the floor, in stillness and in locomotion. The shapes in the air can be motivated and enhanced by arriving on, coming off, or going over apparatus. Working with others can be introduced by having one partner on the floor make a shape with his body while the other jumps or goes over the partner, making a shape in the air.

Advanced work on the relationship of body parts and body shapes leads into the study of symmetrical and asymmetrical shapes. This study can include both locomotor and nonlocomotor situations and the use of apparatus. (Remember that symmetrical movement can be only forward, backward, up, and down. All movement done to the side requires greater effort on one side and becomes asymmetrical.)

Sample Learning Experiences

1. As you travel across the mat, make the shape of your body change drastically at least two times.

2. Find ways to move on your hands and feet when your body is in very wide shapes, followed by a different shape of your own.

3. While jumping and landing softly off and on apparatus, show very clear twisted shapes in the air.

4. Remembering what symmetrical shapes look like, see how you can travel making only symmetrical shapes.

Discussion. Even young children experience the concept of shape early in school. Therefore, the work in gymnastics can reenforce or elaborate learning initiated elsewhere in the school curriculum. The children enjoy the challenges in this theme and are often most intrigued with controlling their bodies while in the air. Some children are extremely earth bound, however. They find it hard to leave the floor and do not jump high but often think they have. It takes time for these and other children to feel comfortable in flight, especially when flight is coupled with the additional task of changing the shape the body makes while in the air.

ACTIONS OF BODY PARTS. When the relationship of body parts is studied in nonlocomotor movement, balance begins to be a major focus.

As balance is introduced, the study of the actions of body parts is closely aligned with it. Recall that body parts can *support the body, lead the action, apply force,* and *receive force or weight.* In balancing, the children must note especially the relationship of the free body parts to those parts that form the base of support. Work proceeds through experiences that develop the ability to change the relationship of the free body parts while maintaining stability on the same base of support.

After considerable experience in balancing on many different body parts in diverse positions, the children can take the body into off-balance as a profitable challenge. Intentionally moving from balance into off-balance occurs when a body part initiating action leads the center of gravity of the body away from the base of support to a point where balance can no longer be maintained on that base. Being able to voluntarily take the body into off-balance is a specific skill that must be developed to a high degree to gain agility and versatility in gymnastics; however, we do not study off-balance by itself, but in conjunction with balance. Eventually, it is logical to study it with locomotor movement, since off-balance always results, at least momentarily, in some form of locomotion. As the body in off-balance hurries to regain stability, a new base is formed. This transference of weight from one base to another is locomotion. If the full expanse of this theme is developed, the child becomes sensitive to controlling the actions of the body in receiving the weight. Experiences primarily have students going from balance, off-balance, and back to balance to gain a feel for moving body parts into position to receive the weight. Receipt of weight can be coupled successfully with many other content ideas, such as flight, step-like actions, and body shapes.

In most cases, learning to receive force is essential—to protect oneself and others and to increase the incidence of success. Both are essential to safe, controlled, skilled performance. In receiving force generated by the body's weight, as in landing, control of the force focuses on absorbing the force to reduce the shock of landing and to diminish the possibility of bruising the tissues and placing undue stress on the joints of the body. Controlled landings can be distinguished by several of the following characteristics.

1. The body gives in many joints sequentially to increase the time to absorb the force.

2. Effort is made to elongate the body before the moment of contact and to make the body more compact upon landing by sequentially bending in the joints to absorb force over greater distance and a longer time period.

3. The body either rebounds resiliently after landing to reduce the time one stays on the supporting body part or transfers weight quickly to new body surfaces to disseminate the force over greater body surface.

4. The body moves in the direction of the force until the momentum of the force is stopped or the direction of the force is altered.

Sample Learning Experiences

1. Try to arrive on the apparatus on different body parts, and carefully let different body parts receive your weight when you first touch the mat or floor.

2. While you practice different step-like actions, let each new body part slowly take your weight. Make each new base a planned movement by carefully placing the new base on the floor.

3. Balance on your head, shoulders, and upper arms (shoulder stand); while your feet are in the air, see how you can change the relationship of your feet (fast–slow; far–near; in different spaces).

4. Take a balance; make one body part pull (lead) you into off-balance and control this position to take you onto a new base in a different balance.

5. Develop a sequence that shows fast and slow movement into off-balance, followed sometimes by a new balance or longer moments of traveling.

Discussion. When teaching the actions of the body parts, such as receipt of weight in task 1, you may need to help the children recognize which body parts can be used safely for different purposes and which ones should be used only with caution or not at all. For example, knees and elbows can be damaged seriously if children fling themselves onto them. They are boney and have no joint action that lets the body give to absorb the force. However, the freedom of movement and the variety in movement can be expanded through opportunities to try to use and to invent the unusual. Inventiveness should reflect sound use of the mechanical principles discussed in Chapter 4.

Tasks like the third one should never be used in classes with children who cannot assume the shoulder position. The task would have to be more open to accommodate individual differences. For example, you can restate the task by saying, "Take a balance position that allows your feet to be free and up in the air." This would open the task sufficiently for most children. The open task makes it possible for all children to work on the change of relationship of the feet. When all children in a class can assume a specific position (shoulder stand) or perform a specific step-like activity (cartwheel), these can be used as content without necessarily compromising your commitment to the individuality of the child.

SAMPLE UNIT PLAN THEME 4

Themes. Introduction to Relationships of Body Parts—Theme 4 (and selected content from Themes 1 and 3).

Unit Focus. Twisting, curling, and stretching to change relationships of body parts and body shapes while balancing.

Appropriate For. Children who can maintain their balance on a variety of body parts and who can work independently.

Length of Unit. Two 30-minute lessons.

Content

    Body—actions: twisting, curling, stretching; shapes: twisted, round, straight, wide
        weight bearing: balancing

    Space—

    Effort—slow-fast; variation

    Relationships—body parts: near–far, together–apart, above–below, behind–in front of

Student Objectives. The students should be willing to try to

1. Increase their flexibility and develop a variety of balances on different bases of support as they intentionally change speed when arriving into and traveling out of balanced positions and when changing relationships of body parts while balanced.

2. Make a continuous change in the base of support by intentionally going to the extremes in twisting, stretching, and curling in order to place new body parts or surfaces in different places on the floor to form new bases of support.

3. Know that different body shapes can be made in the air, while traveling being supported by body parts, or when balancing by involving the actions of the body (twist, stretch, curl, swing) and by changing the relationship of one body part to others.

4. Accept responsibility for improving the range and variety of their movement by exerting a real effort to do their best work and trying to intentionally place body parts on the floor and avoid aimless flinging and flopping.

Teaching Area. Indoor space large enough to accommodate class size.

Apparatus and/or Equipment. Mats—enough for each child to work continuously, if mats are used. (Continuous work in this unit can be done on floor without mats.) Apparatus of children's own choosing.

Learning Experiences (Tasks)

1.0 Take a balance position that is comfortable but somewhat challenging and, without moving your base of support, begin with at least one free body part (a body part not being used for support) and see how you can take it near to the floor and far away from the floor without losing your balance.

1.1 Same as above, but take free body part as far away in all different places about the body. Think about space in back, in front, to the sides, up, down, and keep your balance.

1.2 Change the base of support and make a balance you can hold still where both feet are free and in the air. Play around with all the relationships you can make with your feet, keeping ankles extended. (Then begin to place feet, knees in different relationships to your base and see how many

A Suggested Progression For Sample Gymnastics Unit/Theme 4

Lesson 1		Lesson 2	
Tasks	Teaching Tips	Tasks	Teaching Tips
1.0	It may be necessary in some classes to designate a position or move right along with the students in a "follow me" approach to get them started. Throughout, urge them to hold each new balance only briefly.	2.0	Same as Lesson 1—work on refinement in contracting muscles so each new position becomes held (fixed) as soon as possible.
1.1	Challenge them to use all the space about them, especially in back of them and well away from them. Encourage, from the onset, muscle tension and upness in all balances. Stop them and have them start from a new base to get more variety.	2.1	Speed can help or hinder when achieving balance. Caution them to think ahead when they produce speed to place a new body part on the floor. Often the momentum stopped by the body part that becomes fixed in supporting body can be dissipated in the free body parts by twisting around the base, it may produce moments of spinning, which children enjoy.
1.2	Stress: apart, behind, in front, and different kinds of shapes—round body; tuck to make body parts close to each other.	2.2	Keep their series of changes in relationship of body parts to create new bases short so the changes can be remembered, repeated, and refined. (A sharing time here can help to pace lesson—ask performers to do series twice, observers watch to see whether it is repeated identically.)
2.0	Throughout this and all units, stress muscle tension, getting children to sense tightness of muscles and extensions. Encourage twisting, curling, stretching, and PLACING a surface or body part on floor or mat.	4.0	The use of apparatus—make it your choice or the children's—depending on class needs and amount of time left in lesson.
3.0	Key here is to get the level to change rather frequently, making the change continuous.	4.0	Again, keep series short. Urge copier to note speed and how the body twists, curls, and stretches to get each new body part (surface) down to become base.
3.1	Balances should occur on/off apparatus as well as part of base on mat or floor and part of base on apparatus.		

different ways you can come out of your balance onto your feet or knees.)

2.0 Start with a balance on one hand and one knee and its lower leg. Carefully twist and curl and see if you can get shoulders or back to become the base. Keep twisting, stretching, and curling to constantly change the body parts serving as the base.

2.1 Sometimes, as you change relationships of free body parts, really speeding up the movement helps to put you into a new position, freeing a new body surface for your base. Intentionally think about producing speed but take care—no flopping.

2.2 Once you develop a series of changes in relationships of body parts and bases of support, practice repeating these and make the changes smooth—no stops.

3.0 As you change your base, try to show a change in the level of your body. Frequently select and extend specific body parts to get them as high and as far away from the base as possible.

3.1 You can add a piece of apparatus and see how you can thoughtfully and carefully

travel from the floor onto the apparatus just by freeing different body parts to become new bases of support. Decide whether you are going to start on the apparatus or off and try to travel back and forth from the floor to the apparatus several times. Take care to show tight, clear body lines all of the time—no sagging.

4.0 Start with a balance of your own and see how you can twist, curl, stretch to place different body surfaces and body parts as the base, trying to eventually arrive back onto the original base in exactly the same shape. (You may choose to use apparatus or not.)

4.1 Share your series of changes with the person next to you. One of you be an observing person and watch closely. Then the other person shows. Select one series and see whether the two of you can be look-alike twins and do the changes exactly together. (Then try to duplicate work of the other person.)

Evaluation. Refer to Chapter 10 and either select or adapt one of the evaluative tools or develop a tool that can be used to help assess a specific aspect of the unit that is important to the needs of the children.

GYMNASTICS THEME 5—INTRODUCTION TO WEIGHT

The fifth gymnastics theme shifts the content back to "how the body performs the movement." In the third theme, the effort factor of time or speed was the focal point. Here, the weight factor of effort is studied. This factor seems to present great difficulty to interpreters of Laban's system for analyzing movement until they perceive it as strength, energy, or specifically here in gymnastics as muscle tension. The control of this aspect of effort is closely aligned with achieving finesse, agility, and versatility in gymnastics. Both the efficiency and effectiveness of the movement depend on the ability to produce, select, and regulate strength and energy resulting from varying the amount of muscle tension.

Learners in physical education begin to cope with this factor, perhaps unwittingly, in the first lesson at the earliest age, when the teacher asks them to travel and stop. In order to travel, they have to produce muscle tension. Then they develop an awareness for muscle tension used to maintain a firm, clear position when stopped. The "alert stillness" required engages the muscles in a controlled state of tension, and a feeling for the kinesthetic sense of effort in muscle tension begins if you turn the child's attention to this feeling. From the beginning, muscle tension, strength, and energy should be an ever-present and compelling emphasis as you teach because *no one, no thing* can produce this tension for the learner (except chemicals, electricity, or blows that induce muscle reflexes). The child alone must learn to produce, select, and regulate muscle tension, strength, and energy. What compounds this problem is that different muscles are responsible for moving different body parts in different directions to do different things and at different times. These muscles have to be engaged in sequence with appropriate amounts of tension in order for the movement to be efficient and effective.

This brief exposé on the weight factor should show the importance of Theme 5 to the study of gymnastics. While teaching from this theme, and whenever the occasion presents itself, you should make every effort to develop within the child both an awareness for the feeling of tension and his responsibility for producing and controlling it.

Development of Theme 5

> **Basic Content**
> Weight: firm, strong, tension
> soft, slight, relaxed
> (Revisitation of activities and actions of the body)
> (In conjunction with Theme 1 and other themes.)

WEIGHT (FORCE). Weight, as a factor of movement, includes *firm, strong, tension* at one end of the spectrum and at the other end, *soft, light, and relaxed.* It should not be confused with the usual interpretation of weight as a measurement for the bulk of the body. Neither should it be confused with "weight transference" or "weight bearing." *Weight, the factor of movement, as content in a lesson, focuses on the intensity of muscle tension and the ability to control it.* As in dealing with time and other concepts, the teacher should show the contrast that exists within the weight spectrum. The essence of the challenge is to extend the outer reaches of this spectrum to the full capacity of the individual, so he has a wider range of choice when the concept presents itself in movement. For example, the greater the degree of difference between a child's strongest movement and his very lightest, the greater the choice the child has in being able to vary his movement.

In this theme, the thoughts, actions, and feelings of the individual center on producing, selecting, and regulating muscle tension. In order to be successful in producing and regulating muscle tension, it helps to experience the inner feelings or the kinesthetic sense of muscle tension. Like all themes, it is possible to launch the study of the content in several different ways and at different times in the program. Weight can be studied as the predominating theme or as a supplementary one along with such aspects of the movement content as balance, body shapes, locomotion, locomotion and stillness, actions of the body, and takeoff and landings. Both dance and games teaching have weight as a continuing, visible content focus also. How and where you start with it as a theme in gymnastics perhaps is dependent somewhat on the program area (dance, games, or gymnastics) in which the concept is introduced and whether the responsibility in your gymnastics unit is to introduce the weight factor, to elaborate upon it, or both.

If we are introducing the concept first as content in gymnastics, we can take a brief moment for the children to tense and relax muscles to review the feeling for muscle tension. (This feeling has been introduced much earlier, in conjunction with starting, stopping, and holding the body in a clear position of alert stillness.) One way to proceed is by having the children work on traveling with self-regulated momentary pauses, focusing on the control of tension during the pause. This same kind of experience could be transferred to apparatus where the pause becomes almost an instant of perching on a bench before leaving it. Closely associated with these types of experiences are those that have the mover regulate the intensity of the muscle tension to produce extensive amounts of energy or very little. The study in contrasting muscle tension can be done in a variety of gymnastic settings, on the floor, with apparatus, while working alone or with others.

The work on contrasting and regulating tension is perhaps easiest to feel and appreciate by starting with a single, simple activity (running or jumping for examples), fixing the experience on developing the spectrum of strong and light. Do not misconstrue strong as always associated with loud and fast, with the opposite always characteristic of light. To avoid this misconception, provide experiences that combine strong effort with both ends of the time spectrum (fast-slow) and provide opportunities for moving firmly and quietly.

Essential to developing the capacity for regulating muscle tension is the ability to change the degree of tension within a movement. Changes in tension can be studied in both locomotor and nonlocomotor movement. While teaching muscle tension in balancing (nonlocomotor), you should stress producing muscle tension in an upward direction. The inexperienced tend to demonstrate either insufficient tension or tension in a downward direction, which results in a sagging, heavy appearance rather than a light, buoyant, lifted, upright position. In ad-

dition, emphasize controlling the body as it moves to the next base of support. This feat takes willful control of tension.

Stress should also be placed on the role of the feet, arms, and legs in producing power (momentum) as well as in controlling power. Much attention should also be given to developing a driving, accelerated run and firm takeoffs. Likewise, there must be continued attention to the tension that is essential for controlling the weight upon landing. The children's natural joy and capacity for flinging themselves wildly on the mat or floor must be curtailed and focused toward finding equal satisfaction in the desire and ability to control the landing so movement can continue purposefully and skillfully or a clear position can be maintained.

The ability to vary the actions of the body and activities can be elaborated when the actions and activities are revisited, this time with the purpose of examining energy and strength. The lesson to be learned is similar to those presented earlier. A movement done with differing intensity of muscle tension takes on different characteristics, serves different purposes, and adds to finer selectivity and greater versatility in gymnastics. This axiom related to selectivity and versatility was stressed earlier in relation to time, body actions, relationships, and each of the other aspects of the movement content.

Sample Learning Experiences

1. Right where you are, tighten your muscles and relax; try to feel the differing amount of tension or tightness in your muscles.

2. Travel in any way you like, frequently come to a momentary but complete stop, showing an alert stillness with muscles tight and ready to move again.

3. Select a way of traveling (teacher or student can do selecting); in your own space, make this movement as strong as you can, then make it as fine and gentle as you can.

4. Take a balance you can hold and make your free body parts twist in different directions. Develop a feeling for firmness, then lightness, in your twisting. Feel the body part become very tense and then feel the tension leaving the body part.

5. Approach and mount the bench, touching it lightly with hands or feet. As you go over it, make a clear, strong shape in the air, controlling your landing in either a resilient, springy landing or a still position on your feet.

6. Develop a fast, strong run, mount the box, hold a momentary balance, and then push off

high into the air (controlled landings still emphasized).

7. Travel in and out of balance showing clear moments of firm, upright tension and other moments of released tension.

Discussion. Since the responsibility for producing tension is personal, children may benefit by expressing their feelings of muscle tension verbally. They also need to tell what they do or think about to produce tension. Use their words and phrases in teaching. For example, children have replied with words such as strong, tight, hard, and solid to the query about their feeling of muscle tension. Concerning what they do to produce tension, they have been heard to say, "I tighten my muscles"; "I squeeze"; "I make them hard." Sometimes a difficult concept is easier to communicate when expressed in terms that have a personal meaning and in terms that the children themselves have used.

All of the discussions following each theme should be reconsidered. Ideas related to pacing the lesson, sharing the discussions with the learner, teaching both concepts (firm–fine) in the same lesson for contrast, using apparatus, varying experiences, all apply equally to the teaching of weight. The challenge in teaching is the same; the content is different. The content is used to get children committed to the belief that they are responsible for their movement and can produce, improve, vary, and control it. In Theme 5, this commitment is directed toward the weight factor or intensity of muscle effort. We must revisit this theme again and again as the body grows and develops and as the child matures as a learner. The capacity for controlling muscle tension should develop proportionately with the increasing body mass if the child is to continue to find satisfaction in gymnastic movement.

APPARATUS. Apparatus of all kinds can be used in conjuction with this theme, especially for establishing situations that involve control of tension while in flight. Because this theme is one of the later themes, and the children will be somewhat older and hopefully more skilled in gymnastics, they should be challenged by more diverse use of apparatus as well as by the complexity of the arrangement. Higher apparatus, if available, can be a stimulus for developing greater intensity in movement, which is central to the purpose of this theme. Even if taller apparatus is available, exciting work can be done on the floor and on the lower benches, boxes, and beams as well.

SAMPLE UNIT PLAN THEME 5

Themes. Introduction to Weight—Theme 5 (and selected content from Themes 1, 2, and 4).

Unit Focus. Body shapes in flight, vaulting, or dismounting, with emphasis on strong, firm takeoffs and selecting appropriate muscle tension.

Appropriate For. Children who have regard for safety of self and others and who have managed fixed and resilient landings in gymnastics.

Length of Unit. Six 30-minute lessons.

Content

    Body—flight, vaulting, body shapes in the air; (landings)

    Space—(directions)

    Effort—time: accelerating

    Weight—muscle tension in air to create shapes

    Relationship—legs to hands, legs to each other, to the box; near, far

Student Objectives. The students should be willing to try to

1. Know that selecting and producing different amounts of muscle tension in flight helps

to achieve control of the body and its parts essential to creating different shapes in the air and to changing the relationships of feet to the hands and to the apparatus to create different vaults.

2. Produce acceleration in their approaches to apparatus by lengthening the size of their stride and increasing their speed to develop the momentum essential to creating various body relationships in vaulting (weight transference over apparatus from feet to hands to feet).

3. Vary the direction and kind of landing (fixed or resilient) to achieve greater versatility in managing their bodies in and after flight.

4. Sustain a working atmosphere in class by individually taking a moment to quietly observe work of others, if work becomes exhausting, and spacing themselves away from performers to allow room for others to accelerate.

Teaching Area. Indoor space with apparatus thoughtfully placed to allow groups of children accelerating space free of other groups.

Apparatus and/or Equipment. Selection of vaulting boxes, stools, benches, bars, planks, sufficient mats to allow each four to six children to have several pieces plus mats to protect landing surfaces.

Learning Experiences (Tasks)

1.0 Take care to first *WALK* out a working pathway for you to be sure your path does not cross the path of others. On your pathway, start with a nicely lifted upper body, take light, running steps and finish with a jump, landing on two feet at the end.

1.1 (Use only if [when] students have demonstrated self-discipline and control of directions and speed.) See whether you can find and accelerate into a new pathway and end these short runs with a jump and a vertical, springy landing with a pop-up. Make the landing after the pop-up come right back down in the same spot as your landing from the jump.

2.0 Look about room (there could be a stage, vaulting boxes, stools), find some surface that is stable and is about thigh high or slightly higher. Think; get your lifted start-ing posture, and make short, light, accelerated run toward your table surface. As you approach the surface, take a two-foot takeoff and place your hands on top of the surface, bending at the hips (pike position). See how high you can take your hips in the air over your hands and then bring your feet down softly on your takeoff spot.

2.1 Without the run, place and keep your hands flat on the surface thigh high or higher with feet close to the front of the box, stool, or stage; see how you can do repeated springs into the air, taking hips higher over hands each time.

2.2 Begin with repeated springy jumps, getting hips high over hands, and then make one of these springs take you up, on, or over the vaulting surface. Try to make each landing *light* and *brief*, keeping your hands on the vaulting surface.

3.0 Begin to make your takeoff spring you up onto the vaulting surface, hold a balance, and exaggerating stretching, twisting, and/or curling, make clear body shapes in the air and try to land in a fixed (glued) landing with your back straight with the wall and shoulders over your feet. (Groups of four to six; teacher needs to be sure that safe running room is available for each group.)

3.1 Begin to make your takeoff spring you up onto the vaulting surface, hold a balance, and exaggerating stretching, twisting, and/or curling, make clear body shapes in the air and try to land in a fixed (glued) landing with your back straight with the wall and shoulders over your feet. (Groups of four to six; teacher needs to be sure that safe running room is available for each group.) (Here, teacher can begin to designate shapes to be made in the air, such as wide, twisted, round.)

3.2 After you make the shape in the air and land, sometimes add a roll or sometimes step-like actions and really show distinctly new body shapes while in the air. Do not let yourself make the same shape again and again.

4.0 Combining your best upright starting posture, quick accelerated run, and placement of hands on your apparatus, see how you can take your legs and body over the apparatus, being thoughtful about muscle

Task	Lesson 1 — Teaching Tips	Task	Lesson 2 — Teaching Tips	Task	Lesson 3 — Teaching Tips
1.0	Encourage them to get a strong upward thrust from the thigh of the leg that leaves ground first in jump. Work for *high* jumps *NOT* LONG with landing coming very near takeoff spot.	1.0	Same as Lesson 1, but accent acceleration and building size of steps from small to large.	1.1	Emphasize acceleration—short runs—see 1.0, Lesson 1.
2.0	Demonstration helpful. Stress keeping arms straight, push arms straight—LIFT *HIPS* UP.	2.0	Refine and try to get hips so high, a slight moment of balance occurs when hips are high over hands.	2.1	Landing should be close to box, stool, etc., and springy.
3.0	Urge two-foot takeoffs for those who can stress glued landings—back vertical, trunk not leaning forward.	3.1	During practice, designate fixed and held landings. Watch feet—if too far apart, strain put on knees in landing; stress feeling the contrast between the two.	4.0	Stress tension in landing so the bend in the knees is halted and child does not collapse.
3.1	Keep them working on one shape long enough to explore several ways of making it. Exaggerate shape: make it bigger than life. After a while, have them show resilient landings—popping straight up after dismount.	3.2	Urge maintaining lifted performance posture throughout. Do not let them minimize roll or step-like actions. Comment on shapes in rolls/step-like actions.	4.0	Repeat doing resilient landings.
				4.1	Watch placement of hands—fingers point in direction of vault—forward, sideward.

tension in arms and in the entire legs, straight to the toes. Land on your feet on the mat in a fixed (glued) landing, making an effort to keep trunk vertical so hands do not touch the mat in landing but can be carried out to each side to help in achieving balance on the feet. (Groups of four to six; teacher needs to be sure that safe running room is available for each group.)

4.1 Clearly show the willful control of the relationship of your feet and legs to each other. Sometimes try to vault with legs together, sometimes apart.

4.2 Each person in your group try to make your vault different from all others.

4.3 Each of you try to perform some of the vaults you have seen others do.

4.4 Select a couple of vaults with different leg relationships and refine the muscle tension in the legs/feet as well as the glued landing or a landing followed by a roll or step-like action.

5.0 (For this, task apparatus must be arranged to encourage continuous mounting and dismounting. Place several pieces of apparatus for each group of four to six children in places to elicit changes in pathways.) Take care to do this safely, see how you can mount or vault different pieces in your group working-space intentionally to vault back onto the apparatus so you make a couple of different shapes on each piece.

5.1 As you vault on and off various pieces of apparatus and travel to new pieces—clean up your traveling—look like a GYMNASTIC PERFORMER all of the time and hold an upright position at the end to show your performance is finished.

5.2 Two or more people may be able to work simultaneously, depending on skill of students and amount of apparatus and working space.

5.3 Remembering your entire sequence, really work on maintaining the performance posture and attitude throughout. Take every effort to make those body lines clear in your shapes and your movement springy, light, and lifted throughout.

Evaluation. Refer to Chapter 10 and either select or adapt one of the evaluative tools or develop a tool that can be used to help assess a specific aspect of the unit that is important to the needs of your students.

GYMNASTICS THEME 6—FLOW AND CONTINUITY IN MOVEMENT

The sixth theme, on *flow and continuity*, emphasizing *selection and refinement of gymnastic sequences*, focuses on improving the totality of the movement response—the movements themselves and the way they are linked. The intent of this theme is threefold:

1. To enhance the ability to control the flow of movement.

2. To achieve greater continuity in movement.

Sample Gymnastics Unit/Theme 5

	Lesson 4		Lesson 5		Lesson 6
Task	**Teaching Tips**	**Task**	**Teaching Tips**	**Task**	**Teaching Tips**
2.1	Get as many children doing this at once as space/apparatus permits.	2.2	Try to achieve two-foot landings on vaulting surface, then different body parts, i.e., shins, seats, etc.	2.2	Make takeoffs stronger. Emphasize forceful hurdle.
4.0	Same as Lesson 3—stress tension in legs/ankles/feet to show clarity of body shape.	4.3	Same as Lesson 4, but observe ways to refine.	5.1	Have them select a sequence and work on it.
4.0	Resilient landings, stressing same as 4.0 above.	4.4	Same as Lesson 4. Get them to roll in the direction of their landing.	5.3	Refine sequence.
4.3	Encourage variety. Children tend to pick a favorite.	5.0	Reduce running space between pieces of apparatus. Look carefully to see needed organizational changes for Lesson 6.	5.2	Give *IF* children are ready. (May suggest this only to two to three children.)
4.4	Can also do this with resilient landings.		Urge them to mount/dismount from one piece in a variety of directions and places on apparatus.	5.3	Show sequence.
		5.1	Really stress upness, lightness, and tension in body parts. Avoid moments of sagging.		

3. To highlight the importance of selection and refinement as key ingredients of skill development, learning, and versatility in gymnastic movement.

All three of these purposes are so important they should be stressed often throughout the entire study of educational gymnastics. From the first lesson, the teacher and children working together will focus again and again on flow, selection, refinement, and continuity. In units on content from earlier themes, flow was subordinate to or concealed by a more predominant focus on other movement content. Here, flow, selection, refinement, and continuity play the primary content roles. The addition of any other content to lessons built on Theme 6 is of secondary importance, but is essential content since the students must be doing some form of movement to be able to study flow.

When children begin work on a movement idea, often they are encouraged to find many ways to work with the idea. This kind of work develops self-confidence, builds variety, and increases range of movement. Continuously seeking different ways, however, is not an end in itself in the study of movement or in the study of gymnastics, nor is this process alone likely to result in highly skillful or versatile movement. At some point, the focus must shift, even when the content is from Theme 1, from variety alone to selection and refinement of movement. The movement selected is practiced again and again to improve its execution. Movements should be examined and selected on the basis of the need or effect wanted in gymnastics. Also in relation to selection, when one movement is linked with another, the way they blend—the continuity—has to be studied so the flow in the series of movements can be controlled in a precise way to produce the desired effect. The work introduced more incidentally on flow and continuity now becomes the core of the content, with selection and refinement of movement in sequences the secondary focus.

Development of Theme 6

> **Basic Content**
> Flow: bound, stoppable
> free, ongoing
> (In conjunction with content from Theme 1 and other themes.)

FLOW. The teacher can initiate the use of *flow* in the study of movement by first combining movements with momentary pauses in which the body remains alert and movement resumes shortly. The more simple the movement ideas, the more elementary the experience. For example, beginners can control flow by traveling on different body parts, whereas the more advanced students can examine flow by combining rolling with headstands or more difficult and creative movements of their choice. In any case, one key idea is linking alert pauses with movement. The more deliberately the pauses are planned and controlled and the more selected

and refined are the ways and means of moving, the greater the facility for creating and maintaining continuity in movement.

Further work in flow goes toward a feeling for ongoing movement to add to the more bound movement initiated in the first experiences. Too frequently, work in gymnastics or stunts and tumbling is concentrated heavily on learning, practicing, and refining single stunts or gymnastic skills in isolation. FROM THE VERY OUTSET IN EDUCATIONAL GYMNASTICS, THE EMPHASIS IS ON LINKING ONE ACTION OR MOVEMENT TO ANOTHER. This ability to work and take one movement into the next is just as important as combining movement with alert pauses. Both are essential in the refinement of isolated skills as well as in developing skillful sequences in movement. The facility for controlling flow by making it appear to be ongoing or punctuated with brief pauses creates the picture of the mastery of movement we enjoy seeing in gymnastics and provides the thrill of being able to achieve this flow.

Experiences that demand thought and practice to find different ways of linking two or more movements increase the capacity to create and maintain constant or ongoing movement. Additional work that focuses attention on moving into certain positions in a variety of ways or from a variety of bases of support leads to greater suppleness and agility as well as greater variety in the movement itself. Any of the content introduced earlier could be used in conjunction with flow. The time, space, and weight factors of how the body moves, all the different activities, actions and parts of body, the space dimensions as well as relationships can be revisited singularly or in combination when studying flow.

The more nearly the management of flow is mastered, the more a series of movements becomes a continuous, connected whole. The greater the awareness for the actions and body parts that take one into and out of different phases of the gymnastic sequence, the greater the capacity for controlling continuity. This linking or transitional movement also is an essential part of the study of flow. Sample experiences have been designed for the study of the three aspects of flow: combining movements with no pauses (ongoing), linking movements together, and traveling with alert pauses (bound).

Sample Learning Experiences

1. Travel on your hands and feet, trying to keep your speed the same at all times.
2. See how you can roll and go immediately into transferring weight onto hands, then feet.
3. Develop a movement sequence of step-like actions and flight in which you show brief, planned pauses in your work. Try to include these pauses on the floor and on apparatus.

Discussion. Much of the movement of young children is performed without thinking. They have a knack for flinging themselves into activity without taking a mental inventory. The first responsibility associated with the sixth theme is getting children to willfully preestablish a plan to their movement. The work starts simply by helping them to focus on keeping their movement going. As they show ability in this area, the complexity of the task is extended by asking them to do increasingly more difficult single forms of movement and also more complicated combinations of movements. This skill of planning ahead in movement is then augmented by altering flow through momentary pauses.

Skillfully connecting one movement to another becomes the next focus. Concentration centers on linking one movement to another, with the transitions attempted and altered in a variety of ways. Throughout the study of gymnastics, the teacher and the child can be involved in selecting the content used in the experiences. Both the teacher and the child should play a role in selecting how the linkage of the movements is to take place. The teacher selects the ways to alter the linkage to ensure practice and experiences in specific variations on a theme, whereas the child selects the variation on a theme to gratify his preference and allow his abilities to emerge and flourish.

As the ability to link movement develops, the focus shifts from linking one or two movements to linking several movements to form gymnastic sequences. Early in my introduction to educational gymnastics, someone from England deepened my appreciation for movement sequences by comparing them with sentences and words. The following idea may help you and your students. A series of words goes together to make a sentence as sequences are made up of a series of movements. A sentence has a definite beginning (a capital) and ends with a punctuation mark. *A series of movements becomes a sequence, as discussed in this book in relation to gymnastics, when a clear position designates the beginning, a position is held to punctuate the end of the sequence, and the movements in between can be remembered and repeated in order.* It has been my experience that children have more difficulty with the "capitals" and "punctuation marks" than with the movements in between. They seem to just start without planning what their body looks like, and rather than stopping and maintaining a clear position at the end, they just quit their planned movement and amble back to start again. Also, there has been some tendency to repeat inane, weak, undemanding endings.

In focusing on sequence development, the teacher's and the students' efforts should be directed toward:

—improving the selection and execution of the movement.

—duplicating precisely the series of planned movements.

—developing continuity within the sequence.

—selecting more demanding movements to link together in a series.

Most work done with sequences develops motor memory by helping children prepare and repeat totally planned series of movements. As the work progresses and children get the feel for linking movements together skillfully, they can excel at creating sequences extemporaneously. Attention given to selecting and refining responses is important to either the preplanned sequences or the ones created as the child moves. Children need to be encouraged to

1. practice movement sequences that are difficult for them.

2. practice the transitional movement that links parts of the sequences together.

3. eliminate extraneous movements—those that are not planned or that distract from the sequence.

4. continuously seek ways to vary their efforts.

5. increase the challenge by striving for greater quality, variety, and difficulty in tasks for their sequence.

From the beginning, children should be encouraged not to wait in line for a "turn to learn" but to use every possible moment for movement. The odd moments spent by some children waiting to get on a piece of apparatus, for instance, can be used to refine a movement that is used in their sequences or one they wish to include but have not because they lack skill or confidence in performing it or linking it with other movements. A class or an individual who is personally committed to refinement is more likely to achieve full potential. Working in an environment where refinement is an ongoing challenge can be a thrill for both the children and the teacher.

APPARATUS. Apparatus can be used throughout this theme, but work on the floor should not be neglected. Also, efforts in refining movement are usually investigated, where possible, on the floor and then transferred to apparatus, due

largely to the safety factor. Moreover, the logistics involved in sharing large pieces of apparatus with other members of a class makes practicing on the floor often more practical.

SAMPLE UNIT PLAN THEME 6

Themes. Introduction to Flow and Continuity—Theme 6 (and selected content from Themes 1 and 3).

Unit Focus. Developing gymnastic sequences, intentionally showing a combination of stopped and ongoing movement.

Appropriate For. Children who have developed confidence and skill in balancing and who demonstrate versatility in locomotion in a gymnastic setting.

Length of Unit. Five 30-minute lessons.

Content

    Body—(selected locomotor forms)

    Space—

    Effort—flow: ongoing; stopped; time: (variation in speed)

    Relationships—

Student Objectives. The students should be willing to try to

1. Combine selected forms of rocking, rolling, spinning, hanging, swinging, and/or step-like actions in a variety of speeds to create gymnastic sequences showing planned, ongoing moments combined with balancing and moments of stopped or stoppable flow.

2. Know that momentum in ongoing movement gives the appearance of being continuous with no feeling of hesitating or stopping.

3. Wait to take their turn until the person ahead of them will not cause them to alter their flow of movement and to keep from interfering with other persons working in their group.

4. Begin to combine specialized gymnastic forms of locomotion, nonlocomotion, and/or flight (i.e., round-off, cartwheel, dive-rolls) along with skillful, unnamed, inventive forms of rolling and step-like actions.

Teaching Area. Indoor space large enough to accommodate size of class working in small groups on a variety of prearranged apparatus.

Apparatus and/or Equipment. Wide assortment of benches, beams, boxes, stools, apparatus for hanging/swinging, bars, and sufficient mats to protect landing surfaces where necessary.

Learning Experiences (Tasks)

1.0 Without traveling from your own working space, trying to show upness in the whole body and muscle tension, try to keep your body in constant motion by making gymnastic-like stepping actions from one body part to another.

1.1 Strive for more variety by willfully changing levels, but keep the stepping motion continuous.

1.2 Select a low position, then go to a high position and finish at a medium level, making all the moves that take you from each of the positions step-like and continuous—no stops. Take your time, do not be in a

A Suggested Progression for Sample Gymnastics Unit/Theme 6

	Lesson 1		Lesson 2		Lesson 3		Lesson 4		Lesson 5
Tasks	**Teaching Tips**	**Tasks**	**Teaching Tips**	**Tasks**	**Teaching Tips**	**Tasks**	**Teaching Tips**	**Tasks**	**Teaching Tips**
1.0	Urge the children to show best gymnastic skills. Urge variety by not only mentioning kinds of movement (cartwheels, etc.) but suggest body parts to step on (shins, lower arm, etc.), and encourage original actions.	1.2	If class (or a single child) has difficulty, designate the base for the low starting position.	2.3	Get them to repeat and refine every phase.	4.0	(See 2.0, 3.0) Give them time to try ideas—urge different children to start from different places and to approach apparatus in different directions.	4.2	Refine and share, working for a completed sequence with a continuous, alert gymnastic posture that clearly shows ongoing as well as stoppable flow.
		1.3	Give this to groups or individuals when they are ready—build speed carefully.	3.0	Same as Lesson 1				
1.1	*IF* children are naturally *showing* levels, rather than suggesting they include them, comment on how well they are showing variety by changing levels, and go to 1.2.	2.1	Same as Lesson 1. Work for greater fluidity from one phase of the sequence to the next.	3.1	The pauses can be a definite balance or a "perch or a catch"—a slight pause.	4.0	Children could write their sequences—chart them out—between turns of doing them. Then ask them to check whether they see the same movement repeated too often and suggest they put different actions in for variety.		
		2.2	Make sure movement they add represents their best gymnastic work and continue to stress fluidity.	3.2	Begin to urge change in direction—pathway.				
2.0	(*IF* no hanging apparatus is available, you can substitute a vault/body shape in air for swing.) Stress muscle tension-extension or tightness throughout and teach to get them to feel their movement wanting to go on—to continue. If they land backwards, ongoing movement will likely continue backwards.	3.0	(If no hanging apparatus is available, substitute mounting apparatus and going into a balance instead of a hang.) Stress feeling the difference between this sequence and one completed in 2.2. (This one is stoppable almost at any time; the one in 2.2 was ongoing and fluid.)	3.3	You may need to have some children shorten sequence. Continue with ideas started in 3.2.	4.2	Exaggeration of ongoing moments the key. Urge them to watch each other to see these moments in work of others.		
2.1	Urge them to prepare hands to receive weight for step-like actions after roll—going immediately onto their hands as soon as they arrive on their feet after the roll.								

rush to show all three levels. Try again, but reorder the occurence of the levels.

1.3 Repeat 1.2, have students work on increasing speed, but make the sequence go through each of the levels.

2.0 Arrive onto the apparatus, swing, drop, and roll, making your movement continuous. (Teacher will probably need to select and arrange apparatus carefully to get a piece of swinging apparatus for each grouping of four to six students. A mat placed where the children execute the drop will be needed if apparatus takes the students far off floor.)

2.1 Add step-like actions (may be combined with flight) after roll and then finish with an upright, lifted, standing position. (Can change the ending position to be: one knee, a knee and a stretched leg, a hand and a foot, or a student-selected position.)

2.2 Add any movement you want to your run to *begin* your approach to the apparatus, but select something that will help you develop momentum—it cannot be just a run; arrive, swing, drop, roll, step-like action—hold—all one continuous movement.

2.3 Take out any extraneous movement and speed up your sequence. Make it look as though no one could stop you, but do it safely.

3.0 Arrive on apparatus, hang and/or balance, then drop into a fixed landing on your feet; go into a slow cartwheel and hold.

3.1 Intentionally plan and make two pauses before arriving on apparatus: hang/balance, drop into a fixed landing, into a slow step-like action—hold.

3.2 Add anything at the beginning in your approach but make the entire sequence look like you could stop still or change direction at any time.

3.3 Clean up body lines—make each movement planned and precise. If you are doing some movements that do not challenge you, take them out and put in some of your better work.

4.0 (Teacher needs to plan the arrangement of two to three or more pieces of apparatus for each four to six children. Draw a precise diagram showing the placement of the apparatus on a card for each group. Have each group arrange its gymnastic setting

as diagrammed.) After you have your apparatus arranged, begin to work on a gymnastic sequence that clearly shows real moments of ongoing, unstoppable movement, punctuated with sudden stops or slow movements that could be stopped at any time.

4.1 Take time to think about the kinds of gymnastic skills you are combining and your speed, levels, directions, pathways. Strive for variety in all of these to make your sequence exciting.

4.2 Stop adding new ideas to your sequence; practice and perfect what you are doing, trying to be a light gymnast throughout your sequence—and exaggerate the ongoing moments to make them stand out from the stoppable ones.

Evaluation. Refer to Chapter 10 and either select or adapt one of the evaluative tools or develop a tool that can be used to help assess a specific aspect of the unit that is important to the needs of your students.

GYMNASTICS THEME 7—RELATIONSHIPS TO OTHERS

In the seventh theme, gymnastics leaves the realm of individual activity intentionally to give students the opportunity to combine their work with the work of others. Children learn that the gymnastic ability that they have acquired individually can be even more satisfying and exciting when done in relation to someone else. This work with another person often challenges efforts not used fully when working alone. Also, having someone else to assist with movement allows new movement content to be added. As a result, those movement experiences, which cannot be accomplished individually, enhance and expand the program of gymnastics. Learning to select, adjust, and synchronize movement to correspond with the work of others forms the basis for the additional challenges posed in this theme. In conjunction with these additional movement challenges, reaching mutual decisions, considering the skill of others, and cooperating are important affective or social objectives that often emerge as personal traits for development when the focus is on relationships with other people. Every aspect of movement done in association with another person has to be given consideration in light of the ability of that other person. In other words, the ability of one person may dictate to another what is to be done, the speed and tensions to be used, location of the movement to be performed, as well as the relationships involved. Heretofore, all of these decisions have been based largely on individual desires and capacities. When these decisions are group-oriented rather than personal, one of four things can happen—and all four provide important experiences.

1. Each person may have to subordinate personal ability and not use certain skills or perform or link them in his or her usual way because another person may not be of equal ability or readiness.

2. Each person may have to show greater diligence to achieve some movement heretofore not accomplished if the partner wants to include it in their mutual work.

3. Each person can develop interdependence, confidence, and respect for others.

4. Each person can achieve different gymnastic movements that are impossible to execute alone.

What happens most frequently is a combination of these four. There is a constant flow of give and take when working effectively with others. Also, the dimension of working with others provides a full measure of pleasure for those who enjoy interacting with people.

Development of Theme 7

Basic Content

Relationship of partners and small groups:

    contrasting
    alternating
    successive
    canon
    mirroring—matching
    following—copying
    above—below
    behind—in front of
    near—far
    over—under—alongside
    supporting—being supported
    lifting—being lifted
    (In conjunction with content from
    Theme 1 and other themes.)

Activities of the body:

    counterbalance
    countertension

RELATIONSHIP OF PARTNERS AND SMALL GROUPS. All of the work involved in this theme can be experienced in relation to a partner or with a group. Since group work requires relating to more people, it is more complex. Therefore, in general, movement ideas generating from the content of Theme 7 would be introduced in partner work before they would be considered appropriate for small groups. However, when there are strong social ties or related reasons, or when there are odd numbers in a class, some of the ideas can be studied immediately by selected students working together in groups of three or four.

Copying. Copying (or following) is one manner of relating to others without being dependent on them to assist in the execution of movement. Each person performs the movement independently of the others. One person goes first, initiating the activities, while the other follows or copies the movement. This kind of relationship was introduced in Theme 2, in one of the sample learning experiences, to get the children to focus on the actions of the body parts and the activities being performed. In this theme, experiences that include copying provide more mature students with the social aspect of movement, expand the challenge, and provide yet another motivation scheme to develop more versatility through a group process for selecting and refining movement.

While teaching copying, focus attention on

1. the leader selecting ways to move that the follower can perform.

2. the leader executing the movements at a speed that allows the follower to see and recall the sequence of the movements.

3. the follower observing the movement carefully and duplicating it precisely with regard to the number of movements, the actions of the body parts, the activities being performed, and the sequence in which they are done, as well as the effort and relationships involved.

Children working with copying as a central idea should be encouraged to keep the sequences brief at first. As the ability to observe and duplicate movement improves, both the speed and length of sequence may increase. Initiating the sequence and copying the sequence are both important, although different. Any lesson involving copying as content should provide all children with the opportunity to extend their abilities in both the role of the leader and that of the follower or the copier.

Matching. Matching is similar to copying as each person is independently responsible for all movement. Like copying, two (or more) people must do the same movement. In copying, however, one person moves as others watch and then duplicate the movement. In matching, both (all) people working together perform identical movements at the same time. Thus, the sequence must be determined and then practiced in order for each of those working together to be able to match all aspects of the movement sequence. Again, cooperation is required, especially in the selection of the movements and in the establishment of a flow pattern that all can perform.

Mirroring. What has been said concerning matching is true of mirroring, except for one aspect. In mirroring movement, rather than having partners or groups do identical movement, the actions of the left side of the body of one person or group are duplicated on the right side by the other partner or group, thus creating a mirror image.

Sample Learning Experiences

1. Number one makes a shape he/she can hold. Number two jumps over number one, lands, travels, then duplicates the shape number one made.

2. Two of you try to time a forward roll combined with a cartwheel and see whether you can have hands and feet touch the floor at the same time in the roll and in the cartwheel.

3. Select movements both of you can do and put them in a sequence. Once you both have learned the sequence, try to see whether each can match the other and do the sequence at the same time.

4. Take the sequence you have just perfected; repeat it several times with your partner or group, showing copying–following, matching, and mirroring. When you have shown all three, everyone hold a still, alert position.

Discussion. When introducing copying, matching, or mirroring, teachers should be prepared to see the skill level of the work diminish at first, because yielding to the skill of another and the additional challenges posed in thinking about duplicating or mirroring movement take their toll. Also, the activities selected by the partners or small groups are not likely to be as difficult as those any one person may be able to perform when working without regard for the ability of others. Teachers also need to be alert to encourage children who are getting the feel for matching, mirroring, or copying, and encourage them to include more and more challenging movements in their sequences.

Consideration should be given to elaborating concepts sufficiently before rushing on to new content. Some teachers are overanxious to introduce new content. This tendency causes them to "cover" material and not teach it so that genuine learning takes place and so that each concept becomes a meaningful part of the movement repertoire of the children. You must be just as careful, however, to keep the work on the same concept progressing so the children do not fall victims of repeating work with the same level of aspiration day after day, unit after unit.

Relationships Requiring Body Contact. Several forms of relationships involve interdependency between members of a group or partners as a major criterion to successful execution. Those relationships requiring interdependency are *counterbalance* and *countertension, lifting* or *being lifted,* and *supporting* or *being supported.* In each of these, the work of one person is specifically dependent on the work of another person. Actual body contact must be made in order for the essential relationship involved to be established. Because of the body contact and the interdependency requirements, experiences of this nature should not begin until considerable personal skill has been developed along with respect for each other's safety. Counterbalance and countertension are usually coupled in the same units of work since they represent opposite ends within a concept continuum. In both counterbalance and countertension, the weight of one person counters the weight of the partner to form a mutually interdependent base of support. When two people are involved in true counterbalance or countertension individually, each is off balance. Without the other, each would fall. The weight of one person stabilizes the position of the other by keeping the weight of the other from moving in the direction the body is leaning.

Alternating, Successive, Canon. The relationships to be studied in *alternating, successive,* and *canon* are similar in that one person (or group) moves at a time. These imply working with a group or in partners, taking turns. As the relationship indicates, *alternating* in gymnastics means first one goes, then the second, until each person working on alternating has gone and then the order is repeated.

Successive relationship is one performing right after the other, not necessarily repeating the movement of the person who went first. A relationship performed in *canon* style is a form of copying usually executed by more than two people who, one at a time, repeat a movement sequence with the precise dynamics initiated by the first person.

Sample Learning Experiences

1. Each time you achieve countertension, both of you find a way to move out of it, traveling away from your partner.

2. After you have made your balance on the box (working in partners), one of you dismount, then add height or distance to the dismount of the other by lifting. If you prefer, you can add the lift after both have dismounted. Person doing the lifting, keep in contact with the person you are lifting until you feel your partner stable and able to manage further movement alone.

3. Really being sensitive to the path of others and timing your rolls to avoid each other, see how the four of you in your group can alternate rolls across the mat, starting from different places on the mat.

4. Independently in succession, travel to the turret (platform) and mount it, staying in a balance until all three of you have made a group balance on the turret. Then successively (one after the other) choose your own dismount and pathway and end in an individual balance away from the turret.

5. Somewhere in your group sequence, show a canon relationship, making sure each of you duplicates the dynamics of the movement exactly, and somewhere show two of you being supported.

Discussion. This work on relationships requiring body contact, particularly on counterbalance and countertension, is likely to present new kinds of movement experiences for almost all children in a class. It requires considerable exploration and experimentation to develop any feeling for freedom, variety, or skill in execution. As the uninitiated start to explore countertension, they usually begin by clasping each other's hands. After they get the feel of the proportionate counterpull that both must exert to maintain their mutually formed base, they can find great satisfaction in hooking other body parts and using a variety of bases and positions in demonstrating countertension. In teaching countertension, caution children not to let go of the partner's grasp without the partner being prepared for the release. Also, children need considerable practice and effort in managing their bodies independently immediately following the moment of countertension when a separate base of support is established independently by each person.

In counterbalance, rather than hooking body parts with a partner or partners and pulling away from this point of contact, the direction of the force is applied toward the body parts making contact. In counterbalance, the same mutual interdependency exists as was present in countertension. Children working on counterbalance find great satisfaction early and begin to try more and more daring bases. Soon they discover that the body parts each uses in forming the base can be different. In progressing in the work on counterbalance, children should be encouraged to practice arriving into counterbalance as well as moving away to work independently again. Once either the concept of counterbalance or countertension is learned, it can be used in partner or group work in sequence development. Also, when sufficient skill, respect, and trust have been developed, children can take the work begun on the floor to apparatus.

A feeling for counterbalance and/or countertension can be simulated individually if the performer relies on apparatus to help establish balance. This obviously is done by leaning slightly off balance and placing a part of the body on the apparatus to maintain balance or by securing a body part to a piece of apparatus and pulling away from the apparatus.

APPARATUS. Apparatus can be used in conjunction with this theme; however, extensive work can be done without it since one of the purposes is to have the students use each other's bodies in much the same way as they formerly have used apparatus.

Lifting, being lifted, supporting, and being supported require the children to be fully responsible for the safety of others. Tasks involving these relationships should be reserved for classes or groups of children who have had extensive partner and group work, who have demonstrated unusual gymnastic skill in working independently, and who have matured to the point where they can accept responsibility for managing other people's bodies safely in movement.

When children achieve the level of skill development that warrants concentration on group and partner relationships, they should be capable of exercising considerable freedom in selecting and arranging equipment. Sometimes, you may find it advisable to limit the number of pieces to be used and the amount of time that can be spent in preparing the arrangement to keep the children from spending too much time "moving furniture."

If the apparatus is used in group work, especially when the group is working on a sequence, apparatus often is placed so the children in the group working with it have to interrelate or cross each other's path frequently. When doing matching work, some children find it helpful to have their partner working across from them so they can look at each other as they work separately on their own apparatus. Still other children find it challenging to match the movement of their partner while working side by side on the same pieces of apparatus or on separate but identical arrangements of apparatus. Each arrangement of apparatus offers something new.

SAMPLE UNIT PLAN THEME 7

Themes. Relationships to Others—Theme 7 (and selected content from Themes 1 and 4).

Unit Focus. Partners and/or small groups working together in the development of movement sequences with emphasis on matching, copying, and canon relationships.

Appropriate For. Children who can remain productive in a group setting in gymnastics and who are sensitive to these requisites of safety: watching out for others, managing speed and flow of movement in space restricted by the movement of others.

Length of Unit. Five 30-minute lessons.

Content

    Body—balancing and all forms of locomotion

    Space—managing space to accommodate others

    Effort—managing time, weight, and flow to accommodate others

    Relationships—matching; copying; canoning

Student Objectives. The students should be willing to try to

1. Arrange apparatus in ways that will allow a group of four to six to be productive on and around the apparatus at one time.

2. Know and demonstrate the following relationships in a gymnastic setting with others:

    Matching—two or more people doing exactly the same movement at the same time.

    Copying—one partner moves, and the other partner repeats the performance exactly.

    Canoning—a group sequence in which one person performs a movement and all others, moving one at a time, duplicate the movement.

3. Work independently and as a group to create, practice, and refine a gymnastic sequence highlighting copying, matching, and canon relationships, with members in their group utilizing the floor and the independently selected and arranged apparatus.

4. Increase their skill and versatility in gymnastics by eliminating moments of thoughtless "play" and by intentionally accommodating the flow of movement by others to provide a safe environment for all.

Teaching Area. A space large enough to accommodate arranging several pieces of apparatus for each four to six children, with sufficient working space for each group.

Apparatus and/or Equipment. Selection of mats, vaulting boxes, benches, stools, platforms, and any other apparatus available in the school sufficient in number to allow for each group to create an arrangement of its own.

Learning Experiences (Tasks)

1.0 In your own space on the floor, one person in each group will be the leader and will take a starting position. The leaders then slowly will begin to curl, twist, and stretch to carefully take their weight constantly onto new body parts or surfaces. Group members who are watching the leaders, sharpen your ability to see movement by matching exactly what your leader does. Begin to do the movement right along with the leader. Get into groups of four to six people—the person whose last name is farthest in the alphabet will be the first leader.

A Suggested Progression For Sample Gymnastics Unit/Theme 7*

	Lesson 1		Lesson 2		Lesson 3		Lesson 4		Lesson 5
Tasks	**Teaching Tips**	**Tasks**	**Teaching Tips**	**Tasks**	**Teaching Tips**	**Tasks**	**Teaching Tips**	**Tasks**	**Teaching Tips**
1.0	Encourage movement on the spot and continuous movement. Change leader one or two times.	1.1	You may want to restructure groups from previous day or keep them the same. Reasons for doing either will exist.		(Discuss canon relationship or review if concept is not new.)		(Keep apparatus arranged the same as in Lesson 3.)		(Keep apparatus arranged the same as in Lesson 3.)
2.0	As they repeat this, encourage more complicated forms of movement and a performance posture throughout.	2.1	You may need to emphasize performance posture and encourage them to select their best gymnastic work.	1.2	Give several people opportunity to be leaders—urge each to do movements all can do.	4.0	This will take time. Be alert to groups who have all leaders, no followers, and vice versa—they will need help in sorting out ideas or making decisions. Sometimes it is helpful for the teacher to observe without intervening.	4.0	Work to refine group sequence. Give groups opportunity to see what others have done. Ask observers to be able to tell when they saw:
2.1	Urge the pathways be changed abruptly and directional changes come so forward, backward, and/or sideward movement result.	2.2	(See Lesson 1.) Stress alertness in the air—show muscle tension, clarity of body shape.	3.0	Bodies may be touching or separate. Help students to examine both ideas, or a combination can be exciting.	4.1	Give this if or when work needs variety.		—matching
2.2	This can have a safety problem. Give this task to each group when the group is capable of managing it safely. Do not worry if the whole class cannot experience this, especially during the first lesson.	2.3	Caution children to adapt their speed and flow of movement to accommodate others. If they should need to stop or change pathways or speed for others, ask them to make these changes look like preplanned moves.	3.1	Safety precaution is needed—they do not have to dismount all at the same time or in same direction.	4.2	Give this if and when work needs variety.		—canon
				3.2	Again—dismount can be in twos or threes—does not mean all must match.				Encourage some groups to increase length of sequence, include more difficult gymnastic-like skills, show the relationship more clearly, more often.
				3.3	Urge them to copy not only movements, but speed, direction. Remind them to remember how apparatus is arranged—they will use it for next two lessons.				

*Throughout all lessons, children should be able to arrange apparatus. Teacher may need to monitor the arrangement for safety.

1.1 Leader will do a short series of movements combining step-like actions and flight. All others in the group watch, then try to copy.

1.2 Leader does a short series of movements showing a change in levels, ending in a balance. Others in the group, one at a time, copy the leader's movement in canon style with all holding ending balance until the last one arrives in balance. Then come out of the balance, taking care to avoid others, and look like a gymnast when you do.

2.0 Carefully try to select different starting places away from your apparatus. Combining flight, step-like actions, and/or rolling—looking like performers—each of you, starting when you are ready, arrive onto the apparatus and go immediately into a balance you can hold. When everyone has arrived and is balanced, come out of your balance back onto the floor or mat and hold. (Then go back to your starting positions and start again.)

2.1 As you travel all at one time in your group to your apparatus, try to vary not only *what* you do but also your *directions* and *pathways*—do not all move forward in a straight pathway.

2.2 This will take a lot of caring about each other, so be careful. As you travel to take a balance on a piece of apparatus, take care that each of you tries to include a beautiful vault or a jump onto and off of another piece of apparatus before arriving onto the piece where you are going to balance.

2.3 See whether you all can now start from different places, go onto and over the first piece of apparatus, arrive onto the second piece of apparatus in a balance, and go back to your original spot, without working again on the first piece of apparatus. Watch out for each other—you may start at different times.

3.0 Each of you, starting from a different place, see how you each can mount the same apparatus and create a balance together. Then take care and dismount safely.

3.1 Try different ways of dismounting after all in your group have arrived on the same apparatus.

3.2 Show matching movement as you dismount.

3.3 Select one way of dismounting from your group balance and do it one at a time in canon style. Hold your ending position until all have dismounted.

4.0 Work to show matching and copying relationships, including one group balance where individuals come out of the group balance in canon style. Develop a group gymnastic sequence in which you are all working and sharing apparatus.

4.1 Try to achieve greater variety in your group sequence by changing pathways and directions.

4.2 Begin to take notice of the speed of others in your group sequence and get a contrast in speed.

Evaluation. Refer to Chapter 10 and either select or adapt one of the evaluative tools or develop a tool that can be used to help assess a specific aspect of the unit that is important to the needs of your students.

GYMNASTICS THEME 8—INTRODUCTION TO RHYTHM

The eighth theme refocuses attention on the totality of movement by emphasizing creating, repeating, and refining rhythm patterns in gymnastic sequences. Its primary purpose is to develop a feel for the rhythm that can be created in gymnastic movement. Rhythm patterns can be developed and sensed by those being introduced to gymnastics, especially in short series of movements that are repeated. With the emphasis on rhythm, the content includes time, weight, and flow, with the addition of any other specific content that either the teacher or the student selects. The feeling for rhythm may have been experienced when children were doing a series of movements or when focusing their efforts on developing movement sequences or when repeating certain movements; however, in this theme, rhythm in gymnastics is the chief topic.

Development of Theme 8

> **Basic Content**
> Time: Rhythm (repeating beat pattern)
> Weight: all variations
> Flow: all variations
> (In conjunction with content from Theme 1 and other themes.)

RHYTHM. There is no new content since time, weight, and flow already have been studied independently as well as collectively. The discussion of these three effort qualities is not repeated even though they are basic content. Thus, content in this theme is the study of rhythm patterns not yet examined in relation to gymnastics. Although this theme is the last one in gymnastics, rhythm in connection with dance should have been experienced many times by the children. Therefore, even rhythm may not be a new concept to the students. What may be the only different if not new idea is creating, repeating, and refining gymnastic sequences where the chief purpose is the sensing and development of repeatable rhythm patterns.

Work on this theme usually starts with movement on the feet or on hands and feet as the way to develop a rhythm pattern. These initial responses are not channeled immediately into movement sequences with a definite beginning and a definite ending position. Children are urged to listen to the cadence of the sounds made as their body parts touch the floor. This introductory study of rhythmic flow allows the children to respond to beat patterns developed by the teacher or to create their own patterns and repeat them. When this work is initiated with more mature or experienced children, they soon can be working in partners or small groups, copying and matching the cadences of others. The focus is directed to the time pattern of the sounds, as well as their intensity. By duplicating beat patterns and differentiating between the pauses, the quick and slow moments in the cadences, as well as the soft and strong movements, the child soon learns to hear and repeat the rhythm pattern that is established. Any content introduced earlier can be used in conjunction with this theme. Often, when experienced children are encouraged to select movement to do in a rhythm pattern, a wide variety of skillful gymnastic movement emerges.

The final step in this theme has the children developing gymnastic sequences with a detectable and repeatable rhythmic pattern. The last stages within this final step then would have partners or small groups creating gymnastic sequences containing a rhythm pattern. In any of the stages, including the last, the teacher can stipulate the activities to be performed, the apparatus to be used (if any), and even the rhythm pattern to be reflected in the sequence. Each of these decisions also could be given to the students, depending on the nature of the experience the teacher is trying to provide and the ability of the children to handle the decision-making role.

Sample Learning Experiences

1. Jumping back and forth over your rope on the floor, listen to the sounds your feet make as your feet touch the floor.

2. Try to develop a beat pattern on your hands and feet that you can repeat as you move back and forth over the bench.

3. With one or two others, listen to the beat pattern of one person without watching and see whether those of you listening can put movements together that fit the pattern you hear.

4. Letting only hands and feet touch the floor, experiment with working out a cadence and then repeat it. (Add a roll or rolling.)

5. Add apparatus to your working space and see whether you can repeat your cadence while moving on, over the apparatus.

6. With a partner, develop a cadence, then incorporate it in a sequence that you both can do.

7. In small groups, develop a sequence with a cadence; then see whether you can work out a way in which you repeat this sequence several times. (Later, you might suggest that some in the group hold still balances while others repeat the rhythmic sequence.)

Discussion. Although there is a characteristic rhythm or flow in all movement, the beat pattern in gymnastics is rarely produced intentionally by the uninitiated. If it is audible, many times the children do not hear it or become aware of repeating the beat until emphasis is placed on rhythm patterns. Work starts with stress on rhythm patterns that can be heard, but can progress to where children can retain the identical beat during quiet, inaudible movements as well as during the audible beat. One purpose of this theme is to expand sensitivity for movement. Throughout most of the gymnastic work, extensive effort has been placed on getting children to see and to feel movement. Here, another sense is aroused in order to develop it and add it to those of seeing and feeling in the study of movement. Listening to and hearing rhythm patterns in gymnastics are experiences that can be shared and appreciated by both the performer and those who observe. Children enjoy and learn from hearing the beat of another person's movement without seeing it, duplicating the beat in personally designed movement, and then comparing their responses. This experience is another way of illustrating to the children the amazing variety in movement.

The quality of the response as well as the degree of difficulty present in the movement the children incorporate in their rhythmic sequences can and should increase as the children mature in their gymnastic ability, if the teacher intervenes prudently. Since all movement ability takes time to perfect, this theme should be the focus several times throughout the later years in the elementary school program. THIS WORK CAN SHARE THE LESSON FOCUS WITH ALMOST ANY CONTENT AND ALSO CAN BE USED FREQUENTLY AND SUCCESSFULLY IN RATHER ISOLATED EXPERIENCES WITHIN LESSONS BASED ON EARLIER THEMES.

APPARATUS. The complexity of the arrangement of the apparatus as well as of the types and amount used in conjunction with this theme is largely reflective of the student's ability both to cope with the apparatus and to create and repeat a cadence in gymnastic movement. Use simple apparatus such as ropes on the floor or poles on blocks to introduce the idea if, for example, the movement to be done is jumping. If the class or a child has demonstrated special versatility for step-like actions on feet and hands, perhaps a bench could be used. Also, you can introduce the theme, using no apparatus.

SAMPLE UNIT PLAN THEME 8

Themes. Introduction to Rhythm—Theme 8 (and selected content from Themes 1, 3, and 5).

Unit Focus. Creating and reproducing rhythmic patterns in gymnastics, involving step-like actions, rolling, and momentary pauses.

Appropriate For. Children who have not studied rhythmic patterns in gymnastics but who have developed a repertoire of gymnastic skills involving rolling and step-like actions.

Length of Unit. Three 30-minute lessons.

Content

    Body—rolls, step-like actions

    Space—

    Effort—intentional control of weight and time in developing and repeating rhythm/cadence

    Relationships—gymnastic movement in relation to a rhythmic pattern

Student Objectives. The students should be willing to try to

1. Increase their satisfaction and that of others in a gymnastic setting by hearing and creating audible rhythmic patterns and by reproducing these rhythmic patterns in a gymnastic movement sequence.

2. Challenge themselves to invent, select, and refine more difficult gymnastic responses throughout the unit.

3. Know that time, weight, and flow are the movement dynamics that comprise rhythm in gymnastics, too.

Teaching Area. Indoor space large enough to accommodate class size.

Apparatus and/or Equipment. Simple equipment, such as ropes, for each child and blocks, bamboo poles, and one bench and mat for each four to six children.

Learning Experiences (Tasks)

1.0 Select one kind of step-like action that you can do just on your feet or on hands and feet and quietly, doing your best work, repeat this step-like movement, going back and forth over a rope on the floor in your own space. Listen to and try to feel the rhythm that begins to develop as you repeat your movement.

1.1 Listen to this pattern (slow, slow, quick, quick, pause—♩ ♩ ♫ pause) and try to make this same rhythmic pattern with your body parts touching the floor, going back and forth or alongside the rope.

1.2 Repeat above, giving new patterns such as slow, slow, slow, slow, quick. (Be sure the patterns you, the teacher, develop are repeated and lend themselves to step-like actions.)

1.3 Listen to this pattern and notice the accented beats and try with step-like actions to repeat the pattern, showing the accents. (CLAP, clap, CLAP, clap, CLAP, clap, CLAP, clap, pause.)

1.4 Clap out another beat pattern of your own and see whether you can duplicate the beats and accents with step-like actions.

1.5 Perform your gymnastic rhythmic pattern for a partner. Listener—listen to the rhythmic pattern and see whether you can clap the pattern when performer has fin-

A Suggested Progression For Sample Gymnastics Unit/Theme 8

	Lesson 1		Lesson 2		Lesson 3
Tasks	**Teaching Tips**	**Tasks**	**Teaching Tips**	**Tasks**	**Teaching Tips**
1.0	Children may start out with highly unlike gymnastic responses. You can change this after the rhythmic pattern concept is understood.	1.4	Same as in Lesson 1. Stress also trying to include more difficult step-like actions on a greater variety of body parts.	3.0	Work for quality—stress increasing difficulty of work they choose to do as well as showing more muscle tension throughout entire body to improve the quality of their performance.
1.1	If children are having difficulty with the rhythmic pattern concept, stop—have someone do a single step-like skill like a cartwheel. Have class clap each time a hand or foot touches the floor. Then have them do two in a row and clap.	1.5	LISTENING IS BOTH A SKILL AND AN ATTITUDE. GIVE ATTENTION to the role of the listener and the accuracy with which the partner's pattern is repeated.	3.1	Stress importance of *looking* alike in movement and *doing* every movement in same cadence. Repeat sequence several times.
1.2	Clap the beat out as the children start to work in 1.1 and here in 1.2. Along with the claps, say the appropriate words, i.e., slow, slow, slow, quick.	1.6	Stress here that the *rhythmic pattern* heard is to be duplicated, *BUT* listeners' responses may vary since they did not see the movement.	3.2	Children tend to make sequences too long—watch and suggest shorter ones. Remember *creating* and *repeating* pattern *is* the important content that is being taught.
1.3	See 1.2 comments—add accent with voice and loud claps. Soon drop words to spell out time and go to verbal cues to improve movement response, such as MOVE♩, with ♩, the ♩, beat ♩.	2.0	Emphasize that repeating same kind of movement helps to create and to hear rhythm.	3.3	Handle this completely on individual basis.
1.4	Urge children to keep patterns short and encourage them to repeat the movement several times without stopping so rhythmic pattern is really felt by them.	2.1	Urge them to try different rolls . . and to listen to different rhythms that are created.	4.1	Children likely just to step on and jump off at first. Hands placed on bench with feet going back and forth over the bench might be suggested.
2.0	CHECK and coach for tight, firm bodies—avoid letting them collapse while rolling.	2.2	May want to ask for a variety of rolls here from some children who seem ready.	4.2	Again, keep pattern short and ask them to do it several times in a row to feel and hear the repeated beat pattern.
2.1	Urge them to exaggerate the slap, but still maintain absolute best rolls.	2.3	Refer to listening done at the beginning of the class and highlight this as maturing behavior—being interested in the work of others.	4.3	Continue to work on refinement of movement and clarity in the audible rhythm pattern.
2.2	Stress making no extra pauses but the planned ones.	3.0	Teach out any extraneous unplanned movements and emphasize short sequences with a definite pause at the end. *Stress* repeating these movements several times to *hear* and *feel* the pattern.		
2.3	Being interested in someone else's work *is* important—stress the listening/clapping role.	4.0	Give the children a choice in adding bench or continuing their work without it.		

ished. Performer—check to see whether pattern is clapped accurately. (Change roles.)

1.6 Same as above, but listener turns away from performer and closes eyes. Performer does a short rhythm pattern of step-like actions. Afterward, the listener responds by trying to repeat the rhythmic pattern in a gymnastic sequence of his or her own.

2.0 Select one of your best rolls (forward, backward, straddle) and repeat it three times down the mat. Take care how mats are carried and placed. Get into groups of four to six and begin.

2.1 Each time your hands touch the mat in rolling, accent this, making a sound with your hands, slapping the mat as you repeat your roll.

2.2 Put in a pause as you roll several times on the mat. Still accent the hands touching the mat.

2.3 Listen carefully and clap the beat of the person's movement in front of you. Then create your own rhythmic pattern by accenting rolls and pausing.

3.0 Combine step-like actions and rolling into a rhythmic sequence. Try to accent the pattern with sounds made with body parts touching the floor and with planned pauses.

3.1 Two or more of you might enjoy doing the same gymnastic sequence at the same time. Really listen to the beats and try to be right on beat together.

3.2 Increase the number of times you repeat your pattern (decrease pattern if it is too long).

3.3 Same as 3.1, but ask children to try to perform more complex step-like actions and rolls and/or work on improving their performance by making lines of their bodies clear and increasing muscle tension when appropriate.

4.0 (Add a bench somewhere near the mat.) See how you can incorporate the sounds made when arriving onto and leaving the bench into your rhythmic pattern.

4.1 As you are working to include the bench in your own rhythmic gymnastic sequence, you may want to arrive on and off the bench several times. Be free to experiment.

4.2 Select some of your best ideas for incorporating the bench and now add those to rolling and step-like actions on the mat and floor and make a repeatable rhythmic gymnastic sequence.

Evaluation. Refer to Chapter 10 and either select or adapt one of the evaluative tools or develop a tool that can be used to help assess a specific aspect of the unit that is important to the needs of your students.

PROGRESSION

A thematic approach has been used throughout each of the three program areas as a means to organize the content. While the eight gymnastic themes progress from the simple to the more complex content, **these themes are not presented as color-coded program blocks; therefore you should not teach all of the content ideas centering around one theme before you dare move to the next theme. Progression built from this point of view would fail to recognize the variation of difficulty within the content of each theme, the individual characteristics of both the teacher and the children, and may also not reflect the tremendous variation in facilities, apparatus, and time schedules in the different elementary schools.**

Rather than exhaust one theme before moving to the next, use several appropriate themes for each group of children. Also, since the ideas central to one theme are extensive, themes that are studied earlier at one grade level can be reintroduced for reenforcement. As any theme is revisited, it can be the focus of new units of work, or the content of these former themes can be used in conjunction with new themes as they are introduced and developed. (This has been practiced throughout this chapter when the sample units for Themes 2 through 8 were written.) *Literally dozens of unit plans and scores of lessons can be designed around each of the themes.* Each time a theme is studied, you can approach the program content at a higher level or in a more complicated way to challenge the children to achieve greater skill and a more complete awareness for the content. Instead of having explicit program blocks designated as appropriate for various ages and stages of development, we have illustrated in Figure 8–3 how the themes often overlap for different grades and how several themes serve as sources for content in gym-

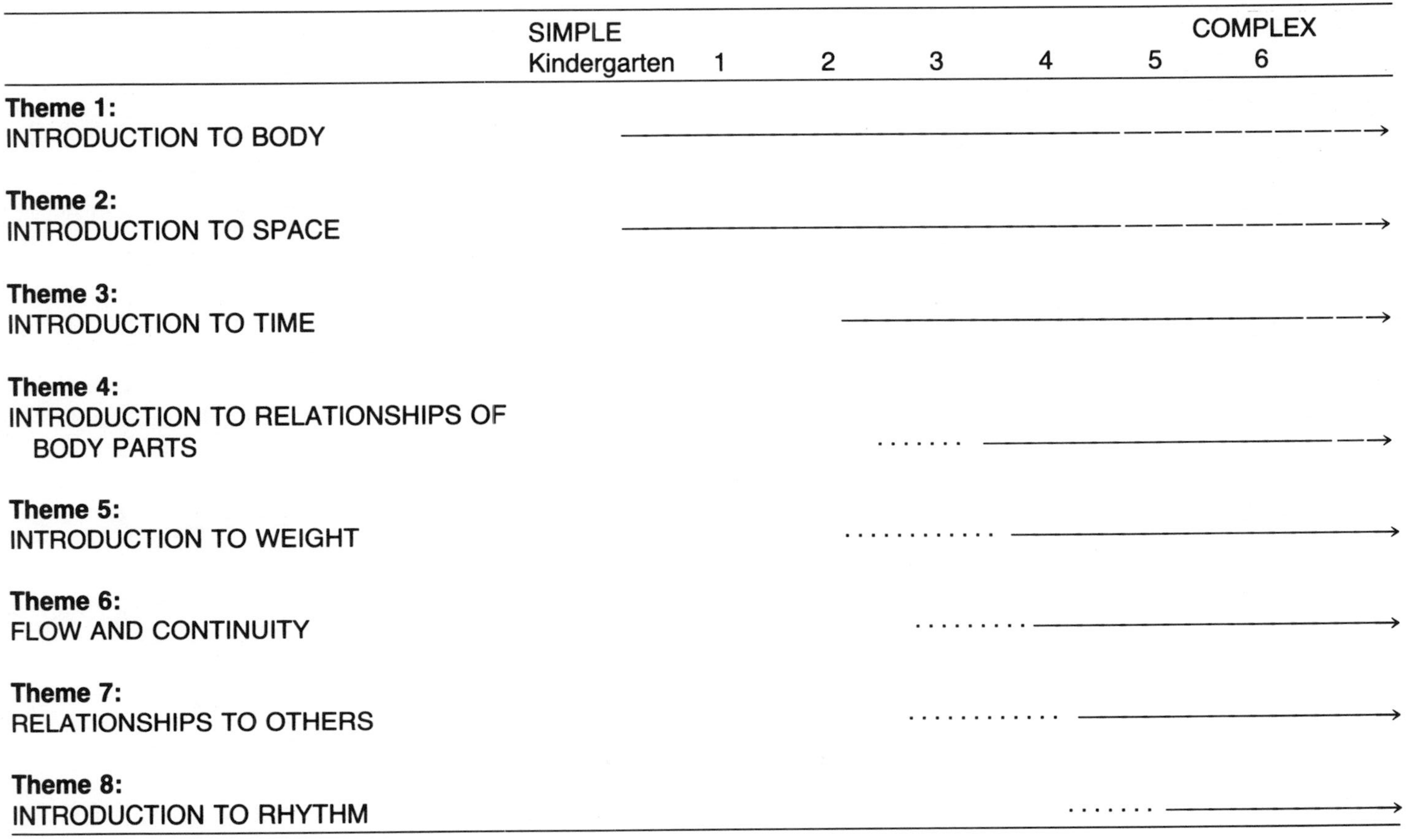

SIMPLE ← → COMPLEX

Kindergarten 1 2 3 4 5 6

Theme 1:
INTRODUCTION TO BODY

Theme 2:
INTRODUCTION TO SPACE

Theme 3:
INTRODUCTION TO TIME

Theme 4:
INTRODUCTION TO RELATIONSHIPS OF
BODY PARTS

Theme 5:
INTRODUCTION TO WEIGHT

Theme 6:
FLOW AND CONTINUITY

Theme 7:
RELATIONSHIPS TO OTHERS

Theme 8:
INTRODUCTION TO RHYTHM

Fig. 8–3. Theme Progression for Educational Gymnastics Program Introduced in the Primary Grades

nastics for each grade, kindergarten through sixth, during any one school year.

Figure 8–3 illustrates how the eight gymnastics themes are phased in gradually over seven years, kindergarten through the sixth grade. It also shows which themes are appropriate for each grade. In the figure, the solid lines indicate when each of the themes is apt to hold great meaning for the children and how long the theme is suggested as a main focus when constructing yearly plans and units of study. The dotted lines indicate times when the content from the themes might be introduced earlier to children needing advanced challenges. The broken lines show that themes can be studied longer, especially with children who are not quite ready for the more complex challenges of the later themes. Also, the broken lines particularly indicate when the themes would be revisited at an advanced level when children have progressed to more complex themes. The implications of the broken and dotted lines can relate either to total classes or to content challenges for individual children.

Some themes come into focus close to one another. This observation prompts two suggestions. First, when the educational gymnastics program is initiated with older children, you must consider their maturity and not treat them as if they were kindergarteners. Therefore, when introducing the program to older children, you can move more rapidly through the first and second themes or eliminate them as initial content to be studied independently. Content in these two themes could be included along with the more advanced themes. Second, you should avoid hurrying children, irrespective of age, through content so rapidly that the various content concepts are not learned, or the subsequent experiences will be beyond their ability. Do not feel compelled by the suggested progression to teach the last two themes especially if your program of physical education is limited to one or two weekly instructional periods. While the progression has been defined rather specifically in the illustration, in the final analysis it has to be tempered and shaped by a sensitive teacher who knows children and movement.

THE INTENT IN PROGRESSION SHOULD BE TO MAKE THE CONTENT FIT THE NEEDS OF THE CHILDREN RATHER THAN MAKING THE CHILDREN FIT A PROGRESSION.

REFERENCES

1. Morison, R.: Educational Gymnastics. Liverpool, I.M. Marsh College of Physical Education, 1956.
2. Laban, R.: Modern Educational Dance, 2nd ed. Revised by L. Ullman. New York, Frederick A. Praeger, 1968.
3. Preston-Dunlop, V.: A Handbook for Modern Educational Dance, 2nd ed. Boston, Plays, Inc., 1980.

SELECTED READING

Briggs, M.: Movement Education. Boston, Plays, Inc., 1975.

Cameron, W., and Pleasance, P.: Education in Movement—Gymnastics. Revised. Oxford, Basil Blackwell, 1971.

Department of Education and Science, Movement Physical Education in the Primary Years. London, Her Majesty's Stationery Office, 1972.

Holbrook, J.: Movement Activity in Gymnastics. Boston, Plays, Inc., 1974.

Mauldon, E., and Layson, J.: Teaching Gymnastics, 2nd ed. London, Macdonald & Evans, 1979.

Morison, R.: A Movement Approach to Educational Gymnastics. London, J.M. Dent and Sons, 1969.

Pallett, D.: Modern Educational Gymnastics. New York, Pergamon Press, 1965.

Parent, S. (ed.): Educational gymnastics. In Elementary Curriculum: Theory and Practice. Reston, VA, AAHPERD, 1982.

Russell, K.: An alternate approach to school gymnastics. In Gymnastics: Everything You Wanted to Know. Edited by Lynn J. Sinclair. Symposium Proceedings. Toronto, Canadian Gymnastic Federation, 1980.

Stanley, S.: Physical Education: A Movement Orientation, 2nd ed. Toronto, McGraw-Hill of Canada, Ltd., 1977.

Williams, J.: Themes for Educational Gymnastics, 2nd ed. London, Lepus Books, 1979.

Chapter 9

The Teacher as Observer, Interpreter, and Decision-Maker

KATE R. BARRETT*

In Chapter 3, a teacher was defined as an observer, an interpreter, and a decision-maker. The challenge of living up to this definition is awesome, but as a definition, it is a good one because effective teachers must be skilled at all three behaviors. For example, in response to a task, a child (Anna) jumps from a Swedish box trying to get height and a stretched body shape while in the air.

As OBSERVERS, we must be able to *see* accurately what Anna is doing:

*All photographs in this chapter not otherwise credited were taken by the author.

How high is the box; how is it placed in relation to the mat?

Where are the other children situated; what are they doing?

What did Anna do to get onto the box, to get to the end of the box, to get off of the box?

What are Anna's arms and legs (head, trunk) doing just prior to takeoff, during flight, upon landing?

What is the shape of Anna's body just prior to takeoff, during flight, upon landing?

As INTERPRETERS, we must be able to *explain* the meaning of what we saw; when Anna jumped she

Was approximately one foot above the top of the box. Why?

Hesitated before jumping; almost stopped. Why?

Held her elbows, knees, trunk in slight flexion. Why?

Looked at mat throughout jump. Why?

As DECISION-MAKERS, we must be able to decide *what to do* once our observations have been interpreted:

Observe Anna try the jump again before giving any feedback.

Give Anna feedback now to help her get more height on her jump.

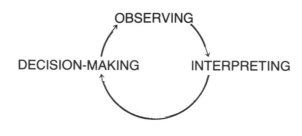

Fig. 9–1. The Interrelationship of Observing, Interpreting and Decision-Making.

Ask Anna what she thinks she could do to improve her body position while in the air.

As teaching behaviors, observing, interpreting, and decision-making are interrelated and occur continuously throughout every lesson. These ideas are used to organize this chapter, but are discussed separately to highlight their uniqueness. When you are studying the material, keep in mind how they are related: teachers observe, interpret what they have seen, and based upon this, decide what to do. Figure 9–1 represents this idea.

THE TEACHER AS OBSERVER

Skillful observation has long been considered one of the most important skills teachers should have if they wish to be effective, thus the idea of the *teacher as observer*. Becoming skilled, though, takes a willingness to practice continuously and to realize that improvement comes quickly when the practice is focused. This is something all teachers need to work on, and they should not be afraid to admit when they need help. The road to improvement begins with the ability to observe objectively.

Observing Objectively

A skilled observer in any field of study has the ability to observe objectively, reserving judgment until the number of observations warrants it. This means observing what is there, not what you think is there. To a teacher in physical education, this implies the ability to see accurately all parts of the movement and how the environment may be affecting it. Compare the two observations opposite and identify which one is "judgmental" and which one is "objective."

Observation A is judgmental because Sandra's position to catch the ball was judged to be "good" and her body was judged to be "well balanced." In both instances, no information supported what was "good" or "well balanced." Observation B describes what Sandra did and does not make any judgment.

Another characteristic of skilled observers is their ability to describe adequately and accurately what they have seen. They can describe all types of movement, not just the movement associated with games or dance, for example. This text is rich in language to help meet this need in that it includes languages of mechanics, development, and Laban analysis; they can be used separately or together, whatever is appropriate.

If observing objectively or having a fluent "movement" vocabulary are not skills you do easily, working with photographs that have "caught" or "frozen" the movement is an excellent way to practice. Two reasons why this is helpful are that (a) the movement "stays put" and therefore gives you time to see it, and (b) the normal stresses of teaching are removed, and therefore, you are less distracted or hurried. The photographs that follow have been selected for this purpose. For each photograph, describe both the environment and the movement of the children. When describing the environment, attend to the physical boundaries, the arrangement, size, and texture of the equipment and apparatus, and the placement of the children and teacher (if one is present). When describing the movement of the children, attend to what the body is doing, where in space it is moving, how the body and body parts are moving, and any significant relationship between and among children, children and equipment and apparatus, and body parts.

Photo from the Agency for Instructional Television

A. Sandra is in a good position to catch the ball; her body appears well balanced.

B. Sandra's hands are directly under the ball and her eyes are looking straight at it; her feet are slightly apart, with one in front of the other.

Photos from the Agency for Instructional Television

Photo from the Agency for Instructional Television

Photo from the Agency for Instructional Television

THE TEACHER AS (OBSERVER) INTERPRETER

Teachers must be able to explain what they observe, thus the idea of the *teacher as interpreter*. When teachers interpret, they explain the meaning of what they saw and make judgments about it. This has to be done throughout a lesson and usually quickly. Let us go back for a moment to Anna, the young child seen jumping off of a box earlier in this chapter. It was observed when Anna jumped that

1. her height in the air was approximately 1 foot above the box height (36 inches).

2. she hestitated, almost stopped before jumping.

3. her elbows, trunk, and knees were slightly flexed; she looked at the mat throughout the jump. As an interpreter, having made these observations, you must now explain them; interpret them. What do they mean, what do they tell you about Anna, what do they suggest?

What do you think they mean, and why? Is Anna afraid of the height? Is she having difficulty timing the thrust of her legs with the lift of her arms? Does Anna have a perceptual problem? Is she tired? Does she lack the body awareness needed to stretch all parts away from her body's center?

Interpreting from a Knowledge Base

Becoming skilled at interpreting takes prac-tice and requires a strong knowledge base. To help support your interpretations, this text emphasizes the necessity to have a working knowledge of child development, motor in particular; basic mechanical principles governing human movement, Laban analysis; principles of skill acquisition, and evaluation. How to use this knowledge is something you learn by experience, *lots of it*, and depends, too, on what you are teaching, your objectives, and the developmental level of the children. These areas of knowledge help you answer why you think something happened. The more you can draw on your knowledge base, the more faith you can have in your interpretations and the more choices you will have about what to do next when in a teaching situation.

As in practicing to observe objectively and to describe what you saw, photographs of movement are very useful when you need practice in interpreting. To help you practice, a series of questions has been designed with each one related to a specific photograph. It is suggested that you study the photographs and answer the questions by yourself first, and then discuss them with others. Because you do not know the children or the situation in which each photograph was taken, all answers have the potential of being "right." Let us agree that the strongest answers are those that can be backed up with the strongest rationale.

Interpretation Task 1

1. Which way do you think this child will roll; why?
2. Will this roll be efficient or inefficient; why?

Notes:

Interpretation Task 2

1. What do you think the child is about to do; why?
2. Do you think she could take her weight on her hands and roll; why? Which directions; why?

Notes:

Interpretation Task 3

1. What movement quality or qualities is this child trying to express; why?
2. Is he being successful; why?

Notes:

Photos from the Agency for Instructional Television

Interpretation Task 4

1. Identify the two offensive players and the two defensive players.
2. Evaluate the receiver's positioning in relation to her teammate (thrower).
3. When could the thrower have released the ball; why?
4. Evaluate the opponent's marking ability throughout the sequence.

Notes:

Interpretation Task 5
1. Which children appear to have the best control of the ball; why?
2. Evaluate the children's use of space in both photographs.
Notes:

Interpretation Task 6
1. With which body part is the child preparing to strike?
2. Will she be successful; why?
Notes:

Interpretation Task 7
1. What do you think each child is trying to do; why?
2. Will they be successful; why?
Notes:

Interpretation Task 8

There are 6 years difference in age between the girl in the first photograph and the girl and boy in the second.

1. Why are the older children jumping higher than the younger child?
2. Why is the older girl jumping higher than the boy?

Notes:

Interpretation Task 9
1. With what body part(s) are these children expressing strength?
2. Which child is being more successful; why?
Notes:

Interpretation Task 10

1. Which child seems to be most successful in dribbling the ball; why?
2. Which child has made the best adjustment to the implement; give reasons for your choice.

Notes:

Interpretation Task 11
1. What have these children been asked to do?
2. What movement qualities are these children trying to use?
Notes:

Interpretation Task 12
1. Was the movement that preceded this one a quick movement; a slow movement; a direct movement; an indirect movement; a strong movement; a light movement; why?
Notes:

Photo from the Agency for Instructional Television.

Interpretation Task 13 (study photos right to left)
Study the three sets of photographs.
1. Which child will most easily come to a standing position; why?
2. Which child appears to be the most advanced; why?
Notes:

Interpretation Task 14

1. What effect does the low hurdle have on this child's takeoff and hand contact with the mat?
2. How will this child finish her roll?
3. Compare the takeoff and hand contact with the mat between these photographs and those used in Interpretation Task 13.

Notes:

THE TEACHER AS OBSERVER *AND* INTERPRETER

Thus far we have described the teacher as both an observer and as an interpreter. For the former, objectivity and a rich movement description were stressed; for the latter, making interpretations from a solid knowledge base was considered important.

The Observation Plan

A major characteristic that is evident among effective teachers is the commitment they have to *planning for observation* when they prepare to teach; they make out a *plan*. How they do this and what they include in the plan differs among them, but they all plan and they all say that planning for observation plays a significant role in their success as teachers.[1] Before the idea of the teacher as a decision-maker is examined, this idea of planning to observe will be presented, because when the plan is used, it requires both observation and interpretation skills.

To introduce the idea of making an observation plan, a series of plans have been prepared as examples. The first plan is accompanied by some brief comments designed to orient you to the basic idea. A set of seven more plans and photographs follows to show how plans might differ for different types of tasks and to give you practice in using plans to guide your observation. Each sample plan has been designed to relate to a single task and not a series of tasks or a lesson. The purpose of using one task is to illustrate a way to approach observation planning; it is expected that you will vary the way you plan to fit your needs.

THE TEACHER AS OBSERVER, INTERPRETER, AND DECISION-MAKER

COMMENTS (See Observation Plan 1)

1. *SITUATION:* Knowing the situation gives you the "boundaries" in which you will be observing. This helps you plan more realistically.

2. *TASK:* Stating the task *clearly* is essential before you begin to design your plan. The effectiveness of your plan depends on the clarity of your task.

3. *TASK CLASSIFICATIONS:* Classifying the task gives you information about it that helps you understand it better. For this plan a task is first being classified as to its type: basic, extending, simplifying, refining, applying, or organizational,[2] and then as to the condition of the environment.[3] The task in this sample plan is considered as a "basic task," a task that could serve as a basis for extending, simplifying, refining, or even applying tasks. (A discussion of these task types comes later.) The environment in this task is considered complex (and therefore will be more difficult to observe) in that

> *the object is in motion:* the object is a ball here and it is being dribbled, hence it will travel through space.
> *the child is in motion:* the child is dribbling a ball and hence will be traveling through space.
> *the teaching environment is in motion:* all the children will be moving at one time by dribbling a ball; and the space in which they are doing this is considered *"in motion."* If the children were working on the spot—no traveling—the teaching environment would be considered *at rest.*

4. *WHAT TO LOOK FOR:* Listing, in order of priority, what you plan to look for specifically is the substance of the plan. There are no set features (what is listed in this column are often called critical features[4]) to be listed here as this will differ from task to task (because needs of the children change) and from teacher to teacher (because teachers do not always agree on what they think is important). What is listed here must be able to be seen and must have a reason for being listed. In this plan, what to look for is stated in the form of a question; answering requires the teacher to observe, *then* interpret.

5. *WHEN/HOW LONG:* Indicating when and for how long you plan to observe a particular feature or set of features helps to organize your observing. The length of time indicates when and how long you will observe that particular feature. In this plan, the teacher begins right away observing for SPEED and SPACING and continues doing this throughout the development of the task. The teacher plans to observe FOOT ACTION and BODY ACTION after the children have begun working and are safe with their speed and spacing; CHANGE OF DIRECTION is picked up a little later. Toward the end of the time period for this task, the teacher will be alert and observing all five features, or those of the five most needed.

6. *STRATEGIES/TECHNIQUES:* Thinking through when you plan to scan the group or to focus on individuals or groups of individuals controls where you let your eyes search. Personal comments are often helpful.

7. *POSITIONING:* Stating where you want to position yourself and how you want to move around and through the group should be done, at least until you are aware of position and move. Many teachers have no recollection of their positioning techniques and are amazed to find out how often they remain in one spot when teaching.

3 TASK CLASSIFICATION: basic

1 SITUATION: Multi-purpose room; 28 children: third grade; each child with a ball (8-inch PG, slightly deflated); task new to children.

2 TASK: Using your own ball, dribble it throughout the space, changing the directions you move often.

	At Rest	In Motion
Object		x
Child		x
T/ Envir.		x

4	5	6
WHAT TO LOOK FOR	**WHEN/HOW LONG**	**STRATEGIES/ TECHNIQUES**
SPACING (of children and balls): is it safe for the situation? does it allow for responses appropriate to the task?	⟶	Scan continuously.
SPEED (of children and balls): is it safe for situation? does it allow for responses appropriate to the task?	⟶	
FOOT ACTION (prior to and at contact): is it in line with the desired direction; is the contact of the foot sudden, firm, direct?	⟶	Scan first, focus on individuals later if spacing and speed are safe. Once I have scanned all these features I will alternate where to observe, depending on results.
BODY: is the weight held over the balls of the feet? when traveling, is there resiliency in ankle joint? is the body alert, ready to move quickly and easily in any direction? when changing directions, is the body balanced?	⟶ ⟶ ⟶ ⟶	
CHANGE OF DIRECTION: are all directions being used? is the moment of "changing" direction sharp, clear? is the body balanced at moment of change?	⟶ ⟶ ⟶	Remember to observe body action in relation to foot action.

7

POSITIONING: I plan to keep myself outside the group, back to the wall and move around entire group. When helping an individual, I will keep rest in view by periodic scanning. If I stay in one place it will only be for a brief moment.

Sample Observation Plan 1

SITUATION: Multipurpose room; 25 children; 14 ropes and 14 hoops well-spaced out; K-1; traveling on different body parts is familiar, but not throughout the space and with small equipment, they are very excited.

TASK: Travel from a rope to a hoop to another rope, taking weight on different body parts.

	At Rest	In Motion
Object	x	
Child		x
T/ Envir.		x

WHAT TO LOOK FOR	WHEN/HOW LONG	STRATEGIES/ TECHNIQUES
SPEED (of children): is it safe for situation; does it allow for responses appropriate to the task?	⟶	Scan continuously then focus:
SPACING (of children/apparatus: is it safe; does it allow for responses appropriate to the task?	⟶	when children seem "focused" and in control of their movements, plan to begin focusing on individuals.
WEIGHT TRANSFERENCE: when weight is on hands is head up? when weight is taken on different body parts is it absorbed carefully (right amount of muscle tension for control)?	⟶ ⟶	
BODY: are children taking their weight on a wide range of body parts?	⟶	
APPARATUS: are children using both types of apparatus?	⟶	
EFFORT: weight—is the right amount of (muscle) tension used for control?	⟶	

POSITIONING: At all times, I will keep the entire class in view. I plan to move quickly around and through group—never staying in the center of the space. When helping individuals, I will continuously scan the group; to do this, my back will have to be toward the wall.

Sample Observation Plan 2

PRACTICE PHOTOGRAPHS

1. Study the plan so you are familiar with it.
2. Observe each photograph, using the plan as your guide. BE CAREFUL not to interpret and make the judgments asked for in the plan TOO QUICKLY. Observe objectively first: see what is there in relation to the situation and task requirements, *then* interpret.

TASK CLASSIFICATION: basic

SITUATION: Gymnasium; 30 children; 15 mats; third grade; mats evenly spaced throughout space; task new to children.

(floor)

TASK: Select a way of transferring your weight from your feet to your hands to your feet; first do it slowly, then fast.

	At Rest	In Motion
Object	x	
Child		x
T/ Envir.	x	

WHAT TO LOOK FOR	WHEN/HOW LONG	STRATEGIES/ TECHNIQUES
SPACING (of work): are children working in a safe relationship to each other?	—————————→	Scan continuously. All related to safety of child.
SPEED (of work): does the speed of work allow children to think about what they are doing?	—————————→	
WEIGHT TRANSFER: when weight is on hands is head up? when weight is taken on hands, feet, is it absorbed carefully?	—————————→ —————————→	
SELECTION PROCESS: can children find different ways to shift weight? does the way chosen have the chance for a smooth transition when refined?	——————→ ——————→	Scan first, then focus on those needing help.
BASIC BODY ACTIONS: when the body or body parts are stretched, curled, or twisted, are these actions clear?	——————→	Scan then focus, then scan. Be sure to focus on different children.
EFFORT: is the right amount of tension used throughout sequence? is there a clear difference between the fast sequence and the slow sequence?	——————→ ——————→	

POSITIONING: Start on outside of group, moving around room slowly. When helping individuals, be certain I can see entire room; move child to better position if necessary. Do not get caught in center or with children working *behind* me.

Sample Observation Plan 3

PRACTICE PHOTOGRAPHS
1. Study the plan so you are familiar with it.
2. Observe each photograph . . .

TASK CLASSIFICATION: Organizational

SITUATION: Gymnasium; 30 children; 30 mats, 10 benches; fourth grade; apparatus and mats placed against a wall, benches together and mats in 3 piles; this type of organizational responsibility is new to the children.

	At Rest	In Motion
Object	x	
Child T/		x
Envir.		x

TASKS: After you have formed groups of two to three, take out one bench and 3 mats and arrange them so you can dismount from the bench by jumping, landing, rolling in three different places. When ready, sit by your arrangement.

WHAT TO LOOK FOR	WHEN/HOW LONG	STRATEGIES/ TECHNIQUES
GROUP FORMATION: can all children find a group?	⟶	Scan continuously.
SPEED (of children): is the pace the children are using in the gym safe to form groups? to take out apparatus and mats? to move apparatus and mats?	⟶	
SPACING (of children and apparatus): is the space between the children and the apparatus adequate when they are forming groups? taking out apparatus and mats? moving apparatus and mats; height safe?	⟶	I will focus closely on the ends of the benches, corners of the mats.
APPARATUS: do their arrangements show safe traffic patterns? room to roll? three landing areas? Are children sitting *next* to apparatus?	⟶	

POSITIONING: Will start with my back to the wall and next to apparatus and mats, facing class. As the apparatus is moved, I will begin to circle the gym, trying not to get at one end, with my back to the wall so I can keep ALL children in view.

Sample Observation Plan 4

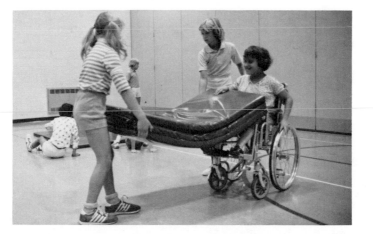

PRACTICE PHOTOGRAPHS
1. Study the plan so you are familiar with it.
2. Observe each photograph . . .

SITUATION: Multipurpose room; 24 children, second grade; this task is new, but the children know how to "experiment."

TASK: Experiment with the effort actions of slashing and gliding and thrusting and floating. Find different ways to put them together while remaining on the spot or traveling.

	At Rest	In Motion
Object	NA	
Child T/	x	
Envir.	x	

WHAT TO LOOK FOR	WHEN/HOW LONG	STRATEGIES/ TECHNIQUES
SPACING: are the children working in a safe relationship to each other?	⟶	Scan periodically.
EFFORT ACTIONS: is the use of time, weight, and space clear enough to distinguish each effort action? Slash: sudden/firm/indirect Glide: sustained/fine/direct Thrust: sudden/firm/direct Float: sustained/fine/indirect	⟶	Scan continuously with periodic focusing, trying to get to see all children at some point. New tasks will develop from this one so it is important to see and take in as much as I can.
BODY: how are the children using their body parts: to lead, to follow, to gesture? what parts are the children using: elbows, knees, head? are they using rising, sinking; opening, closing? what shapes are they using?	⟶ ⟶ ⟶ ⟶	When observing BODY and SPACE, I do not want to make judgments, just see what they do.
SPACE: what levels are the children using? do they move into different directions?	⟶ ⟶	

POSITIONING: I shall begin on the outside of the group, and when they are working, I shall move freely among them. No matter where I go I plan to keep my position such that I can see everyone by scanning.

Sample Observation Plan 5

Photo from the Agency for Instructional Television.

Photo from the Agency for Instructional Television.

PRACTICE PHOTOGRAPHS
1. Study the plan so you are familiar with it.
2. Observe each photograph . . .

TASK CLASSIFICATION: extending

SITUATION: Multipurpose room; 27 children; fifth grade; the children have been working on just meeting and parting; this task takes the idea further; 4 to 5 to a group.

(floor)

TASK: This time, as you meet in the center, add rising and sinking while you mingle. Remember, as you come together and separate, your movements should be firm/sudden; as you mingle, fine/sustained.

	At Rest	In Motion
Object	x	
Child		x
T/ Envir.	x	

WHAT TO LOOK FOR	WHEN/HOW LONG	STRATEGIES/ TECHNIQUES
SPACING: do the children have enough space in which to work freely?	⟶	Scan all groups quickly.
BODY: when meeting and parting do the children use different locomoter patterns?	⟶	Focus on groups but scan within each. Toward second half of period, focus on selected individuals.
when rising and sinking do children: change the body part leading, use turning, have a focus (eye) throughout?	⟶	
SPACE: do children use different directions and levels in their work?	⟶	Center observation on the rising and sinking part as this is new.
RELATIONSHIPS: when mingling, are the children close enough to bring out turning and twisting?	⟶	
EFFORT: do the children show clearly when meeting and parting, a firm/sudden quality?	⟶	
when rising and sinking, a fine/sustained quality?	⟶	

POSITIONING: Begin away from groups so I can easily see that all are working with focus and concentration. Work with each group standing, so that all other groups are clearly in my view.

Sample Observation Plan 6

PRACTICE PHOTOGRAPHS

1. Study the plan so you are familiar with it.
2. Observe each photograph . . .

TASK CLASSIFICATION: refining

SITUATION: Gymnasium; 27 children; 1 ball per child (8-inch plastic); fifth grade; children are organized and understand task; helping each other is new, but striking is familiar; they are trying to improve their striking ability.

TASK: In twos, one person work to improve ability to strike a ball continuously with upper body parts; the other person observe to see the position of the body part at contact. After a short while, have the observer comment on what was seen.

	At Rest	In Motion
Object		x
Child	x	
T/ Envir.	x	

WHAT TO LOOK FOR		WHEN/HOW LONG	STRATEGIES/ TECHNIQUES
SPACING: is it safe; does it allow for responses appropriate to task?		————————→	Scan quickly.
"Observers"	"Movers"		
Are they where they need to be to see partner's movement?		————————→	Scan continuously.
	Are movers: positioning body parts directly under the ball?	————————→	Scan continuously.
	using all their upper body parts?	————————→	Gather information to use in later lessons; emphasis today is on working with observer.
	using a firm, direct, and sudden hit to strike ball?	————————→	
	alert and balanced and ready to shift body position, prior to, during, and after contact?	————————→	
By their comments and answers to my questions: do they understand "body part position at contact"?		————————→	Scan, then focus where needed. *Listen* to observer's comments and answers to questions.
Do they change roles often, but not too quickly?		————————→	
Are they helpful to partner?	improving the position of body part at contact?	————————→	

POSITIONING: I shall start moving around the room, being certain I can scan the entire group. When listening to individual children, I shall still keep rest of group in view by scanning periodically. If a pair is in a bad spot for me to do this, I will move the two of them away from the center.

Sample Observation Plan 7

PRACTICE PHOTOGRAPHS
1. Study the plan so you are familiar with it.
2. Observe each photograph . . .

TASK CLASSIFICATION: applying

SITUATION: Gymnasium or field with markers; 28 children; 1 ball per 10 children; sixth grade; the last 3 lessons have led up to this task carefully; the children are capable of getting into play by themselves. They know the structure of the game, but have not played it long.

TASK: In your groups of 8 to 10, play Field Dodgeball.

	At Rest	In Motion
Object		x
Child		x
T/ Envir.		x

WHAT TO LOOK FOR	WHEN/HOW LONG	STRATEGIES/ TECHNIQUES
SPACING: have all groups arranged their space safely? is there enough space behind the restraining line? behind the base? between other groups?	⟶	Scan quickly.
BASIC IDEA: do all groups have the basic idea of the game?	⟶	Scan all groups first, then focus on each in turn.
BASIC STRATEGIES: do runners move in relation to ball? do fielders throw in relation to movement of runner?	⟶ ⟶	Order of focus dependent on group needing most help first. (Scanning picks this up.)
GAME SKILLS: *runners:* can they handle the locomotor skills required to change directions in relation to ball and fielder's positions? avoid being hit? cross restraining line in control? *fielders:* can they handle the locomotor and manipulative skills required to keep the ball ahead of the runner? throw at runner without losing ball?	⟶ ⟶	As I work with one group, I shall keep other groups in view by quickly scanning.

POSITIONING: At first, I shall place myself so I can see all groups, especially their restraining line. When working with individual groups (basic pattern unless I see a reason to bring them all in), I shall position myself so other groups are in view.

Sample Observation Plan 8

PRACTICE PHOTOGRAPHS

1. Study the plan so you are familiar with it.
2. Observe each photograph . .

Designing Your Own Plan

Planning for observation is in actuality part of the lesson planning process. How each of us uses the information gained from this part of the planning process may be different. Some will use forms such as those in the examples given and attach them to the lesson plan, whereas others might list important things to look for directly onto the lesson plan itself. What is important is that you plan, not the way you report your plan. The steps that follow are designed to guide you through the process of making your own plan. While studying these steps, it might be helpful to refer occasionally to one of the earlier examples. Following steps 1 through 4 will give you the background information necessary to design a plan. The last four steps guide the making of the actual plan.[5]

STEP 1—DESCRIBING THE SITUATION. Identify clearly the situation in which this task will be taught. This will alert you to some potential problems that may influence your final observation plan. This includes such information as teaching area, number of children, grade or age of children, equipment/apparatus, and knowledge of children's backgrounds.

STEP 2—STATING THE TASK. State your task *as clearly as possible* so you know specifically what it is you want the children to do. This is not easy, but an essential part of the preplanning work.

STEP 3—CLASSIFYING THE TASK. Identify first the type of task you have and then the conditions of the environment. When this analysis is complete, it tells you both the purpose of the task and the conditions of the environment. Both will influence decisions about what and how you observe.

Task Types. There are six types of tasks: basic, extending, simplifying, refining, applying, and organizational.[2] A *basic task* is the initial or in-

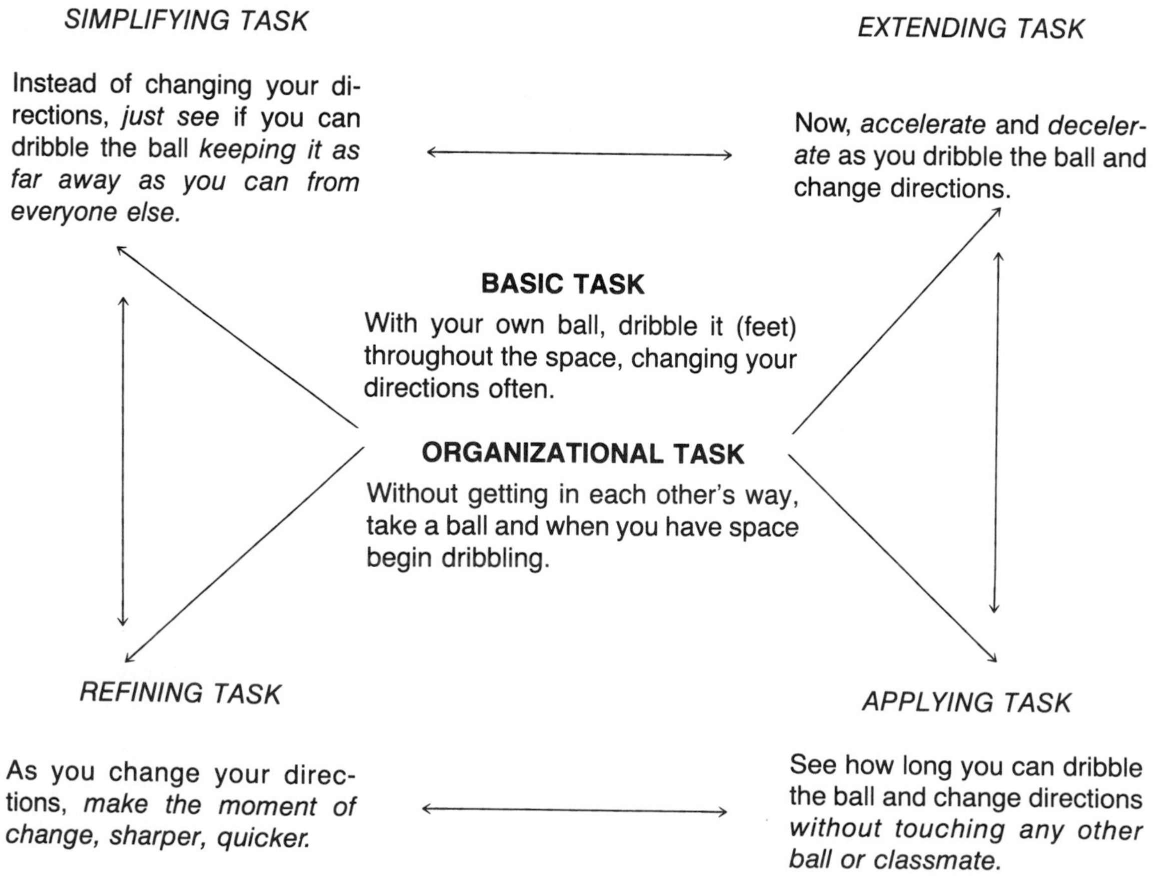

SIMPLIFYING TASK

Instead of changing your directions, *just see* if you can dribble the ball *keeping it as far away as you can from everyone else.*

EXTENDING TASK

Now, *accelerate* and *decelerate* as you dribble the ball and change directions.

BASIC TASK

With your own ball, dribble it (feet) throughout the space, changing your directions often.

ORGANIZATIONAL TASK

Without getting in each other's way, take a ball and when you have space begin dribbling.

REFINING TASK

As you change your directions, *make the moment of change, sharper, quicker.*

APPLYING TASK

See how long you can dribble the ball and change directions *without touching any other ball or classmate.*

Fig. 9–2. Relationship Among Task Types

troductory task given to children when starting a new idea. Other tasks develop from it and in relation to it. A questionable progession would result if you used basic tasks without asking children to extend, simplify, refine, or apply what they were learning. *Extending tasks* are tasks that "extend" the basic task by increasing its difficulty; *simplifying tasks* "simplify" the basic task by decreasing its difficulty. Tasks designed to help children improve some aspect of movement that is a part of the basic task are called *refining tasks*. An *applying task* gives the children an opportunity to use movement skills they have learned in a new situation. Any task designed to influence the way the class is arranged is an *organizational task*. This task is included here because it has been discovered that few teachers have thought about how to observe children "organizing," and it is important they do. Figure 9–2 shows how these task types are related.

Environment. At the top of every observation plan is a box with sections to check, which when completed, describe your situation in terms of whether objects, children, and the teaching environment are "at rest" or "in motion."[3]

Objects refer to all types of equipment: balls, sticks, mats, benches, hoops. When they are *at rest*, they are not moving when children work with them; e.g., mats on the floor, balls placed on a tee, ropes on the floor. When objects are *in motion*, they are moving when children work with them; e.g., thrown, rolled balls; a turned rope; a rolling hoop.

Child refers to the person involved in the class. Children *at rest* are not traveling, not covering space; e.g., tossing and catching a ball "on the spot," striking/hitting a ball off a tee, practicing taking weight on different body parts, rising and sinking without traveling. Children *in motion* are moving through space; e.g., running to catch a ball, traveling on, over, along a bench; meeting, then parting.

Teaching environment refers to what is happening in the space in which the teaching is going on. To decide whether the teaching environment is at rest or in motion you look at where the children are allowed to go. When the environment is *at rest*, the children are working in a designated area, they are not free to use the entire space; e.g., working at dif-

ferent pieces of apparatus or dribbling a ball throughout the entire space.

STEP 4—DECIDING WHAT TO LOOK FOR. This step is both the last and first step before making your observation plan. It is divided into two parts: analysis and selection of critical features.

Part 1: Analysis. Before you can identify what you specifically want to observe, you need to *analyze the movement or movements you wish to teach as well as how the environment might affect the children's ability to respond.* How well you handle this analysis depends on your ability to apply and integrate knowledge synthesized from experiences such as kinesiology, motor learning, motor development, physiology, sport and dance classes, and Laban analysis. A discussion of how to do this is beyond the scope of this chapter, but let this point be made. This analysis is *the turning point* in the process of observation planning, and if you are not confident in doing this, you need to find out why. Everything that follows from this point depends on the *quality* of this analysis. As you gain more knowledge and have more teaching experiences, your ability to analyze the moment(s) and environment should improve.

Part 2: Identification and Selection of Critical Features. The final step before making the decision as to what to look for is identifying what are called *critical features*. These are features or components of the movement and environment that are important to the performance— that when modified or changed affect the outcome of the movement. From your analysis (Part 1), make as complete a list as possible of the critical features you think are important. Because it is impossible to look for all the features at one time, you then select from this list specifically what you want to look for, taking into consideration your objectives for the lesson, the time you have, and the children's ability and experience with the task. When you have arranged the features in an order of priority, the first part of your plan is done. No matter how difficult this seems to you, remember, it is basic to becoming a skilled observer.

The way you actually write down these critical features is up to you. They can be in the form of statements, single words, phrases, or questions. The sample plans here have used the question format that requires you to observe and make an interpretation of what you see. Beginning teachers have found this useful.

STEP 5—DECIDING WHEN/HOW LONG TO OBSERVE. The more experience you have in teaching, the easier this step becomes. (It is difficult to give concrete suggestions because your decisions depend so much on the children's developmental needs.) After you have planned a series of lessons, you will discover your own approach. The approach used in designing the sample plans was guided by a belief that a safe learning environment is a key to a productive one.

The sample plans show this influence by listing as the first features to observe, those directly related to safety. Furthermore, it is usually suggested that they be observed for the entire time the children work with the task. After safety, those features that are considered "critical" to the movement itself are listed and decisions made about when to observe them and for how long. The order for observing is an important consideration, because at first, it is difficult to see more than one or two features at a time. As your skill in observing improves, you will be able to see more features at one time; in fact, you will be able to see how certain movements relate to each other. The latter takes practice, but should be a goal of every teacher. With additional skill also comes the ability to see, and remember, other features not planned for in your original plan.

STEP 6—DECIDING STRATEGIES AND TECHNIQUES FOR OBSERVING. Again, experience is the best teacher. Scanning and focusing are the two techniques suggested. Scanning is usually used for observing the entire class or a group of children when you need to glance from child to child rapidly. You may pick up specific information from individuals, but the purpose is to obtain general or specific information about the group you are observing. Strategies used in scanning vary from observer to observer as perceptual style is unique. Teachers need to discover for themselves the pattern(s) that best allows them to keep the entire group in their view, or under *observational control*.

Focusing is used for observing an individual or small group when you want to obtain detailed information about their progess. Decisions as to where specifically to look are not always easy to

make, but you need to learn to do this. Your understanding of movement and how skill is acquired can provide valuable guidelines. For example, Roberton and Halverson in Chapter 3 point out that, when initially observing for detail, you focus on those components (body parts) that have developmental importance; e.g., the legs in locomotion and the trunk in throwing and striking.

Both techniques are important and should be developed together. With the other parts of the plan well thought through this part is a natural outgrowth.

STEP 7—DECIDING WHERE TO POSITION YOURSELF. Decisions as to where you should position yourself are easy to make, but difficult to act upon—it takes a lot of concentrated practice. Most teachers underestimate the importance of being in a good position for observing and pay little attention to it. Because of this, many teachers find themselves in a poor position to scan the entire class or even to focus on an individual or small group. All teacher/observers should be in a position that allows them *to scan the entire group, "seeing every child," at any time, with the least amount of turning around.* Some suggestions follow that may be of help.

1. Position yourself toward the outside edge of the teaching area (the center is the most difficult place from which to observe).

2. Face the center of the teaching area with your back toward the outside (wall or natural boundary).

3. As you teach/observe, move around and through the children, being guided as to what path to take and how fast to take it by what you are looking for and how well you can see all the children by quick periodic scanning.

4. Bring individual children toward the outside edge of the teaching area if you want to work with them specifically; this will allow you to still scan the entire group without feeling like a human turntable.

5. Use the center of the teaching area sparingly, if at all. It is not a place in which you can afford to get caught, as you cannot observe well from this spot. If you do use it, plan its use so it will not require your physical presence, but rather just your voice.

Deciding where to position yourself should be taken seriously, as it often results in "seeing" or "not seeing." To become skilled takes practice and a strong commitment to "being in the right position at the right time."[6]

Improving Your Ability to Observe and Interpret

One of the most pressing concerns that teachers have is the feeling that they are not taking any steps to improve their observation and interpretation ability. They know of their importance and just hope they will get better with time and experience. This problem is a realistic one and three suggestions follow that may help in beginning to solve it.

TAKE PLANNING TO OBSERVE SERIOUSLY. No matter how you finally approach this task, take it seriously. Do the best job you can. When you plan, you are reviewing all aspects of what is important relative to a given task as well as making specific decisions as to what to look for and possible directions for interpretation. Because of this process, you will understand better what you are teaching and you will "see" more. When you have established an approach that works for you, improvement should be a natural outcome.

TEACH CHILDREN HOW TO OBSERVE AND INTERPRET. Besides being valuable skills for children to learn, teaching them is a wonderful way for you to practice. First, because you will have to evaluate their observations and interpretations, you will tend to concentrate harder. The ability to concentrate and attend to what you are looking at is a characteristic of a more skilled observer. Second, as you will only be looking at one child at a time, or maybe a small group, you have an opportunity to observe and interpret without all the distractions associated with teaching a class of children. The normal distractions in day-to-day teaching often prohibit careful observation and interpretation, especially if you are not that skilled to begin with. As skill improves, it becomes easier to do both without being distracted.

Teaching children to be good observers and interpreters of movement is valuable for many reasons, such as helping them to

1. understand something that is unclear, e.g., what it means to "contact the ball under it," to "concentrate inwardly," or "to counterbalance."

2. appreciate their movement capabilities and those of other children.

3. learn about movement, how it develops, and how this might affect their own progress.

When you teach children how to observe, remember that they have to be in a good position to see and will need help in what specifically to look for. Begin simply, by asking them to focus on one idea at a time; only after they begin to show some skill in observing can you ask them to focus on more than one. For example:

1. For the Beginner: "Look at the body part that Ricky is using and tell me where it is contacting the ball;" and "Is that a good place? Why?" or "Which body part is leading Tommie as he is rising and sinking?" and "How can you tell that a body part is leading and not just being carried?" or "Watch this balance-to-roll sequence that Lenore is practicing and tell me the order of the body parts that take her weight when she rolls," and "Is the roll a safe one? Why?"

2. For the More Advanced: "Observe both Marie and Angie as they dribble the ball with their feet and compare the way both are changing their directions;" or "Observe this group of four as they try to pass the ball ahead of the receiver. Comment on where the ball is being placed when passed and when the receiver moves to ask for it." Because both these questions imply interpretations, help the children observe first, then interpret what they have seen.

"PRACTICE" DURING YOUR LESSON. Besides getting some practice when you help children to observe and interpret, using different organizational patterns offers you additional opportunities. There are times when it is appropriate *not* to have all children participating at the same time. Sometimes, children need more space for responses to a task to be appropriate. At other times, a rest is important, or they are having difficulty staying out of each other's way. At these times, organizing your class so they are not all participating at once will meet the children's needs and give you an opportunity to observe fewer children at one time. Figure 9–3 shows three basic organizational strategies that can be applied to several different situations as well as being varied themselves.

Strategy 1, one half on and one half off, can

1—one half on and one half off

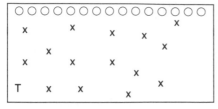

○ = children waiting out of the way
x = children actively participating
T = teacher
Procedures: as soon as the Xs have had ample opportunity to work, they move to the empty side of the space and the ○s move into the open space. Change often and quickly.

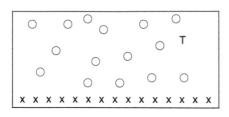

2—one half up and one half down

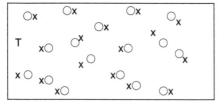

○ = children waiting (seated on the floor/ground)
x = children actively participating
T = teacher
Procedures: as soon as the Xs have had ample opportunity to work, they sit down and the ○s begin working. Make sure those who are seated are evenly spaced out over the teaching area.

3—Snowball

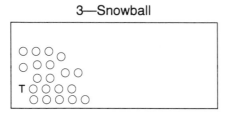

○ = children waiting to begin working
T = teacher
Procedures: when designated, each child goes into the space, begins working. The number of children slowly increases until all are working.

Fig. 9–3. Basic Organizational Strategies.

be used in any situation where the need for space is apparent. Little time is wasted in changing positions because the children do not pass through each other's groups.

Strategy 2, one half up and one half down, is not appropriate for all situations. To be an appropriate strategy to use, the task itself or the skill level of the children must not need much space. This strategy is particularly useful when children are working with a task that does not require traveling.

Strategy 3, slowly adding children, is fun for the children and they love doing it, and you can really practice observing. You do not want to

use it often, because of the three strategies given, this one affords the child the least amount of active participation. This strategy is useful when children are having difficulties staying out of each other's way when working. As the group size increases, you can stop it at any size and talk to both groups: the "observers" with you and the "doers" out in the space. Be sure to change the order of children each time you use it, however; its effectiveness will lessen if the children are always in the same order.

If you are having difficulty in observing some aspect of the children's work, this strategy is appropriate, because you can see each child, one at a time, in quick succession, rather than all together. You do not want to use it for this purpose too often as it does cut down on the children's participation time.

All these strategies can be used equally well with games, dance, and gymnastics, and all can be varied according to individual needs. For example, the snowball strategy could be used with groups as well as with individual children. Instead of the children working one at a time, you would start the groups one at a time.

So that valuable time is not lost, the children should learn how to organize themselves into these patterns. Once they know how to do them, little time is taken when they are used.

THE TEACHER AS (OBSERVER, INTERPRETER) DECISION-MAKER

Teachers must be able to decide what to do after they have interpreted their observations; thus the idea of the *teacher as decision-maker*. When teaching, teachers have to make decisions constantly as well as quickly. To develop confidence in making these decisions, and confidence in the decisions, teachers must be guided by a set of beliefs about physical education, children, and teaching, *together with* their ability to observe and interpret. Chapter 2, Physical Education—A Design for Direction, states the set of beliefs to which this program is committed and discusses its relation to teaching. A review of this chapter will show that the approach taken in this book views

CHILDREN as:
 individuals,
 total persons,
 potential decision-makers and independent learners, having a right to learn how to move in a way that fosters
intellectual and affective growth and a positive self-concept; and

PHYSICAL EDUCATION as:
 learning to move skillfully,
 being aware of the meaning, significance, and joy
of movement, and
 understanding mechanical principles that govern
skillful movement.

It is within this philosophical commitment that the idea of the teacher as decision-maker will be viewed.

It would be naive to think that all decisions that teachers have to make could be identified and then in some way "taught." Because this is neither possible nor desirable, certain "critical" decisions that teachers have to make have been selected for discussion. They have been selected because they are considered "critical." These decisions are related to designing tasks, presenting tasks, reacting to children's responses, and creating an environment for learning.

Task Design

The basic component of the physical education lesson is "the task." A task is what we ask children to do. It indicates the content to be developed and the type of response expected from the children, movement or organizational. Throughout each lesson, teachers are constantly making decisions about what tasks to give children (or a child)—specifically, what to say and how to say it. What this means is that teachers must be adept at designing tasks *on the spot* and *in relation to the immediate situation*. If teachers have made careful lesson and observation plans, this job is made easier. Before this can be done easily and with confidence, certain key ideas about task design need to be understood: tasks have purposes, tasks have content, and tasks have structure.

TASKS HAVE PURPOSE

To review, tasks are of two types, movement and organizational, with movement tasks being designed for five different purposes:
 to introduce content (basic task),
 to extend or elaborate content (extending task),
 to simplify content (simplifying task),
 to refine or practice content (refining task), and
 to use or apply content in different situations (applying task).

To check your understanding of this idea, study the tasks listed below and identify, where appropriate, their type and purpose.

	TYPE	PURPOSE
a. "As you roll out of your balance, curl your body more."	a _____	a _____
b. "Carefully put your equipment away."	b _____	b _____
c. "Let's begin something new. Take a partner and begin tossing to each other, so catching must be done in the air."	c _____	c _____
d. "Practice the part of your dance where all four of you are rising and sinking together. See whether you can make all movements appear as one."	d _____	d _____
e. "Now let's make this harder. This time use all your upper body parts."	e _____	e _____
f. "Using the two effort actions of thrusting and floating, design a short sequence to emphasize their differences."	f _____	f _____
g. "Change your group size from four to two, this should help make this easier. Also, let's only work with jumps and rolls, not balances as well."	g _____	g _____

Answers: (a) movement/refining; (b) organizational/—; (c) organizational/—; (d) movement/basic; (e) movement/extending; (f) movement/applying; (g) organization/—; movement/refining; ment/simplifying.

One might ask at this point, since this is the third time in this chapter that the concept of task purpose has been discussed, why is this idea so important? It is important because when you are able to identify the purposes of tasks, you can then monitor how you are developing your content, in other words, your "progression." The effectiveness of your progession is a direct result of the tasks used and in what order—*over time.* No research has specifically addressed this idea of order and purpose, but based on what we know about children and how they learn physical skills, we should be able to evaluate some combinations as to their potential for effective progression. React to these combinations of tasks and discuss the reasons for your reaction:

> basic, simplifying, extending
> basic, extending, refining
> refining, applying, basic
> basic, applying
> extending, simplifying, applying
> simplifying, basic, extending

TASKS HAVE CONTENT

In addition to tasks having purposes, tasks have content or substance, which needs to be clearly identifiable. In this text, the content of physical education has been identified as movement, with each program area deriving its "own" content by applying Laban's analysis of movement to its uniqueness. The specific content and a suggested progression (the themes) are fully explained in Chapters 6, 7, and 8, so they will not be further discussed here. It is important for our purposes, however, to be able to recognize from the written or spoken task what the content is. Tasks should be designed so the content is *clearly* stated, leaving no doubt as to the material with which the children will be or are working. Recording the content used over time, what it was and how it was sequenced, is another way for teachers to examine their own progression. How much content to include per task is not a question that can be answered without knowing the specific situation. From what we know about how children learn physical skills, however, good advice would be to keep tasks fairly simple in design by focusing on one or two key ideas, adding others only in rare instances.

Consciously being aware of the specific content focus of a task helps teachers state tasks more clearly when teaching. From a number of "teacher behavior" studies it has been found that teachers have *extreme difficulty* in saying clearly what they want the children to do. Their statements are often too long and poorly sequenced. To say the least, they have definitely challenged the researchers. Being able to identify content in both written and verbal situations should help teachers begin to improve their own ability to direct the children. Discuss with someone what you think is the key (movement) content in the following tasks.

1. Develop a short sequence that uses three different methods of weight transference and a change in direction (applying task).

2. This time, still in your group of three, pass the ball among yourselves, always making the receiver jump to catch it (extending task).

3. Travel throughout the space by skipping, turning, and spinning (basic task).

"Answers:" (1) weight transference, directions; (2) passing in relation to a player, jumping; (3) skipping, spinning, turning.

TASKS HAVE STRUCTURE

One of the beliefs that guides this approach to physical education is that children are capable of making decisions about what they learn and how they learn. This implies that both the teacher and the child must be considered as potential decision-makers and that both will have responsibility for significant decisions, decisions that will affect the direction of learning. These decisions, the type and amount, are identified when you analyze the structure of the task. To analyze the structure of the task you have to do two things: (a) identify its "degree of openness" and place it on the teacher behavior continuum and (b) identify the specific decisions and whose responsibility it is to make them by studying the task itself.

Figure 9–4 illustrates the teacher behavior continuum, which indicates the opportunity available to the teacher and child for making decisions relative to content and the learning process.[7]

One end of the continuum is represented by minimum opportunity for the child (the teacher's role in decision-making is predominant); the other end represents maximum opportunity for the child (the child's role in decision-making is predominant).

You will notice that on this continuum there is no labeling or categorizing of teaching patterns, as this would give the impression of a prescription to follow. The ability to react to the emerging situation, a skill necessary to accommodate individual needs and differences of children, is often lost if teaching is thought of as discrete and specific patterns of behavior.

The two examples that follow (Figures 9–5 and 9–6) illustrate the idea of analyzing the structure of a task; understanding them should help you analyze your own tasks as you design them.

To test your understanding of the task structure concept, place the following tasks on the teacher behavior continuum (Fig. 9–7) and analyze their degree of openness in the space on the right.

Minimum opportunity for child to make decisions regarding content and the learning process	←——— TEACHER BEHAVIOR CONTINUUM ———→	Maximum opportunity for child to make decisions regarding content and the learning process

Fig. 9–4. Opportunity Available for Making Decisions Relative to Content and the Learning Process.

EXAMPLE 1

Teacher's Behavior (Tasks)	Analysis
"As you travel throughout the room, change your direction often." (Basic task)	The structure is considered fairly open as the learner has many decisions to make—the way to travel, the directions to travel as well as the moment to change them.
"Now, as you travel, use only your feet, but keep changing direction." (Simplifying task)	The structure is not quite so open; the limitation of using only feet is responsible for this change. The learner has decisions only regarding directions—when and which ones to make.
"Still using your feet, travel first in a forward direction, then backward, then to the right, left, and then repeat from the beginning. Use a quick running action." (Extending task)	The structure is considered tight or closed, with few or no learner decisions regarding either content or the learning process. Figure 9–5 illustrates this pattern. This teaching episode would be described as allowing the child *many* decisions, then *fewer*, and finally even *less*.

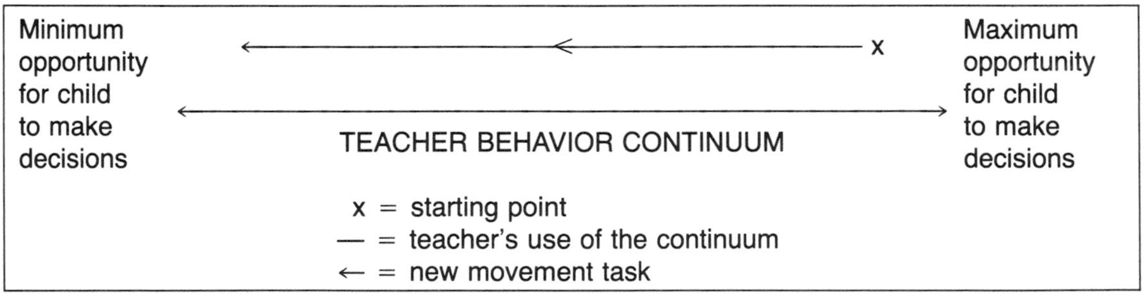

Minimum opportunity for child to make decisions	← ──────────── ← ──────────── x	Maximum opportunity for child to make decisions
	TEACHER BEHAVIOR CONTINUUM	

x = starting point
— = teacher's use of the continuum
← = new movement task

Fig. 9–5. Teacher Behavior Pattern For Example 1.

EXAMPLE 2

"In groups of four, use the Swedish box and the four accompanying mats arranged as you wish, always being careful of each other." (Basic task)

The structure is open, as the only decision the learners did not make was related to the equipment. This type of situation may not always result in productive work by the learners because it is so open—the learners may not know what decisions there are to make. It sometimes results in stereotypic movements.

"For a moment, let's change what we are doing. Keep the same groups and the same equipment, but use them only one at a time. Run, land on the top with only your feet touching, jump with a full stretch, and land softly, letting your body weight be absorbed into a roll." (Simplifying task)

The structure has altered considerably, with few decisions available to the learner. They could arrive on the box facing different directions as well as dismounting with varied stretched shapes. Unless the learners have had considerable experience with using different equipment, or in changing the shape of their body, these variations in responses are not likely to occur, basically because the children are unaware of these decisions. If the teacher observes that the learners are not using the options, he may have to make that clear in the directions he gives them.

"Continue what you are doing, but try to use different directions when mounting and dismounting; if you can, vary your shapes more while in the air." (Extending task)

The learners know specifically what types and how many decisions they have. The structure of this task is still fairly closed, but with the addition of decisions involving directions and shapes, it is beginning to "open." Figure 9–6 illustrates this pattern. This teaching episode would be described as allowing the children many decisions, then very *few*, then a *few more*.

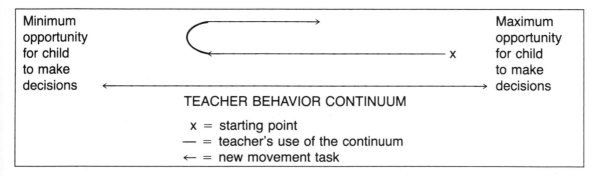

Fig. 9–6. Teacher Behavior Pattern For Example 2.

To test your understanding of the task structure concept, place the following tasks on the teacher behavior continuum (Fig. 9–7) and analyze their degree of openness in the space on the right.

Teacher's Behavior (Tasks)	Analysis
"As you strike the ball with different parts of your body, vary the force you are using." (Basic task)	
"Now, select two body parts with which you feel comfortable and see if you can keep the ball off the floor." (Refining task)	
"With two other children, see how long you can keep the ball going without its touching the floor. You may use all body parts." (Applying task)	

Minimum
opportunity
for child   ←——————————————————→   Maximum
to make   TEACHER BEHAVIOR CONTINUUM   opportunity
decisions   for child
                                                                                         to make
                                                                                         decisions

x = starting point
— = teacher's use of the continuum
— = new movement task

Fig. 9–7. Teacher Behavior Pattern.

This section on the teacher as decision-maker has been specific and detailed in its discussion of the task and its design. This was done deliberately because the task is considered the central component of the lesson and gaining insight into it is critical. To design a task requires synthesizing this information in relation to a particular situation. When designing you own tasks remember: think about their PURPOSE, think about their CONTENT, and think about their STRUCTURE. It is getting the "right" purpose with the "right" content with the "right amount" of structure that results in an appropriate task. The many sample tasks throughout Chapters 6, 7, and 8 can serve as examples.

Task Presentation

Designing a task is one thing, presenting it is another. At first, this might seem to be "splitting hairs;" but focusing on how tasks are presented often alerts you to situations that might ordi-

narily be overlooked. For instance, there are times when the task is considered appropriate for many of the children, but not all; how do you present it? Is there a difference in presenting tasks to individual children as opposed to a total group? What about a complex task, such as a game or game-like task or a gymnastic or dance sequence; how do you present them?

HELP CHILDREN SELECT APPROPRIATE TASK. All tasks should be designed so they allow for children's individual needs and differences. This is accomplished by paying attention to the task's *structure*, a topic just discussed. Sometimes, however, the task as designed, even though its structure allows for individual differences, may still be too hard for some children. In this case, it is the *way you present* the task, that can help the situation. When you are presenting a task that you believe is too difficult for some of the children, begin with a phrase that gives them a choice of whether to attempt it or not. Here are several suggestions:

1. "Some of you may like to try the next task, others may wish to wait awhile. . ."

2. "For those who think they would like to try a harder task. . ."

3. "If you think you would like to try this task. . ."

In all situations, you want to make it clear that the children could continue working on the previous task. It is also possible to give two tasks (if they are *clear* and *short* and the difference in complexity is obvious) and let the children select between them. The latter idea is only appropriate for self-directed children.

MAKE TASKS DESIGNED FOR INDIVIDUAL CHILDREN SHORT. In an approach to physical education that is committed to individual differences, giving separate tasks to individual children or small groups is to be expected. Tasks to individual children are usually given "on-the-run." You observe a child who needs to be challenged more or challenged less and you want to help. Think before you speak. Design the task in your mind first and mentally phrase it, shaping it into something short and clear; then say it to the child. For example, the class has been working on taking their weight on different parts of their bodies while in an inverted position. You see a child you think needs a simpler task, and you say: "Bill, let's try taking your weight on different body parts, but stay upright" (simplifying task).

All types of tasks should be appropriate, their selection being based on the immediate needs of the situation. You want to be "quick, short, and clear" because as a teacher of 30 children you cannot afford, in most situations, to take your eyes off of the group for any length of time. Do remember, too, when giving a task to an individual child or small group, to keep observing the rest of the class.

GIVE ONLY PART OF THE TASK AT A TIME IF COMPLEX. Because tasks can vary so in their form, some tasks are by their nature more difficult to present. In this category fall such tasks as a game, a game-like task, a dance sequence, a dance, or a gymnastic sequence. The key to presenting these types of tasks is to "present" them in parts, not all at one time. The basic principle you want to follow is to give the children only what they need to get started; then, add the rest as needed. It is a bit like cooking.

Let us use as an example a task that is a dance sequence (an applying task).

Task. In groups of four to six, design a short sequence that begins with the group tightly clustered together, then rising and sinking as a group, followed by thrusting and slashing and moving out into the nearby space. The sequence ends with all children, one after the other, returning to their starting positions, using floating and gliding.

"Presenting" the Task. A task of this nature should be presented over a period of time, *throughout* which the children will be moving (not listening to a full explanation). Here is one possible approach that can be adapted to all tasks similar in nature.

1. Tell the children they will be developing a short dance sequence in groups of four to six.

2. Have them get in their groups and sit down close together (remember, *you* know the task and it begins with the children together).

3. "Walk them through" the basic sequence. This means, start them in a close group shape, have them rise and sink (no concern for refinement yet), separate away from group (no mention yet of thrusting and slashing), bring them back in one at a time (no mention yet of floating and gliding). Have them repeat this a few times so they become truly familiar with it.

4. "Walk them through" it again, but this time, adding the effort actions of thrusting, slashing, floating, and gliding in the appropriate places. (Emphasis on starting and finishing positions can come later.)

5. Have them begin to work with the task—it has now been presented.

As the children begin working in earnest, you will need to individualize your work with them. In many instances, you will be designing additional tasks on the spot that reflect the needs of the group or specific individuals. Most tasks should be for refining purposes, for you would not have designed this task if the content within it was not familiar to the children.

Reacting to Children's Responses

Up to this point, the decisions we have been talking about have focused on the task. The point was made that the task is the central component of a lesson and serves specific purposes, has an identifiable structure, and is often difficult to present when complex. Some tasks are designed ahead of time, some tasks are designed during the lesson itself; but other than the first task of the lesson, tasks are most often presented *in reaction* to something the children did. In fact, teachers spend a large majority of their teaching time "reacting."[8] Reacting, then, is a concept that needs some discussion because what teachers say to children and how they say it affects their growth in our classrooms.

WHAT WE SAY

As teachers, we are reacting to what children are doing all the time. Mainly through some of the recent research in teaching physical education, we are becoming aware of several different ways this is done. As a behavior, Anderson says "reacting" usually involved accepting, rejecting, modifying, or expanding what a child is doing.[9] (Many of the modifying and extending behaviors will take the form of our extending, simplifying, refining, and applying tasks already discussed.)

Obviously, one cannot go into much detail about every behavior that might occur when reacting to children's responses, but several general reactions can be discussed so at least we might become aware of them in our own teaching. (The discussion that follows has been influenced by Anderson's Clinical Task-17 Teachers' Reactions to Students and the Fishman Category System for Augmented Feedback.[9])

When we, as teachers, react to children, some general characteristics about these reactions are important to recognize. They are global in nature, but serve as an orientation to the idea. Answer for yourself the following:

How much do you react? Do you think it is enough, too little, too much?

Are your reactions positive, negative, or mixed? Do you know? Can you recognize the difference?

Do you repeat yourself or do you use varied vocabulary? Do you have any verbal "habits" in the way you react?

Are your reactions personal or impersonal? Do you know and call the children by name when reacting to them?

What do your answers tell you, can you answer them from memory? Most research is telling us that we need to make an audio or video tape or have an outside person help us to answer these questions initially.

As this approach to physical education is committed to helping all children become as skillful as they can, it should interest us particularly to become aware of what we say that is a reaction specific to the way children move. In other words, what "feedback" do we give children about their movement responses? Is it POSITIVE, NEGATIVE, GENERAL, SPECIFIC, TEACHER INITIATED, or CHILD REQUESTED?

Positive/general: "That's a good move, Charlie."

Positive/specific: "Melissa, the firm stretched shape of your arms and legs is just what I meant."

Positive/specific/child: "Melissa, I liked what I saw, do you know what you did well this time?"

Negative/general: "Bob, that's not smart!"

Negative/specific: "Marie, the way you landed from that jump was too heavy; you did not bend your hips, knees, or ankles, enough."

Negative/specific/child: "Marie, maybe you could tell me what did not work quite right for you during this jump."

Two basic guidelines are suggested here in relation to this concept. The first is to balance positive and negative feedback, but work on being specific. If children do not know what to work on, how can they improve? The second guideline is obvious: whenever possible, have the children think about how they are responding rather than have you always take the responsibility. This way, you can help them understand movement, particularly theirs, as well as help them take some responsibility for the direction of their learning.

Besides the type of feedback given, it is also important to know TO WHOM IT IS GIVEN: to individuals, to small groups, to an entire class; IN WHAT FORM IT IS GIVEN: verbal, nonverbal, both; and WHEN IT IS GIVEN: while the child(ren) is moving, right after the child(ren) has completed the task, much later?

It is often asked when discussing decisions

made in relation to the above "How do you individualize to a group?" and "Do you ever demonstrate?" In response to the first question, individualizing does not mean working with only one child. It means designing tasks and reactions so the needs of all children can be accommodated. This is why understanding the concept "structure of the task" is so important. You "individualize" to a group of children in the same way you do to an individual; recognizing, however, that it is more difficult to do with a group. This is another reason why skillful observation and interpretation is so important; skill in seeing what is happening in a group is a prerequisite to designing tasks that can be individualized.

When physical educators began using methodologies that encouraged children to think about what they were doing, they thought this meant you were not to use demonstrations. Demonstrations for the purpose of showing "the right way" to do something have little place philosophically; but demonstrations that are *designed* to help children understand movement certainly are a valuable form of feedback. They need to be designed for that purpose. Then, when used, the children must be guided in their observations. Helpful guidelines for this were given earlier when teaching children how to observe was discussed.

HOW WE SAY IT, TO WHOM, AND WHY

Besides being interested in whether we give feedback to individuals or to groups, Martinek, Crowe, and Rejeski have become interested in the *characteristics* of the individuals or groups to whom we give our attention and how they may affect our teaching; for example, do you teach children you perceive as high, low, or averaged skilled differently; boys, girls, white, black? Do you know? The reason these physical educators are interested in these questions is that they believe that as teachers we hold "expectations" about the children's achievement and social behavior, and these influence the way we behave and the way children respond. It is the characteristics of the children, they say, that help form these expectations and influence our teaching behavior.[11]

An important link to make here is between this concept of "teacher expectancies"[11] and the need to learn how to observe objectively and to interpret from a sound knowledge base. Because, as teachers, we often let our biases (nonobjective observations) influence what we see and how we interpret. Biases are a potential source for how our expectations about chidren's achievement and social behavior are formed. Martinek, et al. suggest three in particular: somatotype, physical attractiveness, and sex.[11]

The implication here is that teachers need to develop an awareness of the type of expectations they hold for different children and the ways these expectations might be influencing their behavior. By suggesting this, however, we are not trying to change the positive outcomes achieved by children whom we expect to do well and who do; but rather, to help those children who in physical education may not be reaching their potential because of the expectations teachers may hold. As this approach to physical education is committed to helping *all* children reach their potential in movement and accommodating their individual differences, it is critical that we become aware of this and, if changes need to be made, to make them.

Creating an Environment for Learning

A commitment to helping all children reach their potential for movement is a commitment to creating an environment that OPTIMIZES LEARNING. Children cannot learn how to move unless this occurs. For this to happen children must be safe, on task successfully, challenged, and confident.

BEING SAFE. When children are expected to gain skill in gymnastics, dance, or game settings, they must feel safe and be safe. Children feel and are safe when they themselves, their classmates, and their teacher demonstrate concern for safety. A physical education class is no place for unsafe behavior from the children or from the practices of teachers. A few reminders might be helpful.

1. Sharpen your observation skills so you can *anticipate* unsafe behavior and situations before they happen.

2. Be sure there is enough space if speed is part of the task requirements—space that can be used safely and productively. Always have ample "spillover" space for all tasks that need it.

3. Involve the children in making safety decisions for themselves and for the group; be sure they know the "why" behind them; discuss the concept of risk-taking, an inherent part of physical education and related to safety.

BEING (SUCCESSFULLY) ON TASK. Much is being written and researched now about on-task behavior, active time, or motor-engaged time.[10] These phrases mean more than children just being "on task," "active," or "participating." They mean being *successful* while being *on task* and *active*. To judge whether children are being successful has always been a responsibility of teachers, but it takes keen observation and interpretation ability, because "being successful" may be different for different children. As you get to know the children, this task becomes easier.

The importance of being successful while on task is certainly not a new idea, but over the past several years, we may have become too captivated by the idea of *maximum* participation rather than optimal or successful participation—there is a difference.

Creating an environment that optimizes participation requires strong organizational abilities. Every time you teach a task, the organizational patterns used must optimize the children's participation. This involves considering the following:

1. The number of children moving at once—*all* children cannot be expected to move *all* of the time for every type of task.

2. The way children are spaced and faced—having all children scattered for every type of task is not effective.

3. The way they are grouped—for skillful movement to be an outcome, children will have to be grouped in a number of different ways. It is suggested that, in whatever way the children are grouped, they should know the criteria, why it was done that way and what is expected of them. For example, in a mixed ability level grouping the children should know that

1. The group was designed to mix the more experienced with the less experienced.

2. Both groups have a responsibility and goal: the more experienced to relate their movements to the movements of the less experienced, and the less experienced to take advantage of the help (not to hold back, the more experienced).

3. In gymnastics, dance, games, and other school activities, they will need to work in groups with differing experience levels—it is a valuable skill to learn.

BEING CHALLENGED. When you design tasks that vary in the degree of openness, thus allowing children to make some decisions about how they will perform, be aware that they are challenging themselves. Are they extending themselves, pushing themselves? Tasks with different degrees of openness encourage children to individualize their responses but can, if the responsibility for self-challenge is not fully taken, hold them back. Be alert to this possibility and discuss it with the children. They love to challenge themselves and to be challenged, but they do not always know how to do it—alone.

BEING CONFIDENT. Children need to approach learning with confidence and feeling good about themselves in the physical education class. This is not a new idea, we all know the effects of this. When children are confident and feel good about themselves, it gives them courage to try something a bit harder, something less familiar, without the "fear of failure." Central to this approach is a willingness to experiment, to explore, to inquire, all important to learning, but children must be confident entering the unknown. Making a "mistake" (if this is possible from a developmental perspective) should be seen as important to learning, not something to shy away from. An environment that OPTIMIZES LEARNING "tells" the children just this.

Analyzing Your Own Teaching Behavior

Within the last several years, teachers have become more interested and more at ease with the idea of describing and analyzing the way they teach. This is being done in several different ways, informal to formal, and covering many aspects of teaching. The major purpose of most "observation tools," as they are called, is to describe what a teacher actually does when teaching. The tool(s) is selected because it focuses on behavior the teacher wants described. The basic reason for using these tools is to become aware of what you do, so if you wish to change it, you have a base from which to start.

The six tools that follow have been designed to reflect verbal behaviors considered important to the approach to physical education presented in this text. Some tools require an outside person

Tool 1: Location and Facing of the Teacher[12]

Purpose: To describe where teachers move and position themselves in relation to the class when teaching.

Directions: In the boxes provided, chart the pattern of movement taken by the teacher as he/she moves throughout the space. Use one continuous line in charting the teacher's path; place an arrow (→) in the direction the teacher is observing. If the teacher moves into a position where some of the class are out of view, place a check (✔) in the appropriate places. Place an X where the teacher is at the moment you begin to record.

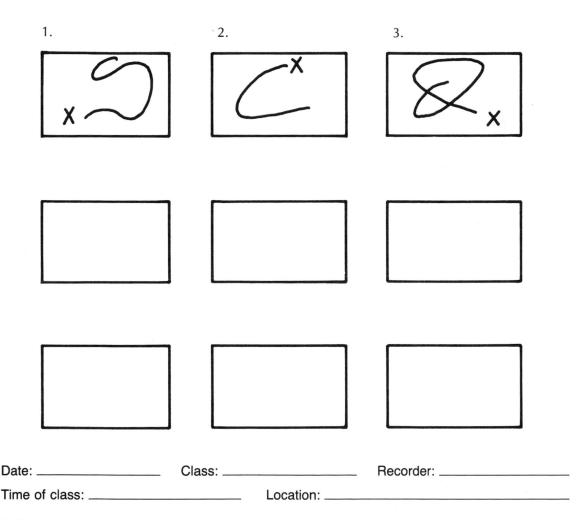

1.

2.

3.

Date: _____ Class: _____ Recorder: _____

Time of class: _____ Location: _____

Follow-up Questions:

1. In what areas of the space did you spend most of your time? Do you know why?
2. Did the physical arrangement of the space have any effect on where you moved? If so, in what way(s)?
3. Did the way you positioned yourself have any affect on the group? Why?
4. Could you observe the class equally well from all positions?
5. What would change, what would you repeat? Why?

Tool 2: Focus of Teacher's Verbal Behavior[12]

Purpose: To identify to whom teacher's verbal behavior was given.

Directions: In each of the columns provided, indicate every 3 seconds to whom the teacher is talking: C = all children in the class; G = a group of children; and I = an individual child.

1	2	3	4	5	6	7	8
C							
C							
C							
C							
C							
C							
I							
I							
C							
C							
C							
I							
G							
C							

Date: _____ Class: _____ Recorder: _____

Time of class: _____ Location: _____

Follow-up Questions:

1. To whom did you direct your verbal behavior? Do you know why?
2. Would you make any changes? Why?

Variations by Adding Subscripts

Indicate: —task (t) or feedback (f) adding subscript, i.e., C_t, C_t, C_f.
　　　　　—different children by adding subscript I_1, I_2, I_3.
　　　　　—sex of child by adding subscript I_b, I_g.

Design additional subscripts relevant to your personal interests.

Tool 3: Type of Task

Purpose: To identify the types of tasks used during a lesson.

Directions: Listen to an audio tape of your lesson, and in the space provided, write down the tasks presented during the lesson. After completing the list, identify the types used.

TASKS	ANALYSIS
1. Dribble the ball, using all parts of your feet.	movement, basic
2. Now, change directions.	movement, extend
3. Still changing directions, try to accelerate and decelerate.	movement, extend
4. Let us go back a bit: keep using all parts of your feet, but only work on acceleration and deceleration.	movement, simplify
5. Better; now, make the acceleration sharper.	movement, refine
6. Put your balls away and come over here.	organizational

Date: _____   Class: _____   Recorder: _____

Time of class: _____   Location: _____

Follow-up Questions:

1. Did you use one type of task more than another? If you did, why; if not, why not?
2. Do you have any pattern to the sequence of tasks used? Would you change it, why; why not?

Tool 4: Content of Task

Purpose: To identify the content of the lesson by analyzing the tasks.

Directions: Listen to an audio tape of your lesson, and in the space provided, write down the tasks presented during the lesson. After completing the list, identify the content of the lesson by analyzing each task.

TASK	ANALYSIS OF CONTENT
1. Travel, contrasting sudden movement with sustained, using all available space.	*Body:* total body (implied), traveling as an activity *Space:* general *Effort:* time: sudden/sustained *Relationship:*
2. Now, as you travel, see whether you can use more individual body parts: elbows, knees, feet, for example.	*Body:* same, with addition of body parts *Space:* Same as *Effort:* for *Relationship:* Task 1
3. Take a partner, and working with the same idea, try to copy each other's movements.	*Body:* Same as *Space:* for *Effort:* Task 2 *Relationship:* copying each other's movement.

Date: _____   Class: _____   Recorder: _____

Time of class: _____   Location: _____

Follow-up Questions:

1. Did the content relate to your objectives?
2. Is there anything in this analysis that surprised you? If so, why did it?

Tool 5: Structure of the Task

Purpose: To describe the position of decision-making responsibility of both the children and the teacher.

Directions: Listen to an audio tape of your lesson, and in the space provided, write down the tasks presented during the lesson. Draw a line after five tasks. For each of the four tasks, draw your pattern of behavior using the teacher behavior continuum. Use an X to indicate the tasks and arrow heads (>) to indicate their sequence.

TASKS	PATTERN OF DECISION-MAKING
1. Find different parts of your body on which you can take your weight.	
2. Now, take your weight on just your shoulders and find different ways to get to your feet.	
3. Start with weight on two hands and one foot; shift to your hips; shift to your hands, head, and one foot.	Minimum opportunity ⟶ ⟵ X Maximum opportunity
4. Now go back to the first task, use different body parts on which to take your weight.	

Date: _____　Class: _____　Recorder: _____

Time of class: _____　Location: _____

Follow-up Questions:

1. Was the "structure" of the task appropriate for your objectives?
2. What other "structure" could you have used?

Tool 6: Dyadic Interactions

Part I: Identification of dyadic interactions. (Interaction between the teacher and one child.)

Purpose: To identify the specific child with whom the teacher interacts.

Directions: In the columns provided, every 3 seconds, write down in order the names of the children with whom the teacher is working: speaks, touches, points, etc. (This may be done by a child who knows the names of all the children in the class or by the teacher listening to an audio tape of the lesson. If the latter is used, the teacher *must* use the children's names when working with them.)

Names	Names	Names	Names
Tom	Dan	Dick	Doris
Pat	Pat	Betsy	Charlie
Walter	Charlie	Bunny	Melissa
Tom	Charlie	Tom	Tom
Bob	Rosemary	Pat	Bil
Sally	Jerry	Walter	Bill
Tom	Pat	Walter	Walter
Melissa	Tom	Marie	Dick
Lynne	Bill	Gail	
Tom	Doris	Betsy	
Marie	Jan	Jim	
	Dick	Jim	

Time: _____ Class: _____ Recorder: _____

Date: _____ Location: _____

Part II: Perceived skill level of children.

Purpose: To identify those children whom the teacher *perceives* to be high skilled, average skilled, low skilled.

Direction: Mark next to a class list those children whom you perceive to be high skilled, average skilled, and low skilled. For example:

Class List
Ms. Price/3rd grade
_____

Patricia Crowe (A)
Thomas Martinek (H)
Walter Rejeski (H)

Part III: Analysis

Directions: After completion of Part I and Part II, use the information recorded to fill out (a) the tabulation chart and (b) the summary chart.

Tabulation Chart

Total Dyadic Interactions	Girls	Boys	High	Average	Low
43	19	24	24	11	8

Summary Chart

Total Dyadic Interactions	% of Total Dyadic Interactions				
	Girls	Boys	High	Average	Low
43	44%	56%	56%	26%	18%

1. What is your reaction to this information? Were you surprised?
2. Based on this information, would you like to make any changes? If so, what changes?

to make the initial recordings, and others do not; you can make the necessary recordings by listening to an audio tape of your lesson. An inexpensive minicassette recorder with a mike worn on your person serves nicely. The tools needing a person other than yourself have been designed so upper elementary children can use them with minimum instruction and practice. Each tool presented includes purpose, directions for use, a recording sheet partially filled out, and follow-up questions to ask yourself. These tools are considered examples and you are encouraged to design your own or use others appropriate to your needs. Anderson's book *Analysis of Teaching Physical Education* has a broad selection of tools covering many aspects of teaching.[9]

Describing and analyzing your teaching behavior is something to consider seriously. The insight gained is well worth the time and energy spent. Do not be surprised, however, if, when you begin, you find out you are doing things you *know you do not do!* It happens to us all, and you have to begin somewhere.

REFERENCES

1. Barrett, K.R.: Personal interviews with Leroy T. Walker and Ellen Griffin, July 1980.
2. Adapted from Rink, J.E.: Observation System for Content Development Physical Education—Manual. The University of South Carolina, Columbia, 1979.
3. Robb, M.D.: The Dynamics of Motor Skill Acquisition. Englewood Cliffs, N.J., Prentice-Hall, 1972; Singer, R.N.: Motor Learning and Human Performance, 3rd ed. New York, Macmillan Publishing Co., 1980; Stallings, L.M.: Motor Learning from Theory to Practice. St. Louis, Missouri, C.V. Mosby Company, 1982.
4. Arend, S., and Higgins, J.R.: A strategy for classification, subjective analysis, and observation of movement. Journal of Human Movement Studies, 2:36, 1976.
5. Adapted from handouts in PE 354—Teaching Elementary School Physical Education, a Junior Physical Education Major Course, The University of North Carolina at Greensboro, 1982.
6. Barrett, K.R.: Observation for teaching and coaching. JOPER, 50(1):23, 1979.
7. Barrett, K.R.: I wish I could fly—a philosophy in motion. In Contemporary Philosophers in Physical Education and Athletics. Edited by P. Lepley and R.A. Cobb. Columbus, Ohio, Charles E. Merrill, 1973.
8. Morgenegg, B.L.: Pedagogical moves. In What's Going On In The Gym. Edited by W.G. Anderson, and G.T. Barrette. Motor Skills Theory Into Practice, Monograph 1:63, 1978.
9. Anderson, W.G.: Analysis of Teaching Physical Education. St. Louis, Missouri, C.V. Mosby Company, 1980.
10. Siedentop, D., Tousignant, M., and Parker, M.: Academic Learning Time—Physical Education Coding Manual, Revised. School of Health, Physical Education and Recreation, The Ohio State University, 1982.
11. Martinek, T.J., Crowe, P.B., and Rejeski, W.J.: Pygmalion in the Gym: Causes and Effects of Expectations in Teaching and Coaching. West Point, New York, Leisure Press, 1982.
12. Adapted from an observation tool used in PER 332/The Teaching Learning Process, Bowling Green State University, Bowling Green, Ohio.

SELECTED READINGS

Barrett, K.R.: Studying teaching—becoming a more effective teacher. In Physical Education for Children—A Focus on the Teaching Process. B.J. Logsdon, et al. Philadelphia, Lea & Febiger, 1977.

Barrett, K.R.: Observing for teaching and coaching. JOPER, 50(1):23, 1979.

Brown, E.W.: Visual evaluation techniques for skill analysis. JOPER, 53(1):21, 1982.

Davis, J.: Learning to see: training in observation of movement. JOPER, 51(1):89, 1980.

Hutslar, S.: The expectancy phenomenon. JOPERD, 52(7):88, 1981.

Mauldon, E., and Layson, J.: Movement observation. In Teaching Gymnastics, 2nd ed. London, Macdonald & Evans, 1979.

Martinek, T.J., Crowe, P.B., and Rejeski, W.J.: Pygmalion in the Gym: Causes and Effects of Expectations in Teaching and Coaching. West Point, New York, Leisure Press, 1982.

Morison R.: A Movement Approach to Educational Gymnastics. Part 3: Observation and teaching; Safety and observation. London, J.M. Dent & Sons, 1969.

Rink, J.E.: The teacher wants us to learn. JOPER, 52(2):17, 1981.

Chapter 10

Evaluation of Processes and Products

ROSEMARY McGEE

Evaluation within the context of physical education for elementary and primary school children should be a continuous process related to the objectives of each lesson. This frame of reference places the emphasis on formative instead of summative evaluation. Although summative evaluation (usually resulting in a final judgment of some sort) is still desirable, it is no longer the primary evaluative procedure. More important is the day to-day progress made through the interaction of the teacher and children in the physical education setting.

Both summative and formative evaluation can be either criterion-referenced or norm-referenced. The criterion-referenced approach bases the evaluation of the child's performance on a predetermined objective or standard; i.e., the child, at the end of this lesson, should be able to balance on at least four different body parts. The child is judged to have met this criterion or not. Such standards can be set for various stages of the unit and also for the completion of the unit. Norm-referenced judgments are made by comparing the child's performance with the performance of other children. They can be in the same class, of the same age generally, in the state, or nation, for example. The child's performance is then reported as a percentile ranking among the group, as highest, average, etc. as the case may be. This norm-referenced concept is also usable in either a formative or summative context.

Summative evaluation takes place when the learning process is completed.[1] It shows the level of achievement of each student as well as of the class as a whole. It permits comparisons of achievement between groups and may result in the establishment of norms and comparisons with predetermined standards of attainment. Summative evaluation is used to establish grades and to meet the school systems' requirements for certain levels of achievement.

Summative evaluations may be established, however, using either a criterion- or norm-referenced framework. Using only summative assessment is no longer considered adequate because summative evaluation tends to serve the system more than the student and its application is not generally as humanistic.

Formative evaluation, on the other hand, is an integral part of the learning process.[1] It identifies the phases of each lesson learned, the parts not yet acquired by the student, and the direction for adjusting the lesson to accommodate the students' needs. Assessment of a formative nature is different for each teacher because the teacher knows the specific objectives for each lesson. Evaluation in this context is usually criterion-referenced because it judges each child in relation to the immediate objectives.

The current philosophy of elementary physical education programs stresses the concepts of alternatives, choices, flexibility, variety, versatility, and other such words that refute the concept of only-one-acceptable-way to do a task. Whereas earlier, a teacher may have been primarily interested in how far a child could jump, now that teacher is interested in the variety of ways the child can jump with good body control. This change in philosophic position, which has changed the methodology and content emphases of physical education in the elementary schools, has likewise changed the role of evaluation. Both product and process evaluation continue to be needed, but the emphasis has changed from a product to a process orientation. The teacher-centered program was generally product-oriented, using summative evaluation. The current student-centered program is process-oriented, stressing formative evaluation. Consequently, the growth process in developing movement patterns is more essential than the final product measure.

Evaluation is a questioning process. Objectives are set, and then questions are posed to see whether the objectives have been met. The questions would be asked at the end of the unit if a summative stance persists. Questions would be posed during and at the conclusion of each lesson if a formative position prevails. In addition, the questions would be open, they would be numerous, and they would be asked to help the child and teacher diagnose the performance so further development could be planned.

Note that the answers to the questions posed would be different for the summative and formative positions. A precise, often numeric, answer would be given to the summative questions. A more subjective, analytic, narrative statement would probably be the response to the formative-type questions.

An understanding of the questioning format used in the presentation of the lesson and in the teacher's dialogue with students is crucial to the evaluative process, because it puts a premium on observational skills and subjective judgments as bases for making decisions. Consequently, the traditional skill test and fitness battery are less prevalent. Instead, such assessment tools as rating scales, anecdotal records, diaries, logs, interviews, and discussions are the data-gathering vehicles for teachers and students to get direction for the ongoing decisions during the lesson.

OBSERVATIONS

The ability to observe well is a developed skill for the teacher and the student alike. Teachers need to understand the mechanical principles of human movement and the total growth and development patterns of children as they relate to movement.[2] They should be able to identify quality movement. These competencies are acquired through study and through working with children in movement experiences. Developing this observational keenness helps the teacher set new problems and plan for future tasks.[3]

The children learn to observe with guidance from the teacher.

> By sensitive observation the teacher can help children to adjust their habits and preferences to achieve more balance ability while strengthening their natural gifts.[4]

The teacher can help children develop this skill in observing by focusing their observations:

> What did you notice about Mary's jumping?
> What do you notice about the way these two children are working together?[5]

As the children become proficient observers, they can analyze their movement patterns more meaningfully. Quality of movement and intent of movement are important for the child to "see" because, once the child observes accurately, he/she is better able to clarify his/her movements.[5,6]

THEORETIC CONCEPTS

Evaluation could be viewed from three theoretic positions. Each would assess the child's movement, but from a different perspective and with a different emphasis. The three positions will be designated as Activity Areas, Movement Elements, and Learning Domains (Fig. 10–1). Because of the interrelatedness of the various viewpoints, the evaluation of movement can be approached from each position.

Activity Areas

The program in elementary school physical education usually centers around movement experiences evolving through dance, gymnastics, and games.

> Dance is concerned with organising and coming to terms with, expressing and commenting on human experience. In these ways it is allied with the other art forms. But dance is also allied with gymnastics and games and athletics in the physical education programme. This, too, is

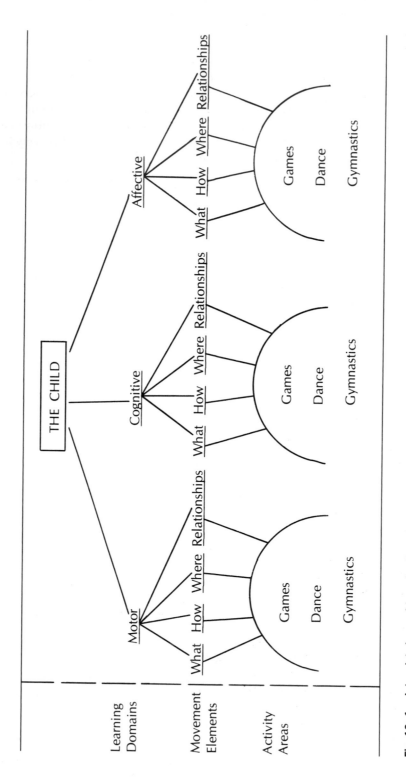

Fig. 10–1. Interrelatedness of Learning Domains, Movement Elements, and Activity Areas

perfectly understandable, for dance is indissolubly linked with all these activities involving human movement. Gymnastics arises from the child's delight in using movement to grapple with problems of mastering the environment—of supporting his body in precarious balance, of leaping on to apparatus, of arriving safely on the floor from heights. Games arise from the child's delight in the skill of using implements to control movement objects such as balls, tops and quoits in competitive situations.[7]

The evaluative processes might be focused on the unique aspects of each type of activity:

1. The adjustment to the accompaniment and a time structure in dance, the expression of feelings and moods, the effort actions, the creativity.

2. The adjustment to the floor, small equipment, and apparatus work in gymnastics, the variety of ways of using them, the daring, the individual challenge for success.[3]

3. The adjustment of implements and objects in games, the strategy involved, the competitive element, and the teamwork necessary.

Movement Elements

Underlying these activity areas of dance, gymnastics, and games are the tenets of Laban, which have been conveniently charted (with slight variations) by several authors.[3,8,9] If the evaluative process is focused on the elements in the movement analysis, a certain type of assessment is appropriate.

1. *How* the body moves, involving time, weight, space, and flow.

2. *What* the body does, involving actions of the body, actions of body parts, activities of the body, and shapes of the body.

3. *Where* the body moves, involving areas, directions, levels, pathways, planes, and extensions.

4. *Relationships* of the body, involving body parts, individuals, groups, and objects.

These "how," "what," "where," and "relationship" aspects of movement might still be addressed within the context of games, dance, or gymnastics, but the evaluation would focus on the elements of the movement as opposed to the unique characteristics of game, dance, or gymnastic movements.

Learning Domains

Barrett suggests three interrelated goals for elementary school physical education.

1. A child should be able to move skillfully. He/she should be efficient and effective in movement situations, both planned and unexpected.

2. A child should develop awareness of the personal value of movement. Also, he/she should become sensitive to how he/she feels about his/her movement as well as the movement of others.

3. A child should have knowledge about movement and the principles that govern it. He/she should understand how this knowledge is applied to his/her movement and that of others.[10]

These goals suggest the three domains of learning as indicated by such writers as Jewett,[11] Harrow,[12] Krathwohl,[13] and Bloom.[14] The motor, affective, and cognitive domains identify another approach to viewing the assessment process.

1. Skill in movement—motor domain.

2. Feelings about movement—affective domain.

3. Knowledge of movement—cognitive domain.

These three domains imply a fragmentation of the child that is not intended. Children move with thought and feeling. Even though assessment tools usually are directed to one of the three domains, the direction suggests an emphasis and not an exclusion of the other two domains. The teacher may use an affective instrument such as an attitude scale, but this choice does not negate the whole-child concept.

The interrelatedness of the three theoretic approaches to examining movement suggests that evaluation processes may be "plugged in" at any point.

1. The teacher or child or children may be interested in pinpointing the gymnastics *activity area* focusing on knowledges and understandings.

2. They may be interested in an overall *attitude* assessment about dance.

3. They may want to know *what* body performance was evident in a game.

SAMPLE TOOLS

Many of the measures presented in this chapter could be used as either process or product evaluation, depending on when and how the teacher uses the information. One of the purposes of evaluation is to make the assessment of student progress as personalized and diagnostic as possible. Thus, numerous measuring tools must be used in a variety of situations. Unfortunately, tools that are compatible with the philosophy of elementary school physical education in today's schools are rare. Because of this sparseness, the teacher must develop new assessment instruments and adapt others.

Rating Scale

This subjective estimate brings order to the process of evaluation and provides for degrees of the quality, trait, or factor being examined.[15]

PURPOSES

1. Evaluate qualities that cannot be easily and efficiently measured objectively.[16]
2. Corroborate assessments from other sources.
3. Systematize observation.

USES

1. Use the rating scale several times during a segment of work to detect changes in performance.
2. Have students view a student, make notations on a rating scale, and then follow up with a discussion involving the raters and the performer. This interaction benefits both the raters and the performer in their understanding and analysis of movement.
3. Use a compilation of rating scale results to assist in the formulation of a narrative assessment of progress.
4. Review results of ratings for individuals or a group for direction in future planning of movement tasks.
5. Ask children to develop rating scales, thereby focusing their attention on the identification of important aspects of the task being rated.

GUIDELINES FOR USE

1. The components of the performance to be rated should be defined clearly.
2. The rater should have adequate time to view the performer.
3. The rater, whether teacher or student, should have prior study, interpretation, and practice with the rating scale.

4. The notations on the rating form should be made during or immediately following the observation.
5. Rating scales should be constructed or adapted by the teacher to fit the objectives being assessed.

EXAMPLE

Based on lesson 9 of "Ready, Set . . . Go!" Level One[8] (Fig. 10–2).
Note that frequency of success implies some facility with the movement task as noted in the response column and that other aspects of quality are built into the scale specifically or by implication. This rating scale relates to the focus of this one lesson, but it might be used following several lessons that employ a bean bag in the tasks. The Comments section may be used by either or both the teacher and the child to note reactions, circumstances, and reminders.

INTERPRETATION

The interpretation of the results can vary from a general impression to a precise score. Visual examination of the notations reflects that the child is more skillful when he/she handles the bean bag himself/herself than when a partner is involved, is progressing in throwing ability, and needs to work more on involving the various parts of the body in the task.

For a more precise assessment, numeric points can be assigned to each frequency:

Usually	3 points
Sometimes	2 points
Seldom	1 point
Never	0 points

The child in Figure 10–2 has scored 15 out of a possible 21 points. This particular scoring system is based on the assumption that all factors are equally important and that all pertinent ones have been included. An adaptation would be for the teacher to arrive at the relative importance of the various factors and perhaps weigh some of them more heavily than others. Whether the results are considered narratively or precisely, the teacher still needs to come to grips with a judgment about the level of performance demonstrated. This decision is based on such points as the developmental level of the child, the

Rating Scale: Handling a Bean Bag with Different Body Parts

Name		Rater		Date	
		Usually	Sometimes	Seldom	Never
The child can					
Catch a bean bag he/she tosses to himself/herself		x			
Catch a bean bag tossed by a partner			x		
Use different body parts to catch a bean bag he/she tosses to himself/herself			x		
Use different body parts to catch a bean bag tossed by a partner				x	
Absorb force effectively when catching a bean bag			x		
Direct the bean bag effectively when tossing it		x			
Smoothly combine the movements of catching and tossing the bean bag			x		

Comments:

Fig. 10–2. Sample Rating Scale

amount of experience with the task, the criterion levels set, and the progress the child had made since the last assessment. The teacher knows the situation and can make the judgment in the proper context.

NOTE. This sample of a rating scale emphasizes the *movement elements* within the *motor domain* of the *gymnastic activity area.* illustrating the theoretic concepts shown in Figure 10–1.

Diary

This written record of the writer's experiences and thoughts is usually noted daily or perhaps weekly, depending on the frequency of the lessons. See example in Fig. 10–3.

PURPOSES

1. Verbalize portions of the lesson that are especially meaningful to the student. Accomplishments, reactions, questions, and understandings might be noted.

2. Record the student's thoughts at regular intervals.

3. Keep a record of the student's experiences and reactions.

4. Communicate with the teacher in a written medium.

5. Help the student have a sense of his/her progress.[17]

USES

The teacher can:

1. Read the diaries periodically for feedback.

2. Obtain guidance for changes in partners, tasks, organization, and content.

3. Get input about the child's progress in motor, cognitive, and affective domains.

4. Correlate the diary material with information from anecdotal records, logs, and rating scales, for example.

5. Communicate with the child in written dialogue.

The child can:

1. Translate movement experiences into cognitive and affective expressions.

2. Express concerns about class incidents.

P.E.

February 28, 1975
Robbie, James, Randy

Our game was to put a rope for a boundary line and have a team on each side of the rope and ~~hit the~~ hit the ball on each side of the rope and when it hits the other side the other team hits it back (using different parts of our bodys). *was this game anything like the game you wanted to play with the whole class? yes* (I think we need more boundary lines so we will not hit it all over the place. *could you use more ropes? Let me know if you need more.*

do you need to think about ball control as well as boundaries? yes

Fig. 10–3. Excerpt from Student Diary (including comments by teacher)[18]
Note: This diary dialogue relates to the cognitive domain of the games activity area as shown in Figure 10–1.

GUIDELINES FOR USE

1. Students should construct, identify, and decorate their diaries so they become objects of interest and importance individually owned.

2. Notating in diaries should be voluntary.

3. Sharing the diaries with the teacher should be the child's decision. The teacher should not share diary notations with other students or teachers. The rapport established between the child and teacher should be protected and will be enhanced as the child learns to trust the teacher.

4. The teacher should not correct the spelling or grammar. The notations must be free expressions and not exercises in writing.

Random teacher comments selected from diaries:

> It seems to me that you worked well today.
> Were you throwing or striking?
> What can you do to be ready for the ball?
> Do you think you can like games?
> Do we need to talk about this?
> If you are having trouble with an idea, ask me and I will try to help.
> I like your drawings very much. Could you draw a picture of your game next time?[18]

INTERPRETATION AND COMMENTS

Diary notations provide the teacher only a fraction of the information needed to evaluate a child's progress. The notations may not be entirely accurate, and they may not be complete. Nevertheless, they inform the teacher of progress as seen by the child.[4] Reading the diaries regularly will give the teacher a longitudinal view of the child's reactions and may reflect a pattern of behavior that is unavailable through other means, or not as clear. One of the benefits of the diary is its versatility in revealing an understanding or a feeling a child has experienced in a motor context.

Anecdotal Record

This document is a written impartial record of an incident in the life of a student as observed by a teacher.[15]

PURPOSES

1. Pinpoint significant occurrences.

2. Focus the teacher's perception of individual children.

USES

The teacher can:
1. Identify patterns of conduct.
2. Correlate anecdotal records with other informational sources, such as diaries.
3. Share information with other school personnel for counseling purposes.
4. Gain direction in the personalization of teaching.

GUIDELINES FOR USE

1. Notations should be concise and value free.
2. Notations should reflect a series of observations.
3. An anecdotal record page should be prepared for each child in the class.
4. Notations need not be made for each child every day.
5. Notations should reflect lack of prejudice.

EXAMPLE

Dated notations about a fifth-grade child:

1/15 Is looking for and sometimes demanding my attention. When she had it, she demonstrated an ability to accomplish the task with reasonable success. When my attention was elsewhere, she caught near her body, often at a comfortable mid-level with minimal enthusiasm.

1/29 Exceptional grasp of reaching, absorbing concept, w/ self she is reaching high and covering a long arc on recovery. Not sure w/ partner's toss.

2/28 Antoinette works w/ a more sustained fine touch which seems to be combined w/ a relaxed, not at all "competitive" outlook. In groups she is more concerned w/ the discussion and design than the play.

3/19 Worked very seriously in ball control. Developed idea of absorbing force. I am trying to push her for more speed.[18]

INTERPRETATION AND COMMENTS

The danger of anecdotal notations is the tendency to make judgments about a child that are based on too little information and isolated from the rest of the school scene. Anecdotal records supply one or two pieces to the puzzle and should be interpreted only in a total context.

Performance Test

A performance test requires the student to make a movement response that is scored. Skill, fitness, and physical factors such as balance, coordination, and agility are examples of the kinds of assessment made by using performance tests. The rating scale technique discussed previously may be considered a performance test. It is one way to score a performance. Later in this chapter, other rating scales will be presented as well as skill, body coordination, motor disability, and fitness tests. These tools assess some of the movement aspects of physical education.

COGNITIVE MEASURES

Assessment of cognitive accomplishments can vary from an informal conversation with a student to precisely administered group tests. Some awareness of understandings is evident through the child's motor performance and through discussions of videotape recordings and demonstrations. A more concrete assessment can be made, however, if the setting is more structured. Cognitive assessment can be a process or product procedure, depending on when it is taken and how it is used. An early assessment could be used in diagnostic, prescriptive, and formative ways. Assessment toward the conclusion of a large segment of work, such as a game segment, might reflect summative, achievement, and product information. The tool could be the same; the application of the results would determine its role in either process or product evaluation.

Dialogue

A flexible conversation, such as a dialogue, permits an individualized assessment that can be refocused in relation to the student's comments. It provides an appropriate avenue of cognitive awareness when written expression tends to penalize the child.

DIALOGUE WITH A KINDERGARTEN STUDENT

Teacher: How can your arms help you jump very, very high?

Child: They went over like that.
Teacher: How can your legs help you land softly?
Child: They are bent when you jump off.
Teacher: Are your legs straight or bent when you land?
Child: Bent.
Teacher's Refocus: Jump and see what your legs are doing.
Watch me jump and see what my legs are doing.[19]

COMMENTS. Notice that the refocusing prolongs the dialogue and gives the child an opportunity to express his/her ideas. Standardized directions probably are not suitable for the very young child. It is helpful to combine the dialogue with the child's performance of what he/she means, and then judge whether cognition is present.

DIALOGUE WITH A SIXTH GRADE STUDENT

T: What kinds of things were you thinking about in class to help yourself improve on the jump, land and roll?
What did you think about in the jump?
S: (answered roll instead of jump)
Get self in a ball to make it better.
To control myself.
T: How would that control it better?
S: Make you roll a lot better instead of hands and feet going all over the place.
T: What would you think about doing with your hands to make the roll better?
S: Get them close to your body.
T: When rolling, what part of the body should touch the mat first?
S: Feet.
Knees—no
Hands.
T: O.K., take weight on the hands: next part?
S: Behind.
T: Should the head touch?
S: Yes
T: What kinds of things did you think about to improve your jump?
S: I tried to get higher.
T: How did you do that?
S: By jumping up and taking my arms with me.
T: Did you really feel like your arms were helping you or did they just go up with you?
S: They helped a little.
T: What about the position of your body?
S: Sometimes it was out of whack.
T: If you want a higher jump, what position would help you?
S: I don't know.
T: The way you jump, you have lots of power, what direction do you want it to go in?
S: Up.

T: Is there anything you can think of that would help you improve your landing?
  S: You can give with it when you are going down.
T: What does that mean "to give with it?"
  S: Let yourself come down with yourself.
T: All right, so your whole body is going to come down; are you going to do anything specifically with your body to give more?
  S: Just put your arms down as you go down.
T: Do you do anything with your legs as you hit the mat?
  S: Yes.
T: What?
  S: They get tight and go into a roll.[20]

COMMENTS. This dialogue was put on cassette, transcribed, and then studied by the teacher. Although this particular inquiry involved only two questions, more or different ones could have been used. A charting of answers could be made if the same questions were posed to each child.

Picture Identification

The teacher collects a variety of pictures showing athletes, dancers, and other people in various positions.[21] In addition, he might collect

space, to skills, and to level—and some to relationships to objects. Ideally, the pictures should be selected to tap the cognitive points to which the teacher is giving attention. The responses could be either written or oral.

SAMPLE QUESTIONS

What body shape is shown?
Is the performance high or low?
A series of pictures may be taken by the teacher to focus on aspects of movement that the child should be able to identify. One such picture series was developed by McCormick[22] to test children's ability to identify directions such as front, behind, over, and under.

Demonstration

This instrument involves sixth-grade students observing and identifying the effort actions demonstrated by the teacher.[23]

SCORING. The teacher demonstrates six effort actions, including duplications. Correct answers are worth 3 points for effort actions and 1 point

---

Observe and identify the effort actions demonstrated (Courtesy Dr. Josephine Sutlive)

EFFORT ACTIONS	*TIME*	*WEIGHT*	*SPACE*
1. _____			
2. _____			
3. _____			
4. _____			
5. _____			
6. _____			

List of Effort Actions:	List of Time Aspects:	List of Weight Aspects:	List of Space Aspects:
Thrusting	Sudden-fast	Fine-light	Direct
Pressing	Sustained-slow	Firm-heavy	Indirect
Floating			
Flicking			

---

photos of children in movement environments. Questions would be posed about each picture. Some questions might relate to shape, to use of

each for time, weight, and space aspects, totaling 6 points for each performance and 36 points for the total.

COMMENTS. This test was administered to 20 sixth graders in 1 hour, testing 4 students at a time. Other effort actions could be included.

Objective Knowledge Test

Cognitive learning takes place in a hierarchy such as the levels suggested by Bloom: knowledge, comprehension, application, analysis, synthesis, and evaluation.[14] The Educational Testing Service in Princeton, New Jersey, identifies the three levels of remembering, understanding, and thinking. Many cognitive measures tap only the bottom level of the hierarchy instead of trying to accommodate the full range of cognition that a child might demonstrate.

READY? SET . . . GO! KNOWLEDGE ACHIEVEMENT TEST

This test developed by Hart is designed to assess knowledges and understandings based on "Ready? Set . . . Go!," a television course for elementary physical education. This test covers the content in the Level One television series.[8]

The instrument is a group paper-and-pencil test consisting of 2 sample questions followed by 33 test questions arranged in approximate order of difficulty. Each item consists of a set of 4 pictures compiled into a test booklet for each child. The statements are read aloud to the children from the test manual, and the children mark an X through the picture that designates their response. Administering the test takes approximately 35 minutes. Transparencies of the responses could be projected if standard answer sheets are available. A sample page of the answer sheet accompanied by the parallel test items has been included. Copies of the examiner's manual, including the item statements and the pictorial answer sheet, may be obtained from Dr. Virginia Hart, Physical Education Department, Mars Hill College, Mars Hill, North Carolina 28754.[24]

Excerpt From Test

Say:
Turn to the next page and fold your booklet back.
Demonstrate. See that all booklets are folded back so that only page 2 is showing. Check to see that each child has turned to the right page. Read the next question number: 4.

Say:
4. Place your marker under the first row of pictures on this page. It is question number 4. Look at the pictures in this row. Find the picture of the child who is *rolling sideward.* Put a mark on the correct picture.
5. Move your marker down and put it under the next row of pictures. Find the picture of the children whose *shapes are the same.* Put a mark on the correct picture.
6. Move your marker down and put it under the next row of pictures. Find the picture of the child who is going *over* the equipment. Put a mark on the correct picture.
7. Move your marker down and put it under the next row of pictures. Find the picture of the child who is *making the ball bounce* from the floor. Put a mark on the correct picture.
8. Move your marker down and put it under the next row of pictures. Find the picture of the child who is *going to throw* the ball. Put a mark on the correct picture.
Say:
Now put your pencil down. Turn to the next page and fold your booklet back.
Demonstrate. See that all booklets are folded back so that only page 3 is showing. Check to see that each child has turned to the right page.

EXERCISE PHYSIOLOGY KNOWLEDGE TEST FOR FIRST GRADERS*

Wilson[25] developed 15 test items for first graders that are based on the *Basic Stuff Series I*[26] and focus on the *Exercise Physiology*[26] component of the series and the *Childhood*[27] age group in the *Basic Stuff Series II.*[27] This work in cognitive assessment is geared to Basic Stuff series similarly to the way the Educational Testing Service developed the AAHPER Cooperative Physical Education Tests in 1970 to parallel *Knowledge and Understanding in Physical Education*[28] published by the AAHPER in 1969. In time, it is hoped that cognitive assessment tools will be developed to tap each of the five content areas in each of the three age clusters presented in the *Basic Stuff Series I* and *II.* Following her initial research, Wilson suggested that using only two choices in each item was probably too easy for first graders and that they probably can make a discrimination among three choices. The test booklets and directions may be obtained from Wilson. The items included here in Figure 10–5 have been used successfully

---

*Used by permission of R. Wilson, doctoral student, School of HPERD, UNC-Greensboro, Greensboro, N.C.

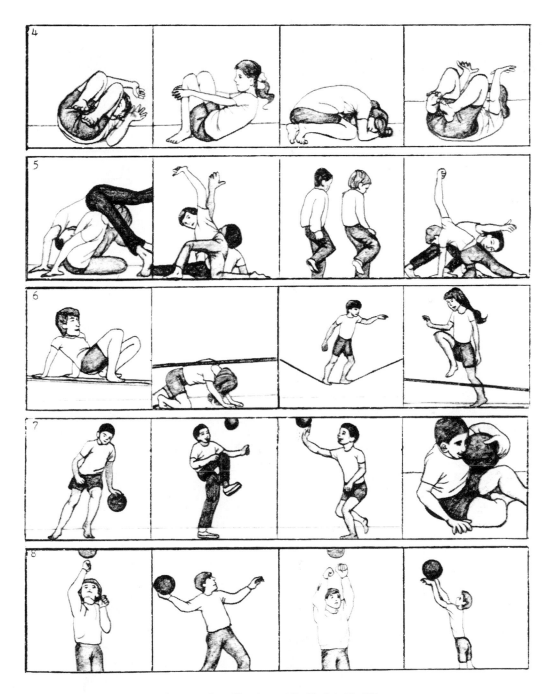

Fig. 10–4.   Page of Answer Sheet from Hart Test (Courtesy of Dr. Virginia Hart)[24]

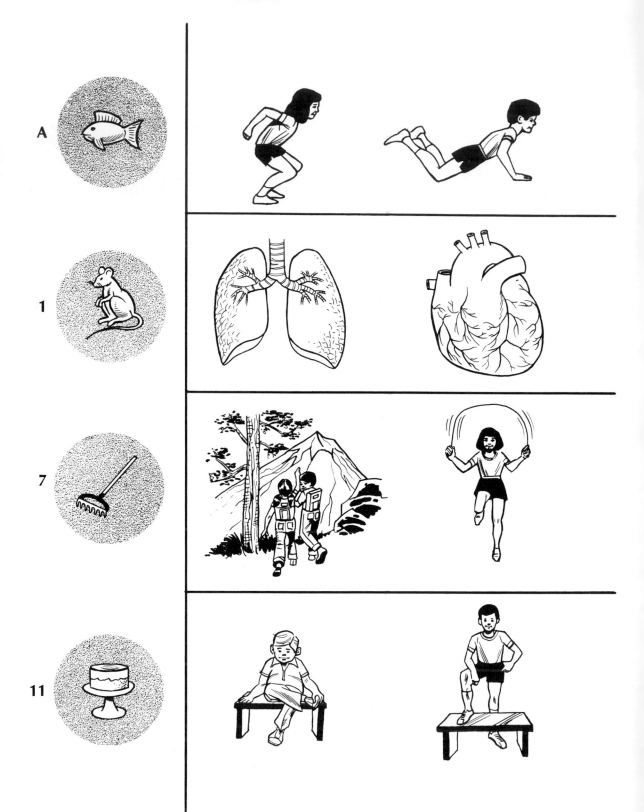

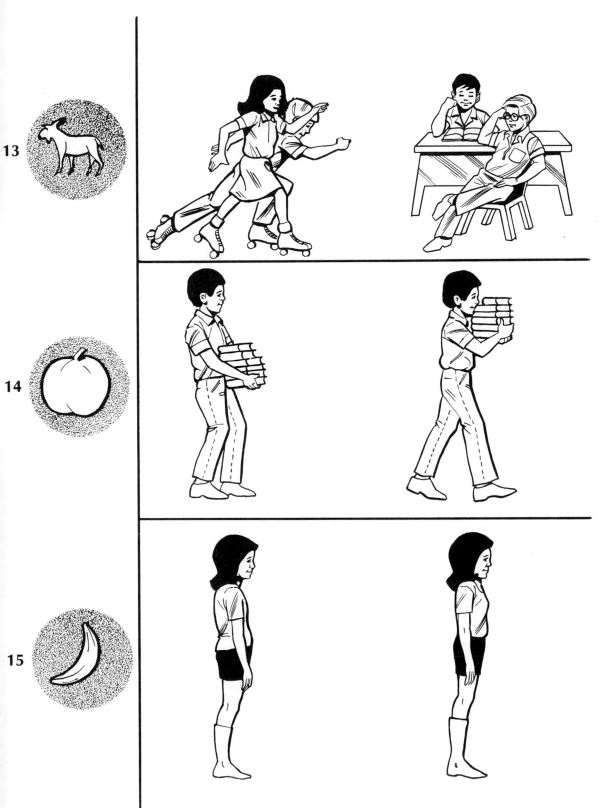

Fig. 10—5. Test Items from Wilson 1st Grade Test on Exercise Physiology

with first graders and are indicative of the type of cognitive assessment appropriate for them. The illustrations are taken from the Basic Stuff Series[26,27] and the North Carolina Achievement Test—Grade 1.[29]

Introducing the Test

Say:

I am going to give each of you a booklet in which we will do some work. See how well you can do. Leave your pencil down on your desk. You will be told what to do just twice. Therefore, you must listen carefully. You will be given one of these booklets (hold up booklet). Do not open it until you are told.

Distribute the test booklets, face up to each student. Make sure that each student receives the booklet with his/her name and information on it.

Say:

Point to the name on your booklet to be sure it is yours.

Say:

You must do the work yourself. Look only at your own booklet. Open the first page.

Be sure each child has the right place. Keep a test booklet in your hand to illustrate each part of the directions.

Students are to mark their answers on the picture. They will use a big X for marking the correct answer on the picture. There is only one correct answer.

Say:

Now, place your marker just below the row with the fish.

The first row of pictures is a sample item that will provide practice in the technique of marking. It will not be scored.

SAMPLE ITEM. Use the transparency to project the sample item on the wall or screen, and the marker to mark the correct picture.

Say:

Look at the pictures in the first row at the top of the page. You will make a big X on the picture that is the correct answer.

Say:

Be sure your marker is under the first row of pictures. Look at the pictures in this row by the fish. Find the picture of the child who is exercising his/her leg muscles. Put a mark on the correct picture. Make your mark like a big X.

Put a big X on the first picture in the test booklet and hold it up for the children to see.

Say:

The first picture is the correct answer. Are there any questions?

Check to see that each student has found the proper picture for the sample item. Then start reading the test questions. It is not necessary to read question numbers.

Say

1 mouse	Move your marker down and put it under the row of pictures next to the mouse. Find the picture of a heart. Put an X on the correct picture.
7 rake	Move your marker down and put it under the row of pictures next to the rake. Find the picture of an activity where the heart will beat the fastest. Put an X on the correct picture.
11 Cake	Move your marker down and put it under the row of pictures next to the cake. Find the picture of the child who has done little exercising. Put an X on the correct picture.
13 goat	Move your marker down and put it under the row of pictures next to the goat. Find the picture of an activity that will burn more calories. Put an X on the correct picture.
14 apple	Move your marker down and put it under the row of pictures next to the apple. Find the picture of the child who looks tired. Put an X on the correct picture.

Say:

Now, put your pencil down. Turn to the next page and fold your booklet back.

Demonstrate. See that all booklets are folded back so that only page 5 is showing. Check to see that each child has turned to the right page. Read the next question, number 15.

Say:

15 banana	Place your marker under the row of pictures next to the banana. Find the picture of the child who has good posture. Put an X on the correct picture.

Say:

Now, put your pencil down. Close your booklet and put it on your table or desk with the front up.

Collect booklets.

Additional Cognitive Test

AAHPER Cooperative Physical Education Test (1970)

Forms 4 A and 4 B for Grades 4, 5, and 6.

Available from Educational Testing Service, Princeton, New Jersey.

AFFECTIVE MEASURES

Assessment with the affective domain covers attitudes, self-concept, social adjustment, and perceptions about behavior. These intangibles are receiving attention because educators are placing more emphasis on the child as a thinking, moving, and feeling person. The tools in this section focus on the "feeling" dimension. The scales have been selected because they represent a grade range, they have been used or seem appropriate for use within the context of elementary physical education, and they are administratively feasible for the classroom teacher or the physical education specialist.

Often, an affective instrument can be used with one or two children: they need not be considered only for total group administration. The user will want to study these examples of affective measures as well as others to select those most appropriate for the purposes of the teacher.

Cratty Adaptation of Piers-Harris Self-Concept Scale*

The Piers-Harris [30,31] scale is based on a compilation of statements made by children concerning their likes and dislikes about themselves. In 1967, Cratty,[32] working at the UCLA Perceptual Motor Learning Laboratory, constructed a scale adapted from the Piers-Harris scale, which could concentrate more on physical ability and appearance. The statement questions are classified into 5 categories: feelings about general well-being, social competence, physical ability, physical appearance, and social achievement. All 20 statements were found to be valid because each one discriminated between the children with high scores and those with low

*From Cratty, B., et al.: *Movement Activities, Motor Ability, and the Education of Children.* Springfield, Illinois, Charles C Thomas, 1970. Used by permission of Charles C Thomas and the author.

SELF-CONCEPT SCALE

NAME _____ DATE _____ GRADE _____ M _____ F _____

Scoring

Key†				
+	1.	Are you good at making things with your hands?	Yes	No
+	2.	Can you draw well?	Yes	No
+	3.	Are you strong?	Yes	No
+	4.	Do you like the way you look?	Yes	No
	5.	Do your friends make fun of you?	Yes	No
+	6.	Are you handsome/pretty?	Yes	No
	7.	Do you have trouble making friends?	Yes	No
+	8.	Do you like school?	Yes	No
	9.	Do you wish you were different?	Yes	No
	10.	Are you sad most of the time?	Yes	No
	11.	Are you the last to be chosen in games?	Yes	No
+	12.	Do girls like you?	Yes	No
+	13.	Are you a good leader in games and sports?	Yes	No
	14.	Are you clumsy?	Yes	No
	15.	In games do you watch instead of play?	Yes	No
+	16.	Do boys like you?	Yes	No
+	17.	Are you happy most of the time?	Yes	No
+	18.	Do you have nice hair?	Yes	No
	19.	Do you play with younger children a lot?	Yes	No
+	20.	Is reading easy to you?	Yes	No

†Questions to which a positive response is expected.

scores on the scale. The 20-item scale involves a yes-no response by the child. It can be read to the children, if reading ability is a factor.

Cratty designed the test for use with children in kindergarten through grade 6. His research showed no significant differences for age or sex within that grade range. The scale can be used to encourage children to talk about their physical abilities and appearance and to identify the children who have low self-concept scores so they can be helped.

DIRECTIONS. You have a questionnaire that will determine how you feel about yourself. Each question will be read and you should then immediately decide how you feel and circle yes *or* no to answer. Ready?

The first question is _____. Now circle "yes" or "no." (The question is repeated and the instruction to circle yes or no given again.) The second question is _____. (Continue through the 20 items.)

SCORING. The Scoring Key has been included with the Self-Concept Scale, but should not be printed in the copy of the answer sheet used by the children. Score 1 point for each response expected. Deduct 1 point for each expected positive answer that was circled no and each expected negative answer that was circled yes. The score is the number of expected responses given for the 20 items.

Tanner's Movement Satisfaction Scale

This attitude scale of 30 items measures the degree of satisfaction or dissatisfaction a child feels with his movement.[33,34] Tanner[33] revised the Nelson and Allen Movement Satisfaction Scale to make it appropriate for primary grade children. The scale items are read to the children who then circle a face, ranging from very happy to very sad that best describes that child's liking or disliking of that particular movement.

DIRECTIONS. The teacher should prepare a series of face drawings, showing reactions from very happy to very sad, to pin to the board.

INSTRUCTIONS TO THE CHILDREN. Do you recognize these pictures? (Point to the wall chart of faces. Response from children.) Yes, of course you do. Do you notice anything about the faces in these drawings? Yes, in some the face is very happy, and in some it is sad; either looking as though the person feels good about

things or bad about them. How does the face look here? (Point to the first drawing.) Yes, very happy indeed; and here? (Point to the second drawing.) Yes, still happy, but not *very* happy like the last one. In this one? (Point to the last drawing.) Oh yes, the person is *very unhappy* isn't he, very sad looking; and here? (Point to the next to last drawing.) He is still sad. Is he as unhappy as the one before? No, he isn't, is he? Now look at this drawing in the middle. (Point to the middle drawing.) He's not happy or sad is he? In fact he looks as though he is not quite sure *how* he feels about things. He really doesn't know how to feel about it all.

Can you really tell how the person feels by these pictures? Yes, I think you can now—so now you are going to use them in a fun way; you are going to use them to show me how *you* feel about some of the things that you do.

You see the papers in front of you: they have faces drawn on them just like these on the board. I am going to ask you some questions about things that you do, and you are to color the face that best shows how *you feel* about doing them.

Let's have a little practice with one or two questions before you start coloring on your paper. If I ask you "How do you feel about eating ice cream?," which one would you color? Yes, nearly all of you would color the very happy one; some might not feel quite so pleased about it and might color just the happy one, but I don't suppose anyone would color the very sad one. Let's try another, "How do you feel about playing the piano?" Some of you may never have had the chance to try this, and so have no idea how you would feel about it. If that is the case, which one would you color? Yes, this one in the middle, the one that is not really sure what to think about how he feels. One more: "How do you feel about having to sit down all day long?" Most of you feel very unhappy when you have to sit still for a long time, don't you?

I think you know how to do this now, don't you? Just remember, you don't have to try to please anyone by your answer; there is no right or wrong answer; you are just showing how *you* feel about the question.

Is your name at the top of your paper? Put your marker pencil beside number one, and listen—now, color the face that best shows how you feel about that. Now put your marker beside number two . . .

Scale Items (Courtesy Dr. Patricia Tanner)

1. How do you feel about bouncing a ball many times without stopping?
2. How do you feel about jumping very high?
3. How do you feel about picking very big things up and carrying them?
4. How do you feel about moving and stopping very suddenly?

5. How do you feel about climbing on very high things?

6. How do you feel about tagging games?

7. How do you feel about playing hard and using lots of energy?

8. How do you feel about stretching your body as far as you can?

9. How do you feel about balancing on one leg?

10. How do you feel about running very fast?

11. How do you feel about jumping over something about as high as your knee?

12. How do you feel about rolling over and over and over?

13. How do you feel about moving in a big space?

14. How do you feel about moving quickly around chairs, tables, or people when you have to?

15. How do you feel about kicking a ball a long way?

16. How do you feel about having to move slowly all the time?

17. How do you feel about running for a very long time?

18. How do you feel about moving to music?

19. How do you feel about running backwards?

20. How do you feel about bouncing a ball quickly lots of times?

21. How do you feel about hanging from things?

22. How do you feel about throwing a ball for someone else to catch?

23. How do you feel about moving when your friends are watching you?

24. How do you feel about playing very hard and fast?

25. How do you feel about jumping on to something about as high as your knee?

26. How do you feel about moving very heavy things?

27. How do you feel about throwing and catching a ball?

28. How do you feel about moving sideways?

29. How do you feel about changing directions quickly when you are moving?

30. How do you feel about jumping a long way, when you get to run before you jump?

SCORING AND ANSWER SHEET. An answer sheet with 30 sets of faces should be prepared and given to the students. There are 30 items, each receiving a possible 5 points for a Very Happy response, 4 points for Happy, 3 for Undecided, 2 for Sad, and 1 for Very Sad.

The range of scores is from 30 to 150, with the larger number representing the more positive attitude of a child about his/her movement.

135–150 points = Very Happy
105–134 points = Happy
 75–104 points = Undecided
 45–74 points = Sad
 30–44 points = Very Sad

Toulmin Elementary Physical Education Attitude Scale (TEPEAS)*

Toulmin[35] conducted both a preliminary and final study to ensure the careful construction of this attitude-assessment tool. For the preliminary study, 365 students from 9 to 12 years of age were used. Revisions in the scale were made and then another group of 315 students was administered the final form of the scale. The final 50 items cover program content, outcomes of program content, self-concept and level of aspiration, peer group relations, teacher, and scheduling and time. The scale may be considered to have construct validity and internal consistency as a measure of expressed attitudes of elementary school children toward the physical education program.

The scale is appropriate for both boys and girls in grades four, five, and six. It can be used to measure the status of attitudes toward the program and to evaluate changes in attitudes about the program.

DIRECTIONS. Please read carefully. Below, you will find some statements about physical education. We would like to know exactly how you feel about each statement. You are asked to think about physical education as it concerns you during your regular physical education class period. Do not consider the statements as after-school activities. Students are not all alike in their feelings. There are no right or wrong answers.

You have been given a separate answer sheet on which to write your feelings to each statement. After reading a statement, you will know at once, in most cases, whether you agree or disagree with the statement. If you agree, then decide whether to place an X under *strongly agree*, *agree*, or *slightly agree*. If you do not agree, then place an X under *slightly disagree*, *disagree*, or *strongly disagree*.

*From Toulmin, M.L.B.: The Development of an Original Instrument to Measure the Expressed Attitudes of Children Toward the Elementary School Program of Physical Education. Master's Thesis, Texas Woman's University, 1973.

Wherever possible, let your own experience affect your answer. Work rapidly. Do not spend much time on any statement. This is not a test, but is simply a way to find out how students feel about physical education. Your answers will not affect your grade. We will keep your answers secret, so please answer each statement exactly the way you feel about it. Be sure to answer every statement.

1. I would like to have physical education every day.
2. We do not get to play what we want to in physical education.
3. Because physical skills are important to youth, it is important for a person to be helped to learn and improve those skills.
4. Physical education teaches you to get along with others better.
5. I am afraid of getting hurt in physical education.
6. Many of the games we play in physical education are a waste of time.
7. Physical education should be only for those who are good at it.
8. Time for physical education is too short.
9. I like to play games in physical education.
10. I never get to be "it" when we play games in physical education.
11. I get enough exercise without physical education.
12. Boys and girls laugh at me in physical education when I cannot do things.
13. Students learn to understand each other better after playing together in physical education.
14. Too often we must go outside in cold weather when we should stay inside.
15. Most of the things I learn in physical education, I can use after school.
16. Our physical education teacher likes children.
17. A person could better control his/her feelings if he/she did not have to take physical education.
18. When I get older, I plan to take band instead of physical education.
19. Physical education teaches us to respect others' rights.
20. Physical education skills bring more enjoyment to life.
21. I get tired in physical education before others do.
22. My parents do not think physical education is very important.
23. Physical education does not help me learn to control my feelings, such as anger.
24. Our physical education teacher knows his/her job well.
25. I like to run.
26. Arguments in physical education have caused me to lose friends.
27. Physical education has helped me set goals to improve my physical fitness.
28. When I grow up I will continue to exercise.

29. My parents often scold me for ruining my clothing in physical education.
30. Physical education teaches you good sportsmanship.
31. I feel so out-of-place in a physical education class.
32. Physical education helps me to relax.
33. Our teacher makes us do dumb things.
34. Physical education has taught me to appreciate the things my body can do.
35. Physical education is a waste of time in improving health.
36. Physical education does not help you to make friends.
37. I learn something new nearly every time I have physical education.
38. I look forward to physical education regardless of the weather.
39. Fat students should not have to take physical education.
40. Physical education encourages boys and girls to cheat.
41. Physical education is just as important for girls as it is for boys.
42. Many physical education activities make me feel clumsy.
43. I would rather not play in physical education if I cannot be on my best friend's team.
44. Physical education activity gets one interested in good health habits.
45. Our grading system in physical education is fair.
46. Physical education is too rough.
47. Tests should not be given in physical education.
48. Most of my friends like physical education.
49. I like to do exercises.
50. There is not enough good coming from physical education class to give it so much time.

SCORING. Toulmin stated that the maximum score possible is 300. Those students scoring 150 and above have expressed a favorable attitude toward the physical education program and those scoring below 150 have indicated attitudes that are unfavorable toward the elementary physical education program.

The 24 positive statements are item numbers 1, 3, 4, 8, 9, 13, 15, 16, 19, 20, 24, 25, 27, 28, 30, 32, 34, 37, 38, 41, 44, 45, 48, and 49. The other 26 statements are negative statements, and the scoring values need to be reversed; i.e., a "strongly agree" response to a negative statement is worth 1 point instead of 6 points.

	Positive Statements	Negative Statements
Strongly Agree	6	1
Agree	5	2
Slightly Agree	4	3
Slightly Disagree	3	4
Disagree	2	5
Strongly Disagree	1	6

For example: The answer sheet has 6 categories

		SA	A	SA	SD	D	SD
Item 1 is positive, so the key would be:	1.	( ) 6	( ) 5	( ) 4	( ) 3	( ) 2	( ) 1
Item 2 is negative, so the response would be scored in reverse:	2.	( ) 1	( ) 2	( ) 3	( ) 4	( ) 5	( ) 6

The key should be prepared by the teacher for ease in scoring, but it should not be printed on the answer sheet used by the students.

A range of scores from 50 to 300 is possible. If intermediate interpretations are desired, they could be designated as follows:

50–74	Strongly unfavorable attitude toward physical education program
75–124	Unfavorable attitude
125–150	Slightly unfavorable attitude
151–224	Slightly favorable attitude
225–274	Favorable attitude
275–300	Strongly favorable attitude toward physical education program

Horrocks Prosocial Play Behavior Inventory (HPPBI)*

Horrocks[36] developed this inventory to measure the prosocial play behavior of fifth- and sixth-grade boys and girls in recreational play situations. Working with teachers, Horrocks developed a set of behavioral attributes associated with successful and cooperative recreational games playing. Ten fifth- and sixth-grade teachers and 6 elementary school physical education teachers observed the students in recreational settings, which consisted of both high and low organizational games, and under conditions that provided extensive, moderate, and limited supervision. The teachers looked for 35 prosocial and antisocial play behaviors that had been identified by Hor-

---

*From Horrocks, R.N.: Relationship of Selected Prosocial Play Behaviors in Children to Moral Reasoning, Youth Sports Participation, and Perception of Sportsmanship. Doctoral Dissertation, The University of North Carolina at Greensboro, 1979. Used by permission of the author.

Prosocial Play Behavior Inventory

Child's Name _____   Teacher _____

INSTRUCTIONS

Please describe as accurately as possible the above student's behavior during recreational game playing activities by circling one of the 4 responses to each statement. Give a response to every item and BASE YOUR RESPONSES UPON YOUR PERSONAL OBSERVATIONS AND EXPERIENCES.

	THE STATEMENT IS:			
	Not at all	*Very little*	*Somewhat*	*Very much*
	like	*like*	*like*	*like*
THE CHILD	*the child*	*the child*	*the child*	*the child*
1. Avoids arguments	1	2	3	4
2. Wins without "gloating"	1	2	3	4
3. Accepts defeat without complaining	1	2	3	4
4. Offers consolation when a group member makes a mistake	1	2	3	4
5. Shares equipment readily	1	2	3	4
6. Abides by the rules of the game	1	2	3	4
7. Shares the game activities (does not "hog" the ball)	1	2	3	4
8. Accepts referee's decisions	1	2	3	4
9. Takes turns readily	1	2	3	4
10. Accepts constructive criticism and suggestions from peers	1	2	3	4

rocks. The behaviors were rated as either easily observable, at times difficult to observe, or very difficult to observe. Only statements on which the teachers could achieve 80% of agreements as "easily observable" were retained in the inventory. This behaviorally anchored rating scale (BARS) approach to scale development has achieved acclaim because it restricts the behaviors to those that can actually be observed. Content validity can be claimed because the scale reflects easily identified behaviors. Horrocks also claimed high internal-consistency reliability of the inventory.

The inventory is appropriate for use with children in the fifth and sixth grades to assess their prosocial behavior in recreational game settings. It can also identify students who need some assistance with moral reasoning and perceptions of the concept of sportsmanship.

SCORING A student's prosocial play behavior score is determined by totaling the points circled for each of the 10 behavior statements. Those children who display prosocial play behaviors receive more points than those who do not display the prosocial behaviors. The score can range from 10 to 40 points. Horrocks identified the following levels within the score range and reported statistically significant differences on both moral reasoning and perceptions of sportsmanship for those students in the upper and low groups:

Upper	37–40
Average	26–36
Low	10–25

The Children's Competitive and Cooperative Attitude Scale (CCCAS)*

Hutchins[37] developed the Children's Competitive and Cooperative Attitude Scale, using 426 boys and girls in grades 3 through 6. Her research utilized the theoretic construct proposed by Johnson and Ahlgren[38] that competition and cooperation are not two extremes of one linear dimension. In other words, a child's attitude could fall into one of four categories:

1. High competitive and high cooperative attitudes

2. High competitive and low cooperative attitudes
3. Low competitive and high cooperative attitudes
4. Low competitive and low cooperative attitudes

The original pool of 49 items was reviewed by 50 teachers to discern appropriateness for age and grade levels. In addition, the scale was field tested and factor analyzed to determine whether clusters of competitive- and cooperative-attitude statements existed. The reliability, using the field tested results, was .695 for the competitive subscale and .692 for the cooperative subscale. Using the competitive and cooperative subscales for the Minnesota School Affect Assessment[39] as validity criteria, the coefficients for both subscales were significant.

The CCCAS is suitable to use with boys and girls in grades 3 to 6. Two scores result: one that is an attitude assessment for competitiveness and one that shows the child's attitude toward cooperativeness. A yes-no response is used with the 21 items. An appropriate answer sheet should be prepared. If group rather than individual attitudes are of interest, the names of the students need not be placed on the answer sheets.

DIRECTIONS FOR CCCAS ADMINISTRATION. "I need to know how boys and girls your age feel and think. I am going to read some statements to you and would like you to decide whether what I say is like you or unlike you. The answer you mark should show how *you* really feel about *yourself,* not how you think you *should* feel. I am the only person who will see your answers so I would appreciate having you give your honest feelings. If you have any questions at any time, raise your hand and I'll come to your desk."

"Now let's go to the answer sheet. Check to make sure you have filled in your age, sex, and grade. Put your pencil on the number 1. The first statements is: I LIKE TO DO BETTER THAN OTHERS. If you feel that you do like to do better than others, fill in the blank on your answer sheet under number 1. If you feel that you do not care whether you do better than others or not, fill in the blank on your answer sheet under number 2. Are there any questions?"

"Because some of you read faster than others,

---

*Hutchins, P.A.: The Relationship of Children's Personality Factors to Their Competitive and/or Cooperative Attitudes. Ed.D. dissertation, University of Maine, 1978. Used by permission of the author.

I will read all the items aloud to you so we can finish at the same time. Remember, there are no right or wrong answers. I need to know what your feelings are. Let us continue."

SCORING. Count the number of yes responses in each subscale. There are a possible of 10 in the competitive subscale and 11 in the cooperative subscale. Hutchins suggested that scores of 7 and above be considered high and that scores of 3 and below be considered low on each subscale. She believed that it is the child scoring in the fourth category, low competitive and low cooperative attitudes, about whom the teacher should be especially concerned.

The Children's Competitive and Cooperative Attitude Scale (CCCAS)

*1. I like to do better than others.
2. I would feel badly if I thought I was letting my parents down.
3. I try hard to please my teacher.
*4. I work hardest when I am trying to do better than others.
*5. I like to be able to do things better than others can.
6. I ask for help from my teacher before starting out on a job I have never done before.
*7. I need to win the games I play.
*8. I work harder at something if I feel others are doing better than I am.
9. I have a lot of fun playing any kind of game with others when there is no winner.
*10. I try harder when I see others doing a good job.
*11. I want to be better at things than most people are.
12. I am good at carrying out what others want me to do.
13. I like to say and do things that will help others.
*14. I like to be told that I have done better than other people.
15. I like to be a member of a group.
16. I enjoy working on a project with a group.
17. I believe what my teacher tells me when I have a problem.
*18. I like to get my work done before any of the other kids do.
19. I think good grades are important for everyone.
*20. I try to be the best person on a team.
21. I follow directions and do what is expected of me.

---

*Competitive subscale.

Johnson Motor Performance Expectancy Scale*

Johnson[40] developed this scale to assess the expectation attitudes of third grade children toward their motor performance. It is a nonverbal instrument consisting of 23 photographs depicting children in different movement situations typically observed in elementary physical education classes. Each child looks at the set of photographs[8] and makes one of three choices regarding his or her expected ability to do what the child in each picture is doing.

Coefficients of stability and of internal consistency were used to examine the reliability of the scale, which proved to be satisfactory. Validity was established by presenting evidence related to content, concurrent, and construct aspects of the scale. This scale (JMPES) is suitable for use with third grade boys and girls and will reveal a self-report score of each child's attitude about his/her expectations to perform motor tasks.

The three choices of responses are represented by cartoon faces:

I think I can do what the person in the photograph is doing (smiling face = 3 points)

I don't know if I can do what the person in the photograph is doing (neutral face = 2 points)

I don't think I can do what the person in the photograph is doing (frowning face = 1 point)

The three faces are placed beneath each photograph in random order to avoid the possibility of all smiles being marked just because they are in the same position. Johnson considers a score of 67 to 69 to be indicative of a child's very good feelings of his/her motor performance abilities. Scores between 55 and 66 are average. Children

---

*Johnson, S.: Student Expectations and Dyadic Interactions with Physical Education Teachers of Third-Grade Children. Ed. D. dissertation, UNC-Greensboro, 1982. Used by permission of the author. Copies may be obtained from the author, who is Research and Training Associate, Institute for Aerobic Research, 12200 Preston Rd., Dallas, Texas 75230.

Photo by Kate Barrett

Photo from the Agency for Instructional Television

Photo from the Agency for Instructional Television

Photo from the Agency for Instructional Television

Photo from the Agency for Instructional Television

Fig. 10–6.   Item from Johnson Motor Performance Expectancy Scale

who score 54 and below should be given special attention and encouragement. Figure 10–6 shows the sample item that is used to help the students understand how to respond to the scale. In addition, the 4 pictures opposite are shown to illustrate the kinds of movement experiences presented in the 23 pictures.

"Me In Dance"*

Carlson[41] developed 3 self-concept scales for second and third grade children in the areas of games, dance, and gymnastics. They are fashioned on the bipolar statement pattern used by Gordon[42] in his Self-Concept Scale. Carlson administered the various scales to from 72 to 107 second and third grade children in 5 different school settings. The physical education specialist reported what he/she thought each child's self-concept would be in each of the 3 movement areas. The correlations between the specialists' ratings and the childrens' scores on the "Me In

---

*Used by permission of the author. All three scales may be obtained from Dr. J.B. Carlson, Elementary Coordinator, Department of HPER, Appalachian State University, Boone, N.C.

Dance" scale ranged from .48 to .62. This exploratory work shows promise even if only as a means of raising the awareness levels of the children in the context of the 3 different forms of movement. The scales could be used (1) to compare the feelings of the children before and after a unit, (2) to determine self-feelings within each of the 3 movement areas, (3) to help the teacher identify students with affective needs, (4) to enhance teacher-student interaction, and (5) to consider implications for curricular revision.

The scale, "Me In Dance," is included along with the directions for administering the scale to children. Carlson stated that a 3-point scale instead of a 5-point one might be more suitable as a response range for children in the lower grades.

INSTRUCTIONS FOR ADMINISTERING "ME IN DANCE"

This is not a test to see how much you know or do not know.

These are statements about you.

They are to learn how you see yourself most of the time in dance experiences.

There are no right or wrong answers.

Only what you feel about yourself is important.

Before you write anything, think about yourself for a little while: not how you think you ought to be; not how the teacher thinks you ought to be; not how you want to be; not how your parents or friends want you to be. This is just how you yourself feel you are most of the time. Please put your name on the paper. Now let us look at the paper.

Look at Number 1. On one side it says, "Making up dances is fun" and on the other side, "It is not fun to make up dances." If you feel that making up dances is fun most of the time, you would circle the 1. If you feel that it is not fun most of the time to make up dances, you would circle the 5. If you feel you are somewhere in between, you would circle the 2, 3, or 4.

Look at Number 4. It is different. On one side it has, "I do not use many different parts of my body when I dance." If you feel that most of the time you do not use many different parts of your body when you dance, you would circle the 1. If you feel that most of the time you do use many different parts of your body when you dance, you would circle a 5. If you feel you fit some-

"Me In Dance"

1. Making up dances is fun.	1 2 3 4 5	It is not fun to make up dances.
2. I enjoy the skipping, leaping, walking, running, galloping, and jumping activities of dance.	1 2 3 4 5	I do not enjoy the skipping, leaping, walking, running, galloping, and jumping activities of dance.
3. Dance movement helps me understand who I am.	1 2 3 4 5	I do not understand who I am when I dance.
4. I do not use many different parts of my body when I dance.	1 2 3 4 5	I use many different parts of my body when I dance.
5. I can be myself in dance.	1 2 3 4 5	I cannot be myself in dance.
6. Moving my body to music or a drum beat does not give me a good feeling.	1 2 3 4 5	I get a good feeling when I move my body to music or a drum beat.
7. I like to travel through space, turning and moving my body in different ways.	1 2 3 4 5	I dislike traveling through space, turning and moving my body in different ways.
8. I do not express my feelings when I dance.	1 2 3 4 5	I express my feelings when I dance.
9. I have good control at moving through space then stopping and starting on signal.	1 2 3 4 5	It is hard for me to move through space then stop or start on signal.
10. I am comfortable moving throughout all the space there is (general space) as well as the space right around me (personal space).	1 2 3 4 5	I am not comfortable moving in all the space there is (general) and the space around me (personal).
11. I do not like moving with a partner or in a small group.	1 2 3 4 5	I like moving with a partner or in a small group.
12. I am good at changing directions when I dance, moving forward, backward, sideward, up and down.	1 2 3 4 5	I am not good at changing directions when I dance, moving forward, backward, sideward, up and down.
13. I enjoy using certain parts of my body to lead my dance movement.	1 2 3 4 5	Using certain parts of my body to lead my dance movement is not enjoyable to me.
14. It is a good feeling when I reach my body as far from the ground as possible, then let it collapse way into the ground.	1 2 3 4 5	Reaching my body as far from the ground as possible, then letting it collapse way into the ground is not a good feeling for me.

where in between, you would circle a 2, 3, or 4. It is very important to think about each statement as I read it. I will answer any questions you need answered, so feel free to ask them. Remember, it is how you feel about yourself in dance that is important. Please be honest in your answer.

SCORING. Items on this scale were randomly reversed to decrease a child's tendency to go down the 5 column marking responses. The first step in scoring, therefore, is to prepare a key so that 5 always represents the positive end of each pair of bipolar statments. Items 1, 2, 3, 5, 7, 9, 10, 12, 13, and 14 would be scored 5, 4, 3, 2, 1, which is the reverse of the 1, 2, 3, 4, 5 printed on the scale used by the child.

Since there are 14 items, scores can range from 14 to 70. Scores around 42 would reflect a neutral feeling; scores of about 49 and above would be indicative of positive feelings. The closer the score is to 70, the more positive the child feels about himself/herself in dance.

Additional Affective Measures

Bolea, A.S., Felker, D.W., and Barnes, M.: Pictorial Self-Concept Scale. Available from Institute for Child Study, University of Maryland, College Park, Maryland 20740.

D'Augell, J.F.: Modified Children's Self-Concept Scale. Unpublished Instrument. Penn. State University, State College, Pennsylvania, 1973.

Farrah, G.A., Milchus, N.J., and Reitz, W.: Self-Concept and Motivation Inventory (1968) "What Face Would You Wear?" Available from Person-O-Metrics, 20504 Williamsburg Road, Dearborn Heights, Michigan, 48127.

Mancini, V.A.: A Comparison of Two Decision-Making Models in an Elementary Human Movement Program Based on Attitudes and Interaction Patterns. Doctoral dissertation, Boston University, 1974. Cheffers and Mancini Human Movement Attitude Scale (CAMHM)

Martens, R.: Sport Competition Anxiety Test. Champaign, Illinois, Human Kinetics Publishers, 1977.

Martinek, T.J., and Zaichkowsky, L.D.: Manual and scale for the Martinek-Zaichkowsky self-concept scale for children. Jacksonville, Illinois, Psychologists and Educators, 1977.

Meyer, J.A.: Physical Education Attitude Inventory for Grades Five and Six. Montgomery, Alabama, Department of Public Instruction, 1970.

Piers-Harris Children's Self-Concept Scale. (The Way I Feel About Myself) (1969) Available from Counselor Recordings and Tests, Box 6186, Acklen Station, Nashville, Tennessee 37212.

Simon, J.A., and Smoll, F.L.: An Instrument for Assessing Children's Attitudes Toward Physical Activity. Research Quarterly, 45:407, December, 1974. Also *In* Barrow, H.M., and McGee, R.: A Practical Approach to Measurement in Physical Education, 3rd ed. Philadelphia, Lea & Febiger, 1979.

MOTOR MEASURES

Evaluation of the motor domain in elementary school physical education is essential because the program is presented through movement, and objectives in all three of the learning domains are reached within the movement context. Instruments need to be developed to fit the type of program that is unique in its attempt to present a variety of movement experiences. Subjective judgments, made through observations and assisted by rating scales, comprise the mainstay of evaluation in this domain. Decisions about movement prescriptions for children and program direction should not be based on the results of any one measure. In other words, a composite evaluation is safer and truer to the aim of developmental movement experiences for all children.

Learning within the usual class procedure need not halt because assessment is taking place. The process of preparing for a test, taking it, and analyzing the results can be meaningful to the students. They should be involved. Measuring is not something a teacher does *to* a student, but a process the teacher goes through *with* the student. Just as the children can be creative and perceptive about gymnastic patterns and videotape analyses, for example, they can be helpful as well in developing rating scales and test items. The instruments presented have been used with a range of grade levels. Some are very specific,

RATING OF A SPECIFIC MOVEMENT TASK			
Name _____ Date _____ Rater _____ Task: Develop a short movement sequence combining three ways of taking yourself into the air. Emphasize a stretched position of your body and maintain a constant speed. Use as much space as possible.	Well Done	Satis-factory	Needs More Work

Body Awareness
    Ability to show a stretched position
       throughout the body
 Space Awareness
    Maximum use of space
 Time Awareness
    Ability to maintain a steady speed			

Comments: (by teacher and/or student)			

Fig. 10–7. Rating Scale for a Specific Movement Task

others are more general. They can be used either as presented or as examples to guide teachers and students who wish to develop instruments that fit their objectives more precisely.

The motor measures included have been grouped to show the instruments appropriate for use within the games, gymnastics, and dance context, the body and motor coordination tests, the perceptual motor training and disabilities tests, and, finally, the fitness tests. Each has been reviewed carefully and selected for inclusion because of its credibility in measuring the performance of children.

Rating Scale for a Movement Task

This rating scale (Fig. 10–7) is adapted from Barrett's ideas and suggestions that rating scales should be developed by teachers related to their particular situations.[2] This one is an example for teachers who wish to develop rating scales to fit their special needs. The task for this rating scale follows: "Develop a short movement sequence combining three ways of taking yourself into the air. Emphasize a stretched position of your body and maintain a constant speed. Use as much space as possible."

The scale may be used appropriately several times within the unit to show developmental, formative assessments. In that case, the dates the assessments were made should accompany the checks recorded in the columns.

DIRECTIONS. Ask each child in turn to perform the task for you as the rest of the class continues to work.

SCORING. The precise numeric scoring is not significant. The rating scale will pinpoint areas of strength and weakness to discuss with the student.

Rating Scale: Performance in Games*

Smith[43] developed a rating scale that includes all four skill components in games and that delineates some subcategories for each component. She suggests that the scale be used by observers who have an understanding of movement education and that the scale can be used in parts or in total. She considers it appropriate for students from 5 to 12 years of age (Fig. 10–8).

*Used by permission of N.L. Smith, Physical Education Specialist, Winston-Salem-Forsyth Schools, Winston-Salem, N.C.

Rating Scale: Performance in Games

Name		Age	Grade		Rater	

Skill Components	Dates of Ratings	Excellent use of skill components with high degree of quality	Exhibited often but with limited degree of quality	Observable at times when child is working on own	Exhibited mechanically/ on teacher command	Exhibited to a limited degree
Body Awareness	locomotor					
	nonlocomotor					
	manipulative					
Space Awareness	directional skills					
	ability to use levels					
	use of pathways					
Effort Awareness	time: sudden–sustained					
	weight: heavy–light					
	space: direct–indirect					
	flow: bound–free					
Relationships	player to self					
	player to equipment					
	player to other players					

Comments

Fig. 10–8. Rating Scale: Performance In Games

Rating Scale: Performance of Selected Game Skills

Game Component: Space Awareness
               1. general space
               2. personal space
               3. directions
               4. extensions

Purpose: The purpose of this rating scale is to determine the child's use of space in relation to: (1) general space, (2) personal space, (3) directions, and (4) extensions, *while playing in a game.*

Name: _____ Date: _____

Directions: Indicate the degree to which this child demonstrates the following *Space Awareness* skills by placing a circle around the number in the horizontal line under the characteristic.

1. To what degree of effectiveness does the child travel through the general space of the game area?

10	9	8	7	6	5	4	3	2	1	0

The child consistently travels through the entire general space.	The child consistently travels through half the general space.	The child travels only in the space close by.

2. To what degree of effectiveness does the child use the personal space while manipulating an object?

10	9	8	7	6	5	4	3	2	1	0

The child consistently reaches far away from his/her body while maintaining contact with his/her base of support.	The child sometimes reaches far away from his/her body but sometimes loses contact with the base of support and moves outside of his/her personal space.	The child rarely reaches away from his/her body without losing contact with his/her base of support.

3. To what degree of effectiveness does the child change direction while manipulating an object?

10	9	8	7	6	5	4	3	2	1	0

The child consistently changes direction when necessary to meet the demands of the game, i.e., in relation to others; for dodging, tackling, shooting, etc.	The child sometimes changes direction when necessary.	The child rarely changes direction.

4. To what degree of effectiveness does the child use different directions while manipulating an object?

10	9	8	7	6	5	4	3	2	1	0

The child consistently uses different directions (forward, backward, sideward) to meet the constantly changing demands of the game.	The child sometimes uses different directions.	The child rarely uses more than one direction.

5. To what degree of effectiveness does the child use extensions while manipulating objects?

10	9	8	7	6	5	4	3	2	1	0

The child consistently uses all the space around the body and over it, as is required by the game.	The child sometimes uses all the spaces of his/her body.	The child rarely uses all the spaces of his/her body.

COMMENTS

Fig. 10–9. Rating Scale: Performance of Selected Game Skills

The scale will provide a profile of the relative performance among the four components. Smith does not provide for a total score on the scale, but one could be implemented by the user if desired.

Rating Scale: Performance of Selected Game Skills*

Hudgens[44] developed a rating scale based on the component of Space Awareness, which includes general space, personal space, directions, and extensions. The 10 to 0 range shown in Figure 10–9 is well defined to assist the rater in making the appropriate assessment. A total score may or may not be important. The scale will show strengths and weaknesses within the space awareness components.

Relationships Rating Scale for Game Play Development†

Irwin, Jewett, and Woodfield[45] used a time-sampling technique as described by Irwin and Bushnell[46] to measure game play development in body awareness, space awareness, and relationships. The scale to assess relationships is included to illustrate the time-sampling technique, which gives an objective dimension to ratings that are usually more subjective. Figure 10–10 shows a copy of the form partially completed. Time sampling in this case means that a notation of the child's performance is made every 3 seconds over a 30-second time period. These notations can be made from a videotape. Live coding is possible, but more difficult for the teacher who is inexperienced in the technique.

The component of relationships focused on the appropriateness of the movement to one of the four aspects of relationship: object, equipment, individual, group. A correct response was coded as one (1), and an incorrect response was coded as a zero (0).

*Used by permission of A. Hudgens, Elementary Physical Education Teacher, Charlotte-Mecklenburg Schools, Charlotte, N.C.
†Used by permission of J. Irwin, S. Jewett, and D. Woodfield, graduate students, School of HPERD, UNC-Greensboro, Greensboro, N.C.

USE OF RATING SCALE TO ASSESS RELATIONSHIPS IN GAME PLAY DEVELOPMENT

1. Select one or more aspects of the rating scale you wish to measure: object, equipment, individual, group.
2. Record the major emphasis(es) on the record sheet.
3. Devise tasks appropriate for (a) the physical and mental development levels of the children, and (b) the selected major emphasis(es). Some tasks are given on the sample form in Figure 10–10. Other task examples:
   (1) Strike the ball to a wall with a short racket. The object is to keep the ball going while aiming for the same area on the wall.
   Relationships: racket to ball, racket to body, body to wall and ball.
   (2) Toss and catch a ball with a partner.
   Relationships: child to ball when catching, child to child when throwing, arm in relation to body when throwing.
   (3) A lead-up volleyball game with a group of six. The object is to keep the ball going among six people by striking it with the hands and arms.
   Relationships: body position to ball when striking, relation of child to the child he/she is sending the ball, relation of the child to the whole group.
4. Record the names of the students to be rated in the Name column.
5. Record the date above the relationship aspects being evaluated. This will permit you to use the same sheet again if only a limited number of aspects are being evaluated at this time or if the same aspects are being evaluated several times during a unit.
6. Film the lesson.
7. Record observations. Code every 3 seconds, for a period of 30 seconds, for *each* aspect being evaluated. There should be 10 notations. Follow the same procedure for each child.
8. Count the number of 1s recorded. Record in the tally section on the form. Divide the tallies by the total number of observations (should be 10). Multiply by 100 to get the percent score for each aspect rated.

Observer: _____ Date: _____ Grade: _____

Major Emphasis: <u>Object and Individual, all 4</u>

Tasks:

1. <u>Strike the ball into the air with different body parts and keep control of the ball</u>
2. <u>Throw the ball so your partner must reach, stretch, or jump to catch it</u>
3. <u>Throw the ball ahead of your partner so he/she must move to catch it</u>

Name	OBJECT	TALLY	EQUIPMENT	TALLY	INDIVIDUAL	TALLY	GROUP	TALLY	TOTAL TALLY	% age RATING	COMMENTS
Alice 4/27	1011000100	4/10			1100000000	2/10					0s were wait time (individual)
Alice 5/21	1011100100	5/10			1111011011	8/10					
Paul 4/27	1001011001	5/10	1101011010	6/10	1011011010	6/10	1010100011	5/10	22/40	55%	
Paul 5/21	1010110111	7/10	1011101011	7/10	1110111011	8/10	1101110101	7/10	29/40	73%	

Fig. 10–10. Relationships Rating Scale for Game Play Development

9. Then calculate the percent rating. When all four aspects have been rated, total all the 1s and divide by the total number of tallies (should be 40). Next multiply by 100. This will give you the percent rating of the total relationship component.

10. A comments area allows you to record any additional information that may be pertinent to your evaluation.

11. Obtain a descriptive interpretation of the score by referring to the following percent level scale:

80 to 100% Superior
60 to 80%   Above Average
40 to 60%   Average
20 to 40%   Below Average
0 to 20%   Needs to try harder

This percent level scale can be used to record percentages for either individuals or whole classes, depending on the requirements of the task.

The sample shown in Figure 10–10 reflects that Alice was rated twice, about a month's time apart, on relationships with object and individual. She improved slightly in her performance related to an object and significantly in relation to performing with another individual. Paul, on the other hand, was rated on all 4 aspects of relationships. Working on these tasks over a period of a month, he improved from 55% to 73%, performing in the appropriate way.

Rating Scales for Phase 1,[47] Manipulative Games Skills: Catching, Striking, Throwing*

Akers, Allison, and Hudgens[48] developed these three assessment instruments and provided a listing of sample tasks appropriate to each scale. The teacher will think of others, as well. The use of a minimal criterion is unique. Unless a child can demonstrate the minimal criterion performance, a rating is not appropriate. For example, the minimal criterion for catching is that the child be able to catch the ball with hands or implement and maintain control. Trapping the ball against the chest would not meet the min-

imal criterion; therefore, the child should not be rated on a catching task using this rating scale. The "Comments Concerning Task Performance" sections of the rating scale permits developmental information to be recorded as well as information about the child's interpretation of the task.

Based on the evidence for reliability and logical validity, these rating scales have value as assessment tools for the teacher. The instructions for a catching task, a list of possible catching tasks, and the rating scale for catching (Fig. 10–11) will be presented first, followed by the same materials for striking (Fig. 10–12) and throwing (Fig. 10–13).

Use of Space and Body Awareness in Games

Williams and Wilson[49] designed two test items in 1973 to assess two of the most basic concepts in an educational movement approach to games, the use of space and body awareness. Irwin[50] revised the items in 1982, refining the procedures for recording and scoring the items. The items are performed within the games context.

Item No. 1, The Use of Space

The task is to travel freely, using as much space as possible within designated boundaries. The space can be a regular-sized gymnasium or as small as an empty classroom. Several students should perform at once. The action can be put on videotape for later analysis, or each child can have a partner record his/her floor pattern on a score card. Three 30-second trials are given with 10- to 15-second rest intervals interspersed.

INSTRUCTIONS Find an empty space away from everyone. Begin traveling in any way you wish. Try to use all the space. Move into empty spaces. Begin working.

SCORING. Each child's use of space is replicated on paper and rated according to the 5-point scale shown on the score card (Fig. 10–14). The score is the average rating points for the three trials. The rating score can be given by the teacher as he/she analyzes the tapes, or the score can be determined by the students as they discuss the performance and floor tracings on the score cards.

*Used by permission of P. Akers, P. Allison, and A. Hudgens, Presently or formerly Elementary School Physical Education Teachers in North Carolina.

Sample Instructions for a Catching Task

Task:	Catch a self-tossed beanbag with one hand, in different places around you.
Equipment:	One beanbag per child.
Practice Trial:	Each child will be given 30 seconds to practice the task before being tested. The test instructions will be read to the child before the practice trial. The test administrator may demonstrate the task.
Test Trial:	The test administrator will give a signal to begin and the child will continuously perform the task for a sufficient amount of time for a rating to be made.
Instructions:	"When I say begin, toss the beanbag so that you will have to catch it with one hand, in different places around you. Remember to catch the beanbag at high levels, medium levels, and low levels, as well as in front of you, behind you, and out to the sides. Always be alert and ready to make the catch. Position your hand in line with the beanbag and absorb the force of the beanbag when you catch it. Are you ready? Begin."
Rating:	The child's performance will be rated on a scale of 1 to 5. Comments will be entered in the two Comment sections.

List of Possible Catching Tasks to be Selected by the Teacher

Movement Aspect	Tasks
Body	1. Catch a self-tossed object with either hand.
Space	2. Catch a self-tossed object in different places around you.
Effort	3. Catch an object tossed to you at different speeds.
Space	4. Catch a ball that has rebounded from the floor.
Body	5. As you travel, catch an object, tossed to you, with either hand.
Space	6. As you travel, catch an object tossed to you from different distances.
Relationship	7. With an implement, catch an object that is tossed to different places around you.
Relationship	8. While moving with an implement, catch an object that is tossed to you at different speeds.
Relationship	9. While moving with an implement, catch an object that is tossed to you from different distances.

Rating Scale for Catching

Name _____ CASSANDRA JONES _____ Age or Grade ___ 5th Grade ___

MINIMUM CRITERION FOR CATCHING: The child is able to catch the ball with hands or implement and maintain control.

MEETS MINIMUM CRITERION: YES __✔__   NO _____

CATCHING RATING CRITERIA

1. Total body is alert and ready for the catch.
2. Hand(s)/implement is positioned in line with the trajectory of the object.
3. Hand(s)/implement is used to catch and keep control of the object.
4. Appropriate force absorption is demonstrated.

5-POINT RATING:

Date(s)	Tasks	Movement Aspect B,S,E,R	Most of the time 5	More than half the time 4	Half the time 3	Less than half the time 2	Rarely 1
Dec. 10	1. Catch a self-tossed bean bag with one hand in different places around you	S				✔	
	2.						

COMMENTS CONCERNING RATING CRITERIA:
   Cassandra did not appear to be ready and alert for the catches. Her movements were stiff
   and bound. Many unsuccessful catches occurred due to her inability to give with the catch.

COMMENTS CONCERNING TASK PERFORMANCE:
   Cassandra failed to use different places around her in which to catch the bean bag. She only
   caught the bean bag in front of her body, at a medium level.

Fig. 10–11. Rating Scale for Catching

Sample Instructions for a Striking Task

Task:	Strike a plastic ball with different body parts sending it straight up.
Equipment:	One plastic ball per child.
Practice Trial:	Each child will be given 30 seconds to practice the task before being tested. The test instructions will be read to the child before the practice trial. The test administrator may demonstrate the task.
Test Trial:	The test administrator will give a signal to begin and the child will perform the task a sufficient amount of time for a rating to be made.
Instructions:	"When I say begin, work in your own space and strike the ball with different body parts, sending it straight up. Be sure to keep the body part you are using firm and get that part under the ball before striking. Please be sure to use different parts to strike. In order to control the ball you may catch it after you strike, let it bounce, or continuously strike it. Are you ready? Begin."
Rating:	The child's performance will be rated on a scale of 1 to 5. Comments will be entered in the two Comments sections.

List of Possible Striking Tasks to be Selected by the Teacher

Movement Aspect	Tasks
Body	1. Continuously strike the ball straight up, using different body parts.
Effort	2. Continuously strike the ball straight up, with different body parts varying the amount of force used.
Space	3. Continuously strike the ball straight up with the hands, contacting the ball at different places around you.
Body	4. Continuously strike the ball against the wall, using different body parts.
Body	5. Continuously strike the ball straight up, using a paddle/racket.
Effort	6. Continuously strike the ball with a paddle/racket, varying the amount of force used.
Space	7. Continuously strike the ball so that you make yourself move to get it.
Space	8. Continuously strike the ball into general space with different body parts so that you are traveling as you are striking.
Space	9. Continuously strike the ball into general space with different body parts so that you are changing directions as you strike the ball.

Rating Scale for Striking

Name _____ STEVE HILL _____ Age or Grade _ 5th Grade _____

MINIMUM CRITERION FOR STRIKING: The child is able to send the object away from the body
with a striking motion.

MEETS MINIMUM CRITERION: YES __✔__   NO _____

STRIKING RATING CRITERIA

1. Total body is alert and ready for strike.
2. Body part/implement is aligned for strike.
3. Body part/implement is firm at contact.
4. Proper range of motion for task demands is used.
5. Body part/implement is perpendicular to line of flight.
6. Object is contacted opposite line of flight.

5-POINT RATING:

Date(s)	Tasks	Movement Aspect B,S,E,R	Most of the time 5	More than half the time 4	Half the time 3	Less than half the time 2	Rarely 1
	Strike plastic ball straight up with different body parts	B		✔			

COMMENTS CONCERNING RATING CRITERIA:
Gets body part under ball almost all the time. Loses "alertness" occasionally, when continuously striking for long time. Has control of effort. Is firm except with knees and elbows.

COMMENTS CONCERNING TASK PERFORMANCE:
Steve tried several different body parts both upper and lower and right and left. Did not attempt to use head.

Fig. 10–12.   Rating Scale for Striking

Sample Instructions for a Throwing Task

Task:	Using an over-arm throw, throw a whiffle ball at the wall target from a distance of 15 feet.
Equipment:	A whiffle ball for each child. A wall target that is a circle, 24 inches in diameter, drawn on the wall. Tape to mark the restraining line.
Practice Trial:	Each child will be given 30 seconds to practice the task before being tested. The test instructions will be read to the child before the practice trial. The test administrator may demonstrate the task.
Test Trial:	The test administrator will give a signal to begin and the child will perform the task a sufficient amount of time for a rating to be made, throwing at his own rate of speed.
Instructions:	"When I say begin, throw the whiffle ball at the wall target from behind the restraining line. You must use an over-arm throw. When throwing, use the proper amount of force needed to get the ball to the wall and follow through with your arm toward the target at the release of the ball. Be sure to be alert and ready for the next throw. Are you ready? Begin."
Rating:	The child's performance will be rated on a scale of 1 to 5. Comments will be entered in the two Comments sections.

List of Possible Throwing Tasks to be Selected by the Teacher

Movement Aspect	*Tasks*
Space	1. Throw the object in the spaces around you.
Body	2. Throw the object while traveling and stopping.
Body	3. Throw the object while running in the general space.
Space	4. Throw the object into the general space so that you have to move to catch it.
Effort	5. Throw the object to the wall while varying the distances the object is thrown.
Effort	6. Throw the object to the wall while varying the force of the throw.
Space	7. Throw the object to a target so that you have to move to catch it.
Space	8. Throw and catch the object while moving and changing direction.

Rating Scale for Throwing

Name ____CHRIS SMITH_____ Age or Grade __5th Grade_____

MINIMUM CRITERION FOR THROWING: The child is able to release the object in the intended
direction of flight.

MEETS MINIMUM CRITERION: Yes __✔__ No _____

THROWING RATING CRITERIA

1. Total body is alert and ready for throw.
2. Body part/implement uses proper amount of extension for task demands.
3. Body part/implement continues in the direction of desired ball flight.
4. Proper range of motion for task demands is used.
5. Total body is aligned for throw.

5-POINT RATING:

Date(s)	Tasks	Movement Aspect B,S,E,R	Most of the time 5	More than half the time 4	Half the time 3	Less than half the time 2	Rarely 1
2/5	1. Using an over-arm throw, throw a whiffle ball at the wall target from a distance of 15 feet.	S		✔			
	2.						

COMMENTS CONCERNING RATING CRITERIA:
 Chris does not show complete trunk rotation, and forearm action is limited.

COMMENTS CONCERNING TASK PERFORMANCE:
 Chris is able to successfully perform the task. The ball lands well within the target area.

Fig. 10–13. Rating Scale for Throwing

Use of Space and Body Awareness in Games*

Name: _____ Date: _____ Rater: _____

Item No. 1
USE OF SPACE
_____

Pathway student takes: Comments

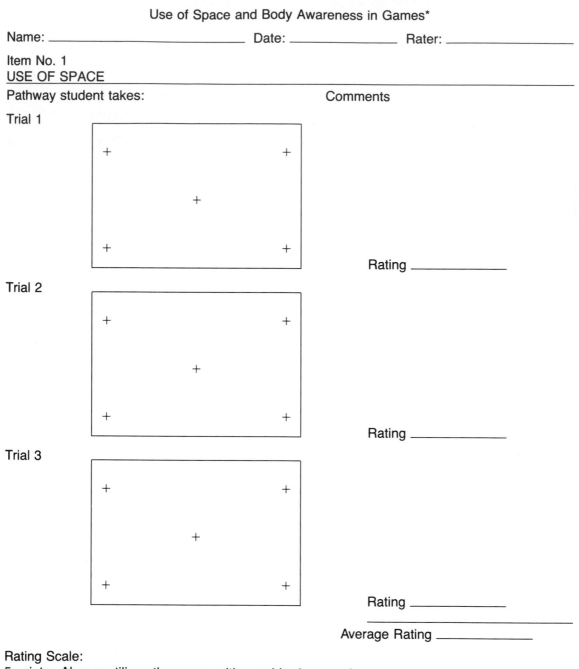

Trial 1

Rating _____

Trial 2

Rating _____

Trial 3

Rating _____

_____

Average Rating _____

Rating Scale:
5 points: Always utilizes the space with good body control.
4 points: Most of the time utilizes the space with good body control.
3 points: Frequently utilizes the space with good body control.
2 points: Sometimes utilizes the space, occasionally bumps into someone.
1 point: Rarely utilizes the space: (a) remains in one area, (b) uses limited amounts of space, (c) remains on the periphery, (d) remains in the middle, and/or often bumps into some-one.

_____
*Used by permission of J. Irwin, doctoral student, School of HPERD, UNC-Greensboro, Greensboro, N.C.

Fig. 10–14. Use of Space

Item No. 2, Body Awareness with an Object (Striking)

The task is to strike the ball (a 9-inch plastic ball) with as many different body parts as possible. The children are given three 30-second trials, with 10- to 15-second rest intervals.

INSTRUCTIONS. Find a space away from everyone. Strike your ball, using as many different parts of your body as possible. Keep control as long as you can but change parts often. If you lose your ball, get it back as quickly as possible and begin again. Be aware of others. Begin working.

SCORING. The different body parts used are checked on the score sheet. Repetitious striking with one body part counts as one body part, and a return to a previously used body part does not count again. The ball may rebound from the floor. The score is the average number of different body parts contacted with the ball during the three trials. A subjective rating can be noted also, using the rating scale on the score sheet.

Older children can score for one another, eliminating the use of the videotape equipment, if each student has two other students working with him/her; one to call out the body parts and one to record. The rating might be more difficult for the students to decide but it would be an interesting analysis for them.

Irwin suggests the use of a composite score, which would encompass both items. This is possible under the assumption that the two items are equally important to the game's content. She further suggests that the recording forms for the two items could be printed on the front and back sides of a score card for efficiency of administration. (Figs. 10–14 and 10–15). Variations could be introduced by changing the task description in the Instructions.

Weatherman Dribbling Test*

The Weatherman Dribbling Test[51] is designed to show developmental levels of dribbling, thus determining the point at which the student experiences difficulty. Its purpose is to determine dribbling proficiency for sixth grade students and

---

*Used by permission of P.G. Weatherman, Physical Education Specialist, Winston-Salem-Forsyth Schools, Winston-Salem, N.C.

may be appropriate for other grade levels as well. The test had concurrent validity with subjective ratings and high test-retest reliability.

The Dribbling Test

EQUIPMENT. Two basketballs, 5 cones, measuring tape, pencils, stopwatch, score cards, time sheet, tape, and a gym or outdoor smooth surface measuring 72 feet in length and at least 10 feet in width.

DIRECTIONS. The student begins by standing with a basketball at point A (see Fig. 10–16). On "Go" signal, student will dribble in place at point A for 10 seconds. On the signal, "Walk," the student will walk and dribble to point B. On the signal, "Run," the student will run and dribble to point C. On the signal "Alternate," the student will continue running and dribbling, alternating left and right hands, while moving in a zigzag pathway around cones to point D, where time is stopped and recorded. Each student will be given 5 trials, 1 practice trial and 4 to be recorded. The performance will be rated on the criteria discussed and timed between sections C and D of the test. These scores are recorded on a score card shown in Figure 10–17.

JUDGING CRITERIA:
1. The body should be in a low, crouched position.
2. The wrist should be relaxed, with the fingers curved for control and force.
3. The eyes and head should be kept up the majority of the time.
4. The height of the bounce should be no higher than waist level the majority of the time.
5. The ball should be kept in front of the body, allowing maximum control.

SCORING. Two scores are possible. One is the average rating of the four trials. Another is the average time to perform the last segment over four trials. Totals of ratings for each segment may provide some diagnostic information about the level of dribbling where difficulty was encountered.

Rating Scale for Dance

Dimondstein discusses criteria for qualitative judgments that reflect the conceptual framework for a child's dance: (1) basic elements of space,

Name: _____ Date: _____ Rater: _____

Item No. 2
BODY AWARENESS WITH AN OBJECT (STRIKING)

Body Parts	Different Body Parts Contacted		
	Trial 1	Trial 2	Trial 3
Head	_____	_____	_____
Shoulder(s)	_____	_____	_____
Elbow(s)	_____	_____	_____
Arm(s)	_____	_____	_____
Hand(s)	_____	_____	_____
Chest	_____	_____	_____
Stomach	_____	_____	_____
Hips	_____	_____	_____
Side(s)	_____	_____	_____
Upper thigh(s)	_____	_____	_____
Knee(s)	_____	_____	_____
Shin(s)	_____	_____	_____
Ankle(s)	_____	_____	_____
Feet	_____	_____	_____
Others	_____	_____	_____

Total Number of Different
Body Parts Contacted   _____ _____ _____   Average Number of Different
Body Parts Contacted: _____

Subjective Rating   _____ _____ _____   Average Subjective Rating:
_____

Comments:

Rating Scale:
5 points: Always has control of his/her body and the ball and uses 10 or more different body
         parts.
4 points: Frequently has control of his/her body and the ball and uses 9 to 6 different body parts.
3 points: Half the time, has control of his/her body and the ball and uses 5 or less different body
         parts.
2 points: Sometimes has control of his/her body and the ball and uses 5 or less different body
         parts.
1 point: Rarely has control of his/her body and the ball and uses 2 or less different body parts.

Rating of Use of Space   _____
Rating of Body Awareness   _____
Total Composite Score   _____

Fig. 10–15. Body Awareness With An Object

Specifications for the Weatherman Dribbling Test

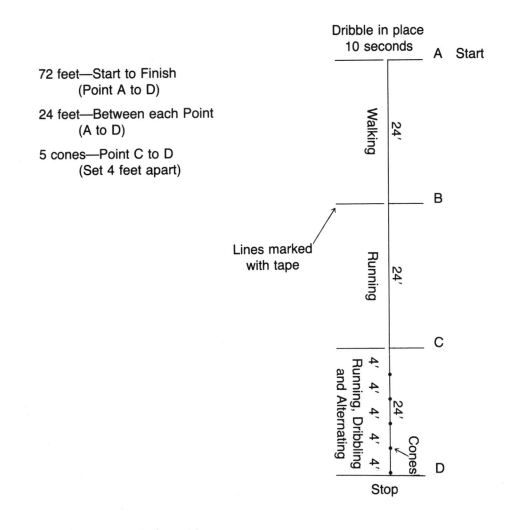

72 feet—Start to Finish
  (Point A to D)

24 feet—Between each Point
  (A to D)

5 cones—Point C to D
  (Set 4 feet apart)

Fig. 10–16.   Specifications for the Weatherman Dribbling Test

Score Card for the Weatherman Dribbling Test

Name _____   Class _____

Age _____   Sex _____   Date _____

Key: 5 points—Fine performance: excellent skill.
  4 points—Good performance: only minor points need attention.
  3 points—Average performance: needs refining; more practice needed.
  2 points—Poor performance: showing progress but much assistance and practice needed.
  1 point —Virtually no performance: special assistance needed.

Trials	Dribbling while standing still	Walking and drib-bling	Running and dribbling	Alternating hands while running and dribbling	Totals of Ratings
				Rating Time	
Trial 1					
Trial 2					
Trial 3					
Trial 4					
Totals				Total Ave.	Total:
Comments:					

Fig. 10–17.   **Score Card for Weatherman Dribbling Test**

time, and flow, (2) total construct of space, time, and flow, and (3) the perception of these elements as aesthetic qualities.[52] In addition to these factors intrinsic to dance, there are generalized behaviors that children reveal through the nature of their involvement in the creative process. These factors, derived from Dimondstein, are used as the basis for the rating scale in dance. The gradations for the ratings are gathered from Schurr.[3]

DIRECTIONS. The teacher should be aware of the focus points of the rating scale throughout the dance unit and then make an overall assessment of the child's performance. This difficult task may require anecdotal notations on the rating scale as the work progresses. The headings on the rating form, as well as the clarifying sub-

points, should be discussed with the child (see Fig. 10–18).

SCORING. The overall impression of the dance expression is more important than the precise numeric score. The teacher should discuss the rating scale notations with the child.

Rating Scale: Performance in Gymnastics*

A form rating sheet can be used to accommodate different pieces of apparatus, small pieces of equipment, and various aspects of performance in gymnastics. Weatherman[53] has devel-

_____

*Used by permission of P.G. Weatherman, Physical Education Specialist, Winston-Salem-Forsyth Schools, Winston-Salem, N.C.

Rating of Child's Performance in Dance					
Name _____ Date _____ Factors	Excellent	Better than average	Average	Slightly below average	Special help needed

1. Emotional involvement
    Necessary impetus for creative work
    Initiates ideas for exploration
    Involvement reaches an intensity
 2. Focus on a problem
    Beginning to structure an idea
    Elaborating, refining
    Making form out of the formless
 3. Development of an idea into an objective form
    Leads to a creative product
    Expression shaped by selected use of movement elements
    Creating something meaningful for the child to externalize
 4. Fulfillment as a result of the release of the imagination
    Fulfillment of child's idiomatic ways of showing emotional
        involvement through facial expressions and gestures
    Tangible evidence of child's imaginative powers					

Comments:					

Fig. 10–18.   Rating Form—Child's Performance in Dance

Rating Scale: Performance in Gymnastics			Date(s)		
Name _____ Teacher _____ Age/Grade _____					
Situation: Task: _____					
Apparatus/Equipment: _____					
1. Introduction to the Body (with emphasis on ways the body can move) Comments:	1 2 3 4 5				
2. Introduction to Space (with emphasis on areas, levels, directions, extensions, and pathways) Comments:	1 2 3 4 5				
3. Introduction to Time (with emphasis on body actions and activities) Comments:	1 2 3 4 5				
4. Relationships of Body Parts (with emphasis on body shapes and actions of the body) Comments:	1 2 3 4 5				
5. Introduction to Weight (with emphasis on activities of the body) Comments:	1 2 3 4 5				
6. Flow and Continuity of Movement (with emphasis on selection and refinement of movement in sequences) Comments:	1 2 3 4 5				
7. Relationships to Others (with emphasis on partners and small group work) Comments:	1 2 3 4 5				
8. Introduction to Rhythm (with emphasis on creating, repeating, and refining rhythm patterns in movement sequences) Comments:	1 2 3 4 5				

Fig. 10–19.   Rating Scale: Performance in Gymnastics

oped a rating scale using the eight movement themes for organizing and developing content for educational gymnastics. It has the potential for a variety of these uses (Fig. 10–19). Only one or two factors might be rated on any one occasion to reflect formative assessments. One factor might be rated several times to show the child's progress. If all the factors were rated toward the completion of the unit in gymnastics, all ratings received on all eight items could be totaled to reflect a summative evaluation. The rating levels could be defined as follows:

5 points: Fine performance; excellent
4 points: Good performance; only minor points need attention
3 points: Average performance; needs more practice
2 points: Poor performance; showing progress but much work needed
1 point: No performance; special help needed

Another type of gymnastics assessment is shown later in the chapter under the section on the Application of Evaluative Information.

Schilling Body Coordination Test*[54]

The purposes of this test are to measure body

---

*Adapted from Schilling, F., and Kiphard, E.J.: *Körper-koordinations-test für Kinder KTK*. Marburg, West Germany, Institute for Medical and Educational Child Guidance of Philipp University, 1974.

control and coordination and to identify motor retardation. It is designed for boys and girls 5 to 14 years of age. They should have separate norms.

A class of normal size can be tested in one period if sufficient leadership and equipment are available to test on a station-to-station basis. If only one station is provided for each of the four items, a small gym or even a play room will afford ample space.

CLASS ORGANIZATION. This battery should be administered on a station-to-station basis. Since the four items are not strenuous, the order of events is not a factor, and therefore a class can be divided into squads with each squad starting at a different station. Individual score cards can be provided. Once the testing is started at different stations, the squads can rotate to the next station upon finishing. If one station seems to be lagging behind the others, a second station may be used to speed up testing procedure, provided enough leadership and equipment are available. Scoring should be done by a trained assistant.

GENERAL PROCEDURE

1. All four items require special equipment. These materials should be provided before the day of testing (Fig. 10–20).
2. All items should be explained and demonstrated before testing is begun.
3. The purpose of the test should be made known to the students.

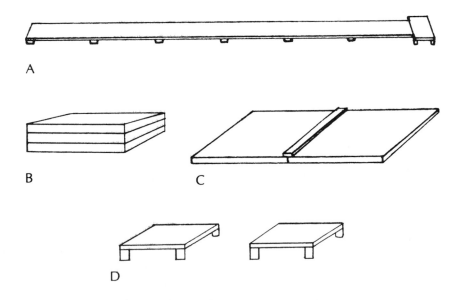

Fig. 10–20. Equipment for the Schilling Body Coordination Test (A, B, C, D)

4. Scores are more reliable when the student wears tennis shoes.
5. Student leaders must be trained in advance of the testing period.

USES. The results of this test may be used to identify the level of retardation of body coordination and for classification and guidance.

TEST DESCRIPTION

Item Number 1—Balance Backward (Fig. 10–21A)

PURPOSE. To measure balance.

FACILITIES AND EQUIPMENT. Three balance beams each 3 meters long and 5 cm from the floor, including the crosspieces for supports. The first board is 6 cm wide, the second is 4.5 cm, and the third is 3 cm (Fig. 10–20). One of the 25-cm-square boards used in Test 4 is placed at the starting end of each beam to be used as a starting platform.

DIRECTIONS. The test consists of three trials of walking backward on each of the three beams. The test director first demonstrates the test; the subjects then have one practice trial of walking forward and backward on each of the three boards. If the subject loses balance in this practice trial, he/she may step back on the board at that point and continue the remaining distance. After this practice trial, the subject then steps back on the starting platform at the widest beam and this time only walks backward for the first test trial. If the subject loses balance and touches the floor with one or both feet, he/she must return to the starting platform and start a new trial. Three trials are permitted at each beam for a grand total of nine trials. The test administrator counts out loud each step as it is taken.

INSTRUCTIONS. First, we want you to practice balancing. Start walking forward from this platform and walk to the end of the beam. Stand there for a few seconds and then walk backward carefully to the starting platform so that you do not step off the beam. After this practice trial, start your first test trial from the platform at the end of the widest beam and this time walk only backwards to the end of the beam. If you step off the beam and touch the floor with one or both feet, return to the starting platform and begin a new trial. You have three trials. When you finish at the wide board, move on to the next one. I will count your score out loud for you as you walk.

SCORING. The final score is the total number of backward steps the subject takes on the 3 trials on each of the 3 boards. Step 1 from the platform on to the beam does not count. The count starts with the second step and continues until the child steps off or reaches the end of the beam. A maximum of 8 points may be awarded for each trial. If the student traverses the full length of the beam in fewer than 8 steps, he/she is awarded the top score of 8 for the trial. The maximum score is 72 points (3 beams × 3 trials × 8 points).

Item Number 2—Hopping (Fig. 10–21B)

PURPOSE. To measure hopping skills along with dynamic balance.

FACILITIES AND EQUIPMENT. Twelve rectangular foam rubber blocks 50 cm × 5 cm thick.

DIRECTIONS. The test consists of hopping over 1 or several stacked blocks on 1 leg. The test director demonstrates the event by hopping on 1 leg to a foam rubber block. He hops over the block and continues hopping for at least 2 more steps, covering a distance of approximately 3 meters. The test is done first on one leg and then the other. Two practice trials are permitted on each leg. Five- and 6-year-old children are given 2 practice trials of 5 hops each without the blocks. If they succeed, 1 block is added for the first test trial. This rule is applied for each leg. Older children are given the 2 practice trials for each leg using 1 block. If a child older than 6 years fails the 1-block test on the practice test, the block is removed, and then, if he/she succeeds, the first test trial begins with the proper level for that age group. Therefore, the starting level of the test trial depends on the outcome of these practice trials and the age of the child, as listed in the following section. After the practice trials, the child starts the test trials. The starting levels are:

5-year-olds	0 blocks
6-year-olds	1 block
7- and 8-year olds	3 blocks
9- and 10-year olds	5 blocks
11-year-olds and older	7 blocks

If a child 7 and older does not succeed at these starting levels, his/her first trial is started using

1 block. Three trials are permitted at each block level. It is a failure when (1) the opposite leg touches the floor, (2) the blocks are kicked over, and (3) after hopping over the blocks, less than 2 hops are taken.

INSTRUCTIONS. Start hopping here on one leg at his starting line. Hop to the block, hop over it, and then hop at least two more times on the same leg before you stop. If you touch the floor wih the other leg or knock over a block, that will count as a failure.

SCORING. Three points are scored for each of the 13 levels of blocks (0 to 12) if the child succeeds on the first trial: 2 points are scored if he/she succeeds on the second trial; and 1 point is scored if the third trial is successful. At beginning heights greater than 1-block level, a successful first attempt is awarded 3 points for each of the underlying blocks. If the child fails the 3 trials at any given level, the test is terminated if he/she has failed to accumulate 5 points on the preceding 2 heights. A maximum of 39 points may be awarded for each leg, for a grand total of 78 points.

Item Number 3—Lateral Jumping (Fig. 10–21C)

PURPOSE. To measure jumping ability.

FACILITIES AND EQUIPMENT. Stopwatch. Two plywood sheets measuring 60 cm × 50 cm × 8 cm, joined by hinges. A small wooden strip approximately 60 cm × 4 cm × 2 cm in size is mounted along the midline of the total surface area of the hinged boards. A lath will serve this purpose (Fig. 10–20).

DIRECTIONS. The test consists of jumping laterally back and forth across the wooden strip. The subject holds his feet together and jumps as rapidly as possible for 15 seconds. The test director demonstrates the task as described. The subject has 5 practice jumps and then 2 test trials of 15 seconds each. Each jump counts 1 point, and it counts as a score even if the legs separate on landing, or the subject slips off the board, or touches the wooden strip, or comes to a brief halt.

INSTRUCTIONS. Stand near the wooden strip, with your feet together. On the signal "Go," jump sideways across the bar and back as fast as you can until I say "Stop." Try to keep your feet together at all times. If you step on the strip or off the platform, do not stop.

SCORING. Each jump is scored one point. The final score is the total number of jumps in the two trials.

Item Number 4—Lateral Movement (Fig. 10–21D)

PURPOSE. To measure the speed of lateral movement.

FACILITIES AND EQUIPMENT. Stopwatch. Two boards 25 cm square and 1.5 cm thick (Fig. 10–21D), with 4 rubber door bumpers fastened at each corner to form a platform 5 cm high.

DIRECTIONS. The test consists of moving the platform sideways as many times as possible in a 20-second time period. For the starting position, the platforms are placed side by side and 1-platform-distance apart. The test director explains and demonstrates the test by showing the starting positions of the platforms and how the subject performs the task. The student starts by standing on one platform with the other platform to his/her left. On the signal to start, the student picks up the platform to his/her left with both hands, places it on the right, then steps to the moved platform, picks up the platform just vacated, and places it to the right, and so on.

One practice trial of 3 to 5 shifts is permitted, where both speed of movement and proper positioning of the platform are emphasized. If the child prefers to move in a straight line to the left rather than right, this is permissible. Two trials of 20 seconds each are conducted, one after the other, with approximately a 10-second pause in between trials. The test director moves in front of the subject and counts the score out loud.

INSTRUCTIONS. Stand on the right platform to begin the test. At the signal "Go," take the other platform in both hands and place it to your other side. Now step to that platform and repeat these movements as many times as you can until I say "Stop." You score one point each time you place a platform on the floor and another point when you step on the next platform to your right with both feet. I will count your score out loud as you move sideward. Try to move the platform as many times as possible. Your feet should never touch the floor.

A

B

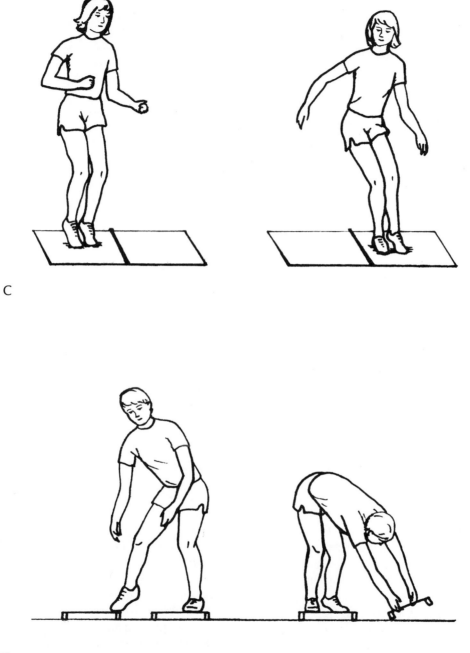

C

D

Fig. 10–21.   Test Items for the Schilling Body Coordination Test (A, B, C, D)

Schilling Test of Body Coordination Score Card							

Date　　Name　　　　　　　　　　　　　　　　　Age　　Grade　　Sex

Motor Ability

	Pretest	Post-test	Test 2 (Hopping):			
Test 1 (Balance):						
Beam 1: Trial 1	_____	_____	_____	_____	_____	
Trial 2	_____	_____	_____	_____	_____	
Trial 3	_____	_____	_____	_____	_____	
			Right Leg:			
Beam 2: Trial 1	_____	_____	_____	_____	_____	
Trial 2	_____	_____	_____	_____	_____	
Trial 3	_____	_____	_____	_____	_____	
			Left Leg:			
Beam 3: Trial 1	_____	_____	_____	_____	_____	
Trial 2	_____	_____	_____	_____	_____	
Trial 3	_____	_____	_____	_____	_____	
			_____	_____	_____	
			_____	_____	_____	
TOTAL	_____	_____	_____	_____	_____	
			_____	_____	_____	

Test 3 (Lat. Jump)　　　　　　　　Test 4 (Lat. Movement)

　　　　　　　　　　　　　　　　　　　　　　　TOTAL　_____　_____

	Pretest	Post-test		Pretest	Post-test
Trial 1:	_____	_____	Trial 1	_____	_____
Trial 2:	_____	_____	Trial 2	_____	_____
TOTAL	_____	_____	TOTAL	_____	_____

BATTERY SCORE: Pretest _____　　Post-test _____

Fig. 10–22. Score Card for Schilling Test

SCORING. A score of 1 is awarded when the platform to one side of the subject is picked up and placed at the other side. The second score is awarded when the student has stepped on the moved platform with both feet. The third point is awarded when the platform is moved again, and so on. The final score is the total number of points scored on the two 20-second trials.

The Charlop-Atwell Scale of Motor Coordination*

The Charlop-Atwell Scale of Motor Coordination[55] is a quick and easy measure of some aspects of gross motor coordination of chil-

dren between the ages of 4 and 6 years. Since the scale is designed to measure gross motor coordination as opposed to fine motor or perceptual, motor coordination, the items are geared toward the use of the entire body. One unique feature of the scale is the inclusion of 2 assessments for each item: the ability of the child to perform a certain task and the quality of the performance. Consequently, there are 3 scores: (1) an objective subtest, which scores the accuracy of performance (38 possible points); (2) a subjective subtest, which measures the quality of the performance (34 possible points); and (3) a total score (72 possible points). The subjective subtest includes 3 factors:

Precision of Movement　—exactness and accuracy of the movement without concern for a completely successful performance

*Reprinted with permission of authors and publisher from Charlop, M., and Atwell, C.W.: The Charlop-Atwell Scale of Motor Coordination: a quick and easy assessment of young children. Perceptual and Motor Skills, 50:1291, 1980.

| Smoothness and Flow | —continuity of movement, lack of pauses or abrupt interruptions |
| Flexibility | —agility and gracefulness |

The six items in the scale are included to fulfill certain functions:

Jumping Jacks	}—coordination of the upper limbs with the lower limbs
Prehistoric Animal	}—speed and accuracy of learning new skills
Jump and About Face	}—coordination of two simultaneous actions
Scarf Twirl	
Hopping	—dynamic balance
Tiptoe Balance	—static balance

The scale has been carefully developed by Charlop and Atwell, who show it to reveal a developmental trend, high test-retest and interobserver reliability, and strong external validity. It is rare to locate a scale of such quality which is also simple to administer and does not require special equipment. The classroom teacher or physical education specialist should be able to administer this scale to each child in 15 minutes. The authors caution that the scale may be inappropriate for an in-depth evaluation of a child's overall motor coordination and for physically handicapped children. The use of a larger and more representative sample will enable further study of the scale. A summary of the mean scores is included in Table 10–1 to allow the teacher to make some norm-referenced comparisons.

TEST ADMINISTRATION

Each child should be tested individually in the company only of the rater. The total time for both scale administration and scoring is approximately 15 minutes per child. Each child receives a standard set of instructions and demonstration for each item. For convenience during the testing situation, the instructions for each item are provided along with the testing criteria on the scale scoring sheets.

In order to attain optimal performance, the rater should establish and maintain good rapport with each child during the administration of the scale. We recommend that raters engage the child in a brief conversation before testing to make the child feel more relaxed and comfortable. It is also desirable for the testers to reinforce the child with praise and offer encouragement throughout the testing procedure. If a child obviously does not understand the instructions, then the instructions should be repeated without penalizing the child's score.

For the scale item Scarf Twirl, the child is permitted to hold the scarf in whichever hand is preferred. The child is also allowed to hop on either the right or left foot for the Hopping item.

For the two items in which scoring is based on a time criterion, a watch or clock that measures seconds is required. A stopwatch is best. For the scale item Scarf Twirl, a scarf or piece of cloth is necessary. It can be of any size, provided that when it is held out perpendicular to the child's body, it does not touch the ground.

The order in which the items are presented is not predetermined. During the provisional standardization procedure, the items were administered in a random order. It is advisable to start the testing procedure with an easier item to allow the child to initially experience success. It is thus recommended to present the Tiptoe Balance or the Jump and About Face as the first item.

Upon completion of the testing, the children should be thanked and reinforced for their cooperation and performance.

Table 10–1. Means for Objective Subtest, Subjective Subtest, and Total Scale Score by Age (N = 201)

	4.0	4.5	5.0	5.5	6.0
OBJECTIVE SUBTEST SCORE					
All Children	21.7	26.3	29.3	29.8	31.3
Boys	20.7	26.2	29.0	29.1	30.5
Girls	22.5	26.5	29.5	30.8	32.2
SUBJECTIVE SUBTEST SCORE					
All Children	20.9	22.9	24.6	25.1	26.4
Boys	19.8	20.8	24.1	24.1	25.1
Girls	21.8	25.2	24.8	26.3	27.9
TOTAL SCALE SCORE					
All Children	42.7	49.2	53.9	55.0	57.7
Boys	40.5	47.0	53.1	53.5	55.6
Girls	44.4	51.8	54.4	57.1	60.1

THE TEST

Name _____ Objective Subtest /38
Age _____ Subjective Subtest /34
Date _____ Total Scale Score /72

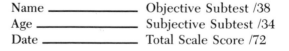

Jumping Jacks

INSTRUCTIONS. We are going to do jumping jacks. Watch me first. You are to jump, putting your feet apart and your arms up so that you can clap your hands above your head like this. Now, you are to jump, putting your feet back together and your arms back down at your side like this. Now you are back where you started from. Watch me again. Jump so that your feet are apart and your hands clap above your head. Then you are going to jump back to how you were before, with your feet together and your arms down at your side. So it is, arms up, legs out, then arms down and feet back together. (Demonstrator is to perform movements as he/she explains what the child is to do.) Now you try it. Arms up, feet apart. Now, arms back down, feet together. (Demonstrator has the child do this a few times.) Now I want you to do the jumping jacks faster by yourself like this. (Demonstrator does three continuous jumping jacks in a row.) Now you try it. (If child cannot perform at least one correct jumping jack, repeat instructions and have the child try again. Allow the child three trials before moving on to the next scale item.)

OBJECTIVE CRITERIA. 1 trial = 5 seconds

6 pt. does one jumping jack on first trial

4 pt. does one jumping jack on second trial

2 pt. does at least one jumping jack on third trial

SUBJECTIVE CRITERIA

Precision of movement

2 pt. arms raised and lowered *and* legs moved out and back together, not necessarily in synchrony

1 pt. arms raised and lowered *or* legs moved out and back together

0 pt. failure to do No. 1 and No. 2

Smoothness and flow

2 pt. continuous movement

1 pt. slight pauses between jumping jacks

0 pt. stops before each jumping jack to return to starting position, then proceeds

Flexibility

2 pt. agile and bendable, not stiff and rigid

1 pt. exhibition of tense and strained movements

0 pt. jerky, robot-like movements

Jump and About Face

INSTRUCTIONS. I want you to jump up into the air, turning around so that you face the wall behind you, and land with both feet on the ground. Watch me. (Demonstrator jumps into the air, turning 180° to face the opposite direction, and lands with both feet touching the ground at the same time.) Now you try it.

OBJECTIVE CRITERIA

4 pt. jumps and lands directly facing opposite direction

2 pt. jumps but does not land directly facing opposite direction

0 pt. fails to turn facing opposite direction when jumping

SUBJECTIVE CRITERIA

Precision of movement

2 pt. appears to land with both feet touching the ground at the same time

1 pt. lands with one foot obviously reaching the ground first, then followed by the other foot

0 pt. steps back or falls when landing

Flexibility

2 pt. arms relaxed

1 pt. arms stiff and rigid

0 pt. arms moved first before the body turns

Hopping on One Foot

INSTRUCTIONS. I want you to hop in place on one foot until I tell you to stop. (Demonstrator hops in place for a few seconds.) Remember to keep hopping, without putting your other foot down, until I tell you to stop. Try to hop in one place, do not hop around the room. Ready? Start hopping. (Demonstrator tells the child to stop after 8 seconds.)

OBJECTIVE CRITERIA

6 pt. hops in place for 8 seconds without putting raised foot down

4 pt. hops in place for 8 seconds, with putting foot down only once after 4 seconds

2 pt. puts foot down within first 4 seconds

0 pt. quits before 8 seconds

SUBJECTIVE CRITERIA

Precision of movement

2 pt. hops relatively in one place without moving about

1 pt. hops within area of 1 square foot

0 pt. hops without staying in area of 1 square foot

Smoothness and flow

2 pt. continuous hopping

1 pt. slight pauses between hops or unclear about pauses

0 pt. long pauses between hops

Flexibility

2 pt. lands lightly on ground

1 pt. unclear or lands moderately heavily
on ground

0 pt. lands heavily on ground

Prehistoric Animal

INSTRUCTIONS. I want you to get down on
your hands and feet like this. (Demonstrator has
both hands and feet on the ground with knees
moderately straight.) Do not bend your knees.
Now, take one step forward with one hand, not
moving your other hand and feet. (Demonstrator
moves one hand a few inches forward, keeping
the other hand and feet in place.) Then move
the other hand forward, then one foot, then the
other. (Demonstrator does this.) So, it is hand,
hand, foot, foot. (Demonstrate series of movements again.) Only move what I tell you to move.
When I say hand, only move one hand. Now
you try it. Get down on all fours. Remember to
keep your knees straight. Now move one hand,
then the other hand, then one foot, then the
other foot.

hand-hand-foot-foot
hand-hand-foot-foot

(If child cannot do at least one of these series,
have him/her stand up and repeat demonstration. If child still cannot perform one series correctly, score accordingly and move on to next
scale item.

OBJECTIVE CRITERIA

10 pt. alternates hand-hand, foot-foot (at
least twice) on first trial of 5-foot distance to be walked

8 pt. alternates hand-hand, foot-foot on first
trial at least once

6 pt. alternates hand-hand, foot-foot on
second trial at least twice

4 pt. alternates hand-hand, foot-foot once
on second trial

2 pt. shows some indication and attempts
to move in sequence

0 pt. cannot alternate hand-hand, foot-foot
on any trial or crawls

SUBJECTIVE CRITERIA
Precision of movement

2 pt. does not bend legs at the knees

1 pt. bends knees some of the time

0 pt. bends at the knees while walking

Smoothness and flow

2 pt. none or slight pauses in between
hand-hand, foot-foot sequences

1 pt. long pauses of 3 seconds or more in
between hand-hand, foot-foot sequences

0 pt. falls in between or during sequences
on hand-hand, foot-foot

Flexibility

2 pt. child gets into position of all fours,
with legs straight, quickly and easily

1 pt. relatively easy for child to get into
position of all fours

0 pt. difficult for child to get into position
of all fours

Scarf Twirl

INSTRUCTIONS. I want you to take the scarf
in your hand and hold that arm straight out from
your side like this. (Demonstrator holds arm with
scarf straight out, perpendicular to body.) While
you are holding your arm out. I want you to
twirl across the room to where I am standing,
like this. (Demonstrator twirls across a distance
of 12 feet toward the child, keeping the arm with
the scarf out from his side.) Remember to keep
your arm up—do not let the scarf touch the
ground. While you are twirling, whenever you
face me, make sure you look into my eyes. That
way you will not get dizzy. (Demonstrator now
stands 12 feet away from the child.) Hold your
arm with the scarf straight out from your side.
Now twirl over to where I am standing. (During
the twirling across, if the child lowers his arm,
remind him to keep his arm up. Also, remind
the child to look into your eyes whenever possible.)

OBJECTIVE CRITERIA

6 pt. does not drop arm and twirls in a
moderately straight line (does not
wander out of 4-foot-wide area of
imaginary straight line between child
and observer)

4 pt. drops arm once and twirls on moderately straight line

2 pt. drops arm more than once, but twirls on moderately straight line

0 pt. drops arm more than once and/or cannot twirl in a straight line

SUBJECTIVE CRITERIA

Precision of movement

2 pt. twirls in complete circles facing initial direction

1 pt. does not twirl in complete circles

0 pt. fails to twirl

Smoothness and flow

2 pt. not stopping between twirls

1 pt. stopping between twirls

0 pt. walking between twirls

Flexibility

2 pt. while twirling, child shows graceful movements, not stiff and rigid

1 pt. child exhibits some tense and strained movements while twirling

0 pt. ungraceful, rigid movements while twirling

Tiptoe Balance

INSTRUCTIONS. I want you to stand on your toes, without moving around or putting your heels down, until I tell you to stop. (Demonstrator stands on toes for a few seconds.) Now you try it. (Demonstrator tells the child to stop after 8 seconds. If the child is wearing heavy shoes, have the child take his/her shoes off.)

OBJECTIVE CRITERIA

6 pt. balances for 8 seconds, without putting heels down

4 pt. balances for 8 seconds, putting heels down after 4 seconds

2 pt. puts heels down within 4 seconds

0 pt. quits before 8 seconds

Charlop-Atwell Scale of Motor Coordination

Name _____ Age _____ Date _____

Directions: Circle the scores.

Items	Objective Criteria						Precision of Movement			Smoothness and Flow			Flexibility			Total
1. Jumping Jacks 1 trial—5 seconds		6	4	2	0		2	1	0	2	1	0	2	1	0	
2. Jump and About Face 1 trial			4	2	0		2	1	0	—			2	1	0	
3. Hopping on 1 Foot 1 trial—8 seconds		6	4	2	0		2	1	0	2	1	0	2	1	0	
4. Prehistoric Animal 2 trials—5 feet	10	8	6	4	2	0	2	1	0	2	1	0	2	1	0	
5. Scarf Twirl 1 trial—12 feet		6	4	2	0		2	1	0	2	1	0	2	1	0	
6. TipToe Balance 1 trial—8 seconds		6	4	2	0		2	1	0	2	1	0	2	1	0	
TOTALS																

Fig. 10–23. **Score Card for Charlop-Atwell Scale**

SUBJECTIVE CRITERIA

Precision of movement

2 pt. stands in one place without moving feet

1 pt. moves feet after 4 seconds

0 pt. moves feet within first 4 seconds

Smoothness and flow

2 pt. exhibits no wobbling of any part of the body while balancing

1 pt. exhibits wobbling after 4 seconds of balancing

0 pt. exhibits wobbling within first 4 seconds

Flexibility

2 pt. child quickly and easily gets on tiptoes on first attempt

1 pt. child takes two attempts to get on tiptoes before balancing begins

0 pt. child needs extra instructions on how to stand on tiptoes

Martin Screening Test for Motor Disabilities*

This screening test, developed by Martin,[56] consists of four items, which take approximately 2 minutes per child to administer. The test taps the areas of balance, body image, coordination, rhythm, and kinesthetic awareness of the body. The test is moderately reliable and valid. Given at the beginning of the year, it will be useful for identifying children whose motor development is below standard so remedial or adaptive physical education programs can be begun at an early age.

> It is imperative that a screening device identifies as many children as possible who really do have problems that should be examined further. To do this a test must be able to accurately label a child as having problems when he truly does and avoid labeling him as not having problems when he truly does. The more efficiently a test can do this, the more value it has.[56]

All directions should be given with the child standing at your side. Each item should be demonstrated correctly, and then the child should be asked to perform the item exactly as shown. Children not taking the test should not be permitted to watch.

It is important that the child understand what he/she is to do. If the child indicates in words or by his/her actions that he/she does not understand the prescribed task, reinstruct him/her in the correct procedure.

TEST ITEMS

1. JUMPING FORWARD FOUR TIMES. The child is told that he/she will be asked to jump forward four times on both feet, keeping the hands on the hips and the feet together. The correct procedure is then demonstrated. Ask the child to jump forward four times exactly as you did.

Errors include hesitation, a break in rhythm, removing the hands from the hips, incorrect number of jumps, separating the feet, and loss of balance.

2. TOE TOUCH AND REACH. Tell the child that he/she will be asked to touch his/her toes and then reach for the ceiling, going up on his/her tiptoes, and to do this several times. Demonstrate the item four times, keeping the feet together while performing. The knees may be bent slightly if difficulty is noticed. Then have the child do exactly as you did. Count only the errors that occur during the first four cycles.

Errors include hesitation, a break in rhythm, separating the feet more than an inch, and loss of balance.

3. BEAM WALK FORWARD (2 INCHES × 2 INCHES × 10 FEET). Tell the child he/she will be asked to walk forward on the balance beam in a heel-to-toe manner. Demonstrate the walking, being sure to touch your heel to your toe as you walk, and move slowly. Have the child do exactly as you did. If the child moves too fast or fails to move in the heel-to-toe manner, ask the child to start over and do it correctly. Correct performance is imperative for proper scoring.

The first eight steps—not counting steps in which an error occurs—are used for scoring. An error is putting one or both feet on the ground.

4. KINESTHETIC ARM SENSE. The child is told that he/she will be asked to close his/her eyes and put his/her arm straight out in front of him/her, straight out to his/her side, and straight up over his/her shoulder, and then to repeat this procedure, using the other arm. He/she is then told that he/she will be asked to put both arms

---

*Used with the permission of the author.

straight out in front of him/her in a parallel manner.

With your eyes closed, demonstrate this procedure to the student. Then tell him/her to do exactly as you did as you direct him/her. Tell him/her to close his/her eyes. Touch the student's right arm and tell him/her to start with this arm. Direct the child to put his/her arm straight out in front, straight out to the side, straight up over the shoulder, then down to the side. Direct him/her to use the other arm now. Repeat the above sequence, using the left arm. Then tell him/her to put both arms straight out in front. Finally, tell him/her to put his/her arms down and open his/her eyes.

An error occurs when the student does not hold the arms in the prescribed position of "straight" out in front, out to the side, or up over the shoulder. It is also an error if the child's arm is bent at the elbow when the child considers the task complete. If the student corrects an improper placement of the arm, do not count this as an error (the examiner is interested in the end result and not how it was obtained).

SCORING. The maximum score for each item is 8. Each mistake noticed is subtracted from the possible total score of 8 for each test item. Mistakes for a particular test item are listed under the description of that item. Each mistake or repetition of the same mistake is counted as an error and should be subtracted from 8. The lowest score given on any item is 1. No zero should be given. Each test item should be scored and recorded separately. The total score of all 4 items

should also be figured. The lowest possible total score will be 4 and the highest will be 32. Figure 10–24 suggests a format for the score card.

The cut-off scores suggested by Martin are between 18 to 21 for kindergarten children, 20 to 23 for first-grade children, and 22 to 25 for second-grade children.

Checklist: Characteristics of Students Who Need Perceptual-Motor Training[57]

A project report by Vodola stated that one of the prime objectives of physical education is the development of fundamental motor patterns.[58] The child who is motorically handicapped should be identified and given specialized instruction. This checklist developed by Sherrill helps the teacher become aware of behaviors that characterize children who may need special help.

SCORING. No scoring is necessary. The checklist will reveal a general pattern of behaviors that will alert the teacher to seek help for the child.

Smith Physical Fitness Test for Elementary Students*

Smith[59] constructed a four-item fitness test by adapting some items from the Glover Fitness Battery[60] and the AAHPERD Health Related Physical Fitness Test.[61] She assessed agility and

---

*Used by permission of N.L. Smith, Physical Education Specialist, Winston-Salem-Forsyth Schools, Winston-Salem, N.C.

Martin Screening Test		
Name _____ Age _____ Date _____ Tester _____		
Items		*Score*
1. Jumping Forward Four Times		_____
2. Toe Touch with Reach		_____
3. Beam Walk Forward		_____
4. Kinesthetic Arm Sense		_____
	Total Score	_____
Comments: (Mistakes, reactions, etc.)		

Fig. 10–24.   Score Card for Martin Screening Test

DIRECTIONS AND CHECKLIST
CHARACTERISTICS OF STUDENTS WHO NEED
PERCEPTUAL-MOTOR TRAINING
(Courtesy Dr. Claudine Sherrill)

NAME _____ AGE _____ SEX ____ DATE _____

SCHOOL _____ TEACHER _____

This checklist is to be completed by the classroom teacher, speech therapist, or physical education instructor. The observations should be made during regular class periods without the knowledge of the student being observed. The observation should be over a period of time sufficient for an objective view of the student.

	Check

1. Fails to show opposition of limbs in walking, sitting, throwing.
2. Sits or stands with poor posture.
3. Does not transfer weight from one foot to the other when throwing.
4. Cannot name body parts or move them on command.
5. Has poor muscle tone (tense or flaccid).
6. Uses one extremity much more often than the other.
7. Cannot use arm without "overflow" movements from other body parts.
8. Cannot jump rope.
9. Cannot clap out a rhythm with both hands or stamp rhythm with feet.
10. Has trouble crossing the midline of the body at chalkboard or in ball handling.
11. Often confuses right and left sides.
12. Confuses vertical, horizontal, up, down directions.
13. Cannot hop or maintain balance in squatting.
14. Has trouble getting in and out of seat.
15. Approaches new tasks with excessive clumsiness.
16. Fails to plan movements before initiating task.
17. Walks or runs with awkward gait.
18. Cannot tie shoes, use scissors, manipulate small objects.
19. Cannot identify fingers as they are touched without vision.
20. Has messy handwriting.
21. Experiences difficulty tracing over line or staying between lines.
22. Cannot discriminate tactually between different coins or fabrics.
23. Cannot imitate body postures and movements.
24. Demonstrates poor ocular control; unable to maintain eye contact with moving objects; loses place while reading.
25. Lacks body awareness; bumps into things; spills and drops objects.
26. Appears excessively tense and anxious; cries or angers easily.
27. Responds negatively to physical contact; avoids touch.
28. Craves to be touched or held.
29. Overreacts to high frequency noise, bright lights, odors.
30. Exhibits difficulty in concentrating.
31. Shows tendency to fight when standing in line or in crowds.
32. Avoids group games and activities; spends most of time alone.
33. Complains of clothes irritating skin; avoids wearing coat.
34. Does not stay in assigned place; moves about excessively.
35. Uses either hand in motor activities.
36. Avoids using the left side of body.
37. Cannot walk sideward to either direction on balance beam.
38. Holds one shoulder lower than the other.
39. Cannot hold a paper in place with one hand while writing with the other.
40. Avoids turning to the left whenever possible.
41. Cannot assemble puzzles that offer no difficulty to peers.
42. Cannot match basic geometric shapes to each other visually.
43. Cannot recognize letters and numbers.
44. Cannot differentiate background from foreground in a picture.
45. Cannot identify hidden figures in a picture.
46. Cannot catch balls.
47. Cannot relate the body to environmental space; is unable to move between or through objects, guided by vision and an awareness of body dimensions.
48. Seems "lost in space;" confuses north, south, east, and west.

body control using a hoop shuttle item similar to the potato-race format found in other fitness batteries. She also included bent-knee sit-ups and seal-crawl items to measure abdominal strength and arm and shoulder girdle strength, respectively. Her aerobic item was a one-half mile run which proved to be a feasible item for elementary children to perform. The AAHPERD Health Related Fitness Test has norms for a 1-mile run for children as young as 5 years. Some training, practice, and discussion about points to consider when running a more lengthy distance should be covered with the children.

DIRECTIONS: ONE-HALF MILE RUN. The students begin from behind a starting line. On the signal, "Ready, set, go," the students begin running the course, going to the right of the orange traffic cones which mark the course. Record time in minutes and nearest tenth of a second from starting time to finish line. The course should be fairly flat and free of rocks and debris.

If the teacher wishes to test half of the class at a time, half of the students can stand at the finish line to hear the times called out by the teacher. Each student notes the minutes and seconds for his/her particular partner. Then the group changes places so the other half of the class can take their turn. One group of fourth graders performed the one-half mile run with an average score of 4:42 and a range of 3 to 7 minutes.

Smith added the unique feature of an effort rating, which accompanied each test item. The effort rating was based on observable characteristics of performance, including noticeable expenditure of energy.

Additional Motor Measures

AAHPERD: AAHPERD Youth Fitness Test Manual, Reston, Virginia, AAHPERD, 1976.

AAHPERD: Health Related Physical Fitness Test. *In* AAHPERD: Lifetime Health Related Physical Fitness Test Manual. AAHPERD, Reston, Va., 1980.

Arnheim, D.D., and Sinclair, W.A.: The Clumsy Child—A Program of Motor Therapy, 2nd ed; St. Louis, The C.V. Mosby Co., 1979. The Basic Motor Ability Tests—Revised, 1978.

Beveridge, S.K.: The Relationship Among Motor Creativity, Movement Satisfaction, and the Utilization of Certain Movement Factors of Second Grade Children. Doctoral dissertation, Ohio State University, 1973. Motor Creativity Test.

Braley, W.T.: Sensorimotor Skills Program. Unpublished Research Study, Dayton, Ohio. Dayton Public Schools, 1970. Sensory Motor Awareness Survey for 4- and 5-year-olds. *In* Barrow, H.M. and McGee, R.: A Practical Approach to Measurement in Physical Education, 2rd ed. Philadelphia, Lea & Febiger, 1979.

California State Department of Education, Sacramento. The Physical Performance Test for California (Revised), 1971.

Developmental Perceptual-Motor Rating Survey, 1970. Reported in September 1, 1970 issue of *The Physical Education Newsletter*, 100 Garfield Avenue, New London, Connecticut 06320.

Grade 3 Health and Physical Education State Assessment of Educational Progress in North Carolina, 1973–1974. Available from the Department of Public Instruction, Raleigh, North Carolina 27602.

Grissom, W.M.: Rhythmic Motor Test. Doctoral study, University of Missouri, 1971.

Hardin, D.H., and Garcia, M.J.: Diagnostic performance tests for elementary children (Grades 1–4). JOPERD, 53(2):48, 1982.

Loovis, E.M.: The Ohio State University Scale of Intra-Gross Motor Assessment. Division of Physical Education Nisonger Center, Ohio State University, Columbus, Ohio, 1975.

McClenaghan, B.A.: Development of an observational instrument to assess selected fundamental movement patterns of exceptional children. Doctoral Study, Indiana University, 1976. Fundamental Movement Pattern Assessment Instrument.

Orpet, R.E., Research Consultant, Marianne Frostig Center of Educational Therapy, California State College, Long Beach. Sensory-Motor and Movement Skills Test Battery, 1972.

Seefeldt, V.: Motor Performance Testing. Institute for the Study of Youth Sports, Room 213, Women's Intramural Building, Michigan State University, East Lansing, Michigan, 48824.

ADMINISTERING TESTS

Many more assessments would be administered to students if their use was not considered

Checklist of Procedures for Administering Tests*

Time	Procedures Related to Students	Procedures Related to the Test
Prior to Administering the Test	Review test Decide on suitability of its use Orient students to purpose, uses Explain and demonstrate test items Provide practice time Get parental permission, if indicated Get administrative permission, if necessary Check for medical restrictions	Schedule space Make a check-off list of all equipment and materials needed Plan and complete floor markings Secure personnel to help administer test Train assistants (judges, scorers) Review: Test directions Set-up procedures Safety precautions Organizational plan Scoring procedures Dismissal Take-down procedures Time to report to help test Determine procedures for incorrect performance or for mistakes during trials Prepare rating forms, score cards, etc. Standardize directions and scoring procedures Arrange stations Decide on class organization: Mass, squad, individual, combination Post diagram of traffic flow and testing order for arrival, during testing, and dismissal Estimate time needed for each item Plan activity for early finishers and uninvolved students Identify testing areas Have spare equipment in reserve
Just Before and During Administration	Tell the students again what the test is and why it is being given Explain testing and scoring procedures Demonstrate the test items, if appropriate Handle any questions Administer practice trials Motivate students to perform well Administer test in a positive and efficient manner Tell students their scores immediately after performance, if possible Provide for students not involved in test If written test, put relevant words on blackboard to help with spelling Provide for students who finish early Supervise whole process	Place equipment Check for proper placement and safety of all equipment Check that all helpers are present and adequately prepared Make mental notes of testing situation, children's reactions, smoothness of administration
Just After Test and Later	Compare results with criterion-referenced preset standards Compare results with norm-referenced standards Interpret results to students as promptly as possible (individually and as a group) Protect privacy of individual scores Do not embarrass any student Share results with parents, if appropriate Discuss the testing process with the students Thank children for their cooperation and motivated performance	Collect score cards Analyze test results Use results for future lesson/program planning Note changes to be made in procedures the next time test is administered Return all equipment and materials to proper storage Evaluate results in relation to purpose of test Thank personnel who helped with administrative procedures

*Appreciation is expressed to Mickie McCormick, Susan Jewett, Gary Sanders, Jane Irwin, and Ann Hudgens, whose ideas were incorporated into the checklist.

Fig. 10–25. Checklist of Procedures for Administering Tests

extra work and nonlearning time by teachers. Careful and detailed planning, student involvement in the process, and the coupling of "testing and teaching" contribute to the efficiency and effectiveness of evaluative procedures. Concerns related to the students and to the assessment tool need to be addressed. The following chart will help the teacher review the steps that should be planned when assessments are anticipated (Fig. 10–25). Some of the preparations must be accomplished well before the test is actually administered; others provide follow-up. Certainly, no well-planned assessment that will provide honest scores can be accomplished on the spur of the moment. Planning for evaluative procedures should be a part of the lesson planning and just as carefully done.

PROGRAM EVALUATION

Much of the evaluative process is directed toward the student or product of the physical education program. Another way to view elementary school physical education, and thus to assess its impact, is to examine the program or the processes that the children encounter. All facets of the program—facilities, equipment, time allotment, progression, lessons—should be evaluated.

Program evaluation scales should provide a basis for improving the quality of the program since the scale provides a systematic look that ferrets out strengths and weaknesses. Thus, steps can be taken to overcome the recognized weaknesses. Most state departments of public instruction supply evaluative scales to be used for accrediting purposes. Program improvements are more likely to occur if the teacher has a positive outlook about these self-evaluations.

Cameron and Pleasance pose some "questions which the teacher may ask to assess the quality of his work and to bring in mind aspects of the lesson which could be improved for more effective teaching." These questions are geared specifically to the gymnastic area, but many of them are applicable to dance and games as well.[62]

1. Do the children change clothes quickly so that only a minimum of time is lost from the lesson?

2. Do the children enter the hall knowing what they are to practice, and are they able to work quietly at their chosen activity without interfering with other children?

3. Am I making the most of the free practice time by seizing opportunities for individual coaching and guidance?

4. Are the individual mats, and the small and large apparatus, distributed round the hall in the best order for ease of collection and return?

5. When I tell the class to collect or exchange pieces of small apparatus, do I also tell them what they have to practice; or do I wait until they have the apparatus before telling them, so that they cannot begin until the slowest child is ready?

6. Is my work presented in such a way that all the children are able to achieve satisfaction and work to the limit of their ability?

7. Are the children working with interest, confidence, initiative, and growing understanding? If not, is this due to

a. the limitation being too difficult for the class at the stage they have reached?

b. the limitation not being clearly expressed?

c. the children not being sufficiently familiar with the vocabulary of the analysis of movement?

d. the limitation being inappropriate to the arrangement of apparatus?

e. insufficient time being allowed for experiment?

f. the lack of pertinent comment and questioning on my part?

g. the lack of my insistence on limitations being accurately fulfilled?

h. the children having to concentrate on finding many different answers to a problem rather than perfecting one solution?

8. Are the children able to work with a partner and in cooperation with a group, subordinating their own inclinations and aspirations to the fulfillment of a communal response?

9. Are the demonstrations

a. the children's?

b. short?

c. purposeful?

d. followed by immediate opportunities for practice?

e. not given by the best performers every time?

10. After demonstrations do I draw comment from the class by skillful questioning?

11. Is there a balance in the lesson between floor and apparatus work?

12. Are there enough groups to enable all the children to be working all the time?

13. Do the children queue to use the apparatus, or do they fully explore its possibilities by approaching it from different directions?

14. Is there variety in the large apparatus situations that I have set, and do I try to make them more interesting by varying the arrangements and combination of individual items of equipment?

15. Is the class able to set up the apparatus safely, correctly, quickly, and is it distributed so as to make the best use of the available space?

16. Once the apparatus has been erected and checked by me, are the children allowed to start work directly?

17. Are the children able to change group places informally without a great loss of time and fuss?

18. Is the apparatus put away carefully and tidily so that the teacher of the next class finds it in good order?

19. Are my powers of observation and imagination sufficient to help the children in the performance and development of their responses?

20. Am I giving the children opportunities to repeat work previously practiced so that they may achieve a satisfactory and satisfying standard of performance, and do I regularly change the apparatus arrangement and lesson content?

21. Have my lessons a relevance to what has gone before? Do I bear in mind the stage that the class has reached and the children's rate of development? In short, am I preparing my lesson thoroughly?

Shurr suggests four questions that the teacher should ask himself/herself immediately following the lesson:

1. Were the objectives of the lesson accomplished? If not, why?

2. Were all of the students actively involved in the lesson?

3. What resulted from the lesson and the student's evaluation that should be incorporated in the next lesson?

4. Was there any particular behavior or improvement in an individual of which I should make special note?[3]

Much of the evaluation of information gleaned by the teacher is subjective and perhaps not recorded. Jordan suggests that the absorption of the children in the lesson is a good barometer of its effectiveness.[4] Although this absorption level is measured through the subjective observation of the teacher, it provides a real sense about the amount of involvement, thinking, and feeling the children are putting into their movement experiences.

A broader evaluation, encompassing the entire year is equally valuable. Students, other faculty members, and parent groups can also be helpful in program evaluation. Following are some general areas that should be explored.

Program of Activities
   curriculum

   variety
   progression
   planned and written
   meets needs of individual children
   enrichment and remedial program
   methods of evaluation
   objectives listed
Leadership
   qualified personnel
   personal and professional growth
   relationships with administration, faculty, parents, community, students
Administration
   time allotment
   budget
   organization and schedule
   medicals, insurance
   records
Facilities and Equipment
   indoor and outdoor space
   safe and clean
   storage space
   amount and variety of equipment, inventory
   media equipment
   care of equipment and facilities
   supplies

The physical education faculty should evaluate the program at the completion of each year to direct the planning for the following year. Program evaluation is a learning experience for the faculty just as student evaluation is a learning experience for the students.

APPLICATION OF EVALUATIVE INFORMATION

The use of assessment information, regardless of the source, can have an impact on different groups within the school setting. The *school administration* and the school system as a whole are concerned with the content and implementation of the program. They need to show parents and the public what is being accomplished.

This evidence of accountability has emphasized summative evaluation in the past and is a management-by-objectives approach to "proving" that certain standards have been met. Summative evidence is easy to produce because it emphasizes numeric answers to show the status of achievement of the group. Summative evaluation can be criterion-referenced as well as norm-referenced. If the school has established certain criterion levels of achievement for each grade level, a report can show the percentage of students that has reached the stated standards at the completion of each school year. This approach is probably more educationally justified than norm-referenced reporting, which compares student achievement with other students. Child-centered programs, with goals for each child, need to be held accountable, but perhaps in a more subjective way than the teacher-centered programs that state goals for all children. Administrators must accept the philosophic position that stresses the individual child and his/her growth. Elementary school physical education teachers must help administrators realize that input from more subjective, ongoing evaluations (such as rating scales, diaries, and discussions) can be used effectively to assess program worth. This formative approach fits the humanistic and personalized emphasis in education today, even though the summative approach is more compatible with the "dollars-and-cents" accountability demands of the public.

Children want to know how they are doing and feel less threatened if they are judged in relation to their own developmental level and changes in performance ability rather than in relation to the accomplishments of other members of the class. This kind of judging places the traditional concept of grading in jeopardy because there would be no universal grade standard for "excellent," "good," "average," "poor," and "unacceptable." It also means replacing the symbols of achievement such as A, B, C with narrative comments. A grade of B in physical education no longer would mean better-than-average performance in relation to established standards for the group: it would mean better than average progress in physical education for that individual child.

> The question of grading children is totally inconsistent with the philosophy of open education. British primary teachers told us they could see no purpose whatsoever in grading children on the work they do. They felt that if children were well pleased with their work, if information was correct, if they took pride in their accomplishments, if they felt they were making adequate progress, and if they continued to maintain a zest for learning, then it was unnecessary and harmful to give children an A, a B, or a 90%. They also believed that the practice of grading or marking puts unbearable pressure on children to achieve what the teacher expects. Rather, they would encourage the child to learn to set up his own realistic standards of what it is he can accomplish.[17]

Evaluation has often had a negative connotation because it was synonymous with grading. This limited perspective of evaluation probably also involves the misuse of evaluative procedures to dehumanize students. The assessment of a child's progress should be done in conjunction with the child because this process, too, can be a growing and meaningful one.

Hudgens[63] has designed an assessment report form for educational gymnastics (Fig. 10–26). Use of such a form enables the child and parents to have a report of achievement without the need to report a single letter or numerical grade representative of achievement. The process of evaluation and the communication with the parents are both healthy aspects of a physical education program.

Evaluation to the *parents* means finding out about the unique strengths and weaknesses of their child and what the school is doing about them. This process is more appreciated and more creditable if the parents realize that their child is more than a number; the information sent home reflects a knowledge of the child as a unique individual. The school accomplishes two important goals with this approach to parents. First, accountability is enhanced because parents come to realize that the teacher knows their child: second, respect for school procedures and philosophy is maintained, thus fostering good public relations for the school system as a whole.

The merits of the evaluative process center around the *teacher* as the implementor. The communications with administrators, parents, and students will reflect the importance of evaluation as viewed by the teacher. Evaluative information helps the teacher justify the program to administrators, interpret it to parents, and plan and replan it with students.

The teacher will be especially interested in the two prongs of the evaluative scheme: the growth of the students and the implementation of the program. In the latter case, regular evaluations of teacher performance and program evaluation of the entire year's work come into focus. The two foci of student and program are interrelated. If "good" things are happening to the students, the assumption is that the program is good. If schools present a "good" program, the public assumes the student is benefiting. Evaluation of both aspects makes assumptions unnecessary and provides a double check that

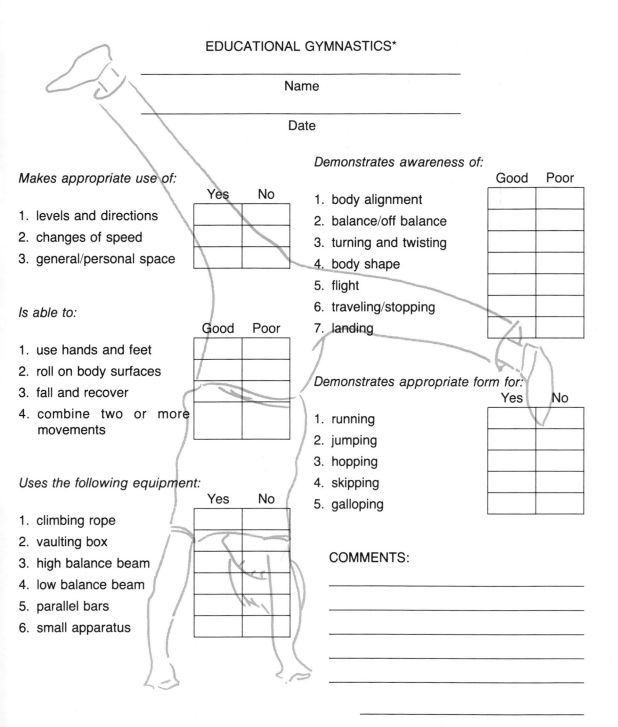

EDUCATIONAL GYMNASTICS*

_____

Name

_____

Date

Makes appropriate use of:

	Yes	No
1. levels and directions		
2. changes of speed		
3. general/personal space		

Is able to:

	Good	Poor
1. use hands and feet		
2. roll on body surfaces		
3. fall and recover		
4. combine two or more movements		

Uses the following equipment:

	Yes	No
1. climbing rope		
2. vaulting box		
3. high balance beam		
4. low balance beam		
5. parallel bars		
6. small apparatus		

Demonstrates awareness of:

	Good	Poor
1. body alignment		
2. balance/off balance		
3. turning and twisting		
4. body shape		
5. flight		
6. traveling/stopping		
7. landing		

Demonstrates appropriate form for:

	Yes	No
1. running		
2. jumping		
3. hopping		
4. skipping		
5. galloping		

COMMENTS:

_____
_____
_____
_____
_____

_____

Physical Education Teacher

*Used by permission of A. Hudgens, Elementary Physical Education Teacher, Charlotte-Mecklenburg Schools, Charlotte, N.C.

Fig. 10–26. Report Form for Educational Gymnastics

both approaches are operational. Consequently, neither the child nor the program suffers.

Teachers are not exempt from evaluation, but they need to become adept in summarizing various types of formative, subjective information to show program value. Some of the formative tools presented in this chapter are more time-consuming than administering a test at the completion of a unit. The teacher must weigh the merits of the various measures and use them efficiently and effectively.

REFERENCES

1. Safrit, M.J.: Evaluation in Physical Education, 2nd ed. Englewood Cliffs, New Jersey, Prentice-Hall, 1981.
2. Barrett K.R.: Exploration—A Method for Teaching Movement. Madison, Wisconsin, College Printing and Typing Co., 1965.
3. Schurr, E.: Movement Experiences for Children, 2nd ed., Englewood Cliffs, New Jersey, Prentice-Hall, 1975.
4. Jordan, D.: Childhood and Movement. Oxford, Basil Blackwell, 1966.
5. Bilbrough, A., and Jones, P.: Physical Education in the Primary School. London, University of London Press, 1968.
6. Stanley, S.: Physical Education: A Movement Orientation. Toronto, McGraw-Hill, 1969.
7. Carroll, J., and Lofthouse, P.: Creative Dance for Boys. London, Macdonald & Evans, 1969.
8. Logsdon, B.J., and Barrett, K.R.: Teacher's Manual for Ready? Set . . . Go!—A Television Course for Elementary School Physical Education. Level One. Bloomington, Indiana, National Instructional Television Center, 1969.
9. Russell, J.: Creative Dance in the Primary School. London, Macdonald & Evans, 1965.
10. Barrett, K.R.: Physical education is movement education (Reprint.) Instructor, 82:47, 1973.
11. Jewett, A.E., et al.: Educational change through a taxonomy for writing physical education objectives. Quest, 15:32, 1971.
12. Harrow, A.J.: Taxonomy of the Psychomotor Domain. New York, David McKay Co., 1972.
13. Krathwohl, D.R., Bloom, B.S., and Masia, B.B.: Taxonomy of Educational Objectives: Handbook II: Affective Domain. New York, David McKay Co., 1964.
14. Bloom, B. (ed.): Taxonomy of Educational Objectives: Handbook I: Cognitive Domain. New York, David McKay Co., 1956.
15. Barrow, H.M., and McGee, R.: A Practical Approach to Measurement in Physical Education, 3rd ed. Philadelphia, Lea & Febiger, 1979.
16. Baumgartner, T.A., and Jackson, A.S.: Measurement for Evaluation in Physical Education, 2nd ed. Boston, Houghton Mifflin Co., 1982.
17. Hertzberg, A., and Stone, E.F.: Schools are for Children. New York, Schoken Books, 1971.
18. Norris, G.L.: Perceptions of an Elementary School Physical Education Learning Environment Reflective of Humanistic Tenets as Seen by Participants and Selected Observers. Unpublished Study. University of North Carolina at Greensboro, 1976.
19. Sasser, C.M.: Cognitive Dialogue. Project for PE 676, Issues in Elementary School Physical Education. University of North Carolina at Greensboro, 1975.
20. Craig, B.R.: Cognitive Dialogue. Project for PE 676, Issues in Elementary School Physical Education. University of North Carolina at Greensboro, 1975.
21. Tatro, V.K.: Picture Identification. Project on Evaluation for PE 470, Specialized Methodology in Physical Education. University of North Carolina at Greensboro, 1975.
22. McCormick, M.R.: Directionality Identification of Four and Five Year-Olds. Project for PE 676, Assessment of Children in Physical Education Class. University of North Carolina at Greensboro, 1982.
23. Sutlive, J.L.: Cognitive Demonstration. Project for PE 676, Issues in Elementary School Physical Education. University of North Carolina at Greensboro, 1975.
24. Hart, V.: Ready? Set . . . Go! Knowledge Achievement Test. Doctoral dissertation, University of North Carolina at Greensboro, 1976.
25. Wilson, R.: Exercise Physiology Knowledge Test for First Graders. Project for PE 676, Assessment of Children in Physical Education Class. University of North Carolina at Greensboro, 1982.
26. Kneer, M.E. (ed.): Basic Stuff Series I Informational Booklet: Exercise Physiology. Reston, Virginia, AAHPERD, 1981.
27. Trimble, R.T.: Age Level Specialist, Basic Stuff Series II: Childhood. Reston, Virginia, AAHPERD, 1981.
28. Larson, L. (ed.): Knowledge and Understanding in Physical Education. Washington, D.C., AAHPER, 1969.
29. North Carolina Testing Program: First Grade, Prescriptive Reading Inventory. Monterey, California, McGraw-Hill, 1981.
30. Piers, E.V., and Harris, D.B.: Age and other correlates of self-concept in children. Journal of Educational Psychology, 55:91, 1964.
31. Piers-Harris Children's Self-Concept Scale: The Way I Feel About Myself. Counselor Recordings and Tests, 1969. Box 6186 Acklan Station, Nashville, Tennessee 37212.
32. Cratty, B., et al.: Movement Activities, Motor Ability, and the Education of Children. Springfield, Illinois, Charles C Thomas, 1970.
33. Tanner, P.W.: The Relationship of Selected Measures of Body Image and Movement Concept to Two Types of Programs of Physical Education in the Primary Grades. Doctoral dissertation, Ohio State University, 1969.
34. Snodgrass, J.E.: Comparison and Relationships of Selected Measures of Self-Concept in Primary Age Children. Doctoral dissertation. University of North Carolina at Greensboro, 1975.
35. Toulmin, M.L.B.: The Development of an Original Instrument to Measure the Expressed Attitudes of Children Toward the Elementary School Program of Physical Education. Master's Thesis. Texas Woman's University, 1973.
36. Horrocks, R.N.: Relationship of Selected Prosocial Play Behaviors in Children to Moral Reasoning, Youth Sport Participation, and Perception of Sportsmanship. Doctoral dissertation. University of North Carolina at Greensboro, 1979.
37. Hutchins, P.A.: The Relationships of Children's Personality Factors to Their Competitive and/or Cooperative Attitudes. Ed.D. dissertation. University of Maine at Orono, 1978.
38. Johnson, D.W., and Ahlgren, A.: Relationship between student attitudes about cooperation and competition and attitudes towards schooling. Journal of Educational Psychology, 68:92, 1976.

39. Ahlgren, A., Christensen, D.J., and Lun, K-S.: Minnesota School Affect Assessment, Minnesota High School Testing Program. Student Counseling Bureau, University of Minnesota, 1977.

40. Johnson, S.: Student Expectation and Dyadic Interaction with Physical Education Teachers of Third-Grade Children. Ed.D. dissertation. University of North Carolina at Greensboro, 1982.

41. Carlson, J.B.: "Me In Dance", "Me In Gymnastics", and "Me In Games" Self-Concept Scales for Second and Third Grade Children. Unpublished Study. Appalachian State University, Boone, North Carolina, 1982.

42. Gordon, I.J.: A Test Manual for the How I see Myself Scale. Gainesville, The Florida Educational and Development Council, 1968.

43. Smith, N.L.: Rating Scale: Performance in Games. Project for PE 676, Assessment of Children in Physical Education Class. University of North Carolina at Greensboro, 1982.

44. Hudgens, A.: Rating Scale: Performance of Selected Game Skills—Space Awareness. Project for PE 676, Assessment of Children in Physical Education Class. University of North Carolina at Greensboro, 1982.

45. Irwin, P.J., Jewett, S.R., and Woodfield, D.W.: Evaluation of Game Play Development. Measurement Tools: Body Awareness, Space Awareness, Relationships. Project for PE 676, Assessment of Children in Physical Education Class. University of North Carolina at Greensboro, 1982.

46. Irwin, D.M., and Bushnell, M.M.: Observational Strategies for Childstudy. New York, Holt, Rinehart, and Winston, 1980.

47. Barrett, K.R.: Games Teaching: Adaptable, Versatile Players. Journal of Physical Education and Recreation, 48(7):21, 1977.

48. Akers, P., Allison, P., and Hudgens, A.: Rating Scales for Phase I Manipulative Game Skills: Catching, Striking, and Throwing. Project for PE 676, Assessment of Children in Physical Education Class. University of North Carolina at Greensboro, 1982.

49. Williams, K., and Wilson, V.A.: Elementary School Physical Education Performance Test. Project for PE 468, Measurement in Physical Education. University of North Carolina at Greensboro, 1973.

50. Irwin, P.J.: Test Revision: Body and Space Awareness. Project for PE 676, Assessment of Children in Physical Education Class. University of North Carolina at Greensboro, 1982.

51. Weatherman, P.G.: Weatherman Dribbling Test. Project for PE 676, Assessment of Children in Physical Education Class. University of North Carolina at Greensboro, 1982.

52. Dimondstein, G.: Children Dance in the Classroom. New York, Macmillan, 1971.

53. Weatherman, P.G.: Rating Scale: Performance in Gymnastics. Project for PE 676, Assessment of Children in Physical Education Class. University of North Carolina at Greensboro, 1982.

54. Schilling, F., and Kiphard, E.J.: The body coordination test. JOHPER, 47:37, 1976.

55. Charlop, M., and Atwell, C.W.: The Charlop-Atwell Scale of Motor Coordination: a quick and easy assessment of young children. Perceptual and Motor Skills, 50:1291, 1980.

56. Martin, L.L.: Construction of a Screening Device to Identify Children with Possible Motor Disabilities in Kindergarten, First and Second Grades. Doctoral dissertation. Purdue University, 1971.

57. Sherrill, C.: Adapted Physical Educational and Recreation: A Multidisciplinary Approach. Dubuque, Iowa, Wm. C. Brown, 1976.

58. Vodola, R.M. (Project Director): Developmental Physical Education: Low Motor Ability. Township of Ocean School District, Oakhurst, New Jersey, 1974.

59. Smith, N.L.: Smith Physical Fitness Test for Elementary Students. Project for PE 676, Assessment of Young Children in Physical Education Class. University of North Carolina at Greensboro, 1982.

60. Glover, E.G.: Physical Fitness Test Items for Boys and Girls in the First, Second, and Third Grades. In Barrow, H.M., and McGee, R.: A Practical Approach to Measurement in Physical Education. 3rd ed. Philadelphia, Lea & Febiger, 1979, p. 193.

61. AAHPERD: Health Related Physical Fitness Test Manual. Reston, Virginia, AAHPERD, 1980.

62. Cameron, W. McD., and Pleasance, P.: Education in Movement. Oxford, Basil Blackwell, 1971.

63. Hudgens, A.: Report Form: Educational Gymnastics. Project for PE 676, Assessment of Young Children in Physical Education Class. University of North Carolina at Greensboro, 1982.

Chapter 11

Creating Materials for Teaching

BETTE JEAN LOGSDON

Organizing the concepts identified in the content chapters on dance, games, and gymnastics into progressively challenging and integrated programs of physical education for children is not an easy task even for the experienced teacher who is fully prepared to teach physical education using the educational approach. For those who are just beginning to develop a commitment to this approach, selecting and organizing content and planning for teaching may be a most foreboding undertaking to launch out on alone with no assistance. This chapter has been designed to SUGGEST guidelines and to provide SAMPLES to facilitate the early learning stages in planning in an attempt to make this difficult task less awesome for beginning teachers.

Planning, as it will be discussed, because the beginning teacher is being served, will appear to some readers to be locked-stepped, one-way oriented, *with no alternatives*. NOT TRUE. Let it be understood early, when reading and studying this chapter, that so long as the philosophic position basic to the educational approach, the content progression present in the movement themes, and the learning principles applied developmentally to motor activities are not violated, planning for teaching can be as individual as the person doing the planning. Teachers and students alike using this text should feel free to design their own formats for planning. Even though the formats may vary widely, the ideas developed in the chapter can be helpful since the processes one goes through in planning should

be similar. Also, let it be known that the formats used in planning are predicted to change as the user matures and becomes more practiced in implementing plans when teaching. The following organized approach to planning has been developed in response to college students and school teachers who have asked for help in formulating the planning processes, saying they need specific guidelines to trigger these thought processes.

PLANNING: QUESTIONS TO GET YOU STARTED

Some questions must be answered before the process of planning begins and you start selecting, organizing, and developing content, if your planning is to be meaningful to you the teacher and challenging for the students you teach. These questions are

WHO AM I TEACHING?

WHY AM I SELECTING THE CONTENT?

HOW WILL I TEACH?

Who Am I Teaching?

Before beginning to plan at any level, try to establish an awareness of the students for whom the plan is to be written. Knowing the following

information about the children will be helpful in planning:
- chronologic age
- grade level
- developmental needs
- special characteristics
- previous experiences

As you write your first plan, whether it be an outline of a total program, a unit, or a lesson plan, you are likely not to know the "WHO," or the children for whom you are writing the plan. In this case, when you do not know the children and cannot get the real data, you need to develop them hypothetically before you go any farther, so as you plan you can identify with specific needs and characteristics of students even if you cannot identify with a specific group of students.

Why Am I Selecting the Content?

Arriving at the answer to this question when you begin to plan for teaching physical education should send you back to the goals of physical education. The goals of physical education for the educational approach as found in Chapter 2 are to

1. MOVE SKILLFULLY, demonstrating VERSATILE, effective, and efficient movement in situations requiring either planned or unplanned responses.
2. Become aware of the MEANING, SIGNIFICANCE, FEELING, and JOY of movement, both as a performer and as an observer.
3. Gain and apply the KNOWLEDGE that GOVERNS HUMAN MOVEMENT.

The decisions relevant to the "Why" you select specific content should always be reflective of these goals, with a concerted effort made to plan for the DEVELOPMENT OF SKILLFUL, VERSATILE MOVERS IN INSTRUCTIONAL, EDUCATIONAL SETTINGS that nurture the joy and understanding of the movement. In addition to attending to the goals of physical education, care must be taken to see that the *content you select is appropriate* for the motor abilities, age group, and social and mental development of the children for whom you are selecting it relevant to the *objectives or purposes* you are trying to achieve.

How Will I Teach?

The philosophic statement given in Chapter 2 lies at the heart of this answer. The beliefs about the individuality of the learner, the commitment to teaching the whole child and helping all children to fulfill their potential, the willingness and ability of the teacher to share the decision-making process with children, and the beliefs about learning will all be reflected in the decisions you will make when planning. How you will teach will begin to surface in your planning when you begin to select content, propose objectives, and select, organize, and develop learning experiences for students. Chapter 9 was devoted to the methodologic decisions, the "HOW?," that are encompassed in the educational approach. Studying the chapter and trying to implement the ideas that are presented when you plan should help you to develop a learning environment when you teach that is in tune with the philosophic position.

PHASES IN PLANNING

There are three phases in planning—three time frames for which planning ultimately must be thoughtfully conceived in developing and implementing a physical education program. These are Program Overview, Unit Plan, and Lesson Plan. The Program Overview is the largest time frame for which plans are written. These plans span the entire time period for which the physical education program is to be taught. For example, in a school that enrolls children from kindergarten through sixth grade, a 7-year Program Overview would be needed.

The Program Overview identifies the content to be taught and projects the sequence and the progression for teaching the content for each grade.

The time frame of the second phase, the Unit Plan, is much smaller than the time frame for a Program Overview. A Unit Plan outlines the content, objectives, and learning experiences, and provides an evaluation tool for a brief period of time during one part of the year for a single grade. The Unit Plan usually projects work for two to six lessons. In conjunction with each Unit Plan, a suggested teaching progression for the unit, charting a lesson-by-lesson development of the unit, may be prepared and attached to the plan to guide your planning when you start to prepare to teach from the unit. Take time to refer back to Chapters 6, 7, and 8. The discussion for each of the themes in all three program-area chapters ends with a sample Unit Plan and a Suggested Teaching Progression for each unit.

The smallest time frame for which planning is usually written is the Lesson Plan. It spans one instructional class period. Lesson plans are prepared to help guide you as you teach one lesson to a group of students.

These three phases in planning, starting with the largest time frame, the Program Overview, and moving through the Unit Plan to the smallest, the Lesson Plan, represent the sequence teachers should follow when developing an instructional, educational program of physical education in which the progression is planned, challenging, and appropriate for the children.

Program Overview—Phase One In Planning

Planning the Program Overview of a total physical education program is perhaps the most difficult form of planning for beginning teachers. This task is difficult largely because beginning teachers often do not have the understanding of the scope and sequence of the entire content to be taught, nor do they have sufficient teaching experience to have derived an appreciation for the learner and the teaching-learning process essential to understanding the problems and the needs inherent in planning for progression. The ability to accomplish long-range planning may be facilitated greatly, however, by personal experience acquired through broad, alert participation in sports, gymnastics, and dance and by studying and understanding movement and the progression that exists in the themes discussed earlier in Chapters 6, 7, and 8.

THEMES—A SCHEME FOR ORGANIZING CONTENT

The dance, games, and gymnastic content was organized into themes in Chapters 6, 7, and 8 in an effort to assist in understanding the sequence in the development of skillful, versatile movement and in selecting and outlining program progression. The following is a complete list of the themes from the dance, games, and gymnastic chapters.

THEMES FOR DANCE, GAMES, AND GYMNASTICS

Dance Themes
  Theme 1: INTRODUCTION TO THE BODY
  Theme 2: INTRODUCTION TO EFFORT
  Theme 3: INTRODUCTION TO SPACE
  Theme 4: THE FLOW OF MOVEMENT
  Theme 5: INTRODUCTION TO RELATIONSHIPS
  Theme 6: INSTRUCTIONAL USE OF THE BODY
  Theme 7: THE BASIC EFFORT ACTIONS

Games Themes
  Theme 1: INTRODUCTION TO BASIC BODY AND MANIPULATIVE CONTROL
  Theme 2: INTRODUCTION TO SPACE
  Theme 3: INTRODUCTION TO MOVEMENT QUALITY (EFFORT)
  Theme 4: MOVEMENT FLOW
  Theme 5: INTRODUCTION TO BASIC RELATIONSHIPS
  Theme 6: ADVANCED BODY AND MANIPULATIVE CONTROL
  Theme 7: INTRODUCTION TO COMPLEX RELATIONSHIPS

Gymnastics Themes
  Theme 1: INTRODUCTION TO THE BODY
  Theme 2: INTRODUCTION TO SPACE
  Theme 3: INTRODUCTION TO TIME
  Theme 4: RELATIONSHIPS OF BODY PARTS
  Theme 5: INTRODUCTION TO WEIGHT
  Theme 6: FLOW AND CONTINUITY OF MOVEMENT
  Theme 7: RELATIONSHIPS TO OTHERS
  Theme 8: INTRODUCTION TO RHYTHM

Figure 11–1 has been developed to aid further in the selection of content needed in the development of the Program Overview. This figure is a composite of each of the theme-progression figures located at the end of the three program chapters on educational dance, games, and gymnastics. It illustrates three helpful suggestions essential in selecting appropriate content when planning for progression.

THEME COMPOSITE: A GUIDE FOR PLANNING

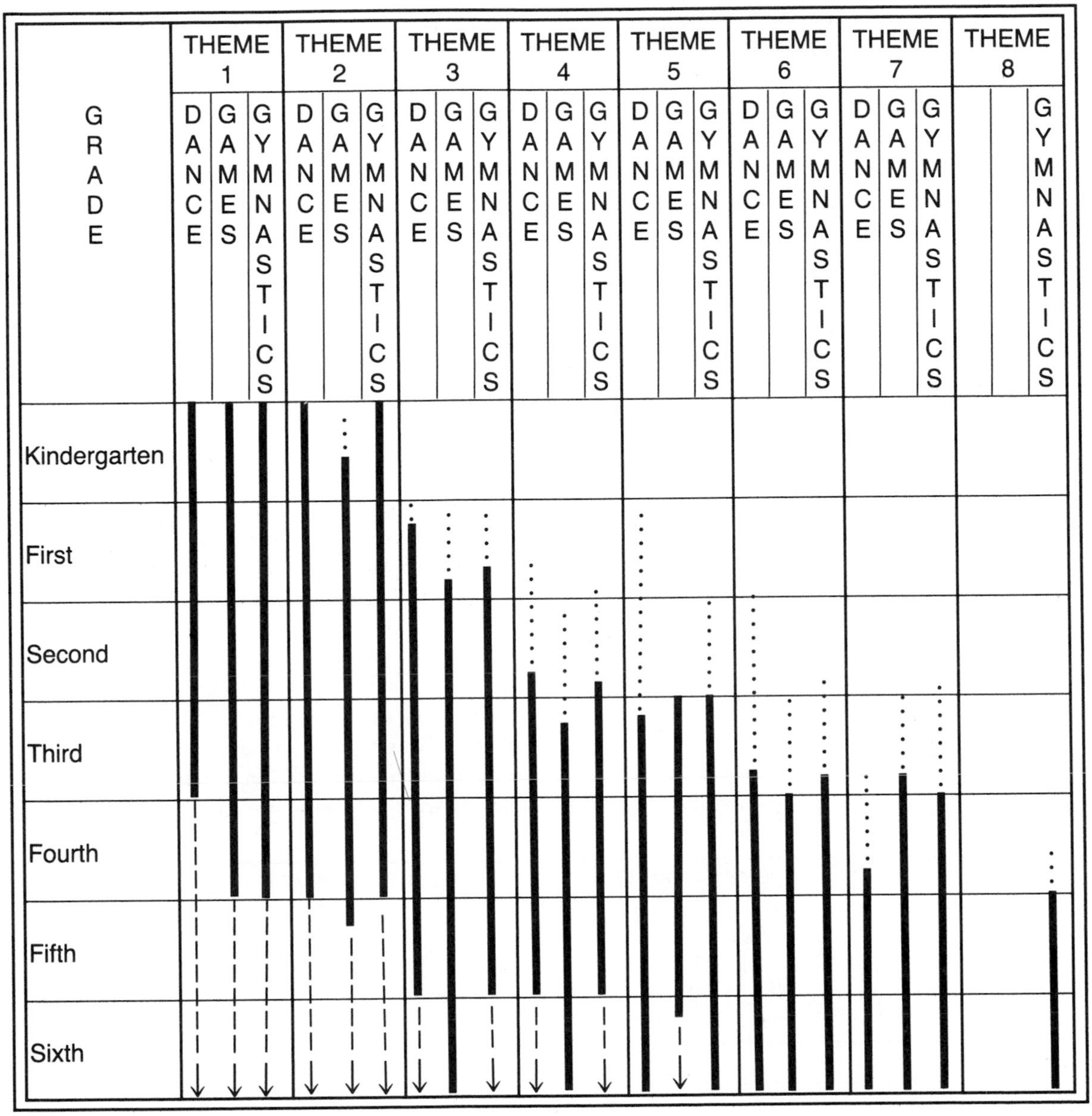

Fig. 11—1. Theme Progression By Grade Level for Dance, Games, and Gymnastics.

Examine the figure closely. The graphics, grade by grade, show the following:

1. when each theme is most appropriate for each grade (illustrated by a solid line ▬).
2. which themes may be phased in earlier to challenge select groups of students needing more advanced work (illustrated by dots · · · · · ·).
3. which themes can be continued to accommodate children who need less complicated challenges rather than moving on to more advanced themes; or when the content of the themes can be selected and used in combination with material from more advanced themes (illustrated by dashes — — — — — —).

These three indicators charted for each theme in dance, games, and gymnastics should be useful in selecting content and determining when each theme is appropriate for the various grades. Look at Figure 11–2. One theme from one program area, Games Theme 2, has been singled out from the progression composite in Figure 11–1 and reproduced to help clarify these three points to aid in understanding progression in content selection. Notice the solid line (▬). It indicates you normally should anticipate kindergarten children being able to handle some of the content from Theme 2 in Games somewhere toward the end of the school year. This solid line further shows the content of Theme 2 being of major significance from late in the kindergarten year through the fourth grade. The dots (· · · · ·) preceding the dark line indicate that content

from Games Theme 2 may be used earlier, approximately midyear, with some kindergarten children who are ready for an extra challenge. The dashes (— — —) opposite the fifth and sixth grades illustrate that advanced content from Theme 2, Games, may be used as the major focus of work with these upper grades *rather* than material from more advanced themes. The dashes also show Theme 2 content may be used in conjunction with work from more advanced themes in the fifth and sixth grades, depending on the capabilities and needs of the children and the amount of instructional time allocated for physical education.

In planning the Program Overview, it is helpful to rely heavily on the content progression inherent in the discussion of the themes in the dance, games, and gymnastic chapters and upon Figure 11–1 to help guide your selection of themes most appropriate for the children for whom you are planning.

STRUCTURING PROGRAM OVERVIEW

One essential in initiating preparation of a Program Overview is figuring the number of instructional periods of physical education that will be taught annually to a class. This number is determined by multiplying the number of weeks in the program by the number of lessons per week. For example, if there are approximately 36 weeks in the school year, the following calculations show the number of lessons needed annually for each grade for programs that have 1, 2, 3, 4, or 5 weekly lessons.

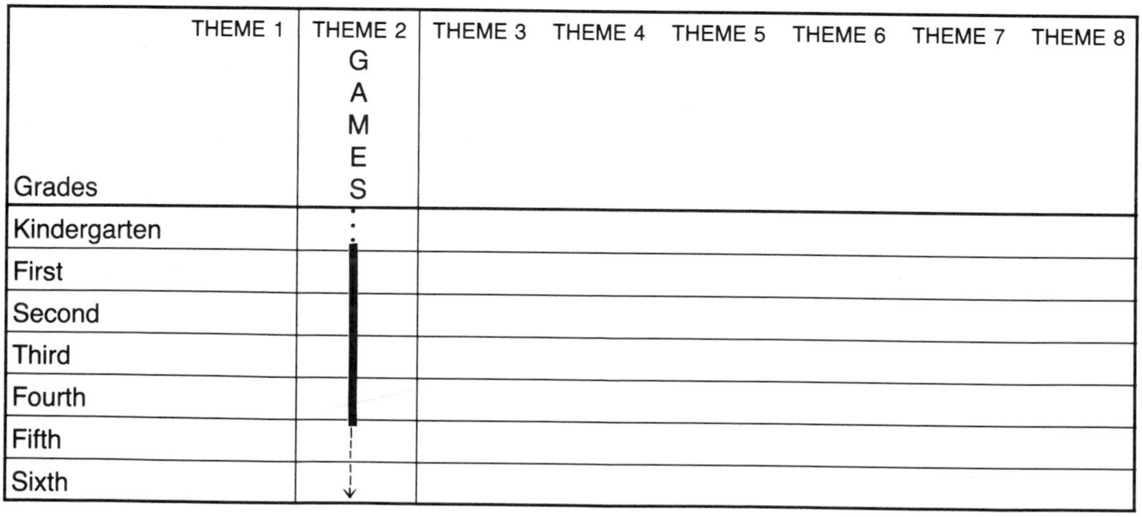

Grades	THEME 1	THEME 2 G A M E S	THEME 3	THEME 4	THEME 5	THEME 6	THEME 7	THEME 8
Kindergarten								
First								
Second								
Third								
Fourth								
Fifth								
Sixth								

Fig. 11–2. Progression for Theme 2 in Games.

Determining Number of Lessons Needed Annually
36 weeks × 1 lesson per week = 36 lessons annually
36 weeks × 2 lessons per week = 72 lessons annually
36 weeks × 3 lessons per week = 108 lessons annually
36 weeks × 4 lessons per week = 144 lessons annually
36 weeks × 5 lessons per week = 180 lessons annually

After the needed number of annual lessons is determined, a series of unit focuses are written for the year in dance, games, and gymnastics, with a specified number of lessons approximated for each unit. The total number of lessons for all of the units should approximate the number of lessons needed annually.

DEVELOPING UNIT FOCUSES

The content for each unit is selected from among the content of the specific themes designated in Figure 11–1 as appropriate for the grade level for which the Program Overview is being developed. A unit focus may be identified specifically with content from *one program area:* dance, games, or gymnastics as illustrated in each of the units written at the end of each theme in Chapters 6, 7, and 8. A unit focus also may be developed around content from *more than one program area;* however, it is rather common for those who are new to program development based on the thematic approach to select content from among the themes in a single program area, i.e., dance, games, OR gymnastics. Usually it is believed to be more difficult for beginners to select a concept and elaborate on it in two or more program areas than it is to teach the concept in a single program area. All sample units in Chapters 6, 7, and 8 focused on content directed toward one program area. An example of a unit focus implemented in two program areas could be, *Body Parts Leading the Action with Emphasis on Body Parts Initiating Direction.* The experiences in this unit could have the children engaged in gymnastics as well as dance. The concept of specific body parts initiating direction to the action would permeate both gymnastic and dance experiences.

A series of unit focuses is written in the development of the Program Overview to identify and to order the content to be taught. Completing the following fill-in-the-blanks statement has helped some beginning teachers in writing their initial unit focuses.

Unit Focus: _____ **with emphasis on** _____ .
　　　　　(selected content from one theme)　　　　　　　　　　(selected content from same
　　　　　　　　　　　　　　　　　　　　　　　　　　　　　　theme or a different theme)

Example:
Dribbling and Passing the Ball with the Feet with *Emphasis* on *Lead Passes.*
(*Dribbling* and *passing the ball* with the feet were selected from Games Theme 1, whereas *lead passes* was selected from content in Games Theme 5.)

It may be helpful when writing other focuses to use *while* or *when* in the place of *with emphasis on.*

A Program Overview is developed by examining the content of the themes designated as appropriate for each grade level in all three program areas. Then you select from among this content and prepare a number of unit focuses. When writing unit focuses, and thereby selecting and deciding on priorities in the content to be taught, it does help if you keep reflecting on what comprises skillful, versatile performance in dance, games, and gymnastics. These focuses should outline the progression for introducing the most significant content from the appropriate themes. Keep in mind the grade level for which the program is being planned and the available instructional time and the number of units needed for each grade.

SAMPLE PROGRAM OVERVIEW

Following is a SAMPLE PROGRAM OVERVIEW for kindergarten through sixth grade for

PROGRAM OVERVIEW SHOWING SCOPE AND SEQUENCE
KINDERGARTEN THROUGH SIXTH GRADE

KINDERGARTEN DANCE

Approx. no. of Lessons	Unit Focus
2	Traveling, with rising and sinking
4	Traveling, with emphasis on locomotor patterns, body parts, rising and sinking
4*	Rising–sinking, opening–closing; traveling and stationary; emphasizing locomotor patterns
4	Sudden, in combination with sustained movement, emphasizing stepping, jumping, running, and rising–sinking, opening–closing
4	Firm, in combination with fine movement, with stepping, jumping, running, with opening–closing
6*	Sudden, sustained, firm, fine while opening–closing, rising–sinking, and emphasizing body parts

KINDERGARTEN GAMES

Approx. no. of Lessons	Unit Focus
6	Traveling and stopping, with and without catching, throwing, and dribbling balls of different sizes and weights
4	Catching, throwing different objects (bean bags, balls of different sizes and weights), use of different body parts for catching
3	Striking, emphasizing feet, hands, knees, heads (balloons) and dribbling with hands/feet
3	Throwing (and catching) different balls, striking (balloons) with different body parts and stationary balls with rackets
4	Traveling by dribbling (hands/feet) and striking (balloons with body parts and stationary balls with rackets)
2	Collecting balls of different sizes and weights, followed by traveling and stopping
2	Throwing, striking, catching, and collecting, using different objects of choice

KINDERGARTEN GYMNASTICS

Approx. no. of Lessons	Unit Focus
5	Traveling and stopping on different body parts with emphasis on a response to a signal; spacing, and independency in moving
3	Changing the body parts touching the floor during stillness and while traveling, with emphasis on holding still positions strong and firm
5*	Traveling on different body parts with emphasis on variety
4	Rolling, jumping, and landing in different ways with emphasis on holding stillness and traveling after landing
4	Introducing the forward roll and taking weight on hands, with emphasis on rolling in own space and landing on feet
3	Moving and stopping while going on, onto, off, over, under apparatus, with emphasis on making different body parts support the weight and spacing for safety

FIRST GRADE DANCE		FIRST GRADE GAMES		FIRST GRADE GYMNASTICS	
Approx. no. of Lessons	Unit Focus	Approx. no. of Lessons	Unit Focus	Approx. no. of Lessons	Unit Focus
4	Traveling, emphasizing different body parts, rising–sinking, opening–closing	4	Traveling and stopping in general space while dribbling with the hands and feet and throwing and catching	4	Traveling on different body parts in own space and general space, with emphasis on showing muscle tension and reviewing starting and stopping
6	Sudden, combined with sustained movement, emphasizing body parts opening–closing, and rising–sinking	2*	Dribbling with feet, hands, and hockey sticks (cut down)	4	Forward rolls and taking weight on hands, with emphasis on coming to the feet quickly while rolling and controlling the placement of the feet after taking weight on hands
3*	Contrasting the difference between firm, strong movement and fine, delicate movement	3	Use of different directions when catching and collecting balls of different sizes and weights	5	Traveling in a variety of ways and pausing, with emphasis on making different body parts form the base and showing clarity in body lines by creating muscle tension
5	Sudden, firm movement combined with sustained, fine movement while traveling, emphasizing body parts and use of rising–sinking and opening–closing	5	Throwing and catching, using levels and extensions	4	Rolling in different directions, followed by brief moments of weight on hands or a balance on selected body parts
6	Sudden, fine movement combined with sustained, firm movement while traveling, emphasizing body parts and use of rising–sinking and opening–closing	5	Catching and striking, using different body parts	3*	Contrasting slow and fast movement, traveling on hands and feet
		5	Throwing, all basic patterns emphasized, and catching and collecting	4	Swinging, hanging, and/or traveling on apparatus with emphasis on resilient and fixed landings on the feet, combined with rolling and a change in direction

*These units have been developed and may be found in Chapter 6, 7, or 8.

PROGRAM OVERVIEW SHOWING SCOPE AND SEQUENCE KINDERGARTEN THROUGH SIXTH GRADE (continued)

SECOND GRADE DANCE		SECOND GRADE GAMES		SECOND GRADE GYMNASTICS	
Approx. no. of Lessons	Unit Focus	Approx. no. of Lessons	Unit Focus	Approx. no. of Lessons	Unit Focus
2	Jumping, turning, spinning, combined with stepping and sudden and sustained movement	4	Catching, throwing different objects (bean bags, balls of different sizes and weights) and use of different body parts in catching	4	Forward and backward rolls, followed by weight on hands, with emphasis on the placement of the hands in rolling and the landings after taking weight on hands
2	Traveling, using all space, combined with moving in personal space	3*	Using directions and extensions while catching and throwing	3	Developing short, gymnastic sequences involving step-like actions, jumps, turns, and rolls, with emphasis on stillness to start and to finish the sequence
3*	Using levels and directions in space while opening and closing, showing changes in speed	3	Striking with different body parts and dribbling with feet and hockey stick while traveling and stopping	3	Showing clarity of body shape and upness in the body when traveling and balancing
3	Rising—sinking, opening—closing using levels, directions, and emphasizing different body parts	4	Traveling with balls of different sizes and shapes, while accelerating and decelerating, using general space, and changing directions	4*	Balancing, rolling, and step-like actions, with emphasis on changing levels and directions
6	Firm, fine, sudden, sustained movement, combined with rising—sinking while traveling, and use of body parts	2*	Striking with emphasis on force production	4	Changing supporting body parts in a balance and ways to travel, with emphasis on creating and controlling speed
4	Combining use of levels and directions with running, jumping, spinning, and stepping, contrasting sudden with sustained movement	4	Catching, throwing, dribbling, striking with the hands and different implements, emphasizing amount of speed and force	4	Changing pathways (with and without a change in body front) with emphasis on constant motion on mat or apparatus, increasing the amount of time and number of children (from 1 to 5) who can work safely and simultaneously
4	Sudden, firm, combined with sustained, fine with rising—sinking, opening—closing, and use of pathways and levels	4	Striking with different body parts and implements and balls of different sizes and weights	3	Exploration of muscle tension when rocking and in extensions of body parts when spinning on different body parts, with emphasis on keeping the momentum going and transferring weight to different body parts

THIRD GRADE DANCE		THIRD GRADE GAMES		THIRD GRADE GYMNASTICS	
Approx. no. of Lessons	Unit Focus	Approx. no. of Lessons	Unit Focus	Approx. no. of Lessons	Unit Focus
5	Traveling, with use of levels, directions, contrasting sudden with sustained movement and firm with fine movement	5	Dribbling with feet and implements, emphasizing acceleration, deceleration, and use of directions	4	Changing the relationship of the legs and feet while rolling and traveling on hands and feet to develop greater variety, with emphasis on the relationships of the legs and feet while rolling, in the air, and landing
4	Spinning, running, twirling freely, combined with stepping, walking while traveling, rising—sinking, and pathways	4*	Controlling the flow of movement when striking, throwing, catching, and dribbling		
6	Direct combined with indirect movement, combined with firm, fine, sudden sustained movement and body parts	6	Striking, with emphasis on force production and direction, using body parts and implements	3	Showing clarity of body shape and upness in the body when traveling and balancing
4*	Experiencing free flow and bound flow and sensing the difference	3	Throwing and catching, with emphasis on force production, use of levels, and directions	4	Arriving on and dismounting from apparatus on different body parts, with emphasis on approaching and dismounting in different directions and traveling in the same or different directions after landing
2	Matching, mirroring, with emphasis on levels, bound and free flow, and traveling	6	Catching, collecting, with emphasis on force absorption with body parts and implements	2*	Twisting, curling, and stretching to change relationships of body parts and body shapes while balancing
3	Contrasting speed and weight while meeting and parting and mingling and matching			4	Relationship of body parts when balancing and traveling, with emphasis on symmetry and asymmetry and clarity of body shape
				3	Changing the base of support while spinning or rocking, with emphasis on developing a sequence incorporating spinning and/or rocking, traveling, and balancing, showing a clear change in levels

*These units have been developed and may be found in Chapter 6, 7, or 8.

PROGRAM OVERVIEW SHOWING SCOPE AND SEQUENCE
KINDERGARTEN THROUGH SIXTH GRADE (continued)

FOURTH GRADE DANCE		FOURTH GRADE GAMES		FOURTH GRADE GYMNASTICS	
Approx. no. of Lessons	Unit Focus	Approx. no. of Lessons	Unit Focus	Approx. no. of Lessons	Unit Focus
3	Meeting and parting as they relate to individual body parts and to others	5	Throwing, catching, collecting, dribbling, carrying, striking, stressing body and implement position prior to contact	4	Matching the work of others, with emphasis on eliminating unplanned movement and observing and duplicating the speed and muscle tension apparent in different body segments
3	Rising–sinking, meeting–parting, and mingling, while contrasting firm with fine movement and sudden with sustained movement	3	Planning where to carry or dribble ball in relation to different sized groups and obstacle courses	3	Intentionally selecting and showing different body parts, leading the body into and out of balances, with emphasis on controlling speed and placement of body parts
5	Use of levels, directions, and pathways while meeting–parting, rising–sinking, emphasizing matching and contrasting	3*	Positioning and repositioning as they relate to teammates and opponents	2	Twisting, curling, and stretching to change relationship of body parts to create different body shapes while balancing
3	Jumping, combined with traveling and use of levels and pathways	6	Striking, using upper body parts, emphasizing positioning before striking and placement of strike in relation to teammates and opponents	4	Step-like actions and moments of flight, with emphasis on perfecting or developing specialized gymnastic patterns (such as cartwheels, round-offs, walk-overs)
6	Rising–sinking, opening–closing, use of levels and directions, emphasizing body shape	4	Striking with rackets, emphasizing body and racket position before contact and hitting in relation to others	6*	Body shapes in flight, vaulting, or dismounting, with emphasis on strong, firm takeoffs and selecting appropriate muscle tension
4	Gesturing, combined with traveling, use of body parts, and clarity of body shape	3	Positioning and repositioning in relation to teammates and passing ahead of a runner	5*	Developing gymnastic sequences, intentionally showing a combination of stopped and ongoing movement

FIFTH GRADE DANCE

Approx. no. of Lessons	Unit Focus
3	Meeting and parting, emphasizing changes in use of time, weight, and levels in space
4	Jumping, emphasizing the five basic patterns, pathways, levels, and gestures
4*	Clarifying shape of the body alone and with others
4	Thrusting, slashing, flicking, and dabbing
4	Wringing, pressing, flicking, and dabbing
3	Matching, contrasting while traveling, using thrusting, slashing, floating, and gliding
2	Meeting–parting, mingling, rising–sinking, using wringing, pressing, flicking, and dabbing

FIFTH GRADE GAMES

Approx. no. of Lessons	Unit Focus
6	Throwing, catching, carrying, collecting, striking, dribbling, using a range of implements and body parts
2*	Catching balls that force running, jumping, and reaching simultaneously
6	Dribbling with feet and implements contacting objects coming at different speeds and in different places
6	Extending and recovering balance while dribbling with feet and with implements, catching, collecting, and striking
4	Throwing, catching, and dribbling with the hand in relation to teammates and opponents

FIFTH GRADE GYMNASTICS

Approx. no. of Lessons	Unit Focus
4	Accelerating, decelerating, and introducing stopping momentum to create visual excitement in a gymnastic sequence by showing variety, with emphasis on controlling muscle tension
3	Balancing on different body parts and a variety of step-like, rolling, and flight activities, with emphasis on creating and changing the base of support on the floor and on the apparatus, showing definite body parts leading body into and out of balance
6*	Body shapes in flight, vaulting, or dismounting, with emphasis on strong, firm takeoffs, and selecting appropriate muscle tension
3	Selecting and refining gymnastic patterns (emphasis on those requiring step-like actions and/or flight), with emphasis on performing the pattern repeatedly two or more times alone, with a partner, and/or in a small group
5	Developing small-group gymnastic sequences, with emphasis on showing twisting and curling to move into and out of balances and simultaneous, alternating, or successive movement
3*	Developing gymnastic sequences, intentionally showing a combination of stopped and ongoing movement

*These units have been developed and may be found in Chapter 6, 7, or 8.

PROGRAM OVERVIEW SHOWING SCOPE AND SEQUENCE KINDERGARTEN THROUGH SIXTH GRADE (continued)

SIXTH GRADE DANCE		SIXTH GRADE GAMES		SIXTH GRADE GYMNASTICS	
Approx. no. of Lessons	Unit Focus	Approx. no. of Lessons	Unit Focus	Approx. no. of Lessons	Unit Focus
4	Traveling, with jumping, spinning, and stepping, emphasizing pathways and variation in time and weight	6	Throwing, catching, collecting, striking, dribbling, carrying, using a range of implements and body parts	4	Combining/refining selected rolls, flight, and step-like activities with emphasis on acceleration, hurdle step, and strong, firm takeoffs to develop momentum
5	Rising–sinking combined with gestures, use of levels, and direct and indirect use of space	4*	Passing to spaces, emphasizing the placement of the ball in relation to the receiver	5*	Partners and/or small groups working together in the development of sequences, with emphasis on including matching, copying, and canon relationships
3*	Thrusting, slashing, floating, and gliding	4	Passing to spaces, emphasizing ahead of and even with teammate, using dribbling with the feet and with implements	3*	Creating and reproducing rhythmic patterns in gymnastics, involving step-like actions, rolling, and momentary pauses
3	Wringing, pressing, flicking, dabbing	6	Passing to dodge an opponent when traveling with a ball along the ground and in the air	4	Developing and refining a gymnastic sequence while manipulating a small piece of apparatus (e.g., hoop, ball, wand)
3	Thrusting, slashing, floating, gliding, combined with questioning and answering, and matching and contrasting	4	Close marking and intercepting when traveling with a ball on the ground or in the air	3	Supporting and/or lifting while working with others to create balances and flight
3	Wringing, pressing, flicking, dabbing, with questioning and answering, matching and contrasting			5	Creating counterbalance and countertension with apparatus and/ or with others, with emphasis on awareness of clarity of body lines and muscle tension
3	Combination of effort actions emphasizing group shapes				

*These units have been developed and may be found in Chapter 6, 7, or 8.

a program of physical education where each grade receives instruction 2 times a week for 36 weeks. Notice that the unit focuses have been grouped separately by program area for each grade level. During the teaching implementing this overview, the units in dance, games, and gymnastics would be selected in the approximate order in which they are presented, with the dance, games, and gymnastics units being intermingled throughout the year in accordance with the needs of the particular grade for which they were written. For example, a teacher might arbitrarily choose to alternate units in dance, games, and gymnastics. The routine may be varied by sometimes allowing the children to decide in which program area they prefer the next unit to be, or at times, for various reasons, the teacher might decide not to follow the arbitrary decision of alternating units in the three program areas.

The following exercise is recommended to aid in knowing the themes and learning their content, and to help beginning teachers appreciate the scope and sequence of the content presented in the sample Program Overview. Take each focus separately and, referring back to the Program Overview and to the dance, games, or gymnastics chapters, study the content and determine the theme or themes that is/are represented in each unit focus. Underline the content in each focus and then write in the theme that each bit of content represents. Then check to see whether the content outlined in the focuses for each grade has been selected from themes designated in Figure 11–1 as appropriate for the designated grade level. As you study these focuses and determine the themes, keep in mind this is a *SAMPLE* Program Overview used to illustrate how an overview may be prepared. It is *NOT MEANT* as an absolute that MUST be followed. Because preparing the Program Overview is the most difficult stage of planning to do, however, you may find it helpful to use the sample overview as a starting point for developing a program for your situation. As you review the themes and the content represented in each unit focus, you may find some gross omissions in content which should be taught. You may also need to alter some of the focuses, reorder some of the focuses, make additional ones and insert them in the progression, or delete focuses that have no meaning for you or the children.

Developing the Unit Plan—Phase Two in Planning

The construction of Unit Plans may be facilitated by first referring to Chapters 6, 7, and 8 and reading the sample unit written for each theme in dance, games, and gymnastics. You will notice that one style of unit planning was developed and used in preparing each unit in these three chapters. This format for unit planning is reproduced here in this chapter in Figure 11–3. The separate discussion on each section of the Unit Plan which follows has been written to help beginners understand some of the processes and procedures essential in developing units.

UNIT PLAN OUTLINE

PROGRAM AREA:
Theme(s).
Unit Focus.
Appropriate For.
Length of Unit.
Content
    Body—
    Space—
    Effort—
    Relationship—
Student Objectives.
Teaching Area.
Apparatus/Equipment.
Learning Experiences (Tasks).
Evaluation.

Fig. 11–3. Format for Unit Plan Construction.

DETERMINING THE PROGRAM AREA. Determining the program area is the easiest of all decisions to be made in unit planning. You merely select and list one of the program areas: dance, games, or gymnastics.

SELECTING THE THEME(S). Focus your attention on these three basic questions when you are considering theme selection:

1. Is this the first time the students will have studied content from this theme?
2. If this is not the first encounter with the theme, what portion of the content of the theme has been experienced previously by the children?

3. Was the previous experience with the content in the same program area as the unit you are writing or was it in a different program area?

Keep in mind that, when you are writing an isolated unit with no knowledge of the program the children have encountered prior to your unit, your answers to these questions will be based on suppositions and not fact. But the answers are essential to progression and good planning, and should be stated before proceeding to the subsequent steps in unit planning. Care should be taken when developing a unit plan not to select content to be taught from too many different themes. Selecting too many sources often results in no focal point and neither you, the teacher, nor the students will really sense any specific accomplishment when the unit is taught. Remember, *we do NOT use THEMES as content. We SELECT CONTENT FROM THE THEMES*. Also, no one class of students studies content from one theme to the exclusion of all other themes. ALL classes of children STUDY CONTENT SELECTED FROM AMONG TWO OR MORE THEMES. Note in Figure 11-1, THE CONTENT FOR EVERY GRADE IS SELECTED FROM CONTENT AMONG TWO OR MORE THEMES.

Another important consideration in theme selection is determining which theme to choose. Make sure the theme is appropriate for the children so their developmental needs will be challenged and the progression inherent in the themes will be followed. Figure 11-1 approximates which specific themes in dance, games, and gymnastics are appropriate for each grade level. The content selected from the theme and the experiences developed on that content should become more complex for the maturing student.

CHOOSING THE CONTENT. This step makes you isolate specific content from among all the content contained in the theme or themes you have selected for the unit. Remember, the content encompassed by one theme is used in the development of many units, so be precise in the selection of content for one unit and list the specific content to be taught. If the children have not encountered the theme content, your selection of the content from the theme should come from among the more simple skills or concepts. If you are providing enrichment for a group

of students on a concept they have studied previously, then the content you select as well as the way you develop it in the unit will often need to be more advanced.

Go back to Chapters 6, 7, and 8, specifically to the theme or themes you have chosen for your unit, and look at the content contained in the theme and read the discussion about the content. Also, referring back to Chapter 5 and reading about the specific content you have selected may help you gain a more complete awareness for this content you plan to teach. Reading about the content in other books also can provide for a deeper understanding.

State the content you plan to teach in terms specific to the program area of the unit. DO NOT PLUCK WORDS FROM THE MOVEMENT FRAMEWORK AND LIST THEM AS CONTENT IF THEY DO NOT SAY CLEARLY WHAT YOU PLAN TO TEACH. Reword the concept. Make it meaningful to you. Extrapolate the idea or movement category listed in the framework so the words you use to describe your content say exactly what you think you mean. DO NOT MAKE THE READER INTERPRET WHAT YOU MEAN.

Notice the outline for unit planning in Figure 11-3 causes you to make specific decisions concerning content to be taught in each of the four aspects of movement. For example, if you want your unit focus to be *Varying the Relationships of the Legs While Rolling*, the content would be listed in the following manner:

BODY—rolling
SPACE—
EFFORT—
RELATIONSHIPS—one leg to the other:
        far–near,
        in front–behind,
        side–by–side,
        apart–together.

Note it is not necessary to have any unit focus cover content from all four movement aspects.

STATING THE UNIT FOCUS. The unit focus will either be copied from the Program Overview, if an overview has been prepared previously, or it will be written when the Unit Plan is being developed. In either case, the focus is written in an attempt to narrow the direction of the unit. Writing the focus sometimes seems to be redundant because the unit focus usually restates the selected content. Reviewing the unit focuses listed in the Sample Program Overview presented earlier in this chapter should provide insight in writing focuses.

STATING FOR WHOM THE UNIT IS APPROPRIATE. Generally, this statement in the Unit Plan identifies the kind of experiences or skills the children need to have had before encountering the content in your unit would be meaningful. Serious consideration of this helps you to reflect briefly on progression and should help to sensitize you to some of the developmental needs of children. Too many teachers of physical education teach the same thing over and over to children at all grade levels. Completing this section thoughtfully may help to eliminate this unsound practice.

STIPULATING THE TEACHING SITE. This decision is often crucial to the success of the unit when it is taught. The selection of the site for the unit should be based on

The nature of the activity
The age and number of students in the class
The content to be taught
The objectives of the unit

Think of the teaching station needed for teaching the unit and raise these questions: Will the unit be taught inside? Will it be taught outside? Part inside, part outside? If outside, what kind of surface—grass or blacktop? In a large space, small space? Will the experiences have special needs such as wall space or electrical outlets? Decisions of this nature, widely matching the objectives of the unit, can enhance the learning potential of a unit. Unwise decisions related to facilities, such as planning a unit to be taught inside that needs a large outdoor teaching area, will lead to feeble attempts at developing challenging game-like conditions needed in skill development. The experiences provided the children will fail miserably in achieving the objectives of the unit. Conversely, some units are taught best in small areas. If the teaching area is limited, the content selected to be taught in that area must be selected carefully, and the learning experience must be developed with those limitations in mind.

Work in many units—the objectives—cannot be achieved in teaching stations unsuitable for the selected experiences. For example, a unit focused on *Lead Passes with the Feet with Emphasis on Creating Spaces* requires a setting that will allow the game-like dynamics of the soccer dribble to develop and to be used and that is large enough for the spatial relationships that must be created between players to be real and "game size." To attempt to teach the content from this unit to a class of children in a limited space can often be ludicrous because neither the dynamics of the dribble nor the essential, spatial relationships basic to the objectives can be practiced or achieved in a restricted area, either indoors or outside. YOU END UP NOT TEACHING THE CONTENT SELECTED FOR THE UNIT. YOU DO NOT ACHIEVE THE STATED OBJECTIVES. When this happens, the chain of progression which you think you have planned in your yearly program fails to materialize because the children will not have achieved the skills and understandings which are basic to further challenges in other units.

LISTING THE APPARATUS AND/OR EQUIPMENT. When selecting and listing the equipment, be specific in stating the quantity, the size, and the kind needed. If your unit is on dance, the equipment might include a list of the percussion instruments, the record player, and any kind of stimulus or materials you or the children would use in the unit, such as the name of a specific phonograph record. Listing these materials makes you arrive at precise decisions early in planning your unit, which will be useful in some of the remaining steps in unit planning and later on in lesson planning.

The American Alliance for Health, Physical Education, Recreation, and Dance (AAHPERD) recommends that enough small equipment (balls, hoops, racquets—things commonly used by individuals to develop manipulative skills) should be available in large enough quantities so that all children in a class may have their own piece of equipment.[1,2] To extend this concept further in supplying adequate learning materials in physical education, it is recommended that large apparatus used in gymnastics, goal standards for games, and the like, should be in sufficient supply so each group of four to six children in the class has the use of the designated apparatus.

DETERMINING LENGTH OF THE UNIT. We suggest the approximate number of lessons in the unit be stated before you start writing. The statement you have just read and all indications thus far in the book, including the units in Chap-

Photo from the Agency for Instructional Television.

ters 6, 7, and 8 and the Program Overview in this chapter, may lead you to believe that the length of the Unit Plan must be rigidly established before you start the writing of the learning experiences, and once established, the length must not be changed. NOT TRUE. Actually, the opposite is true. The length of the unit may be altered. It may be altered two or three times. You may change the length of the unit, thus the number of lessons to be taught from it, as you write the unit. When you prepare the Plan of Progression for Teaching a Unit, you may find you need one or more additional lessons to give the necessary sequence to the experiences and the essential time with the progression to the children to be able to achieve the unit objectives. Also, when you are actually teaching the unit, many reasons occur that require the proposed length of the unit to be altered. Some of these reasons could be the following:

1. *The children you teach:* They may be more or less advanced than anticipated and able to move through the unit faster or may need to go slower.
2. *You, the teacher:* You might inadvertently lose time in class organization, in task development, or you may differ in your ability to deal with the content effectively with different groups of children.
3. *School schedules:* Often, schedules change and present various kinds of problems that trigger the need for altering the planned length of the unit.
4. *The content:* Frequently, the content of the unit becomes exciting and you and the children agree that more time could be spent on the unit in a profitable manner.

For example, the regular school schedule may be disrupted for a day or two because of snow, parent-teacher conferences, or a holiday. When these disruptions occur, sometimes it might be wiser to devote one or two more additional lessons to a unit already started than to introduce a new unit. Of course, this depends on whether you, the teacher, and the children can extend the work effectively for the additional lessons. Care should be taken not to carry on a unit too long. Rather than devoting an excessive number of lessons to one unit, it may be wiser to revisit the content that is deemed to be important more than once during the year rather than extend the length of time devoted to the unit initially.

STATING STUDENT OBJECTIVES. The objectives in the educational approach to teaching physical education are written in a style that tends to be more humane and that accommodates individual differences more than the usual behavioral objectives that state a required, terminal student behavior that must be attained by all students by the end of the unit. The style of objectives being suggested is illustrated, in part, in the unit outline in Figure 11–4, with the phrase: *"The students should be willing to try to."* This phrase is written to acknowledge the individual differences that exist among children in every class. Rather than set an explicit, minimal standard, which must be achieved by all, this phrase states that all students should be willing to try to achieve the objectives of the unit, and it implies that the potential for achieving the objectives will vary among the children.

In writing the objectives for a unit, *keep them few in number.* Make sure that at least one objective identifies the key *motor objective,* one states the key *cognitive objective,* and at least one reflects the key *affective objective.* Objectives should be relevant to the content and to the developmental stages of the children for whom the unit is planned. *Write complete objectives— do not allude to information; provide information. Educate the reader.* The following examples may be of some help in differentiating between objectives which provide information and those which allude to information.

EXAMPLES OF OBJECTIVES
The children should be willing to try to
1. Know how to absorb force when catching.
2. Know that to absorb force when catching a ball with the hands one must give in the elbows and hands in the direction the ball is traveling at the moment the ball contacts the hands.

Which objective gives you, the reader, the most information? Objective number 1 or number 2? Which objective requires the writer to know more about catching? Objective number 1 or number 2? **Number 1 alludes to information. Number 2 spells it out.**

In writing the objectives for a unit, keep in mind that they should serve later as a basis for evaluating the progress the children make during the unit.

PREPARING LEARNING EXPERIENCES (TASKS). Take a moment to turn back to one or two of the sample units in Chapters 6, 7, or 8 and familiarize yourself with the way learning experiences are written and how they are listed in the Unit Plans. When you start to write your first unit or two, you may find it to be a definite advantage to develop the final experience first. Determining this last culminating experience can give direction to each of the learning experiences you plan later. After this last task is written, then write the main tasks, numbered 1.0, 2.0, 3.0, etc., as shown in the sample units in the aforementioned chapters, until you have built a progression that makes your culminating experience a logical next and final step in the unit. Before you actually start to write the learning experiences for a unit, turn again to several units in the earlier chapters: read only the main tasks and look for the progression which builds from one main task to another.

After the main tasks have been written and the progression of the unit has been outlined by these main tasks, go back and develop a series of supplemental tasks, numbered 1.1, 1.2, 1.3, etc., under each of the main tasks. These supplemental tasks are written to

1. Give the children time and practice to acquire the abilities introduced in the main tasks.
2. Encourage children to develop greater versatility in their responses to the main task.
3. Change the environment in which the main tasks are introduced to help motivate the children to stay with a learning situation longer.
4. Refine the movement (skill) introduced in the main tasks.
5. Expand the challenge to stimulate more advanced work on the content.
6. Apply or use the skill (movement) that is identified in the main tasks.

If you take the time to compare several of the Unit Plans found in the content chapters with their respective plan of progression for teaching those units, you will see how the learning experiences found in a Unit Plan could eventually be ordered in planning the several individual lessons from the unit. You should be able to detect from this reading that learning experiences ARE NOT TAUGHT IN THE EXPLICIT ORDER IN WHICH THEY ARE LISTED ON THE UNIT PLAN. The reason becomes more obvious when you reread the plan of progression for the various units. You should be able to see how the same main learning experiences as well as the supplemental experiences are sometimes repeated within a lesson as well as being used in two or more of the lessons. This revisitation of tasks negates the idea of the tasks being used in the order they are written.

Also, notice in your rereading of the plan of progression following some of the units that it is not unusual for other tasks to be introduced before all of the supplemental tasks of the previous experience have been included. This shifting from one main task to another without completing all supplemental tasks and the revisitation of tasks are done to afford children the *practice time* and the *learning time* needed to develop skills basic to the content. The learning achieved during this practice time cannot be rushed; therefore, the supplemental tasks are often distributed over several lessons. This practice of presenting the supplemental tasks over several lessons also aids in pacing lessons and allows for variety within lessons more than would occur if you moved sequentially step by step through each of the supplemental tasks in the order they appear on the Unit Plan.

PREPARING FOR EVALUATION. Each unit should have a plan of evaluation developed for it. This plan should be used to determine the progress the children make toward achieving the objectives of the unit. To prepare a way to evaluate the progress in the first unit or two you write, start by refamiliarizing yourself with the objectives of your unit. Then, as McGee says in Chapter 10, when designing the evaluative tool for the unit, ". . . make the assessment of student progress as personalized and diagnostic as possible." Refer to the evaluation chapter and look at the kinds of tools that are described and, following one of the ideas given there or one of your own, develop a tool to record the progress the children make daily toward achieving one or more of the objectives of your unit.

A SYNTHESIS FOR DESIGNING UNIT PLANS

Figure 11–4 synthesizes the preceding information on Unit Plan construction. It is important to reiterate that unit planning may take many forms. The previous discussion and the synthesis which follows represent but one form for planning units.

PROGRAM AREA:

Here you list the program area(s): dance, games, and/or gymnastics. This helps you narrow the source of the content for the unit and lets any reader of your unit know the type of unit it is.

THEME(S):

If you have developed a Program Overview and are developing a unit from the overview, you check the source of the content in the unit focus by examining the content in the various themes. List the theme(s) from which the unit content has been selected.

CONTENT:
        BODY:
        SPACE:
        EFFORT:
        RELATIONSHIPS:

List only the content that is to be TAUGHT. Most units WILL NOT have content from each of the four movement aspects. Phrase content in terms that make sense to you and to the students. Be specific—make the listing of content identify precisely what you plan to teach. If you have developed a Program Overview, the content will be determined by selecting one of the unit focuses from the overview and then analyzing the content contained in the focus or included in your interpretation of the focus.

UNIT FOCUS:

Pinpoint the direction of your unit, remembering that many units are written from each theme. Keep in mind that the unit will only span several lessons.

APPROPRIATE FOR:

Here, you outline the kind of movement background the students should have in order for your unit to be suitable. If you write this thoughtfully, it should have you reflecting on progression.

TEACHING SITE:

Stipulate the kind of location in which the unit can be taught best. Recommend the size and surface as well as the location of the working area.

APPARATUS AND/OR EQUIPMENT:

List the recommended amount of equipment/apparatus; describing the size, weight, and shape, where appropriate.

LENGTH OF UNIT:

Project the number of lessons that can be developed meaningfully from the unit. Keep in mind that the recommended length of units in the elementary school is approximately two to six lessons, depending on the nature of the content and the abilities of the children and the teacher.

STUDENT OBJECTIVES: The students should be willing to try to:

Make each objective complete the sentence started with the phrase: The students should be willing to try to. Usually, this is accomplished by beginning each objective with a verb. These statements should pinpoint specific affective, cognitive, and motor objectives and should be appropriate for the age group for whom the unit is planned and be achievable in the time allotted for the unit. Be explicit—tell precisely what you expect the students to aspire to, keeping the objectives few in number. Spell out the knowledges and attitudes to be developed or improved as well as the skills to be developed. Do not make the reader fill in information—include the facts; do not make the reader guess.

LEARNING EXPERIENCES (TASKS):

Develop a series of major tasks which, when taught, should accomplish the unit objectives. Under each of these major experiences, prepare a number of subtasks to extend the challenge of the content of the major tasks and provide motivation and more instruction and practice time essential to skill development. As you write, keep in mind that the list of tasks is usually not taught in the exact order in which it is written and it is not organized in lessons. (Reread several suggested progressions for teaching the units in Chapters 6, 7, and 8.)

EVALUATION:

Design and attach an evaluative tool, especially for the unit you have written, which can be used to record daily the extent to which the objectives of the unit have been achieved by each student. Make the tool complete so any reader could use it. Show what is to be assessed and provide an explicit key for assessing it. The tools most helpful in teaching will often be used throughout the teaching of the unit to assess the day-by-day progress being made by the children. (Refer to Chapter 10 to assist in designing tools for evaluation and assessment.)

Fig. 11–4. Hints for Designing Unit Plans.

Preparing Lesson Plans—Stage Three in Planning

Certain mental processes related to planning for teaching, if developed, can facilitate the teaching/learning process and make teaching less traumatic for the teacher and learning more exciting for the students. Thinking through the purpose of the lesson, studying the content to be taught, and attempting to perceive the developmental stages in motor performance of the children in the activities associated with the unit aid in the development of these processes and can help the teacher to develop competence essential in teaching. Outlining a possible progression for teaching the content of a lesson, projecting specifics to be observed in the responses of the children as they work, and de-

veloping pertinent coaching hints to be given to improve the performance of the students also can aid in the development of these processes and can help teachers to develop confidence in teaching. The format for lesson planning outlined in Figure 11–5 has been prepared to help teachers beginning to implement the educational approach basic to this book to develop competence and confidence essential to teaching. This format is an example of the procedure mentioned by Barrett in Chapter 9 whereby pertinent observation points are arranged by priority and included on the Lesson Plan.

The following suggestions for preparing a Lesson Plan outline a step-by-step procedure for planning. Each section of the Lesson Plan in Figure 11–5 has been given a number from 1 through 12. The suggestions which follow have

---

SUGGESTED FORMAT FOR LESSON PLANNING

(1) *LESSON NUMBER.*

(2) *UNIT FOCUS.*

(3) *OBSERVATIONS INFLUENCING THIS LESSON.*

(4) *LESSON PURPOSE.*

(5) *CONTENT*
Body—
Space—
Effort—
Relationships—

(6) *OBJECTIVES.* The students should be willing to try to

(7) *APPARATUS/EQUIPMENT.*

LEARNING EXPERIENCES (TASKS)	WAYS TO CHANGE TASKS TO ACCOMMODATE INDIVIDUAL DIFFERENCES	OBSERVATION PLAN AND FEEDBACK TO IMPROVE AFFECTIVE BEHAVIOR AND/OR KNOWLEDGE	OBSERVATION PLAN AND FEEDBACK TO IMPROVE MOTOR RESPONSES
(8)	(9)	(10)	(11)
	Easier: More difficult:		
(12) *LESSON EVALUATION.*			

Fig. 11–5. Suggested Outline for Planning a Lesson.

been numbered to correspond with the sections of the Lesson Plan.

SUGGESTIONS FOR PREPARING A LESSON PLAN

(Each number corresponds with the same number on the Lesson Plan in Figure 11–5.)

1. *LESSON NUMBER.* You record two numbers such as 1–4, 2–4, 3–4, or 4–4. The first designates the number of the lesson, and the second indicates the total number of lessons projected for the unit.

2. *UNIT FOCUS.* The unit focus is copied directly from the Unit Plan.

3. *OBSERVATIONS INFLUENCING THIS LESSON.* The information called for here comes from the evaluation you have made of previous lessons or insights you have gained from other experiences. Write this, stating factual information, telling what was actually seen, trying to refrain from using judgmental terms.

4. *LESSON PURPOSE.* State briefly the main objective you are trying to accomplish in the lesson. This could be related to either the affective, cognitive, or motor development of the children. At times, it may include a specific idea for improvement of your own teaching behavior.

5. *CONTENT.* First, review the *content of the unit.* List opposite the appropriate aspect of movement *only the content you plan to focus on in the lesson.* (All four aspects, body, space, effort, and relationships, are not usually represented as content to be TAUGHT in either the Unit Plan or in a Lesson Plan.) Phrase the content in words that have real meaning to you. Avoid listing broad categories of movement when you plan to teach specifics and vice versa.

6. *OBJECTIVES.* Reread the objectives of the unit and your lesson purpose. Objectives should be stated clearly and directed toward the development of the affective (attitudes, feelings, social interactions), cognitive (knowledge and understandings), and motor (skillful, versatile movement) domains. Keep your objectives few in number. As you write, do not refer indirectly to information—spell it out, educate those who might read your lesson. Develop objectives that are significant to the developmental stage of the students you are teaching and specifically related to the content of the lesson.

7. *APPARATUS/EQUIPMENT NEEDED.* List all of the materials needed by you and the children. Give the amount, the size, and the kind. If music is to be used, list the name of the record or the tape cassette and the equipment on which it is to be played.

8. *LEARNING EXPERIENCES (TASKS).* Refer to the Unit Plan and to the suggested progression for teaching the unit for the recommended sequence of experiences for the lesson, if one has been developed. THINK OF THE CHILDREN YOU ARE TEACHING AND THEIR DEVELOPMENTAL NEEDS. Feel free to alter the projected lesson progression and prepare new tasks, whenever appropriate. On a separate piece of paper, list all the experiences in the order you plan to teach them. Write these experiences in the language you would use with the students. Watch how you phrase each task. When stating the tasks, following these guidelines may help to keep the students' attention while you state the entire task. First, state WHAT they are to do; then WHERE they are to do it; finish the task by giving the directions related to WITH WHAT and WITH WHOM they are to work. As you write the tasks, try to state them in ways that will accommodate different individual skill levels. (Refer to Chapter 9 to refresh your understanding of the different kinds of tasks.)

   After all the experiences and their chronologic order have been determined for the lesson, copy the first experience onto your plan. Complete parts 9, 10, and 11 for your first task. When all four columns have been completed for the first task, draw a horizontal line across the page to separate the task. This keeps all the teaching material for one task on the same level on your page and visually separated so you can refer to your plan quickly when you are teaching. Then repeat this procedure, completing parts 9, 10, and 11 for each task in your lesson.

9. *WAYS TO CHANGE TASKS TO AC-*

COMMODATE INDIVIDUAL DIFFER-ENCES. Reread the learning experience you have written on the Lesson Plan. Think of the variations that exist among the students for whom you are planning the lesson and how the task could be altered to be meaningful to children at different developmental levels. When appropriate, rewrite the challenge of the task to make it easier for the students needing a lesser challenge (prepare a simplifying task) and prepare something harder for those who quickly achieve the goal in the original task (prepare an extending task).

10. *OBSERVATION PLAN AND FEEDBACK TO IMPROVE BEHAVIOR AND/OR KNOWLEDGE.* This part of the plan calls for two kinds of information to show how you plan to deal with the cognitive and affective development of the students. List, in order, your plan for observation and tell what you plan to observe in each task. (Refer to Chapter 9 for help in observation.) Then, to prepare you to help the children improve their understanding of the concept, mechanics, or strategy, or to improve their attitudes about themselves and others, under each observation focus you have listed, outline the teaching emphases you could stress and the questions you could pose. Referring to Chapters 3 and 4 in addition to the content chapters can help you sort out some of the knowledge inherent in your content that needs to be taught.

11. *OBSERVATION PLAN AND FEEDBACK TO IMPROVE MOTOR RESPONSES.* The fourth column is designed to help you look at the motor performance of the students and their developmental stages in relation to the requisites of the task. It, like column 3, is designed to help prepare you to intervene meaningfully in the learning process of the students when they are working by planning your scheme of observation and preparing ideas for feedback.

First, underline the key content in your task. Next, determine your observation strategy (see Chapter 9), and then list precisely what you are going to look at or look for in their responses. Try to list these in the order of their importance, and there-fore, the order in which you would try to work with the children for improvement. Finally, under each point you are going to observe, develop a series of coaching hints which you could use to help the students modify and improve their performance. Remember again the individual differences of the children and reword and redesign several coaching strategies to accommodate different learning styles.

12. *LESSON EVALUATION.* After the lesson is taught, record pertinent information about the progress the students made toward meeting the lesson objectives. Tell what their performance actually looked like or what they did. Do not use judgmental terms—state facts so a reader would know what the students did, too. This information, if factual and explicit, can be helpful to you in writing the next lesson in the unit. Much of this information may be taken from the notations you record on the assessment tool you developed for the unit when you take time during and after your lesson to note the progress that individual children made. (In addition, you may need to prepare an observation plan as described in Chapter 9 and attach it to the lesson.)

FURTHER INSIGHTS FOR PLANNING A LESSON

NUMBER OF LESSONS IN A UNIT. It is important to know that the number of lessons needed to achieve the objectives of a unit may vary when you are teaching the same unit to two or more classes of children at the same grade level. The number of lessons listed on the Unit Plan and outlined in the suggested teaching progression for the unit is a guide, not a mandate that must be adhered to strictly.

OBSERVATIONS INFLUENCING PLANNING THE NEXT LESSON. As you teach each segment of every lesson, pay particular attention to the responses of the children. Carefully observe their performance as it relates to the requisites of the task, the specific objectives, and their developmental stages. (Keep in mind that beginners cannot become pros in one 30-minute period . . . nor during the teaching of one unit.) Constantly monitor their responses and try to capture the progress they make as well as their existing needs. Jot these observations down as you see them. Then in each subsequent lesson, *teach children* NOT just content; be sure your plans and your teaching reflect the developmental needs of YOUR class and not an etheric class that exists only in the textbook.

SELECTION OF CONTENT. One common error is made frequently in the selection of content for a lesson. When teachers think about the content of the lesson, they tend to anticipate and analyze the movement children will do, thereby listing the entire movement analysis as the content to be taught. *Care must be taken to list only the content to be taught, the prime content you want the children to concentrate on as they move.*

WRITING LESSON OBJECTIVES. Have you considered why each of the objectives in this book has consistently started with the phrase, *"The students should be willing to try to"* instead of *"The students must be able to"*? Read those two phrases again and think of the activity that has been the most difficult for you to learn over the years. Think of the times when you took an activity class and some students at the beginning of the class were already experienced. You or one of your classmates may have been handicapped or had learning disabilities. Which phrase would you have preferred your teacher to have used? We recommend the use of the more open objective reflected in the first phrase to allow for these individual differences which do exist in any required, instructional program where students are given no choice in which activity they enroll.

APPARATUS/EQUIPMENT NEEDED. In selecting the equipment/apparatus to be used, think of the size and the skill level of the children who will be using it. Also, consider the number of students in the class and remember the minimum ratio for gymnastic apparatus and other large pieces of equipment is one piece of equipment to each four to six students in the class. The small pieces of sports equipment, such as balls and racquets, should be in sufficient quantity to supply each child in a class with the equipment. Consider also the texture, weight, shape, and other characteristics of the equipment when making your selection. For example, bean bags or yarn balls might be better in certain throwing and catching lessons than balls that have greater

resiliency. Light, commercially produced plastic racquets or racquets made of coat hangers with nylon hose stretched over them may be more desirable than the conventional tennis racquet. Selecting the right equipment and providing it in the appropriate quantity is a must if the objectives in a lesson or a unit are to be achieved.

LEARNING EXPERIENCES (TASKS). Be sure to review the information in Chapter 9 on teaching. This should help in writing all tasks. Keep in mind all learning experiences are not "motor tasks." Some experiences should be written in the form of discussions, observations to be made by the students, or students critiquing work of others, for example. These kinds of tasks should be planned and thoughtfully executed by the teacher. When experiences of this nature are planned, be sure to think of the various roles required in the experiences to be played by the students. For instance, when students are critiquing the work of others, planning should be directed toward the role of the mover as well as the role of the observer, the one doing the critiquing. The responsibilities of both roles must be clarified when the experience is written in the Lesson Plan. Subsequently, when you start to plan for your observation of the children during this experience and to develop your feedback, children playing both roles will need your attention and guidance. Evidence of your planning for teaching for both roles should appear clearly in your Lesson Plans.

PLANNING OBSERVATION AND PREPARING FEEDBACK. As you plan your observation of either the affective, cognitive, or motor responses, you first must identify what it is you are looking for or what it is you want to look at—and these observation points must be stated clearly (see Fig. 11–5). *These should be related*

Photo from the Agency for Instructional Television.

Photo from the Agency for Instructional Television.

Photo from the Agency for Instructional Television.

closely to the purpose of your task. Then, because learning can be enhanced by feedback and because different teaching cues can help different children to learn, you need to write a series of teaching cues or coaching hints in order to be helpful to all children in different ways. Questions may also be developed to stimulate cognitive processes to encourage children to analyze and to think about their responses. REMEMBER, AS YOU PREPARE THESE QUESTIONS, COACHING HINTS, AND TEACHING CUES, YOU ARE FORTIFYING YOURSELF—THE TEACHER—WITH AMMUNITION TO BE USED WHEN TEACHING TO HELP THE CHILDREN IMPROVE THEIR PERFORMANCE AND INCREASE THEIR UNDERSTANDING OF THE MOVEMENT. Without this pertinent teaching material, your role as a teacher is likely to be too passive after the task is given when the children are working. Knowing what to look for and purposefully helping the children improve their re-

sponses require an active, alert, knowledgeable, involved teacher.

EVALUATION DURING THE LESSON. Each unit should have an evaluative tool designed especially for it. If there is none for a unit you might be teaching, design one using the guidelines given in Chapter 10. This evaluation usually is formative in nature, meaning the tool should be used to continually assess the progress of the children throughout the unit as you teach each lesson. As you assess the responses of the children from lesson to lesson and record their progress on the evaluation tool, you should gain specific information about the progress the children are making if the tool reflects the specific objectives of the unit. This assessment, if recorded, can be of great assistance when writing the next lesson or when preparing and teaching future units.

FLEXIBILITY IN TEACHING FROM A LESSON PLAN. Planning and all the care, thought, and reading it takes is done to help you develop competence for teaching. I call the written Lesson Plan, *thinking you can do on your seat.* It should represent your best ideas for making an instructional period meaningful for every child. When you arrive at the school, this well-conceived Lesson Plan in your hand becomes a guide, an aid—and nothing more. No memorization of the plan is necessary, for once the class begins, you should move from one experience to another based not only on what is in the lesson but also on the observations you make of the children and the needs you see at the moment. Feel free to refer to your tasks on the Lesson Plan. You are likely to feel the need to develop new experiences "on your feet" as you teach to respond to those needs—do it. You may also need to refer to the plan to see the questions or ideas you wrote down to be used in providing feedback—do it. The flexibility you need in teaching is yours—exercise it. Do not be of the opinion that a Lesson Plan, once written, must be followed to the letter. On the contrary, it is written to

help beginning teachers develop the processes essential in teaching. These processes, to be effective, must be executed with sensitive variation and selected in response to the needs of the children as they work. Keep in mind some of the best experiences for you and the children will come as the result of both of you sparking each other's ability during the class period—that is when teaching becomes exciting.

SAMPLE LESSON PLAN. The suggested outline for planning a lesson provided in Figure 11–5 was used in the development of the Sample Lesson Plan that follows. As you read the Lesson Plan, notice especially how and where pertinent information has been included. Try to grasp how this information has had to come from a knowledge base.

Summary

In preparing plans at all levels, Program Overview, Unit Plan, or Lesson Plan, it is essential

Photo from the Agency for Instructional Television.

SAMPLE LESSON PLAN
(Developed from Unit Plan for Gymnastics Theme 5 in Chapter 8)

LESSON NUMBER. 2–6

UNIT FOCUS. Body shapes in flight, vaulting, or dismounting, with emphasis on strong, firm takeoffs and selecting appropriate muscle tension.

OBSERVATIONS INFLUENCING THIS LESSON
1. Children in previous vaulting experiences when executing the approach in the vault tended to run at medium speed, slowing down prior to takeoff.
2. Strides in the approach were often similar in length with the length of the approach often being several steps longer than needed to develop desired momentum.
3. Few children intentionally controlled their forward momentum on landing and either fell forward or saved themselves by rolling immediately after landing.

LESSON PURPOSE. To focus the attention on the speed characteristics of the approach to get the students to build up momentum through an accelerated run and to willfully choose and control two kinds of landings—fixed and resilient.

CONTENT
Body—approach, takeoff, and landings
Space—
Effort—time: accelerating
        weight: muscle tension to control force in landing and shapes in flight
Relationships—

OBJECTIVES. The students should be willing to try to:
1. Understand that momentum is useful in achieving height in the takeoff and can be developed by accelerating to the takeoff rather than hesitating and slowing down before takeoff.
2. Know that the strides in an accelerated approach start small and increase as the vaulter approaches the box and the speed builds (accelerates) throughout the approach, being fastest immediately prior to takeoff.
3. Accept responsibility for giving others in their group running space and for learning through observing/critiquing the speed, size of steps, and landings of others.
4. Improve—their approach through practicing an accelerated run.
        —their landing by selecting to practice fixed landings (staying on the spot where they land) and resilient landings (landing and popping straight up and returning to the initial landing spot).

APPARATUS. A vaulting box (or stool) and large mat for each four to six students.

LEARNING EXPERIENCES (TASKS)	WAYS TO CHANGE TASKS TO ACCOMMODATE INDIVIDUAL DIFFERENCES	OBSERVATION PLAN AND FEEDBACK TO IMPROVE AFFECTIVE BEHAVIOR AND/OR KNOWLEDGE	OBSERVATION PLAN AND FEEDBACK TO IMPROVE MOTOR RESPONSES
1. Take care to first *walk* out your working pathway. Be sure your pathway does not cross the pathway of others. Start with a nicely lifted upper body, do a short run, finishing with a strong lift and two-foot landing, which pops you straight back up in the air.	(Could select a space away from others for those who appear to be a little reluctant.)	**Observe walking out pathway:** –stop class, if necessary, if any dangerous condition exists –make sure you do not cross anyone's pathway –your space must be your own –seek out a clear path no one else is crossing –praise those who have established unobstructed pathway –question those about pathway being clear who cross pathways of others –stress everyone is responsible for own safety and safety of others	**Observe length of pathway:** –pathway should be short –take only about 8 to 10 steps –praise for keeping runs short –suggest to selected children to shorten their run **Focus on lift of chest:** –keep chest up –do not let your ribs sag –maintain upness in the part of your body from your waist to your shoulders **Focus on lift of trailing leg during takeoff:** –swing that thigh of that back leg up –make that swing forceful –swing it fast –make it lift you up high, not out far **Look at landings:** –make two-foot landings –make the landing spring you into the air –try to come down in the same spot as your takeoff
2. Now really show your momentum, your speed, building so your fastest speed helps to lift you in the air.		**Scan for spacing:** –watch your spacing –change your working space to keep the work safe	**Focus on speed:** –your speed should build –start rather slow and accelerate –slow, fast, faster—make it build –do not let your speed be the same throughout the run
3. Think about your stride—the size of your steps. They should get bigger as you run, with the last stride the largest. Making your trailing knee and thigh thrust fast and high to lift you straight into the air, land on two feet and spring high into the air.	(May need to point out to specific children their first steps are too large or too small to help them get started.)	**Focusing on stride size:** –Can anyone tell me where you might see someone building up speed while running by starting with shorter, driving strides? Examples: –track—dashes –ice skating to get started –lay-up shot in basketball –vaulting in gymnastics	**Focus on size of stride:** –start small –build length –do not make leaps –end with a comfortable running stride, not leaps **Focus on thrust of thigh of trailing leg:** –see feedback in Task 1 Focus on landings: –make two landings –land and pop right back up –keep body straight so you can pop straight up –get springs in your landing

LEARNING EXPERIENCES (TASKS)	WAYS TO CHANGE TASKS TO ACCOMMODATE INDIVIDUAL DIFFERENCES	OBSERVATION PLAN AND FEEDBACK TO IMPROVE AFFECTIVE BEHAVIOR AND/OR KNOWLEDGE	OBSERVATION PLAN AND FEEDBACK TO IMPROVE MOTOR RESPONSES
4. Let us keep this accelerating run and strong two-foot springy landing. By placing your hands on the vaulting box, see how high you can take your hips into the air and then have your feet come down in the spot where they took off. Remember, all four people carry mat (so you do not drag it) and add your box. Place your apparatus where you had it yesterday—remembering the pathway. Get in your groups of five or six and begin. Key: ☐ = mat (about 4 feet × 8 feet) → = path of runner ☐ = vaulting box (approximately 30 inches to 38 inches high)	To make task easier: —have those children landing too far away from box watch where the feet of others land —could ask them to place a piece of tape down near the box and see whether they can land between tape and box —have children spring up on box repeatedly from a standing position—no running approach—hands on box, feet close to box.	Question the children on where their feet should land in relation to the box to send hips high over hands when hands are placed on top of box. (Why?) —close to box —places feet (their base) near to the next base of support (the hands) —makes it easier to get weight of hips over the hands because it is closer to hands **Scan for carrying boxes:** —remember to lift with legs—arms and back straight —walk sidewards rather than making others walk backwards—can fall and have box land on them Focus on placement of apparatus: —remember your running space —plan your placement to give you running room	**Focus on relationship of feet to box in takeoff:** —landing should be close to box —close means right next to the box **Focus on hands:** —flat on box —fingers forward —shoulder width apart —push with your hands **Focus on arms:** —elbows straight —arms strong —tighten the muscles in your arms **Focus on hips:** —send hips straight up —lift hips up —stay in pike position in the air —make your pop up take your hips the highest **Focus on making landing go right into the lift:** —as you land, let your pop up start immediately —do not get stuck in your landing —keep those landings bouncy
5. Some of you may like to begin by letting your springy takeoff take you up onto the box. Hold your balance on the box for a moment and prepare a twisted, stretched, or curled stretch in the air, landing on the mat on two feet in a held, fixed landing.		**Focus on children twisting in air:** Ask children if landing from a twist, do you need to land with your feet closer together or a little farther apart? Why? —a little farther apart helps to maintain balance because the upper part of the body tends to continue twisting as the lower part of body stops twisting when the feet land and hold	**Focus on springing up on box:** —can land on feet —can land on lower legs —try to make the spring send your feet high so you can land on the box —do not get stuck in your takeoff —make your takeoff spring you up on your box **Focus on shapes:** —exaggerate your shape —make your shape clear —really twist, stretch, curl

6. Try different shapes and do not forget to watch your landing—back should be straight so you do not tip forward. Prepare those muscles to work to keep you from collapsing.	Some children may find it easier to go into a roll after landing than holding a "stuck," fixed landing. Some children can be encouraged to move on to the next task before it is suggested to the whole class.	**Check on eye focus:** -try to look straight ahead -do not let your head drop unless in a tight curl **Look at feet/landing:** -land on both feet -give in ankles, knees, hips -firm up after you give to keep from collapsing -praise for glued landings **Focus for changing shapes:** -try all three kinds of shapes—curled, stretched, twisted -do not do the same shape twice in a row -in your group, each of you try to do a different shape
7. When you can hold a fixed, glued landing with back straight, add a roll or a step-like action and end with a springy pop up at the end. (suggest a slight pause between landing and the roll or step-like action)		**Focus on muscle tension:** -feel the muscles tighten as you exaggerate your shape -feel the tension in your muscles as you make them strong after you give in your landing to keep you upright -you alone must control the muscles—relax them a bit to give in the landing; tighten to keep from collapsing **Focus on pause:** -think—you can hold your landing. Take your time before going into roll/step-like action -show you really have complete control. You are going into the roll/step-like action when you *decide,* not because your momentum makes you.
8. First four people will be responsible for carefully carrying boxes. Others wait till mat truck comes alongside your mat and lift mat onto truck. Doug and David get the mat truck.		**Focus on those still working on fixed landings—no roll or step-like action:** -comment on position of back—straight, perpendicular to floor -maintaining balance on landing -praise them for working to perfect landing before going on **Focus on springy pop up:** -make that pop up at the end very different from your fixed landing -see how high you can go **Scan the roll/step-like action:** -make your roll or step-like action with clear body shapes -really tuck if tucking -stretch if stretching -twist if twisting **Focus on carrying box:** -praise for working quietly -comment on straight arms, lifting by straightening knees Focus on hanging mats: -all lift from one side -lift together -praise for good "team work"

to read, study, and learn as much about the content and the children you are planning to teach as possible. Obviously, practice and experience in teaching help to develop confidence, but for the beginning teacher, in addition to monitoring and analyzing your behavior as you practice teaching, nothing can be substituted for an in-depth, sensitive approach to planning.

REFERENCES

1. Promising Practices in Elementary School Physical Education (Report of the Conference for Teachers and Supervisors of Elementary School Physical Education). Washington, D.C., American Association for Health, Physical Education, and Recreation, 1969.
2. Essentials of a Quality Elementary School Physical Education Program: A Position Paper. Washington, D.C., American Association for Health, Physical Education, and Recreation, 1981.

Chapter 12

The Challenge of Teaching

or

"I Never Promised You a Rose Garden"

MARGARET AMMONS

A frequent admonishment to my students is that good teaching is the most intellectually, emotionally, and physically difficult job there is; poor teaching, the easiest. What is it about good teaching that is so demanding?

Intellectually, the demands are almost overwhelming. Consider the following: An elementary teacher faces anywhere from 22 to 180 students a day, depending on the organization of the specific school. (A recent graduate of our program reported that as a teacher of mathematics to sixth and seventh graders she saw 180 children a day.) This problem is compounded greatly for some physical education specialists who are assigned to two or more schools and have several hundred children in classes daily. Recall that there will be no carbon copies in any group. There may be areas in which children are similar, but they will not be identical. Now dwell on the number and variety of ways in which children can differ, and multiply that figure by the number of children.

Your task is to create conditions for all children so that they can move appropriately toward predetermined objectives. In order to achieve this aim, you must be able to recognize, for example, many different styles of learning, so that you can provide activities and situations that will accommodate those styles.

Let us suppose that one objective in the classroom is that each child should know a variety of terms. This objective simply requires the child to know the terms. The activity required is memorization. Simple enough. But wait. How do you memorize? Some individuals do this best by writing something over and over. Others do it best by reciting one item in a list, then adding an item and reciting two, and then a third. We do not all go about the job of memorization in the same way. So the teacher's job is to ask children how best they memorize and then to provide opportunities for children to achieve the objective.

If, on the other hand, your objective is at a higher level, the problem is magnified. To illustrate, take an objective from a gymnastics or dance lesson that requires a child to create a movement sequence. This requires of the teacher that he/she truly intends that the children *create something and not that they do something that has been predetermined*. The task then becomes one of being able to convince the children that the teacher is being honest and then to determine precisely what words and questions will support each individual child in this personal creative undertaking.

These are only two examples of the kind of intellectual activity in which a good teacher engages. Jackson once claimed that teachers are arational as they teach.[2] That is, teachers do not think about what they do and say; they simply do and say in a kind of detached manner. But Jackson was not talking about good teachers. You can learn to ask the question or to give the direction that will move each child toward your objective.

A good teacher must have in mind and control many variables: objectives, learning styles of students, a variety of learning activities that will match both objective and student, student abilities, inclinations, and limitations. Then decisions are taken based on the best professional judgment the teacher can make. It goes on continuously, the entire time you are teaching. In spite of the care you take with each decision for each child, you are human and may have misjudged. It then becomes necessary to reassess the factors and to create new conditions as the evidence warrants.

Good teaching is not a mechanical, dull endeavor. It keeps you on your intellectual toes and requires that you have a wide basis for choosing strategies, activities, words. Good teaching offers to you the opportunity to sort out your values, choose from among acceptable possibilities, predict consequences, weigh, evaluate, and continue to learn and to grow.

Emotionally demanding? Most assuredly. While love of children is not enough to be a good teacher, it is certainly a requirement. Here, I am not talking about any romanticized conception of love. Rather, I intend love to mean a view of one's fellows, including children, that is characterized by an unconditional, no-strings-attached concern for the well-being of each individual. This love does not have to be earned. It is simply there. When this love prevails in a teacher and that teacher works with large numbers of children on a daily basis, it is demanding. Such love is essential if children are to achieve what I believe is the legitimate purpose of the elementary school.

If children are to grow into the kinds of human beings who themselves are concerned for others, they must experience such concern in all aspects of their lives—not only at home or in church. For, as many have said, children learn what they live.

To discuss the physical demands upon teachers is to belabor the obvious. In any elementary classroom, teachers who are good teachers are on the move. The classroom in which all children are working at their desks, with the teacher behind his or hers, is the classroom where, in all probability, children are taking a test or are engaged in nonproductive activity. In the first instance, there may be justification for physical inactivity of the teacher. In the second instance, there is none.

If one is to be intellectually and emotionally on top of the teaching situation, one cannot be inert. How can you know with certainty that a particular activity is what a given child needs if you are not near the child? This is true in teaching physical education, too. If you are withdrawn from the situation or from a child for protracted periods of time, how can you determine whether a child needs support?

Extra teaching responsibilities, such as planning, conferring, meeting, are all additional physical demands made upon the teacher. They are all essential to the task. Some 25 years ago, a state legislature decreed that teachers should put in a 40-hour week if they expected to be paid higher salaries. One teacher wrote a letter to a local newspaper saying in response to the decree, "Splendid. Now I'll be through at noon on Thursday."

Now, why would anyone in his or her right mind want to be a good teacher, especially since so many teachers seem to survive as poor ones? Each must answer that poser for her or himself. The only legitimate answer I can give is my own. I would like to share it with you. This is in no way to say that I have succeeded; only that I have wanted to be a good teacher.

As a student all the way through a B.S. degree, I performed well. I enjoyed playing the school game. It was not until I entered graduate school that honest-to-goodness learning played any significant part in my education. Having discovered that learning is exciting, exquisite, and painful, it became obvious to me that what *I had been asking of the children I taught was that they PERFORM rather than that they LEARN.* I had been a poor teacher. It was an unsettling yet provocative discovery.

This enlightenment led me to want to be a good teacher, to offer to students of any age the same opportunity to get as excited about education in schools as I had finally become myself. It was an honest desire to share, not information, but ideas, concerns small and large, ways of knowing, successes, and failures. It was the realization that adults have a responsibility to the generations who follow. It became a commitment to students, a commitment that says "I will do my utmost to see that the time you spend with me will be spent in ways that are worthwhile in your eyes, in ways that make you want to grasp your world and your place in it, and in ways that let you leave my class feeling better about yourself than you did when you arrived."

Sentimental? Perhaps, but I prefer to classify it as a hard-nosed translation of what I believe about people, about the knowable world, and about good teaching into practical, everyday behavior.

How did I come to have such a commitment? It was caught from two teachers, who demonstrated the kind of intellectual honesty and excitement about the field of education in general and about good teaching in particular, and who exemplified in their relations with students a deep and abiding love.

It would be a boon to be able to teach teachers how to have a deep commitment to good teaching. Indeed, if one were able so to teach, he or she could make a million. The best we can do at the moment is to teach as we would have you to teach and hope that to you we will make a difference.

Not all who engage in teaching should. If teaching is pursued without the commitment I have suggested, it is likely to be disenchanting. With such commitment, however, teaching is the most exciting, tantalizing, exasperating, and rewarding way I know to give a life.

REFERENCES

1. Rogers, V.R., and Church, B.: Open Education: Critique and Assessment. Washington, D.C. Association for Supervision and Curriculum Development, 1975, p. 40.
2. Jackson, P.W.: Life in Classrooms. New York. Holt, Rinehart and Winston, 1968, p. 145.

Index

Page numbers followed by "t" indicate tables.